Exceptional Children and Adults

AN INTRODUCTION TO SPECIAL EDUCATION

Exceptional Children and Adults

AN INTRODUCTION TO SPECIAL EDUCATION

Eleanor W. Lynch and Rena B. Lewis, Editors
San Diego State University

Scott, Foresman and Company
Glenview, Illinois   Boston   London

THE SCOTT, FORESMAN SERIES IN SPECIAL EDUCATION

Series Editor: Richard J. Morris
The University of Arizona

DEDICATION

For Our Parents
Virginia and Leo Whiteside
Margaret and Willard Bishopp
and
Our Partners
Patrick Harrison
Jim Lewis

Photo credits are on page 661 and are considered as an
extension of this copyright page.

Library of Congress Cataloging-in-Publication Data

Exceptional children and adults.

Includes bibliographies and
index.
1. Special education—United States. I. Lynch,
Eleanor W. II. Lewis, Rena B.
LC3981.E932   1988   371.9   87-20504
ISBN 0-673-15903-5

1 2 3 4 5 6 7 - RRC - 92 91 90 89 88 87

Preface

Exceptional Children and Adults is about exceptional people as infants and pre-schoolers, as school-age children, and as adolescents and adults. It is designed to provide a sound and comprehensive introduction to the study of exceptionality in relation to both handicapping conditions and extraordinary gifts and talents. Three major aspects of the study of exceptionality are emphasized: characteristics of exceptional people, services provided to these populations, and issues that affect exceptional individuals and the services they require.

Because many disciplines and professions have contributed to the body of knowledge about exceptionalities, the focus of this book is its multidisciplinary emphasis. College and university students preparing to become special educators will find information about educational treatment of the exceptionalities. Those interested in other fields will find information about the contributions made by speech and language pathologists, counselors, school psychologists, vocational rehabilitation counselors, physicians and school nurses, social workers, physical and occupational therapists, and other professionals.

School-age students are not the only exceptional individuals with special learning, social/emotional, or physical/health needs. Exceptional individuals can be found in all age groups. Exceptionalities may be identified at birth; they may continue into adulthood and maturity. In recognition of the lifespan nature of exceptionality, another focus of this book is its coverage of all age groups. Infants and preschoolers, school-age students, adolescents, and young adults are discussed in each of the categorical chapters. In addition, one chapter is devoted to the transition issues that exceptional individuals face as they move from school into young adulthood and the world of work. The book's final chapter is devoted to one of the newest fields of study in exceptionality—the study of aging. This chapter examines issues related to exceptional people as they age.

Cultural and language differences influence the impact of exceptionality. The way in which exceptionality is perceived by families differs from one culture to another, and language differences may change both the services and the way in which they are provided. Because of the increasing cultural and linguistic diversity within the United States, a chapter focusing on multicultural issues and exceptionality has been included.

Exceptional individuals cannot be considered alone; they must be considered within the context of a family. From infancy through adulthood, exceptional individuals (like all people) influence and are influenced by family members. Because of the overwhelming importance of the family's role in the life of exceptional people, one chapter focuses exclusively on families of exceptional children and adults.

These chapters represent an important addition to an introductory textbook because they highlight the impact of exceptionality throughout the lifespan as well as the interaction of cultural heritage, language, family values and beliefs, and exceptionality.

Throughout *Exceptional Children and Adults* are features that highlight some of the important aspects of the study of exceptionality. Most chapters contain "Introducing . . ." sections that provide a personal introduction to an exceptional person or persons. "Assessment Strategies" focus on method used to evaluate exceptionalities; "Promising Practices" describe some of the innovative programs that serve exceptional individuals. "Advances in Knowledge" provide information on breakthroughs in medical research or research on the nature of exceptionality; "Special Education Technologies" describe ways in which current technologies can benefit exceptional people. At the end of most chapters is a list of Resources for further information; a Glossary of special terms appears at the end of the book.

The study of exceptionality is a broad field incorporating many separate areas of expertise. The authors of each of the chapters within this book reflect those areas of expertise, and each has been written by one or more experts in the area.

Acknowledgements

We would like to express our appreciation to our editors, Chris Jennison and Anita Portugal, and to the designer, Jacqueline Kolb. Thanks go to the editor of the Scott, Foresman Series in Special Education, Richard J. Morris, of The University of Arizona, as well as to the reviewers whose suggestions assisted us in the improvement of this text.

Leroy Aserlind, Jr.	*The University of Wisconsin*
Ruth S. Barnhart	*Iowa State University*
Stewart Ehly	*The University of Iowa*
Constance T. Fischer	*Duquesne University*
Gilbert R. Gredler	*University of South Carolina*
Ira Gross	*University of Rhode Island*
Douglas Guess	*The University of Kansas*
Kathleen C. Harris	*California State University*
Marjorie L. Lewis	*Illinois State University*
Gerald Mahoney	*The University of Michigan*
C. Julius Meisel	*The University of Delaware*
Catherine Morsink	*University of Florida*

Virginia L. Pearson — *Wayne State University*
Barbara W. Reeves — *Ohio University*
Stephen Safran — *Ohio University*
Hana Simonson — *York College, City University of New York*
John Umbreit — *The University of Arizona—Tucson*
James M. Van Tassel — *Ball State University*
Lee A. Witters — *The University of Nebraska*

Eleanor W. Lynch
Rena B. Lewis

Brief Contents

ISSUES IN THE PROVISION
OF SERVICES *502*

Contents

Part Two

THE EXCEPTIONALITIES 94

3

7

Hearing Disorders 276

Donald F. Moores and
Julia Maestas y Moores

8

Communication Disorders 318

Carol A. Swift

Part Three

ISSUES IN THE PROVISION OF SERVICES 502

12

Part One

EXCEPTIONAL PEOPLE

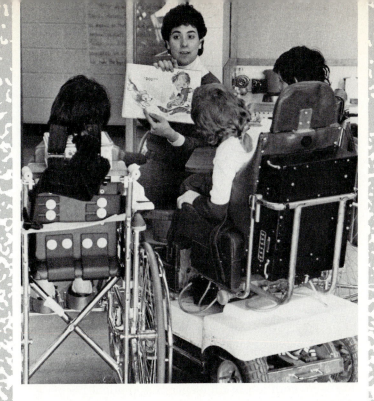

Exceptional people are, first and foremost, individuals. As individuals, they have different hopes and dreams, different aspirations, different personalities, and different needs. What sets them apart as a group is the exceptionality and the effects of that exceptionality on their ability to meet the expectations of their families, the educational system, and society.

Chapter 1, *The Nature and Needs of Exceptional People,* introduces the concept of exceptionality. Among the topics covered are the impact of exceptionality, the number of exceptional people, etiology and prevention of exceptionalities, and special needs of exceptional people. Also discussed are the disciplines that provide services to exceptional individuals. A brief history of society's concern for exceptional people is provided and current practices are described. The chapter ends, like most in this book, by considering future perspectives for the treatment of exceptional people.

In Chapter 2, *Services for Exceptional People,* the focus is on intervention. The types of available services are described, and intervention is considered for each of the three major stages of development: early life, the school years, and adulthood. At the end of this chapter (and all others that follow) is a list of Resources for seeking further information about the chapter's content.

Chapter 1

THE NATURE AND NEEDS OF EXCEPTIONAL PEOPLE

Exceptionality is a condition of difference. Exceptional people are those who differ from other individuals in some important way. They may be perceived as extraordinary because of a disability which hampers their participation in life's common tasks or because of an unusual ability or talent which sets them apart from their peers. Some exceptional persons fail to meet society's expectations for individuals of their age and culture; others exceed these expectations.

Like all people, exceptional ones are individuals. Although they share many characteristics with members of the nonexceptional population as well as with others of the same exceptionality, they remain individuals. The exceptionality only serves to intensify each individual's uniqueness by its interaction with personal traits, life experiences, family background, and cultural heritage.

The study of exceptionality is the study of individuality: Its aim is the understanding of the complexities of the exceptional condition as they affect the individual infant, child, adolescent, or adult. This understanding provides the foundation for the professions concerned with the welfare of exceptional people.

Exceptional people are those individuals whose capability to perform important life activities deviates significantly from the level of performance expected

Eleanor W. Lynch and Rena B. Lewis
San Diego State University

by society. Although all persons deviate in some way from societal expectations, the difference is not considered an exceptional one unless it is of sufficient magnitude to be judged as either a special ability or disability. Society recognizes abilities and talents in many realms of endeavor: scholarship, leadership, sports, the creative and performing arts. With disabilities, however, the difference must occur in a skill area considered critical. Skills such as walking and talking are examples of critical life activities; skills such as dancing and singing are not.

Critical skill domains include communication, self-help, locomotion, interpersonal relationships, and thinking and learning. The ability to perform these important life activities is called adaptive behavior. Adaptive behavior is defined by the American Association on Mental Deficiency as "the effectiveness or degree with which individuals meet the standards of personal independence and social responsibility expected for age and cultural group" (Grossman, 1983, p. 1). Exceptional persons are those whose adaptive behavior calls attention to itself; because of an ability or disability, their performance is discrepant from the standards of society.

Expectations for performance depend upon the age of the individual. In the early childhood years, the concern is development of sensory-motor, communication, self-help, and socialization skills. In the school years, the expectation changes to application of basic academic skills to life situations and, in adulthood, to vocational and social adjustment. The concept of exceptionality also differs from culture to culture. The lack of basic reading and writing skills may be viewed as a major disability in an information-intensive technological society but as a milder problem in an agrarian culture where literacy skills are considered less vital. However, many of the exceptionalities are universally acknowledged, particularly those with physical manifestations and those that are severe in nature.

Exceptional persons include both individuals handicapped by disabilities and individuals distinguished by special talents and gifts. A disability is a physical, sensory, cognitive, or emotional impairment which affects a person's ability to function in some way. Not all disabilities are handicaps since some can be alleviated or corrected. For example, eyeglasses and hearing aids reduce the effects of some sensory impairments. Only when a disability interferes with an important life function does it become a handicap.

The major handicapping conditions are mental retardation, learning disabilities, emotional disturbance (or behavior disorders), communication disorders, hearing impairments, visual impairments, and physical and health impairments. Gifted and talented individuals represent another segment of the exceptional population. These persons stand out from their peers because of their abilities rather than their disabilities.

Exceptionalities may occur in combination. If there is more than one disability, the individual is considered multiply handicapped. It is also possible for an individual to be both handicapped and gifted. Multiple exceptionalities increase the complexity of individuality as do cultural and linguistic differences. An exceptional person whose cultural heritage is at variance with society's primary culture or whose language of communication is other than the standard language is a special challenge to the professions that serve exceptional people.

THE NUMBER OF EXCEPTIONAL PEOPLE

Exceptionality is not rare; exceptional people make up a sizeable proportion of the general population. Kirk and Gallagher (1983) estimate that between 8 and 16 percent of the school-age population of the United States is exceptional.

The number of exceptional individuals can be expressed as either a prevalence or incidence estimate. Prevalence is the number of persons within a defined population who are considered exceptional at any one time. For example, an estimate of the prevalence of learning disabilities would be the number of learning disabled persons living in the United States in January 1988. Incidence, in contrast, is the number of new cases identified within some specified time period (Barker & Rose, 1979). Incidence figures are lower than prevalence figures since they reflect only those persons newly identified as exceptional.

Exceptionality is not necessarily a permanent, lifelong status. Some children are not identified as exceptional until they enter school; others are handicapped only in the school environment and are able to cope successfully with the demands of adult life. Many people, unexceptional as children and in the early adult years, become exceptional as they acquire disabilities as part of the aging process. Among the most common disabilities that affect persons older than 65 are hearing impairments (found in 29% of this population), vision impairments (20%), and restrictions in general mobility (18%) (Harris, 1979).

Exact counts of the number of exceptional people are difficult to obtain. One impediment is the lack of consistency among definitions; different disciplines, professions, and service agencies set different criteria for identification of the various exceptionalities. Another difficulty arises from the diverse methodologies used to collect incidence and prevalence data. Studies using different instruments to gather information from different sources about different samples of exceptional individuals tend to produce varying estimates. A third obstacle to accurate accounting is the variation that occurs due to factors such as age, gender, and socioeconomic status. Estimates of the number of exceptional people vary from one age group to the next, from one gender to the other, and from the less affluent strata of society to the more affluent. With the handicap of mental retardation, for example, greater numbers of exceptional persons are identified among school-age children, among males, and among persons from lower socio-economic groups (Cegelka & Prehm, 1982a).

One source of prevalence information is the database maintained on public education. Although this encompasses only school-age children and youth, it provides one of the more accurate prevalence estimates. According to the information presented in Table 1.1, over four million public school students were identified as handicapped in the 1983–84 school year. This represents approximately 11 percent of the total public school population (U.S. Department of

Table 1.1

Enrollment in Special Education Programs for Handicapped Children, Ages 3–21, During the 1983–84 School Year

Type of Handicap	Enrollment
Learning Disabilities	1,811,489
Speech Impairments	1,130,569
Mental Retardation	750,534
Serious Emotional Disturbance	362,073
Physical and Other Health Impairments	110,830
Deaf and Hard of Hearing	74,279
Visually Handicapped	31,576
Multiple Handicaps (Including Deaf-Blind)	70,049
TOTAL	4,341,399

Source: Adapted from *Seventh Annual Report to Congress on the Implementation of Public Law 94–142: The Education for All Handicapped Children Act* by U.S. Department of Education, Office of Special Education and Rehabilitative Services (1985). Washington, DC: Author, p. 199.

Education, 1985). However, this may be a low estimate of actual numbers because it is probable some handicapped children remain unidentified or unserved. Also, it does not reflect the full range of exceptionality since gifted and talented individuals are not included.

There is variation among the exceptionalities in the numbers of persons each represents. Hearing, vision, physical, health, and multiple impairments are considered low incidence handicaps since each accounts for less than 1 percent of the general school population. High incidence exceptionalities include the gifted and talented as well as the handicaps of mental retardation, learning disabilities, communication disorders, and emotional disturbance; each is estimated to make up between 1 and 3 percent of the general school population. These differences in numbers among exceptionalities are illustrated by Figure 1.1 which presents data on the number of handicapped students (ages 3 to 21) served in special education programs.

Within each exceptionality, there is a continuum ranging from mild to severe. With handicapped individuals, those with mild handicaps are the least disabled. While the terms mild and severe are less appropriate for the gifted and talented group, these persons also vary in the extent to which they are affected by the exceptionality. Across all exceptionalities, individuals at the mild end of the continuum outnumber those at the severe end. Thus, there are greater numbers of mildly retarded individuals than severely retarded individuals and, among the gifted, fewer geniuses than moderately bright persons.

Figure 1.1

Distribution of Children Ages 3–21 Served by Handicapping Condition,
School Year 1983–84

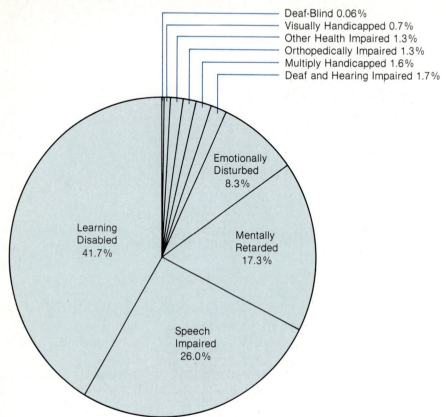

Source: Adapted from *Seventh Annual Report to Congress on the Implementation of Public Law 94–142: The Education of All Handicapped Children Act* by U.S. Department of Education, Office of Special Education and Rehabilitative Services (1985). Washington, DC: Author, p. 199.

ETIOLOGY AND PREVENTION

The search for etiology or cause is an important part of the study of exceptionality. Knowledge of the cause of a condition increases the likelihood that it can be controlled. Once the etiology of a disability is known, it may become possible to prevent the disability or to develop medical or educational interventions to reverse or lessen its effects. With special abilities, knowledge of causation serves a different purpose because the goal is encouragement of the condition and its enhancement.

Etiological research has successfully identified and described a large number and variety of causative agents for exceptional conditions. For most exceptional individuals, however, the specific cause of the ability or disability remains unknown. With mentally retarded persons, for example, the more than 250 identified causes account for only about 10 percent of the population (Maloney & Ward, 1979). Clearly the study of etiology must continue.

The known causes of exceptionality can be categorized by the developmental period in which they occur. For disabilities that become apparent in childhood, causes are differentiated into three periods of onset: prenatal, or while the child is in utero; perinatal, or during the birth process; and postnatal, or after birth. Maternal infections such as rubella which damage the unborn child's sensory and central nervous systems during the early stages of pregnancy are considered prenatal causes. Injury or trauma during the birth process is a perinatal cause, and disabling accidents or diseases occurring after birth are postnatal causes.

Another dimension along which causes can be differentiated is the type of etiological agent. Although exceptionalities may be due to either biomedical or sociobehavioral causes (Cegelka & Prehm, 1982b), most etiological classification systems emphasize the biomedical. One example is the AAMD medical etiological classification, in many ways consistent with the International Classification of Diseases (ISD-9) of the World Health Organization (1977) and the Diagnostic and Statistical Manual of Mental Disorders (DSM-III) of the American Psychiatric Association (1980). The AAMD system (Grossman, 1983) recognizes nine types of causes of mental retardation: infections and intoxications, trauma or physical agent, disorders of metabolism or nutrition, gross brain disease, unknown prenatal influence, chromosomal anomalies, other conditions originating in the perinatal period, retardation following psychiatric disorder, environmental influences, and other conditions. Moore (1982) offers a classification system for biomedical causes of neurological impairment. Included as etiological agents are infectious diseases, gestational and obstetric disorders, disorders related to environmental hazards, genetic disorders and chromosomal abnormalities, and neurocutaneous syndromes.

Although more difficult to substantiate as causative agents, sociobehavioral factors play an important role in the determination of abilities and disabilities. Despite the continuing debate over the relative contributions of heredity and environment, there is general agreement that each of these forces influences performance. Blackhurst and Lewis (1982) discuss this viewpoint:

> . . . there is an interaction between heredity and environment. That is, genetics set the theoretical range for a person's potential, and the quality of the environment determines the behavior patterns that the person develops within this range. Thus, a person with average genetic potential may actually function as mentally retarded if reared in an impoverished environment. (p. 1221)

An impoverished psychosocial environment places its inhabitants in jeopardy. Environments that lack stimulation are not conducive to optimal development in children or peak performance in adults. In situations of poverty, nutrition and health care may suffer, adding the risk of biomedical assault. Poverty is one of the sociobehavioral risk factors identified by Garber and McInerney (1982) which, if extreme, signal the possibility of a threat to normal child growth and development. These factors are: socioeconomic status of the family, the quality of the home environment, the intellectual performance of the mother and functioning levels of siblings, literacy, number of children in the family and their spacing, and parental attitudes of hopelessness or negativism. The environment of the school can also affect a child's level of performance. In fact, it has been suggested that some mild disabilities are the direct result of inadequate classroom instruction (Reynolds & Birch, 1977).

Exceptionalities may be due to more than one cause. For example, a low birth weight infant may suffer a postnatal injury or be reared in an environment of deprivation. In this case, it is probable that the causative factors will interact to increase the severity or scope of the disability. It is also possible for etiological agents to counterbalance one another. While a mild neurological impairment may not respond to medical treatment, its effects may be lessened by the provision of an enriched environment in the home and in the school.

The ultimate aim of etiological research is the prevention of disabling conditions. Some causes of disability, such as the crippling disease of polio, have been virtually eliminated. Advances in early detection allow the diagnosis of other conditions in utero. Amniocentesis, for example, is a medical technique in which a sample of the amniotic fluid surrounding the fetus is collected for chromosomal and other analyses. If abnormalities are detected, the family can then decide whether to continue or terminate the pregnancy. Some potentially disabling conditions respond to medical or surgical intervention. For example, the effects of hydrocephaly can be decreased by a surgical procedure in which a shunt is implanted to drain away the excess cerebrospinal fluid surrounding the brain. This reduces the cranial pressure that causes brain injury.

Environmental causes of disability are also subject to prevention and treatment, but the techniques are socioeducational in nature rather than medical. The goal is the provision of an environment that is a positive influence rather than a neutral or negative one. Training new parents how to care for their infants, extending the experiences of preschoolers through early educational enrichment, and ensuring quality instruction for school-age children and youth are all ways of combating the potentially injurious effects of an unfavorable environment.

SPECIAL NEEDS OF EXCEPTIONAL PEOPLE

Exceptional people may require special attention from society. In addition to support from their families, they may benefit from assistance from community agencies that provide educational, vocational, recreational, medical, and social services. The need for aid may persist throughout the lifespan or be present at only one time; it may extend to all important life activities or be limited to one or two.

Heterogeneity characterizes the exceptional population. As individuals, they are different one from another. As subgroups differentiated on the basis of specific abilities or disabilities, they differ both in the kind and intensity of special assistance that may be needed. However, they share with all persons the potentiality for cognitive, affective, and sensory and physical development. Cognitive development encompasses thinking, reasoning, and judgment and the application of these processes to the learning of new information. In affective development, the concern is the emergence of feelings and emotions, the sense of self, and the building of relationships with others. Development in the physical and sensory areas includes growth and maturation of the body, the acquisition of gross and fine motor skills, and the development of sensory abilities such as vision and hearing.

Three types of needs, which relate to the three areas of development, are common to all persons: learning needs, social and emotional needs, and physical and health needs. For exceptional people, however, this relationship is complicated by the presence of specific abilities or disabilities in one or more of the developmental domains. Mental retardation, for example, is a cognitive deficit, one that makes learning more difficult and thereby intensifies the learning needs of mentally retarded individuals. In contrast, emotional disturbance is an affective disorder which results directly in special social and emotional needs; however, since emotional well-being also affects learning, learning needs are present as well.

Table 1.2 lists the various exceptionalities and the primary developmental area of ability or disability associated with each. Also presented are the critical life skills typically affected and the resulting special needs. Although variation may be expected with each individual, these represent the general characteristics associated with each of the exceptionalities.

There is not always a direct correspondence between the ability or disability area and the special needs experienced by persons of that exceptionality. Some exceptionalities, such as hearing and vision disorders, are physical in origin yet manifest themselves as special learning needs. In global disabilities such as mental retardation, emotional disturbance, and severe multiple handicaps, more than one area of performance is affected. All exceptionalities influence social and emotional development to some extent because they have an effect upon the exceptional person's concept of self and his or her interactions with others.

Intervention programs for exceptional people are designed around their special needs. The goal of intervention depends upon the type and severity of the ability or disability. For gifted and talented individuals, the aim is development and enhancement of abilities. For handicapped persons, the goal is to lessen the effects of the disability to the maximum extent possible.

In some cases, disabilities can be overcome through intervention; for example, intensive educational services may rid young children of certain communication disorders. Many disabilities, however, cannot be cured, and intervention must proceed in other directions. In one intervention approach, compensation, the aim is to bypass the disability rather than ameliorate it. Strengths of the individual are used to compensate for the limits of the disability. Persons who are deaf

Table 1.2

Overview of the Exceptionalities

Exceptionality	Area of Ability or Disability	Critical Life Skills Affected					Primary Needs		
		Communication	Self-Help	Locomotion	Interpersonal Relations	Thinking and Learning	Learning	Social-Emotional	Physical-Health
Mental Retardation	Cognitive Disability	X	X		X	X	X	X	
Learning Disabilities	Cognitive Disability	X			X	X	X	X	
Communication Disorders	Cognitive or Physical Disability	X			X	X	X	X	
Emotional Disturbance	Affective Disability				X	X	X	X	
Hearing Disorders	Sensory Disability	X				X	X		
Vision Disorders	Sensory Disability		X	X			X		
Physical and Health Handicaps	Physical Disability		X	X					X
Severe Multiple Handicaps	Multiple Disabilities	X	X	X	X	X	X	X	X
Gifted and Talented	Cognitive Ability					X	X		

or blind, for instance, are trained to utilize the senses that remain unimpaired. In this way, the effects of the disability are lessened as persons learn alternate methods of accomplishing critical life tasks.

When compensation is not feasible, the goal of intervention becomes acquisition of as many critical life skills as possible. This is a realistic goal because all exceptional persons, whatever the severity of the disability, are able to learn and to develop new skills. Despite intervention, the skill repertoires of some exceptional individuals will remain limited, at least when compared with society's expectations for normal performance. However, intervention can be considered successful if, by promoting the acquisition of new and important life skills, it dispels some of the effects of a severe disability.

DISCIPLINES SERVING
EXCEPTIONAL PEOPLE

No single professional group has the knowledge or training necessary to work with all exceptional people and successfully meet their medical, educational, social, and emotional needs. As a result, disciplines as diverse as medicine, education, nutrition, speech and language pathology, social work, dentistry, nursing, occupational therapy, psychology, audiology, and physical therapy must cooperate in the provision of programs to exceptional individuals. This collaboration across disciplines has been called "multidisciplinary," "interdisciplinary," or "transdisciplinary" practice.

Multidisciplinary generally means that persons representing several different professions work on different aspects of the same case. They may be informed about what each is doing, but each works independently often without exchanging information with the others. For example, Michael is an eight-year-old boy with Down Syndrome. Michael has medical needs because of a heart problem and allergies; he has social/welfare needs because he is a member of a low income family with only a mother in the home; and he requires assistance in learning. In Michael's case, a physician, social worker, public health nurse, and teacher are all involved in assisting Michael and his mother; however, if these professionals are engaged in multidisciplinary practice, they may not know what goals and objectives each other is working toward. This can result in overloading families with service providers and fragmenting services. In Michael's case, the teacher, social worker, and public health nurse may all make home visits. The physician and the public health nurse may both give directions about managing Michael's heart problem and allergies. The social worker, public health nurse, and teacher may all be listening to the mother's concerns and providing information on child management; however, there may be no one helping her to synthesize and use the information that she receives to make decisions. This model can lead to confusion, lack of direction, and lack of follow-through in educational and treatment programs.

In interdisciplinary practice, all of the professionals involved in a case work together with the family to establish priorities and goals and to coordinate services. In Michael's case, his mother and all the professionals would meet or talk together to determine treatment priorities and ways of accomplishing them. They might decide that only two professionals should do home visits to prevent a constant parade of strangers through the home. The public health nurse might help Michael's mother with medical and social service problems; the teacher might assist with educational goals. This model helps to assure that services are coordinated and based on family priorities. The quality of service is improved and less time and money are expended.

The transdisciplinary model, developed in early childhood intervention programs, continues to be used most frequently where the same team works with the child and family over an extended period of time. In this model, professionals representing a wide range of disciplines share information about the case and about their own discipline. Each team member trains the others in the professional skills unique to his or her own discipline. For example, the social worker or school psychologist may train the teacher, occupational therapist, and nutritionist how to listen to family concerns, when to provide supportive counseling, and when to call the psychologist or social worker for help. Likewise, the teacher may train the occupational therapist, nutritionist, or social worker to implement a language program for the child, to demonstrate it, and collect data on its effectiveness. This blending and sharing of professional roles assists each professional in understanding all the child's and family's needs while enhancing the professional's own skills. In Michael's case, one person might be selected to be the home visitor. That person would help monitor all of the programs while meeting frequently with the team for consultation and training. This model requires commitment. The team of professionals must have time to train each other, be willing to trust others enough to share skills, and members must be able to recognize their own limitations when working outside their own area of expertise. When these conditions are met, transdisciplinary practice can provide quality services which blend with family needs.

Professions Concerned with Learning Needs

Special educators, speech and language pathologists, psychologists, adaptive physical educators, and vocational rehabilitation counselors are the professionals most often identified with the learning needs of exceptional individuals. Special educators are usually trained in the generic aspects of exceptionality and then specialize in one area such as physical handicaps, learning disabilities, or giftedness. Special educators are responsible, with other members of the team, for developing, implementing, and evaluating the individualized education program for each student they serve. Formerly, special educators worked in special classes or special schools which served only exceptional students. Now, these professionals often work with regular educators on the campuses of regular elementary and secondary schools. Some teach special classes, but many serve as resource teachers. In this role, they provide supplemental instruction to exceptional students as well as assistance to regular education teachers as exceptional students are integrated into regular classrooms.

Speech and language pathologists are trained in language acquisition and the remediation of speech and language problems in both children and adults. They may work on language skills with individuals or groups or, in school settings, with special class teachers to develop individualized communication programs. Since language and thinking are so closely related, speech and language pathologists often provide assistance in developing academic programs that deal with basic concepts and problem solving. Audiologists, the professionals responsible for assessing hearing, work closely with speech and language pathologists to determine whether hearing aids or other forms of amplification would be effective for students with hearing losses.

Psychologists play many roles in the provision of services to individuals with exceptional needs, but they are most frequently associated with learning and social needs. Some psychologists are certified as school psychologists; they are

A school psychologist meets with a student who has behavior disabilities;
results of their meetings may determine the extent to which special services
are needed.

responsible for evaluating students for admission to special programs and for helping to determine specific learning needs. They may also provide consultation to special educators, other professionals, and parents on issues such as management of behavior at home or in the classroom.

The newest profession concerned with the learning needs of exceptional individuals is adaptive physical education. This discipline developed as physical educators recognized the need for exceptional students to have movement, mobility, and physical conditioning programs as part of their education. Less medically oriented than services such as physical therapy, adaptive physical education adds a strong motor component to the educational program of many students with special needs.

Finally, vocational rehabilitation counselors are concerned with the learning needs of exceptional individuals as these needs relate to independent living and employment. Rehabilitation professionals work with special educators to provide programs that allow for a smooth transition from high school to higher education, employment, or vocational training. They serve exceptional adults who have become disabled as well as those who have had special needs throughout their lives. In addition to providing vocational training, they teach independent living skills to enable their clients to become more fully integrated into their communities.

The social and emotional needs of exceptional individuals are of concern to all professions, but several disciplines are most strongly identified with these two areas. Social workers, guidance counselors, psychologists, vocational rehabilitation counselors, and special educators are concerned with the social and emotional needs of exceptional people.

Social workers become involved with exceptional individuals as caseworkers, group workers, or community workers. Each of these specializations provides services related to social and emotional needs. Caseworkers often serve as case managers for a handicapped individual or for families with a handicapped member. In this capacity, the social worker assists in obtaining needed services whether these be counseling, medical treatment, or financial assistance. The caseworker may also serve as an advocate for the exceptional individual to ensure that his or her rights are protected. Group workers usually work with several individuals in a counseling or problem-solving capacity. They frequently assist adolescents and adults with special needs in areas such as making friends, living independently, sexuality, marriage, and child rearing. Through instruction, modeling, and group process, exceptional individuals learn adaptive ways of meeting their own social and emotional needs. Community social workers are those who have specialized in community organization and administration. Although they may not provide direct services to exceptional individuals, they may be heavily involved in setting policy and developing the community's capacity to provide programs and services for its exceptional citizens. They may set up networks of professionals, contribute to collaborative efforts across agencies, and serve on boards and commissions charged with developing transportation, recreation, or health services that are accessible to exceptional individuals.

Guidance counselors and school counselors generally work within educational systems to assist students to plan their educational programs, make career choices, and develop positive attitudes about themselves and their capabilities. Counselors may aid in the integration of handicapped students in a mainstreamed setting, work with gifted or talented students to plan a program of study that recognizes their special abilities, or help disabled students to acquire appropriate social and interpersonal skills.

Although psychologists are concerned with learning needs, they are also identified with social and emotional needs. As individual, group, or family therapists, clinical psychologists are frequently involved in assisting exceptional individuals and their families. Like psychologists, vocational rehabilitation counselors and special educators are also identified with the social and emotional needs of exceptional people. As special educators work with young children, adolescents, and young adults in school settings, they continually attend to social and emotional development. It is their responsibility to see that the individualized education program addresses skill building in these areas. Rehabilitation counselors, working with adolescents and adults, are concerned with complete habilitation of the individual. Their efforts often focus on the ability to meet people, make friends, work cooperatively, and become a part of the community.

Professions Concerned with Medical and Health Needs

Throughout the history of the treatment of exceptionality, individuals in the medical and health-related professions have been instrumental in initiating and developing programs for exceptional people. Although many of the first schools were begun by physicians, today these professionals are more closely identified with medical and health needs. Included among medical professionals are physicians, nurses, physical therapists, occupational therapists, nutritionists, and dentists.

As with nonhandicapped individuals, the physician's role with exceptional people varies from person to person. Their involvement may be as intensive as restorative surgery and life support or as routine as health maintenance or occasional treatment of acute illness. Medical specialty areas most likely to interact with exceptional individuals and their families include: neonatology, physical medicine and rehabilitation, pediatrics, genetics, neurology, and psychiatry.

Nurses, especially pediatric nurse practitioners and public health nurses, are often involved with disabled individuals and their families. Their role varies but often includes prevention, parent counseling, health screening, and case management. Nurses frequently work with families of young handicapped children with physical and medical problems. They may work in the child's home or in schools, clinics, hospitals, private physicians' offices, or residential settings.

Physical therapists (PTs) and occupational therapists (OTs) are concerned with motoric functioning. Physical therapists have traditionally treated lower extremity problems whereas occupational therapists were more concerned with arm and hand function. In recent years that distinction has blurred, but some specialization has remained with physical therapists more concerned with mobility and large motor activities and occupational therapists more concerned with independent living, sensory-motor, and fine motor skills. Physical therapists have maintained much stronger ties to the medical profession and offer treatment only with a physician's prescription. Although OTs consult with physicians regarding treatment plans, they are not required to practice by prescription. Both OTs and PTs can provide valuable information about typical and atypical motor development, assist in determining an individual's current and potential motor functioning, provide training in the use of appliances or prosthetic devices, and help in preventing further handicaps through correct positioning, relaxation, and range of motion techniques.

Nutritionists who specialize in health and medication-related nutritional problems often work with exceptional individuals and their families. For example, syndromes such as phenylketonuria (PKU) require special diets to prevent further problems and, with chronic health disorders such as cystic fibrosis and diabetes, careful dietary planning and monitoring is necessary. Less well known, but equally important, are the dietary needs created by certain medications. Many drugs used to control seizures deplete the body of needed vitamins and minerals; individuals taking these drugs need to be aware of their supplemental nutritional needs. In addition to helping individuals and families develop special diets, nutritionists provide education about healthy eating habits which can prevent other health problems.

Finally, dentists are often involved with exceptional individuals. Their role may be one of preventive dentistry, patient education, and routine treatment. It may also involve serving with a team of physicians, surgeons, and speech and language professionals to restore or repair cranial and facial anomalies which are a part of some syndromes.

Each of these disciplines makes major contributions to the provision of quality services to exceptional individuals. Their roles vary with the exceptionality and the age of the individual, but they are the core of an interdisciplinary team.

THE IMPACT OF EXCEPTIONALITY

Exceptionality is not a theoretical abstraction but a reality that touches the lives of millions of people. Whether the exceptional ability or disability is heralded as a cause for rejoicing or grief, its impact is felt not only by the exceptional person but also by his or her family and loved ones. The force of this impact is influenced by many factors, not the least of which is the exceptional person's individuality. In addition, the effects of exceptionality differ across the lifespan and in relation to the type and severity of the condition.

Differential Effects Through the Lifespan

The concept of development is usually associated with childhood and adolescence, periods when developmental changes are obvious and dramatic. However, it is equally appropriate to speak of adult development and the changes that occur in the span of time between adolescence and old age. Attention to the adult years is especially germane to the study of exceptionality because it is during this period that persons are expected to function independently.

The lifespan can be separated into three major developmental periods: infancy and the preschool years (from birth to age 5), the school years (from age 5 to age 18 or the completion of formal secondary schooling), and adulthood (beginning at approximately age 18 and extending through old age to death). Since each of these periods is characterized by different sets of developmental issues, each is affected somewhat differently by exceptionality.

The accomplishments of the normally developing child in the years from birth to five are astounding. In addition to impressive physical growth, preschoolers acquire an amazing array of skills. They learn to creep, stand, walk, run, and jump (locomotion); to feed, dress, and toilet themselves (self-help); to laugh and play and interact cooperatively with others (interpersonal relations); to talk and to understand speech (communication); and to match, discriminate, count, and classify (thinking and learning). Exceptionality can affect the acquisition of any one of these types of important skills. However, since developmental areas are interrelated, seldom is the impact of the ability or disability limited to a single realm of functioning.

Children identified as exceptional before the age of five typically represent the more extreme abilities and disabilities. Unusually able preschoolers, characterized by accelerated development, perform at levels expected of older youngsters; they may teach themselves to read and write, learn to play a musical instrument, or begin a study of chemistry, entomology, or a second language. Disabled preschoolers, in contrast, are developmentally delayed and often fail to attain developmental milestones at the expected ages. Severely retarded children, for example, may not yet have learned to walk and talk at age three. Some young children, such as those with visual impairments, acquire many skills at the average rate but are hindered by the disability in the attainment of others.

Of critical importance during this period of the lifespan are the effects of the exceptionality upon the family. Most people do not expect to become the parents of an exceptional child, particularly a disabled one; children do not picture their new brother or sister as deaf, blind, or physically handicapped. When an infant or young child is diagnosed as disabled, parents may react with shock, denial, grief, anger, and depression (Drotar, Baskiewicz, Irvin, Kennell, & Klaus, 1975; Solnit & Stark, 1961). Even the identification of giftedness may be unsettling if this is incongruent with the family's view of the child or its expectations for him or her. Most parents, as they begin to understand the limitations or special abilities of their exceptional child, recognize the importance of providing a warm, supportive home environment to encourage and stimulate early development. Intervention efforts during the infancy and preschool years focus on the needs of the child, the parents as primary caregivers, or both. Typical services include pediatric medical care, intensive early childhood education programs, parenting training, and parent support groups made up of other mothers and fathers of exceptional children.

In the school years, children extend their range of experience from the home and neighborhood to the school and community. Development and physical growth continue while schooling and interaction with other children contribute to the acquisition of many new skills. By the end of the elementary grades, the average child can read, write, spell, and calculate with some facility, and will have some knowledge of science, social studies, history, art, and music. In addition, the child has learned to cope with the behavioral expectations of the school and is well established in a peer group. The teenage years are marked by the physical changes of puberty and emerging sexuality, the growing acceptance of the peer group as the source of approval and behavioral standards, and movement toward the independence of adulthood. Secondary education continues the development of basic literacy skills and content knowledge in subjects such as history and science; new areas of study are introduced including, at least for some students, vocational classes. Throughout the junior high and high school years, the aim is preparation for the future whether that be entry into the workplace or a continuation of formal education in a postsecondary setting.

Exceptional children may begin the school experience already ahead of or behind their age-mates. The precocious child may have mastered the content of the first few grades; the severely disabled youngster at five may be learning the skills average children learn at age two or three. Other less extreme abilities and disabilities first become apparent in the school years when children are confronted with the academic demands of subjects such as reading and writing or when they are expected to conform to the social and behavioral standards of the school environment.

In the elementary grades, intervention typically is educational in nature with the purpose of attending to both learning and social needs. For gifted and talented children, this may mean passage through the grades at an accelerated pace or enrichment of the standard instructional program. With disabled individuals, instruction is geared to the needs of each child whether this requires teaching walking skills, the rudiments of reading, or strategies for making friends. In the high school years, preparation for adulthood assumes major importance, as it does for average adolescents. Gifted students may seek early admission to college. Some disabled students also will prepare for advanced study; others will train during high school for positions in the work force. For those severely handicapped students for whom competitive employment is not yet an option, education continues to stress acquisition of critical skills, particularly those concerned with independent living and vocational readiness.

The role of the family changes somewhat as the child enters the school years. No longer is the home the primary setting for learning; the responsibility for formal education has been assumed by the school (although children of course continue to learn from their parents and siblings). For parents of exceptional children, participation in their child's education may mean continued efforts to advise, to cooperate with, and even to influence the school, particularly if the parents feel the instructional program being provided is not the most appropriate. As the exceptional child becomes a teenager, the family concerns itself with planning for the future. At this time, parents must again come to grips with the very real limitations of some disabilities. If it is not probable that the child will become able to live independently, important decisions must be made about who will care for this person, where he or she will live, and who will take responsibility at the death of the parents.

Adulthood, the period in which persons assume responsibility for the conduct of their own lives, usually begins soon after the completion of high school, although postsecondary training may continue for a number of years. Young adults are expected to support themselves through some type of employment and to set up and maintain a new home environment separate from that of their parents. For many, dating, courtship, and marriage lead to the beginning of a family of their own and the responsibilities of parenting. In the middle years of adulthood, vocational pursuits continue and leisure pastimes begin to assume greater importance as child-rearing duties end and adults prepare for the coming years of maturity. With retirement from the work force, older adults are free to pursue recreational interests and enjoy social interactions with friends and family. In old age, declining health and physical problems may force mature adults to curtail some of their activities and to relinquish a portion of their self-sufficiency.

Some exceptional persons cope with the demands of adulthood so success-fully that society no longer considers them exceptional. Mild disabilities, though they do not disappear, lose their significance if the person is able to secure employment, maintain a home, and raise a family. Gifted and talented individuals cease to be a concern as they blend in with the rest of the adult population; while they may stand out as leaders in the vocations they select, certainly this is not perceived as a reason for intervention. For other exceptional persons, support remains a critical need during adulthood. Intervention may be limited to minimal assistance with tasks of daily living, such as the provision of transportation services to physically handicapped individuals. It may extend to vocational, social, and recreational areas for severely disabled adults unable to work com-petitively or live independently. Residential services become necessary for some disabled adults when their family is no longer able to provide care or as aging intensifies the effects of the disability.

A final factor related to lifespan issues is the age of onset of the exceptionality. Abilities and disabilities present from birth (even though they may not be dis-covered at this time) are considered congenital. Special gifts and talents are usually placed in this category. Adventitious exceptionalities are those that occur at some later point in life. A disability can occur at any age but, generally, the earlier the age of onset, the more debilitating its effects. Persons who sustain disabilities at later ages have the advantage of a period of normal development; they have had the opportunity to acquire a repertoire of skills, some of which may remain unaffected by the disability or serve to lessen its effects. For example, adventitiously deaf persons who experienced normal speech and language de-velopment before the onset of the hearing loss are typically less handicapped in communication skills than congenitally deaf persons.

Effects of Different Exceptionalities

Exceptionalities do not produce uniform effects; they do not have equal impact upon the lives of exceptional persons and their families. Exceptionalities differ in type and severity, and their influence is related to these two dimensions. Type refers to the general nature of the exceptionality (that is, whether it is a cognitive, affective, sensory, or physical condition) and to the specific ability or disability. Severity, in contrast, is a description of the extent or magnitude of the exceptionality.

In general, the more severe the exceptionality, the more influence it will exert. A severe hearing loss, for example, is more limiting than a mild one, a great gift or talent more enabling than a lesser one. The degree of severity affects the intensity with which the condition impinges upon the person's capability to perform important life tasks. More severe exceptionalities spread their effects over more areas of functioning; milder exceptionalities facilitate or hinder the acquisition of fewer critical skills. Thus, it is easier to compensate for the effects of milder conditions since they disrupt development less dramatically.

However, it is important to recognize that abilities and disabilities are considered mild only in relation to other exceptionalities; all exceptionalities represent a significant departure from expected performance. The term mild is a misleading one since it suggests a small or insignificant difference. No person with a mild disability would consider it unimportant; no family of a mildly handicapped child would call the condition insignificant. A disability is mild only in the sense that it is less severe, less debilitating, less serious than other disabilities.

Within each exceptionality, it is possible to describe a range of severity. The condition of mental retardation, for example, is classified into the levels of mild, moderate, severe, and profound, and a similar system is used for hearing losses. Learning disabilities are characterized as mild or severe, and visually handicapped persons are described as either partially sighted or blind. These different levels of performance within each exceptionality point up the important role of severity in determining the effects of the condition.

The type of exceptionality also influences the degree of its impact. One factor relating to type is the visibility of the condition, that is, whether it is immediately apparent to the observer. In general, the most visible conditions are those involving physical or visual impairments. Obvious physical manifestations such as a missing limb or the poor motor coordination associated with cerebral palsy are visible signs of difference, ones that call attention to the person's disability before he or she has had the opportunity to demonstrate competence. Even the presence of a wheelchair, crutches, a white cane, or a guide dog may influence the way in which the person is perceived and create very real barriers to social acceptance. However, there is no relation between the visibility of a condition and the extent of its impact upon important life functions. A person with severe physical involvement may be brilliant, socially adept, and vocationally successful; another, showing no visible signs of exceptionality, may be extremely disabled. It is simply not possible to predict a person's capabilities by outward appearances.

A more important factor than the difference in visibility across types of exceptionalities is the variation in severity. Exceptionalities vary in the comprehensiveness of their impact; those considered more severe influence a greater number and range of important life functions. Among school-age individuals, for example, the conditions of learning disabilities, mild mental retardation, and behavior disorders are sometimes referred to as the mild handicaps. These disabilities are judged to be mild because, in contrast with severe mental retardation and emotional disturbance, their influence is less comprehensive and therefore less debilitating.

Cognitive exceptionalities such as mental retardation are generally regarded as more serious than sensory or physical disabilities. Mental retardation is a global disorder affecting performance of a wide range of critical life activities; physical and sensory disabilities leave some areas unaffected and in these areas performance remains normal. Mental retardation and giftedness are the most intense of the cognitive exceptionalities. Among the sensory impairments, the loss of hearing is considered more disabling than the loss of vision, at least when it occurs in childhood. Although blindness is a more conspicuous handicap, deafness is the more severe because it interferes not only with the ability to hear but also with the development of important language and thinking skills. The affective disorder of emotional disturbance is difficult to characterize in relation to other exceptionalities. At one end of its continuum is the mild disability of behavior disorders; at the other end is severe emotional disturbance, a condition capable of producing devastating effects across all areas of functioning.

When exceptionalities occur in combination, the dimensions of type and severity remain important but it is also necessary to evaluate the interaction between the exceptional conditions. Multiple disabilities are likely to be more serious than single disabilities, particularly if they affect different areas of functioning. For example, when the sensory disorders of blindness and deafness are combined, the effects of both disabilities are aggravated since neither vision nor hearing remains intact to compensate for the loss of the other sense. In contrast, when giftedness occurs in conjunction with a disabling condition, the effects of the ability tend to mitigate the effects of the disability. While giftedness will not completely dispel the limitations imposed by a sensory, physical, or learning disability, it will to some degree lessen its impact.

HISTORY OF SOCIETY'S CONCERN FOR EXCEPTIONAL PEOPLE

The condition of exceptionality has been recognized throughout the world from ancient to modern times, but the treatment of exceptional people has varied significantly from period to period and from culture to culture. The tolerance for difference in any social system is influenced by the society's beliefs and traditions, religious views, economic stability, and confidence in its ability to accommodate change. Exceptional individuals have been protected, if not fully accepted, in periods and cultures in which society has held generally positive attitudes about the human condition, when religious beliefs have portrayed the deity or deities as benevolent, and when the economic base was firm and there was no internal or external threat of change. In less secure times, exceptional individuals have been denied their rights, their dignity as persons, and sometimes their lives by the larger society. Although each area of exceptionality has its own history, general practices in the treatment of exceptional persons can be chronicled from ancient times to the present.

The Early Civilizations

Little is known about the treatment of exceptional individuals prior to Egyptian civilization, but at least one archeological study of Neanderthal people demonstrates that disabled persons existed before recorded history and sometimes occupied positions of influence and respect within their tribes. In a description of the skeletal remains of persons presumed to have lived over 45,000 years ago, Solecki (1971) detailed the disabilities of one of the males: probable blindness; congenital malformation of the right arm, collarbone, and shoulder; damage to the skull; and arthritis. Although this ancient man might be considered multiply handicapped, the burial mound covering his grave and the offerings surrounding it suggest he was an important and revered member of his tribe.

Treatment of individuals with disabilities varied among the early cultures of the Near East. In ancient Egypt, there was a strong taboo against infanticide, yet its practice sometimes resulted in the slaying of newborns with disabilities. Around 2500 BC, Babylon adopted the Code of Hammurabi which protected women and children, but there is no evidence that handicapped individuals were included or that its provisions improved the quality of life of those it protected. Words which express concern about and compassion for those less fortunate can be found in the writings and teachings of all the world's great religious leaders: Confucius (551–479 BC); Siddhārtha Gautama (563–483 BC), founder of Buddhism; Jesus (0–33 AD); and Mohammed (569–622 AD). Yet, when these teachings have been translated into practice, the result for disabled persons has not always been more sympathetic treatment. For example, while the Ten Commandments, the Torah, and the teachings of Jesus advocate humane treatment of the poor and the disabled, interpretation of these words in early civilizations linked disability to sinfulness and the cure of these afflictions to goodness. Disabling conditions came to be viewed as the result of sin, and a cure through faith was the only acceptable treatment; if the individual was not cured, it could only be because he or she still harbored evil or because of lack of faith. This early association of sinfulness with disability has had a profound effect upon society's treatment of handicapped persons throughout the centuries and it has yet to be completely dispelled.

The societies of Greece, Rome, and Sparta valued fitness, intelligence, beauty, strength, and courage and so each attempted to eliminate individuals with disabilities that interfered with the development of a stronger, more perfect population. In Sparta, fathers determined whether newborns lived or died and, if the father decided the child should be allowed to live, the infant was then brought before a council of inspectors who ruled on its fitness. Infants found or suspected to be defective were thrown from a cliff or left to die in the wilderness. Infanticide was also practiced in Greece and Rome, although treatment of disabled babies varied during different periods of history. At the same time that these cultures were making major contributions to law, philosophy, mathematics, art, and science, a common practice was the killing of infants who were female, disabled, or illegitimate. In fact, some of the greatest thinkers of the time were influential in maintaining the practice. The evil nature of the weak and the stupid was often referred to during the Homeric period (1300–1100 BC) in the legends of Odysseus and again by Plato (427?–347 BC) near the end of Greece's major period of influence (Scheerenberger, 1982). Accounts of the Roman Empire describe the use of mentally retarded persons as fools and jesters to entertain in the homes of the wealthy (Kanner, 1964).

Greek and Roman history and mythology frequently mention blind individuals and the use of blinding as punishment. These accounts suggest a large population of blind persons in Greece and Rome; some of these became famous seers venerated by the people while others lived with poverty and persecution (Lowenfeld,

1975). One early forerunner of contemporary social service was a public support system for disabled Athenians. This plan, implemented by the reformer and lawgiver Solon (639?–559? BC), was designed to provide for soldiers crippled or blinded in conquest but was later broadened to include civilians with disabilities. As in modern times, eligibility requirements were stringent and the amount of money was only about half of that needed to maintain a modest standard of living.

In the years that followed, other attempts were made to provide for persons with disabilities. Families sometimes cared for their disabled children; foundling homes were established for children without families; and in some areas such as Geel, in Belgium, the entire community opened its doors to those with disabilities. Treatment during this period was limited to the basics of food, clothing, and shelter. No thought was given to assisting the disabled in any other way, and even this brief respite from persecution was about to end.

The Middle Ages and the Renaissance

During the Middle Ages, many disabled individuals lived as beggars and clustered together in towns or in groups that wandered the countryside. Especially common were blind beggars, frequently the subject of tricks and taunting by townspeople (Lowenfeld, 1975). A few of these persons, gifted in song and rhyme, traveled as troubadours and were known as the "blind bards." Although their skills in music and verse earned them a place in history and legend, their vocation was determined more by their disability than their talents.

In the Renaissance, as in early Rome, handicapped individuals (especially those with mental retardation, emotional disturbance, epilepsy, and physical deformities) served as jesters for kings and queens. These "clowns" of the court entertained the royal family and their guests by antics which drew attention to their disabilities. Some handicapped persons were kept by scientists to serve as diviners. Tycho Brahe (1546–1601), father of astronomy, is said to have kept as a prophet a man described in some accounts as mentally retarded, in others as a catatonic schizophrenic. Brahe believed that this man's gestures and utterances were revelations about the stars and heavens.

The Reformation, with its emphasis upon religious retribution and its reliance on superstition, was a period of great suffering for handicapped persons. The slowness of the mentally retarded, the seizures of those with epilepsy, and the mutism of the deaf were interpreted as clear signs of demonic possession; exorcism was practiced to purge the devils from those afflicted. Both John Calvin and Martin Luther believed that individuals with disabling differences did not have souls and therefore were not people at all (Kanner, 1964); since they were subhuman, society bore no responsibility for their welfare.

Although general treatment of disabled individuals was inhumane, there was some movement to improve the lives of this segment of the population. Juan Luis Vives (1492–1540), a Spanish social reformer and humanist, wrote persuasively of the kinds of useful work that blind people could do if trained. He included not only jobs such as weaving and assisting in a blacksmith's shop but also study of the sciences and arts (Lowenfeld, 1975). In 1620 in Spain, Juan Bonet published the first book on education of the deaf in which he set forth his teaching methods. Although others had also worked successfully with deaf members of the royal family, Bonet's account was the first to survive (Moores, 1978). At about the same time, Georg Philip Harsdorffer of Germany described a way to make letters distinguishable to the blind by writing with a stylus on tablets covered with wax. Francesco Lana-Terzi suggested that symbols consisting of dots and angles be used to represent letters of the Italian alphabet and that these be engraved or embossed so that they could be read by the blind.

The Eighteenth and Nineteenth Centuries

The eighteenth and nineteenth centuries marked the real beginnings of the search for ways not only to care for disabled persons but also to educate them. In 1793, the physician Philipe Pinel (1745–1826) became the superintendent of the asylum at Bicêtre in France (Scheerenberger, 1982). The Bicêtre was originally intended to provide food, clothing, protection, and some education for the retarded persons that it sheltered but, at the time Pinel was placed in charge, it had grown into a large, filthy asylum. Although large institutions such as this often began as sanctuaries from harsh treatment on the outside, they rapidly grew into unmanageable, dehumanizing places in which treatment was far harsher than that in the community. Like the infamous Bedlam in England, the Bicêtre housed the poor, retarded, insane, and other outcasts from society; inmates were shackled in overcrowded cells and corridors, food was limited, medical treatment unavailable, and attempts at treatment nonexistent. Pinel instituted immediate reforms, such as the unshackling of inmates, and attempted rehabilitation of the mentally retarded and mentally ill (MacMillan, 1982).

Within the same period, Jacob Rodrigue Pereire (1715–1780) began work with persons who had been deaf and mute since birth. His methods were successful and influenced the work of Jean Marc Gaspard Itard (1774–1838) with the "wild boy of Aveyron." Itard, Pinel's student and a physician at the Institution for Deaf Mutes in Paris, founded the science of otology, diseases of the ear, but is better known for his efforts to educate Victor, the young boy found wandering alone in the woods of Aveyron, France. When brought to Itard, Victor made only grunting sounds and had no civilized behavior. Itard worked with him intensively for five years, and Victor gained many skills from the enriched environment, interaction, and stimulation. Although Itard himself was disheartened because Victor had learned to speak only a few words and remained limited when compared with normal individuals, the French medical community praised the remarkable changes brought about by Itard's instruction (Kanner, 1964).

Edouard Onesimus Seguin (1812–1880) worked with Itard for a year before Itard's death in an attempt to educate an idiotic child (the term used at the time to describe retardation) and, in 1839, he established a class for "idiots" at Salpetriere in Paris and another at Bicêtre in 1841. Seguin's methods, untested at the time, provided a basis for aspects of instructional practices in use today: observational assessment, practice of activities to be learned, use of concrete objects and "real" learning materials, and commitment to the belief that all children, regardless of their degree of retardation, can learn. Seguin's successes with mentally retarded children were heralded by the Paris Academy of Sciences, and visitors from the United States and Europe came to observe his methods. Following the overthrow of the king in 1848, Seguin emigrated to the United States where, in 1876, he and six American leaders founded the Association of Medical Officers of American Institutions for Idiotic and Feeble-Minded Persons, known today as the American Association on Mental Deficiency.

Louis Braille (1809–1852), who lost his sight in a childhood accident, developed the communication system for the blind which bears his name. By adapting Charles Barbier's technique for sending military messages in the dark, Braille devised the system of reading and writing which gave blind persons access to the world of print (Lowenfeld, 1975). From its initial beginnings in Paris, the system spread to all countries of the world.

In the early 1800s, Thomas Hopkins Gallaudet, a graduate of Harvard about to enter the ministry, became interested in teaching Alice Cogswill, the nine-year-old deaf daughter of his neighbor. Gallaudet's success in teaching Alice reaffirmed her father's commitment to establishing a school for the deaf; money was raised, and Gallaudet traveled to Europe to study the methods in use there. In Great Britain, he was rebuffed by the Braidwoods who considered their system of teaching the deaf a family secret. Gallaudet traveled to France to study with Sicard and then returned to the United States with Laurent Clerc, one of Sicard's instructors who himself was deaf. On April 15, 1817, the American Asylum for the Education of the Deaf and Dumb (later the American School for the Deaf) was opened in Connecticut (Moores, 1978).

In 1829, the New England Asylum for the Blind (later renamed the Perkins Institution and Massachusetts Asylum for the Blind) was incorporated. It opened in 1832 with Samuel Gridley Howe as the first superintendent. Howe believed that blind persons could be educated to become productive and independent adults, that physical education should be a required part of their training, and that they should be expected to learn to care for themselves (Lowenfeld, 1975). The model Howe used in Massachusetts was disseminated throughout the United States.

Maria Montessori (1870–1952), the first woman to receive the doctorate of medicine from the University of Rome, was directress of an experimental school designed for mentally handicapped children. Her methods were so successful that many of her students learned to read and write well enough to pass their public school examinations. In 1907, she organized a school for children from low income families in a tenement house in the slums of Rome. The curriculum was based on three areas she felt were essential: practical life activities, sensory training, and formal academic studies (Gutek, 1972). Modifications of Montessori's original method continue to provide direction to many contemporary programs for both exceptional and nonexceptional children.

The programs developed by Maria Montessori which include systematically arranging a child's environment are effective in teaching exceptional children.

The 1900s

At the turn of the century in the United States, institutions were the major service delivery model for severely handicapped children and youth. Residential institutions located in state capitals served blind and deaf children; mental retardation was not yet differentiated from emotional disturbance and these groups were also removed from their communities and sent to state institutions or training schools. Less severely handicapped persons remained in their home communities and, in larger cities where special education classes were available, they attended school. Where special schooling was not an option, many mildly and moderately handicapped children remained at home with their families and, as adults, took jobs which they could learn to perform.

In the early 1900s, two major influences affected society's views toward handicapped individuals. The first was Darwin's theory of evolution. Social Darwinists argued that heredity alone was responsible for the nature of an individual, only the strong should survive, and defects could be prevented by eliminating imperfect people.

The second influence was the testing movement. In Paris, Alfred Binet developed a measure in which a series of tasks were used to evaluate a child's mental age; mental age predicted probable success in school. The result of Binet's work with Theodore Simon was first published in 1905; it was later revised and a version designed for use in America. The instrument provided a reliable way of comparing the intellectual performance of one individual with that of another. Based on this first intelligence or IQ test, the American Association on Mental Deficiency revised its classification system; "moron" which referred to individuals with mild retardation was added to the traditional levels of "idiot" and "imbecile."

The Eugenics Movement grew out of a combination of forces: the development of intelligence tests, the belief that heredity rather than environment was the primary determinant of intelligence and behavior, and recognition that the educational techniques of Itard, Seguin, and Montessori did not eradicate all effects of disabilities. This movement was also influenced by genealogical studies such as that of Henry Goddard who traced the family history of the Kallikaks and concluded that "feeble mindedness" was hereditary. Proponents of eugenics assumed all social problems were caused by the breeding of inferior or contaminated stock and that elimination of such stock would cure the ills of society; they suggested that people with mental retardation and other disabilities be prohibited from having children. As a result, many states passed sterilization laws. Sterilization programs were carried out in institutions and communities, and thousands of handicapped individuals were sterilized with no regard for their wishes or rights. The eugenics movement did not end in the early 1900s. In Nazi Germany, thousands of mentally retarded, physically handicapped, and emotionally disturbed persons were put to death as part of Hitler's plan to create a master race (Rosen, Clark, & Kivitz, 1976).

School programs for children with disabilities were begun in the United States in the late 1800s and early 1900s; exceptional children were educated in separate special classes segregated from the rest of the school program. Classes for deaf, blind, mentally retarded, and emotionally disturbed children were offered in many large public school systems to prepare students to become contributing members of society. During the years of the Depression in the 1930s, the number of children served in special classes declined, but classes increased with the economic recovery following World War II. MacMillan (1982) estimated that by 1948 approximately 90,000 retarded children were attending special classes in public schools.

During the first half of the twentieth century, professionals interested in the treatment of disabilities began to build upon the work of pioneers such as Itard to develop new methods of education and training. In the early 1950s, public schools began to admit students with more severe handicaps; for example, in 1951, laws passed in California, Minnesota, and Wisconsin provided special programs for trainable mentally retarded students (Scheerenberger, 1982). Although concern was expressed over the segregated nature of special classes, these programs proliferated. The efficacy of special classes was studied and results were equivocal, but the number of separate programs continued to increase.

The dramatic growth in the 1950s and 1960s in educational, vocational, medical, and support services for disabled individuals was due primarily to the efforts

Table 1.3

Litigation Affecting Exceptional Individuals

Case	State	Year	Effects
Brown v. Board of Education	KS	1954	Established as a matter of law that racially segregated education was unequal
Hobson v. Hansen	DC	1967	Abolished the tracking system in public schools
Wolf v. Legislature State of Utah	UT	1969	Mandated public education for all children in Utah regardless of level of functioning
Spangler v. Board of Education	CA	1970	Established that group tests were inadequate for making placement decisions
Diana v. State Board of Education	CA	1970	Settled out of court with six mandates related to assessment of language minority children and their placement in special education classes
Doe v. Board of School Directors of the City of Milwaukee	WI	1970	Placed a temporary injunction on the placement of children on waiting lists for special education
Marlega v. Board of School Directors of the City of Milwaukee	WI	1970	Protected due process rights around exclusion from school on medical grounds
Wyatt v. Stickney	AL	1971	Affirmed that institutionalized individuals have the right to treatment based on an extension of the guarantees of the 14th (due process) and 8th (prohibition of cruel and unusual punishment) amendments
Mills v. Board of Education of the District of Columbia	DC	1972	Supported the right to education for all handicapped children and established the need for a hearing prior to exclusion or classification
Ricci v. Greenblatt	MA	1972	Required a review of institutionalized individuals' medical needs, lifted a hiring freeze, and required that comprehensive treatment programs be established
Pennsylvania Association for Retarded Children (PARC) v. Commonwealth of Pennsylvania	PA	1972	Settled in a consent agreement establishing the right to education for all retarded children in Pennsylvania
Larry P. v. Riles	CA	1972	Prohibited the use of individual intelligence tests in the placement of black children in special education classes

			Table 1.3 (continued)

Litigation Affecting Exceptional Individuals

Case	State	Year	Effects
New York State Association for Retarded Children, Inc. v. Rockefeller	NY	1975	Did not uphold right to treatment, but upheld rights of institutionalized individuals to be protected from harm
PASE v. Hannon	IL	1980	Determined that individual intelligence tests do not discriminate against black children and allowed their use with other measures in special education placement decisions
Pennhurst v. Halderman	PA	1981	Interpreted the Developmentally Disabled Assistance and Bill of Rights Act as a statement of national goals rather than a guarantee of treatment rights
Rowley v. Board of Education	NY	1982	Found PL 94–142 to guarantee procedural safeguards and an individualized education program but not equal educational opportunities for handicapped children

of one major group, parents of handicapped children. Although professionals supported the movement toward improved services, parents were the driving force behind the initiation and maintenance of programs. Parent organizations such as the National Association for Retarded Children and the Association for Children with Learning Disabilities fought on the local, state, and national levels for equal opportunities for handicapped children; their lobbying resulted in funding support for special education and other services. Parents played a major role in strengthening society's acknowledgement of the rights of handicapped persons, and they continue to do so today.

The period from 1960 to 1980, of all times in history, was the most active in the development of programs and assurance of rights of individuals with disabilities. The use of legislation and litigation to accomplish the goals of deinstitutionalization, normalization, and right to treatment is the hallmark of this era. Court cases which have guaranteed the rights of exceptional individuals are highlighted in Table 1.3. Many of these cases contributed to the passage of PL 94–142, the Education for All Handicapped Children Act of 1975, sometimes called the bill of rights for disabled persons. This law, along with Section 504 of the Rehabilitation Act of 1973, guarantees handicapped individuals equal access to programs and services. PL 94–142, the most significant piece of legislation related to the education of handicapped children and youth, provides a free, appropriate, public education to every school-age person identified as handicapped in the United States.

The history of the treatment of exceptional persons is not one of which the world can be proud. In every age and culture, individuals with differences have been stigmatized. Society's treatment of disabled persons has ranged from neglect to persecution and even extermination; only in the last century has there been general support for the education and training of those with disabilities. Throughout history, individuals concerned about the welfare of disabled persons have spoken for those not always able to speak for themselves; rarely, however, have handicapped people been consulted about their own destiny. The future may be different. With the enactment of important human rights legislation, the growing recognition by society that persons with differences are first of all persons, and the increasing visibility and assertiveness of disabled people, the twenty-first century may be one in which differences are not only acknowledged but also appreciated.

CURRENT PRACTICES

The major assumption underlying contemporary practice in the treatment of exceptionality is the principle of normalization. This philosophy, which originated in Denmark (Nirje, 1969) has come to influence policy development in the United States (Wolfensberger, 1972). Normalization, as defined by Nirje (1969), is "making available to the mentally retarded [and other disabled individuals] patterns and conditions of everyday life which are as close as possible to the norms and patterns of the mainstream of society" (p. 181). On the basis of this principle, exceptional individuals have moved from more to less restrictive educational, vocational, and residential settings. During the school years, handicapped students are educated in the mainstream to the maximum extent appropriate. Consistent with the normalization movement is the trend toward noncategorical programming. Since categorical labels such as "mentally retarded" and "physically handicapped" tend to stigmatize the individual while providing little direction for intervention, many programs cut across categories to serve persons with similar needs rather than similar labels.

These directions are reflected in Public Law 94–142, the Education for All Handicapped Children Act of 1975, which has had a profound effect on the detection of disability and provision of services. The law has five major requirements which must be met by any local, intermediate, or state public educational agency receiving federal funds:

1. All handicapped children must be provided a free and appropriate public education;
2. Children must be assessed for special education eligibility using instruments that are free from racial and cultural bias;
3. Each child must have a written individualized education program (IEP) which addresses long- and short-term instructional goals, the services to be provided, and how the child's progress will be evaluated;

4. Every handicapped child must be educated in the least restrictive environment (LRE), with nonhandicapped children to the greatest extent possible;
   and
5. Due process rights are guaranteed to each handicapped child and to his or
   her parent or guardian.

Local and state education agencies must provide a free and appropriate public
education to all handicapped individuals from the preschool years through
young adulthood regardless of the severity of the disability. Children and adolescents suspected of having handicapping conditions are assessed by a team of
trained professionals to determine their eligibility for special education services.
Instruments free of cultural, racial, and linguistic bias must be utilized, and
assessments may only be conducted with parental consent. A "child find" provision of the law requires that public schools seek out and assess individuals
from birth to age 21 who may need special educational services.

Following the multidisciplinary assessment, a meeting to develop the individualized education program (IEP) is convened. The IEP—written jointly by the
teacher, parents, student (when appropriate), and a representative of the administrative or supervisory staff of the school—is a plan describing the student's
placement, program, and services. Others who have conducted assessments such
as the psychologist, speech and language therapist, nurse, or counselor may also
provide input. Every IEP must include: (1) documentation of the student's current
levels of functioning; (2) annual goals or the accomplishments anticipated by the
end of the school year; (3) short-term goals written in instructional terms; (4) a
listing of the special education and related services that the child will be receiving; (5) the extent of integration with nonhandicapped students; (6) the projected
beginning date of services and their duration; and (7) the procedures for evaluating progress on an annual basis (Turnbull, Strickland, & Brantley, 1982). IEPs
must be written at least annually, and comprehensive evaluations conducted
every three years.

Timeliness for each of the procedures in special education assessment, placement, and review as well as procedures for hearings on any decision are included
in the PL 94–142 regulations. These procedural safeguards assure that students
are assessed and placed in a reasonable length of time and that the student's and
parents' rights are protected. If parents do not agree with the assessment, placement, or proposed instructional program, they may refuse to accept the services
and appeal the decision.

Section 504 of the Rehabilitation Act of 1973, as amended, provides the basis
for the enforcement of PL 94–142. Section 504, often referred to as the civil rights
legislation for handicapped individuals, was designed to eliminate discrimination based solely on a handicapping condition. This act applies to all agencies
receiving federal funds (including educational programs from preschool through
college) and contains the same requirements as those in PL 94–142. Additionally,
Section 504 contains fiscal sanctions and penalities for those agencies which do
not comply with its regulations. In combination, PL 94–142 and Section 504

contain provisions which, for the first time in history, guarantee the rights of all handicapped individuals to education, vocational training, employment, and other publicly sponsored services.

These laws provide guidelines for optimal development and delivery of special educational services and have considerably improved services to handicapped children and their families. Legislation, however, cannot guarantee that what actually occurs within a classroom represents the best educational practice. A great deal of work remains to be done to match exemplary instruction to the needs of exceptional students.

Detection of Exceptionalities

The first step in the provision of services to exceptional people is detection of the ability or disability. Some exceptionalities are obvious: blindness and deafness, paralysis or the loss of a limb, a marked delay or precociousness in the attainment of early developmental milestones. Others are less visible or represent more subtle deviations, making them more difficult to detect.

Identification procedures are based upon the assumption that the performance of exceptional persons is in some way discrepant from expected performance. However, expectations vary with the age, gender, and culture of the individual. The unbounded enthusiasm of the toddler for activity and exploration is viewed as inappropriate behavior in an older child who might be termed impulsive, undisciplined, or hyperactive. Rough play and fistfights are considered usual for boys, unusual for girls. Culture also influences behavioral expectations. The Pan-Asian child may sit silently in the classroom not because of an inability to respond but in respectful deference to the teacher (Lynch & Lewis, 1982). In the American Indian culture, cooperation and achievement of the group are valued, rather than competition and individual accomplishment (Pepper, 1976). Thus, standards for appropriate performance vary across cultures; a behavior that calls attention to itself in one cultural milieu may pass unnoticed in another. Because of this, Mercer (1979; Mercer & Lewis, 1977) recommends that exceptionality be determined on the basis of pluralistic standards which reflect not only the expectations of the general social system but also those of the individual's particular cultural group.

Various theoretical models propose differing views of the source of exceptionality, the appropriate criteria for its determination, and the goal of intervention. In the clinical or medical model, the exceptional condition is thought of as pathology which exists within the individual. Disabilities are viewed as diseases to be cured. Identification criteria are statistical with any departure from average or typical performance considered exceptional.

In contrast, the sociobehavioral model views exceptionalities as interactions between the characteristics of the individual and the demands of the environment. The goal of intervention is to improve functioning and this is accomplished through the education of the individual and adaptation of the environment. Multiple criteria which reflect the special needs of the individual and the environmental expectations for age, gender, and culture are used to determine whether or not an exceptionality exists. Kirk and Gallagher (1983) describe the shift from the medical model to the sociobehavioral or ecological perspective:

> As programs for exceptional children gradually expanded and included more children with mild handicaps—such as communication disorders, learning disabilities, behavior disorders, and mild mental retardation—it became clear that the definition of exceptional involved a mix of the individual's characteristics and the special demands the environment made on that individual. This recognition of the role of the environment in defining exceptionality has been widely referred to as moving from the medical model, which implies a physical condition or disease within the patient, to an ecological model, in which one sees the exceptional child in complex interaction with environmental forces. (p. 9)

In detection, it is necessary not only to identify the exceptionality but also to assess its effects upon performance. Merely establishing the existence of an ability or disability does not provide sufficient information for intervention; what is required is information about the exceptional person's special needs. Persons with the same exceptionality often function quite differently. Knowing that persons are learning disabled or mentally retarded, for example, gives little indication of their skill in getting along with others, holding a job, reading the newspaper, or caring for their personal needs.

Assessment is the process of gathering information about exceptional persons for the purpose of making intervention decisions. Assessment includes detection of the ability or disability and, when appropriate, diagnosis of the cause of the condition. Its primary purpose, however, is description of the exceptional person's ability to perform critical life activities and determination of his or her special learning, social-emotional, and physical-health needs.

Assessment begins with a comprehensive study of the individual across the dimensions of cognitive, affective, and sensory-physical growth and development. PL 94–142 guidelines, for example, specify several areas to consider: health, vision and hearing, motor abilities, general intelligence, academic performance, communication abilities, and social-emotional status. The environment in which the person is expected to perform is also the subject of study. Investigation of the ecologies of the home, community, school, and workplace provides important information about expectations and the ways in which environmental demands may exacerbate or lessen the effects of the exceptional condition. Because assessment involves gathering information about a wide variety of ecological concerns and individual characteristics, it is a multidisciplinary undertaking, drawing upon the expertise of several professions.

Assessment can be viewed as a series of steps that provide different types of information for different intervention decisions. McLoughlin and Lewis (1986) identify five steps in assessment: screening, qualification for services, program planning, monitoring progress, and program evaluation. Screening is the process of surveying large groups of individuals to identify persons who may be at risk for certain conditions; public schools, for example, routinely screen pupils for vision and hearing disorders. Individuals identified in screening efforts and those referred by concerned parents, teachers, or others may then be assessed to determine if an exceptionality qualifies them for services. Because it is not possible (and often not desirable) to intervene with all persons, it is necessary to select only those individuals whose special needs warrant extraordinary attention.

Once eligibility is established, the emphasis shifts to intervention decisions. Assessment is directed toward the specific needs of the individual and how these needs can best be met through special educational, vocational, recreational, medical, or social services. The intervention program is carefully planned, then implemented, and assessment continues. The progress of the individual is monitored and the effectiveness of the program evaluated to allow modification of the intervention strategy as needed.

Of the many techniques used to gather assessment information, the most common approach is direct measurement of the individual's performance. The person is presented with one or a series of test tasks in an attempt to elicit a representative sample of behavior. Norm-referenced tests are formal standardized measures designed so that the performance of the individual can be compared to the performance of a specific norm group (such as American children). Less formal criterion-referenced tests assess mastery of specific skill areas. Measures designed for administration to one person at a time are preferred for individuals who may be exceptional because these allow better control of the testing environment and more opportunity for observation of the person's behavior than group tests. Tests are available for a wide variety of purposes including assessment of hearing and vision, motor abilities, general intelligence, academic performance, communication abilities, and vocational aptitude and skill.

Observation is another frequently used assessment technique. No test task is introduced; the individual is simply observed in interaction with his or her environment. Observation is a flexible technique, one that can be used in any ecology: the home, classroom, grocery store, bank, or job site. It is particularly useful for gathering information about interactive skills such as communication and interpersonal relationships. A third major assessment strategy utilizes persons other than the exceptional individual as sources of information. Parents, teachers, friends, employers, or others serve as informants to report their observations, and sometimes evaluations, of the individual's performance in a variety of settings. Information is gathered from informants through interviews, questionnaires, and rating scales. This technique is valuable when observation and direct measurement are not possible (as in tracing a person's developmental, health, or school history) and when it is important to consider the views of important others in the exceptional person's life.

Services for Children and Youth

The primary services needed by exceptional children and youth are diagnostic, educational, medical, therapeutic, and protective. All children suspected of being exceptional need a comprehensive evaluation conducted by professionals in all of the relevant disciplines. Public schools provide developmental, educational, and psychological assessments under the provisions of PL 94–142. Many clinics, notably the university-affiliated programs at large universities, also provide comprehensive, interdisciplinary assessment services which include medical evaluation.

The service delivery system with the most responsibility to exceptional children and youth is the educational system. Within special education, students may be served in a variety of options ranging from the most restrictive (least contact with nonhandicapped peers) to the least restrictive. Although the restrictiveness of an environment is ultimately determined by the student's needs and characteristics, some options are by nature more restrictive than others. Most restrictive is a residential institution where students live and attend school. Although this type of placement is far less common now than in the past, some exceptional individuals—such as those with severe multiple handicaps or severe emotional disturbance whose home care is too difficult for their natural or foster family—are served in institutions.

Special schools serving only handicapped individuals are available for students with severe learning or behavioral problems or those with sensory disabilities. Although this once was a popular delivery system, it is no longer favored. School systems throughout the country are attempting to move students out of the segregated special centers to more integrated normalized educational environments.

Students whose needs cannot be adequately met in a regular classroom may be placed in a special class in an elementary or secondary school. These classes are characterized by nongraded programs with the same students and teacher working together for more than one year. Although this option is less restrictive than placement in a special school, the contact students actually have with nonhandicapped peers varies considerably. In some schools, there is a free flow between regular and special education classes with many combined activities; in others, handicapped students are almost as isolated from the mainstream as they were in segregated schools.

One of the newer arrangements for delivering special education services is the resource room. In this model, exceptional students spend the majority of their school day in a regular classroom with extra help from a special education resource teacher. In addition to providing instruction to students, the resource teacher may help the regular class teacher plan for the handicapped students in the class. This model has aided mainstreaming efforts by providing additional instruction to exceptional students as well as support for regular education teachers.

Many students with learning, physical, or sensory handicaps also get "pull out" services from specialists in their areas of need. For example, a blind student may be integrated into a regular seventh grade classroom with the support of a mobility instructor who provides instruction on cane traveling skills; a physically handicapped student might receive therapy from an OT or a PT while in a program for multiply handicapped students. Because specialists are often assigned to more than one school, they are referred to as itinerant teachers; since the services they provide differ from traditional academic instruction, they are described as support or ancillary services.

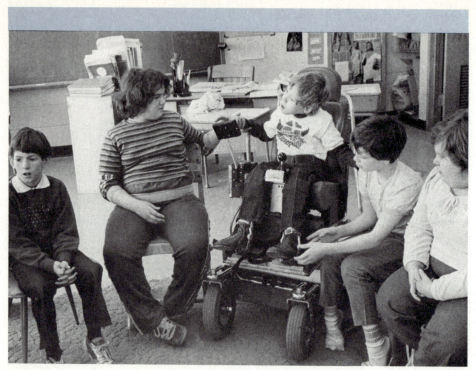

Students needing special services may spend part of their school day in a resource room and be mainstreamed for other classroom activities.

The school services described thus far are designed for individuals with handicaps rather than for those with special gifts or talents. In general, this lack of attention is representative of the services for gifted and talented individuals. Less has been done to enhance the abilities of this group because it has been assumed that they are skilled enough to learn without the benefit of special services. Even PL 94–142 does not address gifted and talented students. It is for handicapped individuals only, and its provisions do not apply to the gifted and talented. There are, however, several educational models used to provide service to gifted students. Some districts have special classes in which gifted students are segregated from their peers and the curriculum is more advanced. In addition, gifted and talented students may attend regular classes but receive special instruction for part of their day in a resource program. Acceleration or grade skipping is used to allow students to enter college at age 15 or 16. Several large cities have developed special high schools which recognize and encourage special abilities. Most well known are schools like the Bronx High School of Science or the School for the Performing Arts featured in the movie *Fame.* Although options do exist, there are generally fewer programs for gifted and talented students than for handicapped students. Fewer still are available for students who are both handicapped and gifted.

Medical services for children and youth are provided through private physicians, clinics, health maintenance organizations, and regional centers for the developmentally disabled. In some states, the Department of Public Health or Maternal and Child Health is charged with conducting screening clinics to detect disabilities. National screening programs such as the Early Periodic Screening, Detection, and Treatment (EPSDT) program are available free of charge to low income families. Medical services are also available from the many university hospitals involved in research and treatment of disabling conditions.

Therapeutic services include occupational and physical therapy as well as psychotherapy. Occupational and physical therapy may be provided through public or private medical facilities or by a unit of the state government. Although the name of the department varies from state to state, the general services are the same. Some school systems employ physical and occupational therapists to work with students in special education programs. Having educators and therapists on the same staff has proven an effective way to provide more integrated services. Psychotherapy for exceptional individuals and/or their families is provided by therapists (clinical psychologists, social workers, psychiatrists) in private practice and through mental health clinics.

All states have some office responsible for protecting the rights of minors. These departments are generally part of the state's social service system and work to protect children from abuse and neglect. They often become involved with exceptional children and youth because of the higher incidence of abuse of this population. They may also oversee the adoption of exceptional individuals and monitor the state's residential facilities.

Services for Adults and the Aged

All adults, handicapped and nonhandicapped, usually need medical, vocational, and counseling services at some time during their lives. Exceptional individuals may need additional support related to housing, transportation, family planning, recreation and leisure, or protection and advocacy.

In many states, medical, counseling, and social services are provided for adults with disabilities through regionalized centers. These centers employ professionals from a variety of disciplines who deliver direct services to handicapped individuals. Departments of Vocational Rehabilitation offer vocational assessment, job training and counseling, and instruction in skills of independent living. Rehabilitation counselors are most involved with clients with acquired disabilities, but in recent years their caseloads have included an increasing number of individuals disabled from childhood.

Disabled adults in many communities have established service centers which provide counseling, assist in finding housing or transportation, or sponsor recreational events. Some, with the help of federal funds, have developed centers for independent living which enable multiply handicapped individuals to live independently in an adapted apartment with a caregiver nearby to assist as needed. Parent organizations have also been instrumental in developing group homes, recreational programs, and transportation services for adults with disabilities.

The financial and protection needs of adults with disabilities are generally served through state governmental agencies. Persons below a specified annual income are eligible for medical insurance and a monthly stipend paid through the social security system. State governments also have an office of protection and advocacy which protects disabled adults from exploitation and lobbies for their rights.

Services for developmentally disabled adults are less well developed than those for children. The resources are not managed by a single agency or regulated by federal law. This results in wide variations in adult services from state to state and from community to community. Recently, disabled adults have organized and become a vocal group lobbying for equal opportunities and basic human rights. Their efforts have created a greater awareness of the needs of disabled individuals and have improved access to programs and services through the reduction of architectural and attitudinal barriers.

Lifespan Services

Programs and services for handicapped individuals are not dissimilar to those for nonhandicapped people. Both groups use educational, medical, social, and vocational services at various times throughout their lives. With the growing recognition that handicapped and nonhandicapped individuals are more alike than different, all services are becoming less segregated; disabled and able-bodied individuals are beginning to be served by the same physicians, social workers, psychologists, and teachers in the same settings. This integration of services has been one of the most important changes in the service delivery system in the past ten years. Segregation because of disability is ending as is segregation by sex, race, color, and age.

The services vary in only three ways: (1) the time that they are first provided, (2) their intensity, and (3) their duration. The case of Emily, presented below, illustrates these variations.

Emily's life is not dramatically different from most of ours. She attended school, took a job, and has begun to live as an adult on her own. The major differences are in the time that she first received services, the intensity of those services, and their duration. After intensive medical intervention at birth, Emily began school in an early intervention program. By age three, she was already in a school program. Throughout her educational career, she had additional services provided by a resource teacher and a physical therapist. In junior high school she was involved in vocational training; and in high school she participated in community-based on-the-job training. As a young adult, a vocational rehabilitation counselor worked with her to find employment. Modified housing available for those with disabilities, wheelchair transportation service, and the aid of a social worker and peer counselor helped make it possible for Emily to live successfully on her own. To achieve this goal of adult independence, Emily required more intensive services over a longer period of time, but the kinds of service—medical treatment, education, career counseling, financial assistance, housing, and transportation—were not so different from those services that all individuals need.

introducing

EMILY

Emily was born with spina bifida, a severe spinal cord defect, and hydrocephalus. Within hours of her birth, the spinal defect was surgically repaired and a shunt was put in place to reduce the intracranial pressure caused by the hydrocephaly. In a stable physical condition at three months of age, Emily was referred to an early intervention program where she and her family received services from a transdisciplinary team. Throughout her first three years, she was followed medically and continued to be a part of an early intervention program.

At age three, Emily still had limited mobility and was not learning as rapidly as would be expected. She was referred to a mainstreamed special education program for preschoolers. Emily attended the preschool class until she was six. At age six she entered a regular kindergarten class. When it was time for first grade, Emily was still behind the other children and it was clear that she would never be able to walk independently. Emily continued in the regular first grade classroom with extra help from a special education resource teacher on a daily basis and a physical therapist twice weekly; this assistance continued throughout elementary, junior high, and high school. During junior high school, she began a vocational training program which included training at school as well as on a job site in the community.

Since Emily was not academically able to complete the regular high school curriculum and continued to receive special education services, she was eligible to stay in a school vocational training program until she became 21.

At age 21, with her vocational skills and the help of a rehabilitation counselor, Emily took a job in the mailroom of a large corporation. She did well in this job and enjoyed the people she worked with and the freedom that her earnings gave her. At this point, Emily decided that she would like to live more independently, to move away from the family home to an apartment of her own. With the help of a social worker and one of the peer counselors at the community's service center for the disabled, Emily located an apartment in a center for independent living. The center had apartments specially designed for individuals with disabilities but included nonhandicapped persons as well. Transportation to the building where she worked was easy to manage using the bus system's van for people in wheelchairs. The counselor and Emily's family helped her complete the rental agreements and develop a budget for independent living. Now, at age 25, Emily is living in her own apartment, working for a large company, and managing her own life with help from her family and a social worker.

FUTURE PERSPECTIVES
FOR EXCEPTIONAL PEOPLE

Since 1970, there has been more interest and progress in the field of exceptionality than in all of the preceding centuries. Law, bioengineering, medicine, and education have all had a major impact on the field. With such rapid growth and development in recent years, what does the future hold? What issues and influences will shape the study of exceptionality in the coming years?

In the next decades, technology will probably be the development with the greatest impact on the lives of exceptional individuals. The microchip which made home computers as accessible as television sets has just begun to affect services for exceptional people (Bennett, 1982; Hannaford & Tabor, 1982). As software improves and special educators gain computer literacy, the use of computers for assessment, management, and instruction will improve the educational programs of both handicapped and gifted students. The importance of the microchip to rehabilitative efforts has already been demonstrated. Individuals with cerebral palsy use computer-synthesized voices to communicate, and reading machines make print material instantly available to people who are blind. Computerized environmental control units make it possible to unlock doors, turn appliances on and off, and use the telephone with a puff of air on a special switch. Yet these advances will probably seem primitive within the next several years. Bionic devices which provide complete, natural control of prosthetic arms, hands, and legs are being used experimentally as are implants which perform the function of damaged muscles and nerves. These devices allow individuals with spinal cord injuries or amputated limbs to move in ways that have not been possible since their injury. Within the next few years, advances in technology will turn science fiction into reality.

The second major influence on the field of exceptionality may be the changing demographics within the United States. By the year 2000, English-speakers will be in the minority in many areas of the country with speakers of Spanish or an Asian language in the majority. Each system that serves exceptional individuals will be forced to develop ways to serve an increasing number of exceptional people from diverse cultures. Another demographic change is the result of the "baby boom" of the late 1940s through the early 1960s which produced the country's largest population cohort. That group of individuals is moving toward maturity. By the year 2015, over 40 million Americans will be age 65 or older (Weller & Bouvier, 1981). The large numbers of adults with disabilities within that group will require changes in the vocational, residential, health, and social service system which may improve services for all exceptional individuals.

A third issue may be the maintenance and expansion of rights for exceptional individuals. Exceptional individuals are a minority; like most minorities, their role in society is defined by the majority. Although disabled consumers have become a vocal group, they must still rely on the larger society to vote on services. These votes are based on national priorities which are often determined by the availability of funds. Reliance on votes instead of rights causes gaps in the service system. When the economy is strong, more money is available for human services; in a weak economy, priorities often shift away from human services. A major task of the 1990s will be to assure that services are provided as a matter of right.

An emphasis on quality services may become the fourth major influence in the field of exceptionality. After services are guaranteed, their effectiveness must be monitored because the existence of services is not a guarantee of quality. Services in the next decade may be improved by the knowledge gained from research and evaluation on current practices.

Study and practice in the field of exceptionality are old, yet never have there been so many new ideas and challenges. Regardless of the professional role that one chooses, there is an opportunity for each person to make a positive difference in the lives of exceptional people.

SUMMARY

Exceptional people differ from other individuals in some important way. Some have disabilities which interfere with their participation in learning or daily activities; others have special talents or abilities which set them apart from their peers. But like all people, those with exceptionalities are individuals first; their exceptionality is just one of their unique characteristics. Although categories of exceptionality do not adequately describe any individual within the category, exceptionalities are often discussed in terms of mental retardation, physical and health handicaps, impairments in vision or hearing, communication handicaps, learning disabilities, emotional or behavioral handicaps, and special talents or giftedness.

The exact number of individuals with exceptionalities is difficult to determine since definitions differ, the methods used to collect data vary, and exceptionalities are affected by age, gender, and socioeconomic status. However, information on handicapping conditions during the school years suggests that at least 11 percent of children and youth in the United States have some handicap, gift, or talent important enough to influence their ability to perform in school.

Many causes of exceptional conditions have been determined through research on etiology, but the cause of many others remains unknown. For disabilities which are detected during childhood, the known causes are sometimes categorized by the developmental period during which they began such as the prenatal, perinatal, or postnatal period. In other instances, causes are differentiated as biomedical or sociobehavioral. Many exceptionalities are a result of more than one cause and it is the interaction of these multiple causes which determines the intensity and scope of the exceptionality. Although etiological research is often far removed from the needs and concerns of an exceptional person's daily life, determining the cause is the first step in finding ways to prevent disabilities and to increase exceptionalities such as giftedness.

All people have common needs, but exceptional people may have some additional ones. Professionals from many disciplines work with exceptional people to meet unique learning, medical, social, and emotional needs. The impact of an exceptionality can be mild or profound depending upon the condition; the characteristics, background, and culture of the individual and his or her family; the services that are available; and the attitudes of society. Although no exceptionality is insignificant to the person affected, negative aspects can be minimized with good services, well-trained professionals, supportive family members, and accepting societal attitudes.

Exceptional people have been recognized throughout history, and their treatment has varied from period to period and culture to culture. The beliefs, traditions, religion, economic stability, and the society's confidence in its ability to accommodate difference and incorporate change have influenced treatment. In some cultures individuals with handicaps have been sought out and destroyed; in others they were elevated to positions of influence and protected.

Recently, treatment of exceptional people has improved as a result of advocacy from parents and exceptional individuals themselves, legislation and litigation which established their rights, and positive changes in society's views of exceptional individuals. One of the most influential pieces of legislation has been PL 94–142 and its subsequent amendments which guaranteed a free and appropriate public education to all handicapped persons.

At the same time, technology has expanded to improve the lives of many handicapped individuals. Medical procedures which improve physical functioning have been introduced. Microchip and computer technology has enabled individuals with cerebral palsy to communicate through speech synthesizers, made print materials immediately accessible to individuals who are blind, and enabled those with physical handicaps to control their environment through a series of specially designed switches and control panels.

The future for exceptional people is brighter now than in the past. New technology, legislated rights, well-trained professionals, strong advocacy, and social commitment to the importance of all people have emerged to improve the lives of many exceptional individuals; but there is much left to be done to prevent disabling conditions, improve the lives of people who are disabled, and encourage those with special talents and abilities. Some of the work will be done in laboratories, hospitals, and therapy rooms, some in classrooms, social service agencies, and recreation programs, and a great deal within the hearts and minds of all of the members of the community.

References

American Psychiatric Association (1980). *Diagnostic and statistical manual of mental disorders* (3rd ed.). Washington, DC: American Psychiatric Association.

Barker, D. J. P., & Rose, G. (1979). *Epidemiology in medical practice* (2nd ed.). New York: Churchill Livingstone.

Bennett, R. E. (1982). Applications of microcomputer technology to special education. *Exceptional Children, 49,* 106–113.

Blackhurst, A. E., & Lewis, R. B. (1982). Mental retardation. In H. E. Mitzel (Ed.), *Encyclopedia of educational research* (5th ed.) (pp. 1218–1224). New York: The Free Press.

Cegelka, P. T., & Prehm, H. J. (Eds.). (1982a). *Mental retardation.* Columbus, OH: Merrill Publishing.

Cegelka, P. T., & Prehm, H. J. (1982b). The concept of mental retardation. In P. T. Cegelka & H. J. Prehm (Eds.), *Mental retardation* (pp. 3–20). Columbus, OH: Merrill Publishing.

Drotar, D., Baskiewicz, A., Irvin, N., Kennell, J., & Klaus, M. (1975). The adaptation of parents to the birth of an infant with a congenital malformation: A hypothetical model. *Pediatrics, 56,* 710–717.

Garber, H. L., & McInerney, M. (1982). Sociobehavioral factors in mental retardation. In P. T. Cegelka & H. J. Prehm (Eds.), *Mental retardation* (pp. 111–145). Columbus, OH: Merrill Publishing.

Grossman, H. J. (Ed.) (1983). *Classification in mental retardation, 1983 Revision.* Washington, DC: American Association on Mental Deficiency.

Gutek, G. L. (1972). *A history of the western educational experience.* New York: Random House.

Hannaford, A., & Taber, F. M. (1982). Microcomputer software for the handicapped: Development and education. *Exceptional Children, 49,* 137–142.

Harris, C. S. (1979). *Fact book on aging: A profile of America's older population.* Washington, DC: National Council on Aging, Inc.

Kanner, L. (1964). *History of the care and study of the mentally retarded.* Springfield, IL: Charles C Thomas.

Kirk, S. A., & Gallagher, J. J. (1983). *Educating exceptional children* (4th ed.). Boston: Houghton Mifflin.

Lowenfeld, B. (1975). *The changing status of the blind: From separation to integration.* Springfield, IL: Charles C Thomas.

Lynch, E. W., & Lewis, R. B. (1982). Multicultural considerations in assessment and treatment of learning disabilities. *Learning Disabilities, 1,* 93–103.

MacMillan, D. L. (1982). *Mental retardation in school and society* (2nd ed.). Boston: Little, Brown and Company.

Maloney, M., & Ward, M. P. (1979). *Mental retardation and modern society.* New York: Oxford University Press.

McLoughlin, J. A., & Lewis, R. B. (1986). *Assessing special students* (2nd ed.). Columbus, OH: Merrill Publishing.

Mercer, J. R. (1979). *Technical manual: System of multicultural pluralistic assessment.* Cleveland, OH: Psychological Corporation.

Mercer, J. R., & Lewis, J. F. (1977). *System of multicultural pluralistic assessment.* Cleveland, OH: Psychological Corporation.

Moore, B. C. (1982). Biomedical factors in mental retardation. In P. T. Cegelka & H. J. Prehm (Eds.), *Mental retardation* (pp. 76–110). Columbus, OH: Merrill Publishing.

Moores, D. F. (1978). *Educating the deaf: Psychology, principles, and practices.* Boston: Houghton Mifflin.

Nirje, B. (1979). The normalization principle and its human management implications. In R. B. Kugel & W. Wolfensberger (Eds.), *Changing patterns in residential services for the mentally retarded.* Washington, DC: The President's Committee on Mental Retardation.

Pepper, F. C. (1976). Teaching the American Indian child in mainstream settings. In R. L. Jones (Ed.), *Mainstreaming and the minority child.* Reston, VA: Council for Exceptional Children.

Reynolds, M. C., & Birch, J. W. (1977). *Teaching exceptional children in all America's schools.* Reston, VA: Council for Exceptional Children.

Rosen, M., Clark, G. R., & Kivitz, M. S. (Eds.) (1976). *The history of mental retardation: Collected papers. Volume I.* Baltimore: University Park Press.

Scheerenberger, R. C. (1982). Treatment from ancient times to the present. In P. T. Cegelka & H. J. Prehm (Eds.), *Mental retardation* (pp. 44–75). Columbus, OH: Merrill Publishing.

Solecki, R. (1971). *Shanidar.* New York: Alfred A. Knopf.

Solnit, A. J., & Stark, M. H. (1961). Mourning and the birth of a defective child. *Psychoanalytic Study of the Child, 16,* 523–537.

Turnbull, A. P., Strickland, B. B., & Brantley, J. C. (1982). *Developing and implementing individualized education programs* (2nd ed.). Columbus, OH: Merrill Publishing.

U.S. Department of Education, Office of Special Education and Rehabilitative Services (1985). *Seventh Annual Report to Congress on the Implementation of Public Law 94–142: The Education for All Handicapped Children Act.* Washington, DC: Author.

Weller, R. H., & Bouvier, L. F. (1981). *Population: Demography and policy.* New York: St. Martin's Press.

Wolfensberger, W. (1972). *The principle of normalization in human services.* Toronto: National Institute on Mental Retardation.

World Health Organization. (1977). *Manual of the international statistical classification of diseases, injuries, and causes of death* (9th ed.). Geneva: Author.

Chapter 2

SERVICES FOR EXCEPTIONAL PEOPLE

Exceptional people require exceptional services. Whatever the origin of the exceptionality—differences in learning ability, social-emotional development, physical and health concerns, or a combination of these—special needs are the result. And, for exceptional individuals, these needs often necessitate the provision of services over and above those required by the nonexceptional population.

That is not to say that specialized services are necessary for all exceptional persons in all areas of development at all times in their lives. Some persons may have need of extraordinary service in only one area at only one period during the lifespan. Others, with more severe and comprehensive disabilities, may require special assistance in several areas on a continuing basis. However, most exceptional persons also participate, at least to some extent, in the services designed for the general population.

Although exceptional people often require special services, the type, intensity, and duration of those services varies with the individual, the family, and the community. In recent years, there has been a shift from segregated service systems to more integrated or generic services. Disabled people of all ages have begun to be more involved in the mainstream of community life participating with their nonhandicapped peers in school, church, sports, and recreational activities.

Rena B. Lewis and Eleanor W. Lynch
San Diego State University

Exceptional and nonexceptional people alike rely upon three major types of human services: educational services, medical and health services, and social services. All persons take advantage of these service delivery systems, whether their involvement is with the generic services offered to the general public or the more specialized services designed for specific populations such as exceptional individuals.

The public school system is the major provider of educational services. Young children begin school at age five or six with kindergarten or first grade and continue through the elementary grades to junior high school and high school. Educational services are also available to young children below the age of five. Most preschool programs, whether they are publicly supported or offered by private agencies, include an educational component. Adults also have access to education and training. Community colleges, junior colleges, trade and vocational schools, four-year colleges, universities, and other public and private agencies provide educational services to adults of all ages. Among the most common educational services are:

- Development of the basic school skills of reading, writing, and mathematics
- Training in English and other languages, the social sciences, the sciences, mathematics, and other bodies of knowledge
- Preparation for citizenship
- Physical education
- Art and music education
- Prevocational training, vocational training, and professional preparation

Medical and health services are provided by physicians and other health care professionals. Unlike educational services, there is no one agency such as the public school system associated with the delivery of medical services. Instead, individuals receive care from a variety of professionals and publicly supported and private agencies: physicians and others in the health care professions, clinics, health maintenance organizations, residential and respite care facilities, hospitals, and trauma centers. These services are delivered to persons of all ages, from the child in utero to the senior citizen. Common medical and health services include:

- Health maintenance and illness prevention
- Treatment for illness, injuries, and physical conditions and disorders
- Emergency medical and surgical services
- Dental care
- Treatment of vision and hearing disorders

Social services are designed to assist individuals in need and to support and enrich community life. They range from public transportation services to the provision of food and shelter for indigent persons to the establishment of parks, libraries, and museums. Sometimes called community services, they are usually publicly supported, although there are many private service organizations. Among the most usual types of service are:

- Financial support for those unable to afford food, clothing, shelter, and medical assistance
- Housing (either temporary shelter on an emergency basis or subsidized permanent residences)
- Counseling services for individuals and families
- Protective services such as centers for abused children or foster child care
- Recreational and leisure time facilities and programs
- Transportation services such as mass transit systems and public roadways

Generic Versus Specialized Services

Within each service delivery system is a range of services, and this range can be conceptualized as a continuum, with one end representing generic services and the other specialized services. Generic services are those intended for the general population. For example, in the public school, the regular classes offered in the elementary and secondary grades are generic services; they are designed for average students who are able to achieve without special instructional or curricular modifications. At the other extreme of the continuum are specialized services, intended to meet the needs of individuals who are unable to benefit from generic services. For example, if a person who travels by wheelchair cannot board a city bus to ride to work, special transportation arrangements are necessary; generic services are clearly inadequate.

Between these two extremes are the service arrangements which combine general with specialized services. A child may participate in regular classroom activities *and* receive special education services on a part-time basis. Or, a person with cerebral palsy may see a family practitioner for routine health care *and* consult a specialist in motor disorders.

There is a continuum of services in each of three major service systems, as Figure 2.1 illustrates. This model is based upon the special education service models proposed by Deno (1970) and Reynolds (1962). At the base of the pyramid are generic services which address the needs of the greatest numbers of persons. When needs become more severe, the intensity of service increases, first to generic services augmented with special services and then to specialized services alone. At the top of the pyramid are the fewest numbers of persons: those with the most severe problems and the most dramatic need for special services.

At any one time, an exceptional individual may be receiving special services from one, two, or all three service systems. The more comprehensive the disability, the more likely that all types of service will be required. The intensity of the services provided can also vary from system to system, depending upon the individual's needs. For example, a young child with cancer may require specialized medical services, generic educational services with the addition of special

Figure 2.1

Continuum of Services

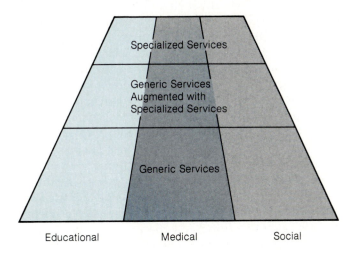

Specialized Services

Generic Services
Augmented with
Specialized Services

Generic Services

Educational   Medical   Social

tutoring for hospital stays, and generic social services. Of course, it is also possible that a person may not need any special services. A blind adult, who has completed formal schooling and now has a successful career and satisfying family life, may be able to use generic medical and social services, at least at this point in his or her life.

Service needs vary throughout the lifespan. A child with learning disabilities may remain unidentified throughout the preschool years and then experience serious educational difficulties upon entry to school; a successful adult who has overcome the effects of childhood polio may begin to experience new symptoms of the disease. In general, persons with the more severe disabilities are identified early in life, and thus those served during the preschool years tend to have intense service needs. The exceptionalities of school-age students range from mild to severe; their service needs span the continuum. However, many persons with mild disabilities require specialized services only during the school years when academic demands intensify educational needs; in adulthood, generic services may be adequate. For those with more severe disabilities, special services remain a necessity into adulthood.

John is an example of a preschool child with intense service needs in several areas. John, now three, is both blind and deaf and his cognitive development appears delayed. He attends a special preschool class three days a week, and his teacher visits him at home every Friday to assist his mother in teaching John self-care and communication skills. The major goal of the home program is to help John learn how to feed himself and to signal his needs to his mother or grand-mother. John's mother is divorced and unemployed; she relies upon governmental assistance to support John and her other two children, a twelve-year-old girl and a six-year-old boy. John was a low birthweight baby and he has had continuing medical problems since his first hour of life. At present, he is under treatment for a cardiac condition.

Sara's needs are less severe, although they are very real to her, her parents, and her teachers. Her preschool years were uneventful but, in the first few grades of school, she began to fall behind her classmates in academic pursuits. Along with the underachievement came inappropriate behavior. When Sara was unable to do classroom work, she reacted by acting out—tearing up her paper, screaming at the teacher, crying, and swearing. Sara's needs are educational and social-emotional ones. She receives special academic assistance each day from the resource teacher, and she visits the school psychologist for counseling twice each week. In addition, her fourth grade teacher has set up a special behavior management program to control Sara's behavior in the classroom.

Henry, a 21-year-old who was paralyzed in a diving accident three years ago, requires only social services but his needs in this area are important ones. Henry does not have use of his arms or legs; he controls his electric wheelchair with head movements. He is enrolled at the local community college where he's studying computer programming. The college campus is accessible to wheelchairs, but Henry needs to use a special van to travel to and from school. Henry lives in an apartment, one of several in a group home for persons with severe physical disabilities. The home is fully accessible, and the staff is available to help Henry with tasks he cannot perform. In addition to special transportation and housing, Henry also needs financial assistance to pay for his living expenses and the cost of his education.

Whether an exceptional individual can benefit from generic services or whether specialized services are necessary depends upon several factors. First and foremost are the needs of the individual. These needs dictate the type of services that are required and the characteristics of those services. For example, in developing the individualized education plan for a student with problems in reading, the educational team may determine that the student's underachievement is so severe that individual tutoring is needed on a daily basis. Because this type of instruction is not possible in the regular classroom, special education services must be provided.

In order to make this kind of decision, it is necessary to understand the nature of the generic services available. Generic services vary in the same ways that specialized services do, and sometimes they are quite adequate to meet special needs. For example, an adult with cerebral palsy may not need to seek out a special dentist or ophthalmologist.

Another factor that must be considered is the principle of normalization. Specialized services can result in the segregation of exceptional individuals; the services may take place in separate facilities, removed from those used by the general population. For example, students who receive their education in special schools may have no opportunity to interact with their age peers in regular grades. For this reason, specialized services should be provided only when they are clearly needed; and, when they are, every effort should be made to combine specialized services with generic services. In addition, services should be delivered in the least restrictive environment, that is, the environment in which generic services take place or the environment that most closely approaches it. For example, if a student's educational needs are so severe that he or she requires the intensive intervention of a special class, that class should be located in a regular school so that its members can participate in regular education activities.

The primary factor in selecting educational and medical services are the characteristics of the individual. Decisions about social services, however, must take into account the characteristics of the individual's family and his or her community. Among the important concerns, in addition to the individual's needs, are the nature of the generic social services available in the community and the types of support that the family is able and willing to provide. For example, if a person's family has sufficient financial resources, he or she may not need special financial assistance. Or, if the city transportation system includes buses with wheelchair lifts, the individual may be able to use this service instead of a more specialized one. Making decisions about social services involves discrepancy analysis (Provus, 1971); the available community and family resources are compared with the needs of the individual and, when a discrepancy results, specialized services are called for.

EARLY LIFE

Exceptionalities which are detected in infancy or the first two years are usually discovered because they are readily visible or so severe that they have a profound effect on the infant or young child's ability to function. Visible exceptionalities are those that can be seen: a missing limb, a physical deformity, or a syndrome such as Down which is characterized by recognizable facial features. Although visible exceptionalities cause an individual to stand out, they may or may not result in severe problems.

The second group of exceptionalities recognized in the first two years are those that are so severe that they have a major impact on the child's ability to survive, grow, and develop. Congenital malformations of the brain, prolonged asphyxia during labor and delivery, or severe cases of neonatal herpes may have devastating effects on development (Blackman, 1983). Although the infant or young child may not look different, he or she has a severe exceptionality which may affect everything from life expectancy to learning.

Mild sensory disabilities, language and learning problems, and some medical and health problems are not detected until the child enters a formal educational program. In these instances, teachers or parents may notice slight delays or differences in the child's ability to use language, solve problems, attend to activities, or coordinate his or her movements. In other instances, children may show delayed physical growth or health problems which interfere with their development. In any case, the first step in the delivery of services is assessment of the child.

Assessment of Exceptionality
in Infants and Preschoolers

There are three primary types of assessment: screening, eligibility or diagnosis, and program development and monitoring. Although these types remain the same regardless of the age of the individual being assessed, they are discussed here in relationship to exceptional infants and preschoolers. Screening is often the first step in determining whether or not an infant or young child is exceptional. Lillie (1977) compared the screening process to pulling a fishing net through the sea. A tightly woven net will catch more fish than one that is loosely woven just as a more comprehensive, in-depth screening procedure will identify more children requiring a complete assessment than one that is less thorough. Because screening procedures are designed to be done quickly and easily and used economically with large groups of people, they must avoid both overidentification and underidentification.

Screening procedures with newborns begin in the first minute of life. At one minute and again at five minutes after birth, infants are screened by the attending nurse or physician using a scoring system developed by Dr. Virginia Apgar (1953). The infant's heart rate, respiratory effort, muscle tone, reflex irritability, and color are each scored on a scale of 0 through 2 (Korones & Lancaster, 1981). Specific criteria are used to determine the score, with a 2 in each category being the highest and a 0 representing a serious problem. Added together, the five scores may total any number from 0 through 10. A score from 7 to 10 represents an infant that is experiencing no distress; a 4 through 6 one with moderate difficulty, and a 0 through 3 severe distress. This very early screening procedure helps physicians determine whether or not it is necessary to conduct further diagnostic assessments. In addition to the Apgar, many states mandate other newborn screening tests to determine the presence or absence of disorders which result in handicapping conditions. The most common of these is the screening test for phenylketonuria (PKU), an enzyme defect which can be effectively managed if treatment is begun early. If it is not discovered and treated, it results in severe mental retardation (Moore & Moore, 1977).

As infants grow into preschoolers, they routinely receive vision and hearing screenings as well as checks for general growth and development. In most areas of the country these screenings are conducted by the child's pediatrician or a nurse practitioner. For children from low-income families without a primary care physician, Medicaid's Early Periodic Screening, Detection, and Treatment program (EPSDT) and the Child Health and Disability Program (CHDP) have been organized to provide routine screening. In addition, most school districts conduct screening clinics prior to kindergarten entrance to determine the need for further assessment.

Emphasis on screening programs is based on the premise that early detection leads to intervention which in turn reduces the effects of handicapping conditions or encourages the development of special talents (Horowitz, 1982; Trohanis, Meyer, & Prestridge, 1982). If, through screening, problems or special talents and potentials are detected, a diagnostic or eligibility assessment is conducted. This type of evaluation is used to determine whether or not the individual qualifies

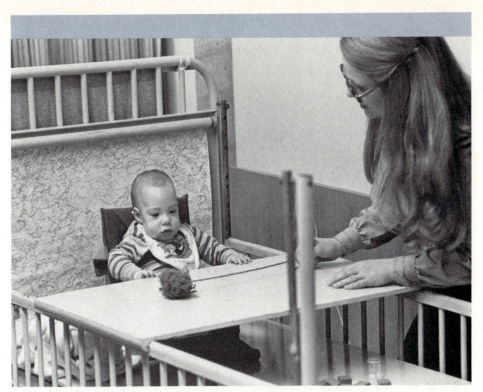

A baby who was born prematurely is given a vision test as part of a follow-up screening program.

for special services and to provide a diagnosis. In infancy and early childhood, accurate assessment is especially difficult. Infants have limited ways of demonstrating their competence requiring that the assessor be a careful, knowledgeable observer. Whether they are delayed, normally developing, or precocious, infants should be assessed only by those who are familiar with infant development, experienced in handling and observing infant behavior, and willing to engage in an interactive process which is controlled by the infant's temperament, cooperation, and state (Ulrey & Rogers, 1982). Unlike their school-age peers, infants and preschoolers have little need for getting the right answer or pleasing adults with their responses (Lidz, 1983; Ulrey & Rogers, 1982). Their language and attending skills are limited and sitting quietly at a table while the examiner presents test item after test item is out of the question. When a young child has severe handicaps, the task is even more complex (DuBose, 1981; Rogers, 1982). Thus, the examiner must be highly skilled and attuned to both the child's performance and the possible reasons for it.

In a diagnostic or eligibility assessment, the primary questions are: (1) Is this child exceptional? (2) Does the child qualify for special programs or services based on the exceptionality? Professionals from a wide range of disciplines work with the child's parents to answer these questions. The development of the interdisciplinary team is a recent trend in the assessment of infants and preschoolers (Bailey & Wolery, 1984; Mulliken & Buckley, 1983). This change in the service delivery system came about in two ways. Professionals recognized that a wide range of disciplines was necessary to adequately assess and serve high-risk and handicapped young children; and as this was being discussed in the field, the regulations of PL 94–142 requiring a multidisciplinary team assessment became law (Orlando, 1981). This change has brought many diverse disciplines together to assess and program for young children. It is not uncommon to find professionals from pediatrics, occupational therapy, nursing, physical therapy, neonatology, special education, child development, speech pathology, psychology, and social work collaborating to discover and meet the needs of a high-risk or handicapped infant or preschooler.

The questions of whether or not a young child is exceptional and whether he or she qualifies for special services and programs are answered differently in the fields of health, education, and social service. Each system and the professionals within it has procedures for determining exceptionality and the eligibility for programs. The answers depend upon the diagnosis, the exceptionality, and the service mandates of each of the systems.

The third type of assessment is conducted to determine service and program objectives and to monitor the program after it has been developed. In medicine, physicians may determine that a young child needs supplemental oxygen which is supplied through a ventilator. In education, a team of professionals including the parents may decide from their assessment that the child needs to develop specific skills in the areas of self-feeding, mobility, and communication. Working with a family counselor using a family needs assessment, the parents may decide that they would like to work to improve their skills in child management. Although each of these programs and services is quite different, each is based on a careful assessment of what needs to occur and how it should be accomplished. In each instance, the success or failure of the service is monitored by documenting the intervention and measuring its effectiveness. Has the child's physical status improved with the use of the ventilator? Is the child acquiring the self-feeding, mobility, and communication skills being taught? Are the parents more effective in managing the child's behavior? If the expected changes are not occurring, the treatment and the way that it is being carried out need to be reviewed and revised.

Early Intervention Goals

Although early intervention is most often thought of in terms of the educational services provided to exceptional infants and their families, it represents a much broader range of medical, educational, and family support services. Regardless of the system delivering the service, the goals may be to: (1) prevent, (2) facilitate, (3) maintain, (4) compensate, or (5) accelerate. These goals are not mutually exclusive. They may be used in combination and may change as the needs of the child and family change.

Prevention of handicapping conditions is a primary medical, educational, and social goal. All three systems have worked singly and in collaboration to prevent handicapping conditions through research and public awareness. Research findings have been shared through campaigns which educate the public about the importance of prenatal care, good nutrition, and the avoidance of substances harmful to the fetus such as nicotine, alcohol, prescription and nonprescription drugs. Massive immunization programs against infectious diseases such as rubella have been mounted to reduce the likelihood that a pregnant woman will contract the disease and pass it on to the unborn child.

In addition to the efforts made to teach people about risk factors, new technologies have been developed to provide direct intervention with the developing fetus. Medical procedures such as amniocentesis, ultrasonography, fetoscopy, and alpha fetoprotein determination are used to detect problems in utero (Menolascino, 1983). These techniques are considered preventative since they contribute to the overall reduction of potentially handicapping conditions. Over 100 inborn errors of metabolism and many chromosomal abnormalities can be detected in the developing fetus through amniocentesis (Menolascino, 1983; Milunsky, 1983). In some instances treatment can be initiated during fetal life. In other instances there is no treatment, but parents have information to determine whether or not the pregnancy should be continued.

Direct intervention with infants and families is often conducted by early intervention teams to prevent the acquisition of additional handicaps (Fraser & Hensinger, 1983). Deafness affects social skill acquisition as well as speech acquisition (DuBose, 1981); early intervention directed at both of these areas can help to prevent major deficits in communication and social functioning. Without therapy and proper positioning, many young children with cerebral palsy would develop contractures. This permanent shortening of the muscle causes imbalances in the pull of muscles on joints and bones leading to skeletal deformities which result in even more limited movement (Fraser & Hensinger, 1983). Thus, prevention is the primary goal. Of course, if it is possible to treat and cure a disability, that will be the goal of intervention.

A second major goal of intervention is facilitation. Simply put, the goal is to promote development or make it easier to achieve. In early educational intervention programs for children with handicaps, task analysis and behavioral principles applied within a functional, developmental framework are used to help the child learn. In other words, a skill such as eating with a spoon is broken down into small, teachable steps. When one step has been mastered, the next is added. In addition to using task analysis to determine skill sequences, early interventionists arrange the learning environment to facilitate skill acquisition. Young children are properly positioned (Finnie, 1975); the child's attention is captured; materials and verbal cues are designed to focus the child on the task; and reinforcers are used to increase the rate or strength of the behavior (Alberto, Briggs, & Goldstein, 1983; Bailey & Wolery, 1984). In programs for gifted or talented young children, the interventionist facilitates learning by providing opportunities for growth in an enriched environment.

In general, facilitation is a goal of most early intervention programs. Although there are slight variations in the way the term is used across disciplines, in each context it is used to describe a program which is designed to improve the child's functioning.

Early intervention programs may also focus on maintenance, compensation, and/or acceleration, and, in many cases, these goals would be used in combination. Maintenance goals are probably most familiar to those who have been on a diet. In most weight reduction programs, participants remain on a maintenance diet after they have reached their weight goal. This maintenance diet allows them to maintain their loss through a controlled, though less restricted, eating plan. The same is true for maintenance goals in early intervention. After any skill has been learned there must be adequate opportunities to practice it if it is to be retained. Maintenance goals in early intervention may include continued therapy or exercises to maintain mobility and flexibility of muscles and joints, practice and instruction in dressing, recognizing letters and numbers, or continued opportunities for social interaction.

Compensation was the primary goal of many of the first early intervention programs designed for low-income children in the 1960s. Programs, such as Head Start, for young, low-income children were designed to compensate for the presumed lack of experience and opportunity in their home environment. Although the cultural deficit model on which the programs were based has since been discounted (Martin & Martin, 1978), the notion of compensation remains. In contemporary early intervention programs, compensation suggests an alternative mode or method of learning used to make up for physical or performance deficits (Safford, 1978). A child with visual impairments may be taught how to use other sensory systems to compensate for limited sight; a child with a missing arm may be shown ways to dress using only one hand; and a child with severely limited speech and movement may learn to use a computer to speak and signal for him.

In almost every program designed to provide early educational intervention, a primary goal is to accelerate the child's rate of development. Whether the program is for gifted preschoolers or severely handicapped infants, interventionists are interested in increasing the child's rate of development and skill acquisition.

Early Intervention Models

Models used in early intervention can be described along multiple dimensions. In this section, early intervention will be described in terms of the system providing the intervention, the theoretical model, and the location of the program or service. Because services for infants and preschoolers with handicaps are more predominant than those for gifted children, services for handicapped children will be described.

Although the health, educational, and social welfare systems are all involved in the provision of early intervention services to exceptional infants and preschoolers, the health care system is often the first to diagnose a problem and provide services. Identification of a medical problem before or at birth necessitates immediate, in-hospital intervention which may take place in the delivery room or the neonatal intensive care unit (Klaus & Fanaroff, 1979; Korones, 1981). In these units, the latest technology is used to support and sustain critically ill infants (Cole & Frappier, 1983; Goldberg & DiVitto, 1983; Klaus, Fanaroff, & Martin 1983). Though life-sustaining, the environment is characterized by bright lights, high sound levels, invasive procedures, and multiple caretakers. In recent years, controversy has arisen over the long-term effects of this early environment on the exceptional newborn. Because of this concern, many neonatal intensive care units have begun to normalize the environment by encouraging parents to hold and feed their infant, reducing the numbers of caretakers involved with each baby, and establishing rhythms by lowering lights and sound levels at night (Korones & Lancaster, 1981).

Health care may continue to be the predominant system in the first months or years of life, or the emphasis may shift to a more comprehensive service delivery system. An infant diagnosed as handicapped or at risk for a handicap may be referred for comprehensive, early intervention services as soon as he or she is medically stable. It is these comprehensive, inter- or transdisciplinary services that represent the ideal in early intervention for high-risk and handicapped infants, preschoolers, and their families (Fewell, 1983). These programs include professionals from a variety of disciplines with expertise in motor, language, cognitive, and social development as well as skill in working with families.

The way in which services are provided in these comprehensive programs is dependent on theoretical orientation since the theoretical model dictates the curriculum content, program structure, and day-to-day implementation (Linder, 1983). Several theoretical models are used as a basis for designing programs and services for infants and preschoolers with handicaps. Although different theorists and authors have used different names to refer to the same model, the principles described in each have been consistent. The four most frequently occurring models are: the normal developmental model, cognitive interactional model, behavioral model, and developmental learning or cognitive learning model.

Using the developmental model, it is the interventionist's role to facilitate learning through modeling and imitation. Emphasis is placed on age-appropriate materials and concepts with instruction being informal and activity centered (Linder, 1983). This model assumes that all children develop in the same sequence regardless of their rate of development and attempts to adapt to the special needs of handicapped infants and preschoolers with as little adult direction as possible. In this model, few adaptations would be made for a handicapped child and instructional objectives would not be specified. Instead, it would be assumed that the child would eventually learn whatever he or she needed to learn by interacting with the materials and people in the environment. In this model, learning how to set a table would be expected to occur as the child plays in the housekeeping center of the classroom.

The cognitive interactional model combines principles from both education and psychology. Most closely associated with Piaget, the model actually represents a synthesis of the work of Jean Piaget, John Dewey, Anna Freud, Erik

Erikson, and others (Linder, 1983). In this model, development is viewed in stages that are sequential, hierarchical, and without variation; only the rate of development differs from one child to another. Learning takes place as a result of the interaction between the child and the environment, and it is the interventionist's job to provide experiences and challenging opportunities for learning and practice through manipulative activities, language, and play. In this approach, children are encouraged to attempt novel tasks appropriate to their developmental level and allowed to learn through their successes and failures. In this model, the teacher has specific, age-appropriate objectives in mind and develops activities or units to teach these objectives. If learning how to set the table were an objective, the teacher might bring out all of the necessary materials, ask the children to name and talk about them, and then demonstrate how to place them on the table. After discussions and modeling, the children would be encouraged to set the table themselves each day at snack time. Since failure is viewed as one way to learn in this model, the children would be allowed to set the table in their own way, then be given feedback on their performance. Children who placed the cup on top of the plate would be told, "The cup goes here, not on the plate."

The behavioral model, unlike the developmental model, provides a controlled setting in which the interventionist directs the learning. Learning objectives are clearly targeted and specified, task analyzed, taught to criterion in small sequential steps which eliminate failure, and reinforced. Data collection is an integral part of the system, and all decisions are based on the results of the data (Halle & Sindelar, 1982). This approach is used to strengthen desired behaviors and to reduce undesired or maladaptive behaviors. Behavioral techniques have been demonstrated to be effective for changing a wide range of behaviors in children of all ages, and have been found to be particularly successful with more severely handicapped young children. In this model learning to set the table would be highly structured and taught in an error-proof way. The teacher would break the skill down into small parts and teach one part at a time. At first, the teacher might arrange everything but the cup on the table, then tell the child to "put the cup here." To reduce the chances for failure, the spot for the cup might be marked with a circle or drawing of a cup. If the child still seemed to be having difficulty, the teacher might physically move the child's arm and hand to the correct spot. Every attempt or trial is recorded, and new tasks are added only when a child has mastered earlier steps.

The developmental learning or cognitive learning model represents a blending of the cognitive developmental and behavioral models. Thus the interactional aspects of Piagetian theory as well as the behavioral principles of task analysis, data collection, and specific instruction are combined. In this model, the interventionist's role is one of training and facilitation, and the goals of the program include increasing the children's repertoire of necessary skills, mastery of their environment, and use of these skills in different situations and locations (Linder, 1983). In this model, table setting would be taught through modeling, practice, and direct behavioral intervention. The teacher first might demonstrate and then physically help the child set the table correctly. Whenever the child was having difficulty learning a task, the instruction would more closely approximate the behavioral model.

In addition to describing early intervention programs by the system that provides services and the theoretical model utilized, programs are also described by the location of the services. Programs may be either home-based, center-based, or a combination of the two. As the name suggests, home-based programs are carried out in the child's home. The interventionist usually visits weekly or biweekly to work with the child on developmental activities and provide support and information to the family. These programs are most common in rural areas where transporting the child for long distances is not feasible and for children under the age of two. Bailey and Wolery (1984) list the following as advantages to home-based delivery models: families without transportation can be served; there is no cost to the program for large, expensive facilities; children are being taught in their natural setting, increasing generalization; and parents receive personalized attention and support. Disadvantages include: heavy dependence on the parent as the primary teacher, lack of respite for the family, lack of peer interaction for children as they reach the preschool years, and extensive professional travel time which reduces the time available for program planning and implementation (Bailey & Wolery, 1984).

Center-based programs occur in schools, hospitals, or clinics. Children are transported to the program where interventionists work with small groups of children. In their discussion, Bailey and Wolery (1984) detail the advantages and disadvantages of center-based programs. Advantages include: efficient use of interventionists' time, ease of administrative supervision, increased opportunities for public relations, availability of other professionals for consultation and teaming, opportunities for children to interact with peers, and service availability to those whose parents cannot be involved. They cite the following as disadvantages: transportation problems, building costs, and decreased parental involvement.

Because of the range of advantages and disadvantages in these models, and varying needs of different children and families, many programs combine home and center-based programming. Children may receive home visits until they reach a certain age, then be gradually incorporated into the center-based program. Or a child of any age may attend the center-based program several days a week and receive home visits once or twice each month. A major advantage of this model is the flexibility that it provides to meet the diverse needs of various children and families.

Services to Young Children and Their Families

Regardless of who provides early intervention services or where those services are located, programs usually include services to the child and services to the family. This is especially true for programs which serve children under age three. Services to children usually include educational and therapeutic objectives derived from the following areas of development: cognition, self-care, fine motor/perceptual, gross motor, social/emotional, and language. Depending upon the child's current level of functioning and needs as determined by the family and professionals involved, a written plan is developed to guide the intervention and monitor its effectiveness. In programs operated by school systems, the written plan is an Individualized Education Program; in programs sponsored by other agencies, it may have a different name but would include similar information. For an 18-month-old who does not yet walk, use words, or eat solid food, the objectives might include pulling to a standing position holding onto a small table, imitating vowel/consonant sounds such as "ba ba," "ma ma," and "da da," and accepting food with some texture such as a banana, pudding, or blended carrots. In the written plan, each of these objectives would be stated more precisely and include criteria for acceptable performance. In consultation with the parents, the interventionist would develop activities, games, and specific instructional strategies to help the child accomplish the objectives. Objectives for most preschoolers are usually more academically and socially oriented. A plan for a preschooler might focus on matching letters; recognizing examples of basic concepts such as *more, less, up, down, above, below*; taking turns on an outdoor swing; and naming body parts.

In recent years, the concept of functionality has emerged in determining curriculum for individuals with severe handicaps (Guess et al., 1978). Functionality refers to the usefulness of the skill being taught in current and future environments as well as to its appropriateness to the individual's chronological age. For example, teaching a severely handicapped 10-year-old how to stack blocks is neither functional nor chronologically age appropriate. Block-stacking is not a skill that is needed in daily life, and a normally developing 10-year-old would never be seen playing with blocks. Thus, this objective would not be selected. This same notion has been suggested as a way to determine curricular objectives for handicapped infants and preschoolers. Although this approach has been useful in developing programs for older individuals with handicaps, it has been less useful in the early years when differences between chronological and developmental age are less pronounced (Bagnato & Neisworth, 1981; Johnson & Jens, 1982).

In addition to child services, a growing number of early intervention programs provide support services to families. Although parents and professionals rate the impact of a handicapped child on the family differently (Blackard & Barsch, 1982), there is little question that the impact is significant (Olshansky, 1962; Perske, 1981; Turnbull & Turnbull, 1978). Initially, programs were developed to serve the child, but as the literature on the importance of attachment and early family experience was incorporated (Schaefer, 1975; Skeels, 1966), programs began to involve parents. Early attempts at parent involvement varied widely from the Portage Project in which parents were their child's primary teacher (Shearer & Shearer, 1972) to the Milwaukee Project in which mothers were trained in job skills and children participated in a structured daycare and nursery school program (Heber, Garber, Harrington, Hoffman, & Fallender, 1975). Others attempted to involve parents through parent education and support groups, as participants in center-based programs, or as case managers for their child.

Most recently, programs have begun to view the family as a complex system in which each part is affected by changes in any other part (see Chapter 12). This perspective has caused many early intervention programs to recognize the importance of the entire family system—parents, siblings, and other extended family members—and to work with the entire system to develop an effective approach to their needs (Lamb, 1983; Pedersen, 1982; Seligman, 1983). This approach assists the family to identify their needs, develop ways of meeting them, and monitor their own progress (Rubin & Quinn-Curran, 1983) shifting the focus from the handicapped child to the needs of all family members (Lynch & Stein, 1982; Turnbull & Turnbull, 1982).

The Efficacy of Early Intervention

No program can be adequately judged by its appeal or what appears to be inherent logic; instead, all programs for exceptional individuals need to be evaluated to determine their short-term and long-term effectiveness. Because of the relative newness, the research orientation of some of the pioneers in the field, and the accountability movement that paralleled the development of early intervention programs, the effectiveness of early intervention has been well documented (Karnes & Teska, 1975; Lazar, Darlington, Murray, Royce, & Snipper, 1982; Linder, 1983; Schweinhart & Weikart, 1981; Yarrow, Rubenstein, Pedersen, & Jankowski, 1982). Although research needs to continue in the investigation of the effects of early intervention on specific types of handicapping conditions, the models which are most successful, and effects on the family system, completed studies have provided useful information.

The first studies of the effectiveness of early intervention were conducted in the 1930s (Skeels & Dye, 1939; Skodak & Skeels, 1949). Infants with low intelligence living in an orphanage were transferred to a state institution for retarded women. In the institution, the infants were cared for by the ward attendants and residents. The infants were held, talked to, given play materials, and taken on outings by their caretakers. In approximately 18 months, the infants' IQs had increased significantly. When their progress was compared to a group of infants of near normal intelligence left in the orphanage where there was little stimulation, the infants who received early intervention were superior in all ways. Furthermore, these gains were maintained into adulthood (Skeels, 1966).

Later studies examining the efficacy of early intervention were conducted with low-income infants and preschoolers (Lazar, Darlington, Murray, Royce, & Snipper, 1982). More recently, additional studies examining the effects of early intervention on handicapped children have been carried out. Since early intervention is designed to produce positive changes for the child and society at large, researchers have examined the following variables after intervention: (1) differences in measured IQ or rate of development (Bricker & Sheehan, 1981; DeWeerd, 1981; Hanson & Schwartz, 1978; Simmons-Martin, 1981); (2) differences in later school performance (Karnes, Schwedel, Lewis, Ratts, & Esry, 1981; Moore, Fredericks, & Baldwin, 1981; Schweinhart & Weikart, 1981); and (3) differences in cost to society (Schweinhart & Weikart, 1981; Wood, 1980). A research design comparing an experimental group which had participated in an early intervention program to a control group that had not would be the ideal way to study these variables. However, such clearly defined groups have not always been available; and when they have been, the numbers of children involved have usually been small. This lack of research precision has been a result of two primary factors. Early intervention programs were designed to deliver service, not to serve as research programs. Therefore, service delivery needs were met before those of research. Second, withholding a treatment or intervention which is believed to be positive has been viewed as unethical by research committees throughout the country; this stance has prevented researchers from maintaining control groups in which children received no services. Despite these constraints, data supporting the effectiveness of early intervention with young children with handicaps have been collected. The findings of several studies support the position that early intervention services can accelerate development in infants and young children with a wide range of handicapping conditions.

Bricker and Sheehan (1981) reported results of an integrated, noncategorical, early intervention program that included children with a wide range of cognitive, motor, and sensory handicaps. Based on norm-referenced and criterion-referenced measures, the 63 children studied showed statistically significant improvement in their rate of development and skill acquisition regardless of their level of functioning. In an evaluation of an early intervention program for deaf children, Simmons-Martin (1981) found that the 44 children who were enrolled in a program at an average of 26 months of age experienced continuous and consistent growth in language development. The Battelle Institute study (1976), described by DeWeerd (1981), included 129 children from 29 early intervention projects. Results of pretests and posttests indicated that many of the children gained 1.5 to 2 times what would have been expected based on predicted rates of development without intervention. Finally, Hanson and Schwartz (1978) documented that 12 Down Syndrome children served by an early intervention program since early infancy achieved developmental milestones somewhat later than nonhandicapped children but consistently earlier than those Down Syndrome children who had not participated in an early intervention program.

The effects of early intervention programs have also been studied in relationship to the child's later school performance. Improvement in academic or social functioning which results in a less restrictive classroom placement is viewed as a positive outcome. Eighty-six children who had participated in the University of Illinois and rural Champaign County's Joint Early Education Program for young children with handicaps were followed into elementary school. Approximately one-half of the sample had speech and language disorders, and the other half were mildly to moderately cognitively impaired, motor impaired, emotionally impaired, or had specific learning disabilities (Karnes, Schwedel, Lewis, Ratts, & Esry, 1981). In the follow-up study, 80 percent of the sample were enrolled in regular classes. Of the 20 percent enrolled in special education classes, almost half were placed there directly from the preschool program. Of the 80 percent in regular education classes, 82 percent were promoted on schedule suggesting that most of the children were performing at or near grade level. Although 60 percent of the children in regular classes received some form of support service with speech and language being the most common, 40 percent were functioning without any extra services.

Moore, Fredericks, and Baldwin (1981) conducted an ex post facto study which compared the functioning of over 1200 nine, ten, and eleven-year-olds in Oregon, most of whom were moderately to severely mentally retarded. The Student Progress Record, a criterion-referenced skill inventory, was administered to all of the students. Within each chronological age level, three subgroups were established: a group which had not attended preschool, a group which had attended one year of preschool, and a group which had participated in two years of preschool programming. Results showed that students who had attended two years of preschool were significantly ahead of those who had not or attended only one year in language, academics, self-help, and motor skills. No significant differences were found in social skills.

In a comprehensive, longitudinal study of students who attended the Perry Preschool in Ypsilanti, Michigan, Schweinhart and Weikart (1981) have developed one of the most credible sources of information about the effects of early intervention programs. The study began in 1962 when subjects were three years old. At that time, 123 children considered to be at risk for educational problems because of borderline mental retardation and low income environments were randomly assigned to an experimental group which received preschool education and home visits or a control group which received neither. At the time of the 1981 report, these students were 19 years of age; those who had participated in the preschool program had maintained consistently higher levels of academic achievement, a stronger commitment to school, and less need for special education services or placement.

A third way to measure the efficacy of early intervention is by cost. Can the cost of early intervention be justified on the basis that it will reduce future costs to society? This has become an important indicator in all areas of service during a time of increasing need and declining resources. Since the measurement of cost benefit is relatively new in human service fields, fewer studies have been conducted; but some important work has begun. In the longitudinal study conducted by Schweinhart and Weikart (1981), the economic benefits of preschool education for at-risk preschoolers were calculated to be $14,819 for a $5,984 investment (in 1979 dollars). This 248 percent return on the original investment was derived by looking at benefits in cost of education, increase in projected earnings, and value of mothers' released time when the child was in preschool. Fewer children who attended preschool required more costly special education services; their lifetime earnings were projected to be higher because of their academic achievement; and mothers released from child care could contribute to the family income. Wood's (1980) study of the cost of services to 940 multiply handicapped children resulted in major differences in the overall educational costs of programs for students who received early intervention services and those who did not. The later the intervention, the greater cost for the student's education to age 18.

Although research needs to continue on the effects of intervention at different age levels, for different handicapping conditions, and for various program models, findings of studies thus far have been quite promising suggesting that early intervention does make a difference.

THE SCHOOL YEARS

Although many children attend nursery and preschools before they enter elementary school, the school years are generally considered to begin at age 5 or 6, when a child enters kindergarten or first grade, and end at age 17 or 18, with the completion of high school. Compulsory education laws vary by state but most require school attendance between the ages of 7 and 16 (Heddens, 1982). Young handicapped children may begin their formal schooling with a special preschool experience (as the last section described), and some states continue to provide special education services to handicapped youth until age 20, 21, or even 25 (U.S. Department of Education, 1985). In the United States, most students of school age attend public rather than private schools. In 1981, for example, almost 90 percent of those enrolled in elementary and secondary grades attended publicly controlled schools (Grant & Snyder, 1983-84).

During the school years, the educational system becomes the focal point of special services for exceptional children and youth. Education is the primary life task expected of this age group, and society's expectations for school-age individuals are tied to educational goals. In addition, public schools are bound by law to provide identified handicapped students with special instructional services. That is not to say that educational needs are the only ones to occur during the school years. When physical-health and social-emotional needs arise, they are dealt with within the context of the interdisciplinary educational program. This may involve providing selected medical or social services within the school setting or working in cooperation with outside medical or social agencies.

Some children—those with visible disabilities and severe developmental delays—enter school already identified as exceptional. Youngsters who are highly gifted or talented may also have been identified during the preschool years. When an exceptionality is dramatic enough to draw attention to itself before the child reaches school age, it is likely that the child will continue to experience special needs in the first few years of school.

Another group of individuals is served during the school years: those with more subtle handicapping conditions, gifts, and talents. In general, the milder handicaps such as learning disabilities, mild mental retardation, and behavior disorders are not identified until children reach school age and begin to experience difficulty with the academic and/or behavioral demands of the school environment (Kauffman, 1981; MacMillan, 1982; Smith, 1983). Some of the less severe speech and language problems may not become apparent until the school years, and mild vision and hearing disorders may be discovered in school screening programs. Also, disabilities may be acquired through illness or injury at any time during a student's school career.

Assessment of School-Age Individuals

The provision of special services is a systematic process in which assessment information is collected to aid in making decisions about eligibility for service,

Figure 2.2

Steps in the Provision of Special Education Services

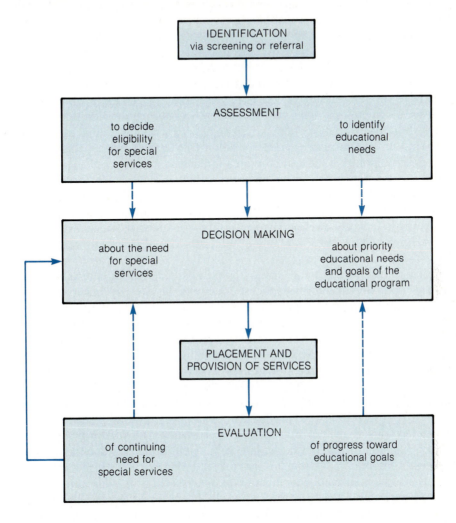

Source: From *Assessing Special Students,* Second Edition, by James A. McLoughlin and Rena B. Lewis. Copyright © 1986 by Bell & Howell Company. Reprinted by permission of Charles E. Merrill Publishing Company.

priority service needs, and the necessity of continuing service. This model, shown in Figure 2.2, includes five major steps: identification of the exceptional student, assessment of the student's needs, determination of the student's eligibility for special programming and selection of the goals and objectives for that program, placement and the provision of services, and evaluation of the student's progress and the effectiveness of the program.

The two major strategies used to identify exceptional individuals during the school years are screening and referral. On a routine basis, schools conduct screening programs to locate students at risk for various handicapping conditions. For example, vision and hearing checks are conducted at regular intervals through the grades and, in many districts, entering kindergarten or first grade students are screened for developmental delays by means of parent interviews and formal or informal measures of current performance. Students are also identified as potential candidates for special services by means of referrals from teachers, other professionals, and parents. A teacher may notice that a child is having difficulty with classroom activities or is experiencing some sort of social-emotional or health-related problem; when this occurs, the teacher refers the child for consideration for special education assessment.

The second step in the provision of services is in-depth assessment. This has two purposes: to assist in determining whether the student meets legal criteria for special services, and to identify the student's special educational needs. According to federal law, students are eligible for special services when there is a school performance problem and when that problem is related to a handicapping condition.

Assessment is planned and conducted by a multidisciplinary team which may include professionals such as special educators, school psychologists, speech-language clinicians, school nurses or physicians, and others. The multidisciplinary composition of the assessment team is only one means of attempting to ensure that the eligibility decision will be a fair one. Eligibility assessment is one of the most controversial aspects of special education, and much criticism has been leveled at assessment practices, particularly in relation to students from minority groups. In the 1960s and early 1970s, professionals, parents, and others interested in the welfare of children took notice of the disproportionate numbers of minority group children identified as mentally retarded and placed in separate, segregated special classes. Special educators such as Lloyd Dunn (1968) called attention to this in his landmark article "Special Education for the Mildly Retarded—Is Much of It Justifiable?" as did Jane Mercer (1973) in her research on the ethnic composition of special education classrooms. In addition, court cases were filed to protest the use of English-language intelligence tests with non-English-speaking children (*Diana v. State Board of Education,* 1970) and the discriminatory nature of intelligence tests for minority culture children (*Larry P. v. Riles,* 1972). In an attempt to prevent the misuse of standardized tests and to encourage nondiscriminatory assessment, the Education for All Handicapped Children Act of 1975, PL 94–142, set forth specific guidelines for conducting eligibility assessments:

1. Parents must give their consent before a child is evaluated.
2. The assessment must be conducted by a multidisciplinary team.
3. Tests and other assessment devices must not discriminate against the student on the basis of race, culture, or handicapping condition.

4. The student must be assessed in his or her own language, unless this is clearly not feasible.
5. Tests and other procedures must have been validated for the specific purpose for which they are used, and they must be administered by trained professionals.
6. Eligibility for special education cannot be determined on the basis of only one assessment procedure, such as an intelligence test.

Despite these safeguards, data compiled by the Office for Civil Rights indicate that minority children continue to be overrepresented in special education programs for mentally retarded students (Messick, 1984). In 1978, for example, 38 percent of the students in classes for the mildly retarded were black, although black students made up only 16 percent of the school population. These findings led to the establishment of the National Academy of Sciences Panel on Selection and Placement of Students in Programs for the Mentally Retarded. The Panel's report, *Placing Children in Special Education: A Strategy for Equity* (Heller, Holtzman, & Messick, 1982), recommends a two-phase assessment process. The first phase of assessment is a study of the effectiveness of the student's learning environment, and the second phase is a study of the learning characteristics of the student. In essence, the report calls for schools to exhaust generic service options before considering special education placement. Eligibility assessment should not take place until the following criteria are satisfied:

- *There should be evidence that schools are using curricula known to be effective for the student populations they serve. . . .*
- *There should be evidence that the teacher has implemented the curriculum effectively for the student in question. . . .*
- *There should be objective evidence that the child has not learned what was taught. . . .*
- *There should be evidence that, when early problems were detected, systematic efforts were made to locate the source of the difficulty and to take corrective measures. . . .* (Heller et al., 1982, pp. 69–70)

Current assessment practices in special education tend to focus on the characteristics of the learner rather than on those of the learning environment. In general, three areas are assessed: general intelligence, current school performance, and the area of suspected disability. General aptitude for learning is assessed with individual measures of intellectual performance such as the *Wechsler Intelligence Scale for Children–Revised* (Wechsler, 1974). General intelligence is of interest with all exceptionalities; it is one of the major factors considered in the identification of mental retardation and giftedness, and average intellectual performance is an important characteristic of other handicapping conditions such as behavior disorders and learning disabilities.

Individual tests of academic achievement are used to evaluate the current school performance of students with mild learning difficulties. Among the most common instruments (McLoughlin & Lewis, 1986) are the *Peabody Individual*

Achievement Test (Dunn & Markwardt, 1970), the *KeyMath Diagnostic Arithmetic Test* (Connolly, Nachtman, & Pritchett, 1976), and the *Woodcock Reading Mastery Tests* (Woodcock, 1973). For students with more severe disabilities who have not begun academic study, current performance is defined in terms of functioning in areas such as cognitive, language, motor, and self-help skill development.

The area or areas of suspected disability is also a concern in assessment. For example, classroom behavior and social-emotional status are the major emphases in assessment of behavior disorders, whereas the student's vision or hearing is the focus in the study of sensory handicaps. However, with most students referred for special education evaluation, assessment is comprehensive to the extent that all areas of potential disability are taken into consideration at some time during the data-collection process. The student's school records are reviewed for results of recent hearing and vision screenings; the student's classroom teachers (and possibly his or her parents) are consulted to determine the student's typical behavior patterns; the student's speech and language is observed and evaluated as part of the testing process; and so on. As necessary, these areas are studied in depth: health, vision, and hearing; motor abilities; speech and language abilities; and social-emotional status.

Not all students who undergo special education assessment are found eligible for special programs. According to a 1980 study reported by the U.S. Department of Education (1982), approximately 20 percent of the students assessed are found *not* to be in need of special education services. When students do meet eligibility criteria, an Individualized Education Plan is developed, based on assessment data and input from professionals, the child's parents, and when appropriate, the students themselves. Another important feature of PL 94–142 is its guarantee of a free, appropriate, public education to all students identified as handicapped. No student can be denied an education because of the severity of his or her disability.

Assessment continues when the student is placed in the special education program. Special education teachers monitor the progress of their pupils on a regular basis and, at least once each year, the educational plan is reviewed and modified. Every three years, or more frequently if necessary, the student's need for special programming is reevaluated.

Intervention Goals for the School-Age Population

With school-age exceptional individuals, as at all age levels, the major purposes of intervention are to lessen the effects of disabilities and to encourage and facilitate the development of gifts and talents. These purposes can be described in terms of several types of intervention goals: prevention, remediation, facilitation, maintenance, compensation, and acceleration.

The prevention programs of the medical, social, and educational service systems continue during the school years in an attempt to reduce the number of acquired disabilities. Among these efforts are safety programs aimed at preventing accidents and injuries (e.g., compulsory seatbelt laws), services for neglected and abused children, and programs designed to educate young people about alcohol and drug abuse (Nolte, 1982). Early identification of handicapping conditions is also viewed as a preventive measure. The earlier in the school years that students with mild learning handicaps are identified and provided with appropriate services, the more likely that the effects of the disabilities can be minimized.

Remediation, a second intervention goal, refers to the "remedying" or curing of disabilities. In medicine, this is the primary goal of intervention whenever a condition is amenable to treatment. For example, if a young child's hearing loss is due to a middle ear infection (otitis media), the physician's response may be to treat the infection with medication. If the condition is chronic, a surgical procedure called a myringotomy may be performed; in this procedure, a small tube is inserted in the eardrum so that the fluid that has collected can drain (Green, 1985). Whatever the treatment regime, the goal is the same: elimination of the cause of the disability.

Remediation is sometimes an educational goal, also. In fact, the term is an educational rather than a medical one, and it is most closely associated with mild learning handicaps. For example, many of the early treatments of learning disabilities (e.g., Frostig & Horne, 1964; Roach & Kephart, 1966) focused on perceptual and motor deficits that were presumed to be the causes of academic learning problems. These treatments were based upon the premise that, if the cause of the learning problem could be remediated, the student would then be able to acquire school skills with the ease of a normal learner. Although the early approaches to the remediation of learning disabilities were not found effective (Arter & Jenkins, 1979; Lewis, 1983), research continues today on the development of techniques to teach this population of schoolchildren new strategies for learning (Deshler, Alley, Warner, & Schumaker, 1981). In addition, remediation is the goal for students whose learning problems stem from poor instruction or the lack of adequate opportunity to learn.

Facilitation of growth and development is a goal for all school-age individuals, including those with exceptionalities. In special education, that goal translates to special instruction designed to meet the unique needs of each learner. Each handicapped student's education is based on an individual program plan which specifies the special services needed by that student. The major goal of that educational program is facilitation of the student's achievement of his or her instructional goals. To accomplish this, specially trained teachers deliver individualized instruction in settings with small numbers of students.

Maintenance and generalization are also important goals. Once students have acquired a new skill or learned a new concept, they must be provided with sufficient opportunities for practice so that they will retain what they have learned (Lewis & Doorlag, 1987). In addition, if students are expected to apply their new skills in a variety of settings or situations, generalization becomes a goal of instruction. Generalization cannot be assumed, particularly with retarded learners and others who have difficulty applying what they have learned to new situations (Stokes & Baer, 1977).

With some learners, compensation is an educational goal. When disabilities cannot be remediated, they can sometimes be compensated for or bypassed. For example, students who have lost function in one sense can learn to use other abilities; although a blind student cannot see a textbook in order to read it, that student can read a braille text or listen to a tape-recorded version of it. Compensatory strategies are also taught to students with academic difficulties, particularly when these students take part in regular education classes. A student with poor arithmetic skills may use a calculator for computation; one with poor writing skills may type homework assignments or tape-record them.

Acceleration is a goal for all exceptional individuals. For gifted and talented students, one of the ways in which the educational experience may be tailored to their special needs is by acceleration through the curriculum at a faster pace than the regular classroom allows. In contrast, handicapped students begin school with fewer skills than their regular class counterparts or they quickly fall behind. For these students also, the goal is to increase the speed with which they learn. Polloway, Payne, Patton, and Payne (1985), in their discussion of effective teaching, maintain that effective teachers not only help students learn more, they also accelerate the rate with which students acquire new skills and information.

Models for School-Based Services

Models for the provision of special educational services vary on many dimensions, but two of the most important are curriculum (or the body of skills and information taught in the educational program) and the instructional methods used to teach that curriculum.

The three curricular models that serve as the foundation for current school practice are the developmental model, the remedial-compensatory model, and the functional life skills model. These models share a common purpose—to assist exceptional children and young people to reach their fullest potential so that they will be prepared to live successfully in the adult world—but the ways in which the models go about achieving that goal are markedly different. However, in each of the models, there is a division between the types of skill areas emphasized for mildly handicapped students and those emphasized for severely handicapped students. Curricula for mildly handicapped children and youth stress the development of academic and behavioral skills; those for students with more debilitating handicaps stress the development of language, social, and daily living skills.

Developmental curricula are based on the premise that there is a set sequence of steps that children go through as they develop, that each step is built on the previous step, and that all children follow the same developmental sequence. The regular education curriculum is one that is developmental in nature; the curriculum of the first grade provides the foundation for that of the second grade, grade 2 builds upon grade 1 and prepares students for grade 3, and so on. For some students with mild handicapping conditions, the primary focus of the special education program is to assist students to achieve the goals of the regular curriculum (and, if possible, to do this at the same rate as that of their nonhandicapped peers). Developmental programs of this type teach the same skills and information as the regular curriculum, and the sequence of instruction is the same. If a student has mastered grade 3 arithmetic, the next step in instruction is to teach grade 4 arithmetic.

The developmental model is also used in some programs that serve more severely handicapped students. With this population, the developmental sequence that is the basis of instruction is not the regular education curriculum. Because of the serious delays many of these students show in a variety of developmental domains, instruction is based upon the stages of normal development for infants and young children. In this type of program, developmental skills are taught in sequence: crawling before walking, walking before running.

In the remedial-compensatory model, development is not viewed as an invariant sequence of stages and steps. The milestones of development are considered important, but achievement of those milestones is approached in a different manner. If walking is an instructional goal, then walking skills are taught, whether or not the student has mastered the developmental prerequisites. Remedial education seeks to teach skills that students did not acquire as they passed through the preschool years or the regular school curriculum; its goal is to fill in the important gaps in the student's development. When this is not possible, the goal of education shifts to compensation. If a student's physical condition precludes the possibility of learning to walk, he or she is taught another way to move about and explore the environment.

The functional life skills model is more future-oriented and less concerned with the developmental tasks of childhood. Its thrust is the development of skills that will benefit students in their future environments. Curricula based upon this model often emphasize self-help and independent living skills, prevocational and vocational skills, and functional academic skills. If skills from the normal developmental sequence or the regular curriculum are taught, it is because they serve some important purpose in adult life.

To clarify the differences among these three curricular models, consider this example. Alex is a mildly handicapped student who is in the seventh grade; he is one year older than his classmates because he was retained in third grade due to poor achievement in reading and spelling. Alex continues to have difficulty with these subjects and his current educational program plan calls for special instruction in reading and spelling. Alex is comfortable reading material written at the fourth grade level; with fifth grade material and higher, he can read the words correctly but shows poor comprehension of what he has read.

In a developmental special education program, reading instruction would begin with fifth grade material, and Alex might even read from the standard fifth grade textbook. The teacher would use special instructional methods to facilitate Alex's progress through the regular scope and sequence of reading skills as quickly as possible.

A remedial-compensatory program would focus on Alex's specific problem in reading, that of comprehension skills. Although fifth grade textbooks might be used for instruction, the goal would be to perfect Alex's ability to understand what he has read, not to teach all of the reading skills included within the fifth grade curriculum. The special program might also attempt to provide Alex with compensatory strategies for accomplishing his reading assignments in the regular classroom.

In a special education program based on the functional life skills model, reading for meaning would be emphasized and instruction would focus on realistic reading tasks. Instead of reading textbooks designed for younger students, Alex would practice his comprehension skills with the reading materials most often encountered in daily life: restaurant menus, newspapers and magazines, job applications and other types of forms, television schedules, and the like. Alex would be learning skills to enable him to cope with the adult world, not attempting to meet the academic requirements of the regular school curriculum.

These three curricular models, though quite different, are not necessarily mutually exclusive. A developmental program might be appropriate for a student in one curriculum area but a remedial one necessary for another skill domain. In addition, the three models form a hierarchy. Special education programs based on the developmental model are most similar to the regular curriculum provided to nonexceptional students. Remedial-compensatory programs represent a more drastic type of intervention, and functional life skills programs are the most radical departure from regular school services.

In general, the younger the child and the milder the disability, the more likely it is that the developmental or the remedial-compensatory model will govern the provision of special services. With older students with persistent disabilities and with students with severe handicaps, there is a more marked discrepancy between their level of performance and that expected in the regular classroom. The greater the magnitude of this discrepancy, the more pertinent the functional life skills model becomes.

In schools today, programs for mildly handicapped students tend to emphasize the developmental and remedial models. For example, Deshler, Lowrey, and Alley (1979) reported that the most common program for adolescent students with learning disabilities was one that provided remedial instruction for skill deficits in reading and mathematics. Programs for severely handicapped students have historically been developmental in nature, but current theorists urge movement toward the functional life skills approach (Guess et al., 1978). Skills should be included in the curriculum only if they are important in the student's current and future environments, and these skills should be taught in the environments in which they are to be performed. In addition, students should participate in learning activities appropriate to their age, not their developmental level.

The career education curriculum in special education is based to some extent upon the functional life skills model. According to the Council for Exceptional Children (1978), "career education is concerned with the total person and his/her adjustment for community working and living." One focus of this approach to special education is preparation for the world of work; students progress through the stages of career awareness, career exploration, career preparation,

The functional life skills approach is the model followed at the Life Experience School, a school for multiply handicapped students.

and career placement (Brolin, 1982; Cegelka, 1985). Career education programs also prepare students for the other important roles of adulthood: self-care, independent community living, social pursuits, marriage and family, and use of leisure time. For example, the life-centered curriculum developed by Brolin (1978) addresses daily living skills, personal-social skills, and occupational guidance and preparation.

Whatever theoretical model underlies the special education curriculum, instruction is the process by which that curriculum is implemented. There are many models of instruction available in special education, but current programs tend to be based upon a behavioral view of instruction. The major premise of this view is that behaviors are learned and thus are amenable to instruction (Alberto & Troutman, 1982; Skinner, 1953; Sulzer-Azaroff & Mayer, 1977). Measurement is an important component of this model; the student's current levels of performance are assessed to determine an appropriate starting place, and assessment continues during instruction to monitor the effects of intervention.

The educator influences learning in two ways: by arranging the instructional environment to facilitate learning and by providing students with appropriate consequences for their actions. In doing this, the teacher manipulates the events which precede the student's behaviors (the antecedents) and the events that follow it (the consequences).

The behavioral model, sometimes called applied behavior analysis, can be used with any age or type of student and any curricular content. Once the goals of instruction are determined, these are translated into specific instructional objectives. The learning tasks targeted in each objective are analyzed and complex tasks are broken down into simpler subtasks. Instruction then proceeds in small, incremental steps. The student learns each step to a prespecified mastery level before moving on to the next step. The teacher closely monitors the student's performance in order to provide feedback on response accuracy, reinforce correct responses, and ensure that the student maintains a high rate of success.

Instructional programs with a behavioral emphasis appear to be effective in promoting student growth. Leinhardt and Pallay (1982), in a review of research on effective special education programs, reached these conclusions:

> Successful programs seem to have a number of elements in common. The majority have a distinctly behavioristic approach. Goals and objectives are clearly specified; instructional devices for obtaining objectives are also specified; overt contingency management systems are operating; and mastery learning techniques are used.   (p. 573)

Another instructional approach that is beginning to influence special education programming, particularly for mildly handicapped students, is direct instruction (Lewis, 1983). This approach is based on the findings of the effective schools research in regular education (e.g., Anderson, Evertson, & Brophy, 1979; California State Department of Education, 1977; Soar, 1973; Stallings & Kaskowitz, 1974). This body of research has identified several instructional factors that appear to contribute to successful school achievement. Among the important factors are a focus on academic learning, teacher-directed learning activities, high teacher expectations for academic progress, and student accountability and cooperation (Weil & Murphy, 1982). In applying these results to special education, Stevens and Rosenshine (1981) suggest that effective instructional programs are individualized, teacher-directed, and academically focused.

Services During the School Years

In the 1983–84 school year, almost 11 percent of the school-age population received special education services because of an identified handicapping condition that interfered with school performance (U.S. Department of Education, 1985). According to federal law, special education must be provided to all handicapped students in need of this service. Although it is possible that some handicapped students remain unserved, it is likely that most are identified and participating in some sort of special program. The current service picture for gifted and talented students is very different; there is no federal law mandating special services for this population. Depending upon the incidence figure used, from 39 percent to 63 percent of gifted and talented students are not identified or are not the recipients of specialized instruction (Thomason, 1981).

The most typical special education service for school-aged individuals is instruction. An Individualized Education Program is prepared for each student and that program is carried out by a specially trained teacher in the student's regular classroom, in a resource room, or some other educational setting.

In addition to the special instructional program, related services may also be provided if these are necessary to assist the student to benefit from special education. Related services include transportation, school health services, medical services for diagnostic or evaluation purposes, speech pathology and audiology, psychological services, counseling and social work services, physical and occupational therapy, and parent counseling and training. Whereas special instruction is aimed primarily at meeting learning needs, related services extend intervention to social-emotional and physical-health needs as well as to the needs of parents of handicapped children.

Instructional programs in special education are usually described in terms of the setting in which instruction takes place. A continuum of service options is available, ranging from placement in the regular classroom with no specialized service to a full-time residential program in a special school, hospital, or other treatment facility. However, the most common placements are resource services and special classes. With resource services, the student spends the majority of the school day in the regular classroom but also receives part-time services from a special education resource teacher; this option is most often used with mildly handicapped students. It is considered one of the least restrictive placements because handicapped students are integrated with nonhandicapped students in the regular classroom. The process of integrating special students with the regular school population is called mainstreaming. According to Kaufman, Gottlieb, Agard, and Kukic (1975), mainstreaming is not just the physical placement of exceptional students in the same classroom as nonhandicapped peers; it is also "temporal, instructional, and social integration" (p. 35).

Special classes are classes within regular schools that contain only handicapped students. These students spend the majority of the school day in this special setting. However, there is opportunity for special class students to interact with their nonhandicapped peers in general school activities and some may be mainstreamed into regular classes for a portion of the school day. Special classes tend to serve students with severe and comprehensive educational needs.

Approximately 70 percent of school-age handicapped students are served in regular classrooms with supplementary resource services (U.S. Department of Education, 1985). Special classes are the next most common setting, serving around 25 percent of handicapped students. Only around 5 percent of handicapped students between the ages of 6 and 17 receive their education in special schools, hospitals, and other separate environments. The picture changes, however, when specific disabilities are considered. The regular class is the most common educational placement for only three groups of exceptional students: those with learning disabilities, speech impairments, and visual handicaps. The majority of students identified as mentally retarded, emotionally disturbed, other health impaired, multihandicapped, deaf and hard of hearing, orthopedically impaired, and deaf-blind are educated in special classes, special schools, or other restrictive environments.

Another way of viewing instructional services is whether they are categorical or noncategorical. With categorical services, students with the same type or category of disability are grouped together for instruction. For example, a school might offer a resource room for learning disabled students, a special class for mentally retarded students, and a special class for physically handicapped students. Categorical programs have several drawbacks, according to Smith and Neisworth (1975). Disability labels are not useful educationally; they do not provide sufficient information for planning instruction. In fact, labels can result in lowered expectations for student performance. In addition, categorical groupings overlap; a child might show characteristics that indicate several different disabilities.

In noncategorical programs, students are grouped according to their learning needs, not type of disability. Thus, a noncategorical resource program might serve any exceptional student who requires assistance because of an academic learning problem. The most typical noncategorical service is a resource room for mildly handicapped students (U.S. Department of Education, 1985). The non-categorical movement in special education has had an impact not only on direct services to students but also on the preparation of teachers. As Blackhurst (1981) observed, noncategorical teacher training programs are becoming more common and "there is a trend toward generic [teacher] certification in special education . . . at least 40% of the states are currently committed to this concept" (p. 199).

The Effectiveness of School-Based Services

Professionals have been interested in the effectiveness of special education programs for handicapped students since the 1930s when these programs began to emerge in public schools (Bennett, 1932; Pertsch, 1936). In the decades before the 1970s, program effectiveness was studied by comparing the performance of handicapped students who received special education services with that of handicapped students who remained in regular classes and received no special services. This type of comparison was possible before special programming became mandatory; at that time, many handicapped students remained in regular classes and neither they nor their teachers were offered any type of special assistance.

The most typical comparison study examined the academic and social status of mentally retarded students placed in special classes and those who remained in the regular classes with no special services. In general, results did not support the value of special class placement. Strain and Kerr (1981), in a review of this body of research, conclude that "EMR children in special classes do not appear to demonstrate significantly better educational achievement than EMR children in regular class placement. In fact, the dominant trend in efficacy research has favored regular class children" (p. 8). In addition, EMR children in integrated settings appeared to show higher self-concepts than those in special class settings. This body of research has been criticized for its methodological flaws and its failure to account for curricular differences between regular and special programs (MacMillan, 1971). However, the findings clearly did not provide empirical support for the benefits of special education services to mildly handicapped youngsters.

In the 1970s, better designed research studies began to amass evidence that special education interventions are effective for school-age children. Among the educational environments compared in these studies were special classes, resource programs, regular classes with support services, and regular classes with no special services. Leinhardt and Pallay (1982) summarized the results of this research:

> There were several examples of successful programs for mildly handicapped students that used isolated environments. Among the two isolated environments, resource rooms and self-contained classes, there is weak evidence that the less restrictive of the two, the resource room, may be superior. There are also examples of successful programs which help nonachieving students in the mainstream without removing them from the regular class.   (p. 564)

Carlberg and Kavale (1980) used a technique called meta-analysis (Glass, 1976) to synthesize the results of 50 studies of special versus regular class placement. They report negative effects of special class placement for students with low IQs but positive effects for learning disabled and behaviorally/emotionally disturbed pupils.

Today, professionals are beginning to approach the efficacy question from a new direction. Forness and Kavale (1984) point out that study of the relative effectiveness of different educational placements may be the wrong question. They say, "Where we teach may not be as important as what and how we teach" (p. 242). Leinhardt and Pallay (1982) concur, and they identify several curricular and instructional factors found effective in promoting student growth. These include small class size, consistency between curricular goals and instructional activities, mastery learning and a formal management system, increased time for cognitive activities, and increased instructional time.

Much of the research on the implementation of mandatory school services for handicapped students has focused on the effects of mainstreaming. According to Madden and Slavin (1983), "research favors placement in regular classes using individualized instruction or supplemented by well-designed resource programs for the achievement, self-esteem, behavior, and social emotional adjustment of academically handicapped students" (p. 519). That is, placing students in an integrated environment is not sufficient; that placement must be accompanied by special services to students and/or their teachers to facilitate academic growth and social acceptance. Social acceptance is a particular problem. Handicapped students in regular classes are less well accepted and more often rejected than their nonhandicapped peers (e.g., Bryan, 1974, 1976; Bryan & Bryan, 1978; Drabman & Patterson, 1981). In addition, handicapped students placed in integrated environments do not automatically begin to interact with nonhandicapped students. Gresham (1981) maintains that "handicapped students do not vicariously acquire social skills via observation of nonhandicapped models unless they are instructed, trained, or reinforced for doing so" (p. 139).

Another method for gauging the effectiveness of special education is to conduct longitudinal studies of students who are program graduates. This type of research evaluates the adult performance of persons who received special services as children, and the results of such studies are reviewed in the next section. However, it is not yet possible to investigate what effects mandatory services will have upon the adult adjustment of handicapped children. The provisions of PL 94–142 did not take effect until 1978 and the cohort of children who began first grade at that time will not complete 12 years of schooling until 1990.

ADULTHOOD

For some, exceptionality is a lifelong experience; for others, exceptionality is acquired. Injuries and aging account for the largest number of acquired disabilities inflating the number of adults who are exceptional; however, the actual number of adults with exceptionalities is difficult to determine. In infancy and early childhood, many young children with exceptionalities are identified and followed through the education or health systems. During the school years, students with handicapping conditions or children who are gifted or talented receive special education services; but when an exceptional individual reaches adulthood, there is no common comprehensive system of tracking and service delivery. This, combined with the increase in disabilities associated with aging, makes it difficult to estimate the number of adults who might be considered exceptional. It is clear, however, that on a worldwide basis, disabling exceptionalities are increasing. It is estimated that by the year 2000, 846 million (13.5 percent) of the world's population will be disabled and that more than four-fifths of those individuals will live in developing countries (Hammerman & Maikowski, 1981). Although the picture in the United States is less overwhelming, a Social Security survey conducted in 1972 estimated that more than 15 percent of the adults between the ages of 20 and 64 were disabled (Krute & Burdette, 1978). Since these estimates were based upon noninstitutionalized persons, a large number of more severely disabled adults were not included in the estimate.

The identification of gifted and talented individuals in adulthood is equally complicated because the definitions of this exceptionality are not easily agreed upon for adults. Assessing adults to determine whether or not they are intellectually gifted is not done; adults seldom take IQ tests. Instead, special talent and giftedness are more often inferred from performance. Nobel laureates are usually considered to be gifted, but they include only a small number of outstanding scholars and diplomats. Artists, musicians, inventors, athletes, individuals who have distinguished themselves in management, or those who are noted for their foresight and vision are often considered to be gifted or talented. However, there is less consensus about adults than children. Many would argue that all composers are talented while others would contend that the composer of an opera is talented but that the composer of the best-selling popular song is not. To some, an Olympic record holder would be talented, but the world's best bowler would not be. Television or film stars may be considered talented by some; by others, they would simply be considered examples of good marketing techniques. Many people would agree that some teachers are gifted or that some people seem to be especially gifted in rearing children; but since there are few forums for recognizing these kinds of talents, they are often overlooked.

Children are often encouraged by supportive parents and teachers to use their talents, but many adults do not have mentors who encourage them. Lack of educational opportunities and self-confidence or life decisions which interfere with achievement limit the number of adults who are recognized as gifted or talented.

Needs of Exceptional Adults

Exceptional adults have the same needs as all adults. They need housing, transportation, access to medical services, vocational and avocational pursuits, and opportunities to develop and maintain relationships. The kinds of assistance that exceptional adults may need to achieve independence varies with their exceptionality, personality, educational or skill level, whether the exceptionality is long-standing or acquired, and the way that they have been parented.

Achieving maturity is not an easy task for anyone; for adults with disabilities, it is further complicated by society's attitudes toward them. During childhood and adolescence when nonhandicapped children are encouraged to challenge limits and develop independence, handicapped children are often sheltered and protected from competition. They may even be infantilized, that is, treated like a young child who needs constant care. Well-meaning parents may be fearful of allowing their handicapped son or daughter to take the kinds of risks that promote learning. Teachers, too, may resist challenging handicapped students thus reducing their opportunities to learn how to cope in the world that they will face as adults. This deprives handicapped individuals of the opportunities to acquire the range of personal, social, and academic skills that are needed to succeed in adulthood (Dickerson, 1981; Lowenfeld, 1975). Many physically handicapped students entering universities report that they were never prepared for the competition of the college classroom nor the physical demands of negotiating a large campus in a wheelchair (R. B. Brady, personal communication, April 18, 1984).

Although society's attitudes about disabled individuals have become more positive over the past few years, attitudes continue to be the most serious barrier for handicapped individuals (DeLoach & Greer, 1981). These attitudes and the treatment that they engender have been described as handicapism. According to Biklen and Bodgan (1977), "Handicapism can be defined as a theory and set of practices that promote unequal and unjust treatment of people because of apparent or assumed physical or mental disability. Handicapism manifests itself in relations between individuals, in social policy and cultural norms, and in the helping professions as well" (p. 206). Some of the handicapist attitudes that have been identified include: viewing people with handicaps as sad people; pitying those with disabilities; seeing only the disability, not the person; avoiding disabled individuals; telling handicapist jokes; and speaking about handicapped people in their presence rather than to them. Stereotypes about individuals with disabilities are as dangerous as stereotypes about any other minority.

Services for Adults with Disabilities

The principle of normalization (Wolfensberger, 1972) posits that individuals with disabilities have the right to live, work, play, and learn in environments as close to those of their nonhandicapped peers as possible. This suggests that the services for adults with handicapping conditions should be the same as those that are available to nonhandicapped adults. For example, handicapped adults should be eligible to participate in the same vocational programs, attend the same churches, live in the same neighborhoods, and use the same recreational facilities as adults without handicaps. The segregationist views of the past which created recreation programs for the blind, medical clinics for mentally retarded patients, and sheltered workshops for mentally ill, mentally retarded, or visually handicapped clients are slowly giving way to integrated, generic programs where all individuals, handicapped and nonhandicapped, can receive services.

Within these generic services, however, there sometimes need to be special adaptations or modifications for individuals with handicaps. For example, public transportation systems should be designed so that they can be used by individuals who are blind and those in wheelchairs. Apartment complexes can have ramps and include some units that have been modified for individuals in wheelchairs. Businesses and industries also need to review their employment practices so that they can take advantage of the skills of handicapped workers. As all community recreation centers, churches, and parks are built, planners should be aware of the modifications that will make them accessible to people with handicaps. Until adaptations are made which allow access to all people, there will continue to be gaps in services.

For some exceptional adults, adapted generic services will never be adequate; more specialized services are necessary. Some adults, especially those who are more severely mentally retarded or emotionally disturbed, need more supervision in their daily lives than a supervised apartment complex can offer. Group homes, located in regular neighborhoods with 24-hour staff, allow individuals

An American Sign Language interpreter is utilized to aid hearing impaired employees in an industrial training class.

with greater needs to live in a near-normal setting with ongoing support and supervision. For adults who are not yet able to function in competitive employment, sheltered workshops can provide opportunities to work for pay outside the home. Many communities have developed transportation systems such as Dial-A-Ride specifically for individuals in wheelchairs or for those with more severe disabilities. Supplemental Security Income, paid through the Social Security Administration, is available to handicapped individuals to provide a very modest income; and other social service agencies often provide recreational opportunities for adults with disabilities. Although PL 94–142 mandates education only through age 21, many community colleges and universities have developed special programs for students with handicaps. Some community colleges have developed life skills programs for retarded adults, and most colleges and universities have Disabled Student Services offices on campus to assist disabled students. These programs provide readers or computer braillers for blind students, assist learning disabled students to improve their study habits, counsel handicapped students as they try to adjust to the demands of campus life, and work with professors to help them understand the special needs of handicapped students.

Longitudinal Studies of Exceptional Adults

Since exceptional adults constitute such a diverse group of individuals, less is known about them than about children who are exceptional. No single agency or organization follows exceptional adults, making it more difficult to collect information about their progress. As a result, what is known has come from longitudinal research studies or anecdotal accounts of small numbers of exceptional individuals. Two of the classic studies have described mildly mentally retarded (Edgerton, 1967) and gifted individuals (Sears, 1979; Terman & Oden, 1947).

Edgerton, an anthropologist, studied mildly mentally retarded individuals who had been released from a large California institution for the mentally retarded after successfully completing a vocational training program. These individuals had completed the training program between 1949 and 1958 and had been discharged without restrictions or continued monitoring by the institution. The 110 subjects of this ethnographic study were equally divided between male and female. They ranged in age from 20 to 75 with a mean age of 35 and a mean IQ of 64. Approximately 74 percent were Anglo, 20 percent Mexican-American, 5 percent black, and 1 percent of other racial and ethnic backgrounds. After six months of searching in the latter half of 1960, 85 percent of the individuals had been located. The search for those remaining continued for another six months, and all but 12 of the original 110 former residents had been located. Those who were never located did not differ from those located in terms of their preinstitution and institution experiences. Researchers contacted the 53 subjects who were still living within a 50-mile radius of the hospital, and made repeated contacts with 51. These 51 were observed and interviewed extensively during a 12-month period about their lifestyles, vocation, relationship to others in the community, personal life, free-time activities, self-perceptions and presentation, and the problems that they encountered functioning in the community.

What became clear in the study was that, although there was great variation in the way these individuals lived, all were living at the bottom end of the social and economic continuum. Even though they were only mildly mentally retarded, had been successful in a job training program, and returned to the community during a time of national prosperity, they were economically and socially impoverished; and the stability which they did achieve was due more to associations with a benevolent benefactor than to their own abilities.

Despite this, their central concerns related to ways to make a living, manage sex, marriage, and reproduction, and what to do with leisure time, concerns which are central to all adults. The difference which Edgerton (1967) reported as having the most impact on the lives of these individuals was the stigma of mental retardation. To succeed in a society which values intelligence, they often denied their retardation and tried to pass as "normal." They invested considerable energy trying to hide their past. The individuals studied had developed excuses to explain their institutionalization, had searched for a marriage partner that was not retarded, and had collected the memorabilia and souvenirs that are part of the accumulation of normal life. Although most read only magazines and newspapers, they had purchased all kinds of books to keep in their homes. Many displayed their mail conspicuously, and one woman even searched for discarded mail to display as another sign of her normalcy. The examples provided by Edgerton (1967) are powerful statements about the stigma of retardation and segregation from society. Among the adults that he studied, their retardation itself presented far fewer problems than their fear of being viewed as retarded. But, regardless of the cause, these problems were pervasive and continuing. In a later follow-up of 30 of the subjects by Edgerton and Bercovici (1976), their situations had not improved significantly.

Another classic study of exceptional individuals was conducted by Terman and his colleagues (1947). In 1921, over 1000 gifted children from large and medium-sized urban areas of California were selected for the study. These subjects have been followed for over 50 years, and a great deal has been written about their achievement, adjustment, and success in adulthood. Although this study represents a landmark in longitudinal data collection, the outcomes must be viewed with skepticism because of the methods used to select the original sample. The longitudinal data have, however, suggested that children with high IQs are generally superior in physique and general health and that their achievement through high school tends to be superior in all academic areas. In particular, those who were accelerated through the grades showed superior academic and life outcomes. In general, the gifted persons in this sample were above average in character and personality. Although this early work does not address or adequately answer all of the questions about giftedness, it clearly dispels many of the myths.

Because of the many changes in programs, services, and attitudes in the past few years, research is needed to determine the characteristics and needs of the disabled and gifted adults of the 1980s and beyond. Early identification, intensive education, increased integration, new curricular emphases, and expanded vocational and life opportunities may make the old ideas obsolete.

FUTURE PERSPECTIVES FOR SERVICES FOR EXCEPTIONAL PEOPLE

Today, exceptional individuals and their families have available to them a wide range of educational, medical, and social services. These services span the age range from infancy to adulthood, and they include both generic services and those designed specifically for exceptional people.

However, appropriate services are not available to all exceptional persons who need them. This is due, in part, to a decline in fiscal resources for human service programs. It is also due to gaps in the service delivery system. For example, while there are many services for handicapped children and adults, there are few for persons with special gifts and talents. Likewise, while school-age individuals have access to numerous types of special programs, the service options for adults are more limited.

This picture may change as the generation of exceptional children moving through the schools today reaches adulthood. This group of children and their families are the first to benefit from PL 94–142's guarantee of appropriate school services for handicapped individuals. As a result, these families are more aware of their rights than any previous group, and they have come to expect special services. When the children finish their public schooling, they and their families will expect to find an array of community services for the benefit of young adults. If these services are not available, this group is likely to exert pressure upon community leaders, social agencies, and legislators to develop appropriate services.

Another factor that will influence the availability of services for adults is the "graying" of America. The average age of the American citizenry is increasing. The lifespan is also increasing, resulting in a national population with a greater concentration of mature adults. And, as persons age, they are more likely to acquire a disability: a physical impairment or health problem, a loss of hearing, impaired vision, even cognitive losses. Thus, changes in national demographics will result in greater numbers of handicapped persons, which will call attention to the need for special medical and social services for disabled adults.

Planning for transitions is another critical issue in service delivery. Among the most important transition points for children and their families are entry into school, puberty, and the completion of formal schooling. These transition points are universal; all families experience them. For families with a handicapped child, however, these changes influence special needs and transitions may involve moving from one set of services to another. To facilitate this, planning must occur and that planning needs to involve collaboration among service agencies. For example, if a student is to make a smooth transition from a high school special education class to a vocational rehabilitation program, the agencies involved must communicate and cooperate with each other and with the student and his or her family.

One of the most important issues facing both children and adults with handicapping conditions are the attitudes of the nonhandicapped population toward persons with disabilities. For mainstreaming programs to be effective, both teachers and students must be prepared to accept handicapped students as full-fledged members of the regular classroom. For deinstitutionalization efforts to be successful, members of the community must be prepared to accept handicapped persons as neighbors, shoppers, bus-riders, and employees. Although handicapped persons today are less likely to be educated and to live in separate segregated environments, negative attitudes persist. These attitudes must be dispelled if the goals of normalization are to be achieved.

SUMMARY

Exceptional people require exceptional services; but the type, intensity, and duration of those services varies with the individual, the family, and the community. The school system is the major provider of educational services for exceptional individuals from preschool through age 21. Medical and allied health professionals provide routine and specialized services throughout the individual's lifespan, and social service professionals and agencies assist exceptional people and their families obtain services which enable them to participate in community life.

For many exceptional individuals, regular community services are adequate for most of their needs. They use the same generic services used by other members of the community. However, more specialized services such as wheelchair accessible transportation, modified educational programs, or babysitting services designed specifically for handicapped individuals may also be needed.

Specialized services for handicapped individuals begin in infancy and extend throughout the lifespan. Medical and educational early intervention programs begin as soon as the disability is diagnosed. The goals of early medical intervention for handicapped children are to prevent disability or reduce the effects of handicapping conditions. Early educational intervention programs are based on a variety of theoretical models; but all are designed to reduce the effects of handicapping conditions, maintain skills, and accelerate development.

During the school years, exceptional students receive special educational services designed to increase their achievement, accelerate their development, improve their social skills, and prepare them for a vocation. The curriculum varies with the student and the exceptionality. For some pupils with learning problems, the curriculum will focus on functional skills such as dressing, eating, and toileting independently; for others, the curriculum will focus on basic academic skills and vocational preparation. For gifted and talented students, the curriculum may focus on advanced skills in a variety of subjects, leadership, or the performing arts.

During the adult years, services for exceptional individuals may include specialized housing, transportation, vocational training, social skills training, counseling, or special aids and devices which allow them to function independently. Professionals from medicine, health, speech and language, social work, counseling, psychology, and vocational rehabilitation often work with adults with disabilities.

Regardless of the type of program and the professional providing the service, all services are based on assessment procedures which examine the needs of the exceptional individual and his or her family. Programs for handicapped individuals are also based on the principle of normalization, the belief that services for handicapped individuals should be as similar to those provided to nonhandicapped individuals as possible.

During the last decade services for exceptional individuals have improved dramatically. In many parts of the country services start in infancy and follow the individual throughout the lifespan; but in many communities the full range of services is not available. Within the next decade the emphasis will shift to assuring that quality services are available as a matter of right.

References

Alberto, P. A., & Troutman, A. C. (1982). *Applied behavior analysis for teachers*. Columbus, OH: Merrill Publishing.

Alberto, P. A., Briggs, T., & Goldstein, D. (1983). Managing learning in handicapped infants. In S. G. Garwood & R. R. Fewell (Eds.), *Educating handicapped infants* (pp. 417–454). Rockville, MD: Aspen.

Anderson, L. M., Evertson, C. M., & Brophy, J. E. (1979). An experimental study of effective teaching in first-grade reading groups. *Elementary School Journal, 79*, 193–222.

Apgar, V. (1953). A proposal for a new method of evaluation of the newborn infant. *Current Researches in Anesthesia and Analgesia, 32*, 260–267.

Arter, J. A., & Jenkins, J. R. (1979). Differential diagnosis-prescriptive teaching: A critical appraisal. *Review of Educational Research, 49*, 517–555.

Bagnato, S. J., & Neisworth, J. T. (1981). *Linking developmental assessment and curricula*. Rockville, MD: Aspen.

Bailey, D. B., & Wolery, M. (1984). *Teaching infants and preschoolers with handicaps*. Columbus, OH: Merrill Publishing.

Battelle Institute of Columbus, Ohio (1976). *A summary of the evaluation of the Handicapped Children's Early Education Program*. Columbus, OH: Author.

Bennett, A. (1932). *A comparative study of subnormal children in the elementary grades*. New York: Teachers College, Columbia University.

Biklen, D., & Bogdan, R. (1977). Handicapism in America. In B. Blatt, D. Biklen, & R. Bogdan (Eds.), *An alternative textbook in special education* (pp. 205–215). Denver: Love Publishing.

Blackard, M. K., & Barsch, E. T. (1982). Parents' and professionals' perception of the handicapped child's impact on the family. *The Journal of the Association for the Severely Handicapped, 7* (2), 62–70.

Blackhurst, A. E. (1981). Noncategorical teacher preparation: Problems and promises. *Exceptional Children, 48*, 197–205.

Blackman, J. A. (Ed.) (1983). *Medical aspects of developmental disabilities in children birth to three*. Iowa City: Division of Developmental Disabilities, Department of Pediatrics.

Bricker, D., & Sheehan, R. (1981). Effectiveness of an early intervention program as indexed by measures of child change. *Journal of the Division of Early Childhood, 4*, 11–27.

Brolin, D. E. (1978). *Life centered career education: A competency-based approach*. Reston, VA: Council for Exceptional Children.

Brolin, D. E. (1982). *Vocational preparation of persons with handicaps*. Columbus, OH: Merrill Publishing.

Bryan, T. (1974). Peer popularity of learning disabled children. *Journal of Learning Disabilities, 7*, 621–625.

Bryan, T. (1976). Peer popularity of learning disabled children: A replication. *Journal of Learning Disabilities, 9*, 307–311.

Bryan, T. H., & Bryan, J. H. (1978). Social interactions of learning disabled children. *Learning Disability Quarterly, 1* (1), 33–38.

California State Department of Education (1977). *California school effectiveness study: The first year, 1974–1975.* Sacramento, CA: Author.

Carlberg, C., & Kavale, K. (1980). The efficacy of special versus regular class placement for exceptional children: A meta-analysis. *Journal of Special Education, 14,* 295–309.

Cegelka, P. T. (1985). Career and vocational education. In W. H. Berdine & A. E. Blackhurst (Eds.), *An introduction to special education* (2nd ed.) (pp. 573–612). Boston: Little, Brown.

Cole, J. G., & Frappier, P. (1983). *Developmental intervention in a special care nursery: A new approach to providing care for the preterm infant.* (Available from Center for Parenting Studies, Wheelock College, 200 The Riverway, Boston, MA 02215)

Connolly, A. J., Nachtman, W., & Pritchett, E. M. (1976). *KeyMath diagnostic arithmetic test.* Circle Pines, MN: American Guidance Service.

Council for Exceptional Children (1978). *Position paper on career education.* Reston, VA: Author.

DeLoach, C., & Greer, B. G. (1981). *Adjustment to severe physical disability.* New York: McGraw-Hill.

Deno, E. (1970). Special education as developmental capital. *Exceptional Children, 37,* 229–237.

Deshler, D. D., Alley, G. R., Warner, M. W., & Schumaker, J. B. (1981). Instructional practices for promoting skill acquisition and generalization in severely learning disabled adolescents. *Learning Disability Quarterly, 4,* 415–422.

Deshler, D. D., Lowrey, N., & Alley, G. R. (1979). Programing alternatives for LD adolescents: A nationwide survey. *Academic Therapy, 14,* 389–397.

DeWeerd, J. (1981). Early education services for children with handicaps—where have we been, where are we now, and where are we going? *Journal of the Division of Early Childhood, 2,* 15–24.

Diana v. State Board of Education (1970). C. A. No. C-70-37 (N.D. Cal. 1970).

Dickerson, M. U. (1981). *Social work practice and the mentally retarded.* New York: The Free Press.

Drabman, R. S., & Patterson, J. N. (1981). Disruptive behavior and the social standing of exceptional children. *Exceptional Education Quarterly, 1* (4), 45–56.

DuBose, R. F. (1981). Assessment of severely impaired young children: Problems and recommendations. *Topics in Early Childhood Special Education, 1* (2), 9–21.

Dunn, L. M. (1968). Special education for the mildly retarded—Is much of it justifiable? *Exceptional Children, 35,* 5–22.

Dunn, L. M., & Markwardt, F. C. (1970). *Peabody individual achievement test.* Circle Pines, MN: American Guidance Service.

Edgerton, R. B. (1967). *The cloak of competence.* Berkeley, CA: University of California Press.

Edgerton, R. B., & Bercovici, S. M. (1976). The cloak of competence: Years later. *American Journal of Mental Deficiency, 80,* 485–497.

Fewell, R. (1983). The team approach to infant education. In S. G. Garwood & R. R. Fewell (Eds.), *Educating handicapped infants* (pp. 299–322). Rockville, MD: Aspen.

Finnie, N. R. (1975). *Handling the young cerebral palsied child at home* (2nd ed.). New York: E. P. Dutton.

Forness, S. R., & Kavale, K. A. (1984). Education of the mentally retarded: A note on policy. *Education and Training of the Mentally Retarded, 19,* 239–245.

Fraser, B. A., & Hensinger, R. N. (1983). *Managing physical handicaps: A practical guide for parents, care providers, and educators.* Baltimore: Paul H. Brookes.

Frostig, M., & Horne, D. (1964). *The Frostig program for the development of visual perception.* Chicago: Follett.

Glass, G. V. (1976). Primary, secondary, and meta-analysis of research. *Educational Researcher, 5,* 3–8.

Goldberg, S., & DiVitto, B. A. (1983). *Born too soon.* San Francisco: W. H. Freeman.

Grant, W. V., & Snyder, T. D. (1983–84). *Digest of education statistics 1983–84.* Washington, DC: National Center for Education Statistics.

Green, W. W. (1985). Hearing disorders. In W. H. Berdine & A. E. Blackhurst (Eds.), *An introduction to special education* (2nd ed.) (pp. 183–230). Boston: Little, Brown.

Gresham, M. (1981). Social skills training with the handicapped: A review. *Review of Educational Research, 51,* 139–176.

Guess, D., Horner, R. D., Utley, B., Holvoet, J., Maxon, D., Tucker, D., & Warren, S. (1978). A functional curriculum-sequencing model for teaching the severely handicapped. *AAESPH Review, 3,* 202–215.

Halle, J. W., & Sindelar, P. T. (1982). Behavioral observation methodologies for early childhood education. *Topics in Early Childhood Special Education, 2* (1), 43–54.

Hammerman, S., & Maikowski, S. (Eds.) (1981). *The economics of disability: International perspectives.* New York: Rehabilitation International.

Hanson, M., & Schwartz, R. (1978). Results of a longitudinal intervention program for Down's syndrome infants and their families. *Education and Training of the Mentally Retarded, 13,* 403–407.

Heber, R., Garber, H., Harrington, C., Hoffman, C., & Fallender, C. (1975). *Rehabilitation of families at risk for mental retardation. The Milwaukee Project.* Madison, WI: University of Wisconsin.

Heddens, J. W. (1982). Elementary education. In H. E. Mitzel (Ed.), *Encyclopedia of educational research* (5th ed.) (pp. 543–555). New York: The Free Press.

Heller, K. A., Holtzman, W. H., & Messick, S. (Eds.) (1982). *Placing children in special education: A strategy for equity.* Washington, DC: National Academic Press.

Horowitz, F. D. (1982). Methods of assessment for high-risk and handicapped infants. In C. T. Ramey & P. L. Trohanis (Eds.), *Finding and educating high-risk and handicapped infants* (pp. 101–118). Baltimore: University Park Press.

Johnson, N. M., & Jens, K. G. (1982). Infant-centered curricula. In J. D. Anderson (Ed.), *Curricula for high-risk and handicapped infants* (pp. 25–30). (Available from TADS, Frank Porter Graham Child Development Center, 500 NCNB Plaza, Chapel Hill, NC 27514)

Karnes, M. B., Schwedel, A. M., Lewis, G. F., Ratts, D. A., & Esry, D. R. (1981). Impact of early programming for the handicapped: A follow-up study into the elementary school. *Journal of the Division of Early Childhood, 4,* 62–79.

Karnes, M. B., & Teska, J. A. (1975). Children's response to early intervention programs. In J. Gallagher (Ed.), *The application of child development research to exceptional children* (pp. 198–243). Reston, VA: The Council for Exceptional Children.

Kauffman, J. M. (1981). *Characteristics of children's behavior disorders* (2nd ed.). Columbus, OH: Merrill Publishing.

Kaufman, M. J., Gottlieb, J., Agard, J. A., & Kukic, M. D. (1975). Mainstreaming: Toward an explication of the construct. In E. L. Meyen, G. A. Vergason, & R. J. Whelan (Eds.), *Alternatives for teaching exceptional children.* Denver: Love Publishing.

Klaus, M. H., & Fanaroff, A. A. (1979). *Care of the high-risk neonate* (2nd ed.). Philadelphia: W. B. Saunders.

Klaus, M., Fanaroff, A., & Martin, R. J. (1979). The physical environment. In M. H. Klaus & A. A. Fanaroff, *Care of the high-risk neonate* (2nd ed.). Philadelphia: W. B. Saunders.

Korones, S. B., & Lancaster, J. (1981). *High-risk newborn infants: The basis for intensive nursing care* (3rd ed.). St. Louis, MO: C. V. Mosby.

Krute, A., & Burdette, M. E. (1978). *Chronic disease, injury and work disability: 1972 survey of disabled and non-disabled adults* (Report #10). Washington, DC: United States Social Security Administration.

Lamb, M. E. (1983). Fathers of exceptional children. In M. Seligman (Ed.), *The family with a handicapped child* (pp. 125–146). New York: Grune & Stratton.

Larry P. v. Riles. (1972). 343 F. Supp. 1306 (N.D. Cal. 1972).

Lazar, I., Darlington, R., Murray, H., Royce, J., & Snipper, A. (1982). Lasting effects of early education: A report from the consortium for longitudinal studies. *Monographs of the Society for Research in Child Development, 47* (2–3, Serial No. 195).

Leinhardt, G., & Pallay, A. (1982). Restrictive educational settings: Exile or haven? *Review of Educational Research, 52,* 557–578.

Lewis, R. B. (1983). Learning disabilities and reading: Instructional recommendations from current research. *Exceptional Children, 50,* 230–240.

Lewis, R. B., & Doorlag, D. H. (1987). *Teaching special students in the mainstream* (2nd ed.). Columbus, OH: Merrill Publishing.

Lidz, C. S. (1983). Issues in assessing preschool children. In K. D. Paget & B. A. Bracken (Eds.), *The psychoeducational assessment of preschool children* (pp. 17–27). New York: Grune & Stratton.

Lillie, D. L. (1977). Screening. In L. Cross & K. W. Goin (Eds.), *Identifying handicapped children: A guide to casefinding, screening, diagnosis, assessment and evaluation* (pp. 17–24). New York: Walker.

Linder, T. (1983). *Early childhood special education—program development and administration.* Baltimore: Paul H. Brookes.

Lowenfeld, B. (1975). *The changing status of the blind.* Springfield, IL: Charles C. Thomas.

Lynch, E. W., & Stein, R. (1982). Perspectives on parent participation in special education. *Exceptional Education Quarterly, 3* (2), 56–63.

MacMillan, D. L. (1971). Special education for the mildly retarded: Servant or savant. *Focus on Exceptional Children, 2* (9), 1–11.

MacMillan, D. L. (1982). *Mental retardation in school and society* (2nd ed.). Boston: Little, Brown.

Madden, N. A., & Slavin, R. E. (1983). Mainstreaming students with mild handicaps: Academic and social outcomes. *Review of Educational Research, 53,* 519–569.

Martin, E. P., & Martin, J. M. (1978). *The black extended family.* Chicago: University of Chicago Press.

McLoughlin, J. A., & Lewis, R. B. (1986). *Assessing special students* (2nd ed.). Columbus, OH: Merrill Publishing.

Menolascino, F. J. (1983). Conclusion. In F. J. Menolascino, R. Neman, & J. A. Stark (Eds.), *Curative aspects of mental retardation* (pp. 73–84). Baltimore: Paul H. Brookes.

Mercer, J. (1973). *Labeling the mentally retarded.* Berkeley: University of California Press.

Messick, S. (1984). Assessment in context: Appraising student performance in relation to instructional quality. *Educational Researcher, 13* (3), 3–8.

Milunsky, A. (1983). Genetic aspects of mental retardation. In F. J. Menolascino, R. Neman, & J. A. Stark (Eds.), *Curative aspects of mental retardation* (pp. 15–25). Baltimore: Paul H. Brookes.

Moore, B. C., & Moore, S. M. (1977). *Mental retardation—causes and prevention.* Columbus, OH: Merrill Publishing.

Moore, M. G., Fredericks, H. D., & Baldwin, V. L. (1981). The long-range effects of early childhood education on a trainable mentally retarded population. *Journal of the Division of Early Childhood, 4,* 94–110.

Mulliken, R. K., & Buckley, J. J. (1983). *Assessment of multihandicapped and developmentally disabled children.* Rockville, MD: Aspen.

Nolte, A. E. (1982). Health education. In H. E. Mitzel (Ed.), *Encyclopedia of educational research* (5th ed.) (pp. 769–777). New York: The Free Press.

Olshansky, S. (1962). Chronic sorrow. *Social Casework, 43* (4), 190–193.

Orlando, C.(1981). Multidisciplinary team approaches in the assessment of handicapped preschool children. *Topics in Early Childhood Special Education, 1* (2), 23–30.

Pedersen, F. A. (1982). Mother, father, and infant as an interactive system. In J. Belsky (Ed.), *In the beginning: Readings on infancy* (pp. 216–226). New York: Columbia University Press.

Perske, R. (1981). *Hope for families.* Nashville, TN: Abingdon.

Pertsch, C. F. (1936). *A comparative study of the progress of subnormal pupils in the grades and in special classes.* New York: Teachers College, Columbia University.

Polloway, E. A., Payne, J. S., Patton, J. R., & Payne, R. A. (1985). *Strategies for teaching retarded and special needs learners* (3rd ed.). Columbus, OH: Merrill Publishing.

Provus, M. (1971). *Discrepancy evaluation for educational program improvement and assessment.* Berkeley, CA: McCutchan.

Reynolds, M. C. (1962). A framework for considering some issues in special education. *Exceptional Children, 28,* 367–370.

Roach, E. G., & Kephart, N. D. (1966). *The Purdue perceptual-motor survey.* Columbus, OH: Merrill Publishing.

Rogers, S. J. (1982). Assessment considerations with the motor-handicapped child. In G. Ulrey & S. J. Rogers (Eds.), *Psychological assessment of handicapped infants and young children* (pp. 95–107). New York: Thieme-Stratton.

Rubin, S., & Quinn-Curran, N. (1983). Lost, then found: Parents' journey through the community service maze. In M. Seligman (Ed.), *The family with a handicapped child* (pp. 63–94). New York: Grune & Stratton.

Safford, P. (1978). *Teaching young children with special needs.* St. Louis, MO: C. V. Mosby.

Schaefer, E. S. (1975). Family relationships. In J. J. Gallagher (Ed.), *The application of child development research to exceptional children* (pp. 138–171). Reston, VA: The Council for Exceptional Children.

Schweinhart, L., & Weikart, D. (1981). Effects of the Perry preschool program on youths through age 15. *Journal of the Division of Early Childhood, 4,* 29–39.

Sears, P. S. (1979). The Terman genetic studies of genius, 1922–1972. In A. H. Passow (Ed.), *The gifted and talented: Their education and development.* Chicago: University of Chicago Press.

Seligman, M. (1983). Siblings of handicapped persons. In M. Seligman (Ed.), *The family with a handicapped child* (pp. 147–174). New York: Grune & Stratton.

Shearer, M. S., & Shearer, D. E. (1972). The Portage project: A model for early childhood education. *Exceptional Children, 36,* 210–217.

Simmons-Martin, A. (1981). Efficacy report: Early education project. *Journal of the Division of Early Childhood, 4,* 5–10.

Skeels, H. M. (1966). Adult status of children with contrasting early life experiences. *Monographs of the Society for Research in Child Development, 31* (3, Serial No. 105).

Skeels, H. M., & Dye, H. B. (1939). A study of the effects of differential stimulation on mentally retarded children. *Proceedings of the American Association on Mental Deficiency, 44,* 114–136.

Skinner, B. F. (1953). *Science and human behavior.* New York: Macmillan.

Skodak, M., & Skeels, H. M. (1949). A final follow-up study of one hundred adopted children. *Journal of Genetic Psychology, 75,* 85–125.

Smith, C. R. (1983). *Learning disabilities.* Boston: Little, Brown.

Smith, R. M., & Neisworth, J. T. (1975). *The exceptional child: A functional approach.* New York: McGraw-Hill.

Soar, R. S. (1973). *Follow through classroom process measurement and pupil growth (1970–71): Final report.* Gainesville, FL: University of Florida Institute for Development of Human Resources.

Stallings, J., & Kaskowitz, D. (1974). *Follow through classroom observation evaluation, 1972–73.* Menlo Park, CA: Stanford Research Institute.

Stevens, R., & Rosenshine, B. (1981). Advances in research on teaching. *Exceptional Education Quarterly, 2* (1), 1–9.

Stokes, T. F., & Baer, D. M. (1977). An implicit technology of generalization. *Journal of Applied Behavior Analysis, 10,* 349–367.

Strain, P. S., & Kerr, M. M. (1981). *Mainstreaming of children in schools.* New York: Academic Press.

Sulzer-Azaroff, B., & Mayer, G. R. (1977). *Applying behavior-analysis procedures with children and youth.* New York: Holt, Rinehart and Winston.

Terman, L. M., & Oden, M. (Eds.). (1947). *The gifted child grows up: Genetic studies of genius, Vol. 4.* Stanford, CA: Stanford University Press.

Thomason, J. (1981). Education of the gifted: A challenge and a promise. *Exceptional Children, 48,* 101–103.

Trohanis, P. L., Meyer, R. A., & Prestridge, S. (1982). A report on selected screening programs for high-risk and handicapped infants. In C. T. Ramey & P. L. Trohanis (Eds.), *Finding and educating high-risk and handicapped infants* (pp. 83–100). Baltimore: University Park Press.

Turnbull, A. P., & Turnbull, H. R. (1978). *Views from the other side of the two-way mirror.* Columbus, OH: Merrill Publishing.

Turnbull, A. P., & Turnbull, H. R. (1982). Parent involvement in the education of handicapped children: A critique. *Mental Retardation, 20* (3), 115–122.

U.S. Department of Education. (1982). *Fourth annual report to Congress on the implementation of Public Law 94–142: The Education for All Handicapped Children Act.* Washington, DC: Author.

U.S. Department of Education. (1985). *Seventh annual report to Congress on the implementation of Public Law 94–142: The Education for All Handicapped Children Act.* Washington, DC: Author.

Ulrey, G., & Rogers, S. J. (1982). *Psychological assessment of handicapped infants and young children.* New York: Thieme-Stratton.

Wechsler, D. (1974). *Wechsler intelligence scale for children–revised.* Cleveland, OH: Psychological Corporation.

Weil, M. L., & Murphy, J. (1982). Instruction processes. In H. E. Mitzel (Ed.), *Encyclopedia of educational research* (5th ed.) (pp. 890–917). New York: The Free Press.

Wolfensberger, W. (1972). *The principle of normalization in human services.* Toronto, Canada: National Institute on Mental Retardation.

Wood, P. (1980). Cost of services. In C. Garland, N. Stone, J. Swanson, & G. Woodruff (Eds.), Early intervention for children with special needs and their families: Findings and recommendations. *Interact* (Newsletter of the National Committee for Very Young Children and their Families).

Woodcock, R. W. (1973). *Woodcock reading mastery tests.* Circle Pines, MN: American Guidance Service.

Yarrow, L. J., Rubenstein, J. L., Pedersen, F. A., & Jankowski, J. J. (1982). Dimensions of early stimulation and their differential effects on infant development. In J. Belsky (Ed.), *In the beginning: Readings of infancy* (pp. 183–193). New York: Columbia University Press.

Resources

Organizations

American Coalition of Citizens with Disabilities
1200 15th Street, N.W.
Washington, DC 20036

Consumer group which provides information and advocacy for individuals with disabilities.

Council for Exceptional Children
1920 Association Drive
Reston, VA 22091-1589

Professional organization which publishes journals, disseminates information on best educational practices for exceptional individuals, lobbies for legislation and services, and conducts annual meetings to discuss research and practice in the education of exceptional individuals. State and local chapters are also very active in many areas of the country.

National Association of Private Schools for Exceptional Children
P.O. Box 34293
West Bethesda, MD 20817

Provides information about private school programs for individuals with exceptional needs.

National Center for Law and the Handicapped
University of Notre Dame
P.O. Box 477
Notre Dame, IN 46556

Provides information, policy analyses, and policy studies on legislation and litigation related to individuals with handicapping conditions.

National Committee on Arts for the Handicapped
1825 Connecticut Avenue, N.W.–Suite 418
Washington, DC 20009

Supports and encourages the involvement of handicapped individuals in the creative and performing arts.

Journals

Exceptional Children
Council for Exceptional Children
1920 Association Drive
Reston, VA 22091-1589

Professional journal focusing on research and policy analyses about the education and development of exceptional children and youth.

Education and Treatment of Children
Pressley Ridge School
530 Marshall Avenue
Pittsburgh, PA 15214

Professional journal focusing on issues of teaching and treatment effectiveness.

Remedial and Special Education
PRO-ED
5341 Industrial Oaks Blvd.
Austin, TX 78735

Publishes reviews, research, and research syntheses of issues involving the education of individuals requiring special instructional methods.

Teaching Exceptional Children
Council for Exceptional Children
1920 Association Drive
Reston, VA 22091-1589

Targeted for special education teachers, it includes practical articles on teaching methods and strategies for exceptional children and youth.

Part Two

THE EXCEPTIONALITIES

Each exceptionality is actually a field of study in and of itself. Although there are many commonalities among exceptionalities, each is characterized by the types of special needs it imposes.

In Part Two, each of the chapters is devoted to a different exceptionality. Each chapter, however, is organized around the same major questions: What are the effects of the exceptionality? What are its causes? What are the characteristics of individuals with this exceptionality? How is the exceptionality detected? How is it treated?

Chapter 3 describes the handicap of mental retardation. In Chapter 4, physical handicaps and health conditions that may impose limitations are considered. Chapter 5 deals with severe multiple handicaps, a group of exceptionalities that may combine mental retardation with physical and even health handicaps.

Sensory limitations are the subject of the next two chapters. Chapter 6 describes visual impairments, and hearing disorders are the subject of Chapter 7.

Communication disorders are discussed in Chapter 8, learning disabilities in Chapter 9, and behavior disorders in Chapter 10.

Chapter 11 dealing with giftedness and talent comes last in this section.

Chapter 3

MENTAL RETARDATION

Mental retardation is a label used to describe individuals who have difficulty thinking, learning, solving problems, and remembering. Like many labels, it is often more misleading than descriptive. Assuming that all mentally retarded people are alike is as inaccurate as the assumption that all Americans or all football players are alike. Although mentally retarded people have deficits in their cognitive abilities, they are all unique individuals. The majority are limited only by the difficulty they experience learning academic subjects such as reading, arithmetic, and spelling. A much smaller group needs assistance throughout their lives with basic tasks such as eating, toileting, walking, and talking (MacMillan, 1982).

INDIVIDUALS WITH MENTAL RETARDATION

The diversity of the population labeled mentally retarded makes generalization difficult; however, four overlapping subgroups—mild, moderate, severe, profound—are defined in the most commonly used classification system. In practice, the four subgroups are often combined into two broader groups which are referred to as mild and severe. Even though the majority of mentally retarded people are only mildly retarded, retardation is considered to be a severe disability because the effects of cognitive deficits are global. They interfere with the individual's

Eleanor W. Lynch
San Diego State University

ability to think, learn, relate, and communicate. The individuals described in the following section (see p. 98) illustrate these points.

Determining the prevalence of mental retardation depends upon the definition used to include or exclude individuals and on the accuracy of current census data on those who are classified as mentally retarded. In MacMillan's (1982) discussion of prevalence studies in the United States during the 1960s and 1970s, he points out that estimates "consistently yielded a figure close to 1 percent of the general population" (p. 66). The best data on the numbers of people identified as mentally retarded during the elementary and secondary school years come from the U.S. Office of Education. Their figures show that almost 800,000 students between 3 and 21 years of age were served in programs for the mentally retarded during the 1982–83 school year making it the third largest category of exceptionality (U.S. Department of Education, 1984).

Mental retardation is not equally distributed across gender, age, and socioeconomic status. There are more males than females with mental retardation (Abramowicz & Richardson, 1975; Mumpower, 1970; Singer, Westphal, & Niswander, 1968). Two different theories have been suggested to explain this discrepancy. The first is the higher incidence of sex-linked recessive conditions in males. There is a higher probability that males will exhibit sex-linked recessive traits than females making them more vulnerable to some types of neurological impairment with accompanying mental retardation (Moore, 1982).

The second explanation, proposed by Masland, Sarason, and Gladwin in 1958, is known as the expectation hypothesis. They suggested that environmental expectations for boys and girls may explain the differences in prevalence between the two groups. It was their contention that boys were shaped to behave more aggressively than girls and were consequently more frequently identified as mentally retarded and placed in special education classes. The quieter, well-behaved girls were never identified. In 1973, Mercer suggested that society is more tolerant of lower levels of achievement in girls than in boys causing fewer girls to be identified as mentally retarded. Many years have passed since the expectation hypothesis was first suggested, and there has been some blending of male and female roles and responsibilities. In the coming years, gender-based expectations may be less of a factor than they have been in the past.

Variations in prevalence also occur with age. Mildly handicapped individuals are most likely to be identified during the school years when their learning difficulties become apparent in the classroom. As preschoolers and adults, they may not be identified as mentally retarded. Moderately, severely, and profoundly retarded individuals are usually identified in the preschool years and continue to require special services throughout their lives. Since the majority of mentally retarded individuals are mildly retarded and identified only during the years they attend school, the prevalence of mental retardation is highest between the ages of 6 and 18 (MacMillan, 1982).

Prevalence is also influenced by socioeconomic status and race. Children from low income families are more likely to be diagnosed as mildly mentally retarded than their more affluent peers (Tarjan, Wright, Eyman, & Keeran, 1973). Since much of academic learning is based on motivation, experience with language,

introducing

BARBARA AND PAUL

Both Barbara and Paul are mentally retarded, but they function at very different levels. Barbara, seventeen years old, is mildly mentally retarded. She attends a regular high school in the morning and spends the afternoon in one of the special education, on-the-job training programs. At school she takes physical education with her nonhandicapped peers and goes to a special education resource specialist who works with her on survival academics and career orientation. Her afternoons are spent at a local beauty shop where she is being trained as an assistant. At the shop, she is learning to greet the customers, drape them and do the hair washing, restock each cosmetologist's case of beauty products, and clean the combs, brushes, and curlers. She has friends from school that she spends time with at the end of the day and on weekends. They often go to a nearby shopping center to browse or to a community recreation center. Although Barbara does not drive, she would like to get her license and is studying to pass the written exam. In many ways Barbara's life is similar to that of her nonhandicapped peers; she is outgoing, attractive, and enjoys the same activities. The primary differences are her ability to achieve academically and her deficiency in problem solving which place limits on some aspects of her life.

Paul, however, is more limited by retardation. He is eight years old, severely mentally retarded, and enrolled in a self-contained special education class at a regular elementary school. The curriculum in his class is based on learning skills which will help the students function as independently as possible. Paul's IEP objectives include learning to dress and toilet himself independently, "talking" by pointing to pictures on a communication board, playing cooperatively with a classmate with plastic building blocks, and going through stores without touching all of the merchandise. At school, Paul has contact with his nonhandicapped peers every day on the playground and in a second grade classroom. He goes to the second grade class for a fifteen minute story period, a time when the teacher reads to the children. In addition, student tutors from the regular classes come to Paul's room to work with the children every day. At home, Paul's brother and sister include him in their play and he is able to entertain himself for short periods. On weekends, the family often goes to a large city park where Paul enjoys feeding the ducks, swinging, and watching the mimes. Paul will always need support and supervision because of his limitations, but he is involved in home and community life.

and opportunities to use newly acquired information, children from middle and upper income homes have an advantage unavailable to many of their classmates. Severe forms of mental retardation are more evenly distributed across socioeconomic levels with only a slightly higher percentage among low income families. This slightly higher percentage may be the result of lack of prenatal care, inadequate nutrition, more frequent, closely spaced pregnancies, or mothers much younger or older than the norm.

Minority children have traditionally been overrepresented in special education classes for the retarded. Changes in legislation as well as changes in assessment practices were initiated to correct this imbalance, but those changes have not always had the intended outcome. The National Academy of Sciences report on special education (Heller, Holtzman, & Messick, 1982) found that, despite the remedies, minority children were still overrepresented. Conversely, MacMillan (1982) has stated that "there seems to be no basis for the accusation sometimes heard that minority children are sought out by psychologists for labeling; on the contrary, they tend to be overlooked" (p. 75). Thus the controversy continues. On the one hand, there is concern that minority students are inappropriately placed in classes for the retarded; on the other hand, there is concern that many minority students are not being identified and not receiving services which they need. As we move into the new decade, perhaps the focus should be on the child's need for service and a range of options for providing it rather than on minority versus majority and special versus regular education.

Estimates of the incidence of mental retardation made by Goddard in 1911 and Terman in 1919 are not dramatically different from current figures. Even with the advances in prevention, diagnosis, medical and educational intervention, the incidence of mental retardation remains at 2 to 3 percent of the population.

Definition of Mental Retardation

The definition of mental retardation developed by the American Association on Mental Deficiency (AAMD) and incorporated into PL 94–142 is the one most commonly accepted and used (Grossman, 1973, 1983; Heber, 1961). It is based on a clinical perspective which views mental retardation as pathology and attributes the deficits to a defect within the individual. This definition specifies criteria for measuring the level of retardation based on the extent to which the individual's measured intelligence (IQ) deviates from the norm as well as deviations from the norm in adaptive behavior. The definition also specifies an upper age limit for the first diagnosis of mental retardation. According to the current AAMD definition (Grossman, 1983):

Mental retardation refers to significantly subaverage general intellectual functioning resulting in or associated with concurrent impairments in adaptive behavior manifested during the developmental period. (p. 11)

In this definition "significantly subaverage general intellectual functioning" refers to an IQ of 70 or below on a standardized test of intelligence such as the *Stanford-Binet Intelligence Scales for Children* (Terman & Merrill, 1973) or one of the Wechsler intelligence scales. This score represents performance that is two standard deviations below the mean, or average score, on these tests. The AAMD Manual states that an IQ of 70 should be viewed only as a guideline; in some school placement decisions it might be extended upward to 75.

"Impairments in adaptive behavior" refers to an individual's ability to meet the developmental, academic, personal-social, and vocational demands appropriate for someone of his or her chronological age and culture. Adaptive behavior for preschoolers includes learning to walk, talk, communicate, and get along with others. During the school years, adaptive behavior is linked to school performance and one's ability to master academic subjects. In adulthood, it includes living independently, working, and more sophisticated interpersonal skills. Because adaptive behavior changes with chronological age and cultural group, it is difficult to measure. Several assessment instruments such as the *AAMD Adaptive Behavior Scale* (Nihira, Foster, Shellhaas, & Leland, 1974), the *AAMD Adaptive Behavior Scale, School Edition* (Lambert, Windmiller, Tharinger, & Cole, 1981), and the *Vineland Adaptive Behavior Scales* (Sparrow, Bala, & Cicchetti, 1984) are used in combination with clinical judgment to determine levels of adaptive behavior.

The "developmental period" refers to the period between conception and age 18. An initial diagnosis of mental retardation can only be made during this period.

To be identified as mentally retarded, all three of the above conditions must be met: an IQ below 70 or in some instances 75, impairment in adaptive behavior, and first identification by age 18. The following case examples illustrate the interaction among these criteria:

Rafaela is an active four-year-old referred for a comprehensive evaluation. Her performance on the Stanford-Binet intelligence test places her IQ between 45 and 53. Interviews, observations, and criterion-referenced measures of her language, social, self-care, motor, and play skills suggest that her performance is more like a two-year-old's than a child of four. Since there is no evidence that Rafaela has emotional problems or that she is being deprived of the experiences that would allow her to acquire these early skills, the assessment team agrees that she is mentally retarded. This diagnosis is consistent with the three criteria: Rafaela's measured intelligence is below 70; her adaptive behavior is below expectation for her chronological age; and Rafaela is still within the developmental period.

Brad was nineteen and in his second year of college, when he was thrown from his sports car in a head-on collision in which he sustained serious head and neck injuries. After two years of recovery and rehabilitation, Brad can walk but is impulsive, easily angered, confused, and forgetful. His reading and math skills are at the third grade level, and he has forgotten much about his life before the accident. His performance on intelligence tests places his measured IQ between 60 and 68, and he is not able to live independently, maintain a job, or interact with others appropriately for more than a short time. Although Brad's measured intelligence is below 70 and he has impaired adaptive behavior, he is not mentally retarded since his disabilities occurred after the developmental period.

Nathan is 10 and in the fourth grade. He is not doing well academically, and his teacher has referred him for a special education evaluation. Following a comprehensive evaluation, the assessment team determines that Nathan's measured IQ is between 70 and 80, that he is several years behind in academic skills, and his ability to make judgments and get along with others is severely limited. However, the team determines that Nathan is not mentally retarded. His academic and social difficulties stem from a behavior disorder, not mental retardation.

Table 3.1

Terminology Used in Several Definitions of Mental Retardation

Organization	Generic Term	Levels	IQ Range for Level	Includes Adaptive Behavior
American Association on Mental Deficiency (Grossman, 1983)	Mental Retardation	Mild Moderate Severe Profound	50–55 to approx. 70 35–40 to 50–55 20–25 to 35–40 Below 20 or 25	Yes
American Psychiatric Association *DSM III* (1980)	Mental Retardation	Mild Moderate Severe Profound	50–70 35–49 20–34 Below 20	Yes
World Health Organization (1975)	Mental Subnormality	Mild Moderate Severe Profound	50–70 35–49 20–34 Under 20	No

These examples demonstrate the number of factors that must be considered and the criteria that must be met before an individual can be diagnosed as mentally retarded. It is a complex task requiring the expertise of a team of professionals, observations of the individual in a variety of settings, and input from the parents.

Professional groups and international organizations other than the American Association on Mental Deficiency have also developed classification systems which describe mental retardation. Table 3.1 depicts the similarities, differences, and terminology in those most widely recognized.

Although the definitions developed by the American Association on Mental Deficiency and other professional groups continue to be the ones most commonly used, they do not represent the thinking of all of those who work in the field. Several alternative ways to view mental retardation are described below.

The behavioral view describes mentally retarded individuals as people with limited behavioral repertoires which have been shaped by the events in their lives (Bijou, 1966). There is no attempt to look for the cause of the individual's behavior or to determine a level of functioning. Instead, interveners identify behaviors which need to be increased or decreased and use reinforcement and other behavioral strategies to teach these behaviors.

In the social system view, societal factors determine the definition of mental retardation; and the definition varies with the culture and its demands. Mercer (1973) describes it as a social status that has been achieved rather than something inherent in the individual. Since this perspective relies on an individual's ability to fit into the society, a streetwise teenager might not be considered retarded in his own neighborhood where he has learned how to survive; but he may be considered retarded at school where he has difficulty reading and doing multiplication.

The social responsibility view, like the behavioral and social system views, emphasizes factors external to the individual. In 1980, Gold proposed a definition which focuses on the society's inadequacies in the training and treatment of individuals labeled mentally retarded rather than on the shortcomings or inherent deficits of the individual. His definition presents a highly optimistic counterpoint to the image of retardation in the AAMD definition:

> *Mental retardation refers to a level of functioning which requires from society significantly above average training procedures and superior assets in adaptive behavior, manifested throughout life. The mentally retarded person is characterized by the level of power needed in the training process for (the person) to learn, and not by limitations on what (the person) can learn. The height of a retarded person's level of functioning is determined by the availability of training technology, and the amount of resources society is willing to allocate and not by significant limitations in biological potential.* (p. 148)

The struggle that has surrounded the development and acceptance of a definition of mental retardation has not been an academic exercise. Each definition represents a philosophy about mental retardation which shapes attitudes, determines services, and dramatically affects the lives of mentally retarded people and their families.

Concerned Professionals

Because of the global impact of mental retardation on the individual and the family, many disciplines are involved in education, treatment, and advocacy activities. Special educators are involved from the preschool years through early adulthood. Psychologists (both clinical and school) provide formal assessments, work with teachers and families on management techniques, and sometimes provide family or individual counseling. Physicians may provide diagnostic information, routine health care, or specialized treatment for mentally retarded individuals with medical and health-related problems. Nurses, especially public health nurses and pediatric nurse practitioners, often work with families whose child has just been diagnosed; they may provide guidance, referral, or teach parents specific management techniques that relate to handling and feeding. Nutritionists are often consulted about special diets or obesity control. Occupational and physical therapists along with adaptive physical educators contribute their expertise to motor development and functioning; and speech and language clinicians and audiologists work with the individual, teachers, and parents to develop communication skills. Social workers and rehabilitation counselors also provide counseling and training to mentally retarded clients and their families.

In recent years, lawyers have become involved in the education and treatment of mentally retarded individuals. Acting as advocates for retarded clients and their families, attorneys have assisted in obtaining rights to education and treatment. Researchers from many disciplines have contributed to the understanding of mental retardation, and medical research in particular has had a significant impact on early detection and prevention of certain types of mental retardation.

ETIOLOGY AND PREVENTION

Discovering the causes of mental retardation is the key to prevention. As researchers learn more about etiology, prevention programs can be initiated to reduce or eliminate some types of mental retardation. The sections that follow highlight some of the work that has been done in these areas.

Etiology

The causes of mental retardation can be grouped into two primary categories: biological and sociobehavioral. Mental retardation that is biologically caused can be divided into two categories: genetically determined conditions and damage to the central nervous system (MacMillan, 1982). Conditions that are determined genetically are a result of inheritance, chromosomal errors, or chromosomal aberrations. As of 1978, over 1000 genetic disorders had been identified averaging more than two new discoveries per week over a twelve year period (Moore, 1982). Although the majority of these disorders do not cause mental retardation, it is estimated that one-half to one percent of the cases of mental retardation are caused by genetic disorders (Berlin, 1978).

Genetic material is stored in the nucleus of each cell on particles called chromosomes. Each chromosome is made up of many genes carrying chemical codes which program cell growth, define cell function, and determine specific characteristics such as hair and eye color. Each cell has 23 pairs of chromosomes (46 in all) with half of each pair donated by each parent (Berlin, 1978). From the point of conception to the birth of the infant, there are many opportunities for errors to occur which could result in birth defects including mental retardation (Batshaw & Perret, 1981).

Down Syndrome is the most frequently occurring genetically determined cause of mental retardation (Smith & Wilson, 1973). The most frequently occurring type is called Trisomy 21 since a third chromosome is attached to the twenty-first pair giving individuals with this syndrome 47 chromosomes instead of the usual 46. Although individuals with Down Syndrome are quite individual in their needs and personalities, they share many similar physical characteristics such as upslanting eyes with epicanthal folds at the inner corner of the eye, a somewhat flattened facial contour, and a tendency toward a protruding tongue. Their hair is usually straight and fine, and their hands are small with stubby fingers. Infants with Down Syndrome have reduced muscle tone causing them to be floppy, but tone usually increases as they grow. Many Down Syndrome infants have heart and/or intestinal defects which require repair in the first few days of life (Smith & Wilson, 1973). Although health problems among Down Syndrome individuals occur more frequently than in the nonhandicapped population, the majority of individuals with Down Syndrome are healthy and can participate

Table 3.2

Common Biomedical Causes of Disability

Type	Examples
Infectious Diseases	Congenital rubella, an infection transmitted from the mother to the fetus during the first trimester of pregnancy, may lead to deafness, mental retardation, heart disease, or visual impairment; this common form of childhood measles is preventable by immunization with rubella vaccine.
	Meningitis, an inflammation of the tissues covering the brain, may result in mental retardation, learning disability, neuromotor dysfunction, or hearing impairment.
	Encephalitis, an inflammation of the brain, may produce mental retardation.
Gestational and Obstetric Disorders	Prematurity and low birth weight are terms referring to infants born before the usual end of the gestational period and/or those whose weight at birth is considered low; such infants are at risk for mental retardation and other handicapping conditions.
	Rh incompatibility between mother and infant may result in the production of maternal antibodies which cause the release of bilirubin, a substance poisonous to the newborn; sequelae include deafness, cerebral palsy, mental retardation, speech disorders, and learning disability; by preventing the sensitization of Rh negative mothers at the birth of the first Rh positive child, Rh disease in later children can be avoided.
	Perinatal injury and anoxia (lack of oxygen) resulting in damage to the central nervous system can lead to serious consequences including mental retardation and cerebral palsy.
Environmental Hazards	Radiation of the mother or the child in utero may cause mental retardation or a variety of birth defects; effects are prevented by limiting exposure to radiation sources.
	Poisoning from lead, mercury, or other environmental toxins may cause permanent central nervous system damage; lead-based paint ingested by young children, lead from auto exhaust, and industrial pollutants containing mercury are sources of metal poisoning.
	Fetal alcohol syndrome, the result of alcohol consumption by the mother during pregnancy, may produce growth deficiencies, mental retardation, or other birth defects; research continues to determine the amount of alcohol capable of producing prenatal effects.
	Injury due to accidents or child abuse may lead to disabling conditions; head injuries caused by auto accidents or physical abuse can result in retardation; emotional injuries caused by psychological abuse or neglect (considered a sociobehavioral etiology) may precipitate behavior disorders.

Table 3.2 (continued)	
Type	Examples
Genetic and Chromosomal Disorders	Down Syndrome (previously known as mongolism), a condition resulting from an extra chromosome, produces mental retardation and characteristic physical features; women over 40 are more likely to produce Down Syndrome offspring.
	Cranial aberrations and hydrocephalus may cause neurological impairment; cranial abnormalities are due to premature closure of the cranial bones; in hydrocephalus, the head is enlarged due to an excess of cerebrospinal fluid.
	Phenylketonuria is an inherited disorder of metabolism which if untreated can produce retardation; this disorder can be detected in newborns and its damaging effects prevented by dietary intervention.
Neurocutaneous Syndromes	Neurofibromatosis, the most common of the disorders which affect both the skin and nervous system, involves the growth of tumors within the nervous system; it may result in spinal defects, childhood leukemia, or hydrocephalus.
	Tuberous sclerosis, a progressive neurological disorder, is associated with mental retardation and epilepsy.

Source: Adapted from Moore, B. C., (1982), Biomedical Factors in Mental Retardation. In P. T. Cegelka and H. J. Prehm (Eds.), *Mental Retardation* (pp. 76–110). Columbus, OH: Merrill Publishing. Copyright © 1982 by Bell & Howell Company. Reprinted by permission.

quite fully in normal activities. With early intervention and the recognition that people with Down Syndrome can acquire a wide range of skills, it is not uncommon to see these children in mainstreamed classrooms learning to read, playing with their peers, working in nonsheltered environments, and living in group homes or supervised apartments.

The second category of biological causes of mental retardation are those that are the result of damage to the central nervous system. Lack of oxygen during labor and delivery, complications of the neonatal period, head trauma, and a variety of other problems may also result in mental retardation. (Batshaw, Perret, & Harryman, 1981). These causes are not genetically determined, but they are biological. Child abuse is another causative factor in mental retardation. One government study (Krug & Davis, 1981) reports a serious increase in child abuse in the United States and estimates that from 1 to 2 percent of the nation's children will be abused by their parents at some time during their childhood. Physical abuse results not only in severe psychological damage but is often the cause of retardation as well.

Table 3.2 describes the most common biological causes of mental retardation and related disabilities. Although the etiology of mental retardation may not be important in developing ways to teach or interact with individuals with retardation, research on the causes of mental retardation leads to knowledge about its prevention.

Sociobehavioral retardation, formerly called cultural-familial or psychosocial, accounts for 70 to 80 percent of the known causes of mental retardation (Garber & McInerney, 1982); yet a clear definition of it is elusive. Unlike biological retardation in which a single causative agent can often be identified, sociobehavioral retardation is more often the result of multiple environmental factors acting synergistically (Grossman, 1983). Poverty, poor nutrition, inadequate parenting, substandard housing, and lack of environmental stimulation or enrichment combine to depress the developing child's cognitive and adaptive behavior. Mildly mentally retarded individuals, those whose performance is between two and three standard deviations below the mean on a standardized test of intelligence (IQ approximately 50 to 70) with impairment in adaptive behavior, are those most often diagnosed as sociobehaviorally retarded.

Since sociobehavioral retardation is found most often among families at the lowest end of the socioeconomic scale, there has been a classic controversy about its cause. This debate, referred to as the nature-nurture controversy, was based on a view of the world which ignored the complexity of both heredity and environment. Those who believed that nature was the primary determiner of intelligence argued that sociobehavioral mental retardation was hereditary. The proponents of this view pointed to the higher incidence of poverty, crime, and social assistance required by these families as evidence that they were genetically inferior and did not have the intelligence to improve their lives. Those on the nurture side of the debate argued that environment was the primary determiner of intelligence and cited lack of education and poverty as the primary causes of sociobehavioral mental retardation.

Although this debate is not yet over (Gould, 1980, 1981; Jensen, 1969, 1981, 1982), it has been overshadowed by another perspective. Data from studies of twins reared apart, adopted children, and instances in which children have developed in isolation suggest that both heredity and environment influence functioning, making each individual a product of the interaction of the two (Garber & McInerney, 1982). Our inherited genetic makeup provides broad boundaries within which the experiences and events of our lives shape our intelligence and personality.

Prevention and Cure

Preventing mental retardation requires efforts in three major areas: medical research, social support services, and public education. To date, advances in medical science have done the most to prevent mental retardation. Through research on etiology and improved diagnostic procedures, many problems which cause mental retardation can be determined in utero. Amniocentesis, ultrasound, and fetography can be used to detect abnormalities of the fetus in mothers who are identified to be at risk (Hayden & Beck, 1982). Amniocentesis, performed early in the second trimester of pregnancy, involves inserting a needle through the

Treatment of Hydrocephalus

Hydrocephalus, an enlarged head caused by the build-up of cerebrospinal fluid, is often associated with mental retardation. In the past, this condition often led to institutionalization. The head often reached proportions that made it impossible for the individual to walk or sit; and the damage which resulted from the pressure on the brain resulted in severe mental retardation. Now, because of break-throughs in medical technology, a shunt can be surgically implanted shortly after birth allowing the excess fluid to drain out of the brain and into the body for disposal. Recently, a shunt was successfully implanted in a fetus in utero using ultrasonic techniques to guide the placement. Although mental retardation was not avoided in this particular case, the surgery did demonstrate the feasibility of the procedure and lend promise to even earlier diagnosis and prevention.

mother's abdomen and withdrawing a small amount of amniotic fluid. The amniotic fluid contains fetal cells which can be tested for various disorders.

Ultrasound is a totally nonintrusive procedure which uses sound waves to outline the shape of the fetus. Since the sound waves respond to different tissue and bone densities, a fairly detailed picture of the fetus can be seen and printed out for more detailed study. This procedure is especially useful for detecting physical malformations and growth retardation (Batshaw & Perret, 1981). Fetography, or microphotography of the fetus, is a developing science which will allow even more definitive diagnosis of some congenital problems. In some cases, immediate steps can be taken to eliminate or reduce the potential hazards to the developing embryo or fetus. In other cases, there is no medical treatment, but parents will be in a position to decide whether to continue or to terminate the pregnancy.

Newborn screenings have gained wide acceptance within the last few years. These tests, performed within the first few minutes and days of life, can accurately diagnose serious metabolic disorders, respiratory problems, and abnormalities of muscle tone. Intervention in the form of surgery, life support, special diets, or educational and medical therapies can be initiated to ameliorate the effects of the handicapping condition. Infants with hydrocephalus (an enlarged head usually caused by an excess of cerebrospinal fluid) often undergo surgery in the first few hours of life. In the surgery, a shunt to drain the fluid is implanted reducing the size of the head and the pressure on the brain. This procedure has significantly reduced the numbers of children with hydrocephalus resulting in severe retardation.

Phenylketonuria, a metabolic disorder which causes severe to profound mental retardation, can be detected within the first few days of life by a blood test developed by Dr. Robert Guthrie (1972). When treated with a special diet, its effects can be dramatically reduced. Although there is no medical treatment for Down Syndrome, Fetal Alcohol Syndrome, or other syndromes associated with delayed development, early detection can lead to educational intervention which reduces the effects of the delay.

Prevention of mental retardation is also dependent upon the improvement of social and financial support services. Infants and young children living in homes in which nutrition is inadequate, interaction with a loving caretaker is not available, stimulation is limited, and abuse and violence are common occurrences are at risk for sociobehavioral retardation. Although intervention programs which work directly with the children have been shown to be effective in reducing the negative outcomes of an inadequate environment, problems of such magnitude must also be tackled in a broader social context. Sociobehavioral retardation can be reduced only through the improvement of overall quality of life, the elimination of poverty, and the protection of children whose parents are not able to provide a physically and emotionally safe environment for them.

Finally, public education is a powerful tool in the prevention of mental retardation. Making people aware of genetic causes of mental retardation which they may carry allows individuals to estimate their chances of having a retarded child and to make more considered decisions about childbearing. The importance of prenatal care in reducing the incidence of mental retardation has been clearly stated by Korones and Lancaster (1981):

> Neonatal intensive care programs have diminished mortality and the incidence of brain damage among survivors, but much if not most of their activity could be eliminated by optimal delivery of prenatal care. Usually the sick neonate was a distressed fetus whose mother's vulnerability to perinatal misadventure could have been identified in 60% to 75% of cases.   (p. 32)

Pregnancies that are medically monitored are far less likely to result in a child with mental retardation or a related disability than those that are not. Public awareness encourages other important medical interventions such as immunizations. Innoculations against rubella (a form of measles which can cause multiple disabilities in the developing fetus) and other infectious diseases in the entire population help to prevent retardation by reducing the likelihood that a pregnant woman will be infected and infect the child that she is carrying. Public education which provides information about positive childrearing practices also assists in reducing retardation.

All of these efforts have helped to reduce the occurrence of many types of mental retardation, yet the incidence of retardation has not changed over the years. In many cases, biological retardation is still unpredictable. No test or procedure can accurately predict who will have a retarded child and who will not; but with the advances in medical technology and the increasing awareness about the effectiveness of medical, social, and educational intervention, the future is very promising. In their discussion of future prospects for curing mental retardation, Menolascino, Neman, and Stark (1983) highlight that promise:

> Time has a way of solidifying scientific assumptions and turning them into "facts." Indeed, the "fact" of irreversibility in mental retardation has been with us so long it has generated an almost automatic counter-reaction: reluctance

to accept the possibility of advances in this area. There is, of course, prece-dence for these attitudes. Historically, ideas and proposals that conflict with established beliefs have often been greeted with reservation, fear, or skepticism. For example, Louis Pasteur, discoverer of the rabies vaccine, was ejected from the French Academy of Sciences in 1867 when he proposed the "radical" theory that germs cause diseases. Then there was the German physicist who, with the advent of the railway, argued that trains traveling in excess of 20 miles per hour would rupture the blood vessels of the passengers. Our own century is not without its skeptics. Not long ago, some authorities claimed that pilots who attempted to break the sound barrier might be "turned into jelly." (p. 302)

Research and practice have dispelled the myths about train travel and breaking the sound barrier. In the years to come, there may be cures for mental retardation; and its irreversibility may no longer be viewed as a "fact."

CHARACTERISTICS OF MENTALLY RETARDED INDIVIDUALS

The primary characteristic of individuals labeled mentally retarded is an impaired ability to learn, remember, reason, and solve problems. Because of this, there has been considerable research on the learning characteristics of people with mental retardation. Problems in methodology in which major variables were ignored have left gaps in our understanding of the learning characteristics of mentally retarded individuals. For example, subjects living in institutions and subjects living at home were not differentiated; levels of retardation were not clearly specified; and subjects with biological types of retardation were grouped with subjects with sociobehavioral retardation. In addition, much of the research has been carried out in controlled laboratory experiments which have focused on narrow questions. Although tightly controlled research assists in theory building, it is often far removed from what a teacher, speech therapist, or parent needs to know to plan a program for a particular student.

Learning Characteristics

Despite these problems, some generalizations about the learning characteristics of mentally retarded individuals have implications for programming. These characteristics relate to the retarded individual's ability to attend to relevant cues, organize information, remember, and apply past learning to new situations. Discrimination learning has been a major focus of research with mentally retarded individuals. Performance is judged by determining how long it takes in a controlled experiment for the individual to consistently respond correctly. For example, in sorting tools to be packaged for sale, it would take longer for retarded students to sort the tools correctly; but once they had learned, their accuracy

Information to be remembered and used in out-of-school situations is practiced many times in the classroom.

would approximate that of someone with average intelligence. The most recent work in this area suggests that retarded individuals have more trouble determining what is expected in a task and more difficulty focusing on the relevant dimensions or cues than their nonretarded peers (Mercer & Snell, 1977; Zeaman & House, 1979). However, once they understand the nature of the task, their performance is only minimally different from that of nonretarded individuals. In other words, though it may take much longer and require more practices for a retarded student's performance to improve, when improvement begins it is comparable to that of nonretarded students (MacMillan, 1982). In recent years, individuals with retardation have successfully learned a variety of complex tasks such as assembling bicycle brakes, operating power equipment, and working in service positions in hotels and restaurants which require adaptation and simple decision making. Although these new levels of achievement are promising, the time and instructional technology needed to teach highly complex skills which require flexibility, judgment, social sophistication, and considerable knowledge do not exist.

Memory is a major element in learning. To learn efficiently, one must recall what has been learned and apply it to new situations. A variety of hypotheses have been suggested to explain the memory deficits in mentally retarded individuals. Bray (1979) has attributed memory deficits to inadequate rehearsal strategies. Nonretarded individuals develop ways to remember information spontaneously. These strategies may include repeating something over and over until it is learned, saying it aloud, associating the material to be learned to something already known, or using other mnemonic devices. Retarded individuals do not rehearse material spontaneously and must be taught to practice information to be remembered.

Memory is also related to the way material is organized to be learned. Imagine two different kinds of filing systems. In one system, files are organized alphabetically by topic and stored neatly in a drawer. In the other system, all of the material is thrown into a box as it is gathered. The way one organizes information as it is being learned is similar to the file systems. If information is clustered, organized, and classified as it is learned, it is much easier to retrieve than information that is added randomly one piece at a time. Work by Spitz (1966, reviewed in Mercer & Snell, 1977) and many others has demonstrated that retarded individuals do not organize information for input which interferes with their ability to retrieve or remember what they have learned.

Some of Spitz's later research (1979) has moved from a focus on learning and memory to an investigation of retarded individuals' ability to think and reason. The ability to use logic and apply previously learned information to novel situations characterizes reasoning; his studies suggest that retarded individuals are most deficient in this area. Even when they are taught specific strategies for attending, organizing, and remembering, they are not able to generalize what they have learned to new situations. This difficulty with generalization includes learning in all skill areas both academic and social (Stokes, Baer, & Jackson, 1974). A mildly retarded student may learn to successfully complete worksheets of addition problems in the classroom, but that does not guarantee that the same student will recognize the need to add the prices of items at the grocery store to determine the total bill. An individual with moderate mental retardation may become quite proficient at ordering lunch at a nearby hamburger chain but may be unable to give the same order at another chain that looks different and has a slightly different menu display.

These difficulties in cognition characterize individuals with mental retardation at all levels with variations only in degree. These characteristics are pervasive, affecting not only school learning but learning in the home, community, and workplace as well. Although difficulty meeting academic demands may only be apparent in the mildly retarded during the school years, their deficiencies in problem solving may continue to be apparent. Moderately, severely, and profoundly retarded individuals experience more difficulty learning, remembering, and solving problems than their mildly retarded peers. The literature supports the belief that all retarded people can and do learn throughout their lives (Ellis et al., 1982; Silverstein et al., 1982), but the instruction must be more specific, the practices more frequent, and the time allowed for learning longer.

Individuals who are mentally retarded are not alike; each one is unique. Yet within this diversity, there are several characteristics which seem to be common among such individuals. Through observation and systematic research, mentally retarded individuals have been described as having reduced motivation, an external locus of control, and deficiencies in social discrimination (Schloss & Sedlak, 1982). All of these shape the way that they interact. For example, reduced motivation may make it more difficult to get individuals with retardation to participate in social activities. They may be less apt to seek out friends, to establish and maintain relationships. An external locus of control (letting outside influences determine your behavior) and poor social discrimination sometimes interact to produce serious problems for retarded individuals. If the crowd that they are with suggests stealing a car for a joyride, they may accede to the wishes of the crowd because of their external locus of control and poor judgment about what is socially (or legally) appropriate.

Social competence for all individuals increases with age and practice, and increased competence leads to willingness to take on new challenges. Mastery of new skills is pleasurable, and the satisfaction resulting from the successful completion of a challenging task is referred to as "effectance" (Harter & Zigler, 1974; White, 1959). Many mentally retarded individuals perform poorly and never experience satisfaction from a job well done. This reduces effectance motivation and causes them to be reluctant to engage in new learning. It also reduces their expectations for success resulting in a variety of behaviors designed to help them avoid doing anything which may produce failure. Students may withdraw, become hostile, or feign lack of concern. These avoidance behaviors, used by all of us sometimes, may become a way of life for retarded individuals.

The construct of locus of control also relates to an individual's expectancies. Described in Rotter's (1954) theory of social learning, locus of control is a continuum of personal responsibility. Young and very outer-directed individuals attribute the events in their lives as totally beyond their control. With personality development, this belief gives way to taking responsibility for successes but attributing failure to powers and events beyond our control. Further along the continuum individuals take responsibility for failure but only modestly claim successes until total self-reliance emerges in which they accept equal responsibility for both the positive and negative events in their lives. According to Schloss and Sedlak (1982), mentally retarded persons seldom progress beyond the first two or three stages on the locus of control continuum. Tymchuk (1972) described the extrinsic motivational orientation of mildly retarded children and Zigler (1966) and others have studied retarded students' reliance on cues from others rather than the task in problem-solving situations. It has been hypothesized that retarded individuals have learned not to trust their own solutions to problems because of their failure, thus making reliance on cues from others an adaptive strategy.

Knowing what to do and when to do it in social situations requires fine discriminations based on relevant social cues (Schloss & Sedlak, 1982). Perhaps because of their difficulty in determining these cues in any learning situation, retarded individuals have difficulty. Consequently, their interpersonal skills may be deficient, and their behavior may seem strange or even offensive in some situations. This is especially true for moderately, severely, and profoundly mentally retarded individuals who have less understanding of social expectations and their own impact on others.

Although studies of self-concept in the mentally retarded have been conducted, the findings have been equivocal. In some instances, mildly retarded individuals were found to have low opinions of themselves while in others they overrated their actual ability to perform specific tasks. Self-concept is extremely difficult to measure, yet it influences all other aspects of one's life. At this point, a great deal of work remains to be done to further our understanding of retarded individuals' feelings about themselves.

During the early 1970s the United States, following the lead of the Scandinavian countries, initiated two major reforms in the field of mental retardation. Pioneered by Wolfensberger (1969, 1972), the ideologies of normalization and deinstitutionalization were introduced. The principle of normalization states that individuals with mental retardation should have the same opportunities and rights of everyday life that are afforded to others: the right to live in their home community, to attend school, to participate in social and recreational activities, to hold a job, and to establish relationships. When this concept was first introduced, the idea was revolutionary. Many retarded individuals lived in large state institutions where the most basic human and civil rights were denied. As human service professionals worked to "normalize" the lives of retarded citizens, it became apparent that deinstitutionalization was necessary (Blatt, 1970; Blatt & Kaplan, 1966). For the past two decades through education, litigation, and advocacy, large institutions have been depopulated. Many retarded people have been returned to their home communities, but a great deal of work remains to be done. According to a 1982 study of residential facilities, approximately 105 out of every 100,000 U.S. citizens is institutionalized because of mental retardation; and over 58 percent of those are living in institutions with more than 64 residents (Hauber, Bruininks, Hill, Lakin, Scheerenberger, & White, 1984). During the next few years, a major thrust in advocacy will, no doubt, be focused on increasing the number and quality of community-based options for retarded individuals and providing support to families who choose not to place a retarded family member outside the home.

Normalization and deinstitutionalization changed the role of society in the treatment of individuals with retardation. A variety of community options including group homes, vocational training programs, and education programs were created; and efforts to increase acceptance were launched. Although early studies of the integration of mildly retarded students were not always positive, more recent work has lent support to mainstreaming (Logan & Rose, 1982). It has become apparent that the attitudes of nonhandicapped students toward their handicapped peers is often related to the attitudes the teacher communicates (Foley, 1979). Research by Hamre-Nietupski (1981), Stainback and Stainback (1981), Voeltz (1982), and others suggests that even students with severe mental

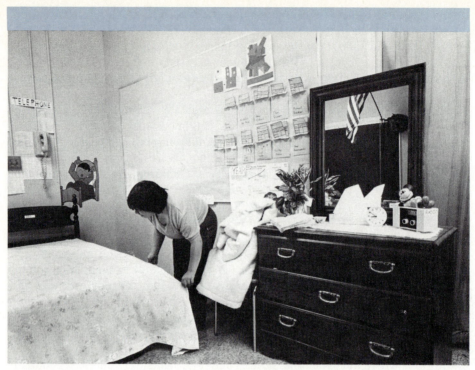

A young woman living in a group residential home takes pride in maintaining a neat room.

retardation can be successfully integrated onto regular school campuses and into community-based recreational and vocational activities. As teachers, parents, and the public become more comfortable with mainstreaming, and the procedures and curricula necessary to help retarded students progress are utilized, mentally retarded students will gain greater acceptance in the world in which we all live.

Medical/Health Characteristics

The medical needs and health of mildly mentally retarded individuals tend to be no different than those of the majority of the population. They benefit from the same kinds of preventive practices and routine health care recommended for all individuals. The primary issue is to assure that they are informed about prevention, the signs and symptoms of disease which should be treated, and where treatment can be obtained. This is especially important for retarded individuals who choose to become parents so that their children's health will be cared for from the prenatal period through young adulthood.

The medical and health needs of moderately, severely, and profoundly mentally retarded individuals are greater than those of their nonhandicapped age peers. Although the days of limited life spans for retarded persons have passed, the more severely handicapped an individual is, the greater the likelihood of associated medical problems. These problems are often apparent early and persist throughout the lifespan. In general, development is delayed; muscle tone may be altered and general physical growth significantly delayed. In some instances, surgery to correct problems or reduce the effects of a problem may be necessary. In others, prosthetic devices which replace a body part (such as an artificial limb) or orthotic devices which prevent deformities or improve functioning (such as braces, splints, or speech synthesizers) are used to help the individual manipulate the environment. Frequently, severely retarded individuals have seizure disorders which require medication, and they may be taking one or more kinds of medicine for seizure control.

Genetic disorders often alter body structures causing problems which require medical treatment, and many syndromes have concomitant physical or health problems. Heart problems are often associated with Down and other syndromes (Lemeshow, 1982). In others the kidneys, liver, or spleen are damaged resulting in recurrent health problems. Upper respiratory problems of varying severity and dental problems are common among individuals with syndromes affecting the structure of the head and face. In a few instances, severely multiply handicapped individuals must rely on tracheostomies (holes made in their windpipes) for breathing, must be fed through tubes, and assisted to eliminate body waste through tubes such as catheters. In all individuals with limited mobility, the maintenance of vital capacity is an important issue. Those individuals who spend long periods of time in wheelchairs or lying down need to be checked for abrasions (bedsores) and need to be helped to find ways to exercise to keep their heart and lungs healthy. In these cases, as well as in those that require daily medication, it is important to have a health professional available to the teachers and therapists.

DETECTION OF MENTAL RETARDATION

The identification, diagnosis, and screening of individuals with mental retardation is a three-step process leading to the provision of appropriate services.

Identification and Screening

Mild mental retardation is usually recognized when a child enters kindergarten or first grade and is unable to keep up with his or her classmates on academic tasks. Since most mild retardation is first diagnosed in the school setting, teachers and school psychologists are the professionals who are usually involved. They may suspect retardation from their observations and confirm it from the child's performance on measures of intelligence, achievement, and adaptive behavior. In some communities, school districts or other agencies conduct widespread screening programs for preschool children. Children who do not have the skills expected for their chronological age may be enrolled in a skillbuilding program which usually includes opportunities for parent education. Programs such as these help prepare mildly mentally retarded children for the demands of formal education.

Severely and profoundly mentally retarded individuals are usually identified within the first two years of life by parents and health professionals. Because of the physical characteristics associated with many types of severe and profound retardation, some infants are diagnosed within hours after birth. Others are diagnosed at five to six months of age when they are not growing at the expected rate, mastering the milestones expected for that age period, and when primitive reflexes dominate their movement patterns (Fink & Cegelka, 1982). Many moderately retarded children are diagnosed between 24 and 36 months when they don't develop speech or understand language like their chronological age peers. At whatever age moderate to profound retardation is suspected, the young child is evaluated by a team of professionals with expertise in early development. By assessing the child's performance in the areas of gross and fine motor functioning, cognition, language, self-care, social/emotional functioning, and physical growth and development, the team makes the diagnosis of retardation.

Criteria for Determination of the Exceptionality

The criteria most commonly used to determine mental retardation are those included in the definition developed by the American Association on Mental Deficiency. The three criteria detailed in an earlier section of this chapter are: subaverage intellectual functioning, impairment in adaptive behavior, and diagnosis during the developmental period. Although there is some variation among professions in interpretation of these criteria, there is general agreement with this definition.

Common Methods for Diagnosis and Assessment

In assessment to diagnose mental retardation, a team of professionals and the parents work together. Parents contribute the developmental history and current observational information to the results of intelligence tests, adaptive behavior scales, and observations done by a school psychologist. The psychologist or psychometrician plays a critical role because of the instruments used to determine intellectual functioning. IQ tests such as the *Stanford-Binet* (Terman & Merrill, 1973), *Wechsler Preschool and Primary Scale of Intelligence* (Wechsler, 1967), *Wechsler Intelligence Scale for Children–Revised* (Wechsler, 1974), *Woodcock-Johnson Psycho-educational Battery* (Woodcock & Johnson, 1977), and *Wechsler Adult Intelligence Scale–Revised* (Wechsler, 1981) are used most frequently. The *Stanford-Binet* (Terman & Merrill, 1973) includes items which measure vocabulary, problem-solving skills, general information, and comprehension from the two-year-old to superior adult level. It relies heavily on verbal ability and the use and understanding of language. The three Wechsler Scales of Intelligence are designed for different age groups as their titles indicate. In addition to including items that measure verbal aspects of intelligence, they also include items which examine aspects of performance such as picture completion, object assembly, and reproduction of geometric designs. Measurement of adaptive behavior is usually done through observation and report using a standardized scale such as the *Vineland Adaptive Behavior Scales* (Sparrow, Balla, & Cicchetti, 1984), the *AAMD Adaptive Behavior Scale* (Nihira, Foster, Shellhaas, & Leland, 1975), or the *Adaptive Behavior Inventory for Children*, a component of the *System of Multicultural Pluralistic Assessment (SOMPA)* (Mercer, 1979). These instruments measure the day-to-day behaviors associated with effective functioning from preschool through adulthood.

To determine whether or not an individual is mentally retarded, a combination of intelligence and adaptive behavior measures as well as observation and parent reports are used. If the findings are consistent with the definition being used, the diagnosis of mental retardation is made which makes the individual eligible for a variety of special educational, vocational, and financial services.

In mental retardation as well as other exceptionalities, the instruments and procedures used to identify the exceptionality provide diagnostic rather than prescriptive information about the individual's skills. Precise information about what the individual can and can't do, and the conditions under which he or she can do it are necessary to plan the instructional program. This kind of information is usually gathered using a combination of formal and informal techniques— achievement and diagnostic tests as well as behavioral checklists, systematic collection of behavioral data, and ecological inventories. Teachers may assess their mentally retarded students' word recognition using one of the many diagnostic reading inventories or test their students' skills in math using a math achievement or diagnostic test. Informal behavioral checklists or task analyses may be used to guide the teacher's observations of the student's eating, street crossing, or vocational skills. As programming for students with mental retardation moves from the classroom to "natural" settings in the community such as restaurants, parks, and job sites, teachers are using ecological inventories to determine which skills should be taught. These inventories take different forms but often include a parent interview which details the student's daily activities and elicits the parents' programming priorities. Others task analyze the skills that it takes to perform successfully in an environment by observing what a nonhandicapped person does. The retarded student's performance in the same situation is observed and compared. For example, a teacher may record sequentially all of the skills that it takes to ride the city bus from a local shopping center to a city pool. After that inventory is completed, the teacher would observe one of the students taking the bus from the shopping center to the pool. The discrepancies between what the student can do and what is needed to make this trip would indicate what specific skills need to be taught in order for the student to make the trip independently. Both formal and informal, commercial and teacher-made assessment strategies are used to help determine what the student needs to learn, the most effective ways of teaching those skills, and the method for determining when the skills have been mastered.

Identifying Deficits
in Adaptive Behavior

For a diagnosis of mental retardation to be made, an individual must show deficits in adaptive behavior. Adaptive behavior varies with age and culture but can generally be described as those behaviors which allow one to function adequately in the world. For very young children, adaptive behavior includes learning to move around, communicate, increase their independence, solve problems, and develop relationships. For students in school, adaptive behavior is related to school performance, the ability to learn basic academic skills, develop and maintain friendships, and increase their mastery of the world. For adults, adaptive behavior is related to successful performance in the world of work, in relationships, and in being a dependable, productive person. Although adaptive behavior reflects an increased mastery of the world and effective performance within it, it is also related to cultural norms. In some countries, few children have the opportunity to attend school and learn basic skills. In others, women may work in the home but are prohibited from having occupations outside the home. In the United States, culture also influences opportunities. Some cultures discourage teenage daughters from achieving independence; others have only limited expectations for infants and preschoolers and do not expect them to develop self-help skills until they enter school. In measuring adaptive behavior in these situations, the cultural issues would be considered, and the individual would not be penalized for deficits in areas in which there had been no opportunities for learning.

The *AAMD Adaptive Behavior Scale, School Edition* (Lambert, Windmiller, Tharinger, & Cole, 1981) is used frequently to measure adaptive behavior. It has been designed to be used with students from 3 to 16 years of age. Part One includes skills in ten behavioral domains: Independent Functioning, Physical Development, Economic Activity, Language Development, Number and Time, Domestic Activity, Vocational Activity, Self-Direction, Responsibility, and Socialization. Part Two includes the following domains: Aggressiveness, Antisocial versus Social Behavior, Rebelliousness, Trustworthiness, Withdrawal versus Involvement, Mannerisms, Interpersonal Manners, Acceptability of Vocal Habits, Acceptability of Habits, Activity Level, Symptomatic Behavior, and Use of Medications. For each item in each domain, the examiner circles the statement that most closely corresponds to the student's functioning. Ideally, the instrument should be completed by someone who is thoroughly familiar with the student's performance. If that is not possible, it may also be completed by asking a number of people who know how the student performs on various items. A third, but less recommended way of gathering information, is through an interview which includes open-ended questions about each of the areas of functioning. Following such an interview, the examiner would complete the inventory from the information gathered.

Factor analytic studies of the instrument have identified five factors which can be scored: personal self-sufficiency, community self-sufficiency, personal-social responsibility, social adjustment, and personal adjustment. The scaled scores for each of these factors can then be compared to scores of students in regular classrooms, those in programs for the mildly mentally retarded, and those in programs for the moderately mentally retarded. Although these comparison scores have promise for determining appropriate placement, they must be used with caution until further research on their reliability and validity has been completed.

Special Considerations with Preschool Children

Making the diagnosis of mild mental retardation is most difficult during the early years. Although parents may notice that children later diagnosed as mildly retarded are slower to master the developmental tasks of early childhood, few are diagnosed before kindergarten or the primary grades. In retrospect, it is usually clear that the child was not developing normally, but these minor developmental deviations were overlooked. Although parents may have expressed concern to a professional about the child's development, they were probably told that the child would outgrow the problem, that it was too soon to tell, or that they were being overanxious.

More severe retardation is usually evident earlier; but because individual infants and preschoolers develop at such different rates and have more limited behavioral repertoires to assess, many professionals hesitate to diagnose mental retardation until a child is three to six years of age. The child is often described as "developmentally delayed," a more benign label suggesting a more optimistic outcome than mental retardation.

Professional reluctance to diagnose mental retardation in infants and preschoolers is based on real issues. The lack of predictive validity of infant tests with infants with mild delays, concern about limiting opportunities and expectations because of a label, and a generally optimistic view of the malleability of young children all contribute to this hesitancy. Although caution should be exercised in making any diagnosis, withholding judgment is not always in the best interests of the child or family. Early accurate diagnosis increases the likelihood of early intervention with both child and family, resulting in more positive outcomes for all.

CONSIDERATIONS IN INTERVENTION

Like all people, individuals with mental retardation have needs that change with time, life circumstances, and age. This section focuses on academic, social, and medical needs throughout the lifespan.

The Preschool Years

All babies need food, shelter, a nurturing, safe environment, and loving caretakers; it is no different for a baby with mental retardation. As infants grow and develop into toddlers and preschoolers, their needs increase to include opportunities to learn, to practice what they are learning, and to experience the world outside their own home and family. Mildly retarded young children are so similar to their nonretarded age peers that they are usually treated no differently. Variations in their upbringing are more a function of the family's desires and attitudes than differences in the child. However, young children with moderate, severe, and profound mental retardation present a much more complex profile of medical, social/emotional, and learning needs. Because of the demands that they make from the first few days of life, this section will focus on more severely retarded young children.

For a few babies who will later be diagnosed as mentally retarded, the first need is medical treatment. Those born prematurely, small for gestational age, in a complicated delivery, or those with congenital deformities or defects require immediate and intensive medical intervention. For many, this intervention is life sustaining; without it, they could not survive their first few hours. The most

This Down Syndrome preschool child is served best in a center-based program where interaction with other children is encouraged, but she may also receive some services at home.

frequent medical interventions include resuscitation, stabilizing breathing, maintaining body temperature, and providing a way for the infant to be fed. Newborns requiring continued medical intervention are usually transferred from the delivery room to a newborn or neonatal intensive care unit (Rudolph & Kenny, 1979), a technologically sophisticated setting supervised by a neonatologist and neonatal intensive care nurses. Some infants with mental retardation require surgery to repair or correct congenital defects in vital organs. These medical procedures are the beginning of early intervention for some mentally retarded young children.

After the infant is physically stable, interventions related to social/emotional and learning needs can be considered. They may be instituted in the neonatal intensive care unit or begun several months later. Intervention is based on the needs of the family, the child, and the availability of services in the community. Early intervention has been demonstrated to be effective in enhancing development and containing later costs for specialized services (Bricker & Sheehan, 1981; Hanson & Schwarz, 1978; Karnes, Schwedel, Lewis, Ratts, & Esry, 1981; Moore, Fredericks, & Baldwin, 1981; Schweinhart & Weikart, 1981). However, today it is still not available in all areas of the country.

Early intervention programs which serve children from birth through age three usually have two goals: (1) to ameliorate the handicapping condition and reduce

Early Intervention

For the past decade the number of infant and preschool programs for mentally retarded young children has increased dramatically. Although the specific goals for each child and family vary, all programs have the common goals of providing educational services to increase the child's skills, preventing further disability, and providing support and information to families. These programs may take many forms. They may include service from a large interdisciplinary team or from a single professional or paraprofessional. They may take place in the home, in schools, hospitals, churches, or a variety of other community settings. Philosophically, they represent many points of view from strictly behavioral,

to developmental, to a blend of theories and practices; and their curricula reflect a broad range of perspectives about the learning tasks in the early years.

Despite this broad range of differences, one thing is clear. Early intervention and preschool education for mentally retarded children improves their later performance. Studies have shown gains in language, self-help, academics, and motor skills that were still apparent at age 11 for those children who had at least two years of preschool experience. Starting to work with retarded children early pays off by improving their ability to function and saving costs for later services.

its negative effects on the child, and (2) to provide support and assistance to parents as they deal with the special difficulties of parenting a handicapped child (Linder, 1983). Programs are designed to teach the child functional, developmental skills such as walking, talking, and self-help. In instances in which the child will never be able to function independently, interventionists attempt to modify the environment so that the child can do as much as possible independently. The concept of partial participation (Baumgart et al., 1982) acknowledges that complete, independent performance of all tasks is not possible for many severely retarded individuals but that skills can be taught which allow them to participate in age-appropriate, socially valued ways. For example, most of us will never have the skills to become professional athletes; but many of us will learn to partially participate by attending games, cheering for our favorite team, and following their progress. Likewise, we may teach a severely retarded young child who will never be able to swim to enjoy the water using a flotation device, or we may move the pieces in a checkers game at the direction of a multiply handicapped player who cannot use arms and hands to move them. This allows the individual to participate in enjoyable, socially valued activities with nonhandicapped peers.

Early intervention program models are often described by the way in which services are delivered. Young children (from birth to 18 months or three years) are usually served in their homes by a home visitor. The visitor may be a special educator, occupational or physical therapist, speech and language therapist, nurse, psychologist, social worker, or paraprofessional. The home visitor brings ideas and activities, demonstrates them to the family, and monitors the child's progress. The visit may also include time for the parents or other family members to share their concerns and needs with the home visitor and to use him or her as a link to other resources. Services delivered in this way are referred to as "home-based."

As infants become toddlers and can profit from interaction with other children, they are often served in small groups in a center-based program. Although several toddlers may be grouped together in a center, these should not be viewed as typical classroom programs. Working with toddlers and preschoolers is qualitatively different from working with school-age children. Academically oriented, physically restrictive programs that are characteristic of many kindergarten and first grade programs are quite inappropriate for young retarded children.

Many programs have found that the most effective way to serve infants and toddlers is through a combination of home and center-based programming. This option includes home visits to work with the child and family in the natural environment but also provides opportunities for the child and family to be with others who may have similar needs. Many parents report that talking with other parents of retarded children has been the most helpful part of early intervention. Recognizing that they are not alone and that many others have found ways to solve the problems that they are confronting seems to be crucial to most families (Rubin & Quinn-Curran, 1983).

Preschool programs for moderately, severely, and profoundly retarded children are mandated in most states as part of PL 94–142. These programs are far more variable in their philosophy and implementation than those for younger children. Some are child-centered recognizing that all young children need time to explore and learn; others are highly structured and teacher-centered with a heavy emphasis on performance. The special needs of retarded preschoolers require a balanced educational program which includes opportunities for play, language learning, problem solving, skill development, experimentation, and socialization. All preschoolers, whether handicapped or not, need opportunities to practice the things that they are learning and to get constructive feedback from adults in a safe, supportive environment. Since the basic skills learned in early childhood are the building blocks for future learning, it is important that retarded preschoolers have high quality educational programs.

Both mainstreaming, or integration, and reverse mainstreaming are used extensively in preschool programs for retarded preschoolers. Preschool mainstreaming, like mainstreaming for older students, is a service delivery model which brings handicapped preschoolers into programs designed for the non-handicapped. Head Start programs have mainstreamed handicapped children since the mid 1970s, and many other public and private preschools have followed their lead. Reverse mainstreaming is defined as bringing nonhandicapped children into a program for handicapped children. Preschools around the country have created integration opportunities by inviting neighborhood preschoolers to attend their special education programs.

The School Years for Mildly Mentally Retarded Students

During the last decade, there has been considerable research, program expansion, and legislation directed toward improving programs for students with severe mental retardation. During that same period, interest in, research about, and programs for mildly mentally retarded students have been decreasing (Polloway & Smith, 1983). These opposing trends have resulted in positive changes for severely retarded individuals but few positive outcomes for those with mild retardation. Because of these differences, each group will be described separately.

During the traditional school years of kindergarten through the twelfth grade, the learning, social/emotional, and vocational needs of mildly retarded children differ from those of their nonretarded peers. Although mildly retarded students are a heterogeneous group of individuals with distinct strengths and weaknesses, some of the learning characteristics cited earlier suggest that carefully planned instruction can increase their achievement (Rose & Logan, 1982).

Through the years, two positions about the nature of mild mental retardation have guided curriculum development. Some researchers have felt that educable mentally retarded students differ only in terms of speed of cognitive skill acquisition (Zigler, 1969, cited in Rose & Logan, 1982). Curricula based on this theoretical position tend to assume that mildly retarded students learn in the same way as their nonretarded peers but at a slower pace. Consequently, the same material that is presented to regular class students is presented to mildly retarded students more slowly in less depth. Since students are not expected to master as much content, this type of curriculum has been described as "watered down" (Kolstoe, 1972, p. 159). Another approach to curriculum for educable mentally retarded students is a functional one. This approach (Rose & Logan, 1982) focuses on those basic academic, personal, social, and vocational skills needed to be effective in current and future environments. The assumption is that, since retarded students have more difficulty generalizing and learn at a slower rate, it is important to maximize their time in school by teaching those skills which help them survive in adult life. Thus, the curriculum is broadly defined to include many of the skills that enable one to function as an independent adult such as learning how to manage money, enter into contracts, apply for jobs, establish and maintain constructive relationships, and enjoy leisure time. With adolescents, the primary emphases would be on career and vocational education to improve the students' chances for getting and keeping a job.

With the current emphasis on integrated classrooms where mildly mentally retarded students are involved in regular classes for most of the school day and receive only limited services from special education resource teachers, the implicit assumption is that they will learn as much as their nonhandicapped peers. Unfortunately, this has not proved true; and many mildly retarded students are failing the regular curriculum and not being taught the skills that they will need to be successful in adulthood (Forness & Kavale, 1984; Gottlieb & Alter, 1984).

Specific content to be taught and the instructional methods and strategies for teaching it are determined through a careful assessment of the student and the application of principles of learning. Wehman and McLaughlin (1981) describe instructional principles which aid in the acquisition of new material and are especially applicable to the mildly mentally retarded. They include:

1. letting students know what they are learning, what tasks they are expected to perform, and how they will be evaluated;

2. using a combination of whole and part instruction, whole for learning material which is not too long and part for learnings which have clearly defined, sequential steps;
3. distributing practice based on the child's characteristics with shorter practices for children with shorter attention spans and longer practices for children who need a warm-up period before peak performance;
4. presenting material in small chunks which do not overwhelm the learner;
5. providing time for reciting or rehearsing material being learned using a 1:4 ratio (four times as much time in rehearsal as in presentation of new material);
6. providing corrective feedback which tells students what they have mastered and what errors they have made;
7. scheduling class time to allow for the maximum number of minutes of time on each task;
8. presenting material both verbally and visually or in a manner that is easiest for the child to comprehend;
9. teaching children to orient and attend to the task at hand, highlighting relevant cues;
10. using advance organizers such as overviews, outlines, introductions, or routines to help students structure material being learned.

After learning has taken place, mildly retarded students may need help in remembering what they have learned or utilizing it in new situations. Teachers can facilitate recall in several ways. Students need to overlearn material to make it a part of their repertoire. Researchers have suggested that once mildly mentally retarded students have learned the material, they must spend half as long again in practice as it took them to learn the material in order to retain it over a long period of time (Blake, 1974). They may also need to be taught strategies to aid in recalling what they have learned. Transferring new knowledge to a novel or altered situation can be facilitated by providing for instruction in multiple settings under varying conditions.

There is considerably more empirical data on *how* mildly mentally retarded should be taught than on *where* the instruction should take place. From Dunn's article in 1968 to the present day, there has been controversy about the integration of mildly handicapped students into regular education programs. Philosophically, integration has been supported and encouraged through the enactment of PL 94–142. There is, however, little empirical evidence that mildly mentally retarded students perform significantly better academically and socially in a mainstream setting (Carlberg & Kavale, 1980; Forness & Kavale, 1984; Sabornie, 1985). This is not to say that mainstream education is inappropriate but that its effects must be examined. Students' gains, academically, socially, and vocationally, should be the primary determiner of where special education services are delivered. If one assumes that the primary purpose of education is to prepare students for successful functioning in adulthood, the focus must shift to the curricula and settings which are most likely to foster those outcomes.

Computer-Assisted Instruction

Although computer-assisted instruction (CAI) is not in itself a new technology, the availability of microcomputers with improved programs has made it a more useful technology for students with mental retardation. For mildly retarded students who need to overlearn basic academic skills, computer programs can provide the drill and practice that they need and keep track of their progress, freeing the teacher to provide instruction. For students who need help getting along with others, computer games can teach teamwork. For students with fewer skills, computer programs can teach cause and effect and discrimination skills in ways that are motivating and reinforcing. Microcomputers in classrooms have greatly increased the amount of time that can be spent on instruction, drill, and practice, making them a useful tool in programs for students with mental retardation.

The School Years for Moderately, Severely, and Profoundly Mentally Retarded Students

Because moderate, severe, and profound mental retardation affects more aspects of development, many individuals have health problems which need attention during the school years. Severely retarded students may have concomitant physical disabilities which require occupational or physical therapy or surgery to maintain mobility. Others have problems with vital organs or are less resistant to disease and infection. Many take medication to control seizures; and in rare instances, basic body functions are maintained by catheters, ventilators, or tracheostomies. Medical care is provided by physicians or allied health professionals. At school, the nurse and therapists often work with the teacher to monitor the student's physical and health needs.

Students with moderate, severe, or profound mental retardation usually start school early in their lives. As six-year-olds, they may already have been participating in educational programs for one to six years. Because of their more intensive special needs, their school years are often eleven, rather than nine, months.

Severely mentally retarded students have the same needs that all students have; however, the limitations they bring to any situation require more creativity in helping them meet these needs. The concept of partial participation (Baumgart et al., 1982) mentioned earlier in this chapter is one of the hallmarks of model programs for severely retarded students. A primary goal of the school curriculum is to assist students to meet their social, emotional, and recreational needs through direct teaching, the use of adaptive devices, and the concept of partial participation.

Within the past five years, there have been major changes in programs for more severely retarded students. The almost exclusively behavioral programming which relied on targeting a specific behavior, breaking it into smaller chunks, teaching the smaller chunks in a series of discrete trials, and rewarding correct performance taught professionals that even the most severely retarded individual could learn. That approach has now been tempered with a broader view of curriculum, a more functional approach to selecting the skills to be taught, and an emphasis on selecting the most appropriate setting in which to teach them (Baumgart et al., 1982; Brown et al., 1983; White, 1980). Four principles now guide programming in school systems which have model programs for moderately, severely, and profoundly retarded students. These principles are:

1. serving students on integrated school sites;
2. providing opportunities for retarded and nonhandicapped students to interact;
3. developing instructional plans based on functional, age-appropriate skills required in students' current and predicted future environments;
4. teaching skills in the settings in which they are used.

Within the past few years, there has been a major effort to move moderately, severely, and profoundly mentally retarded students out of segregated school sites and onto regular school campuses. The first efforts toward educating more severely retarded students in the least restrictive environment placed them into closer physical proximity to nonretarded students, but did not achieve the intended goal of closer interaction (Hamre-Nietupski & Nietupski, 1981). Retarded students often remained isolated with no opportunities for shared activities with students in regular classrooms.

The current emphasis is on the development of programs which facilitate interaction between retarded and nonretarded students in school and in community settings. These efforts have been successful in many areas of the country, and have shown that the results are positive for both retarded and nonretarded students (Brown, Ford, et al., 1983; Hamre-Nietupski & Nietupski, 1981; Stainback, Stainback, & Hatcher, 1983; Taylor, 1982; Voeltz, 1982).

The curriculum for moderately, severely, and profoundly mentally retarded students is undergoing a dramatic change in model school programs. Traditional educational efforts were focused on a developmental approach using the student's mental age as the measure of development. This resulted in teaching school-age children and adolescents skills that are taught to normally developing children in the preschool years. It was not uncommon to see a classroom of moderately retarded 14-year-olds stacking blocks or coloring in preschool coloring books. This approach wasted hours of instruction on skills which have little use in adult life and on skills which were not appropriate for the student's chronological age. Even severely retarded students share many of the interests of their chronological age peers and as teenagers would rather be listening to the latest rock band than recordings of "Old McDonald." Recent effort has been directed toward teaching skills which are more appropriate to chronological age and those which will have future utility to the student (Baumgart et al., 1982; White, 1980). These skills are usually determined through extensive ecological interviews with the student's parents or primary caretakers and form the basis for the IEP.

The final principle which has guided the change in programs for students with moderate, severe, and profound mental retardation is the utilization of nonschool environments for instruction (Brown, Nisbet, et al., 1983; Freagon & Rotatori, 1982; Hamre-Nietupski, Nietupski, Bates, & Maurer, 1982). Much of what mentally retarded students need to learn cannot be taught effectively in the classroom. Students who have trouble generalizing behaviors learn more effectively when the behavior is taught in the context and in the place where it will be used. For example, it is much more effective to teach students how to wash their hands using a kitchen or bathroom sink than it is to simulate the situation in a room without a sink. In addition, classrooms were not designed to teach life skills such as crossing the street and taking the bus, grocery shopping, or working. Although they may be introduced through simulation, these skills need to be taught and practiced in the settings where they typically occur. For example, instruction on how to purchase a new shirt can be conducted much more effectively in a clothing store than in a simulated store in the classroom.

These four concepts are the guiding principles of education for more severely retarded students. Although they are not yet common practice throughout the United States, they provide a framework for the development of quality programs.

Retarded Individuals as Adults

Adults with mental retardation can generally be divided into three groups which parallel the extent of their disability. Many individuals with mild mental retardation are assimilated into the community after high school. They are no longer identified as having special needs and no longer require special services. A second group comprised of some individuals with mild retardation and the majority of those with moderate retardation continue to need special services throughout their lives. They may live in a supervised apartment complex, require help managing money, need counseling around family planning or in finding and keeping a job. With this extra support, they can be successfully integrated into the community. The third group includes those with severe and profound mental retardation. As adults, they can participate partially in many activities, but do not achieve complete independence. Many need continual supervision and assistance in all aspects of their daily lives.

In response to the normalization and deinstitutionalization movements discussed earlier in this chapter, the integration of more severely handicapped individuals into the community has increased. Through groups such as the Association for Retarded Citizens as well as through proprietary groups, new residential options have been created. Group homes with a manager and staff on shifts provide a boardinghouse setting for older adolescents and adults. These homes, located in residential areas, provide opportunities for natural integration in the neighborhood (Perske, 1980). Even the medical facilities for those retarded adults who are extremely medically fragile are being scaled down from large institutions to small centers. Opportunities to work and be paid are also being developed in many communities. Moderately and severely retarded individuals are moving from segregated sheltered workshops and activity centers into community jobs. As special education and vocational rehabilitation work together, more and more retarded adults will be competitively employed in service positions in restaurants, hospitals, and other businesses busing tables, sorting medical supplies, and working as housekeepers in hotels, motels, and dormitories. Perhaps the areas in which the most remains to be done are those of recreational and leisure opportunities and social relationships. Despite increased opportunities for meaningful work, most retarded adults will have more free time than work time. Options for using that free time are still limited as is support for establishing and maintaining long-term relationships.

Although the amount of intervention varies considerably from one group to another, the needs of all people are more alike than they are different. Retarded adults need meaningful relationships with people of their own choosing, opportunities to participate in a variety of recreational and leisure activities, and opportunities to contribute to the community through work that is valued. Contemporary practice with retarded adults emphasizes vocational education, movement from sheltered to competitive employment, a range of least restrictive housing options away from the family home, and the use of generic community services for health care, recreation, housing, and employment. This move toward complete integration into the community involves professionals in many related disciplines including social work, vocational rehabilitation, health, and education.

FUTURE PERSPECTIVES FOR THE TREATMENT OF MENTAL RETARDATION

Professionals who work in the field of mental retardation grapple with a wide range of issues. Paramount among them are those of prevention, intervention, and attitude change. While medical researchers and geneticists work to discover the causes of mental retardation, health educators disseminate the information that is already known about prevention. A major goal of all who work in the field is to reduce the incidence of mental retardation.

Developing educational interventions that have a positive effect on the lives of mentally retarded students is a second major goal. Traditional classroom instruction must be balanced by community-based instruction for students with retardation, and educators are studying ways to broaden their impact through life skills training for all retarded students.

Changing attitudes about retardation is another major goal. Integrating mentally retarded individuals into all aspects of community life beginning in infancy will help to dispel the fears and myths that have surrounded this disability. As people begin to understand more about mental retardation, integration will become more widespread.

Although there have been major advancements in the field of mental retardation in the past few years, there is much that is still unknown. Among the unknowns are its causes. New syndromes are defined yearly, but the understanding of how they occur lags behind their identification. Despite mental retardation's long recorded history, there is still relatively little data on how much retarded individuals can learn. Formerly assumed performance ceilings are being exceeded daily in classrooms, in the community, and on the job. At this point in the development of the field, far more is known about professionals' expectations of performance than the actual capability of retarded individuals. Until there is a better understanding of the causes as well as capability, a great deal remains to be done.

Early intervention, integration of retarded individuals into the community, and chronological age-appropriate skill training will affect future treatment of individuals with mental retardation. Beginning training early, teaching skills that are needed and valued, and including mentally retarded individuals in all aspects of community life, will afford retarded individuals the opportunity to become more effective and decrease society's negative perceptions.

The future is full of challenges which will affect the treatment of retarded citizens. The following are among the most important:

- Conducting basic research which leads to understanding of the causes of mental retardation and their prevention;
- Developing educational programs which address the needs of mildly mentally retarded individuals;
- Bringing all programs for moderately, severely, and profoundly retarded individuals up to model program standards;
- Utilizing technology to increase severely retarded students' independence;
- Helping society understand that people with mental retardation can be valued, contributing citizens if they are given the chance.

SUMMARY

Mental retardation is an exceptionality that affects an individual's ability to think, learn, remember, and solve problems. The range of mental retardation varies from mild to profound. Those with mild mental retardation are often identified only during the school years and blend into the community when they leave high school. Those with moderate, severe, and profound mental retardation have special needs throughout their lives, but can be successfully integrated into community activities. Many individuals who would have been institutionalized several years ago are now working, living in supervised apartments, and participating in the recreational activities of their neighborhood.

There are many causes of mental retardation; but in most instances, the precise cause of an individual's retardation cannot be determined. Chromosomal anomalies, infections in utero, gestational disorders, and environmental hazards have all been identified as causes of mental retardation. In recent years, ways to eliminate or reduce the effects of some disorders have been discovered, and work on others is being carried out in laboratories throughout the world.

In addition to the advances in prevention, there have been some relatively recent advances in the way that people with mental retardation are treated. The moves toward deinstitutionalization and normalization have significantly improved the lives of many individuals who had been deprived of all civil rights for many years. At the same time, systematic instruction using the principles of applied behavioral analysis demonstrated that the most profoundly retarded individuals could learn. The passage of PL 94–142 with its mandate for services for all handicapped children and its emphasis on the unserved and the underserved gave further impetus to the development of programs for moderately, severely, and profoundly mentally retarded students. After nearly ten years of implementation of the law, programs for more severely retarded individuals have begun to emphasize the need for training in chronological age-appropriate skills which will help the individual function more effectively now and in the future. These programs also emphasize the need for training to take place in integrated school settings as well as in the community.

At the same time that programming for more severely retarded students has gained acceptance and shown rapid expansion, programs for mildly mentally retarded students have lost ground. Many students with mild mental retardation have been returned to regular classrooms without the needed support. Those students whose chances of being assimilated into the mainstream after high school have traditionally been high are now having more difficulty competing for jobs and fitting into the mainstream. A major problem in the field of mental retardation relates to the lack of adequate programming and assistance for mildly retarded individuals.

Mental retardation describes a wide range of performance, expectations, and outcomes. It also represents an area which has been surrounded by fear and misinformation. However, as mentally retarded individuals become integrated into the mainstream of life, these myths can be dispelled, enriching the lives of all.

References

Abramowicz, H. K., & Richardson, S. A. (1975). Epidemiology of severe mental retardation in children: Community studies. *American Journal of Mental Deficiency, 80*, 18–39.

Batshaw, M. L., & Perret, Y. M. (1981). *Children with handicaps—a medical primer.* Baltimore, MD: Paul H. Brookes.

Batshaw, M. L., Perret, Y. M., & Harryman, S. (1981). Cerebral palsy. In M. L. Batshaw & Y. M. Perret, *Children with handicaps—a medical primer* (pp. 191–212). Baltimore, MD: Paul H. Brookes.

Baumgart, D., Brown, L., Pumpian, I., Nisbet, J., Ford, A., Sweet, M., Messina, R., & Schroeder, J. (1982). Principle of partial participation and individualized adaptations in educational programs for severely handicapped students. *The Journal of the Association for the Severely Handicapped, 7* (2), 17–27.

Berlin, C. M., Jr. (1978). Biology and retardation. In J. T. Neisworth & R. M. Smith (Eds.), *Retardation: Issues, assessment, and intervention* (pp. 117–137). New York: McGraw-Hill.

Bijou, S. W. (1966). A functional analysis of retarded development. In N. R. Ellis (Ed.), *International review of research in mental retardation* (Vol. 1) (pp. 1–18). New York: Academic Press.

Blake, K. A. (1974). *Teaching the retarded.* Englewood Cliffs, NJ: Prentice-Hall.

Blatt, B. (1970). *Exodus from pandemonium: Human abuse and a reformation of public policy.* Boston: Allyn & Bacon.

Blatt, B., & Kaplan, F. (1966). *Christmas in purgatory: A photographic essay on mental retardation.* Boston: Allyn & Bacon.

Bray, N. W. (1979). Strategy production in the retarded. In N. R. Ellis (Ed.), *Handbook of mental deficiency* (2nd ed.) (pp. 699–726). Hillsdale, NJ: Lawrence Erlbaum Associates.

Bricker, D., & Sheehan, R. (1981). Effectiveness of an early intervention program indexed by measures of child change. *Journal of the Division for Early Childhood, 4,* 11–27.

Brown, L., Ford, A., Nisbet, J., Sweet, M., Donnellan, A., & Gruenewald, L. (1983). Opportunities available when severely handicapped students attend chronological age appropriate regular schools. *The Journal of the Association for the Severely Handicapped, 8* (1), 16–24.

Brown, L., Nisbet, J., Ford, A., Sweet, M., Shiraga, B., York, J., & Loomis, R. (1983). The critical need for nonschool instruction in educational programs for severely handicapped students. *The Journal of the Association for the Severely Handicapped, 8* (3), 71–77.

Carlberg, C., & Kavale, K. (1980). The efficacy of special versus regular class placement for exceptional children: A meta-analysis. *Journal of Special Education, 14,* 294–309.

Dunn, L. M. (1968). Special education for the mildly retarded—is much of it justifiable? *Exceptional Children, 35,* 5–22.

Ellis, N. R., Deacon, J. R., Harris, L. A., Poor, A., Angers, D., Diorio, M. S., Watkins, R. S., Boyd, B. D., & Cavalier, A. R. (1982). Learning, memory, and transfer in profoundly, severely, and moderately mentally retarded persons. *American Journal of Mental Deficiency, 87* (2), 186–196.

Fink, W., & Cegelka, P. (1982). Characteristics of the moderately and severely mentally retarded. In P. Cegelka & H. Prehm (Eds.). *Mental retardation: From categories to people* (pp. 231–259). Columbus, OH: Merrill Publishing.

Foley, J. M. (1979). Effect of labeling and teacher behavior on children's attitudes. *American Journal of Mental Deficiency, 83,* 380–384.

Forness, S. R., & Kavale, K. (1984). Education of the mentally retarded: A note on policy. *Education and Training of the Mentally Retarded, 19,* 239–245.

Freagon, S., & Rotatori, A. F. (1982). Comparing natural and artificial environments in training self-care skills to group home residents. *The Journal of the Association for the Severely Handicapped, 7* (3), 73–86.

Garber, H. L., & McInerney, M. (1982). Sociobehavioral factors in mental retardation. In P. Cegelka & H. Prehm (Eds.). *Mental retardation: From categories to people* (pp. 111–145). Columbus, OH: Merrill Publishing.

Goddard, H. H. (1911). Two thousand normal children measured by the Binet measuring scale of intelligence. *Pedagogical Seminary, 18,* 231–258.

Gold, M. C. (Ed.) (1980). *"Did I say that?" Articles and commentary on the try another way system.* Champaign, IL: Research Press.

Gottlieb, J., & Alter, M. (1984). Perspectives on instruction. *CEC Monograph, 1* (1, Serial No. 1).

Gould, S. J. (1980). *The panda's thumb.* New York: W. W. Norton & Company.

Gould, S. J. (1981). *The mismeasure of man.* New York: W. W. Norton & Company.

Grossman, H. J. (Ed.) (1973). *Manual on terminology and classification in mental retardation.* Washington, DC: American Association on Mental Deficiency.

Grossman, H. J. (Ed.) (1983). *Classification in mental retardation.* Washington, DC: American Association on Mental Deficiency.

Guthrie, R. (1972). Mass screening for genetic disease. *Hospital Practice, 7,* 93.

Hamre-Nietupski, S., & Nietupski, J. (1981). Integral involvement of severely handicapped students within regular public schools. *The Journal of the Association for the Severely Handicapped, 6* (2), 30–39.

Hamre-Nietupski, S., Nietupski, J., Bates, P., & Maurer, S. (1982). Implementing a community-based educational model for moderately/severely handicapped students: Common problems and suggested solutions. *The Journal of the Association for the Severely Handicapped, 7* (4), 38–43.

Hanson, M., & Schwarz, R. (1978). Results of a longitudinal intervention program for Down's Syndrome infants and their families. *Education and Training of the Mentally Retarded, 13,* 403–409.

Harter, S., & Zigler, E. (1974). The assessment of effectance motivation in normal and retarded children. *Developmental Psychology, 10,* 169–180.

Hauber, F. A., Bruininks, R. H., Hill, B. K., Lakin, C., Scheerenberger, R. C., & White, C. C. (1984). National census of residential facilities and residents. *American Journal of Mental Deficiency, 89,* 236–245.

Hayden, A., & Beck, G. R. (1982). Epidemiology of infants at risk. In C. T. Ramey & P. L. Trohanis (Eds.), *Finding and educating high-risk and handicapped infants* (pp. 19–51). Baltimore: University Park Press.

Heber, R. A. (1961). A manual on terminology and classification in mental retardation. *American Journal on Mental Retardation,* Monograph Supplement.

Heller, K. A., Holtzman, W. H., & Messick, S. (Eds.) (1982). *Placing children in special education: A strategy for equity.* Washington, DC: National Academy Press.

Jensen, A. R. (1969). How much can we boost IQ and scholastic achievement? *Harvard Educational Review, 39,* 1–123.

Jensen, A. R. (1981). *Straight talk about mental tests.* New York: The Free Press.

Jensen, A. R. (1982). Changing conceptions of intelligence. *Education and Training of the Mentally Retarded, 17* (1), 3–5.

Karnes, M., Schwedel, A., Lewis, G., Ratts, D., & Esry, D. (1981). Impact on early programming for the handicapped: A follow-up study into the elementary school. *Journal of the Division for Early Childhood, 4,* 62–69.

Kolstoe, O. P. (1972). *Mental retardation: An educational viewpoint.* New York: Holt, Rinehart and Winston.

Korones, S. B., & Lancaster, J. (1981). *High-risk newborn infants.* St. Louis: C. V. Mosby.

Krug, D., & Davis, P. (1981). *Study findings: National study of the incidence and severity of child abuse and neglect.* (DHHS Publication No. OHDS 81-30325). Washington, DC: U.S. Government Printing Office.

Lambert, N., Windmiller, M., Tharinger, D., & Cole, L. (1981). *AAMD adaptive behavior scale, school edition.* Washington, DC: American Association on Mental Deficiency.

Lemeshow, S. (1982). *The handbook of clinical types in mental retardation.* Boston: Allyn & Bacon.

Linder, T. (1983). *Early childhood special education.* Baltimore: Paul H. Brookes.

Logan, D. L., & Rose, E. (1982). Characteristics of the mildly mentally retarded. In P. Cegelka & H. Prehm (Eds.). *Mental retardation: From categories to people* (pp. 149–185). Columbus, OH: Merrill Publishing.

MacMillan, D. L. (1982). *Mental retardation in school and society* (2nd ed.). Boston: Little, Brown.

Masland, R. L., Sarason, S. B., & Gladwin, T. (1958). *Mental subnormality.* New York: Basic Books.

Menolascino, F. J., Neman, R., & Stark, J. A. (1983). Future prospects for curing mental retardation. In F. J. Menolascino, R. Neman, & J. A. Stark (Eds.), *Curative aspects of mental retardation* (pp. 301–321). Baltimore: Paul H. Brookes.

Mercer, C. D., & Snell, M. E. (1977). *Learning theory research in mental retardation*. Columbus, OH: Merrill Publishing.

Mercer, J. (1973). *Labeling the mentally retarded*. Berkeley: University of California Press.

Mercer, J. (1979). *System of multicultural pluralistic assessment: Technical manual*. Cleveland, OH: Psychological Corporation.

Moore, B. C. (1982). Biomedical factors in mental retardation. In P. Cegelka & H. Prehm (Eds.), *Mental retardation: From categories to people* (pp. 76–110). Columbus, OH: Merrill Publishing.

Moore, M., Fredericks, H., & Baldwin, V. (1981). The long-range effects of early childhood education on a trainable mentally retarded population. *Journal of the Division of Early Childhood, 4*, 94–110.

Mumpower, D. L. (1970). Sex ratios found in various types of referred exceptional children. *Exceptional Children, 36*, 621–622.

Nihira, K., Foster, R., Shellhaas, M., & Leland, H. (1974). *AAMD adaptive behavior scale: Manual* (rev. ed.). Washington, DC: American Association on Mental Deficiency.

Perske, R. (1980). *New life in the neighborhood*. Nashville, TN: Abingdon.

Polloway, E. A., & Smith, J. D. (1983). Changes in mild mental retardation: Population, programs, and perspectives. *Exceptional Children, 50*, 149–159.

Rose, E., & Logan, D. (1982). Educational and life/career programs for the mildly mentally retarded. In P. Cegelka & H. Prehm (Eds.), *Mental retardation: From categories to people* (pp. 186–226). Columbus, OH: Merrill Publishing.

Rotter, J. B. (1954). *Social learning and clinical psychology*. Englewood Cliffs, NJ: Prentice-Hall.

Rubin, S., & Quinn-Curran, N. (1983). Lost, then found: Parents' journey through the community service maze. In M. Seligman (Ed.), *The family with a handicapped child: Understanding and treatment* (pp. 63–94). New York: Grune & Stratton.

Rudolph, A., & Kenny, J. (1979). Anticipation, recognition, and care of the high-risk infant. In M. Klaus & A. Fanaroff (Eds.), *Care of the high-risk neonate* (2nd ed.) (pp. 45–65). Philadelphia: W. B. Saunders.

Sabornie, E. J. (1985). Social mainstreaming of handicapped students: Facing an unpleasant reality. *Remedial and Special Education, 6*, 12–16.

Schloss, P. J., & Sedlak, R. (1982). Behavioral features of the mentally retarded adolescent; Implications for mainstream educators. *Psychology in the Schools, 19* (1), 98–105.

Schweinhart, L., & Weikart, D. (1981). Effects of the Perry program on youths through age 15. *Journal of the Division of Early Childhood, 4*, 29–39.

Silverstein, A. B., Pearson, L. B., Colbert, B. A., Cordeiro, W. J., Marwin, J. L., & Nakaji, M. J. (1982). Cognitive development of severely and profoundly mentally retarded individuals. *American Journal of Mental Deficiency, 87* (3), 347–349.

Singer, J. E., Westphal, M., & Niswander, K. R. (1968). Sex differences in the incidence of neonatal abnormalities and abnormal performance in early childhood. *Child Development, 39*, 103–112.

Smith, D. W., & Wilson, A. A. (1973). *The child with Down's syndrome*. Philadelphia: W. B. Saunders.

Sparrow, S. S., Balla, D. A., Cicchetti, D. V. (1984). *Vineland adaptive behavior scales*. Circle Pines, MN: American Guidance Service.

Spitz, H. H., (1979). Beyond field theory in the study of mental deficiency. In N. R. Ellis (Ed.), *Handbook of mental deficiency* (2nd ed.) (pp. 121–141). Hillsdale, NJ: Lawrence Erlbaum Associates.

Stainback, W., & Stainback, S. (1981). A review of research on interactions between severely handicapped and nonhandicapped students. *Journal of the Association for the Severely Handicapped, 6* (3), 23–29.

Stainback, S., Stainback, W. C., & Hatcher, C. W. (1983). Nonhandicapped peer involvement in the education of severely handicapped students. *The Journal of the Association for the Severely Handicapped, 8* (1), 39–42.

Stokes, T. F., Baer, D. M., & Jackson, R. L. (1974). Programming for generalization of a greeting response in four retarded children. *Journal of Applied Behavior Analysis, 7,* 599–610.

Tarjan, G., Wright, S. W., Eyman, R. K., & Keeran, D. V. (1973). Natural history of mental retardation: Some aspects of epidemiology. *American Journal of Mental Deficiency, 77,* 369–379.

Taylor, S. J., (1982). From segregation to integration: Strategies for integrating severely handicapped students in normal school and community settings. *The Journal of the Association for the Severely Handicapped, 7* (3), 42–49.

Terman, L. M., (1919). *The intelligence of school children.* Boston: Houghton Mifflin.

Terman, L., & Merrill, M. (1973). *Stanford-Binet intelligence scale, 1972 norms edition.* Boston: Houghton Mifflin.

Tymchuk, A. J. (1972). Personality and sociocultural retardation. *Exceptional Children, 38,* 721–728.

U.S. Dept. of Education (1984). *Sixth annual report to Congress on the implementation of Public Law 94–142: The education for all handicapped children act.* Washington, DC: Author.

Voeltz, L. M. (1982). Effects of structured interactions with severely handicapped peers on children's attitudes. *American Journal of Mental Deficiency, 82,* 380–390.

Wechsler, D. (1967). *Manual for the Wechsler preschool and primary scale of intelligence.* Cleveland, OH: Psychological Corportion.

Wechsler, D. (1974). *Manual for the Wechsler intelligence scale for children-revised.* Cleveland, OH: Psychological Corporation.

Wechsler, D. (1981). *Wechsler adult intelligence scale—revised.* Cleveland, OH: Psychological Corporation.

Wehman, P., & McLaughlin, P. J. (1981). *Program development in special education.* New York: McGraw-Hill Book Company.

White, O. (1980). Adaptive performance objectives—form versus function. In W. Sailor, B. Wilcox, & L. Brown (Eds.), *Methods of instruction for severely handicapped students* (pp. 47–69). Baltimore: Paul H. Brookes.

White, R. W. (1959). Motivation reconsidered: The concept of competence. *Psychological Review, 66,* 297–333.

Wolfensberger, W. (1969). The origin and nature of our institutional models. In R. Kugel & W. Wolfensberger (Eds.), *Changing patterns in residential services for the mentally retarded* (pp. 59–171). Washington, DC: President's Committee on Mental Retardation.

Wolfensberger, W. (1972). *The principle of normalization in human services.* Toronto, Canada: National Institute on Mental Retardation.

Woodcock, R. W., & Johnson, M. B. (1977). *Woodcock-Johnson psycho-educational battery.* Hingham, MA: Teaching Resources.

Zeaman, D., & House, B. J. (1979). A review of attention theory. In N. R. Ellis (Ed.), *Handbook of mental deficiency* (2nd ed.) (pp. 63–120). Hillsdale, NJ: Lawrence Erlbaum Associates.

Zigler, E. (1966). Research on personality structure in the retardate. In N. R. Ellis (Ed.), *International review of research in mental retardation* (Vol. 1) (pp. 77–108). New York: Academic Press.

Resources

Organizations

American Association on Mental Deficiency
1719 Kalorama Road, N.W.
Washington, DC 20009

Interdisciplinary organization which publishes a professional journal of research in the area of mental retardation, disseminates information, advocates for individuals with mental retardation, holds annual national meeting, and maintains active state chapters.

Association for Retarded Citizens National Headquarters
2501 Avenue J
Arlington, TX 76011

Organized and operated by parents, this group provides information, advocates for citizens with mental retardation, and supports local chapters in many communities. Local groups vary in their scope but frequently provide direct services.

Division on Mental Retardation
Council for Exceptional Children
1920 Association Drive
Reston, VA 22091-1589

Publishes a professional journal and conducts annual meetings at the CEC annual meeting. State divisions are also active in some areas of the country.

Down's Syndrome Congress
1640 W. Roosevelt Road
Chicago, IL 60608

Conducts and disseminates information and research on Down Syndrome

Parents of Down's Syndrome Children
3358 Annandale Road
Falls Church, VA 22042

Organized and operated by parents, this group publishes a newsletter and provides support to parents of Down Syndrome children.

Journals

American Journal of Mental Deficiency
1719 Kalorama Road, N.W.
Washington, DC 20009

Publishes results of empirical research, theory, and research reviews on specific aspects of mental retardation.

Education and Training of the Mentally Retarded
1920 Association Drive
Reston, VA 22091-1589

Publishes research, theory, and policy related to individuals with mental retardation with special emphasis on the utilization of research findings.

Mental Retardation
1719 Kalorama Road, N.W.
Washington, DC 20009

An interdisciplinary journal devoted to publishing research-based articles about effective ways to help mentally retarded individuals and their families.

Chapter 4

PHYSICAL AND HEALTH HANDICAPS

As a group, persons with physical and health handicaps vary in the nature of their medical disabilities, mental and social skills, and cultural backgrounds. A common factor sets them apart: each has a medical disability that somehow limits his or her ability to function in specific life activities. Persons with severe multiple handicaps or severe retardation also may have accompanying physical handicaps, but schools generally classify them as multiply handicapped or severely retarded for legal or funding purposes.

The current trend in education, rehabilitation, and social service is to emphasize the individual's ability to function in important life situations rather than focus on his or her medical diagnosis. Although grouping persons for service by diagnosis may facilitate medical treatment and the organization of medical research, it does not enhance educational programming or rehabilitation services. Furthermore, it may have detrimental social consequences such as arbitrary restriction of activity and inappropriate program placement; denial of educational, vocational, and social opportunities; as well as self-limitations set by persons with physical and health handicaps.

Richard C. Brady
San Diego State University

INDIVIDUALS WITH PHYSICAL
AND HEALTH HANDICAPS

Professionals working with persons with physical and health handicaps have become increasingly sophisticated and concerned about the social and psychological consequences related to arbitrary labeling and categorizing. Professionals are beginning to make a careful distinction between the disabilities designated by medical diagnosis and the resulting handicapping conditions (Best, 1978). The word "disability" refers to a medical problem caused by a physical impairment or condition. On the other hand, the word "handicap" refers to the inability of a person to function in a specific situation as a result of the disability. The extent to which medical disabilities have handicapping potential for a given individual will vary depending upon the severity of the disability, the age of onset, the duration of the disability, and the visibility of the problem. In addition, the demands of the environment in which the individual must operate and the effect of the individual's perceptions of social feedback will affect how handicapping the disability will be. The following are common instances where disability and environment interact to produce physical handicapping conditions:

1. Limitations in mobility—the lack of access to transportation and inability to overcome architectural barriers in the environment.
2. Excessive losses of time and disruptions of life—often the effect of frequent hospitalization, continuing health problems, and lack of efficiency in performing routine daily living tasks.
3. Public stereotypes and misconceptions concerning physical and health problems—usually a result of prejudice leading to artificial barriers to educational, vocational, and social opportunities.
4. Self-devaluation and underestimation of potential—usually includes a lack of motivation to achieve, lack of endurance to complete tasks, and forfeiture of opportunity resulting in a dependent status.

Recent federal and state laws have alleviated many of the restrictions which limited the opportunities of persons with various physical and health handicaps. The *Rehabilitation Act of 1973* (PL 93–112) sets forth the rights of handicapped persons and addresses the problems of arbitrary discrimination. The key sentence in this law states:

> No otherwise qualified handicapped individual in the United States . . . shall, solely by reason of his handicap, be excluded from participation in, be denied the benefits of, or be subjected to discrimination under any program or activity receiving federal financial assistance. (Section 504)

Three of the administrative regulations which were used to implement the *Vocational Rehabilitation Act of 1973* were especially significant to persons with

JAN

At four and one-half years of age, Jan was involved in an automobile accident which left her in a coma for almost three months. No one could predict the extent or permanence of brain damage she would retain when she regained consciousness. As she recovered, it became evident that she had a relatively rare spastic double hemiplegia. All four of Jan's limbs were affected by her spastic body movements. However, unlike quadriplegia, her right side was more affected than her left.

Jan needed intensive speech, physical, and occupational therapy to help her learn to walk, use her hands, and speak again. To obtain these services, her parents enrolled her in a special school for the physically handicapped at five years of age. In the first two years, academic work had to be constantly interrupted as the necessary medical therapies were stressed. Jan's physical abilities continued to improve. By the third grade, she could walk without crutches, although her spasticity was still quite visible. She could speak with difficulty and could use her left hand to perform some tasks.

In the fourth grade, it became evident that Jan's primary problems were now more social and academic than medical. More time was concentrated in trying to improve academic and communication skills. Her education, however, was often slow and inefficient. Writing remained difficult. She had learned to write before the accident and would often be frustrated as she switched from her more functional left hand back to the right. Reading and spelling began to improve but lagged behind normal expectations. She had lost over three years of academic time with her medical recovery and therapy. She seemed to need more time to think than the normal child before making a response. In addition, the physical handicaps of her classmates required time from her teacher and aide which meant, in turn, that she often had to wait for long periods before receiving help or the next assignment.

During the fourth grade, Jan began to spend increased time in a regular class in the elementary school that adjoined her special school. At first, the children in the regular class were distant, often ignoring her or disparaging her contributions. The teacher seemed to be at a loss since this was the first child with a serious physical handicap to be placed in her room. Soon, however, Jan learned to be more socially appropriate in responding, and both her teacher and peers began to accept her.

In the fifth grade, Jan was able to return to her neighborhood school where she was placed in a special class with children who had mild learning handicaps. She since has transferred to a similar class in a middle school and now she is preparing for high school next year. Her reading and spelling are at a fifth grade level; however, math is at the second grade level in spite of the best efforts of special education teachers and her mother's help.

Although Jan is still bothered by her spastic movements and speech problems, socially she does well with both peers and adults. Recently, she began piano lessons; although she has trouble maintaining proper tempo, her tunes are becoming more recognizable. She is proud of her accomplishment. Jan's grooming is impeccable, and she is becoming an increasingly attractive adolescent. With her parents and teachers, Jan is beginning to think about adulthood and the vocational, social, and recreational skills she wants to develop in order to function independently as an adult.

Efforts continue to be made to improve her academic skills; however, it is beginning to appear that her slow progress in traditional math does not warrant the continued effort now being made. Now the plans are to stress more functional ways to survive in society, such as the use of direct read-out clocks and calculators. On the other hand, Jan is beginning to become proficient with the word processor on her microcomputer. This skill with increased reading ability may allow her to function in many regular high school classes with a resource teacher's support.

With the help of his canine companion pulling his wheelchair and carrying his books, this boy is able to attend school as a member of a regular classroom.

physical and health handicaps. The regulations required newly constructed public facilities and transportation to be accessible, prohibited discriminatory practice in admission to public schools and institutions of higher education, and ensured fair practices and nondiscrimination in employment.

The Education for All Handicapped Children Act (PL 94–142), enacted in 1975, provides for placement in the least restrictive environment and the rights to educationally related medical services such as occupational and physical therapy. Before this legislation, many individuals with physical and health handicaps who could have benefited from regular schools were arbitrarily placed in segregated facilities where their medical differences were emphasized instead of their potential to learn (Barsch, 1968). Segregation for medical reasons is also apt to result in an overly protective environment which may leave students ill-prepared to compete as adults with their nonhandicapped peers.

New professional approaches, enlightened legislation, the high-technology revolution, and medical advances have begun to change the outlook and service possibilities for persons with physical and health handicaps (Bleck, 1979). These changes have resulted in the elimination of many medical disabilities, decreased medical disability from the remaining impairments and diseases, and improved opportunities for persons with disabilities to participate in society.

The actual number of children with physical handicaps in schools is hard to estimate since many disabilities do not require reports by medical practitioners. Estimates of orthopedically handicapped children in special education range from .3 to .5 percent of the K–12 school population (Kirk and Gallagher, 1983). More persons with physical and health handicaps are now accommodated in the mainstream of education while segregated programs for the physically handicapped are reserved for those students with medical disabilities which result in severe and multiple handicaps accompanied by extraordinary special needs.

The numbers of students in segregated special education programs with handicaps associated with polio, tuberculosis, heart disorders, uncontrolled epilepsy, and juvenile rheumatoid arthritis have dwindled until they have almost disappeared. However, medical disabilities resulting from head and spinal cord trauma have risen because they are the most likely to produce multiple handicaps and are the most resistant to medical treatment. A modern day anomaly is that, while medical science has limited the disabilities resulting from many diseases, disorders, and impairments, the ability to maintain life has actually increased the number of people surviving with other disabilities.

ETIOLOGY AND MEDICAL CHARACTERISTICS

In the past, teachers and other professionals required only a cursory knowledge of medical disabilities and the resulting handicapping potential of these conditions. Persons with serious medical problems were seldom far from medically trained personnel. Most service was provided at medically oriented centers which tended to place a priority on the person's medical problems often at the expense of other areas of life. However, modern practice focuses on normalization and service provision in the mainstream of human activity. Thus, service providers in education, social work, and rehabilitation are working further from medical support. They now need to have a greater knowledge and understanding of medical conditions in order to adequately serve those with physical and health handicaps.

There are many more medical disabilities that have handicapping potential than can be covered in this chapter. Those selected for review represent the disabilities most frequently encountered by professionals who serve children and youth with physical and health handicaps.

Disabilities of the Central Nervous System

Disabilities resulting from disorders, deficiencies, or an insult to the central nervous system are the most common physical and health handicaps. Persons with physical handicaps secondary to central nervous system problems represent over 55 percent of the physical and health handicapped population found in special education programs. The most common medical disabilities resulting from nervous system damage are cerebral palsy, epilepsy, and spinal cord damage.

Cerebral Palsy.   Cerebral palsy is a general term that describes a syndrome of motor disabilities. There are several types of cerebral palsy that result in different manifestations of the motor disability. The word "cerebral" refers to the brain while "palsy" indicates a motor dysfunction that affects body movement. Any disorder caused by brain dysfunction and resulting in motor dysfunction is cerebral palsy if it meets two additional specifications. First, it must be nonprogressive; that is, the damage to the brain that caused the motor dysfunction remains static and does not worsen. Although the results of the neural dysfunction caused by the brain damage may worsen and often does, the damage to the brain itself does not. Second, the age of onset must be in childhood. The exact age at which a diagnosis of cerebral palsy can be made is not clearly designated in the literature. Bleck (1982a) indicates that it must occur before the end of childhood; Malamud, Itabashi, and Castor Messenger (1964) state that it must be before the fifth birthday; while Scherzer (1974) specifies "congenital" cerebral palsy must originate at or before birth and "acquired" cerebral palsy must be diagnosed in the early developmental years.

Each person that has cerebral palsy will have a different set of symptoms and associated disorders. To describe a given individual's condition, the diagnosis of cerebral palsy is accompanied by a designated clinical type based upon the person's abnormal body movement. The common types of cerebral palsy are spastic, dyskinetic, ataxic, or mixed. Two other descriptors that generally accompany the diagnosis of cerebral palsy indicate which part of the body is involved and the degree of severity. Terms like quadraplegia, hemiplegia, and paraplegia refer to areas of the body; the degree of severity is designated by mild, moderate, or severe. See Table 4.1 for illustrations of the common clinical types, body area designations, and degrees of severity.

To further complicate a diagnosis of cerebral palsy, as many as 80 percent of those affected manifest related disorders such as epilepsy, retardation, or other associated problems. Jones (1983) stresses that those who work with cerebral palsied persons should be aware of the possibility of speech disorders, eye-muscle control problems, visual deficit, hearing loss, visual-perceptual difficulties, poor ability to concentrate, extreme slowness in responding, and behavioral problems.

Any condition that results in brain damage in the prenatal, perinatal, or postnatal periods of development is a potential cause of cerebral palsy. During the prenatal period, diseases, toxic conditions, or lack of oxygen in the mother can result in brain damage to the developing embryo or fetus. In rare instances, hereditary defects will also result in cerebral palsy. Problems in the birth process (perinatal period) which result in intracranial hemorrhage or anoxia are contributors to the numbers of children who have cerebral palsy. After birth (postnatal period), children acquire cerebral palsy most commonly from head traumas, infections, toxic conditions, or anoxia.

The specific types of cerebral palsy and their causes and physical manifestations are presented in the following sections:

1. *Spastic cerebral palsy* is the most common clinical type of cerebral palsy. Spasticity results from a dysfunction of the pyramidal (motor nerve) tract in the brain. The dysfunction is usually located in the motor cortex, the brain center

Table 4.1

Diagnostic Designations for Cerebral Palsy

Types of Cerebral Palsy	Physical Manifestation	Area of Brain Dysfunction
Spastic	Increased muscular tone and exaggerated reflex reactions	Pyramidal tract (motor nerves)
Dyskinetic (Athetoid)	A succession of slow involuntary movements of fingers, toes, hands, and other parts of the body.	Extra-pyramidal system (modifies and refines pyramidal tract impulses).
Ataxic	Lack of muscular coordination and ability to balance.	Cerebellum

Paralysis	Area of Body Affected
Paraplegia	Legs only
Hemiplegia	Leg and arm on the same side of the body.
Quadriplegia	Both legs and arms. Often involves trunk, neck, and face.
Diplegia	Both legs and arms but more involvement in legs.

Severity	Result
Mild	Little limitation of muscular activity.
Moderate	Movement disrupted enough to require canes, wheelchairs, etc. May also disrupt communication.
Severe	Almost totally unable to move or communicate.

Typical Medical Diagnoses

Cerebral Palsy, Spastic, Hemiplegia, mild, secondary to cerebral hemorrhage.

Cerebral Palsy, Athetoid, Quadriplegia, moderate with attending hearing loss, secondary to Rh factor (blood type) incompatibility.

that instigates motor commands to the different motor muscles in the body. This results in faulty transmissions of motor impulses to the muscles that control body movement. Spastic muscles usually become tight and strongly contracted when quick motions or stretches are attempted. The typical spastic movement is initially difficult for the person to begin but then the muscles overreact much as a pocket knife blade initially resists pressure to close, but then suddenly releases and snaps shut. In a given individual, some muscles may be spastic, others may lack strength, and others will be normal. Each person will have a different pattern and degree of spasticity.

In addition to problems with muscle control, persons with spastic cerebral palsy tend to retain infantile reactions and primitive reflexes that are controlled in individuals developing normally in the first years of life. For example, spastic

Figure 4.1

Key Positioning Points to Control Abnormal Reflexes and Reactions Common to Persons with Cerebral Palsy

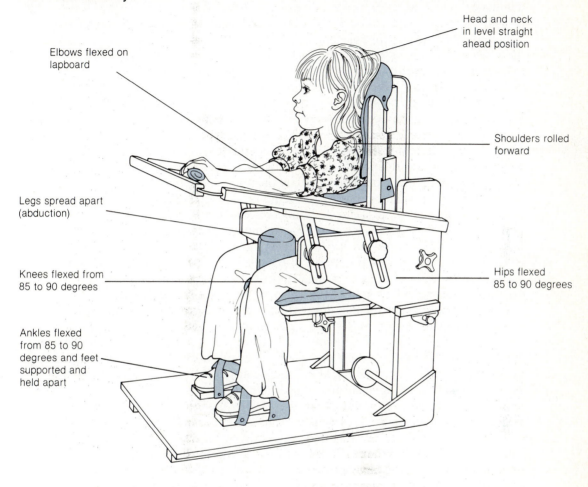

Elbows flexed on lapboard

Head and neck in level straight ahead position

Shoulders rolled forward

Legs spread apart (abduction)

Knees flexed from 85 to 90 degrees

Hips flexed 85 to 90 degrees

Ankles flexed from 85 to 90 degrees and feet supported and held apart

children may go into extension thrust; their back arches, shoulders pull back, and neck stretches upward (see Figure 4.1). A normal child might have an extension thrust as an infant and use it as a way to strengthen muscles and to start a movement such as turning over from stomach to back. Children with cerebral palsy will begin a similar movement but will not be able to release themselves, remaining locked into the extension thrust position. The lack of ability to control extension thrust immobilizes the child and can cause discomfort that will disrupt education.

To control extension thrust, persons working with those who have spastic cerebral palsy keep the student's joints bent in a flex position. Keeping the head tipped forward and the shoulders rolled forward are particularly critical in controlling extension thrust (Finnie, 1975). Many other primitive reflexes which dominate the individual's movement patterns must also be managed in the classroom if the student with cerebral palsy is to profit from the education program.

Lack of ability to control lips, tongue, and swallowing muscles frustrates many individuals with severely involved spastic conditions. Even professionals experienced in working with persons who have severe spastic conditions find that it may take over an hour to help with a meal. Eating can become a major frustration to the severely spastic person as he or she attempts to chew and swallow without gagging. The nearly complete dependency on another for even this simple life function can have a demoralizing effect.

The body of an infant with spastic cerebral palsy may appear quite normal at birth; but, as the individual matures, the body is apt to become increasingly deformed. Much of the work performed by therapists and doctors with children with spasticity is centered upon preventing or slowing deformity. Patterns of muscle spasms and the persistence of uncontrolled primitive reflexes combine to abnormally affect physical growth. The symmetrical muscle tone of the body in the normal child shapes the development of the skeleton within normal parameters; however, the abnormal patterns of muscle tone in the child with spastic cerebral palsy work to cause deformity. For instance, the muscles of a child with spastic hemiplegia will tend to curve the spine toward the affected side.

In addition to the detrimental effects of abnormal patterns of muscle spasms and uncontrolled primitive reflexes on the growth of the body, muscle spasms tend to lead to muscle contractions and a resulting loss of range of motion of the joints. In time, the contractions and continued pull on muscles can result in dislocations at the joints. Dislocation then contributes to added restriction of body movement and more deformity (Bleck, 1982a).

The degree of deformity and restriction of body motion in any given person with a spastic condition is dependent upon age, degree of body involvement, and severity. Proper medical intervention at an early age and continuous treatment can make a marked difference in the amount of deformity and the functional level of a person throughout life. Physical and occupational therapists working with orthopedists try to prevent contractions, dislocations, and skeletal deformities from developing through range of motion and stretching exercises, proper positioning, and bracing. Orthopedic surgery can now correct many of the problems that led to body deformity in the past.

2. *Dyskinetic cerebral palsy* is a result of a malfunction of the extra-pyramidal system of the brain. This system filters extraneous impulses from the pyramidal (motor nerve) tract helping the body make smooth and coordinated muscle movements. The most handicapping type of dyskinetic cerebral palsy is athetosis. In athetoid cerebral palsy, the basal ganglia, located in the mid-brain/brainstem area, do not properly filter the extraneous impulses generated naturally in the pyramidal tract resulting in involuntary and purposeless motion which distorts and frustrates purposeful movement (Bleck, 1982a). The harder a person with

athetoid cerebral palsy attempts to execute purposeful movement, the more extraneous movement is generated. Often speech is difficult and distorted as the person struggles to control tongue, lips, and breathing. In sleep the athetoid condition is not apparent (Jones, 1983), since no purposeful movements are being attempted.

Most persons with athetoid cerebral palsy are quadraplegic with muscle movement problems involving all four limbs. In rarer cases, a person may be hemiplegic, manifesting athetosis only on one side of the body. The infantile reactions and primitive reflexes that plague the person with spastic cerebral palsy can also remain throughout the lifetime of the person with athetoid cerebral palsy.

3. *Ataxic cerebral palsy* results from a disruption of cerebellar function. Trouble balancing, sensing their position in space, and uncoordinated movement are characteristics of individuals with ataxia (Bleck, 1982a). In order to walk and balance at the same time, the person walks with feet wide apart, holds his or her arms out, and may weave in attempts to balance causing the person to look like a child who spins until dizzy and then attempts to walk.

Ataxic cerebral palsy usually accompanies spastic or athetoid cerebral palsy; it seldom is found in a pure form. Therefore, the problems of ataxia become mixed with the problems associated with spastic or athetoid cerebral palsy (Jones, 1983).

4. *Mixed cerebral palsy* is a combination of other types. Since brain damage seldom affects one discrete function of the brain, cerebral palsy often includes a mixture of symptoms. When one type of cerebral palsy is identified, diagnosticians routinely look for mixed varieties as well as related problems such as mental retardation and epilepsy, since persons with cerebral palsy are at higher risk for speech, visual, perceptual, hearing, and behavioral disorders.

Each person with cerebral palsy is unique in his or her physical abilities and adaptations to the environment. The possibilities for various types and mixtures of type, areas of body involvement, degrees of severity, and accompanying disorders are almost infinite. When environmental factors such as educational quality, availability of medical services, and differences in parenting are added, the differences in the actual handicapping potential varies greatly among persons with cerebral palsy.

Epilepsy.   Although figures vary, as many as one in 50 people may have some form of epileptic seizure at some time. Fortunately, medications control the majority of recurring cases allowing most people with epilepsy to pursue nearly normal lives.

Historically, epilepsy was thought to be a result of a person being seized by a devil or possessed by an evil spirit and the prescription was commitment to an asylum or a long fast. In both cases, seizures were reduced since meager or no food created biochemical reactions in the body known to reduce seizure activity. Unfortunately, persons with epilepsy continue to suffer from a history of fear and prejudice which has resulted in unwarranted limitations (Nealis, 1983).

Seizures may be caused by structural damage or chemical imbalance that affects the brain. The specific cause of an individual's seizure is diagnosed in only about half of the cases (Berg, 1982), but what occurs physiologically is known. The neurons in the brain are interlinked, and under normal conditions when one neuron becomes electrically charged, the connecting neurons react by either transmitting or inhibiting the reaction of the charged neuron. Through a series of synapses that connect each of the neurons, neutral messages are sent throughout the nervous system. When these transmitters are "short-circuited" an epileptic seizure occurs.

The type of seizure is determined by the place of origin in the brain, the type of discharge occurring, and the severity of the discharge. As in other central nervous system disorders, each individual with epilepsy manifests a different behavioral pattern during seizures, and the types of seizures may be mixed. The following paragraphs describe the seizures most commonly seen in school settings:

1. *Grand mal.* The grand mal seizure is the most common seizure in school-age students and is the most dramatic in appearance. Typically, the person loses consciousness and drops to the floor. Occasionally a person may sense the beginning of a seizure, but often there is no warning. In the first stage of the seizure muscles are pulled tight, the back is arched, and the face and extremities may turn bluish because of the temporary cessation of breathing. This is followed by writhing, contracting muscles, and jerking motions. On occasion the person may froth at the mouth, vomit, lose bladder or bowel control, or bleed because of a bitten tongue. Usually seizures subside spontaneously within three to seven minutes, leaving the person in a deep sleep or extremely tired and groggy during the post-convulsive period. Since persons lose consciousness at the onset, there is no memory of the seizure.

Grand mal seizures can be frightening in their sudden and dramatic presentation; however, first aid procedures are relatively simple and seizures seldom result in emergency situations. The Epilepsy Foundation of America (1973) suggests that anyone witnessing a seizure should keep calm, clear the area around the person to prevent injury, and refrain from forcing anything into the person's mouth. If breathing is difficult, the person should be rolled to his or her side and tight clothing loosened. If the individual appears to pass from one seizure to another without regaining consciousness, an emergency requiring a physician's attention exists, and an emergency team should be called at once.

Grand mal seizures are usually treated with medication. A combination of dilantin and phenobarbital is a common prescription although several alternative prescriptions are possible. These medications may have side effects that influence classroom performance. Sedatives and tranquilizers can lower efficiency in cognitive learning and cause drowsiness. In some cases, the same medications can have an almost opposite effect upon behavior causing excitability and hyperactivity (Nealis, 1983). Physicians attempt to find a balance of medications and dosages that will control the seizure activity while minimizing side effects.

2. *Petit mal.* Petit mal seizures generally begin at younger ages (Livingston, 1972) but have a lower incidence than grand mal. The most common variety appears as a short stare, which lasts for 5 to 10 seconds. Sometimes they occur in a series of short lapses of attention. The child is unconscious during the seizure

activity and may appear to be daydreaming or in a trance. Since the symptoms are often so ambiguous, diagnosis may take time. Petit mal can be treated with medications and can often be controlled and prevented from becoming more general in its effects (Livingston, 1972).

Akinetic and myoclonic seizures are rare but have more dramatic manifestations. During an akinetic seizure, an individual suddenly loses all muscle tone and drops to the floor. In a myoclonic seizure, the abdominal muscles contract violently pitching the person forward headfirst. Both types are medically distressing because they expose the person to dangerous falls and are often resistant to treatment (Berg, 1982).

3. *Psychomotor seizures.* Psychomotor (temporal lobe) seizures, are more common than petit mal but less common than grand mal. Psychomotor seizures vary. They may appear to be a petit mal seizure in some individuals; in others, the seizure results in a complex automatism in which the person may wander and move about in a manner that seems natural except for its inappropriateness. While individuals of any age may have psychomotor seizures, the onset is often at or after the onset of puberty (Livingston, 1972).

When persons have psychomotor seizures, it is best not to interfere with automatism unless they are endangering themselves or others since restraint can cause agitation or aggression. In some cases, a person can sense the coming of a psychomotor seizure from an aura that precedes the seizure. The aura may take many forms but usually is a false sensation of distorted vision, music, or a familiar smell. An aura may allow the person to seek help or to withdraw from a threatening situation before losing consciousness. Psychomotor seizures, as other types, are treated medically with prescribed medications (Berg, 1983).

Spinal Cord Damage.   The spinal cord carries most of the neural messages transmitted from the brain to the rest of the body. Therefore, the spinal cord is not only vulnerable to damage but can cause serious disability if it malfunctions. The common sources of spinal cord damage are disease, congenital abnormalities, and trauma. The extent of disability depends upon the area of damage and the specific nervous tissue that loses its functioning ability.

Disruption of neural innervation affects muscle tone and alters the development of the skeletal structure. Alterations in the skeletal structure depend upon the extent of damage to the motor nerves and how high on the spinal column the injury is. Physical therapy, bracing, and orthopedic surgery may be used to prevent or minimize skeletal deformity.

In addition to mobility impairment and orthopedic problems that accompany muscle dysfunction, bladder and bowel control may be impaired necessitating the use of diapers, catheterization, or collection bags. Inability to feel sensation secondary to loss of sensory nerve functioning may require protection from extreme heat and cold and from skin irritation. The possibility of sexual impairment requires a sensitivity particularly with adolescents and newly injured adults.

Several conditions can cause impairment of the spinal cord. The most common causes result from disease, congenital abnormality, trauma, or dislocation

introducing

DON

Don is approaching 40 years of age; he is employed, married, and the stepfather of two teenage girls. He has been quadriplegic since age 16 when he severely damaged his spinal cord in a surfing accident. He was left paralyzed from the shoulders down. He is at risk for developing decubitis ulcers (bedsores) and he has neither bladder nor bowel control. His sweat glands do not function, producing a life-threatening situation in excessively warm environments.

After a year of recovery and rehabilitation, Don entered a special school for the physically handicapped. Today he would probably return to his regular high school; then, it was not accessible and there were rules against admission of students with serious medical problems. He was frustrated and quickly became angry at the attempts of many to devalue his potential for future achievement.

Don had taken college preparatory courses before his injury and was now even more determined to attend a university. However, many courses he needed were not offered in the special school; others were "watered down" in comparison to the work he had completed before his accident. Don channeled his frustration toward changing conditions in his special school. His engaging personality enabled him to become student body president and he led a successful student-initiated movement to change the name of the special school. He felt that it was inappropriate and represented a form of "handicapism."

Upon graduation, Don was not academically prepared for entrance to the local university. He applied and was accepted, however, at a local community college. He quickly discovered that although the state rehabilitation services would provide for his education expenses, they refused to fund a specially equipped van for $12,000. Without the van he could not get to school in his electric wheelchair. This forced his family to divert funds from the "in-home

support monies" provided them to cover extra costs for his care to the van's purchase.

Now Don had the van but could not drive it. While most people were learning to drive, he was in the hospital. His special school had not offered driver training. Don had to return to the state rehabilitation services to ask for driver training or money to hire a driver. His request was honored since he owned the van. In the first semester, he hired a driver and took driving lessons. By the second semester, he had obtained his driver's license.

Don stayed active in handicapped rights organizations and campaigned for better accessibility in his community college. During his first year, he had to delay taking classes in his psychology major because classes were on the second floor. The fact that an elevator was under construction made the wait to take his classes bearable. When the elevator was ready, a lock was put on the elevator door and keys were issued only to handicapped students. Don could not manipulate the key with his hands. Three weeks passed before the school administration ruled that the elevator could be open to all students. This delay and similar problems forced Don to drop classes to lighten his load. As a result, it took him three years to complete a two-year course.

Don applied and was accepted in the psychology department at the university of his choice. For the first time, he had to find adequate and accessible housing for himself. Only 2 percent of the housing in the university town was accessible and Don missed a semester just hunting for housing.

Next, Don had to hire an attendant and prepare to financially support himself. Both the money for the attendant's wages and the rent took time to arrange. Social Security income and Medicaid benefits continued to come. In the meantime, Don had to apply for the "in-home support services" funds which had been going to his family until he moved out. However,

Don's family had become somewhat dependent upon this extra outside income.

With Don's tenacity, the strength of his family, and a friend's loan he resolved the day-to-day living problems necessary to continue his education. Again he lost almost a full year in the process. This problem was compounded in his senior year when his attendant fractured Don's arm by applying too much pressure during daily exercises. Don had to withdraw from classes and begin the coursework again when his arm had healed.

While completing his education, Don learned to deal effectively with the "system" to obtain his rights. This led to a job as client's right advocate at his university's Disabled Student Center. He continued to work at the center after graduation, carefully limiting his hours and income so as not to lose his handicapped support benefits.

Don's life recently became unsettled when he fell in love. Marriage meant that his income would be combined with his wife's, disqualifying him from many benefits while simultaneously increasing his income tax. While marriage was an economically unsound decision for Don, he and his fiancée decided that independence and a normalized life was worth the risk.

Don now has a new job in order to increase his income. He worries because his employer has extended his probation period past the six months required of most employees in spite of a good performance record. Don sometimes feels that he must be a "super-crip" just to get an even chance at vocational opportunities. However, he is proud that he lives independently and his tax and economic contributions have more than paid for the benefits he has received.

of vertebrae. When working with young children, congenital disorders are most common. However, with increase in age, the body is subject to more exposure to disease and more possibility of accident and trauma. Following are commonly encountered conditions that lead to spinal cord injury in schoolchildren:

1. *Spina bifida.* Spina bifida is a congenital disorder resulting in a hole forming in the vertebrae of the developing fetus leaving the spinal cord unprotected. Although genetic factors are suspected, all that is known is that, in the fourth week after gestation, the spinal tract in the embryo does not completely close (Bleck, 1982b).

There are three forms of spina bifida: occulta, meningocele, and myelomeningocele. Occulta is common in the general population, usually goes undetected, and seldom results in neurological damage. Meningocele describes the condition in which the meninges which surround and protect the spinal cord are forced out through the hole in the spine by the pressure of the spinal fluid. This causes a "cele" or swelling, vulnerable to injury and disease, to form on the person's back. Without corrective surgery, spinal cord injury and infection are likely.

Myelomeningocele causes the most neurological problems and results most frequently in special education placement because of associated congenital defects. The spinal cord with the meninges are forced out into the "cele" through the spina bifida, but the spinal cord may adhere to the vertebrae causing neural tissue to sustain damage when the body moves. In 80 to 90 percent of the cases, there is a blockage of the flow of spinal fluid in the cranial area resulting in hydrocephalus (Mitchell, Fiewell, & Davy, 1983). The increased pressure of the spinal fluid caused by the blockage simultaneously pushes against the brain and the skull causing brain damage and an enlarged head if left untreated.

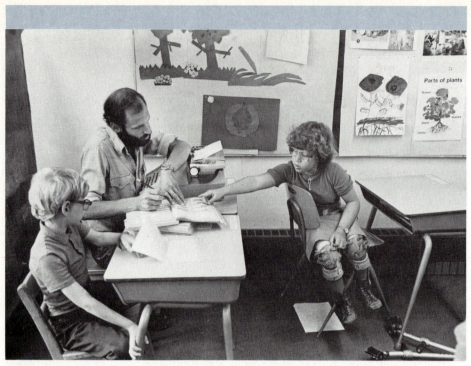

A 10-year-old girl with spina bifida is mainstreamed into a regular school program; she is able to fully participate in school activities.

In the past, the child born with myelomeningocele was given little chance for survival. If the pressure on the brain from an accompanying hydrocephalic condition was not fatal, infection or kidney problems secondary to bladder and bowel dysfunction would be. Today, however, the myelomeningocele will be surgically repaired soon after birth and a shunt will be surgically placed to relieve hydrocephalus. The surgery is designed to permanently correct the spina bifida condition preventing any further damage to the spinal cord and relieving the threat of infection. The shunts placed to relieve hydrocephalus must be monitored and cleared or replaced if they malfunction.

Although persons with a surgically corrected myelomeningocele will suffer no further spinal cord damage, damaged neural tissue does not regenerate leaving the person with an inability to feel sensation or control motor movement below the point of injury.

2. *Poliomyelitis.* Before the development of polio vaccine, polio was one of the most common disability-causing diseases. With mandatory immunization, polio had been virtually eradicated in the United States until the influx of immigrants from Third World nations brought scores of children and adults who had not been immunized.

Medical Breakthroughs in the Treatment and Prevention of Physical Handicaps

Innovations in medicine have continually changed the nature of students found in special education programs for the physically handicapped. With the development of antibiotics and other drugs, large hospital schools for children with tuberculosis and teachers working in terminal wards for children with leukemia have disappeared. Development of new immunization techniques eliminated post-polio students who, at one time, comprised over one-fifth of the students in special schools for the physically handicapped. The vaccine for rubella has reduced the children whose mothers contracted the disease during the first trimester of pregnancy with often serious physical and mental consequences for the children.

Recent developments resulting from better treatment regimens and better technology in developing orthotic and prosthetic devices have not been as dramatic as the discovery of a new drug or vaccine. However, as an example of the effects of advancements in medical treatment, children with muscular dystrophy are kept mobile longer and subsequently have longer life expectancies. Children with cystic fibrosis have had their life expectancies significantly extended into adulthood. For these students, the objectives and expectations for education need to be revised as the medical prognosis improves.

One of the advancements on the horizon of medical research that could further change the types of students in educational programs for the physically handicapped is gene therapy. Disabilities resulting from muscular dystrophy, cystic fibrosis, hemophilia, certain metabolic disorders, and other problems resulting from genetic inadequacies may disappear for the classrooms of the physically handicapped.

As scientists decode the genetic system, they are beginning to identify genes in the organism that are missing or defective. Once a gene is identified, it is becoming increasingly possible to re-create the gene in the laboratory and subsequently use it to replace the missing or defective gene in the organism.

Currently gene therapy has been limited to animal experimentation. However, with the advancement of knowledge and the settlement of ethical considerations in gene therapy, medical scientists are rapidly becoming ready to begin work on some of the genetic disorders that have plagued the human race from the beginning of time.

Polio is caused by a virus that enters the body through the intestine and spreads to the spinal column via the bloodstream attacking the anterior horn cells that connect the motor nerves in the spinal cord with the motor nerves in the peripheral nervous system. Destruction of the anterior horn cells permanently interrupts the transmission of motor impulses to the muscles connected through the affected motor cells.

Little can be done for a person in the acute stages of polio other than relieving the symptoms of the disease, providing assistance in breathing if the thoracic area is involved, and applying heat to the muscle spasms. The extent of permanent damage depends upon which anterior horn cells are destroyed. Polio usually permanently affects the lower extremities and sometimes the trunk. It can leave a person with a spotty pattern of muscle dysfunction with some muscles totally flaccid, some weakened, and others not affected (Bleck, 1982c).

Treatment focuses upon physical therapy, mobility, orthopedic bracing, and occasionally corrective surgery. Since sensory nerves remain intact, there are usually no problems related to malfunctioning of the bladder, bowels, and sensory nerves (Bleck, 1982c).

3. *Spinal muscular atrophy* (SMA). SMA is similar to polio in that it affects the anterior horn cells and thus the motor muscles. The immediate cause of the deterioration of the anterior horn cells is not known, although the genetic link to the disease is recognized. SMA is manifested in severe, intermediate, and mild forms. Infants with the severe form seldom survive beyond the first year.

Children with the intermediate form may exhibit normal motor development in the first months of life but soon show weakness, particularly in the pelvic and body areas. The infant will not gain enough strength to stand or walk. Survival for children with the intermediate form of SMA generally does not extend beyond adolescence or young adulthood.

Children with the mild form will walk as infants but develop weakness in the thighs and pelvic areas that makes ambulation increasingly difficult. There is a normal life expectancy with the mild form; however, continued physical therapy, bracing, and corrective surgery will generally be necessary to prevent deformity and extend the ability to ambulate (Goldberg, 1983).

4. *Spinal cord trauma.* Automobile accidents, recreational mishaps, and falls combined with the medical technology to maintain life has increased the numbers of persons with spinal cord injuries. The older the person, the more exposure to injury, and therefore the higher the incidence of spinal cord injury.

Spinal cord damage secondary to trauma provides the same possibilities for disability as damage secondary to a congenital disorder such as spina bifida. The extent of the disability depends upon the area of the trauma and the amount of nerve damage sustained.

Persons who sustain an injury later in life have established many of their aspirations, attitudes toward work, academic background, and social identity in the mainstream of life. Although many adjustments will be needed, good coping skills and positive attitudes established prior to the handicap will increase the chances of a successful rehabilitation.

Improvements in medical practice have increased the numbers who survive high-spinal-column injury. These persons are usually quadraplegic and in some cases require respirator assistance for breathing. Due to the availability of motorized wheelchairs, specially equipped vans, and carryout respirators, many people with severe spinal cord injuries are able to participate fully in the mainstream of life.

Muscular Dystrophy

Except for central nervous system-related disabilities, childhood muscular dystrophy is the most prevalent medical disorder in special education programs for persons with physical and other health handicaps. The disease appears between three and five years of age with death occurring in the late teens or early twenties. Beginning in the calves of the legs and moving upwards, the muscles deteriorate and waste away. Death usually results from pneumonia or heart failure associated with the weakening of the respiratory and heart muscles (Lyle & Obringer, 1983).

The progress of childhood muscular dystrophy is relentless in spite of medical care and physical therapy. In the primary grades, the child is generally still ambulatory, but by about the tenth year, the child will be in a wheelchair. From the wheelchair, the child will progress to positioning equipment and then to bed.

In most cases, the cause is a sex-linked genetic defect. Almost all cases are boys who inherit the defective gene from their mother. When a girl has childhood muscular dystrophy, it is caused by a defective recessive autosomal gene from a non-sex-linked chromosome. Where no family link is identified, genetic mutation is suspected (Bleck, 1982d). Although no successful medical treatments have been developed to halt or retard the disease, recent research provides hope that the defective genes can be identified in women who are carriers and in the fetus.

Since childhood muscular dystrophy results in continuous weakening, increased disability, and early death, professional personnel need to be aware of signs of psychological stress in both family and child. At first, parents may be reluctant to accept the medical diagnosis and shop for further medical opinions or deny the presence of the disease (Lyle & Obringer, 1983).

Other Health Problems

Although neurologically-related problems now account for the majority of disabilities found in special education programs for those with physical and other health handicaps, there are several other chronic disorders that may impair school functioning to the point that special help is necessary. Because of medical advances, many of the health problems that used to result in special education placement can now be managed in regular classrooms except during acute periods. When there is cooperation among medical personnel, teachers, and families, the potential for social and educational handicaps can be substantially reduced.

Asthma.   Asthma results when the airways in the lungs are constricted by inflammation, enlarged blood vessels, increased mucus, and spasms of the smooth muscles in the breathing tubes. The person suffering an asthmatic attack has difficulty inhaling and exhaling air, causing a characteristic wheezing and panting sound. When specific substances are breathed by the asthmatic, they combine with the antibodies coating the mast cells which line the air passages of the lungs to cause an allergic reaction (Kraemer & Bierman, 1983).

Harvey (1982) reports that asthma was found to be the most common cause of absence from school of any chronic disease reported in studies in Colorado and Texas and it is estimated that at least 2.5 percent of the population has asthma. The severity, frequency, and onset of attacks varies with individuals. Children may grow out of the attacks in adolescence, may have symptoms remaining into adulthood, or show the first symptoms of asthma at adolescence.

Treatment consists of medication and attempts to keep asthmatics away from the allergens which may trigger an attack. Since rapid breathing is also associated with asthma attacks, the individual's exercise may need to be monitored.

In attempting to protect children with asthmatic conditions from attacks, care should be taken to avoid unnecessary social isolation of the child from nonhandicapped children. Children who are not allowed to participate in games or who avoid games with other children risk isolation. Children with asthmatic conditions may be quite sensitive to social rejection, particularly as a result of wheezing during attacks, and thus avoid situations that may bring on an attack where peers are present (Kraemer & Bierman, 1983).

Cancer.   A diagnosis of cancer in a child results in strong psychological reactions from the family, professionals working with the child, and the child. The fact that the chance for long-term remission and survival of the child has significantly increased with the improvement of medical procedures may not be well understood by the general public. Cancer still evokes fears among most people.

Cancer is relatively rare in children with approximately one case per 10,000 children under the age of 15. The most common type is in the leukemic lymphoma group, with tumors of the nervous system and bone the second most common. The causes of most cancers remain unknown; however, various environmental agents have been shown to have a relationship to various types of cancer (Hutter & Farrell, 1983).

A child with a diagnosis of cancer provides a challenge to educators. In spite of the fact that long-term survival is probable—leukemia results in over 60 percent long-term survival—all involved with the child have to deal psychologically with problems related to dying. Close contact with the family and sensitivity to their emotions is recommended. Discussions in class that allow the other children to understand the treatment of the disease (hair loss, etc.) and deal with their feelings of grief may be necessary.

Beyond the emotional factors involved, children are apt to be absent for long periods of time. Makeup work and remedial tutoring may be necessary to minimize the result of lost educational time. If a hospital teacher or home teacher is provided, it will be necessary for the regular teacher to keep in close contact to ensure that appropriate work is completed.

Diabetes Mellitus.   Diabetes mellitus affects about one in 600 children. It results from a deficiency of insulin supplied to the body by the pancreas. This, in turn, prevents the body from metabolizing the glucose needed to fuel the body's cells. Unmetabolized glucose circulates in the blood until excess blood sugar levels cause the kidney to release the glucose into urine and the body to dehydrate. The cause of this condition is not clear although genetic factors are suspected in many cases (Winter, 1983).

Diabetes becomes life-threatening if the body is producing little or no insulin and the disease is not treated. Medical treatment focuses on diet, exercise, and prescription of insulin. In severe cases, insulin must be injected into the body. New developments in testing blood sugar level and the use of insulin pumps that better keep the insulin levels in balance have recently been introduced and should become more commonly used in the future.

The treatment of diabetes is a constant effort to hold a balance between the glucose and the insulin in the bloodstream. Occasionally after exercise or before a meal, the glucose and insulin become imbalanced. Usually, the individual knows the signs and adds sugar or insulin as needed; however, if the person loses consciousness, he or she should receive immediate medical treatment. Symptoms of an insulin reaction include hunger, sweatiness, rapid heart rate, weakness, or anxiety. The treatment is ingestion of sugar.

The realization of having a chronic disorder which needs constant management of diet, exercise, and insulin is a heavy psychological burden for some children. The added weight of the possibility of long-term effects such as loss of sight, kidney dysfunction, and vascular disorders may result in negative behavioral responses, particularly during adolescence. Teachers also need to be aware that a child with low blood sugar levels may be irritable and moody at times.

CHARACTERISTICS OF INDIVIDUALS WITH PHYSICAL AND HEALTH HANDICAPS

Learning, emotional, and health characteristics vary among individuals with physical and health handicaps. It is difficult to predict the effect that a given medical disability will have upon an individual since the nature, severity, visibility, duration, and age of onset are all factors in the effect of a medical disability upon one's life as is the individual's ability to cope. Some persons are ingenious at overcoming mobility problems, loss of efficiency, and negative social feedback while others may be defeated by the same problems.

Learning Characteristics

By educational definition, the medical disabilities and health problems that are the hallmarks of students with physical and health handicaps are not supposed to interfere with intellectual abilities. If retardation or learning disabilities accompany the medical disability, the educational designation is supposed to be multiply handicapped or sometimes severely handicapped. In practice, however, the criteria for placement of persons with medical disabilities are both broad and gray. Some medical disabilities such as cerebral palsy have a high potential for associated learning problems while other medical disabilities have little physical reason to affect brain function.

Most research on the learning characteristics of students with physical and health handicaps has been limited to those placed in special schools and classes. Little empirical study has been devoted to the effects of mainstreaming on the learning characteristics of students with physical and other health handicaps. Thus, much is left to conjecture when trying to determine whether the mainstream produces superior cognitive and social learning to segregation in special classes or schools.

Studies of intellectual functioning of students placed in schools for individuals with physical and health handicaps consistently indicate that these students place within the normal range of IQ scores, but that their scores are skewed to the low side of the curve. This is particularly true in studies of children with cerebral palsy (Connor, Rusalem, & Cruickshank, 1971; Cruickshank, Hallahan, & Bice, 1976; Nelson & Ellenberg, 1978).

In a study of the students placed in a California school for physically handicapped persons, Best (1978) presents the distribution of children by medical disability and IQ score. Although the IQ scores ranged as high as 149, the majority scored below 87. While the potential for test bias to cause spuriously low test scores is recognized, general experience would indicate that children in these types of schools tend to have math and reading scores which are also skewed below the norms expected in regular schools.

Several hypotheses have been presented to explain the relatively low cognitive functioning of children in schools for physical and health handicaps. In 1972 Kirk described the increase in the number of brain-damaged children placed in special classes. Best's (1978) data provides a way to test Kirk's (1972) hypothesis that the influx of more students with brain damage-related disorders results in lower cognitive functioning than in the past. The mean score for the 46 students (ages 3 to 13 years) with physical disorders clearly involving brain dysfunctions (cerebral palsy, epilepsy, post-meningitis, etc.) was an IQ of 79. The mean IQ score of the 25 students (ages 3 to 13) with little possibility of associated brain dysfunctions (hemophilia, Leggs-Perthes, muscular dystrophy, bone tumors, osteogenesis imperfecta, etc.) was 92.

As Kirk (1972) would have predicted, the students with brain damage-related disabilities did score significantly lower on IQ measures than those without brain-related disabilities. However, the higher mean IQ of 92 for the students with medical disabilities with no relationship to brain damage is still below the expectations for regular students indicating that factors beyond physiological brain dysfunction are operating.

Best (1978) theorized that physical disabilities can disrupt the development of motor patterns in children that are seen by some theorists to be precursors to cognitive development and stressed the need to attend to motor development in children with motor disabilities as a precursor to cognitive ability. Throughout the years physical and occupational therapists as well as educators have advocated various sensory-motor approaches to overcome cognitive deficits. However, appealing as these approaches may be, there is not enough known to reliably prescribe them as treatment for cognitive problems. In a review of several of these approaches, Bleck (1982c) found little support in the research literature indicating that sensory-motor therapies have reduced learning problems or increased cognitive development.

Rather than emphasizing sensory-motor or psycholinguistic approaches, Bigge (1976) focuses on task analysis to increase efficiency of instruction to overcome cognitive deficits in children with physical and other health handicaps. She suggests that instruction which is efficient and direct is the most effective.

Many aspects of cognitive functioning in children with physical and other health handicaps are similar to those in children who have learning disabilities (Bigge, 1976). Lewis (1983) found that research supports that (1) learning disabilities are related to the ability to deploy cognitive resources effectively and efficiently; (2) learning strategies can be trained; and (3) direct training in selection and use of task-performance strategies is most apt to be effective. Children with physical and health handicaps who have cognitive difficulty may show problems in deploying their cognitive resources effectively and efficiently. Constant interruptions in programs during the day because of medical therapies, lost time because of medical problems or illness, having to wait for assistance from others before proceeding on projects, lack of exposure to competitive and task-oriented experience, and low expectancies for productivity can all work to inhibit the development of effective and efficient deployment of cognitive resources.

Lewis (1983) makes several research-supported recommendations to offset some of the cognitive problems encountered by children with learning disabilities that would seem equally applicable for children with physical and health handicaps. First, a concerted effort needs to be made to maximize the time that children are directly involved in instruction. Second, skills should be taught directly in desired subjects avoiding extraneous activities. Third, students need to be taught to focus on the relevant features of the learning task and monitor their own progress. Fourth, students need to develop learning strategies to use in study and problem solving. Fifth, skills must be taught so they can be done quickly and accurately in a variety of environments.

Social/Emotional Characteristics

Although physical and other handicaps affect the lives of individuals and their families, there are no social or psychological patterns that are universally applicable to given individuals. Most problems that do exist are a result of an interaction between a specific situation and the individual's response to that situation. The degree or type of medical disability does not seem to be the major variable in predicting social or psychological problems. A person dependent upon the dexterity of his or her body (such as a professional athlete) may show more negative behavior because of a minor injury that affects career plans than another person with a serious injury that results in little or no social or vocational loss.

Development of Dependent Behavior Patterns.
Lack of opportunity and encouragement to develop independence as the child matures is apt to foster dependent behavior patterns such as overreliance upon others, lack of self-motivation to achieve self-sufficiency, and inappropriate social behaviors employed to manipulate others or to create a false image of independence. Dependent patterns of behavior in individuals with physical handicaps may result either from the lack of opportunity to gain social, motor, and cognitive skills or from reinforcement of nonproductive behavior by overprotective adults. Whatever the source, dependency results in abnormal social and psychological development that may continue throughout the life of the child.

During the elementary school years, normal children are becoming increasingly competent physically, cognitively, and socially. Children with physical and health handicaps can become equally involved in exploring their potential and gaining the skills and behavior that lead to overcoming dependent patterns of behavior. The child with a physical or health handicap may need significant support from parents, teachers, and other adults who understand the handicapping condition and the limitations that the medical disabilities may bring, but disabilities should not be allowed to become excuses not to learn the cognitive and social skills required of most children in the society.

Mainstreaming has the positive potential to place children in environments where developmental demands are high and where the accomplishments of normal children serve as models for children with handicaps. Parental support is a key to successful mainstreaming and may require the control of impulses to overprotect and reinforce dependent behavior patterns (Karnes & Esry, 1981).

Adolescence can be difficult for all young people as they adjust to rapid physical and social change while attempting to become psychologically and socially independent. How well a youth with physical and health handicaps adjusts during this period of life depends heavily upon the cognitive, physical, and social skills developed earlier. A person with poor social skills will be particularly handicapped at an age when peer acceptance becomes important. Lack of ability to compete academically or socially undercuts the person's assurance that he or she can become an independent adult.

Preparing to Function as an Adult.   Many medical disabilities have implications for future functioning as an adult member of a family. Beneath doubts about whether they will be an acceptable partner for a member of the opposite sex, adolescents with medical disabilities may worry about their ability to function sexually, rear children, and the genetic consequences and physical aspects of childbearing. These concerns have implications for sex and family education programs and counseling for youth. The best basis to help young people adjust to limitations is the provision of timely and accurate information. Even so, young adults may have to adjust to losses from a medical disability that they either had not been aware of as children or that had not seemed important before adolescence or adulthood.

As individuals with physical and health handicaps enter adulthood, they have many of the same emotional and psychological problems that most persons in our society face. There are the desires to achieve rewarding vocational directions, date and mate, and develop a fruitful social life (Sirvis, Carpignano, & Bigge, 1976). However, for many persons with physical and health handicaps, prejudice interferes with their ability to get employment and insurance, and transportation may be frustrating. Lewis (1977), in a study of persons with visual and physical handicaps, reported an average of 37 percent unemployment, with nonambulatory persons having the highest rates of unemployment among those studied. Postsecondary education can also be frustrating to young adults attempting to use it as access to the social and vocational mainstream. Often physical and health problems slow achievement of goals for those enrolled in higher education.

Laws, social services, and education for those with physical and health handicaps are improving. However, dependent behavior patterns, frustration in achieving life goals, and social discrimination can still result in psychological and social problems for some persons with physical and health handicaps. Jourard (1958) described several maladaptive behaviors observed in individuals with physical and health handicaps including denial of the disability and its limitations, resignation and hopelessness, viewing one's self as a victim, being arrogant and rebellious, viewing the disability as a punishment, and remaining helpless to assure attention.

Dealing with Death.   For all involved in work with children who have physical and health handicaps, death is an ever present possibility. Death is a reality of life; however, when a child dies it can be especially difficult for all who have been involved (Sirvis, Carpignano, & Bigge, 1976). Professionals working with children where death is apt to occur need to be aware of the child's understanding and feelings about death, respond to the concerns of the child's peers, and be able to comprehend the feelings of the family. Above all, the professional needs to manage his or her own feelings in order to appropriately interact with the child, peers, and family.

As parents begin to deal with the imminent or actual death of their child, they are apt to behave as if they are guilty, angry, sorrowful, and/or just overwhelmed. In their anxiety and feelings of helplessness, parents may find it difficult to accept medical diagnoses, talk with people about the death of their child, and may strike out emotionally and blame persons irrationally. As parents adjust, they may appear to go through steps similar to those that Kübler-Ross (1969) describes for adults with terminal illness: denial, anger, bargaining, depression, and finally acceptance.

Medical/Health Characteristics

Although the medical and health characteristics of the most commonly encountered diseases and impairments have been detailed earlier in the chapter, two themes need to be reiterated. Misconceptions about people with physical and health handicaps persist despite knowledge to the contrary, thereby limiting their educational, vocational, and social opportunities. The first misconception relates to intelligence. The degree of physical impairment does *not* have a direct relationship to intelligence (Lewis & Doorlag, 1987). Although reinforced dependency, loss of productive schooltime, and associated brain damage interfere with cognitive functioning, many severely physically handicapped persons have above average intelligence and should not be judged by the seriousness of their physical disability. The second misconception relates to the need to protect physically handicapped individuals because of weakness, fatigue, and pain. Although some medical disabilities are accompanied by chronic weakness, fatigue, and pain, many are not and others are debilitating only in an acute phase. In fact, some physical disabilities cause people to develop above average strength and endurance, such as a paraplegic who develops exceptional upper limb strength and endurance to efficiently operate a wheelchair on a large college campus. Since World War II, paraplegics have participated competitively in wheelchair basketball, endurance swimming, marathons, and other strenuous sports. Irrationally restricting or overprotecting physically and health handicapped persons exacerbates their problems.

DETECTION OF THE EXCEPTIONALITY

A thorough diagnosis and development of a comprehensive treatment program requires cooperation from various professionals including medical personnel, psychologists, rehabilitation specialists, and special educators. A review of the issues and approaches involved in the identification and prescription of programs will be presented in this section.

Identification and Screening

Medical Problems. While the detection and confirmation of the diseases and impairments which can lead to physical and health disabilities and handicaps are primarily a medical function, teachers and other professionals who work with children over long periods of time play an important role. For example, a kindergarten teacher noted that a child seemed clumsy compared with other children in the class and suggested a medical examination. Leggs-Perthes disease, a disorder of the pelvic joint which can result in severe crippling if not properly treated during the acute period, was diagnosed; and the early referral for medical examination prevented unnecessary damage to the pelvic joints.

A basic knowledge of medical problems and their symptoms can help in early detection. In one instance, a teenager developed a limp in the left leg and had some attending behavioral problems. The parents did not seek medical help because they thought the limp was a result of a Little League injury that could not be remedied and the behavior change to be expected from an adolescent. An alert school counselor with some knowledge of neurological problems noted that an arm was also involved suggesting a mild hemiplegia. This led to a referral to a neurologist. The problem was not a Little League injury but a tumor which was developing in the brain.

Cognitive, Social, and Psychological Problems. When cognitive, social, or psychological problems are observed with children who have physical and health handicaps, they are often attributed to the medical disability. Problems may be erroneously accepted as educationally or psychologically unremediable or may be seen as a problem for the medical profession to resolve. However, many observed problems may be the result of environmental conditions that interact with medical disabilities and can be remediated by educational procedures or counseling.

Identification of problems in children with cerebral palsy can be particularly perplexing. Poor performance on tests or in classroom activities may be attributed to mental processes or brain dysfunction; however, many can be alleviated by altering the environment. For example, the child may not be positioned in a way which controls primitive reflexes and reactions affecting his or her ability to attend and respond. If the task requires fine motor control, speech responses, or rapid answers, the child may appear to be having cognitive problems that in reality are resulting from physical inefficiency.

Abnormal social behavior is often easy to identify, but difficult to understand. It may be due to lack of social experience, frustration from the inability to perform a task, or a long-standing behavioral pattern resulting from long-term social devaluation.

When identifying and screening cognitive, social, and psychological problems, it is usually best to assume that what is seen is a result of learned behavior or immediate environmental problems and, hence, subject to straightforward home or classroom remediation. However, many times consultants experienced in the problems of individuals with physical and health handicaps will be helpful in prescriptions for persistent maladaptive behaviors.

Criteria for Determination of the Exceptionality

The major criterion for determination of a physical or health handicap is the presence of a medical disability that impairs the ability of an individual to function in school, vocational, or social environments. Professional focus in recent years has shifted from the medical disability itself to the handicapping effects of the disability. A person with a severe physical or health problem need be seen as handicapped only in those areas of life where the medical disability works to the individual's disadvantage.

An analysis of a person's ability to function in the environment is an essential ingredient in the determination of the handicap and its scope. Physical and health handicaps cannot be seen as general and pervasive. They need to be defined in terms of specific environmental situations at given times. The determination of a handicap, then, is not a static procedure.

Personality factors, the availability of prosthetic technology, family and community support systems, and cognitive ability all interact with the limitations caused by a medical disability to determine the parameters of an individual's handicap. A person who is not particularly handicapped at one time of life or in a given situation may be handicapped in another time or place. For instance, a child with a spinal cord injury may do well socially and academically in elementary school, with medical problems only affecting participation in physical education and playground games. However, as the child grows to adolescence and young adulthood, the medical disabilities resulting from the spinal cord injury may interfere with normal dating and marriage patterns. Inability to perform sexually, reactions from the opposite sex, and the person's self-devaluation could all contribute an increased degree of handicap although the medical disability remains as it was when the person was a child.

Common Methods for Diagnosis and Assessment

Medical Problems.   In most instances, diagnosis and assessment begin with medical personnel. The physician makes a medical diagnosis and prescribes the treatment and related services. Related services might include physical, occupational, and/or speech therapies. The physical therapist may be asked to assess the range of motion, presence of contractures, and need for wheelchairs or other specialized equipment. The occupational therapist may assess fine motor skills in relation to the individual's ability to perform vocational or daily living skills. Sometimes occupational therapists suggest hand splints or other special equipment to improve functioning. Prosthetic equipment, bracing, splinting, or special procedures recommended by occupational or physical therapists usually require a physician's prescription.

Speech therapists assess speech and language ability including the ability to make the necessary sounds, control breathing, and perform the other components of speech. When speech is not possible, speech therapists assess the individual's ability to use alternate types of communication such as communication boards, manual signs, or voice synthesizers. In assessing the potential for speech and language development, the speech therapists may rely upon the reports of psychologists or other specialists since cognitive ability is an important consideration in determining corrective programs.

Cognitive, Social, and Psychological Problems.   The assessment of cognitive, social, and psychological characteristics—integral parts of traditional speech, rehabilitation, and educational assessment—are sometimes problematic when applied to individuals with physical and health handicaps. Discretion in the use of tests and testing procedures is necessary since, in some cases, they must be materially altered to provide useful information that fairly and appropriately represents the needs and abilities of those with physical and health handicaps.

Use of standardized tests and assessment procedures can be particularly misleading when applied to persons with cerebral palsy and other severe physical involvements. Slow reaction times and inability to respond efficiently because of physical, rather than mental, problems can depress test scores and negatively influence evaluation by inexperienced examiners. Slow motor maturity and persistence of infantile reflexes and reactions compound the limitations of a person's ability to explore and learn; hence, information items that are common to the normal person may be beyond their experience (DuBose, 1981; Simeonsson, Huntington, & Parse, 1980). The results of artificially depressed test scores and evaluations with subsequent mislabeling can have detrimental effects upon individuals. They may result in overprotection, lack of exposure to environmental stimuli, and lowered expectancies, which in turn can lead to self-fulfilling prophecies (DuBose, 1981).

Recently, innovations in assessment approaches have begun to remedy some of the negative aspects of more traditional approaches. Simeonsson and others (1980) advocate a multivaried approach to assessment relying on several methods instead of one. They find that the use of standardized tests and developmental scales is inadequate and suggest more use of criterion-referenced tests and functional analyses.

Criterion-referenced tests focus on the individual's ability to perform tasks important to functioning in a specified environment. For instance, the requirements of fifth grade math would be analyzed to ascertain the steps needed to perform in school. Then, children would be tested to see which of these tasks they could individually perform. There would be little interest in how the children compared to each other.

Gauging the True Abilities of the Physically Handicapped

Accurate assessment of children with physical handicaps can be difficult. Results from standardized instruments such as IQ tests and achievement tests which are normed with nonhandicapped populations can be misleading. Children with physical handicaps may respond much slower than the nonhandicapped, lack equivalent social and environmental experiences, or be unable to perform with the physical dexterity or strength necessary for specified test items. Thus, assumptions about intelligence and ability to perform academic tasks can be underestimated.

To avoid underestimation of the abilities of children with physical handicaps, several informal procedures are used by educational assessment specialists. One method is the adaption of criterion-referenced techniques. Criterion-referenced tests for evaluating school achievement are available commercially and often accompany a series of texts in reading and mathematics. In these procedures, the focus is not upon a comparison of a child's performance with that of the child's peers, but an attempt to see how a child can perform various tasks associated with a particular area of skill. For instance, mathematics skills can be logically broken down into discrete steps which can then be used to analyze the child's ability at each of the steps of an operation.

The specialist must go one step further when assessing the child with a physical handicap and consider how the child can best perform the task given his or her particular physical limitations. For instance, a child may not be able to efficiently use a pencil and paper. When one considers the aid to the thinking process in mathematics that a normal person gains when solving a math problem with a pencil and paper, it is easy to see how a teacher or other professional could underestimate a child's ability if tasks were required that would normally be done with a pencil and paper. Even if a child with a physical handicap could use the pencil and paper with an extra effort or given extra time, the added effort needed to manipulate these instruments could distract from concentration on the mathematics or may lead to excessive fatigue.

In recent years, with the development of microcomputers and other technology, specialists have attempted to adapt the use of these devices to compensate for the inability of children with physical handicaps to perform a given task on a criterion-referenced test. Thus, a criterion-referenced test may be altered to allow the child to perform a similar operation using a microcomputer or other device.

The individual nature of the effect of a physical handicap on a given child continues to frustrate assessment efforts to make comparisons between these children and others, whether they have similar handicaps or not. The accuracy of assessment relies heavily on the knowledge and the ability of the assessment specialist to match a given test task with existing technology available to help the child with the physical handicap. Even when requisite tasks are generally agreed upon as necessary to performance in a given skill area, the prescription of technology to allow the individual child with a handicapping condition to best perform the task still requires an idiosyncratic judgment by the assessment specialist. The potential of the adaptation of technology to task performance as a factor in assessment is gaining the attention of researchers. Developments in this area could have a future impact in both the assessment procedures and prescription of education for children with physical handicaps.

Functional analysis is an assessment procedure which employs an approach similar to that used in criterion-referenced tests. However, it can be made specific to an individual and a given situation. First, the environments in which the person must function are identified. Second, an ecological survey is conducted to identify the skills needed to function successfully in those environments. Third, the discrepancy between the person's ability to function and the requirements of the environment are noted. The discrepancies form the bases for educational programs, environmental restructuring, or the prescriptions of prosthetic devices necessary to reduce the handicapping effects of any medical disability (Simeonsson et al., 1980).

Functional analyses can be broad or specific to a particular domain of activity. An examiner performing a functional analysis may focus on a school, recreational, or home environment—or all depending upon the assessment needs. Information is specific to prescription of programs and does not rely on assumptions and inferences that are inherent in many standardized tests (Simeonsson et al., 1980; Wehman & Schlein, 1980).

Special Considerations with Preschool Children

The assessment of cognitive and psychological characteristics of preschool children presents special challenges. Predicting potential or present ability for young normal children can be a precarious venture; however, when a physical or health handicap is involved, it becomes even more precarious. All the assessment problems presented in the previous section apply plus some extras that make the task more unsure. Developmental milestones which were observed and studied by Gesell, Piaget, and other developmental theorists form the basis for many of the developmental scales used to assess infants and preschoolers today. The fact is, however, the developmental theorists did not study the effect of medical disabilities on the development of a child. Little is known about the sequences and chronologies of development for children with various physical and health handicaps. The use of developmental scales standardized with normal children can be both reliable and valid when assessing the developmental progress of such children, but questionable when applied to children with physical and health handicaps. Two reputable developmental scales used to assess the development of a child with a severe physical handicap are apt to produce divergent results with some children (DuBose, 1981).

Factors such as inability to physically explore the environment, the possibility of hidden hearing and vision defects, and the results of overprotection are apt to depress scores or change normal developmental patterns (DuBose, 1981). Inaccurate assessments and the assumptions made from them can be particularly detrimental to the very young child.

CONSIDERATIONS IN INTERVENTION

Intervention programs and physical facilities for individuals who have physical and health handicaps need to be designed to accommodate medical problems and the cognitive and social deficits that may be secondary to them with the degree of accommodation dependent upon the type and severity of the medical disability. If wheelchairs are involved, buildings need to be barrier-free. If people require extensive therapy, activity schedules may have to be altered and therapy areas provided. If individuals need medications or have frequent medical emer-

Classes in a hospital school benefit those children who are hospitalized for long periods of time as well as those who are recuperating and will soon return to school.

gencies, staff must be trained to respond competently and record pertinent medical data.

The variety of school programs for physically and health handicapped students illustrates the types and degrees of accommodation for medical disabilities sometimes required in intervention. The following are common school interventions that may be provided:

1. *Hospital schools.* When children are confined to a hospital for a prolonged period, it is often necessary to provide an educational program within the medical facility. In a hospital, school activities have a lower priority than medical activities. The educational goal is to provide interim instruction so that the child can progress academically and keep up with schoolmates. To achieve these goals, a hospital school teacher generally divides instructional time between a classroom and the bedside. A teacher in a hospital needs to be adaptable, tactful, and often ingenious since children may be acutely ill or recuperating, therapies may interrupt instruction, lessons may differ for each child, and children and families are separated and easily upset.

2. *Homebound instruction.* Homebound teachers may be provided for children confined to their home for medical reasons. These teachers travel from home to home providing lessons and leaving assignments. Teleteaching, which uses tele-

phones to allow several students to talk to each other and the teacher, is sometimes employed to increase the efficiency of homebound instruction and allow children to interact with classmates. This approximates a classroom situation and allows the teacher to provide group instruction. Typically, teleteaching is done in the morning and home visits are made in the afternoon to pick up assignments and tutor individuals.

3. *Special schools for physically handicapped students.* Traditionally, most children with physical and health handicaps were placed in special schools. These schools were generally in or close to the community but separate from regular school facilities. Special school buildings were designed to be barrier-free and provided areas within the schools for medical therapists. Special transportation and equipment were provided and educational programming was adapted. In recent years, many students who would have been placed in these schools are being mainstreamed into regular classrooms, and students who remain are more severely and multiply handicapped than in the past.

4. *Programs in regular schools.* Increasing numbers of students with physical and health handicaps are being educated in regular schools by regular education teachers. Schools have adapted physical facilities by removing barriers and medical technology has provided special equipment that helps students be more independent. The amount of special education support provided the student depends upon the student's specific needs. For one, the support may include a medically trained aide that accompanies him or her at all times; for another, it may only require a piece of special equipment. School-related medical therapies may be provided by itinerant therapists using space in the school. This allows the student to mix and compete with peers in a normalized environment. Most regular schools have a variety of academic programs and support systems to individualize schoolwork. Some students may need to join a special education class or be assigned a resource teacher while others may need minimal or no extra academic support.

The Preschool Years

Young children with physical and health handicaps are often diagnosed at birth or in early infancy. In many cases, the potential for handicapping which accompanies a given medical disability is known. At the preschool age, many handicaps can be averted or mitigated before they develop. Therefore, preschool intervention is becoming a common part of the life of many young children with physical or health handicaps.

Both health and educational agencies cooperate in many states to provide an interdisciplinary approach to treatment. Early bracing, orthopedic surgery, physical therapy, or other interventions may be necessary to prevent medical disabilities from becoming more pronounced with age. Some schools have lowered the age for mandatory special education to three years or younger, recognizing that many cognitive, psychological, and social problems that could be averted with early intervention are apt to be well established when a child reaches kindergarten.

The School Years

Programming for children and youth with physical and health handicaps through the school years requires a great deal of flexibility. Different physical disabilities create different handicapping conditions which must be dealt with to ensure that the benefits of the educational experience are maximized. With the increased realization that most of the life of a person with physical or health handicaps will be lived in a normal environment, educational programs are being designed to normalize the school experience to the greatest extent possible.

When the areas in which a child is handicapped by medical disabilities are ascertained, a further assessment is made to prescribe what is needed to remove or mitigate the handicapping condition. The modifications may include removal of physical barriers, provisions to supply prosthetic equipment, arranging for ongoing therapy, or individualizing the curriculum. Programs are seldom static. Children's needs for special services change with age and medical condition.

Removing Architectural Barriers.

With the advent of Sections 501 and 502 of the Rehabilitation Act of 1973, schools were required to remove architectural barriers or provide alternative ways to provide services. Thus, if a student qualified for the honors English class, it would be unlawful to teach the class where the student could not reach it because of a disability. If steps impede a wheelchair, the school either must have someone lift the student and the chair, move the class to an accessible place, or remove the steps and provide a ramp.

While the law provides for the removal of architectural barriers, educators and others are often unaware of many of the things in an environment that are obstacles to persons with physical handicaps, especially when the person is in a wheelchair. Lewis and Doorlag (1987) suggest that all areas of the school and classroom be checked for accessibility, including chalkboards, bookcases, storage cupboards, etc.; that seating arrangements allow students to slide under tables or have lapboards for working; and that storage be provided for the student's aids and equipment.

Using Special Equipment.

A variety of medical and educational equipment has been designed to assist physically handicapped children improve mobility, remain in body positions that relieve the effects of abnormal reflexes, strengthen and support the body, and assist in completing schoolwork. Positioning chairs, braces, and some other specialized medical equipment may require a doctor's prescription. Occupational and physical therapists may purchase, construct, or modify equipment which helps the child be more mobile or move muscles in specified movement patterns.

Educators and speech therapists may also purchase or construct equipment that facilitates communication for nonverbal persons. Communication boards may be as simple as a chart taped to a wheelchair lapboard that allows the nonverbal individual to point to pictures or words or as complex as scanning equipment operated by specially adapted switches. A communication board mounted upright may be used for individuals with severe quadriplegic cerebral palsy allowing them to indicate words or symbols with eye movement alone.

With the advent of electronics and the use of microchips, devices which synthesize speech can be carried by nonverbal persons. A message can be typed on keys either during or before conversation is begun and a voice synthesizer can then do the talking. Microcomputers are being adapted to enhance verbal communication. During the general session of the National Convention of the Council for Exceptional Children in 1983, a young woman who was a quadriplegic and nonverbal moved her electric wheelchair to the microphone and delivered a twenty-minute address to the large audience in attendance. Using a portable microcomputer equipped with a voice synthesizer, many of her remarks could be given extemporaneously.

Microcomputers which can read voice prints are being developed to control a variety of equipment with voice commands. In the near future, individuals with quadriplegia or other severe physical disabilities will be able to control wheelchairs, phones, word processors, household appliances, and accessories in automobiles. The development of high technology such as voice-activated equipment has the potential to revolutionize the ability of persons with severe physical handicaps to participate in education, compete vocationally, and live independently in the community.

Educators who work with students having severe physical disabilities are becoming increasingly proficient in the use and modification of electrical and electronic equipment. Teachers devise remote switches purchased from electronics shops which are wired into battery-operated toys, electrical appliances, or microcomputers to allow physically handicapped students to operate various pieces of equipment.

Adapting Curriculum.   The primary challenge in adapting curriculum for students with physical and health handicaps is to maximize learning efficiency requiring flexibility and ingenuity on the part of the education team. Students themselves may lack strength, be unable to move efficiently, or require inordinate amounts of time and energy to complete ordinary daily living tasks.

The degree of inefficiency which may be encountered varies from normal to excessive depending upon the problems of the student. The daily schedule of a severely involved child with spastic cerebral palsy provides an example of the daily routine involved for some seriously handicapped children. This child must start a day at 4:30 a.m. with a bath and dressing since this procedure takes about an hour with the constant help of the child's mother or father. Breakfast begins at 5:15 a.m. and requires another hour since the child must be carefully fed and helped to chew and swallow food correctly. By 6:30 a.m. the school bus picks up the child. At about 7:30 a.m. the child is unloaded and brought to the classroom. After the long bus ride, it will be necessary to help the child and the rest of the children in class with their toileting needs. Therefore, serious academic work will not begin until about 8:30 a.m., four hours after the child got up. The child's day will include one-half hour of physical therapy and one-half hour of speech and language therapy plus a morning nutrition period and recess, more interruptions for toileting needs, and a one-hour lunch period. At 2:00 p.m., the child leaves on the bus for the return home at 3:00 p.m.

Removing the Barriers of Physical Limitations

The development of the semiconductor chip (micro-chip) in the 1970s began a revolution in technology for use of microcomputers by the handicapped. These small chips allowed powerful microcomputers to be developed that were lightweight, durable, portable, and relatively inexpensive. The microcomputer technology has been applied to development of artificial arms that are controlled by impulses from a person's nervous system, speech synthesized from word processors for communication, and many applications that accelerate school instruction. In the near future, increasingly powerful and lightweight computers may allow transmission directly to the human nervous systems. Experimentation with computer direction of neurostimulation which allows people with motor nerve dysfunction to walk, the blind to see, and the deaf to hear is presently underway.

Although the use of microcomputers to stimulate nerves to promote ambulation, sight, and hearing are good prospects for the future, several microcomputer applications are currently removing traditional barriers for the handicapped. One such development is the "Single Switch Augmented Communication System." This system allows a person without the use of any limbs or speech to adapt microcomputers (i.e., Apple, IBM, and IBM compatibles) for use as word processors and as voice synthesizers.

The main barrier to word processing for people without the use of their arms is that they can't use the standard keyboard. The "Single Switch Aug-mented Communication System" combines software with electronic dictionaries of words and phrases commonly used in English with a variety of on/off switches which a person can activate to command the computer.

One of the most technically advanced on/off switches is fitted on an eyeglass-like mounting (Words + Infrared Switch).* It produces an infrared beam which, if broken with a blink of an eyelash, raise of an eyebrow, or eye movement, will signal the computer to choose a letter, word, or phrase as the person scans the dictionaries.

The software is also designed to allow the person with the on/off switch to send commands to the computer. The computer, in turn, can command the printer to type letters or activate the speech synthesizer.

Persons using these systems can type as fast as 14 words per minute. By storing pretyped messages, communications can become even quicker.

This device provides a way for a person who has lost almost all body functioning but has retained his or her cognitive ability to communicate with the world. This technology could easily be expanded with existing microcomputer accessories to allow a person to dial a phone, water a lawn, or select reading material from electronically stored materials.

*Equipment and software available from Words +, Inc., 1125 Stewart Court, Suite D, Sunnyvale, CA 94086

Although all students with physical and health handicaps do not require as much time for nonacademic activities as the child described above, the case is not atypical. The teacher has only three to four hours to provide a full school experience which must include adaptive physical education, enrichment activities to compensate for lack of environmental experience, and instruction in the required 3 R's.

The educational team begins individualizing curriculum with the assessment report which includes information about the child's present functional and academic needs. The need areas and the discrepancies between the child's ability to perform define the parameters of instruction. The program is finalized on the Individual Education Program (IEP). Teachers plan the daily steps of instruction, schedule the day's activities, and monitor progress with the help of the team.

Teachers need to be mindful of the future environment of the student. For instance, if a student will be integrated into regular secondary schools and institutions of higher learning, academic and social skills cannot be allowed to lag in spite of the difficulties encountered. Children must often become proficient with equipment which will help them become more independent. Young children's introduction to switches which control battery-operated toys can lead to uses of microcomputers and word processors. Computer games may be designed to enhance the ability to control electric wheelchairs and specially equipped vans later.

Many times teachers adapt existing curriculum and materials. For instance, programmed instruction that requires writing with a pencil is revised to allow a child with poor hand control to respond verbally. Children who cannot use their hands to write may be taught to type or use a word processor at a young age in order that they may be more efficient.

The key to selection and modification of instruction is to provide experiences which will maximize the student's independence in the normal society. Selection of instructional sites in the least restrictive environment possible for the student maximizes experiences with regular students. Development of attitudes and work skills that encourage efficiency and production in spite of medical disabilities and handicaps prepares a student for competition with normal peers for academic and career opportunities. The adaptations of special equipment and use of various medical therapies enhance the use of the body and ability to live more normal and independent lives.

The Adult Years

The adult with a physical or health handicap has social, vocational, and daily living needs that are similar to the normal adult. One of the keys to a satisfying life in this society appears to be the ability to provide income or useful service in order to achieve a degree of economic independence. This, in turn, can provide a degree of social acceptance and self-worth that seems to be the foundation for successful participation in family units and other social groups (Brolin & Kokaska, 1979). Although adults with physical and health handicaps have not had a high degree of vocational success in the past (Bachman, 1972; Lewis, 1977), there is hope for the future with improved education, technological breakthroughs, and increased public acceptance of individuals with handicaps.

An ongoing problem for many with physical and health handicaps is securing adequate and dependable transportation. Without transportation, it is difficult for a person to go to training sites, seek employment, or hold a job. In addition, in today's society, transportation is also the key to social interaction and recreation. The car is the most versatile form of transportation, and with improved technology more persons with severe physical handicaps have had vehicles modified so that they are able to operate them.

Many quadriplegics with electric wheelchairs are able to drive vans with modifications such as hydraulic lifts to allow access for electric wheelchairs, wheelchair lock-downs in place of seats, hand-operated controls sensitive to

Mainstreaming in Action

In recent years, many exemplary programs have provided people with physical handicaps the opportunity to participate with their normal peers in educational, recreational, and vocational settings. Developing such programs has often required imagination and flexibility to overcome administrative and social resistance. The Physically Handicapped/Designated Instructional Services program represented pioneering effort by the San Diego Unified School District to mainstream students with physical handicaps.

San Diego Unified School District operated a large, segregated school for the physically handicapped and bused nearly all students with physical or health problems to that location. However, many of the district's special educators began to question the educational benefits of segregation for many of the students and could not justify the segregated, special school as the least restrictive environment for them as required by federal law (PL 94–142).

The district special educators were sure that the best place to educate many of the students with physical handicaps was in regular schools preferably in their own neighborhoods. They conceived of a plan where each regular school in which a student with a physical handicap was placed would have a trained paraprofessional on-site. The paraprofessional's responsibilities were to maintain communication with the regular school staff, expedite the removal of barriers to classroom access, provide needed help with daily living problems of the students, and support the academic program for each student. A certified specialist in education of the physically handicapped was provided to supervise and train each ten of the paraprofessionals on staff. The specialist also helped with educational assessment and the planning of the listed programs for each student with a physical handicap to ensure the quality of the regular school program.

Although the conceived ideas seemed logical, the proponents soon encountered obstacles to implementation. Routes for the buses with wheelchair lifts would have to be completely revised, and the transportation staff was not sure that it would be possible with existing personnel and equipment. The superintendent's office was not sure that they could staff the new program with their short budget. Principals surveyed their schools and reported that alterations to make each school completely accessible would require considerable expense, and their faculties would require extensive in-service training to ready them for these new students. School nurses raised the problems of medical liability.

The special education staff solved each problem on a separate basis. First, a few students were selected as candidates for mainstreaming. With specific students designated for specific locations, the superintendent's office found that the reduction of staff necessary to serve the students at the special school more than offset the cost of mainstreaming. The transportation staff, with exact addresses and destination times, found that the alterations of the schedules were manageable. Principals and school staffs, when introduced to students and parents on a case-by-case basis, gained confidence and enthusiasm in the program—especially when they were assured that the necessary support staff would follow each student. School plants were altered only to meet the specific needs of each child instead of the large architectural modifications that were first envisioned.

Once the precedent was set and the program's feasibility demonstrated, it was relatively easy to expand the numbers and the severity of handicapped individuals that could be educated in the mainstream with the support of the Physically Handicapped/Designated Instructional Services program.

persons with limited dexterity, and a variety of adaptations for control of accessories.

Public transportation such as buses and trolleys with vehicle lifts have improved accessibility for the handicapped. While persons with wheelchairs still encounter problems with bus, train, and plane travel, vehicles are more accessible than in the past. Individuals who cannot drive private vehicles such as those

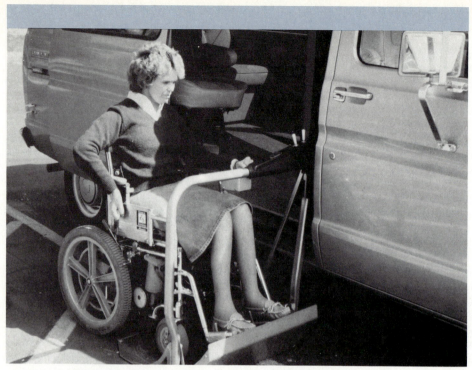

Using a specially equipped van with a hydraulic lift for her wheelchair, this young woman is able to drive herself to her job as a schoolteacher.

with severe physical handicaps, uncontrolled epilepsy, or other medical conditions must rely upon common carriers. Finding someone else to drive or having to rely on a taxicab can be inhibiting.

Financial problems can be a burden to individuals with physical and other handicaps. A diabetic with a medical disability that has a low handicapping potential may find the costs of insulin and needles a constant drain on finances. Those that face surgery or ongoing medical therapy can incur major financial costs. Special equipment such as braces, prosthetic limbs, and modified vehicles are often prohibitive in cost. There are several sources of revenue to aid those with physical or other health handicaps. Rehabilitation will finance training, transportation, or medical equipment if expenditures are likely to lead to employment. Supplemental Security Income provides stipends for persons with handicaps who are unemployable or who cannot maintain a minimum level of employment. Medicaid is available to defray medical costs if individuals qualify, and volunteer agencies such as the Easter Seals Society or United Cerebral Palsy will provide a variety of medical and social services for individuals. Support from private agencies are provided through a mixture of charitable donations, fees charged to governmental agencies for contracted services, or fees paid by families who can afford services. Generally services from private volunteer agencies are provided to the qualified person at little or no cost.

A good deal has been written about the vocational and financial needs of the adult with a physical or health handicap. As important as these aspects of life are, they are not the only consideration. Life without recreation would not be a pleasant contemplation. Persons with physical and health handicaps have developed a wide range of interests. Paraplegics participate in sports activities such as wheelchair basketball, tennis, and marathon racing. The stereotype that the leisure activities of handicapped persons are limited to nonactive pursuits is not true. Adults with physical and other handicaps participate in a range of active recreations such as bowling, archery, fishing, skiing, off-road racing, and camping.

FUTURE PERSPECTIVES FOR THE TREATMENT OF PHYSICAL AND HEALTH HANDICAPS

Several converging trends are changing the way in which society provides for individuals with physical and health handicaps. Although predicting the future is a precarious undertaking, the trends are well established at the present time and public policies and laws have been enacted that will dictate predictable changes. The following are the key trends which are remolding practice:

1. *Human rights for the handicapped.* The second half of the twentieth century has been marked with struggles for civil rights designed to ensure equal opportunity and protection against discrimination by race, color, sex, or handicapping condition. Although discrimination still exists, it is contrary to public policy and public laws in education, employment, construction, and transportation.

2. *High costs of programs that support dependency.* There is a growing concern about the rise in expenditures of programs designed to support dependent populations. Social Security Insurance (SSI) costs have risen until the financial foundations of the system have been threatened. Thus, programs that have potential to create a more independent citizenry from groups that have traditionally been dependent are gaining public support. With increased sophistication and understanding of the dynamics of handicaps, there is a growing recognition that persons with physical and health handicaps represent a potentially valuable source of production rather than a continual drain on resources.

3. *Advances in medical science and technology.* Diseases and impairments of the past which were the sources of handicapping conditions are being removed as threats by increasingly rapid advances in medical science and technology. Many diseases and conditions which formerly removed persons from productive lives are now no longer a threat or may only be a temporary problem. In addition, medical technology has developed prosthetic and other devices which remove and relieve handicapping problems for many with medical disabilities. With the advent of microcomputer and other technologies and advances in medical science, there should be continued change in the population of persons who are classified as physically handicapped.

4. *Advances in special education.* The expertise and sophistication of special education in the United States has improved with consistent federal support for training and research in the second half of the twentieth century. Some of the advances that are presently occurring are incentives for the development of infant programs, the establishment of mandated preschool programs, increased mainstreaming of handicapped with nonhandicapped students, and improved career and vocational education. The combination of these trends points to an optimistic future.

To ensure an optimistic future, research and improved practice is necessary in several areas. Medically, if there were major breakthroughs in our ability to prevent or cure neurological damage, the numbers of physically and health handicapped children would be greatly reduced. The improved use of microchips and other emerging technologies should continue to improve prosthetic and other devices. Educational research is necessary to enhance the development of cognitive and social skills of children with a variety of physical and health handicaps. Administrative and teaching efficiency needs to be improved to support mainstreaming efforts and to maximize the productive learning time in which a student is concentrating on school subjects.

The development of an enlightened and aware general public is the key to the future. It is hoped that favorable publicity in the media, mainstreaming in the schools, and more contact with persons with handicaps in society will provide the basis for improved public awareness and understanding. The future for individuals with physical and health handicaps is dependent upon continued public support to provide the new impetus for technologies, the funds for medical research, and the insurance of free access to the normal society.

SUMMARY

Persons with physical and health handicaps comprise a heterogeneous group of individuals of all ages, cultural backgrounds, and socioeconomic levels. They are similar only in that they share a physical or medical disability that impairs their ability to function in specific life activities. Definitions of physical handicaps and health impairments used by schools usually exclude students with mental retardation or severe multiple handicaps even though these students often have physical or health problems accompanying their primary disability. In settings other than schools, physical and health handicaps are usually identified in medical terms.

In the past, students with physical and health handicaps were often grouped in classrooms by their diagnoses or disabilities; but recently, the focus has shifted to the individual's skills and ability to function in society. This shift in emphasis is part of a movement to protect individuals from arbitrary discrimination due to their medical diagnosis and to assure that they are integrated into the mainstream of society. Public laws and policies reflect the philosophy of integration through the requirement that physical barriers be removed from public buildings, a mandate that students have an appropriate school placement in the least restrictive environment, and a prohibition against discrimination on the basis of a handicap.

Changes in social conditions and major breakthroughs in medical treatment have changed the nature of the population of physically and health handicapped individuals who require service. For example, cases of polio, heart problems caused by diseases in early childhood, and tuberculosis are rare; but the percentage of individuals with neurological disorders such as cerebral palsy, spina bifida, and spinal cord trauma has increased. Medical science has found ways to prevent or cure many diseases that were previously debilitating, and it has found ways to prolong life in many who are terminally ill.

Although there is no direct relationship between physical and health handicaps and intelligence, the group as a whole manifests higher percentages of learning deficits, social/emotional problems, and physical limitations than expected in the general population. In the past, many of these problems were seen mainly as side effects resulting naturally from specific medical disabilities; but more recently, attention has focused on the environmental and medical factors which interact to worsen the handicap.

In addition to medical and health interventions for physically and health handicapped individuals, educational programs serve important functions. School programs designed to prevent learning, social, and vocational deficits begin in infancy or the preschool years and continue through postsecondary education. These programs focus on preacademic and academic skills as well as helping students decrease their dependency, reduce emotional frustrations, and increase their ability to compete in society.

Improvements in social conditions, education, and medical treatment are resulting in better opportunities for individuals with physical and health handicaps to compete and participate in society. Current trends indicate that more persons will be educated in regular classrooms, live in nonrestrictive and barrier-free communities, and be fully employed in the nation's work force. These trends have positive implications for the quality of the lives of persons with physical and health handicaps and for society in general which benefits from the contributions of all of its members.

References

Bachman, W. H. (1972). Variables affecting postschool economic adaptation of orthopedically handicapped and other health-impaired students. *Rehabilitation Literature, 33,* 635–647.

Barsch, R. H. (1968). *The parent of the handicapped child.* Springfield, IL: Charles C Thomas.

Berg, B. O. (1982). Convulsive disorders. In E. E. Bleck & D. A. Nagel (Eds.), *Physically handicapped children: A medical atlas for teachers* (2nd ed.) (pp. 171–180). New York: Grune & Stratton.

Best, G. A. (1978). *Individuals with physical disabilities.* St. Louis: The C. V. Mosby Company.

Bigge, J. L. (1976). Task analysis. In J. L. Bigge & D. A. O'Donnell, *Teaching individuals with physical and multiple disabilities* (pp. 5–22). Columbus, OH: Merrill Publishing.

Bleck, E. E. (1979). Integrating the physically handicapped child. *The Journal of School Health, 49* (3), 141–146.

Bleck, E. E. (1982a). Cerebral palsy. In E. E. Bleck & D. A. Nagel (Eds.), *Physically handicapped children: A medical atlas for teachers* (2nd ed.) (pp. 59–132). New York: Grune & Stratton.

Bleck, E. E. (1982b). Myelomeningocele, meningocele, and spina bifida. In E. E. Bleck & D. A. Nagel (Eds.), *Physically handicapped children: A medical atlas for teachers* (2nd ed.) (pp. 345–362). New York: Grune & Stratton.

Bleck, E. E. (1982c). Poliomyelitis. In E. E. Bleck & D. A. Nagel (Eds.), *Physically handicapped children: A medical atlas for teachers* (2nd ed.) (pp. 419–422). New York: Grune & Stratton.

Bleck, E. E. (1982d). Muscular dystrophy—duchenne type. In E. E. Bleck & D. A. Nagel (Eds.), *Physically handicapped children: A medical atlas for teachers* (2nd ed.) (pp. 385–394). New York: Grune & Stratton.

Brolin, D. E., & Kokaska, C. E. (1979). *Career education for handicapped children and youth.* Columbus, OH: Merrill Publishing.

Connor, F. P., Rusalem, H., & Cruickshank, W. M. (1971). Psychological considerations with crippled children. In W. M. Cruickshank (Ed.), *Psychology of exceptional children and youth* (3rd ed.). Englewood Cliffs, NJ: Prentice-Hall.

Cruickshank, W. M., Hallahan, D. P., & Bice, H. V. (1976). The evaluation of intelligence. In W. M. Cruickshank (Ed.), *Cerebral palsy: A developmental disability* (3rd rev. ed.). Syracuse, NY: Syracuse University Press.

DuBose, R. F. (1981). Assessment of severely impaired young children: Problems and recommendations. *Topics in Early Childhood Special Education, 9*–18.

Epilepsy Foundation of America (1973). *Recognition and first aid of those with epilepsy.* Washington, DC: Author.

Finnie, N. R. (1975). *Handling the young cerebral palsied child at home.* New York: E. P. Dutton.

Goldberg, M. J. (1983). Spinal muscular atrophy. In J. Umbreit (Ed.), *Physical disabilities and health impairments: An Introduction* (pp. 147–154). Columbus, OH: Merrill Publishing.

Harvey, B. (1972). Asthma. In E. E. Bleck & D. A. Nagel (Eds.), *Physically handicapped children: A medical atlas for teachers* (2nd ed.) (pp. 255–263). New York: Grune & Stratton, Inc.

Hutter, J. J. Jr., & Farrell, F. Z. (1983). Cancer in children. In J. Umbreit (Ed.), *Physical disabilities and health impairments: An introduction* (pp. 185–194). Columbus, OH: Merrill Publishing.

Jones, M. H. (1983). Cerebral palsy. In J. Umbreit (Ed.), *Physical disabilities and health impairments: An introduction* (pp. 41–58). Columbus, OH: Merrill Publishing.

Jourard, S. (1958). *Personal adjustment.* New York: Macmillan.

Karnes, M. B., & Esry, D. R. (1981). Working with parents of young exceptional children. *Educational Horizons, 59* (3), 143–149.

Kirk, S. A. (1972). *Educating exceptional children* (2nd ed.). Boston: Houghton Mifflin.

Kirk, S. A., & Gallagher, J. J. (1983). *Educating Exceptional Children* (4th ed.). Boston: Houghton Mifflin.

Kraemer, M. J., & Bierman, C. W. (1983). Asthma. In J. Umbreit (Ed.), *Physical disabilities and health impairments: An introduction* (pp. 157–166). Columbus, OH: Merrill Publishing.

Kübler-Ross, E. (1969). *On death and dying.* New York: Macmillan.

Lewis, J. P. (1977). *A preliminary survey of the postsecondary educational status of physically disabled adults.* Harrisburg, PA: Pennsylvania State Department of Education (Eric Document Reproduction Service No. ED 146 368).

Lewis, R. B. (1983). Learning disabilities and reading: Instructional recommendations from current research. *Exceptional Children, 50,* 230–240.

Lewis, R. B., & Doorlag, D. H. (1987). *Teaching special students in the mainstream* (2nd ed.). Columbus, OH: Merrill Publishing.

Livingston, S. (1972). *Comprehensive management of epilepsy in infancy, childhood and adolescence.* Springfield, IL: Charles C Thomas.

Lyle, R. R., & Obringer, S. J. (1983). Muscular dystrophy. In J. Umbreit (Ed.), *Physical disabilities and health impairments: An introduction* (pp. 100–107). Columbus, OH: Merrill Publishing.

Malamud, N., Itabashi, H. H., & Castor Messenger, H. B. (1964). Etiologic and diagnostic study of cerebral palsy. *Journal of Pediatrics, 65,* 270–293.

Mitchell, D. C., Fiewell, E., & Davy, P. (1983). Spina bifida. In J. Umbreit (Ed.), *Physical disabilities and health impairments: An introduction* (pp. 117–131). Columbus, OH: Merrill Publishing.

Nealis, J. G. T. (1983). Epilepsy. In J. Umbreit (Ed.), *Physical disabilities and health impairments: An introduction* (pp. 16–28). Columbus, OH: Merrill Publishing.

Nelson, K. B., & Ellenberg, J. H. (1978). Epidemiology of cerebral palsy. *Advances in Neurology, 19,* 421–435.

Scherzer, A. L. (1974). Early diagnosis, management and treatment of cerebral palsy. *Rehabilitation Literature, 35,* 194–199.

Simeonsson, R. J., Huntington, G. S., & Parse, S. A. (1980). Assessment of children with severe handicaps: Multiple problems—multivariate goals. *Journal of the Association of the Severely Handicapped, 5* (1), 55–72.

Sirvis, B., Carpignano, J. L., & Bigge, J. L. (1976). Psychosocial aspects of physical disabilities. In J. L. Bigge & D. A. O'Donnell (Eds.), *Teaching individuals with physical and multiple disabilities* (pp. 79–107). Columbus, OH: Merrill Publishing.

Wehman, P., & Schlein, S. (1980). Assessment and selection of leisure skills for severely handicapped individuals. *Education and Training of the Mentally Retarded,* 50–57.

Winter, R. J. (1983). Childhood diabetes mellitus. In J. Umbreit (Ed.), *Physical disabilities and health impairments: An introduction* (pp. 195–205). Columbus, OH: Merrill Publishing.

Resources

Organizations

American Cancer Society
90 Park Avenue
New York, NY 10016

Funds research, advocates for legislation, provides public information and services to individuals with cancer.

American Heart Association
7320 Greenville Avenue
Dallas, TX 75231

Conducts research and provides information about heart disease and heart disease prevention.

Association for the Care of Children's Health
3615 Wisconsin Avenue, N.W.
Washington, DC 20016

Interdisciplinary group which provides information, advocates for health services for children and families, publishes a professional journal, and conducts an annual meeting highlighting research and best practices in child health care.

Asthma and Allergy Association
1302 18th Street, N.W.
Washington, DC 20036

Supports research and disseminates information about asthma and allergies.

Cystic Fibrosis Foundation
6000 Executive Boulevard—Suite 510
Rockville, MD 20852

Funds research and provides public information about cystic fibrosis.

Epilepsy Foundation of America
4351 Garden City Drive
Landover, MD 20785

Provides public education, advocates for legislation, and provides services to persons with epilepsy.

Juvenile Diabetes Foundation
60 Madison Avenue
New York, NY 10010

Funds research and provides information about diabetes.

Leukemia Society of America
733 Third Avenue
New York, NY 10017

Funds research, disseminates information, and provides services to individuals with leukemia.

Muscular Dystrophy Association
810 Seventh Avenue
New York, NY 10019

Funds research, conducts medical clinics, and provides services to persons with muscular dystrophy.

National Center for a Barrier-Free Environment
1140 Connecticut Avenue—Suite 1012
Washington, DC 20036

Investigates environments for accessibility, advocates for legislation and monitoring of current laws regarding accessibility, and provides public information.

National Easter Seal Society for Crippled Children and Adults
2023 Ogden Avenue
Chicago, IL 60612

Provides support services, medical treatment, special equipment, and advocacy for persons with a wide range of orthopedic handicaps.

Spina Bifida Association of America
343 South Dearborn Street—Suite 319
Chicago, IL 60604

Provides information, supports research, and assists individuals with spina bifida.

Sick Kids (need) Involved People, Inc.
216 Newport Drive
Severna Park, MD 21146
>Advocates for the needs of children with chronic illnesses and provides information.

United Cerebral Palsy Association
666 E. 34th Street
New York, NY 10016
>Advocates for legislation, provides public information, and provides a wide range of services to individuals with cerebral palsy and their families.

Magazines

Mainstream
861 6th Avenue—Suite 610
San Diego, CA 92101
>Articles directed toward persons with handicaps and those interested in handicapped individuals.

Chapter 5

SEVERE MULTIPLE HANDICAPS

Within each type of exceptionality, some individuals manifest the most severe, or disabling, characteristics of that handicapping condition. There are also individuals who show characteristics of more than one condition, that is, they have multiple handicaps. The range of functioning levels, prognoses, and service needs among all individuals with severe and/or multiple handicaps is so diverse that common characteristics among them are not always discernible. However, "severely handicapped" is one of the educational categories included in PL 94–142. The criteria used to identify people as severely handicapped will be explored in this chapter.

INDIVIDUALS WITH
SEVERE MULTIPLE HANDICAPS

A great deal of time, energy, and debate has been put into operationally, accurately, and purposefully defining the category of severe handicaps. In the past, individuals could be identified as severely handicapped based on their almost total exclusion from educational and habilitative services and segregation from society. However, integrated school and adult services are now mandated

Ian Pumpian
San Diego State University

throughout the country making exclusionary definitions less relevant now than in the past.

Individuals are typically identified as severely handicapped when the severity and/or multiplicity of their handicap(s) pose major challenges to them, their families, and society in general in nearly all aspects of growth, development, and functioning. Persons with severe handicaps face these challenges throughout their lifespan. Using this approach, not all individuals with a severe handicap (e.g., total blindness) or with multiple handicaps (e.g., cerebral palsy and deafness) would necessarily be identified as severely handicapped. In this chapter the term "severe handicaps" will be discussed from an educational perspective.

Van Etten, Arkell, and Van Etten (1980) observed that, as the severity of a handicap increases, the greater "the impact on the total life and development of the individual and it should be noted on the family members as well. The more severely impaired the individual, the more problems associated with multiple disabilities will be found . . . and more specific training is required to assure that even the most basic skills are acquired" (p. 2). Thus, Van Etten et al. (1980) differentiate individuals with severe handicaps from those with mild handicaps partially on the notion that the person is not a "six hour child," a term used by the President's Committee on Mental Retardation (1970) in relationship to difficulty in a school context. Instead, it may be accurate to assume that problems associated with severe multiple handicaps may manifest themselves across environments and throughout the individual's lifespan. The diversity of learning, social, and physical problems individuals may have requires the functional expertise of educators; doctors; physical, occupational, and speech therapists; psychologists; social workers; and other professionals. The expertise of each of these service providers must be brought to bear on all the significant environments, activities, and persons in which, and with whom, these individuals function (Brown, Ford, et al., 1983). Finally, the professional community is just beginning to appreciate the needs of the families of these individuals and the critical roles they assume. Parents need services, understanding, and opportunities—not mere sympathy.

To define this population by service need is consistent with Guess and Mulligan's (1982) use of the term "functional retardation" (not to be equated with mental retardation) in that ". . . it suggests that a definition of severely handicapped must be based on goals of programmatic instruction and environmental modification and adaptation" (Sailor & Guess, 1983, p. 8). Furthermore, it suggests that individuals with severe handicaps can be identified on the basis of instructional needs in basic functional life skill areas versus primary needs in remedial academic instruction. Finally, the term implies that professionals from nearly all disciplines need to work together and with families in order to create an effective and efficient service delivery model.

As will be discussed later in this chapter, no single etiology can be identified with this category. While any trauma or debilitating disease could result in severe handicaps, most individuals are identified at birth and will have learning, social, and/or physical problems throughout their lives.

introducing

PEOPLE WITH SEVERE HANDICAPS

Each reader of this text may have very different impressions of the population of people referred to as having severe handicaps. A number of examples follow:

Jane A. relates the term "severe handicaps" to her 20-year-old cousin who is deaf and blind and severely intellectually impaired. Jane has been told that her aunt contracted rubella (German measles) during the first trimester of her pregnancy. Apparently in the 1960s this resulted in numerous children being born with "severe handicaps."

Juan M. relates the term "severe handicaps" to his co-worker's new baby who was born with cardiac, limb, and other physical defects and presumed severe intellectual impairment. It is rumored that the co-worker's wife drank moderately during her pregnancy and the baby had been diagnosed as having fetal alcohol syndrome.

Marie J. relates the term "severe handicaps" to a neighbor's child who has Down Syndrome. Since the child always went to a different school Marie never knew much about him except he didn't talk very clearly and rode his bike around the neighborhood. Marie remembers her parents talking about the fact that the neighbor's parents were quite old when the child was born.

Sue T. remembers a presentation by a parent of a 14-year-old child who had very little volitional movement, was extremely small for his age, and needed to be fed, dressed, and diapered. The parent explained that it had always been difficult to assess his intellectual functioning and in school her son was learning to use his eyes and a board with pictures to communicate with others. Her son's condition was a result of mistakes made in the delivery room.

Sylvia H. has a sister who had a normal pregnancy and delivery, yet the child is extremely resistant to physical contact, flaps his hands a lot, and engages in bizarre verbalizations. One label that has been used to describe her nephew is "autism."

Scott A. has an older brother who lives in a state-operated institution for the severely retarded. His family used to visit him once a year. Scott's brother is nonverbal, not toilet trained, drools a great deal, and often hits and bites himself. Recently there has been talk of the state moving his brother into a community group home with three other persons with various handicapping conditions.

Anton S. has substituted in a school in which a class of students labeled severely handicapped is located. He is aware that many of the regular education teachers in the school do not see a reason for the class to be there and feel the class placement in their school is counterproductive.

Mrs. B. has a nonhandicapped fourth grader who attends a school in which a class of students labeled severely handicapped is located. She has seen a change in her child's attitude and behavior. Where the child used to talk about those weird kids who drool and can't talk, now she comes home and talks about what her handicapped friends are learning to do, who she helps eat lunch, what cerebral palsy is, etc. Mrs. B. shares her daughter's excitement about the ongoing program of structured interactions that has been developed in the school.

Finally, Mike C. does not know how to relate to the term "severe handicaps" at all. Since he has always been isolated from persons with such handicaps he is aware of some vague stereotypes and reluctant feelings but little more.

Which of these images is correct? The fact is these, and many more examples, could accurately represent individuals with severe handicaps. It should be clear to all readers that the diversity of this population and the progressive changes in public policy and service delivery limit any attempt to describe a "typical severely handicapped person."

Population Diversity

The category of severe handicaps encompasses a wide range of ages, functioning levels, discernible handicaps, and diagnostic categories. Guess and Horner (1978) concluded that physical and social behavior differences among this population can be greater than the similarities. This makes defining the population difficult in that it must be recognized as an open-ended rather than a discrete category (Sailor & Guess, 1983).

This diversity has led to various agencies, states, and organizations using many terms in reference to this population. As Lehr (1982) noted, some persons, groups, and agencies use the range of terms interchangeably and others use the range of terms to designate specific subgroups. These terms include expansions, modifications, or permutations of phrases such as: severe multiple handicaps, profound handicaps, severe and profound handicaps, severe and profound multiple handicaps, developmental disabilities, severe disabilities, severe retardation, severe and profound retardation, and so forth. Justen and Brown (1977) concluded that there was very little consensus in terms across state departments of education but that definitions generally fit into one of two categories: (1) severe and profound mental retardation; or (2) severe multiple handicaps.

It should be noted that mental retardation probably constitutes the largest single characteristic among people within the severely handicapped population (Van Etten et al., 1980). However, the converse is not true. That is, not all individuals who are identified within the severely handicapped population are mentally retarded. In addition, most persons who are identified as severely or profoundly retarded manifest at least one other serious handicap (Snell, 1982; Writer, 1981). Even though all of the individuals are not mentally retarded, current limitations in technology often make assessment of intellectual functioning extremely difficult across this population.

Federal Definitions

The most widely used approach to define the term severe handicaps is to operationally define the population according to common physical and behavioral characteristics exhibited by many persons who have severely handicapping conditions. The United States Department of Education, Office of Special Education and Rehabilitation Services, currently utilizes this approach. The definition, repeated below, is essentially derived from a combination of definitions included in PL 94–142:

1. *As it is used in this part, the term "severely handicapped children and youth" refers to handicapped children and youth who, because of the intensity of their physical, mental, or emotional problems, need highly specialized educational, social, psychological, and medical services in order to maximize their full potential for useful and meaningful participation in society and for self-fulfillment.*

2. The term includes those children and youth who are classified as seriously emotionally disturbed (including children and youth who are schizophrenic or autistic), profoundly and severely mentally retarded, and those with two or more serious handicapping conditions, such as the deaf-blind, mentally retarded blind, and the cerebral-palsied deaf.
3. Severely handicapped children and youth—
    (i) May possess severe language and/or perceptual-cognitive deprivations, and evidence abnormal behaviors such as:
    (A) Failure to respond to pronounced social stimuli;
    (B) Self-mutilation;
    (C) Self-stimulation;
    (D) Manifestation of intense and prolonged temper tantrums;
    (E) The absence of rudimentary forms of verbal control;
    (ii) May also have extremely fragile physiological conditions.

(20 U.S.C. 1424)

In paragraph one of the definition printed above the legislators recognized the need to base the definition on the dramatic need for services which characterizes individuals within this population. In paragraph two the legislators delineated a nonexhaustive listing of subgroups and clusters of categories typically found within this population. Paragraph three includes examples of the types of behaviors and conditions persons with multiple handicaps may manifest. Many researchers have seriously questioned this attempt to delineate a set of "may include" characteristics to define this population (Haring, 1978; Sailor & Guess, 1983; Van Etten et al., 1980). However, by emphasizing the need for services along with a common but in no way exhaustive list of descriptors, the definition appears to be a reasonable attempt to define this heterogeneous and diverse population.

The reader should be aware that there are other professionally accepted definitions. For example, vocational rehabilitation counselors have delineated a definition for the category "severely disabled" and in the Developmental Disabilities Act of 1970 the term "developmentally disabled" is defined. Both of these definitions are more inclusive than the one used by the Department of Education in that individuals with severe handicaps are a subset of the population these other definitions describe.

A History of Exclusion

Basing the definition of severe handicaps on the dramatic need for services is a relatively new approach. It represents important changes in public attitudes and policies as well as improvements in instructional technology, service delivery, and professional preparation.

In the past, people with severe handicaps were identified and thus could be defined by one general yet pervasive characteristic. This characteristic was their almost total exclusion from public education, community programs, and services: "an unserved education population" (Van Etten et al., 1980). The compulsory education statutes of most states permitted schools to exclude individuals from attendance who were considered unable to benefit from the instruction being offered. These statutes resulted in the large-scale exclusion, removal, segregation, and institutionalization of children with severe multiple handicaps (Sailor & Guess, 1983).

In fact, Laski's (1979) review of services offered to persons with severe handicaps illustrates that laws of ensuring public policy have in the past:

1. Characteristically excluded many handicapped individuals from services, benefits, and protections provided, as a matter of course, to all other persons;
2. Were enacted to protect many handicapped individuals based on notions of charity rather than entitlement;
3. Were implemented so as to segregate many handicapped individuals from nonhandicapped persons;
4. Suffocated the ability of many handicapped individuals to participate in society as well as stifled the development of services which would have allowed them to appropriately do so;
5. Lagged behind up-to-date service concepts and current understandings of the abilities and learning potentials of handicapped individuals;
6. Reflected common stereotypes of handicapped individuals as uneducable, dependent and inferior.

Public Law 94–142 followed a series of substantial court decisions and legislative enactments affirming a recent shift in public policy attempting to correct massive past discrimination against handicapped persons of all ages (Haring, 1978). This shift has significantly influenced the extent to which people with severe handicaps benefit from new options in care, education, and other habilitative services. Not only is public education now recognized as an inalienable right for all individuals with severe handicaps, increasing numbers of those individuals now and in the future will attend the same public schools as their nonhandicapped age-peers (Gilhool, 1976). Therefore, the exclusionary characteristic is no longer a viable means for identifying individuals with severe handicaps.

The Impact of Definitions on Service Improvements

The recognition of the need to provide rather than deny public education and integrated community services to persons with severe handicaps led to a new approach for defining the population. This new approach has posed new challenges to educators and others who must "not only refine their theories about the learning process but also alter their conceptions about what is possible for the severely handicapped population" (Haring, 1978, p. 1).

Improvements in instructional technology, service delivery, professional preparation, and the provision of community based residential, vocational, recreational, and educational programs are occurring daily. Based on these improvements the following points are now well recognized within the field:

1. Families, the professional community, and our society in general significantly control the choices and opportunities afforded persons with severe handicaps. Stated another way, a person's level of functioning and achievement may be more a factor of technological advances, resource allocations, and societal attitudes than of biological limitations (Gold, 1980).
2. Persons with severe handicaps by definition manifest a variety of educational, social, physical, and/or health problems. Therefore it should be clear that the roles assumed by educational, social, and medical service providers have a significant impact on the total life space of these persons. The need to coordinate these services utilizing an effective transdisciplinary approach is also becoming more and more clear.
3. The significant and often extended role the parents and family of an individual with severe multiple handicaps assume in acquiring, providing, and utilizing resources can no longer be ignored. Professionals are much more sensitive to the need families might have for various kinds of support services. Professionals are also becoming more competent at securing and maintaining the critical involvement of parents and families in service planning and delivery.
4. New organizations to help foster such developments and coordinate the efforts and involvement of educators, parents, politicians, and other service providers have been formed, such as The Association for Persons with Severe Handicaps (TASH), first called the American Association for the Education of the Severely and Profoundly Handicapped (AAESPH) (Lehr, 1982).

Consequently, numerous empirical investigations have demonstrated that, provided appropriate services, individuals with severe handicaps far exceed functioning limits previously presumed (O'Neil & Bellamy, 1978). Therefore, a definition used in reference to this population must be flexible and cannot presume potential and limitations (Haring, 1975). That is, there must be a clear recognition that abilities and behavioral repertoires are not static. As Van Etten et al. (1980) wrote: "The state of being severely or profoundly handicapped, then, is a changing one—one that can be favorably manipulated through educational and vocational training and environmental modifications" (p. 39).

ETIOLOGY AND PREVENTION

Severe handicaps can be caused by a single factor or multiple factors. Individuals with severe handicaps represent an extremely varied etiological picture and typically exhibit more intellectual, motoric, chromosomal, and sensory abnormalities than other handicapped populations (Snell, 1982). Causes may be attributed to prenatal, perinatal, neonatal, and/or postnatal factors. These factors may be induced by genetic and/or environmental events. However, the majority of severe handicaps are caused by serious brain damage before or during birth or infancy. Snell (1982) reviewed etiological studies done with profoundly retarded populations finding that an estimated 75 percent of the causes were organic, 21 percent unknown, and 5 percent attributed to other events. However, she cited studies which reported that in some institutions as many as 60 percent of the cases were recorded as unknown etiology.

A Varied Etiological Picture

It is relevant to note that the range of causes discussed in the other chapters of this text is applicable here and therefore will not be restated. Of particular relevance is the classification of causes cited in the chapter on Mental Retardation. In addition, information on causation and prevention delineated in the chapter on Physical and Health Handicaps is related and relevant for individuals diagnosed with particular physical and health impairments. The major difference with the individuals discussed in this chapter is that those causes have had an even more profound effect on the individual's overall growth, development, and functioning.

Currently many causes of severe and multiple handicaps have been identified and effective approaches to eliminating or greatly reducing their prevalence are widely used. Some of these major accomplishments will be reviewed in this section.

Infections and Intoxications.   Within the general American Association on Mental Deficiency (AAMD) category of Infections and Intoxications, several major advances are worthy of notation. First, rubella, commonly known as German measles, is a viral disease. In 1964, there was an epidemic of rubella. A significant relationship was discovered between birth defects and maternal rubella especially during the first trimester of pregnancy. Birth defects included a high frequency of deafness, blindness, and retardation. In 1969, an effective rubella vaccine became available which, if used, could prevent these handicaps. Rubella is particularly dangerous because many women may not even know they have contracted the disease. Therefore, the vaccine is now recommended for all children after the age of one and for all young women. Although this disease could be eradicated, many children and young women are still not protected.

Second, hemolytic disease (destruction of red blood cells) has been largely attributed to RH incompatibility between the fetus and the mother. This is a major reason why states require blood tests prior to marriage. Many remedies had been used in the past to treat this condition. These past remedies had marginal success and posed dangerous side effects of their own. Currently, however, a RH gamma globulin injection is available which has been extremely successful in reducing the incidence of this disease.

Other advances in this area relate to poisons. First, in the early 1970s, it was discovered that children eating chips of paint were ingesting toxic quantities of lead. Lead poisoning was identified as causing retarded growth and development.

In the early 1970s, legislation and other related actions were implemented which began the identification and elimination of lead-based paints and other lead toxic materials. Although the situation has improved, the problem will persist until sources of lead-based materials (e.g., older painted homes) are effectively controlled. In addition, public education has focused on parents being aware of other poisons within reach of their children. When awareness leads to preventive action, the possibility of eliminating a handicap is increased. Guthrie (1984), a pioneer in the development of infant screening tests, advocates testing all preschool children for lead poisoning and foresees the development of regional periodic screening of preschool children to detect lead and other environmental hazards.

Finally, the relationship between alcohol and drugs and severely handicapping conditions is being widely confirmed. For example, mothers who use narcotics during pregnancy may give birth to an infant addict (Hearings before the Select Committees on Narcotics Abuse and Control, 1980). An area that is receiving a great deal of public attention is Fetal Alcohol Syndrome (FAS). Some researchers report even moderate levels of alcohol consumption during pregnancy can cause FAS which is often characterized by cardiac, limb, intellectual, and/or other impairments (Moore, 1982).

Disorders of Metabolism and Nutrition.   Another AAMD category of causal classification includes Disorders of Metabolism and Nutrition. One major advance concerns a metabolic disease known as phenylketonuria (PKU). Untreated PKU has been highly correlated with severe retardation and other disorders including motor coordination deficits, microcephaly, convulsions, and eczema (Moore, 1982). PKU is now a well known but rare enzyme deficiency. It is inherited as a recessive gene from healthy parents (Tourian & Sidbury, 1983). Basically in PKU the enzyme phenylalanine hydroxylase fails to convert phenylalanine, an essential amino acid, into tyrosine. This results in a toxic build-up of phenylalanine in the blood. However, PKU continues to be uncontrolled in many developing countries where screening techniques are not known or used. Guthrie's noteworthy work in the development of screening tests to detect rare metabolic conditions in infants developed the screening test for PKU (Guthrie & Susi, 1963). What is particularly exciting about this screening test is that if treatment is begun early, PKU can be successfully controlled and the deleterious effects avoided. Treatment is basically the use of a phenylalanine-restricted diet in order to avoid this build-up and prevent the neurological damage (Moore, 1982). Improved screening and dietary restrictions have resulted in improvements of other metabolic diseases as well (e.g., galactosemia).

Trauma and Physical Agents.   Other advances in treatment and prevention can be identified under the AAMD categorical heading Trauma and Physical Agents. Specifically, the improvements in child carseat restraints and growing legislation requiring their use promises to significantly reduce the frequency and magnitude of serious handicaps and deaths resulting from car accidents (Agrin, from car accidents (Agrin, 1982). Also, increased public attention and programs focused on preventing child abuse are the first steps toward preventing this cause of severe physical and emotional injuries and handicaps (Christianson, 1980).

Unknown Prenatal Influences.   Snell (1982) reported that as much as 60 percent of the time severe handicapping conditions are recorded as unknown etiologies. Under the AAMD category of unknown prenatal influence is a condition called hydrocephalus. Hydrocephalus has many causes, some of which can be identified (Moore, 1982). Hydrocephalus generally refers to a significant enlargement of the cranial vault which can be caused by excess, nonabsorbed, or blocked cerebrospinal fluid (Moore, 1982). This condition, if untreated, can lead to serious physical and intellectual impairments including paralysis, visual defects, convulsive disorders, and retardation (Moore, 1982). Surgical techniques have been very effective in treating and managing this condition. Permanent drainage systems, called shunts, are implanted to allow fluid to drain from the brain into the abdomen (Bleck, 1982). Shunts consist of plastic tubes and valves which regulate the drainage with the effectiveness largely dependent upon early detection and treatment.

Chromosomal Abnormalities.   A major cause of mental retardation and other handicaps under the AAMD category of Chromosomal Abnormalities is Down Syndrome. This syndrome has been recognized and researched for over 100 years. The reader is probably familiar with many stigmata that are commonly associated with this syndrome such as a round, flat face; slanted eyes with speckling of the iris; a fissured, usually protruding tongue; a high-arched palate; short feet, hands, and fingers; and poor articulation (Moore, 1982). The most common chromosomal disorder leading to Down Syndrome (90–95 percent of the cases) is an extra chromosome connected with the 21st chromosome (Abroms & Bennett, 1983). This type of Down Syndrome called Trisomy-21, arises *de novo* and is typically not hereditary.

Research related to this syndrome has demonstrated high correlations between maternal age and frequency of Down Syndrome. Hanson (1977), in her excellent guide for parents of children with Down Syndrome, reported the following statistics:

Maternal Age	Risk of About 1 in
20–24	2500 births
25–29	1500
30–34	750
35–39	280
40–44	100
over 45	35 (increasing with age)

In addition, Moore (1982) reported a high risk associated with mothers under the age of 20. Abroms and Bennett (1983) reviewed literature in order to emphasize that the extra chromosome does not originate solely in the mother. They found that the extra chromosome originated in the sperm in 20 to 25 percent of the cases in which karyotypes were informative. They cited studies reporting a statistically significant relationship between paternal age and the incidence of Down Syndrome. Specifically, they reported that men 41 years and older have an increased risk of fathering a child with Down Syndrome regardless of the age of the mother. Thus special consideration should be made by parents who are in an at-risk age. Although the correlation between Down Syndrome, mental retardation, and health impairments is high, not all individuals with Down Syndrome would be considered severely handicapped.

Other Considerations

Finally, issues regarding causation, prevention, and treatment have risen from medical advances and life-saving procedures which are keeping more at-risk children alive. In the 1980s many court cases began to be heard regarding whether parents could choose not to allow these life-saving techniques to be used on their handicapped children. Notable are the Phillip Becker Case (Powell, Aiken, & Smilie, 1982) and the Bloomington, Indiana, Baby Doe Case (Hardman, 1984). The Association for Persons with Severe Handicaps (TASH) (1983) has made the following resolution on this topic:

> . . . The Association for the Severely Handicapped opposes the withholding of medical treatment and/or sustenance to infants when the decision is based upon the diagnosis of or prognosis for mental retardation or related handicapping conditions.
>
> And furthermore this association reaffirms the right to equal medical treatment for all infants in accordance with the dignity and worth of these individuals as protected by the Constitution and Bill of Rights of the United States of America. . . .
>
> And furthermore the Association for the Severely Handicapped acknowledges the obligation of society to provide for the lifelong, medical, financial, educational support to handicapped persons, to extend to them the opportunities to achieve potential, equal and equivalent, to those opportunities offered other/all members of our society.

Thus it is apparent that many causes of severe multiple handicaps can be eliminated or at least attenuated. What continues to be necessary is education to make the public aware of new findings in research and advances in treatments.

CHARACTERISTICS OF INDIVIDUALS WITH SEVERE MULTIPLE HANDICAPS

In the past, persons with severe handicaps were treated as if they could not learn. It is now recognized that all individuals can learn but that learning requires teaching. Although achieved levels of functioning vary considerably within this population, improved instructional technology and service delivery have made gains possible. Limiting services to custodial care and perceiving individuals as children and others as "vegetables," "basket cases," and "infrahumans" indicates a lack of sophistication or a lack of awareness of functional curriculum development strategies, prosthetic devices, and applied behavioral analyses and intervention (Snell, 1982).

Achieved levels of functioning for individuals with severe handicaps must be evaluated on an independent, rather than categorical, basis. Such an evaluation only provides a review of what an individual is currently able to do, not what his or her potential may be. There are persons with severe handicaps who have learned to perform many tasks adaptively in integrated community settings. For example, studies have demonstrated that many persons with severe handicaps can learn to ride city buses (Coon, Vogelsberg, & Williams 1981), use fast-food concessions (Christoph, Nietupski, & Pumpian 1979), engage in age-appropriate leisure activities (Stainback, Stainback, Wehman, & Spangiers, 1983; Voeltz, Apffel & Wuerch, 1981), cross streets (Vogelsberg & Rusch, 1979), and engage in meaningful work (Brown, Shiraga, et al., 1983; Wehman, 1981). The volume and variety of these demonstrations make it extremely unlikely that such success represents exceptional cases of ability (Bellamy, Rhodes, Bourbeau, & Mank, 1982). Instead, Bellamy and his colleagues (1982) concluded that the range of current services and placements afforded persons with severe handicaps have failed to keep pace with the growing number of empirical demonstrations of the potential of these individuals.

A small percentage of severely handicapped persons have multiple sensorial deficits, little if any volitional movement, and are extremely sedated with chemicals. For individuals who are on life support or in such states of biological distress, attempts to maintain life are supplemented by opportunities to participate in normal environments and activities whenever possible. Snell (1982) estimated that only about 7 percent of individuals characterized as profoundly handicapped fit the description by Landesman-Dwyer and Schuckit (1976) as being "(1) incapable of moving through space, even with prosthetic devices and physical assistance; (2) totally lacking all adaptive behaviors as measured by instruments such as the AAMD Adaptive Behavior Scale; and (3) being extremely small for their chronological age (i.e., below the third percentile for height, weight, and head circumference)" (p. 56).

Learning Characteristics

In this population the attainment of ordinary skills requires sophisticated instructional techniques, inordinate instructional time, and attention to each individual's learning and performance characteristics. Nisbet et al. (1982) delineated several typical learning characteristics of severely intellectually handicapped students. Since not all persons with severe handicaps are intellectually impaired, these characteristics cannot be universally assumed; nevertheless, the characteristics have educational implications for a large percentage of the severely and multiply handicapped population. Nisbet et al. (1982) stated that the more impaired the student, the greater the effect on: (1) The amount of skills the student is capable of learning and the rate of learning; (2) The ability to generalize learned skills; (3) The ability to retain and relearn skills; (4) The ability to synthesize skills and generate new skills. Each of these characteristics will be discussed and exemplified below in greater detail.

1. The Amount of Skills the Student is Capable of Learning and the Rate of Learning.

In general the more severely handicapped the student, the longer it will take to learn to perform a skill or skill sequence at a meaningful performance level. That is, students require more direct instructional trials to learn a skill than their less handicapped and nonhandicapped peers. This characteristic alone could account for the assumption that in a given period of time students are capable of learning fewer skills than their less handicapped and nonhandicapped students.

For example, when Sweet et al. (1980) identified the need for a group of severely handicapped 12- to 20-year-olds to use a vending machine, they recognized that nonhandicapped children typically learn basic vending machine skills with very few direct instructional trials. They also recognized that it was likely that their handicapped students would require many direct instructional trials over many days in order to learn the basic vending machine skills. Therefore a decision to teach the skills also meant a commitment to devote a great deal of instructional time to the program each day over the instructional year.

In this case it would have been naive to assume that the students involved in this study would have learned these skills if the program was limited to giving the students, with help, a chance to buy a soda during a couple of field trips.

2. The Ability to Generalize Learned Skills.

The more handicapped the student, the greater the difficulty he or she will have demonstrating skills, which have been learned in one situation, in a new situation (Stokes & Baer, 1977). That is, these students often manifest problems performing learned skills in front of different people, in different environments, with different materials and/or with different language cues provided (Williams, Brown, & Certo, 1975). This is often referred to as difficulty generalizing learned skills or transferring training. Currently a great deal of research is being conducted relative to the contributing factors involved in this phenomenon and instructional strategies which minimize their deleterious effects (Horner, Sprague, & Wilcox, 1982). However, it is sufficient to understand that the more the learning environment is dissimilar to the environments in which learned skills will be expected to be performed, the less likely such performance will occur (Williams et al., 1975).

For example, when Sweet et al. (1980) designed their program to teach vending machine skills, they acquired a vending machine to use in the classroom. This allowed each student to be given many instructional trials. However, in order to promote the transfer and generalization of these skills, Sweet and his colleagues recognized the need to provide students ongoing vending machine use instruction in a variety of vocational, recreational, and community environments in which the students functioned and in which vending machine skills would be useful.

3. The Ability to Retain and Relearn Skills.
Maintenance or retention of a learned skill refers to the period of time which follows the actual acquisition and performance of a skill at acceptable criteria. Persons with severe handicaps often have more problems maintaining skills than their less and nonhandicapped peers. That is, the more severely impaired the students, the greater the likelihood that they will forget the skills they have learned. Forgetting is exacerbated when long periods of time elapse in which the acquired skill is performed either infrequently or not at all. In addition, reteaching the skill takes much longer with severely handicapped individuals (Nisbet et al., 1982).

For example, Sweet et al. (1980) were not interested in wasting valuable instructional time to merely demonstrate skill acquisition for their study. Instead they wanted to make sure their program would result in the development of useful skills for the students involved. The vending machine use program was selected because it was believed that the skills could be used on a regular basis in many environments in which the students functioned and would continue to function for many years to come. Involving the parents in the selection of vending machine use as an instructional priority further substantiated this belief. The selection of functional skills for instruction that could be used regularly minimized the chance that students would forget the skills they learned.

4. The Ability to Synthesize Skills and Generate New Skills.
Skill synthesis refers to the ability to take skills acquired in isolation and integrate them together in skill sequences. One of the major learning and performance characteristics manifested by students with severe impairments is the inability to adequately synthesize within one activity skills that have been learned in isolated skill classes. That is, if communciation skills are only taught in communication class, behavior skills in behavior class, and motor skills in motor class it is likely that a student will have difficulty engaging in an activity which requires performing communication, behavior, and motor skills together. Furthermore, severely handicapped students often have extreme difficulty generating new skills from already acquired skills. That is, the more severely handicapped the student, the more difficulty that student may have appropriately solving practical problems without direct instruction related to those problems (Nisbet et al., 1982).

For example, these characteristics can be exemplified by using the vending machine program again (Sweet et al., 1980). These educators recognized they could not teach vending machine skills in isolation. While they taught students the specific skill sequence for using the vending machine, they also incorporated other skill instruction. That is, if one student used a picture communication book to communicate with others, then relevant vending machine use pictures and symbols of money, breaktime, vending machine choices, and vending machines were placed in the book and used during instruction. Another student who was in a reading program was taught vending machine sight words in reading class as well as during classroom and community vending machine instruction. Other students did not have the money skills to use a vending machine so various coin counting and adaptive money management techniques

Skills learned in the classroom such as locating items on a "grocery shelf" will be used later on a shopping expedition to a local supermarket.

were taught as an ongoing component of the program. Finally, individual students manifested particular behavior problems. Therefore, individualized programs developed to manage these behaviors were implemented and integrated into the vending machine program whenever possible or necessary.

Sweet et al. (1980) also recognized that a student who demonstrated the ability to use a vending machine would require additional instruction to deal with selection changes, price variations, and coin returns that do not work! That is, it was believed that many problem-solving skills would need to be a part of instruction rather than an assumed outgrowth of it.

Service Implications.   Nisbet et al. (1982) concluded that when all of these learning characteristics are considered together several implications become obvious. First, educational and other habilitative services must be directed toward the development of useful, meaningful skills, i.e., functional skills. Second, services must be provided in the environments in which skill use is required. Stated another way, valuable instructional time cannot be wasted on skills which are not normally used, desired, and required in our daily lives. Furthermore, instructional services must be provided in the variety of normalized community environments in which a student currently functions or will function in the future. Therefore, instructional objectives should relate to functional skill development and instructional strategies should result in functional skill use. Instructional strategies will be discussed in greater detail in the intervention section of this chapter.

Social/Emotional Characteristics

The social behavior of many individuals with severe handicaps can often be characterized as socially maladaptive and inappropriate. They may act extremely withdrawn and inattentive toward others or be excessively social (e.g., hugging strangers, always holding hands with others). Other behaviors which some of these individuals manifest that ultimately affect their acceptance may include stereotypic behavior which is repeated excessively and draws negative attention. Examples of stereotyped behaviors include handflapping, body rocking, teeth grinding, and other oral noises. More serious types of stereotyped behavior can be grouped together under the label of self-injurious behavior (Sailor & Guess, 1983). For example, some individuals repetitively slap their face, bite their hands, lips, and arms or even bang their heads against tables, walls, and other objects.

Other persons with severe handicaps may act predictably or unpredictably aggressive toward or in the presence of others. Such behaviors may range from screaming, crying, and noncompliance to pushing, biting, and hitting of both familiar and unfamiliar persons. Finally, according to Sailor and Guess (1983), this population is often characterized by their failure to have learned socially adaptive behaviors and responses. For example, many lack basic self-care skills, continually drool, and exhibit other behaviors expected only of much younger children. These behavior deficits often limit social acceptance.

There are many theories and possible explanations for the development and demonstration of inappropriate behavior. Sailor and Guess (1983) cite growing empirical studies which suggest that such behaviors are often learned and function to terminate and/or increase contact with others. It is also likely that many of these behaviors are maintained when the individual is not taught more socially acceptable behaviors for terminating and/or engaging in interactions with others.

Many investigators now suggest that segregated, handicapped-only environments increase the likelihood that maladaptive social behaviors will be learned and maintained (Sailor & Guess, 1983). For example, Berkson and Davenport (1962) reported that two-thirds of institutionalized residents studied engaged in some type of stereotypic behavior and the longer a child was institutionalized the greater the likelihood he or she would learn stereotypic behaviors. Eyman and Call (1977) found that the frequency of maladaptive behaviors was highest among the institutionalized subjects studied. Brown et al. (1983) also suggested that the environments in which individuals live, work, learn, and play significantly affect the development of appropriate behavior repertoires. Specifically, they concluded that in segregated, handicapped-only environments:

employees often desensitize to, learn to tolerate, ignore, reinforce, and even attempt to justify many maladaptive actions such as nosepicking, public mas-

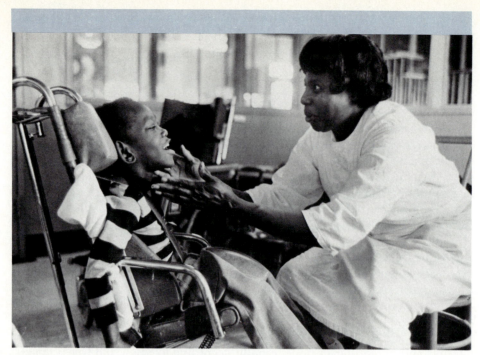

Children with severe handicaps who are hospitalized much of the time will benefit socially from interaction with a caregiver who spends a great deal of time with them.

> turbation, body rocking, childish play, and incessant irrelevant verbalizations. Sooner or later, the pressure from these different kinds and intense degrees of deviant actions wears down, overwhelms, and otherwise discourages or depresses direct care personnel.   (p. 19)

However, Brown et al. (1983) suggested that in normalized integrated environments direct care personnel can become more aware of and responsive to age norms and develop effective programs to teach and maintain socially acceptable behaviors.

What becomes extremely clear from this emerging empirical data base is that individuals with severe handicaps may in fact perform or learn to perform behaviors which are chronologically age inappropriate and socially maladaptive. However, high levels of maladaptive behaviors need not be expected and such behaviors can be reduced, controlled, eliminated, or replaced by more socially acceptable ones (Snell, 1982). Service providers now recognize their responsibility to teach these individuals socially acceptable behaviors (Certo & Kohl, 1983). The behaviors taught should replace or reduce the frequency, duration, and magnitude of less acceptable behaviors.

Gaylord-Ross, Haring, Breen, and Pitts-Conway (1984) conducted a series of studies involving a group of students labeled autistic. These students demonstrated a range of maladaptive behaviors such as social withdrawal, excessive humming, striking self and others, facial grimacing, hand biting, finger twirling, object breaking, jumping, and talking loudly to themselves. Gaylord-Ross and his colleagues developed a social skills training package to teach these students appropriate social responses with nonhandicapped peers in leisure settings. In these experiments inappropriate social responses were displaced by a significant increase in initiating and maintaining appropriate social interactions between these autistic youth and their peers. They concluded that the social training package was responsible for a range of social interaction skills that were acquired.

Voeltz (1983) emphasized that other persons including nonhandicapped peers, parents, teachers, and administrators of both handicapped and nonhandicapped students must and can be prepared to facilitate the social development and acceptance of individuals with severe handicaps. Voeltz specifically described strategies to prepare both severely handicapped and nonhandicapped peers for day-to-day, meaningful interactions in integrated environments. The approaches described have been extensively field-tested and enhanced within the Special Friends and Hawaii Integration Projects. Voeltz (1980, 1982) conducted a series of studies in which structured interactions and interventions to facilitate social integration of severely handicapped students were demonstrated to positively affect the social acceptance of the nonhandicapped students toward their peers. Brown et al. (1983) further described the positive effects of planned integration on instructional personnel, related services staff, and parents.

Brown and his colleagues at the University of Wisconsin-Madison have consistently offered the position that the best way for severely handicapped and nonhandicapped persons to learn to live with, tolerate, accept, and understand each other is through longitudinal interaction during school years. Furthermore, the future service providers and parents of severely handicapped children are the students attending public schools today. Educators must prepare these future service providers and parents to accept and interact effectively with people with severe handicaps. Thus, although a majority of severely handicapped students are still educated in handicapped-only schools, programs which provide for the school and community integration of this population represent the "state of the art" and do have a direct effect on social acceptance (Certo, Haring, & York 1984).

Finally, since parents or guardians are likely to be the key decision makers, resource seekers, and resource linkers throughout their children's lives, establishing a close working relationship between professionals and the family is critical in order to adequately develop resources and opportunities for social acceptance and integration.

Medical/Health Characteristics

Since the term severe handicaps refers to an extremely diverse group, the range of medical and health impairments manifested is also quite extensive. While it is true that some severely handicapped individuals are in generally good health, this group can be characterized by having a larger number and more severe medical and health problems than their less and nonhandicapped peers.

The number and type of medical and health problems this group may manifest are too numerous to delineate in this chapter. It would probably be more efficacious for professionals working with this group to identify each individual's unique disabilities in terms of implications for services. What is important to emphasize here is the potential for primary physical and health impairments to develop secondary ones. Consider a few of the many examples:

1. Individuals who have general mobility problems and spend a great deal of time in wheelchairs or lying in bed have an increased chance of having muscles atrophy and developing bedsores. In addition these persons have an increased risk of their overall growth, development, stamina, and endurance being impaired. This is also true of individuals with various heart and lung diseases and impairments;
2. Individuals who take medication to control seizures and other disorders are also at risk of suffering the many negative side effects of prolonged drug usage such as reduced and/or altered levels of functioning, abnormal hair growth, and inflammation of the gums (gingiva);
3. Individuals who are constantly subjected to needed doctors' appointments, surgeries, treatments, and prolonged hospital stays face an increased chance of having their normal development and education continually interrupted, not to mention the associated pain, suffering, and risks which are likely to the immediate results of these interventions;
4. Individuals who have medical and physical conditions which restrict the way in which they eat and the type and kinds of food they can eat or who do not know how to control their eating habits have an increased chance of having nutritional and weight problems;
5. Individuals who continue to reside in public and private institutions have a greater chance of being exposed to and contracting infectious diseases;
6. Individuals with limited self-care and self-help skills have an increased chance of having various hygiene-related health problems.

It should be clear that individuals with severe and multiple handicaps manifest a range of mobility, heart, respiratory, eating and digestive problems, as well as other syndromes, conditions, and diseases. These conditions and the limitations they impose on an individual's growth and development must be minimized by service providers. Poor physical and health status and lack of fundamental self-care skills do not imply a lack of potential to learn skills, maintain proper diet and exercise, and receive valuable education and habilitative services. What is implied is the need to develop and utilize sophisticated instructional technology and individualize adaptations in order to maximize performance and participation in healthy activities and necessary services. Service providers must be competent and creative:

1. in designing and using specialized equipment;
2. in utilizing various positioning, transferring, feeding, toileting, and dressing techniques;

3. in recognizing the symptoms of medical disorders;
4. in applying a variety of first aid techniques;
5. in communicating and working cooperatively with professionals from various disciplines.

Finally, minimizing physical and health impairments and maximizing growth and development can be most efficiently and effectively accomplished when parents and all service providers have the attitudes, skills, and support to function in a coordinated, comprehensive, and transdisciplinary manner (Hart, 1977).

DETECTION

Due to the severe medical conditions often manifested within this population, the individual is usually identifiable at birth if the handicap(s) are congenital. Thus, the professionals most likely to identify an individual's handicap(s) are doctors and nurses.

Identification and Screening

First screening procedures used include identification of prenatal and neonatal complications, prenatal screening (e.g., amniocentesis and ultrasound), visual observation of the newborn, and the Apgar Evaluation Score for Newborn Infants. Advances in medical technology have led to earlier and more sophisticated identification and treatment of infants with severe multiple handicaps and have made it possible for many more severely handicapped newborns to survive.

After identification of actual and suspected handicaps has been made by the medical staff, the infant and his or her family should have access to professionals from many disciplines to further assess the child and help the family identify and acquire necessary support services. The transdisciplinary approach is widely accepted as an effective model to integrate program goals from various disciplines (Sailor & Guess, 1983). The model is intended to coordinate expertise beginning with screening and continuing through programming. Screening in early childhood programs is primarily to assess sensory, motor, and cognitive skills. This screening provides the framework for more intensive assessments and intervention. Thus parents, educators, social workers, therapists, audiologists, ophthamologists, etc., may become directly involved in the early identification of a child's handicaps and early intervention needs. Again it must be emphasized that prognosis and other attempts to presume future potential of a newborn are extremely limited and should be approached in a cautious and tactful manner. It is clear, however, that the sooner needed transdisciplinary services are made available and provided for the newborn and his or her family, the greater the likelihood that the severity of an individual's handicap(s) can be attenuated (Lyon & Lyon, 1980).

Criteria for Determination of Severe Handicaps

The criteria for determining the existence of severe handicaps in an infant are based on the presence of severe medical disorders and complications and severe lags in normal growth and development in various cognitive, motor, social, and physical domains. The criteria for determining the existence of severe multiple handicaps during school age have been extensively discussed earlier in this chapter. Specifically, it has been suggested that the definition for severe handicaps be functionally based on educational need. Individuals will typically be associated with this population when their primary educational need is an individualized program of functional life skills vs. remedial academics. This determination accentuates the need for professionals from all disciplines to provide services which facilitate the normal growth, development, and functioning of an individual throughout his or her life.

Common Methods for Diagnosis and Assessment

The typical approaches to diagnosis and assessment of this population include a combination of the procedures described in the chapters on Physical and Health Handicaps (Chapter 4) and Mental Retardation (Chapter 3) and will therefore not be repeated here. Furthermore, it should be obvious that procedures used with young children are identical to the ones described in the early intervention section of Chapter 2. Due to the nature and range of possible handicaps, most would agree that a group of professionals representing various professional disciplines should be involved with the parents in all aspects of assessment and intervention (Sailor & Guess, 1983). Vincent et al. (1984) have developed a format for parents to provide critical information about skills being demonstrated by the young child at home. This information can be invaluable both for assessment and program purposes.

In the past, there has been an overreliance on standardized assessment instruments and the test scores produced (Van Etten et al., 1980). In many cases, these assessment procedures, especially when used with older children, adolescents, and adults, fail to provide useful programmatic information, exclude the individual from the environments, activities, and services from which he or she could benefit, and result in the provision of services and curricula only appropriate for young nonhandicapped children (Baumgart et al., 1982). One of the major problems associated with these assessments is that test scores have been used to imply potential (Gold, 1980). However, when appropriate training and experience are provided, many of these individuals continue to achieve beyond their presumed limitations (O'Neil & Bellamy, 1978).

Finally, Gold (1980) emphasized that our focus must be on teaching, not testing and evaluation. "When training is the focus of attention, evaluation must occur. So, train, don't test" (p. 148). In order to adhere to this rule of thumb, further discussions of current assessment strategies considered appropriate for this population will be included in the Intervention section of this chapter.

In summary, greater emphasis is now being placed on assessment strategies, especially with adolescents and adults, which:

1. are criterion vs. norm-referenced;
2. provide specific information about the skills an individual cannot perform related to the task-analyzed activity;
3. are generally conducted by observation within a natural context and can be repeated as a regular and ongoing component of an instructional program.

CONSIDERATIONS IN INTERVENTION

In many parts of the country, services lag seriously behind up-to-date practices. In such places, service needs are presumed to be limited to meeting basic custodial care needs, adults are thought of and treated as children, and functioning is limited to a few large, segregated "handicapped-only" environments. In such places it is presumed that this is all that is possible, necessary, and reasonable for severely handicapped individuals. In such places, they typically don't learn, don't grow, and don't develop socially acceptable adaptive behaviors. Thus, the providers' attitudes are reinforced and the limited nature of services is further justified and perpetuated. Attempts are conscientiously made to keep the facilities clean, attractive, and "modern looking" as possible; however, segregation and "herding" are pervasive. Programs and services confined to large, segregated environments fail to meet the criteria associated with the principles of normalization.

Quality Service Indicators

It is exciting to report that in many other parts of the country increasing numbers of persons with severe handicaps are functioning in a wide range of environments and activities and interact regularly with families, peers, and professionals. In such places there is a prevailing belief that level of functioning is in large part a product of what and how we teach, the services we provide, the adaptations we develop to compensate for major performance deficits, and the way we work together to creatively maximize an individual's participation in a functional, age appropriate, and socially acceptable behavior.

As stated by Pumpian, MacFarlane, and Kalan (in press), ultimately the criteria for evaluating the effectiveness of educational and other habilitative services must be based on whether a student, regardless of functioning level, can be considered an integral and productive part of his or her home and community. That is, services afforded these individuals must be specifically designed to prepare them to participate meaningfully in the environments in which their nonhandicapped peers live, work, play, and learn. This is not to imply that every severely handicapped student will be prepared to live independently, shop independently, work at competitive hours and wages, or for that matter dress, feed, and/or toilet him/herself. It is, however, a reasonable goal to expect that each student will have an individually designed program to enhance his or her participation in such normal activities and environments. This functional preparation is one of the major principles upon which all educational and other habilitative services must be developed and evaluated. The term "criterion of ultimate functioning" has been used to refer to this principle. Brown, Nietupski, and Hamre-Nietupski (1976) defined this principle as referring to: "the ever changing, expanding, localized, and personalized cluster of factors that each person must possess in order to function as productively and independently as possible in socially, vocationally, and domestically integrated adult community environments" (p. 8).

Approaches to designing and evaluating programs and services logically should vary based upon chronological age. Therefore, aspects of programs and services related to preschool and early elementary years, school years, and post-school years will be reviewed individually later in this chapter. There are, however, several quality indicators that should be evident in any comprehensive service delivery model. These indicators relate to both the criterion of ultimate functioning and the typical learning and performance characteristics reviewed earlier. Some of these major quality indicators (listed below) have been identified, exemplified, and emphasized widely in the literature (Certo, Haring, & York, 1984; Donnellan et al., 1980; Laski, 1979; Sailor & Guess, 1983; Snell, 1982) and have served as the basis for curriculum guides, preservice and inservice texts and coursework, research studies, IEP development, and right to education court cases. Thus, as acknowledged by increasing numbers of service providers, parents, and other advocates, these indicators represent current legal and professional opinion of minimal criteria for quality programming. The nonexhaustive listing of quality indicators that should be evident in a comprehensive service delivery model for individuals with severe handicaps includes:

1. functionality
2. chronological age-appropriateness
3. partial participation
4. individualized adaptations
5. coordinated, comprehensive, and future-oriented services
6. interactions with nonhandicapped peers
7. systematic instruction
8. home-school cooperation
9. instruction and assessment in a variety of environments

Each of the characteristics is further described below prior to a description of curriculum development approaches and their uses at different age levels.

Functionality.   Services provided must be functional. Functionality implies that services must be related to teaching, preparing, and otherwise enhancing the acquisition and utilization of useful, meaningful skills. That is, if the student does not perform these skills, someone else would need to perform them for the student. Performing these skills results in increased, meaningful participation in normal nonclassroom activities appropriate to his or her age. Since students with severe handicaps are typically capable of learning less in a given period of time than their peers, and take more direct instructional trials to learn, it should be obvious that service providers must use resources and instructional time wisely by teaching useful, meaningful skills as early as possible (Nisbet et al., 1982).

Chronological Age-Appropriateness.

Services provided must be chronologically age-appropriate. The skills severely handicapped students have mastered are likely to be substantially different from those of nonhandicapped peers of the same age. As a result, individuals with severe handicaps are often provided programs, services, curricula, materials, and interactions appropriate for considerably younger nonhandicapped children (Baumgart et al., 1982). This approach becomes less acceptable and eventually intolerable as students become adolescents and young adults. This practice has perpetuated the perception of individuals with handicaps as "eternal children" (Wolfensberger, 1972). Relating to individuals as eternal children systematically thwarts efforts to prepare them to interact and function alongside their peers as adults. That is, unless chronological age is used as a basis for program development, the delivery of instruction is likely to be nonfunctional, artificial, and inappropriate (Brown et al., 1979).

Partial Participation.

Baumgart and others (1982) define partial participation as an affirmation of the fact that it is possible to teach students skills and provide opportunities to participate in activities and environments from which they are not excluded. The reader should think about the differences between a goal of total independence for an individual versus maximal participation. Many severely handicapped individuals have tremendous performance deficiencies and lack prerequisite skills typically associated with functional activities and natural environments. Therefore, instructional design must include strategies which facilitate or allow the participation of an otherwise excluded child. For example, a student may be taught skills related to the following:

a. boarding a bus, even if she will probably always require assistance to manipulate the stairs;
b. paying bus fare, even if she will probably always depend on others to count out the exact amount;
c. sitting while the bus is in motion, even if her present behavior requires someone to monitor her;
d. pulling the buzzer, even if she needs to be told when to do so;
e. exiting the bus, even if she needs to be accompanied by another person to her destination.

If bus riding objectives were included in this student's program they would be oriented to increasing her participation and giving her, her family, and her service providers a transportation option. Such goals would be appropriate even if it is

A student with limited use of his hands is able to draw on a computer that is adapted with a pneumatic remote control switch.

felt the student may never have the skills to ride the bus independently. This principle of partial participation increases the likelihood that ways will be found to develop age-appropriate and functional programs for very severely involved individuals.

Individualized Adaptations. In order to compensate for substantial skill deficits and the absence of significant prerequisite skills, individualized adaptations must be designed and used. Baumgart et al. (1982) provide a detailed discussion of adaptations in the form of physical assistance, materials, devices, skill sequences, physical environments, traditional rules and policies, and attitudes. New developments in this area will make the habilitative prognoses of individuals with severe and multiple handicaps virtually limitless. The following examples of some of the different types of individualized adaptations are provided by Baumgart et al. (1982):

   a. Personal Assistance: . . . *a job at the supply center of a large general hospital consists of opening perforated boxes of bandages and dumping them onto a supply tray. Matt, who is 17, totally deaf, totally blind, and severely intellectually handicapped, is able to perform many of the skills required by the job.*

However, Matt is currently not able to locate or set up the materials and probably will not acquire these skills. It is unacceptable to exclude him from this job without considering personal assistance adaptations. Instructional personnel could locate the materials and set up the work area during training, and the noninstructional personnel typically present can be taught to locate and set up the materials. (p. 21)

b. Materials and Devices: *Examples of such materials and devices include wheelchairs, hearing aids, orthopedic braces, nonverbal communication systems, and adapted eating utensils. Often, such materials and devices can result in participation becoming both possible and practical. An electric wheelchair that allows a student to ambulate at rates and distances not previously possible and an enlarged portable switch to activate a record player, tape recorder, television set, and/or a blender are but a few examples.* (p. 21)

c. Skill Sequence Adaptations: *. . . most persons lower their pants before sitting on a toilet. For a student with severe motoric and balancing difficulties, it may be more efficient to sit on the commode first and, when in a more stable position, lower his pants.* (p. 21)

Coordinated, Comprehensive, and Future-Oriented Services.   Given the diversity of needs, individuals with severe handicaps typically require access to a network of professional support services throughout their lives. Since these individuals often have problems synthesizing skills learned at different times, isolated therapy approaches are being widely criticized. Instead, approaches which coordinate the expertise and services provided by professionals from different disciplines are being developed (Sternat, Messina, Nietupski, Lyon, & Brown, 1977). Bricker (1976) suggested that one of the roles of the teacher is to act as the educational synthesizer within these transdisciplinary models. Each service provider must facilitate smooth transitions from one environment and/or activity to the next regardless of the instructor(s) and discipline(s) involved and should directly relate to the demands of the current as well as future needs of the student. In addition to teaching a student skills to participate more effectively in environments and activities in which he or she currently functions, service providers must be constantly preparing individuals to function in environments and activities in which they will function in the future. One of the greatest challenges currently facing service providers is assuring an individual's smooth transition from current to subsequent environments and services (Brown et al., 1981). Brown et al. (1982) emphasized the need for current service providers (the senders) and future service providers (the receivers) to jointly design and implement these transition plans. Not only should transition planning be evident in IEP goals and objectives but the critical longitudinal role of parents and families in this process cannot be overstated.

Interactions with Nonhandicapped Peers.   The purpose and positive benefits of social interaction have already been stressed in this chapter. Voeltz, Johnson, and McQuarter (1983) provided a comprehensive review of research and an annotated bibliography related to the integration of school-age children and youth with severe disabilities. Certo, Haring, and York (1984) edited a comprehensive text presenting critical programmatic and administrative issues also related to this topic.

Systematic Instruction.
In order to teach students new skills and evaluate the effectiveness of instruction, educators and other service providers must be powerful technicians (Gold, 1980). Service providers working with this population must be afforded preservice, inservice, and other professional growth experiences which build and improve their competency in using skills and principles associated with learning, behavior, and task analysis.

Home and School Cooperation.
The importance of the home-school partnership has been emphasized throughout this chapter and the text. The curriculum development strategies now being used by educators and other service providers have been developed to facilitate a cooperative relationship between school and home. In addition, it must be emphasized that physical distance creates barriers to home/school cooperation. Long bus rides create distance and cost money. For these reasons, advocates now stress that programs be located in facilities and community environments as close to home as possible.

Instruction and Assessment in Variety of Environments.
Most severely handicapped students have trouble generalizing, transferring, and performing skills in integrated community environments (Warren, Rogers-Warren, Baer, & Guess, 1980). It is now recognized that a significant portion of instructional time should be spent teaching and assessing skills where they are expected to be performed. Increasing numbers of service providers are realizing that the community is an ideal classroom and are allocating resources for instruction in the community in spite of issues concerning insurance and liability for community programming.

Approaches to Curriculum Development

The effectiveness of intervention programs should be determined by systematic evaluation of the results, or outcomes, of the program. Specifically, program evaluation should describe how an individual has benefitted from the intervention. Therefore, before ascribing to a specific intervention approach, it is important to establish criteria that will be used as a basis for program evaluation. It has already been suggested that the criterion of ultimate functioning (Brown, Hamre-Nietupski, Pumpian, Certo, & Gruenewald, 1976) serves this function. Furthermore, quality indicators which can be associated with these criteria have also been delineated. With these criteria and qualities in mind, a critical review of the three major approaches used to generate curricula and associated educational experiences can be conducted.

Certainly there are more than three approaches to curriculum development and none need be mutually exclusive of the other. Here, the developmental, remedial education, and community-referenced functional approaches will be discussed in detail.

The Developmental Model.

Many programs, services, and instructional sequences have been determined by and drawn from observations of normal infant and child development. These observations have been used to generate standardized assessments and have been presented in the form of checklists, tests, and scales. These assessments represent "slices" of average development across a number of dimensions such as self-help, motor, socialization, communication, and cognition (Sailor & Guess, 1983). The findings from these assessments then serve as the source of instructional objectives.

Although the model has an important function in preschool and early elementary years, its exclusive use can no longer be considered appropriate for older students and adults (Wilcox & Bellamy, 1982; Sailor & Guess, 1983; Brown et al., 1976; Snell, 1982) since it focuses on the milestones of early development such as social, motor, language, etc., instead of integrated, functional activities; it is based on prerequisite skills which severely handicapped students may never attain; it includes skills which are not functional in daily use, such as stacking blocks; and it tends to overlook the student's chronological age.

In summary, the developmental approach was used as the basis of developing special educational services. Its use continues to be an appropriate tool with young children but can no longer be considered acceptable as the major approach with older children, adolescents, and adults. Sailor and Guess (1983) conclude:

> . . . the field of education for severely handicapped students is far from any stage of development that would benefit from standardized, general curricula. The individualization that accrues to a teacher-generated curriculum appropriate for each student in an educational program is currently worth ten published curricula and this state of affairs is not likely to change for some years. (p. 135)

The Remedial Education Model.

The remedial academic approach is similar to the developmental approach in that it concentrates on traditional academic skill building (Wilcox & Bellamy, 1982). This skill building often relates to the "basic skills" or "3 R's." Depending on student abilities, curricular content is usually limited to early academic and preacademic instruction which has translated into teaching students number, color, and shape recognition regardless of their chronological age (Brown, Scheuerman, Cartwright, & York, 1973). In this approach, teenagers might spend instructional time using manipulative preschool toys to teach basic concepts, reading preprimers, and touching circles, squares, and red and blue blocks on command (Writer, 1981).

Although academic instruction should be an integral component of most severely handicapped students' instructional programs, providers must be careful that the instructional approach does not result in the same shortcomings typical of other developmentally sequenced curricula. Specifically, attention must be given to chronological age and functional applications. For example, Wilcox and Bellamy (1982) contrasted a traditional timetelling objective, i.e., counting by fives to 55, vs. time management strategies which require secondary age students to match-to-sample a clock, a picture of a clock, and a picture designating the time to perform an activity (Carney, Menchetti, & Orelove, 1977). Thus, as a student becomes older, concentration must shift away from traditional academic curricula to a curriculum which teaches and/or provides the opportunity for functional applications of academic skills. Unfortunately, a curriculum based on academic instruction is typically sequenced too rigidly to allow for such applications and instead results in adults learning their ABC's and learning to read "See Spot run." Since students with severe handicaps are those who will not be adequately prepared for life if merely afforded a remedial academic program (Wilcox & Bellamy, 1982), academic instruction should be used to functionally supplement and enhance the student's individualized educational program.

The Community-Referenced Functional Model.

Thus far, we have rejected reliance upon a developmental curriculum and the remedial academic curriculum. Brown et al. (1976) presented an alternate approach to curricular development described as the community-referenced curriculum (Snell, 1982), based on the demands of adult life (Wilcox & Bellamy, 1982), current and subsequent needs, and individualized critical skills (Sailor & Guess, 1983).

Unlike the previously described approaches, community-referenced functional approaches require an analysis of the student's skills compared with the actual demands of desired environments. Curriculum development is based upon analyses of the discrepancies between the students' present abilities and those required in the environments in which they now function and/or will function in the future.

Sailor and Guess (1983) identified this as a mismatch/match model which analyzes the student's current abilities to function in the world at large. Matches or student skills are identified and used as the bases for strengthening a student's independence and areas of mismatch are used as the bases for generating instructional objectives. Mismatches are broken down into two groups: First, skills which the students do not demonstrate but appear ready to learn are identified. Second, skills that students probably cannot acquire are identified so that individualized adaptations can be developed to compensate for skill deficits.

Curricular content is generated by assessing the student and the actual environment in which he or she will be expected to function. Falvey, Brown, Lyon, Baumgart, and Schroeder (1980) defined ecological inventories as the process used to collect information about environments of concern.

Brown, Falvey, et al. (1979) suggested a six-phase process for developing individualized instructional programs based on the community-referenced approach. Pumpian et al. (in press) presented a seven-phase modification of that process. The reader is cautioned not to conceptualize the seven phases as a rigid vertical hierarchy of activities; each represents activities which should be ongoing and overlapping.

I. A Functional Curriculum Domain Organization
II. A Family Inventory
III. A Lifespace Student Profile Inventory
IV. Ecological Inventories
V. Prioritization Strategies
VI. Functional Student Assessment Strategies
VII. Design in Instructional Programs

Since the community-referenced approach uses strategies most appropriate for school-age, severely handicapped students, each of the seven phases delineated above will be described in the "Intervention During the School Years" section of this chapter.

Intervention at the Preschool and Early Elementary Years

If society is willing to allocate services to very young children and their families, if service providers are willing to work in coordinated and complementary ways, if the meaningful involvement of families is secured, and if critical services are afforded an individual throughout his or her lifespan, the severity and multiplicity of an individual's handicap(s) can be significantly ameliorated. Young, severely handicapped children can learn many skills in areas such as interaction, functional object use, motor, cognitive, and self-help domains. The involvement of a transdisciplinary intervention team will not only facilitate the development of these skills, but also reduce the likelihood of learning maladaptive behaviors and developing secondary handicaps from lack of stimulation, movement, and interaction.

Sailor and Guess (1983) thoroughly reviewed the nature and advantages of the transdisciplinary approach as an attempt to provide a coordinated model for working with children with severe handicaps. The approach is consistent with current understanding of learning theory and the learning characteristics commonly associated with this group. Conner, Williamson, and Siepp (1975) recognized this in the following excerpt:

> Just as human development is the coordination and integration of a variety of physical, mental, emotional, and social processes, so must intervention to aid that development be a coordinated and integrated effort.   (p. 273)

The major curricular approach used in preschool is typically based on the developmental model. At this age the model tends to represent age-appropriate skill development. Curricula are commonly organized into gross motor, fine motor, communication, social, self-help, and cognitive domains. However, there is a need to provide variations within the normal developmental curricula (Sailor & Guess, 1983). For example, activities which incorporate and integrate objectives from several skill domains need to be incorporated into the curriculum and early interventionists need to further sequence and task analyze activities (Connor et al., 1975). Vincent et al. (1980) also stressed the need to further individualize, modify, and supplement early intervention programs with skills and services that directly prepare children for their next educational program. Finally, it should be clear that even at this age service providers must develop interventions which are designed to improve each child's performance with his or her family in both the home and community at large. Thus, ecological inventories of the environments and activities in which young children function should be used to impact the early intervention program.

Interventions During the School Years

As previously mentioned, students with severe handicaps should be afforded services which maximize their performance in a wide range of natural environments. The community-referenced functional approach has been described as representing activities directly related to this type of preparation. A seven-phase process (Pumpian et al. in press) was delineated which utilizes this approach. Each of these phases is described below.

Phase I: A Functional Curriculum Domain Organization.

Although motor, cognitive, social, self-help, academic, compliance, etc., skills are critical for functioning in most activities, the organization of curricula under those domains has led to curricula which are fragmented, age inappropriate and primarily concerned with prerequisite skill development (Baumgart et al., 1982). In order to identify and organize these skills in a manner which directly results in functional skill instruction, Brown et al. (1979) proposed utilizing life space domains to develop individual program and service plans for older children, adolescents, and young adults. The four life space curricular domains suggested are the domestic domain, the vocational domain, the recreational/leisure domain, and the general community functioning stores and services domain. These life space domains have been suggested in order to increase the likelihood that service providers address the comprehensive life space needs of each severely handicapped individual. The organization of curricular content within these domains also increases the likelihood that instruction will directly prepare each individual for maximal participation in the environments and activities in which his or her nonhandicapped peers live, work, play, and otherwise function.

Phase II: Parent/Guardian and Family Inventories.

Many strategies and formats are being developed in order to secure critical involvement or/and information from parents/guardians and other family members in curriculum development.

The State of California Severely Handicapped Teacher Training Resource Network has developed some exceptional formats for soliciting and documenting these kinds of information from families. Figure 5.1 provides an example of a completed set of forms a teacher might use to collect basic information about what a student currently does outside of school hours.

Figure 5.1

PARENT INVENTORY

Student: _P.H._   D.O.B.: _February 3, 1969_

Address: _4531 Bond Street San Diego, CA 92115_

Parent/Care Provider: _Patti -- mother_

Telephone: (home) _619 265-6630_   (work) _619 243-1210_

Interviewer: _Holly Shepard_   Interview Date: _December 17, 1986_

1. Where are some of the places you take _P.H._ in the community?
   Ralph's, Target, Bank, Park

2. How does _P.H._ participate?
   just follows along with me (mother) at the park, she swings.

3. Are there any behaviors that bother you or others?
   biting her hand when frustrated playing with shoes.

3a. What do you do when this happens?
   biting - sign no and take away hand from mouth, shoes - take away shoes.

4. What are things _P.H._ enjoys?
   rocking chair little children going places.

4a. What are things _P.H._ does not enjoy?
   having her hair washed.

5. How does _P.H._ communicate at home?
   We will use signs or pictures with her. She will usually lead us to something if she wants it. Very limited communication.

6. What type of toileting schedule is _P.H._ on?
   2 hour -- habit trained

7. How does _P.H._ get along with brother(s) and sister(s)?
   loves to be around brother; likes to go places with him.

8. Does _P.H._ have any chores to do around the house?
   clears table after dinner.

9. Are there any medical considerations?
   deaf (profoundly deaf) 2 hearing aids

10. Is there any information regarding _P.H._ that we have not talked about?
   Very frustrated with the lack of communication. Concerned with what would be available for P.H. when she leaves public school.

Figure 5.1 (continued)

AFTER SCHOOL ACTIVITY FORM

Week Day (e.g., Monday) _____

Time

3:00 PM   Where _bathroom_
              What _uses restroom_
              With Whom _Mom takes her to bathroom_

4:00 PM   Where _Backyard_
              What _watches kids play outside (neighbors)_
              With Whom _alone_

5:00 PM   Where _livingroom_
              What _watch T.V._
              With Whom _alone, sometimes with brother_

6:00 PM   Where _kitchen_
              What _dinner_
              With Whom _Mom and brother and sister_

7:00 PM   Where _bathroom_
              What _takes bath_
              With Whom _Mom or sister helps with bath_

8:00 PM   Where _bedroom_
              What _plays with toys_
              With Whom _by self_

9:00 PM   Where _bedroom_
               What _goes to sleep_
              With Whom _alone -- own room_

Phase III: A Functional Student Profile. Conducting and updating a life space student profile represents an attempt to succinctly present information regarding a student's current skill development and the environments and activities in which that student currently functions. This information is available from several sources including: the student's cumulative educational record, family interview inventories, current environments being used for instruction, and past service providers. The profile is used to further prioritize and communicate areas relevant for instructional concern and develop a functional relationship between instruction in basic skill areas (e.g., reading) and environments where these skills will be used (e.g., restaurant). Figure 5.2 provides an example of a guide, developed by Brown, Shiraga, York, Zanella, & Rogan (1984) that a teacher might use to assist in constructing a student profile.

Figure 5.2

STUDENT PROFILE GUIDE (*Not* a Working Form)

1. PERSONAL STATUS

   Name: _____ S.S.#: _____

   D.O.B.: _____ C.A.: _____

   School: _____ Date of placement: _____

   Years left in placement: _____ In school: _____

   Address: _____

   Names of parents/guardians: _____

   Others at same address, including:

   Name: _____ Age: _____ Relationship: _____

   _____   _____   _____

   _____   _____   _____

   a. Educational History

       School and City: _____ Dates: _____

       _____   _____

   b. General Health and Medical Information (Historical as pertinent)

       Allergies: _____

       Activity restrictions: _____

       Medications and Reasons: _____

       Surgery: _____

       Others: _____

       _____

2. SKILLS INTEGRATED ACROSS DOMAINS

   a. Motor Skill Information _____

   b. Sensory Skill Information _____

   c. Communication Skill Information _____

   d. Social Skill Information _____

   e. Reading Skill Information _____

   f. Money Handling Skill Information _____

   g. Time Skill Information _____

3. LEARNING STYLE/CHARACTERISTICS

4. BEHAVIOR CHARACTERISTICS

5. DOMESTIC FUNCTIONING

   a. Personal Care/Grooming _____

   b. Housekeeping _____

   c. Meal Planning and Preparation _____

   d. Clothing Care _____

   e. Other Domestic Functioning Information _____

Figure 5.2 (continued)

6. RECREATION/LEISURE FUNCTIONING

  a. Home/Neighborhood

    1. With others _____

    2. Alone _____

  b. Community

    1. With others _____

    2. Alone _____

  c. School

    1. With others _____

    2. Alone _____

  d. Other Recreation/Leisure Functioning
    Information _____

7. COMMUNITY FUNCTIONING

  a. Outdoor Safety _____

  b. Mobility _____

  c. Shopping _____

  d. Restaurant Utilization _____

  e. Other Community Functioning Information _____

8. VOCATIONAL FUNCTIONING

  a. Training History (including dates, environments, primary activities) _____

  b. Current Training Site and Performance _____

  c. Other Vocational Functioning Information _____

9. OTHER

Source: From L. Brown, B. Shiraga, J. York, K. Zannella, & P. Rogan (1984). *Curriculum Outline.* Unpublished manuscript, University of Wisconsin-Madison. Reprinted with permission.

Phase IV: Ecological Inventories. As previously reviewed, strategies for conducting ecological inventories refer to actions service providers take to gain critical information about the environments and activities in which students do or may function. Ecological inventories are conducted within each curricular domain. For example, in the recreation/leisure domain, information about environments and activities in which the student, his or her family and his or her peers use for recreation would be delineated. Basically, an ecological inventory consists of:

  1. delineating a relevant environment;
  2. describing the physical layout such as the rooms, areas called subenvironments;

Figure 5.3

ECOLOGICAL INVENTORY

Environment _Bowling Alley - Pioneer Lanes_

Subenvironment _Cashier area._

Activity _get bowling lane and shoes_

Skill Clusters: 1. _ask clerk for available lane_

    2. _ask for shoes_

    3. _go to correct lane_

Activity _pay for bowling_

Skill Clusters: 1. _finish game - go to cashier_

    2. _return shoes_

    3. _pay for game - leave_

Subenvironment _bowling lane area_

Activity _locating a bowling ball_

Skill Clusters: 1. _go to ball racks_

    2. _find correct size ball_

    3. _take ball to lane_

Activity _bowling_

Skill Clusters: 1. _go to ball holder when it's your turn_

    2. _pick up ball and bowl two frames_

    3. _check score and wait for next turn_

3. delineating major age-appropriate activities and activity sequences which occur there;
4. developing a detailed sequential skill (or task) analysis of the activities that are being considered for instructional purposes.

Figure 5.3 provides a partial example of a simple ecological inventory conducted at a particular bowling alley. The inventory was conducted in order to provide a basic listing of skills performed in the different areas of the bowling alley.

Phase V: Prioritization Strategies.   Many dimensions have been suggested as ways to prioritize what content to include on a student's individual educational plan. The reader is referred back to the quality indicators presented earlier in this chapter. Brown et al. (1979) delineated 18 priorization dimensions which included parental and student preferences, social significance, functionality, and chronological age-appropriateness.

Phase VI: Student Assessment Strategies. After specific environments and activities have been prioritized for a student in each domain, his or her skills and skill deficiencies can be identified by comparing his or her performance directly to the nonhandicapped person ecological inventories. Thus the ecological inventories become a criterion-referenced assessment tool. The discrepancies in performance between the student and the nonhandicapped person inventory should lead directly to designing individualized program objectives, and associated instructional approaches and individualized adaptations, which are presumed to allow and enhance participation. Figure 5.4 provides an example of a completed form a teacher used to assess a student's current grocery shopping skills and to generate adaptation and teaching ideas.

Phase VII: Designing Instructional Progress. After inventories of normalized community environments have been made and organized, family input has been secured, content has been prioritized, and the present level of performance of the student has been assessed, an individualized instructional program must be designed to teach the student the skills to function in the environments and activities of concern.

After initiating the seven-phase process delineated above for each student, the intervention team can then begin to organize staff resources and schedule students together who have priorities in the same environments and activities.

Programming Over the Lifespan

Individuals with severe, multiple handicaps will most likely require some degree of direct support services provided throughout their lives. There will always be a need to consider support services relative to home, work, recreation, and general functioning. There will most likely be a continuing need for individuals from various disciplines to jointly identify and plan for the provision of necessary services.

This chapter has stressed the responsibilities service providers have during school years to prepare individuals with severe handicaps to function in a wide range of integrated environments. In order for these youth to truly benefit from these preparatory services and experiences, it is equally important to stress the need for developing community support systems to maintain and enrich their lives as adults (Sailor & Guess, 1983).

Systems and options are necessary to provide a range of normalized domestic living options. Institutional placements of adults are an indication of insufficient community alternatives. Intagliata, Wilder, and Cooley (1979) reported that various kinds of community living arrangements were all significantly less expensive than institutional placements. There are a variety, rather than a finite set, of existing and potential kinds of alternative community living arrangements which may be appropriate for particular individuals in particular communities (Skarnulis, 1976). Sailor and Guess (1983) provided a listing and description of possibilities which included natural family homes, foster homes, group homes,

Figure 5.4

INSTRUCTIONAL PLANNING FORM

Student: _P.H._

Environment: _Ralph's Superstore_ Date: _9-17-86_

Major Activity (or Activity Sequence) under consideration:

buying an item at the store

Submitted by: _Holly Shepard_ Date: _9-27-86_

Independent (I) Indirect Verbal (IV) Gesture (G) Direct Verbal (DV) Model (M) Physical Prompt (PP)

Nonhandicapped Person Inventory	Discrepancy Analysis for _____ Student/Date	Adaptation/Hypotheses and other comments
Subenvironment: _shopping aisle/cashier_		
Skill Cluster #_1_		
Skill 1. _read list_	_DV_	_use pictures of actual items for list (e.g. use a coupon of the item)_
2. _go to correct aisle_	_DV_	_direct instruction in store, practice with a model layout at school_
3. _locate item_	_G_	_direct instruction in store, and in class (practice)_
4. _pick-up item_	_PP_	_direct instruction in store, and in class (practice)_
5. _put in cart_	_I_	_independent_
6. _go to cashier_	_DV_	_direct instruction in store_
Subenvironment: _same_		
Skill Cluster #_2_		
Skill 1. _locate cashier_	_DV_	_direct instruction in store_
2. _wait in line_	_IV_	_direct instruction in store_
3. _locate seperator bar_	_G_	_direct instruction in store_
4. _put bar on counter_	_G_	_direct instruction in store_
5. _take item(s) from cart_	_G_	_direct instruction in store_
6. _put item(s) on counter_	_G_	_direct instruction in store_
7. _push cart forward_	_PP_	_direct instruction in store_
8. _get out wallet_	_PP_	_new wallet with easier opening (zipper)_
9. _pay when given cue_	_PP_	_predetermined amount of money_
10. _take change, leave_	_DV_	_direct instruction in store, and classroom_

clustered apartments and duplexes, and staffed apartments. It should be clear that in any of these situations the unique physical, medical, behavioral, and other social needs of each individual must be identified. Then formal and informal support systems and services must be designed to ensure a quality of home life.

It has also been stressed in this chapter that the preparatory services provided during the school years include vocational training. In fact, as the adolescent individual gets closer to leaving public school more and more of his or her instructional day should focus on vocational preparation. In the past, vocational preparation and placement was rarely considered a priority, if considered at all. However, recent changes in attitudes, program goals, and associated instructional approaches have resulted from numerous demonstrations of vocational potential existing within this population. These demonstrations have not only proved that adults with severe handicaps can perform complex vocational tasks but are also able to perform those tasks at production levels which justify remuneration. Furthermore, demonstrations have not only proven that it is viable and advantageous to provide job placements in actual integrated community businesses but also that such a service delivery system is more cost efficient than training and maintaining these persons in segregated "activity centers" and "workshops for the handicapped."

The development of normalized work opportunities will provide a better context for developing appropriate living and recreational opportunities for adults with severe handicaps. As previously mentioned, there is a recognized need to develop and improve transition plans between school and postschool agencies. The more these plans focus on the smooth transition from school to a wide range of normalized adult environments, the greater the likelihood that adults with severe handicaps will have the support and training necessary to function in those integrated environments.

FUTURE PERSPECTIVES FOR THE TREATMENT OF SEVERE MULTIPLE HANDICAPS

The provision of quality services to persons with severe handicaps has always depended upon a coordinated relationship between advocacy, demonstration, and research efforts. It appears that an optimistic perspective for the future depends upon all of these efforts continuing in a coordinated manner. Advocates, researchers, and exemplary service providers must continue to keep both progress and obstacles in the foreground of professional and public attention. This will serve as the primary vehicle for the administration of programs and services based on best existing technological advances and practices. Successful integration of individuals with severe handicaps into schools, neighborhoods, workplaces, and communities will require continued quality preservice, inservice, and direct service activities.

Research and demonstrations and replications of innovative services will continue to focus on the theoretical and practical issues and problems to be solved

Community Integration

In many communities, it is not unusual to see people with severe handicaps out in the community—at the shopping center, at movie theaters, grocery stores, church services, in neighborhood schools, and on the job. Individuals who were once institutionalized for life are now participating in the mainstream of society with the help of new legislation, changing attitudes, technological advances, and people who care. Perhaps the most significant change in services for persons with severe, multiple handicaps has been their integration in recent years as well as the increased opportunities and acceptance from their nonhandicapped peers.

in meeting educational and related service needs. There will continue to be a need to produce and document sets of validated interventions related to these solutions. Funding and creative regulation for these program activities and services will continue to be the shared responsibility of local, state and federal agencies. Priorities will continue to focus upon the development and interrelationship between the following:

1. transition of severely handicapped children from restrictive to normalized school, living, and other environments;
2. transition of severely handicapped adolescents from educational settings to integrated work environments;
3. development of early intervention service networks;
4. development of supportive adult services networks;
5. development and functional application of communication, social, cognitive, and psychomotor skills;
6. generalization of learned skills to various natural environments;
7. continued preparation and training of educators, therapists, counselors, administrators, parents, and other professionals and paraprofessionals;
8. applications of high technology;
9. advances in prevention and medical treatment and support.

If progress continues to be made in the areas listed above, parents, service providers, and individuals with severe handicaps should be able to look to the future with optimism. However, all concerned must realize the need to concentrate on both technological as well as attitudinal advances. Research and demonstrations of important technological advances must also relate to educating and involving society as a whole. With the commitment of society and its vast resources and the creativity of families and service providers, increasing numbers of individuals with severe handicaps will have these benefits in the future:

1. live in homes and apartments throughout our communities;
2. receive educational and other habilitative services at birth and throughout their lives;
3. attend school with their nonhandicapped age peers;
4. be afforded functional and chronological age-appropriate curricula;
5. successfully make transitions from school to a variety of normalized environments in which they will work, play, live, and otherwise function alongside their nonhandicapped peers;
6. be recognized, accepted, tolerated, and supported as productive, integral members of their communities regardless of the severity of their handicaps, and regardless of their geographic residence.

SUMMARY

Individuals with severe handicaps are those whose disability has a major impact on all aspects of their functioning throughout the lifespan. In many instances, individuals with severe handicaps have more than one disability; thus, they are described as multiply handicapped. For example, in addition to limited movement the individual may also be unable to speak; or a person may be both deaf and blind. Because of the diversity of handicapping conditions, diagnostic categories, functioning levels, and social behavior included within the category of severe handicaps, the differences among individuals can be greater than their similarities. Although mental retardation is the most common single characteristic among severely handicapped individuals, not all persons classified as severely handicapped are mentally retarded.

The range and intensity of services needed by most severely handicapped individuals is extensive. Most need specialized educational, medical, social, and community services throughout their lives. In the past, these services were typically offered in segregated facilities—schools for handicapped children, institutions, sheltered workshops, and even hospitals built only for handicapped people. However, with changes in legislation, public policy, and the attitudes of the general public, severely handicapped people are far less segregated. The trend is for severely handicapped people to live with their family or in a small group home in their home community, to be educated in public schools, to participate in community services, events, and recreation programs, and to work at some job with training and support.

Severe handicaps can be caused by a single factor or multiple factors. Although etiological research has determined the cause of some severely handicapping conditions, the majority of causes are still unknown. Continued research in this area is critical since prevention efforts can begin only after the cause is known.

Severely handicapped individuals are characterized by limitations in how much and how quickly they learn, difficulty in generalizing what they have learned from one setting to another, poor retention, and limited ability to synthesize skills and generate new skills. But despite the limitations imposed by severe, multiple handicaps, severely handicapped individuals grow and learn.

A recent emphasis on functional curriculum, prosthetic devices, technology, and applied behavioral analysis techniques has enabled many severely handicapped people to increase their skills and independence. School curricula now incorporate the skills and behaviors that will help severely handicapped students to function more independently and effectively in their current or future environments. Students are encouraged to participate as fully as possible in the routines of daily living, and technology such as adapted switches and speech synthesizers are used to compensate for skills the individual does not have.

Services for severely handicapped individuals have changed more in the past decade than those provided to any other group of handicapped people. A philosophy of integration has replaced one of segregation; and medical, behavioral, and educational technologies have enabled even the most severely handicapped individuals to acquire new skills. These changes have had profound effects on severely handicapped individuals, their families, and the people who live and work with them in the community.

References

Abroms, K., & Bennett, J. (1983). Current findings in Down Syndrome. *Exceptional Children, 49,* 449–450.

Agrin, P. (1982). *Motor vehicle occupant injuries to children: Final report.* Office of Traffic Safety Public Policy Research, University of California, Irvine.

Baumgart, D., Brown, L., Pumpian, I., Nisbet, J., Ford, A., Sweet, M., Messina, R., & Schroeder, J. (1982). Principle of partial participation and individualized adaptations. *The Journal of the Association for the Severely Handicapped, 7* (2), 17–22.

Bellamy, G. T., Rhodes, L. E., Bourbeau, P. E., & Mank, D. M. (1982). *Mental retardation services in sheltered workshops and day activity programs: Consumer outcomes and policy alternatives.* Eugene, OR: Center on Human Development.

Berkson, G., & Davenport, R. K. (1962). Stereotyped movements in mental defectives: I. Initial survey. *American Journal of Mental Deficiency, 66,* 849–852.

Bleck, E. E., (1982). Myelomeningocele, meningocele, and spina bifida. In E. E. Bleck & D. A. Nagel (Eds.), *Physically handicapped children, a medical atlas for teachers* (pp. 345–362). New York: Grune & Stratton.

Bricker, D. (1976). Educational synthesizer. In M. A. Thomas (Ed.), *Hey, don't forget about me!* (pp. 84–97). Reston, VA: The Council for Exceptional Children.

Brown, L., Falvey, M., Vincent, L., Kaye, N., Johnson, F., Ferrara-Parrish, P., & Gruenewald, L. (1979). Strategies for generating longitudinal and age appropriate individual educational plans. In L. Brown, M. Falvey, D. Baumgart, I. Pumpian, J. Schroeder, and L. Gruenewald (Eds.), *Strategies for teaching chronological age appropriate and functional skills to adolescent and young adult severely handicapped students* (Vol. IX, Pt. 1, pp. 30–60). Madison, WI: Madison Metropolitan School District.

Brown, L., Ford, A., Nisbet, J., Sweet, M., Donnellan, A., & Gruenewald, L. (1983). Opportunities available when severely handicapped students attend chronological age appropriate regular schools. *The Journal of the Association for the Severely Handicapped, 8* (1), 16–24.

Brown, L., Hamre-Nietupski, S., Pumpian, I., Certo, N., & Gruenewald, L. (1979). A strategy for developing chronological age-appropriate and functional curricular content for severely handicapped adolescents and young adults. *Journal of Special Education, 13,* 180–190.

Brown, L., Nietupski, J., & Hamre-Nietupski, S. (1976). Criterion of ultimate functioning. In M. A. Thomas (Ed.), *Hey, don't forget about me!* (pp. 2–15). Reston, VA: The Council for Exceptional Children.

Brown, L., Pumpian, I., Baumgart, D., Van Deventer, P., Ford, A., Nisbet, J., Shroeder, J., & Gruenewald, L. (1981). Longitudinal transition plans in programs for severely handicapped students. *Exceptional Children, 47,* 624–630.

Brown, L., Scheuerman, N., Cartwright, S., & York, R. (1973). *The design and implementation of an empirically based instructional program for young severely handicapped students.* Madison, WI: Madison Metropolitan School District.

Brown, L., Shiraga, B., Ford, A., Nisbet, S., Van Deventer, P., Sweet, M., York, J., & Loomis, R. (1983). Teaching severely handicapped students to perform meaningful work in nonsheltered vocational environments. In L. Brown, A. Ford, J. Nisbet, M. Sweet, B. Shiraga, J. York, R. Loomis, & P. Van Deventer (Eds.), *Educational programs for severely handicapped students* (pp. 1–100). Madison: University of Wisconsin and Madison Metropolitan School District.

Brown, L., Shiraga, B., York, J., Zannella, K., & Rogan, P. (1984). *Curriculum outline.* Unpublished manuscript, University of Wisconsin, Madison.

Carney, I. H., Menchetti, B. M., & Orelove, F. P. (1977). Community transportation: Teaching moderately handicapped adults to ride the Champaign-Urbana Mass Transit System. In B. Wilcox, F. Kohl, & T. Vogelsberg (Eds.), *The severely and profoundly handicapped child: Proceedings from the 1977 Statewide Institute* (pp. 160–173). Springfield, IL: State Board of Education.

Certo, N., Haring, N., & York, R. (Eds.) (1984). *Public school integration of severely handicapped student: Rational issues and progressive alternatives.* Baltimore: Paul H. Brookes.

Certo, N., & Kohl, F. (1983). A strategy for developing interpersonal interaction instructional content for severely handicapped students. In N. Certo, N. Haring, & R. York (Eds.), *Public school integration of severely handicapped students: Rational issues and progressive alternatives* (pp. 221–244). Baltimore: Paul H. Brookes.

Christianson, J. (1980). *Education and psychological problems of abused children.* Saratoga, CA: Century Twenty-One Publishing Company.

Christoph, D., Nietupski, J., & Pumpian, I. (1979). Teaching severely handicapped adolescents and young adults to use communication cards to make purchases at a fast food counter. In L. Brown, M. Falvey, D. Baumgart, I. Pumpian, J. Schroeder, & L. Gruenewald (Eds.), *Strategies for teaching chronological age appropriate functional skills to adolescent and young adult severely handicapped students* (Vol. IX, Pt. 1, pp. 333–386). Madison, WI: Madison Metropolitan School District.

Conner, F. P., Williamson, G. G., & Siepp, J. M. (1975). *Program guide for infants and toddlers with neuromotor and other developmental disabilities.* New York: Teachers College Press.

Coon, M., Vogelsberg, R., & Williams, W. (1981). Effects of classroom public transportation instruction on generalization to the natural environment. *Journal of the Association for the Severely Handicapped, 6,* 46–53.

Donnellan, A., Ford, A., Nisbet, N., Pumpian, I., Baumgart, D., Schroeder, J., & Brown, L. (1980). A strategy for evaluating educational programs for students with autism and other handicapping conditions. In L. Brown, M. Falvey, I. Pumpian, D. Baumgart, A.

Ford, J. Schroeder, & R. Loomis (Eds.), *Curricular strategies for teaching chronological age appropriate and functional skills* (pp. 206–272). Madison, WI: Madison Metropolitan School District.

Eyman, R. K., & Call, J. (1977). Maladaptive behavior and community placement of mentally retarded persons. *American Journal of Mental Deficiency, 76,* 692–698.

Falvey, M., Brown, L., Lyon, S., Baumgart, D., & Schroeder, J. (1980). Strategies for using cues and correction procedures. In W. Sailor, B. Wilcox, & L. Brown (Eds.), *Methods of instruction for severely handicapped students* (pp. 109–135). Baltimore: Paul H. Brookes.

Gaylord-Ross, R., Haring, N., Breen, C., & Pitts-Conway, V. (1984). The training and generalization of social interaction skills with autistic youth. *The Journal of Applied Behavior Analysis, 17,* 229–247.

Gilhool, T. K. (1976). Education: An inalienable right. In F. Weintraub, A. Abeson, J. Ballard, & M. LaVor (Eds.), *Public policy and the education of exceptional children* (pp. 14–21). Reston, VA: The Council for Exceptional Children.

Gold, M. W. (1980). *Did I say that?* Champaign, IL: Research Press Company.

Guess, D., & Horner, R. D. (1978). The severely and profoundly handicapped. In E. L. Meyen (Ed.), *Exceptional children and youth—an introduction* (pp. 218–262). Denver, CO: Love Publishing.

Guess, D., & Mulligan, M. (1982). The severely and profoundly handicapped. In E. L. Meyen (Ed.), *Exceptional children and youth* (2nd ed.) (pp. 262–300). Denver, CO: Love Publishing.

Guthrie, R. (1984). Explorations in prevention. In B. Blatt & R. J. Morris (Eds.), *Perspectives in special education: Personal orientations* (pp. 157–172). Glenview, IL: Scott, Foresman.

Guthrie, R., & Susi, A. (1963). A simple phenylalanine method for detecting phenylketonuria in large populations of newborn infants. *Pediatrics, 32,* 338–343.

Hanson, M. J. (1977). *Teaching your Down's Syndrome infant.* Baltimore: University Park Press.

Hardman, M. (1984). The role of Congress in decisions relating to the withholding of medical treatment from seriously ill newborns. *The Journal of the Association for the Severely Handicapped, 9,* 3–7.

Haring, N. G. (1978). Progress and perspectives. In N. G. Haring & D. D. Bricker (Eds.), *Teaching the severely handicapped* (Vol. III, pp. 1–7). Columbus, OH: Special Press.

Hart, V. (1977). The use of many disciplines with the severely and profoundly handicapped. In E. Sontag, J. Smith, & N. Certo (Eds.), *Educational programming for the severely and profoundly handicapped* (pp. 391–396). Reston, VA: The Council for Exceptional Children.

Horner, R. H., Sprague, J., & Wilcox, B. (1982). General case programming for community activities. In B. Wilcox & G. T. Bellamy (Eds.), *Design of high school programs for severely handicapped students* (pp. 61–98). Baltimore: Paul H. Brookes.

Intagliata, J., Wilder, B., & Cooley, F. (1979). Cost comparison of institution and community based alternatives for mentally retarded persons. *Mental Retardation, 17,* 154–156.

Justen, J. E., & Brown, G. E. (1977). Definitions of severely handicapped: A survey of state departments of education. *AAESPH Review, 2,* 8–14.

Landesman-Dwyer, S., & Schuckit, J. J. (1976). Behavioral changes in nonambulatory profoundly mentally retarded individuals. Preliminary findings of the survey of state institutions for the mentally retarded. Department of Social and Health Services, State of Washington. In C. E. Meyers (Ed.), *Quality of life in severely and profoundly mentally retarded people: Research foundations for improvement.* Washington, DC: American Association on Mental Deficiency.

Laski, F. L. (1979). Legal strategies to secure entitlement to services for severely handicapped persons. In G. T. Bellamy, G. O'Connor, & O. C. Karan (Eds.), *Vocational rehabilitation of severely handicapped persons: Contemporary service strategies* (pp. 1–32). Baltimore: University Park Press.

Lehr, D. H. (1982). Severe multiple handicaps. In E. L. Meyen (Ed.), *Exceptional children in today's schools* (pp. 455–484). Denver, CO: Love Publishing.

Lyon, S., & Lyon, S. (1980). Team functioning and staff development: A role release approach to providing integrated educational services for severely handicapped students. *Journal of the Association for the Severely Handicapped, 5,* 250–263.

Moore, B. C. (1982). Biomedical factors in mental retardation. In P. T. Cegelka & H. J. Prehm (Eds.), *Mental retardation: From categories to people* (pp. 76–103). Columbus, OH: Merrill Publishing.

Nisbet, J., Brown, L., Ford, A., Sweet, M., Shiraga, B., Johnson, F., & Loomis, R. (1982). *The critical need for nonschool instruction in education programs for severely handicapped students.* Unpublished manuscript, University of Wisconsin, Madison, and Madison Metropolitan School District.

O'Neil, C. T., & Bellamy, G. T. (1978). Evaluation of a procedure for teaching saw chain assembly to a severely retarded woman. *Mental Retardation, 16,* 37–41.

Powell, T. H., Aiken, J. M., & Smilie, M. A. (1982). Treatment or involuntary euthanasia for severely handicapped newborns: Issues of philosophy and public policy. *The Journal of the Association for the Severely Handicapped, 6,* 3–10.

President's Committee on Mental Retardation (1970). *The six-hour retarded child.* Washington, DC: U.S. Government Printing Office.

Pumpian, I., MacFarlane, L., & Kalan, D. (in press). *Functional curriculum guide for San Diego City School District.* San Diego, CA: San Diego City Schools.

Sailor, W., & Guess, D. (1983). *Severely handicapped students: An instructional design.* Boston: Houghton Mifflin.

Skarnulis, E.(1976). Less restrictive alternatives in residential services. *AAESPH Review, 1,* 40–84.

Snell, M. (1982). Characteristics, education and habilitation of the profoundly mentally retarded. In P. T. Cegelka & H. J. Prehm (Eds.), *Mental retardation: From categories to people* (pp. 291–342). Columbus, OH: Merrill Publishing.

Stainback, S., Stainback, W., Wehman, P., & Spangiers, L. (1983). Acquisition and generalization of physical fitness exercises in three profoundly retarded adults. *Journal of the Association for the Severely Handicapped, 8* (2), 47–55.

Sternat, J., Messina, R., Nietupski, J., Lyon, S., & Brown, L. (1977). Occupational and physical therapy for severely handicapped students: Toward a naturalized public school service delivery model. In E. Sontag, J. Smith, & N. Certo (Eds.), *Educational programming for the severely and profoundly handicapped* (pp. 262–278). Reston, VA: The Council for Exceptional Children.

Stokes, T. F., & Baer, D. M. (1977). An implicit technology of generalization. *Journal of Applied Behavior Analysis, 10,* 349–367.

Sweet, M., Shiraga, B., Ford, A., Pumpian, I., Loomis, R., & Brown, L. (1980). Curricular strategies to teach vending machine use skills. In L. Brown, M. Falvey, D. Baumgart, I. Pumpian, J. Schroeder, & L. Gruenewald (Eds.), *Strategies for teaching chronological age appropriate and functional skills* (Vol. IX, Pt. 1). Madison, WI: Madison Metropolitan School District.

TASH: The Association for Persons with Severe Handicaps (1983). *Resolution on infant care*. Policy Statement passed at their Spring Executive Board Meeting, San Francisco, California.

The Select Committee on Narcotics Abuse and Control, U.S. House of Representatives, Ninety-Sixth Congress (1980). *The use of drugs during pregnancy: Committee hearings* (SCNAC REPORT NO. 96-2-21). Washington, DC: U.S. Government Printing Office.

Tourian, A., & Sidbury, J. B. (1983). Phenylketonuria and hyperphenylalaninemima. In J. B. Stanbury, J. B. Wyngaardne, D. S. Fredrickson, J. L. Goldstein, & M. S. Brown (Eds.), *The metabolic basis of disease* (5th ed.) (pp. 270–286). New York: McGraw-Hill.

Van Etten, G. V., Arkel, C., & Van Etten, C. (1980). *The severely and profoundly handicapped*. St. Louis: The C. V. Mosby Company.

Vincent, L., Davis, J., Brown, P., Broome, K., Funkhouser, K., Miller, J., & Gruenewald, L. (1984). *Parent inventory of child development in nonschool environments*. Madison, WI: Madison Metropolitan School District.

Vincent, L., Salisbury, C., Walter, G., Brown, P., Gruenewald, L., & Powers, M. (1980). Program evaluation and curriculum development in early childhood/special education. In W. Sailor, B. Wilcox, & L. Brown (Eds.), *Methods of instruction for severely handicapped students* (pp. 227–258). Baltimore: Paul H. Brookes.

Voeltz, L. M. (1980). Children's attitudes toward handicapped peers. *American Journal of Mental Deficiency, 84,* 455–464.

Voeltz, L. M. (1982). Effects of structured interactions with severely handicapped peers on children's attitudes. *American Journal of Mental Deficiency, 86,* 380–390.

Voeltz, L. M. (1983). Program and curriculum innovations to prepare children for integration. In N. Certo, N. Haring, & R. York (Eds.), *Public school integration of severely handicapped students: Rational issues and progressive alternatives* (pp. 155–184). Baltimore: Paul H. Brookes.

Voeltz, L. M., Apffel, J. A., & Wuerch, B. B. (1981). *Leisure activities training for severely handicapped students*. Honolulu: University of Hawaii, Dept. of Special Education.

Voeltz, L. M., Johnson, R. E., & McQuarter, R. J. (1983). *The integration of school-aged children and youth with severe disabilities: A comprehensive bibliography and a selective review of research and program development needs to address discrepancies in state-of-the-art*. Minneapolis: University of Minnesota–Minneapolis, Minnesota Consortium Institute.

Vogelsburg, R. T., & Rusch, F. R. (1979). Training severely handicapped students to cross partially controlled intersections. *AAESPH Review, 4,* 264–273.

Warren, S. F., Rogers-Warren, A., Baer, D. M., & Guess, D. (1980). Assessment and facilitation of language generalization. In W. Sailor, B. Wilcox, & L. Brown (Eds.), *Methods of instruction for severely disabled* (pp. 227–258). Baltimore: Paul H. Brookes.

Wehman, P. (1981). *Competitive employment: New horizons for severely disabled individuals*. Baltimore, MD: Paul H. Brookes.

Wilcox, B., & Bellamy, G. T. (1982). *Design of high school programs for severely handicapped students*. Baltimore: Paul H. Brookes.

Williams, W., Brown, L., & Certo, N. (1975). Components of an instructional program. In L. Brown, T. Crowner, W. Williams, & R. Lock (Eds.), *Madison alternative for zero exclusion* (Vol. III, pp. 8–28). Madison, WI: Madison Metropolitan School District.

Wolfensberger, W. (1972). *Normalization*. Toronto, Canada: National Institution of Mental Retardation.

Writer, J. (1981). *Severely/multiply handicapped students: Definitions, characteristics, prevalence and incidence*. Unpublished manuscript, University of San Diego.

Resources

Organizations (See also Chapter 3)

The Association for Persons with Severe Handicaps (TASH)
7010 Roosevelt Way, N.E.
Seattle, WA 98115

Professional and parent organization that publishes a journal and newsletter, advocates for individuals with severe handicaps, and holds annual national, and state conferences.

National Society for Children and Adults with Autism
1234 Massachusetts Avenue, N.W.–Suite 1017
Washington, DC 20005

Focuses on issues related to autism from a research, service, and advocacy perspective.

National Genetics Foundation
555 W. 57th Street–Rm. 1240
New York, NY 10019

Dedicated to research and prevention, this organization provides information about genetic causes of handicapping conditions.

Journal (See also Chapter 3)

Journal of the Association for Persons with Severe Handicaps

Publishes original research, comprehensive reviews, conceptual papers on best practices, and descriptions of effective program models and intervention techniques.

Newsletter

TASH Newsletter

Reports on the organization's activities, effective practice, legislation, and other topics of interest to parents and professionals working with individuals with severe handicaps.

Chapter 6

VISUAL IMPAIRMENTS

Vision is the primary information organizing and integrating sense for the sighted person. Lack of, or reduced, vision alters the visually impaired person's orientation to the world influencing the development of cognitive, linguistic, psycho-social, and motor abilities. Systematic learning, which does not occur spontaneously or incidentally, must be facilitated by specifically trained personnel.

This chapter discusses the special needs of individuals who are classified as visually impaired. More specifically, the focus will be on factors which must be considered to determine appropriate services. The discussion opens by defining the population and proceeds through a brief description of the eye, some of the major visual disorders, important characteristics, identification and evaluation, considerations for intervention, and future trends in education and rehabilitation.

INDIVIDUALS WITH VISUAL IMPAIRMENTS

Defining visual impairment is more complicated than one might suppose. As with other handicapping conditions, there is great diversity in the severity of impairment among the visually impaired population. Historically there has been confusion in professional terminology. Barraga (1976) identified 19 terms in the

Ivan S. Terzieff
Western Michigan University

literature to describe the population. The large number of terms leads to limitations in defining the population and planning appropriate intervention programs, as well as in accumulating more precise information through research. Recently there has been a move toward refining and limiting the number of terms to facilitate the communication among the various professionals concerned with the area of visual impairment.

Definition of Visual Impairment

In defining the visually impaired, one must consider several factors such as degree of visual impairment, onset of visual impairment, and functional visual ability of the individual. Each of these factors, separately or in combination, affects the development of appropriate intervention and programming.

The legal terminology for classifying the visually impaired stems from the definitions proposed and approved by the American Medical Association (AMA) in 1934 for economic, vocational, and educational blindness. These definitions emphasized the disability, thus separating those with visual impairments from the general population. Perhaps the economic depression and high unemployment rate contributed to the acceptance of definitions which overlooked other abilities a person might have and how one might function visually in spite of restricted central visual acuity or field of vision.

The following year (1935), the Social Security Board modified these definitions by specifying a visual acuity of 20/200 or less in the better eye after correction and/or a visual field of 20 degrees or less (Schloss, 1963). A visual acuity rating of 20/200 can be interpreted as the ability to see at 20 feet what a person with normal vision can see at 200 feet. Visual field refers to how wide an area can be seen without movement of the eyes or head; tunnel vision is one name for a limited visual field. Today, for legal purposes, the modified AMA definition is still the sole criterion for eligibility for service provision:

> The legally blind are defined as those with a central visual acuity for distance of 20/200 or less in the better eye with correction or, if greater than 20/200, a field of vision no greater than 20 degrees in the widest diameter. (Hatfield, 1975, p. 4)

Many individuals who do not meet the criteria for "legal blindness" experience visual limitation. Those individuals are classified as partially sighted based on visual acuity between 20/70 and 20/200 in the better eye after best possible optical correction.

Many professionals today question such arbitrary limits obtained by the use of static measures. Visual acuity provides no information on functional potential, the effects of the environment on vision, nor the perceptual ability of the individual. The majority of the "legally blind" have considerable useful vision and should not be considered as blind.

The onset of visual impairment provides yet another classification. Individuals who were born with or acquired the impairment shortly after birth are referred to as congenitally visually impaired, while those who acquired the impairment later in life are referred to as adventitiously visually impaired. Both groups share many characteristics. The major difference seems to be in the use of information based on previous visual experiences.

The term visual impairment is currently accepted as the generic term to include the total group of persons with structural and/or functional impairment of the visual sense organ regardless of the nature or degree of impairment. However, this term does not distinguish among individuals with varying degrees of impairments within the total group. Barraga (1976) differentiated three groups within the visually impaired:

1. Individuals who are totally without the sense of vision or have only light perception are referred to as *blind*. These individuals learn primarily through the tactile and auditory senses, although perception of light, when present, might be useful for orientation and mobility purposes.
2. Individuals who have limitations in distance vision, but are able to see objects and materials within a few inches or feet are referred to as *low vision*. These individuals can use their visual sense for many daily activities and perhaps for print reading under varying individual and environmental conditions.
3. Individuals who, in some way, are limited in their use of vision under normal conditions are referred to as *visually limited*. These individuals may need special lighting, special materials, and may use optical and/or other aids in order to function visually; however, they should be considered as seeing persons.

These terms provide consistency and clarify the confusion brought about by the use of diverse terminology. They facilitate the communication among professionals and chart a course for more consistent and appropriate programming for visually impaired individuals.

As with other handicapping conditions, there is no agreement among various sources as to the number of visually impaired individuals. It is generally agreed, however, that visual impairment is at the low end of the incidence continuum. Reynolds and Birch (1977) estimated that approximately one fifth of the U.S. population have some visual anomaly. A majority of these are correctable and do not constitute educational or vocational handicap. Gearhart and Weishahn (1976) estimated that about 55,000 or 0.1 percent of the school age (5–18) population is visually impaired and requires special services and materials. The American Foundation for the Blind (1976) indicated that 1,756,000 individuals in the United States are visually impaired. Of these, more than 50 percent are over the age of 65. It is estimated that as the lifespan increases the number of visually impaired individuals will also increase as aging is closely associated with visual problems.

To the general public, blindness means the inability to see; however, 83 percent of all legally blind individuals have useful vision, with 7 percent considered totally blind and the remaining 10 percent having at least light perception (American Foundation for the Blind, 1976).

introducing

CARA

I have been totally blind since birth, so I don't feel I am missing anything by not seeing. I don't feel handicapped. The only things I can't do are drive a car and pick up a print book and read it. It bothers me when people refer to me as handicapped. Some people really think that, because I am blind, I am totally helpless. They don't know what to do around me. Some people say, "Oh, it's wonderful that you are able to do this," like crossing a street or getting around by myself. It sort of puts me on the spot and makes me feel as if I were an exhibit.

I went to a school for the blind. I feel I received a good education. The thing that was really hard at school was that we had no contact with sighted kids. If I had to do it over again, I probably would have gone to public school instead.

When I go shopping sometimes people will speak louder, as if I were deaf, or if I am with a sighted person, the clerks will ask my companion what I want as if I were mute. It irritates me, especially when I am paying, and I am the one to wear the clothes.

I am now a special education teacher. I feel I am able to relate to kids and understand how they feel.

I want people to understand that when they meet a blind person, that person is normal. Blindness is just a characteristic, not a personality. Treat the blind person as normal and it will be a lot easier for both of you.

Like all disabilities, the handicap of the visually impaired person consists of the cumulative effects of the disability and its inherent limitations, the social misconceptions, and the self-concept of the individual. Lowenfeld (1975) identified three major areas affected when vision is impaired: (1) range and variety of experiences, which affect motor, cognitive, and psychosocial development; (2) mobility, which includes orientation and locomotion and limits the experiences; and (3) interaction with the environment, both physical and social. Information acquisition from the physical environment will be limited to the degree the functional vision is limited. When social interaction occurs, the visually impaired individual may miss much of the subtle information communicated through nonverbal gestures, facial expressions, etc.

The variety of social misconceptions which result in social practices are reflected in the employment market. The visually impaired, characterized as dependent on others and helpless, are often not provided the opportunity to develop and exercise the skills and competencies which will lead to independence.

Although visual impairment is low on the incidence continuum, the diversity and severity of the impairment require the involvement of ophthalmologists, optometrists, teachers, orientation and mobility specialists, low vision specialists, and vocational specialists. Each of these individuals must contribute his or her expertise.

Figure 6.1

Anatomy of the Eye

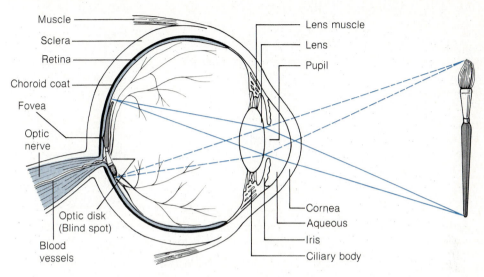

Source: From *Biosphere: The Realm of Life* by Robert A. Wallace, Jack L. King, and Gerald P. Sanders. Copyright © 1984 Scott, Foresman and Company.

ETIOLOGY AND PREVENTION

This section briefly reviews the anatomy of the visual sense organ and discusses the type of loss of functional vision that may occur when the various ocular structures are affected. The human eye is a complex system of interrelated structures (Figure 6.1). Any part of the eye may become nonfunctional through disease, hereditary anomalies, accidents, aging, and other causes.

Structure of the Visual Organ

Table 6.1 provides an outline of the parts of the eye according to three structural layers. Each part of the eye has a very specific function in the process of vision. It must be stated, however, that for perfect vision to occur four conditions must be met: (1) presence of light; (2) intact visual organ (eye) and its muscles; (3) intact optic nerve system; and (4) intact visual cortex. If there is any deviation from these conditions, vision will be adversely affected ranging from total blindness to limited vision. Light reflected from objects enters each eye through the cornea and is refracted, passes through the pupil and the lens where it is further refracted and directed to the fovea (center for most acute and detailed vision). Photochemical and photoelectrical responses in the retina convert the light rays

Table 6.1

Outline of Parts of the Eye According to Layers

Outer Coat	Middle (Uveal) Coat	Inner Lining
1. **Sclera** Tough, opaque covering, except for small area in front. It surrounds the eyeball. The visible white part of the eye. 2. **Cornea** Clear, transparent tissue that completes the sclera.	1. **Choroid** contains (a) blood vessels (b) dark brown pigment which reduces reflection and scattering of light after it has fallen on the retina. 2. **Ciliary Body** (a) Ciliary muscle—originates from the sclera near its junction with the cornea. (b) Ciliary ligaments—emerge from the ciliary muscle and attach to the lens, changing lens shape. 3. **Iris** (including pupil) (a) colored portion of eye (b) a muscular diaphragm with a hole (pupil) in the middle. The iris consists of: (a) circular fibers—cause pupil to constrict in bright light. (b) radial fibers—cause pupil to dilate in dim light.	1. **Retina** An expansion of optic nerve. (a) rods—receptors for colorless and twilight vision. (b) cones—receptors for color and bright day light vision. 2. **Optic Nerve** An extension of the visual cortex. (a) blind spot (b) optic chiasm 3. **Lens** Lies just behind iris and pupil. Held in position by ciliary ligaments. Divides the eye into anterior and posterior chambers. (a) anterior chamber is filled with aqueous fluid. (b) posterior chamber is filled with vitreous fluid.

to electrical impulses which are transmitted through the optic nerve fibers to the visual cortex where actual interpretation occurs (Figure 6.2). Thus, visual disorders may occur whenever and for whatever reason this sequence is interrupted.

Causes of Visual Impairment

Table 6.2 (page 234) gives a summary of common disorders by affected area, cause, visual effect, mode of detection, treatment, and prognosis. An inspection of this information will reveal that by far the major cause of visual impairment in children is of hereditary nature.

Figure 6.2

The Process of Seeing

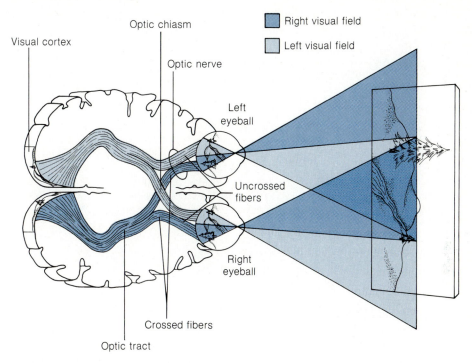

Optic chiasm

Visual cortex

Optic nerve

Left eyeball

Right visual field

Left visual field

Uncrossed fibers

Right eyeball

Crossed fibers

Optic tract

Source: Adapted from *Psychology and Life,* 11th Edition, by Philip G. Zimbardo. Copyright © 1985 Scott, Foresman and Company.

Other causes of blindness have been listed in broad categories to include infectious diseases, poisoning, tumors, and prenatal influences. In recent years, aging has become one of the leading causes of visual impairment primarily because of the increased number of elderly individuals.

All types of visual loss are determined by the site of the affected structure of the visual system. Primarily, there are three types of losses other than total blindness: (1) loss of *clarity*; (2) loss of *field*; and (3) loss of *central vision.*

Loss of clarity is primarily due to opacity in the cornea and/or the lens (cataracts). These conditions can be corrected through surgical procedures of corneal transplants and cataract removal replaced by intro-ocular lens transplant or optical aids. Cataracts vary in degree of density and may be due to a variety of causes; however, they are usually associated with the aging process. They appear to be a common occurrence among persons over age 70 (Jose, 1983).

Loss of visual field is generally due to an affected pathway to the visual cortex or the cortex itself. Some retinal diseases may also result in loss of the visual

Table 6.2

Overview of Ocular Diseases and Disorders

Condition	Affected Area	Cause	Visual Effects
Albinism (total or partial lack of pigment)	Macula (underdeveloped)	Hereditary	Decreased visual acuity (20/200 to 20/70), nystagmus, photophobia, high refractive error, and astigmatism. Visual fields variable and color vision is normal.
Cataracts (congenital)	Lens (opacity)	Hereditary, congenital anomalies (rubella, Marfan Syndrome, Down Syndrome), infection or drugs during pregnancy, and severe malnutrition during pregnancy.	Decreased visual acuity, blurred vision, nystagmus, squint, photophobia, slight constriction in the peripheral visual fields is possible, but visual fields are generally normal.
Cataracts (senile)	Lens (opacity)	Age	Progressively blurred vision; near vision is better than distance vision.
Diabetes Mellitus	Retina	Hereditary	Diplopia, inability to accommodate, fluctuating vision, loss of color vision or visual field, refractive error, decreased visual acuity, hemorrhaging of blood vessels in the retina, retinal detachment. Secondary complications: glaucoma and cataracts. Associated conditions: cardiovascular problems, skin problems, and kidney problems.
Glaucoma (congenital)	Tissues of the eye damaged from increased intraocular pressure.	Hereditary	Excessive tearing, photophobia, opacity or haze on lens, buphthalmos, poor visual acuity, and constricted visual fields.

Table 6.2 (continued)

Mode of Detection	Treatment	Prognosis
Family history and occular examination.	Painted or pinhole contact lenses, absorptive lenses, optical aids, and dim illumination.	Nonprogressive
Ophthalmoscopy and slit-lamp biomicroscope.	Surgery as early as possible in cases of severe visual impairment.	After surgery, inability to accommodate; problems with glare which are corrected with spectacles or contact lenses. Complications from surgery: secondary cataracts and detachment of the vitreous or retina.
Same as for congenital cataracts.	Surgery, with resultant cataract spectacles, contact lenses, lens implant (IOL, intraocular lens).	Same as for congenital cataracts. Complications from surgery: glaucoma, retinal detachment, hemorrhage of the vitreous, infection. Better candidate for intraocular lens (IOL) implants.
Ophthalmoscopy; reports of fluctuating vision.	Insulin injections, dietary controls, spectacles, and laser-beam surgery. Various illumination control aids.	Variation in acuity common.
Tonometry, study of the visual fields, and ophthalmoscopy.	Eye drops; surgery as soon as possible to prevent extensive damage.	With treatment, depends on the innate resistance of the structures of the eye. Blindness if not treated.

Table 6.2 (continued)

Overview of Ocular Diseases and Disorders

Condition	Affected Area	Cause	Visual Effects
Glaucoma (adult)	Same as for congenital glaucoma.	Hereditary or the result of changes in the eye after surgery.	Headaches in front portion of the head, especially in the morning; seeing halos around lights; decreased visual acuity, loss of visual fields, photophobia, and constricted peripheral fields in severe cases.
Glaucoma (acute attack)	Same as for congenital and adult glaucoma.	Inability of the aqueous to drain.	Nausea, severe redness of the eye, headache, and severe pain.
Retinal Detachment	Retina (portions detach from supporting structure and atrophy)	Numerous, including diabetes, diabetic retinopathy, degenerative myopia, and a blow to the head.	Appearance of flashing lights; sharp, stabbing pain in the eye; visual field loss; micropsia, color defects, and decreased visual acuity if the macula is affected.
Retinitis Pigmentosa	Retina (degenerative pigmentary condition)	Hereditary	Decreased visual acuity, photophobia, constriction of the visual fields, (loss in the peripheral field), and night blindness. Usher's Syndrome, Laurence-Moon-Biedl Syndrome, and Leber's Syndrome are associated with R.P.
Retinopathy of Prematurity	Retina (growth of blood vessels) and vitreous.	High levels of oxygen administered to premature infants; occasionally found in full-term infants.	Decreased visual acuity, severe myopia, scarring, and retinal detachment, with resultant visual field loss and possible blindness. Secondary complications: glaucoma and uveitis.
Rubella	Various parts of the eye.	Virus transmitted to the fetus by the mother during pregnancy.	Congenital glaucoma, congenital cataracts, microphthalmia, decreased visual acuity, and constriction of the visual fields. Associated conditions: heart defects, ear defects, and mental retardation.

Developed by Dr. R. T. Jose and Ms. Nancie Bauman, O.T., at the Pennsylvania College of Optometry.

Table 6.2 (continued)

Mode of Detection	Treatment	Prognosis
Same as for congenital glaucoma.	Eye drops, optical aids, sunglasses.	Same as for congenital glaucoma.
Same as for congenital and adult glaucoma.	Emergency surgery	Without emergency surgery, permanent damage to the ocular tissues and loss of visual acuity and peripheral vision.
Ophthalmoscopy and an internal eye examination.	Laser-beam surgery and cryosurgery, depending on the type and cause of the detachment; optical aids; and usually high illumination.	Guarded
Electrodiagnostic testing, especially ERG, and ophthalmoscopy.	Optical aids, prisms. No known medical cure; genetic counseling is essential.	Slow, progressive loss in the visual fields that may lead to blindness.
Ophthalmoscopy	Optical aids and illumination control devices.	Poor, in severe cases, where further detachments can be expected in third decade.
Ophthalmoscopy, slit-lamp biomicroscope, tonometry, and family history.	Surgery for glaucoma and cataracts, optical aids, establishment of appropriate educational goals.	Poor; post-surgical inflammation.

Source: From *Foundations of Education for Blind and Visually Handicapped Children and Youth: Theory and Practice,* edited by Geraldine T. Scholl (New York: American Foundation for the Blind, Inc., 1986). Reprinted by permission of the American Foundation for the Blind, 15 West 16th Street, New York, NY 10011.

Intraocular Implants

Medical advances are, perhaps, best exemplified by microsurgery. In ophthalmology, the microsurgery procedure is most often used for intraocular implants.

An intraocular implant is a surgical procedure in which the lens of the eye is removed and replaced with a manmade lens. A small incision is made in the upper portion of the eye (directly under the upper eyelid). The lens is removed either as a unit, or it is broken into small particles and "vacuumed" out. The implant lens then is positioned in place of the eye lens. The implant is made of transparent plastic material (to allow light to enter the eye) with a filter for filtering out ultraviolet light (which can be damaging to the retina). It is equipped with flexible loops for attachment to the eye without any sutures.

The surgical procedure is 90–95 percent successful; however, the long-term effects are still unknown. Approximately 50 percent of ophthalmologists will not perform the surgery on individuals who are under the age of 50. Further research needs to be conducted to study the effects of rejection and life expectancy of the implant.

The plastic material of the implant does not allow it to change its shape, thus accommodation is impossible. The implant is functional only for distance or near vision. Often, ophthalmologists will use an implant in one eye for distance and an implant for near vision in the other eye. In these cases the individual must suppress vision in one or the other eye depending upon the task he or she is performing at the time.

Although the procedure is new, many ophthalmologists feel that in the near future it could be successfully used with young visually impaired children. If the procedure proves to be successful with children, as it is with the elderly, it will provide them with an early opportunity for visual experiences, thereby limiting the effects of visual impairment on development.

---

field. Generally, field losses are unnoticed until mobility is adversely affected. Two major disorders limiting the visual field and often leading to total blindness are glaucoma and retinitis pigmentosa.

According to the National Society for the Prevention of Blindness (1966), 95,000 persons lose some vision as a result of glaucoma. There are many types of glaucoma, and successful treatment is dependent upon early detection of the condition. The most common treatment is drug therapy, although in many cases, primarily with congenital glaucoma, surgery becomes necessary.

Retinitis pigmentosa is a retinal pigmentary degeneration of unknown etiology acquired through genetic transmission. The first symptom is night blindness and usually occurs in the early teens. There is no specific treatment at this time.

Loss of central vision is due to disorders affecting the macular area of the retina as well as disorders associated with the uveal (middle) tract of the eye. A common disorder in people aged 65 and over is macular degeneration. The disease progresses gradually, resulting in a dense central scotoma (blind spots). It must be noted, however, it does not usually lead to total blindness.

Three other disorders must be mentioned. Retrolental fibroplasia (RLF) and congenital rubella have been greatly reduced due to medical advances, while diabetes mellitus is currently the leading cause of visual impairment in the U.S. (National Society for the Prevention of Blindness, 1980). It is a systemic condition resulting from lack of insulin which controls the amount of sugar circulating in the bloodstream. The major visual problems stem from changes in the blood vessels of the retina. Visual impairment ranges from insignificant to total blindness. Treatment generally depends on the severity of the condition and the age of the individual. Generally, however, it may be treated to some extent with insulin injections and controlled diet. Laser beam surgery is sometimes used to retard the progression.

Retrolental fibroplasia (RLF), also called retinopathy of prematurity, is a bilateral retinal condition seen in some prematurely born infants who are administered high concentrations of oxygen while in the incubator. The high oxygen level prevents the normal development of the retinal vascular system. After the infant is removed from the incubator, the existing blood vessels in the retina cannot supply the necessary level of oxygen which causes a proliferation of new blood vessels and development of fibrous tissue through the retina extending into the vitreous. These, in turn, cause stretching of the retina leading to retinal detachment. The condition is also dependent upon the duration of oxygen treatment and the birth weight of the infant. Each of these factors acts independently and may increase the risk for development of RLF.

Changes in the retina are observable with an ophthalmoscope as early as one month of age. The condition may be prevented or minimized by careful and continuous monitoring of the oxygen level in the incubator. Visual damage due to RLF may range from mild to severe. Visual acuity is dependent upon the severity of the condition. It is usually associated with retinal detachment, high myopia, nystagmus, and strabismus, while glaucoma and cataracts may appear as secondary disorders.

Congenital rubella is caused by exposure of the fetus to the rubella virus. The severity of the condition is dependent upon the time of exposure. The first trimester, particularly the first four weeks of pregnancy, is critical; i.e., the earlier the fetus is exposed to the virus, the more severe the impairment. The virus interferes with the division and multiplication of the cells, thus causing nonspecific chromosomal changes that are responsible for the resultant birth defect. Generally, a triad of visual impairment, auditory impairment, and cardiac abnormalities are associated with the congenital rubella syndrome. The visual impairment is usually due to cataracts, glaucoma, and opacity on the cornea.

Treatment through surgery, although commonly employed, is discouraging and prognosis is usually poor because of the possibility of subsequent viral inflammation of various parts of the eye. The only sure treatment is prevention of viral infection during pregnancy through vaccination prior to conception.

Although low in prevalence, visual impairment is one of the most severe handicapping conditions. It may occur at birth or at any time in the lifespan. Its effects on the individual are detrimental to both education and rehabilitation.

CHARACTERISTICS OF VISUALLY IMPAIRED INDIVIDUALS

The environment that surrounds us makes up the personal and moving space in which we live. When this space cannot be interpreted and utilized, we tend to lose confidence in ourselves as well as the surroundings.

There is a general agreement among researchers that development is influenced by the interaction between the organism and its environment as the organism matures physically. During the first four months, both the visually impaired and the sighted infant are equally restricted in their physical interaction with the environment. The presence of vision affords the sighted infant internal organization of the environment with which he or she will be actively engaged later. The visually impaired infant must accomplish the same task through the remaining sensory channels. The success achieved by the visually impaired has led to the common misconception of sensory compensation, i.e., when vision is deficient, the other sensory channels will be automatically strengthened. The visually impaired individual, therefore, has better hearing, taste, smell, etc. The truth is, however, that he or she must make better use of the remaining sensory channels if he or she is to function on an equal basis with the sighted in a visually oriented world.

Research indicates that visually impaired children develop along the same patterns as the sighted. However, due to many factors, the development is significantly delayed in some areas (motor, cognitive, etc.). This section discusses those delays and proposes some reasons for it.

Learning Characteristics

Higgins (1973) suggests that visually impaired people do not show significant deficits in intellectual processes, but that they might be handicapped in fully utilizing their capabilities because of their inability to abstract the "prerequisite data" from the environment. Lacking the "prerequisite data" leads the individual to arrive at incomplete conclusions registered as a developmental lag. Three areas in which a lag in cognitive development is most evident are object permanence, classification, and conservation.

The literature on object permanence is rather scanty. One major reason may be that the testing procedure utilized with sighted children is not easily adaptable for visually impaired children. Researchers have yet to come up with an alternate methodology suitable for the visually impaired. The existing literature (Fraiberg, 1977; Swallow & Poulsen, 1983) indicates that there is a significant delay in the development of object permanence, and this lag is attributed to inappropriate early experience. Visually impaired infants use the systems related to their own bodies (mouthing, sucking, etc.) for object manipulation for a longer period of time than their sighted counterparts. What is observed then is a slowdown in the development of hand manipulation and exploratory behaviors. Moreover, the infants are not imitating and actively searching the environment because of the absence of visual stimuli. Auditory stimuli do not provide directional cues for search until the last quarter of the first year (Fraiberg, 1977). Thus, the visually impaired child fails to actively interact with his or her environment, resulting in a failure to recognize that objects exist outside the body. However, once the child is engaged in active exploration of objects in the environment, the object permanence concept quickly develops (Swallow & Poulsen, 1983).

The research on classification shows that there are selective developmental lags, but more importantly, that training can ameliorate these lags and bring the classification skills to the level demonstrated by sighted children. Most of the difficulties lie in the interpretation and organization of distinguishing characteristics of objects through sensory channels other than vision. Hearing, smell, taste, and touch provide separate distinguishing features of objects not necessarily able to be integrated simultaneously. To be successful, the child must develop thorough exploratory behaviors. Lowenfeld (1971) delineated two types of tactual exploratory behaviors: (1) synthetic exploration where the entire object is explored at once, i.e., the object must be small enough to be held in and manipulated by one or two hands; and (2) analytic exploration where parts of the object are explored separately and then the entire object is reconstructed, i.e., the object is too large to be held and explored at once. Thus, the visually impaired child must develop the ability to focus on exploration of distinguishing characteristics (Davidson, 1973) as well as the ability to abstractly organize those characteristics.

Conservation may be explained as maintaining an equilibrium between one's schemas and his or her perceptual information about the world. Since the lack of vision limits the perceptual information, it would be reasonable to assume that visually impaired children will demonstrate a delay in conservation tasks. Hatwell (1966) reported a three-year delay in conservation of substance and a four-year delay in conservation of weight. Miller (1969) found that among 6- to 10-year-old visually impaired children, only those with "partial sight" showed evidence of conservation skills, suggesting that vision may be an important determinant to the development of conservation skills.

Delays in various areas of cognitive development may suggest a lower academic achievement; however, the research suggests that the educational achievement does not seem to differ significantly in early school years. In the middle school years, when abstract concepts replace concrete experiences, educational achievement is adversely affected; but by the later school years (high school), visually impaired students have developed the ability to deal with abstract concepts and achieve on the same level as the sighted.

The research seems to indicate that there are significant lags in some areas of cognitive development (Gottesman, 1973, 1976; Friedman & Pasnak, 1973; Higgins, 1973; Stephens & Grube, 1982; Swallow & Poulsen, 1983). These lags are more evident in the early stages of development due to restricted experiences during the sensorimotor, preoperational, and concrete operational stages of development. As those experiences broaden and allow the visually impaired child to actively interact with and organize the environment in a more meaningful way, he or she seems to progress to a comparable level (Boldt, 1969). There is evidence, however, that cognitive styles may differ (Cramer, 1973). In organizing and interpreting the environment, the sighted individual progresses from global to articulated (from the whole to its parts), while the visually impaired person proceeds from parts to the whole (Witkin, Brinbaum, Lomonaco, Lehr, & Herman, 1968). Thus, both arrive at the same conclusions utilizing different thinking processes. Visual impairment, in itself, does not result in lower intelligence (VanderKolk, 1981), nor does it adversely affect academic achievement (Cramer, 1973).

Social/Emotional Characteristics

The social/emotional development of visually impaired individuals may, in part, be affected by the disruption of the mother/child relationship in the early years as well as the attitudes of the community toward the handicapping condition. However, it must be noted that there is no "typical" blind personality. The visually impaired are an extremely heterogeneous group and therefore experience the same variation in the socialization process as the sighted population.

Social concept begins at birth, is related to the needs, feelings, and potential of parent and infant, and is contingent on family attitudes and personal involvement. By six months, the infant is strongly attached to the caregiver and by nine months exhibits a fear of strangers. The infant's awareness of the distinction between attachment and separation has a great deal to do with extending his or her interest to the external world (Barraga, 1976).

During the first six months, vision plays an important role in establishing a healthy bond between mother and infant. Sustained eye contact during feeding and reciprocal smiling, in addition to cuddling, stroking, and rocking allow the infant to develop physical and emotional security. These feelings of trust and security strengthen the parent/child bond without suppressing interest in the external world (Jackson, 1983). Lack of vision, however, diminishes interest in the external world and modifies the interaction with the caregiver and other significant persons, leading to a delay in psychosocial development. For example, smiling is viewed as an indicator of social contact and reciprocal smiling as social interaction. While visually impaired infants smile on schedule, the frequency and use of reciprocal smiling to initiate and maintain social contact is restricted as a result of the visual impairment. Obviously, a circular system is set up—diminished initiation of social contact leads to diminished response from others (Fraiberg, 1977). Thus, the visually impaired infant may have fewer opportunities to experience the emergence of social interaction. Restricted exploration of the environment contributes to a delay in development of play patterns. Play patterns in all children seem to follow similar progression: from solitary to parallel to cooperative play, and from lesser to greater peer interaction (Hull, 1983). A delay in early exploratory behavior results in longer periods of solitary and parallel play and a delay in cooperative play. In addition, restricted mobility contributes to the isolation of the visually impaired infant. The inability, or the lack of opportunity, for the child to partake in many of the physical activities that sighted children and adults engage in contributes to feelings of inadequacy and/or dependency and adversely affects his or her self-esteem. Thus, disruptive patterns of affective development have their beginnings at the very early stages of life.

Having established a secure bond, the child will venture from a dependent to an independent state. The venture to independence for the visually impaired is encountered by many roadblocks. Some of those are a direct result of the visual impairment, others from the effects of parental and social attitudes. As Scott (1969) points out, self-concept is not given at birth, rather it is something acquired:

There is nothing inherent in the condition of blindness that requires a person to be docile, dependent, melancholy, or helpless, nor is there anything about it that should lead him to become independent or assertive. Blind men are made, and by the same processes of socialization that have made us all. (p. 14)

Children learn about themselves from the way others react to them. Parents are the first teachers of feelings. Therefore, parental attitudes influence the child's psychosocial development. Sommers (1944) distinguished four types of parental attitudes toward visual impairment: (1) punishment; (2) fear of the community's belief that blindness is caused by a social disease; (3) feeling guilty of having violated some moral or social code; and (4) feeling personally disgraced. Although these attitudes have altered over the years, parents still report adjustment reactions in the form of denial, overprotection, disguised and overt rejection, and acceptance. Thus, the parents' psychological well-being and the ease or difficulties with which they decipher the cues that facilitate the socialization process influence the personal and social development of the child (Tait, 1972).

Socialization is also dependent upon the attitudes and expectations of others. The visually impaired may experience some social problems during the schooling period when acceptance by peers and participation in social and school activity become important to every teenager. Peer acceptance requires a degree of conformity in dress, behavior, skill, and contribution to the group. Parallel to this, the needs for independence, respect and understanding, mobility, privacy, and feelings of accomplishment are more difficult to meet with impaired vision and further contribute to the emergence of social problems. Concerns about the future, vocational decisions, and questions regarding marriage and family are the same for all, but the degree of concern may be greater for the visually impaired (Scholl, 1973).

McGuinness (1970) compared the social maturity of visually impaired children enrolled in residential and public schools and concluded that those in the public schools had a higher social maturity score. McGuinness attributed the low scores of residential school children to the lack of contact with age-appropriate social behavior, and the greater availability of special help. Schindele (1974) supports those findings, particularly in the older age group, and suggests that it may be the result of a sheltered and unrealistic environment provided by the special school.

Scott (1969) suggests that the basis for social adjustment is the development of a positive self-concept acquired, in large part, through the interaction with others and the expectations others have of the visually impaired individual. The implications of Scott's hypothesis are quite apparent. The psychosocial development of the child is influenced by the expectations others hold for him or her. It would seem that it is a case of self-fulfilling prophecy. Scott's hypothesis was indirectly supported by McGuinness' (1970) findings that children from the public school setting have less opportunity to receive special help and thus may be forced to work out problems for themselves. Acceptance of such a hypothesis, however, must be with caution. It is not clear whether the behavior is influenced by the expectations of others, or whether those expectations are shaped by the pattern of the behavior.

When visual impairment occurs later in life, the greatest difficulties are in the acquisition of alternative ways to carry out some tasks in already established patterns and to accept the curtailment of others. The sequence of reaction to the onset of visual impairment has been described as, and compared to, that of terminally ill patients. The change from one established pattern in one established sensory modality (vision) to a modified or new pattern in another modality (touch, hearing) is often accompanied by deep depression (Valvo, 1971). The process of depression and later recovery has been viewed as death of the sighted person and rebirth of the visually impaired (Carroll, 1961; Cholden, 1958). However, as Schultz (1958) points out, this process does not disrupt the basic personality; whatever disruption or disorganization occurs, it is usually "transient." Indeed, the onset of visual impairment may bring out personal problems, but it is the pre-existing personality that influences the adjustment and rehabilitation processes.

The majority of the research in psychosocial development has looked at early experiences, mother/child relationships, and differences between children placed in residential and public school settings. Some studies have looked at the influence of expectations placed upon the visually impaired by the sighted, while others have investigated the adjustment process of individuals who become visually impaired later in life.

There is substantial evidence that the pattern of social development is not different. Indicators of social attachments and acquisition of social skills (eating, toileting, and dressing) proceed at a slower rate. However, this does not denote a disturbed personality nor a less adequate socialization.

Motor Development

The initial, purposeful, physical activities are dependent, to a large extent, on the ability to see and react to external stimuli. The infant lifts his or her head and sees a toy. The interest in the toy motivates the infant to repeat the action and later to attempt to secure that toy. These initial activities facilitate contact with the environment and provide the incentive for reaching out and extending the trunk leading to a purposeful locomotor sequence. The visually impaired infant must rely on auditory cues to perform a motor task similar to that of the sighted infant. Fraiberg (1977) indicates that the visually impaired infant does not reach out on auditory cues until the last quarter of the first year. Thus, a significant delay is already observed that will result later in a delay of the more complex motor behaviors.

Research suggests that postural developmental milestones (sitting, standing, etc.) are within the normal developmental range, while locomotion items (creeping, crawling, walking, etc.), which normally follow each postural achievement, are significantly delayed. This hypothesis is tenable since achievement on postural items is dependent on the physical capability of the infant, while locomotion is initiated in an interactive manner between the infant and the environment.

introducing

BOBBY

When Bobby was born the doctor said that there is something wrong with his eyes and it is difficult to predict if he will be able to see or not. I thought that my life was shattered, but I did not give up. I took Bobby to another doctor and he told me that medically he couldn't do anything to help him, and didn't know what I could do. Bobby was a quiet and lovable baby. He was very easy to take care of, but I was afraid of what might happen to him in the future.

As Bobby was growing up at times he would reach out toward some things, as if he could see them. He never followed me around the house, but almost always reached for my face when I was close to him.

By the time he was one year old, he would pick up objects and toys and move them in front of his eyes, as if he could see them. I was sure that Bobby could see, but I didn't know how much vision he had.

I hated it when people said that he was blind. I wanted to take him with me everywhere I went, but I was also very embarrassed and sometimes wanted to scream at people.

One day I got a call from a woman asking me to join her and some other parents of blind kids at a meeting in her house. I wanted to tell her that Bobby is not blind, but instead, I accepted the invitation. Am I ever glad I did!

Bobby is five years old now and attending kindergarten. He wears glasses and is beginning to read. All the work seems to be paying off now. I am no longer ashamed, I am proud of him and his progress. Oh, I still worry about him once in a while, but I do that with his sister too.

The visually impaired infant, although physically capable and developmentally ready to initiate locomotion, reaches a plateau with the achievement of each postural stage. The ensuing locomotor stage requires the infant to give up a major portion of his or her physical contact with the surface. The unwillingness to abandon this contact may account for the plateau. The duration of each plateau is dependent upon the quality and quantity of external stimulation as well as the amount of residual vision. When the plateau is overcome through systematic stimulation, the subsequent mobility will occur.

Some researchers advance other, but related, reasons to account for these delays. VanderKolk (1981) suggests that, since the visually impaired child is unable to model the motor behaviors and is unable to see objects in the environment, that child will lack incentive for motoric actions upon the environment. Scholl (1973) postulates that parental overprotectiveness and misunderstanding of the motor needs limit the opportunity for interaction with the environment. Campbell (1970) and Freedman and Cannady (1971) argue that the lack of early visual and motor stimulation results in the delays experienced by visually impaired children. Perhaps it is not any one, but a combination of the above, that accounts for the delay in motor development. As the child matures, the delay in motor development disappears, while difficulties of movement through the environment persist.

Blind students are able to participate in a number of sports;
an example is this high school wrestler.

Early delays in motor and cognitive development result in significant deficits
in environmental orientation and acquisition of spatial concepts. Warren,
Anooshian, and Bollinger (1973) provide an extensive review of the literature
dealing with the role of early vision in spatial relationships and resultant mobility behaviors. Much of the evidence supports the notion that early visual experiences and interaction with the environment may provide the basis for later
spatial organization. Cratty (1971) postulates that, for the totally blind child, the
body is the "central platform" from which movement and acquisition of spatial
concepts is attained. Successful movement through physical space is dependent
upon the child's understanding and control of his own body and the environment.
Therefore, orientation and mobility for the visually impaired begins with the
acquisition of body knowledge (relationships and function of body parts and
body planes) and is extended to the environment (relationships among objects)
(Lydon & McGraw, 1973).

The process of using the senses to establish one's position and relationship to
objects in the environment is referred to as orientation, while the movement from
one point in the environment to another is referred to as mobility. The orientation
and mobility process requires the ability to integrate sensory data from the
environment into patterns of movement behaviors (Hill & Ponder, 1976; Lydon &
McGraw, 1973). This process involves gathering information; organizing the in-

formation in categories according to constancy, dependability, and familiarity; selection of relevant information for the orientation needs; the design of a course of action based on selected information; and the performance of the locomotor activity.

The visually impaired are not incapable of mobility; rather they are restricted in their orientation. Successful mastery of orientation skills enables the individual to exercise some control over the environment and, therefore, move through it with relative ease.

Several reasons have been advanced for the delay in motor development. The delay is more evident during the transitional period from the postural to the locomotor stage and is overcome through external stimulation and increased interaction with the environment. Delays in motor and cognitive development result in deficient orientation and mobility skills. These skills can be developed through the systematic instruction provided by an orientation and mobility specialist.

Communication Development

Communication development takes place within the context of interpersonal relations. Its acquisition is an active process demanding participation by the infant and those around him or her. Generally, visually impaired children demonstrate little developmental differences from sighted children (Warren, 1976). However, there is evidence to suggest that visually impaired children are at a greater risk in the early stages of communication development than at the later stages of language acquisition (Rogow, 1983). Stern (1974) indicates that visual gaze and fixation provide the direct contact with the parent and become the primary signals for interaction. The parents in turn respond to those signals and a base for communication is established (Adamson, Als, Tronick, & Brazelton, 1977).

Visually impaired infants also provide signals, but they are generally unrecognized by the parents. Fraiberg (1977) found that the hands of visually impaired infants are the primary tool for expression. That is, visually impaired infants express with their hands what sighted infants express with their eyes and facial expressions. Parents should use the information provided by the infant's hands as cues to interpret his or her intentions and meanings and engage the infant in communicative activities. Unfortunately, some parents are unable to interpret those signals.

Visually impaired infants live in a restricted environment. They are dependent upon their parents to introduce the people, objects, and events in their environment to them. When and how parents make these introductions is very important. Often parental overprotectiveness restricts the infant's interaction with the environment, thus increasing the possibilities for restricted communicative abilities.

The meaning attached to objects by the visually impaired and the image of these objects may differ from those of a sighted child. However, the child's "understanding of the objects is equally real in terms of his own experiences"

(Rogow, 1983, p. 60). Since those experiences may be limited, the issue of "verbalism" (use of words for which one has no firsthand sensory base) has often been discussed in the literature. Cutsforth (1951) argued that the use of such words leads to "incoherent and loose thinking." Dokecki (1966) in an extensive review of the literature argued that sighted individuals also use such words and that there is no evidence that these words are meaningless or involve "loose thinking." A number of studies (Anderson & Olson, 1981; Burlingham, 1961, 1965; DeMott, 1972; Harley, 1963; Nolan, 1960) have unsuccessfully attempted to resolve the issue.

Although communicative efficiency is enhanced by nonverbal cues, research in this area is scanty. Obviously, a totally blind individual will not be able to interpret unseen nonverbal messages; however, the ability to use such messages will enhance his or her communication interaction with the sighted. In a review of selected literature, Apple (1972) concluded that nonverbal expressiveness is learned and is age related. Although use of nonverbal messages may be learned, the expressions themselves are visually mediated and may provide difficulties with the nuances of communication between the visually impaired and the sighted population.

Evidence presented in the literature on language development in visually impaired children indicates: (1) the acquisition process is different, but it is not necessarily deviant or delayed; (2) environmental factors play a major role in determining the course of language development; (3) intervention should begin at the earliest possible time; and (4) intervention should focus on cognitive, social, and motor activities to enrich the use of communicative competence. Although the unresolved issue of "verbalism" has received substantial attention in the literature, the use of such words does not seem to interfere with the communication process.

Overall, the research indicates that the characteristics of the visually impaired are essentially the same as those that describe the sighted population. While there is some evidence of developmental delays in the early years of life, these delays seem to disappear or become insignificant in later life.

DETECTION OF VISUAL IMPAIRMENT

Visual impairment may occur at any time in the lifespan of any individual. Some are born with the impairment; others acquire it later in life. The identification of those who are totally blind could and often occurs at birth or shortly after. The identification of those who have some residual vision is a more difficult task, especially for the very young. The standard screening tools (Snellen Chart in Figure 6.3 or similar subjective instruments) require the child to respond to the demands of the examination and report accurately his or her visual experiences. For many children, identification of the visual impairment does not take place until the school years when visual screening is mandated by state laws. For still others, detection of the impairment occurs later in life. Visual screening is

Figure 6.3

The Snellen Chart

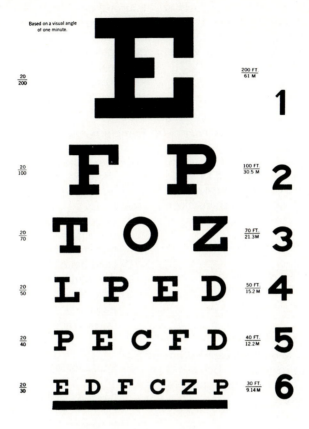

usually performed by the school nurse using the Snellen Chart that measures central distance visual acuity. The typical screening procedure will not identify individuals whose visual problems are related to visual field or near vision loss. It is quite possible that many such individuals will not be identified. Those suspected of having visual problems are referred for in-depth evaluation by an ophthalmologist, who determines the cause, treatment, and prognosis of the impairment.

The procedure for detection of visual impairment is a primitive one at best and the ensuing report has very little educational and/or rehabilitational meaning. For those who are totally blind, the development of the remaining senses becomes important for education and rehabilitation. However, for those with residual vision, further visual evaluation is necessary to determine visual functioning.

Evaluating Functional Vision

Efficient use of vision in low vision individuals is dependent upon several environmental and psychological conditions such as auditory and/or visual distractions, lighting, location, attitudes, beliefs, values, etc.

Tool

The *Diagnostic Assessment Procedure* (DAP) is developed specifically for the visually impaired individual as a part of the Program to Develop Visual Efficiency (American Printing House for the Blind, 1980), which is packed in a kit designed for visual training. DAP identifies specific gaps or weaknesses and strengths in visual functioning which may form the basis for appropriate visual training.

Purpose

To assess the ability to use vision for a variety of tasks and identify visual concepts understood by low vision individuals.

Administration Time

No specific time indicated. May vary for each individual. Multiple sessions may be required. Duration of sessions are determined by fatigue, developmental level, attention span, anxiety, etc.

Format

Assessment kit consisting of laminated cards, needed materials, record booklet, and summary table. Each card corresponds to an assessment task and contains: (a) visual task, (b) required materials, (c) directions for administration, (d) behavioral description of expected response, and (e) approximate developmental level.

The Record Booklet provides space for mastery (+), nonmastery (−), and observational comments. Materials included in the kit range from concrete (objects) to symbolic (pictures, letters, words, etc.).

The DAP is administered individually. Mastery of visual tasks may not be sequential, therefore it is expected that all items be presented. The testee is allowed to self-correct during a response and should receive appropriate credit.

Interpretation and Use of Data

The summary table shows at a quick glance the individual's performance across eight categories of developmental milestones. The results are used for developing a visual training program specifically for that individual. Although not intended for use in selection of appropriate reading medium, results may be one source of information for this purpose.

Sample Items

Item No. 11

Objective: Learner will discriminate missing parts
Visual Task: Recognize distinctive features visually
Material: Doll
Directions:

1. Choose a quiet area with favorable lighting and a table or desk. Be seated directly across from the learner.
2. Hold the doll under the table out of sight of the learner and remove the right arm.
3. Hold doll in front of learner at a distance of about 2 ft. (.6m). If learner is unable to see doll at 2 ft. (.6m), reduce distance to 1-1/2 ft. (.5m) or 1 ft. (.3m), or closer. Say:
    "LOOK AT THE DOLL."
   Pause for learner to look. Then say:
    "TELL ME WHAT IS MISSING."
   If learner responds "shirt or eye," say:
    "WHAT ELSE IS MISSING?"
   If the learner cannot respond by naming what is missing, pointing to the place where arm is missing is acceptable.
4. With the doll under the table, attach the arm and remove the *left* shoe.
5. Hold the doll upside down and repeat direction #3.

Response: LEARNER POINTS TO APPROPRIATE AREA(S) OR NAMES MISSING PARTS.
Developmental Level: 1–3 yrs.

Item No. 31

Objective: Learner will match letters and numbers
Visual Task: Select like symbols
Materials: Vinyl (light side up)
Two strips:
a. letters
b. numbers

1. Choose a quiet area with favorable lighting conditions and a flat working surface. Be seated directly across from the learner.
2. Place the strip with letters in front of learner with the first letter to the learner's left. (Learner may hold strip and bring as close as desired.)
3. Point to the first letter on the left and say:

   "LOOK AT THIS LETTER CAREFULLY."

   After about 15 seconds, point to the other letters in the row and say:

"SHOW ME THE ONE THAT LOOKS JUST LIKE THE FIRST ONE. BE SURE IT IS THE SAME."
4. Repeat direction #3 using the strip of numbers and substituting the word number(s) for letter(s).

Response: LEARNER SELECTS IDENTICAL LETTER AND NUMBER.

Developmental Level: 4–5 yrs.

Criteria for Determination

Vision, as most other skills, is learned. The development of visual skills is influenced to a large extent by environmental, physical, and mental characteristics. Research has demonstrated that visual perceptual abilities and visual efficiency can be facilitated through visual training (Ashcroft, Halliday, & Barraga, 1965; Barraga, 1964, 1976; Jose, 1983). A training program, however, must match the characteristics and abilities of the individual. It is therefore important to assess the total visual system. Such assessment should include:

1. Ocular motor functions: pupillary response, muscle imbalance, convergence, tracking, etc.
2. Functional use: eye preference, lighting conditions, near and far point, field of view, etc.
3. Use of low vision aids: glasses, magnifiers, etc.
4. Visual perceptual skills: visual discrimination, memory, closure, sequencing, etc.
5. Spatial awareness: part/whole and whole/part relationships, self to object, object to object relationships, etc.
6. Visual motor skills: general body movements and coordination, eye-hand, gross motor, fine motor coordination, etc.

Recently, several functional visual evaluation instruments have been developed and widely used for evaluation of the total visual system (Barraga, 1980; Efron & Duboff, 1976; Ficociello-Gates, 1979; Langley & DuBose, 1976).

Diagnosis and Assessment

Determining the extent of visual impairment and visual functioning is only one aspect of the diagnostic process. In programming for education and/or rehabilitation, assessment of all areas of development and functional skills is necessary. However, lack of appropriate instruments hampers valid measurements (Stogner, 1970). Frequently, the visually impaired are penalized because most of the standardized tests are developed for the sighted population. Items of such tests are either directly related to vision or indirectly related to experiences dependent upon vision and/or normal mobility skills. Thus, assessment of the visually impaired often yields questionable and unreliable results. This is particularly true when psychological, educational, and vocational evaluation is used for predictive purposes. The performance of a visually impaired individual on such instruments may not be a reflection of his or her intelligence, learning potential, or vocational ability, but an indication of the individual's sensory intactness, perceptual organization, and amount of social exposure. Furthermore, information regarding the similarities between visual and tactual/auditory experiences is still lacking. It is possible that various sensory systems process incoming information differently and, therefore, could influence learning styles (Barraga, 1976). Thus, appropriate assessment is possible only when there is a recognition of the individual's unique characteristics and needs, and when appropriate instruments are available. Bauman (1980) describes the scarcity of appropriate assessment instruments for visually impaired individuals and points out some of the difficulties in adapting those developed for the sighted population. Adaptations could involve change in the characteristics of the stimulus object from visual to tactual. For example, it is easy enough to make blocks that differ in texture instead of in color, or to convert print into braille. In many ways, such adaptations have been successful; however, it is evident that new elements such as the requirement for tactual discrimination, knowledge of braille, and different reading rates have been built into the adapted tests. For some visually impaired individuals, these tests become measures of tactual discrimination, reading in braille, and rate of reading rather than task performance. In any case, such adaptations do not account for the different life experiences of the visually impaired individual from that of the normative group. Test adaptations violate the norms and any interpretation of the results must be treated with great caution.

The lack of assessment instruments specifically designed for and normed on the visually impaired population is an issue that still remains to be resolved. The process of developing such tests is a lengthy one and riddled with problems. Although the number of visually impaired individuals is relatively small, it is an extremely heterogeneous group. Variables such as age of onset, degree of impairment, utilization of remaining vision, etc., contribute to the difficulties in developing norms for that population. However, if appropriate instructional and training programs are to be designed, a thorough assessment must take place. Table 6.3 represents the most often used instruments in evaluation of visually impaired individuals of all ages.

Studies by Bauman (1968) and VanderKolk (1981) show that the most widely used and perhaps the most reliable tests are verbal measures of mental ability from the Wechsler Scales (*WPPSI, WISC-R,* and *WAIS-R*). The performance sections of these scales are usually replaced with the *Haptic Intelligence Scale* (Shurrager, 1961; Shurrager & Shurrager, 1964) or the *Stanford Kohs Block Design Test* (Suinn & Dauterman, 1966), both normed on the visually impaired ages 16 and above. For the younger age level, the *Non-Language Learning Test* (Bauman, 1947; Bauman & Hayes, 1951) is often used.

Table 6.3

Assessment of Individuals with Visual Problems

Area of Assessment	Tests Most Often Used	Information Obtained	Professionals Involved
Ophthalmological	Snellen Chart, ophthalmoscope, electroretinogram, slit lamp, etc.	Visual acuity, nature and severity of visual impairment, prognosis, treatment, optical aids, etc.	School nurse, ophthalmologist, optometrist
Visual Perceptual	Diagnostic Assessment Procedure-Low Vision, Visual Assessment Kit, A Vision Guide for Teachers of Deaf/Blind Children, etc.	Visual efficiency, visual functioning, visual discrimination, memory, closure, sequencing, etc.	Teacher, rehabilitation counselor, low vision specialist
Developmental Skills	Vineland, Maxfield-Buchholz, Overbrook, Uzgiris and Hunt, Bayley, Denver, Concept Development, RDT, etc.	Special competency, independent living skills, motor skills, cognitive skills, orientation and mobility readiness skills, language development, tactual dissemination skills, etc.	Teacher, rehabilitation counselor, psychometrist, psychologist
Specific Areas	WPPSI, WISC–R, WAIS–R, HIS, Perkins-Binet, SAT, CAT, Metropolitan Math, Key Math, WRAT, etc.	Intelligence, aptitude, achievement, etc.	Psychologist, psychometrist, teacher, rehabilitation counselor
Vocational	Minnesota Rate of Manipulation, Pennsylvania Bi-Manual Work Sample, Kuder Preference Record, California Occupational Interest Inventory, etc.	Manual skills, manipulation rate, occupational interest, attitudes to employment, etc.	Vocational counselor, rehabilitation counselor, teacher

Special Considerations

Braille reading requires intact tactual receptors and coordinated hand use. The *Roughness Discrimination Test* (RDT) (Nolan & Morris, 1965) assesses tactual discrimination ability. Nolan and Morris (1965) tested first grade visually impaired students at the beginning of the school year and successfully predicted (70–75%) whether students would be in the upper or lower half of their braille reading group at the end of the school year.

The *Scholastic Aptitude Test* is the most widely used at the junior and senior high school level. The adaptations made are transcription from print into braille and elimination of the time limitations. The procedures for administration and evaluation follow those applicable for the sighted population. In the area of achievement, a variety of assessment tools, with minor adaptations, are generally used with successful results. Social competency in the early ages is generally assessed by the *Maxfield-Buchholz Scale* (Maxfield, 1957) while the *Overbrook Social Competency Scale* (Bauman, 1971) and the *Vineland Adaptive Behavior Scales* (Sparrow, Balla, & Cicchetti, 1984) are used with visually impaired adults. Administration is through interviews of caregivers, teachers, and parents, as well as direct observation of the subject's behaviors.

Vocational evaluation of visually impaired individuals grew largely as a result of the rehabilitation of blinded World War II veterans. Measures of manual speed and dexterity—i.e., *Minnesota Rate of Manipulation Test* (Betts & Ziegler, 1946), *Pennsylvania Bi-Manual Work Sample* (Roberts, 1945), and *Crawford Small Parts Dexterity* (Bauman, 1958)—appear to be the best predictors for orientation in a work space, success in manipulative jobs, and use of tools.

Because of the various test adaptations and status variables of the visually impaired, the interpretation of test results must be made in light of the individual background, rather than through comparisons with the norms. Despite the inadequacies of testing instruments, evaluation, counseling, rehabilitation, and instructional planning are not only possible but well established professional offerings (Bauman, 1980).

CONSIDERATIONS IN INTERVENTION

Organized education for visually impaired children began about 200 years ago in Paris with the establishment of the first school by Valentin Hauy in 1784. Hauy believed that education of visually impaired children should parallel that of the sighted. Following Hauy's example, Samuel Gridley Howe established the first school in the United States in 1832, located near Boston (now known as the Perkins School for the Blind). Like Hauy, Howe strongly believed that education for the visually impaired should be patterned after that of the sighted. Farrell (1976) summed up Howe's philosophy as follows:

1. *Each blind child must be considered as an individual and be trained according to his personal ability.*
2. *The curriculum of a school for the blind should be well rounded and conform as much as possible to that of the public schools.*
3. *The main objective must be to train blind youths to be able to take their places in the social and economic life as contributing members to their home communities.* (p. 45)

By 1876, at the time of Howe's death, more than 20 residential schools had been established (Lowenfeld, 1973). Currently, 41 states have at least one residential school.

A low vision student does her homework with the aid of a device that magnifies print and projects it onto a television screen.

Despite Howe's philosophy of education for the visually impaired, it was not until 1900 when the first public school class for visually impaired children opened in Chicago. Following the example of Chicago, by 1910 eight other cities had organized such classrooms. By 1948, about 10 percent of the visually impaired children attended public school classes (Lowenfeld, 1973). The increased awareness that visually impaired children can be successfully taught along with their sighted peers and, more recently, the mandate of PL 94–142 have altered dramatically the educational placement. At present, about 80 percent of all visually impaired children are educated in the public school system (American Printing House for the Blind, 1983).

The education of "partially seeing" children followed a similar pattern. In the early stages, along with the totally blind, they were taught braille. Many of them were reading braille with their eyes. This realization led to the establishment of the first classroom for "partially seeing" children in Boston in 1913, followed by a number of other classrooms across the nation (Lowenfeld, 1973). These were commonly known as "sight saving" classrooms. It was believed that holding the printed material too close to the eyes and prolonged use of the eyes caused visual deterioration. Hence, the emphasis in those classrooms was on the preservation of sight. Advances in ophthalmology and educational practices within the last 20 years have shown that children with residual vision should be encouraged and can be trained to use their vision more efficiently (Barraga, 1964; Barraga & Collins, 1979; Collins & Barraga, 1980).

Figure 6.4

The Braille Alphabet

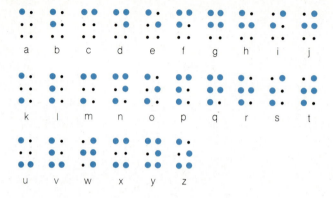

The tendency to parallel the academic curriculum and to make education comparable to that of the sighted necessitates the provision of different materials, equipment, teaching devices, and perhaps most important, a workable system of reading and writing. Historically, many forms of tactile communication systems have been tried, including writing on wax plates, forming letters with wire, embossed and raised letters, etc. (Lowenfeld, 1973). By 1834, Louis Braille had worked out a system of raised dots for reading and writing currently known as braille. Braille's system was based on the concept of Charles Barbier, a French officer who used embossed dots to be read by touch for the transmission of military messages. Barbier's system consisted of twelve dots, six vertical dots in two columns. The vertical six-dot arrangement was too high to be tactually perceived by the fingertips and presented difficulties in reading. Louis Braille reduced it to six dots in a two-column arrangement and designed an alphabet within the six-dot cell. It became officially accepted in France in 1854, and in 1869 at the Missouri School for the Blind. However, the final adoption and modification in this country did not occur until 1932 when the Standard English Braille was officially accepted as the uniform system. The approved system includes grade 1 braille (letters of the alphabet, numbers, and special composition signs) and grade 2 braille, consisting of grade 1 and 189 contractions and short form words. Music, mathematics, and scientific notation codes are based on the same system. Figure 6.4 illustrates the braille alphabet.

The Perkins Brailler and the slate and stylus are the two primary tools for writing braille. The Perkins Brailler invented by Frank Hall in 1862, has six keys, one for each of the six dots. The keys, when depressed in combinations, leave an embossed character that stands for a letter, contraction, short form word, composition sign, punctuation mark, or a numeral. The slate and stylus are easily stored and portable, but more difficult to use. The stylus must be pressed through the opening of the slate in reverse order.

A computer with a braille keyboard and an electronic Perkins Brailler are two instruments that aid blind individuals in their work.

Learning to read braille is a more difficult process than learning to read print. Braille contractions are not logical and do not follow any phonetic rules. Research has shown that reading braille is much slower than that of print (Ashcroft, 1961). Ashcroft found that high school braille readers average about 90 words per minute, while Anderson and Olson (1981) noted that the rate varies according to the material being read. However, it is consistently lower than that of print reading. The single most important factor for the lower reading rate is the single cell as the perceptual unit, rather than words or sentences (Nolan & Kederis, 1969). Because of that, the reader is forced to be much more sequential in perception of the material rather than perceive a number of words at once, as the sighted reader does.

Intervention programs for the visually impaired should strive to meet their present, as well as future, needs. In addition to the regular academic curriculum, individual persons may need specific instruction in the areas of activities of daily living, orientation and mobility, social adjustment, communication, and vocational and career counseling. These areas are generally considered to be critical for, and an integral part of, the education and rehabilitation process for the visually impaired.

Educational Settings

As in the other areas of exceptionality, there is no one educational setting most appropriate for all visually impaired children. A diversity of settings is desirable and necessary in order to meet individual needs. The recognition of the variability of needs has led to a continuum of services. Organizational programming and service provision differ from community to community and are often based on the availability of trained personnel.

Teacher Consultant.   Students are enrolled in a regular classroom and require minimal support services. These services are provided by a teacher consultant who spends less than 50 percent of the school day in direct instruction to students. More than 50 percent of the time is in indirect service provision, such as consultations to parents or regular classroom teachers, procurement of materials, coordination of support services and administrative abilities, and assessment.

Itinerant Teacher.   Students are enrolled in a regular classroom and require instruction in the development of special skills associated with the visual impairment. The itinerant teacher spends more than 50 percent of the time in direct instruction to the student and moves from school to school, serving different students.

Resource Room.   Students are enrolled in the regular classroom in a school that includes a special classroom for use by visually impaired students who require daily support services and specialized instruction. These services and instruction are provided by a teacher of the visually impaired according to individual needs.

Special Class.   Students are enrolled in a special classroom for all or most of the school day. Instruction of these students is provided by a teacher of the visually impaired in concert with other specialists and emphasizes subject matter and developmental skills. Such students may profit by participating in the regular school classes in selected areas as appropriate to the changing needs of the student.

Special School Program.   Students who require specialized instruction and support services beyond that which can reasonably be provided in the public school programs are enrolled in a special day or residential program. These students have access to the educational programs in the local school district either in a part-time or full-time basis.

Mainstreaming of the visually impaired has been a part of the educational program since the turn of the century, and has been reflected in the educational philosophy since the inception of formalized educational programs. Nevertheless, regular classroom teachers still have limited experience with, and many misconceptions about, visual impairment. A number of publications have been developed to help regular classroom teachers become more knowledgeable about instructional strategies and use of special devices (Bookbinder, 1978; Corn & Martinez, 1978; Johnston, 1978; Orlansky, 1977).

Education of visually impaired children, regardless of educational placement, needs to follow three basic principles as outlined by Lowenfeld (1973):

1. *Concrete Experiences.* To enhance the understanding of the real world and lessen the limitation in the range and variety of experiences, visually impaired students must be provided with concrete objects that can be manipulated. Concrete experiences are necessary for learning about the environment. Concreteness in teaching is achieved essentially in two ways: by having the child observe and/or manipulate an object, or by providing a model of the object. Whenever possible, the first is preferred. Very often the size, texture, and shape of a model are so different from reality that children may acquire a distorted concept of the real object.

2. *Unifying Experiences.* Visual experiences unify information from the environment and organize discrete impressions received through the other sense organs. A visually impaired child cannot achieve this unification unless the teacher presents "units of experiences" and unifies them through explanation and sequencing.

3. *Learning by Doing.* Learning about the environment is accomplished primarily through self-initiated activities. The visually impaired child in general has significantly fewer opportunities for such activities. Therefore, visually impaired children must be encouraged to do as many things for and by themselves as possible. Early stimulation and deliberate introduction of motivational situations will enhance the learning potential of the child.

The application of these principles to the educational process of the visually impaired child will ensure later success in academic, social, and employment endeavors. Therefore, the teacher must organize the material better, be specific in explanations, and be knowledgeable of the specific needs of the child.

Preschool Programs

Children up to age five who are identified as visually impaired need to be provided with a qualified teacher and the necessary services. Early intervention should include sensory stimulation; development of body image, gross and fine motor skills, cognitive and language skills and social skills; and parent education. Such intervention will divert the educational and emotional ramifications resulting from the impairments.

Sighted children absorb a great deal of information and experience from the environment. The visually impaired child is at a disadvantage from the very first week after birth. The visual impairment restricts the access to the environment and can have serious consequences for cognitive, motor, and psychosocial de-

Table 6.4

Special Programming for Visually Impaired Infants

Developmental Areas	Normal Child Expectation	Special Adaptation for Blind
Human Attachment	Vision plays a crucial role in the establishment of human bonds.	Stress the importance of "learning to know" through tactile and auditory experience. Encourage holding and talking to the baby during feeding and also creating "social" times of holding, singing, and playing lap games as the baby's awake time is increased.
Discovery of Objects	Eye-hand coordination in the sighted child forms a nucleus from which many patterns of infant learning and development evolve.	Encourage parents to introduce some form of cradle gym or hanging apparatus over the crib of the baby. Such a toy may be lowered over the baby so that random small movements will bring about touch and sound sensations.
Prehension	Prehension—the activity of the baby's hands, their organization, and progressive development—is intimately related to each of the other areas discussed.	Suggest patty-cake games and other informal, improvised lap games that bring the hands together at midline repeatedly. The hands exploring the face of the mother unite other sense impressions of the mother with the tactile experience.
Locomotion	It is the reach for the out-of-range object that initiates the pattern for creeping.	When a baby can demonstrate postural readiness for creeping and reach on a sound cue alone, initiate the pattern for creeping by providing a favorite sound toy just beyond reach.

velopment (Warren, 1981). Systematic intervention for visually impaired infants and their families must begin as early as possible. This early intervention places emphasis on parental involvement. Much of the work of the teacher consists of training family members to interact more effectively with the infant. Table 6.4 illustrates specific adaptations carried out by family members for the accomplishment of key developmental milestones.

Visually impaired infants are basically like all other infants. Many of their needs are the same; however, the process of satisfying these needs may be different and may require consistent parental attention and specialized knowledge. Most parents experience feelings of anger, guilt, etc. They may have the tendency to leave the child alone and struggle with their own feelings. This tendency adversely affects "the first level of affective development—human attachment" (Barraga, 1976, p. 20). Thus, parents need to learn that a dialogue consisting of body play and sound stimulation is essential in developing the sense of security, inner control, and environmental exploration.

Having established strong relationships, the toddler is free to search actively and exercise control over the world of concrete objects. This process facilitates the development of the self as an independent being and the ability to interact with the environment. Spatial orientation and concept formation require a long and tedious learning process but ensure the potential for independent functioning at a later date.

Children with limited vision may be able to use that vision to facilitate their knowledge of the environment. Intervention with these children requires systematic visual training, beginning with visual awareness and fixation, to visual motor coordination. The development of stable visual skills and self-assurance in the ability to use vision in the early stages of development may be the single most important difference between functioning as a totally blind or a sighted individual in later life (Barraga, 1976).

The School Years

The emphasis on early childhood education and the development of technology have prompted educators to recognize that simply substituting tactual, auditory, or enlarged visual materials is no longer appropriate for the education of visually impaired children. In addition to the academic training necessary for all children, there are some specialized aspects of the curriculum for visually impaired students. The following four broad areas have been adapted from Barraga (1976):

1. *Personal competencies and self-adjustment* need to be heavily stressed during the school years. In some cases, the acquisition of functional skills such as grooming, social interaction, home management, and preparation for marriage and family life may take precedence over academic learning for a period of time.

2. *Orientation and mobility* encompass basic concepts in orienting the body in space and moving through the environment. Orientation and mobility skills determine the individual's social competence and future employment. The acquisition of these skills requires sometimes long and intensive training by a mobility specialist. Unfortunately, because such training is provided on a one-to-one basis and the reluctance of many school districts to employ a mobility specialist, a large number of students are not receiving consistent training.

3. *Communication skills* are the first component in the academic curriculum. Although much greater emphasis is placed in the early school years on reading, writing, listening, and speaking, differences of opinion about the medium for reading and writing continue. For those who are totally blind, the primary reading skills to be developed are tactual. Deciding which medium is more appropriate for the low vision student is a more difficult task. Sometimes the decision made is not based on the student's visual abilities but on the teacher's assumption of what is a more efficient medium. Jones (1961) in studying the reading medium

Starting Early with Visually Impaired Children and Their Families

The Child Development Center operated by the New York Association for the Blind was organized as an intervention center to meet the needs of visually impaired infants, preschoolers, and their families. The program is center-based with an outreach component. It consists of a parent-infant training group for infants under the age of two, and a preschool group for children over the age of two. The purposes of the program are to facilitate: (1) parent-infant interactions; (2) maximum growth of infants and preschoolers in all developmental areas; (3) school readiness; and (4) the mainstreaming process of visually impaired children. The Center is a part of a multiservice agency and draws on the agency's resources to provide a comprehensive individualized program.

Every child entering the program is evaluated by a social worker, an infant/preschool education specialist, a pediatrician, a psychologist, a low vision specialist, a speech and language pathologist, an audiologist, and a physical and occupational therapist. All evaluations are conducted at the Center, making it possible for parents to secure those services without traveling to many different locations. Following the evaluation, staff members meet with parents to discuss their findings and develop an intervention program. Each child remains in the program until he or she is placed in a regular school program.

The Center recognizes the important role of the parents in the development of visually impaired children and makes all efforts to involve them in the development and implementation of the IEP Parents and their infants meet in small groups twice a week at the Center with the infant specialist and are visited at home three times a week initially, and once a week later by an outreach teacher. The meetings at the Center encourage parents to discuss their own needs and develop strategies to meet those needs. Parents provide support for each other by sharing experiences and take an active role as teachers. During the home visits, parents are helped with strategies to work with their infants for normal infant development.

When a child reaches age two, he or she becomes eligible for the preschool program. The preschool classes meet five days per week. Each class consists of a maximum of six children, with a full-time teacher, an assistant teacher, one or more volunteer(s), and a student intern. The low child-adult ratio facilitates individualization and provides an opportunity for every child to work on his or her level. Children are provided with experiences in self-help, social, gross and fine motor, language, and cognitive development. The teacher maintains an up-to-date profile in all areas for each child. This provides for continuous progress monitoring and for emphasizing instruction in areas that are most needed.

A mainstreaming placement is secured for every child ready to enter a regular preschool program. In some cases, the child may attend the Center in the mornings and a public preschool program in the afternoon, thus facilitating the transition into the public school setting. In other cases, the child may be placed in a public preschool program full-time with support services provided by the outreach teacher. In either case, the Center staff provides inservice training for all staff at the mainstream site and continuously monitors the child's progress and placement.

The Child Development Center has evolved in response to the needs of visually impaired children and their families. Thus far, it has been very successful in preparing these children to function within the regular school setting.

(print or braille) found a wide variation in children with various degrees of visual acuity. Some students with very low vision were found to be print readers, while others with high visual acuity were braille readers. However, the current emphasis on visual efficiency training has provided an impetus toward print reading for all those who have some residual vision. The medium selected should help the child achieve the highest possible efficiency in information acquisition. Unfortunately, reading rates for braille, as well as print, are quite slow. Differences of reading rates between visually impaired and sighted elementary children are minimal and rarely present any significant educational deficits; however, in the upper grades (high school), the sighted read at a rate three times greater than that of the visually impaired. Consequently, completing an assignment requiring extensive reading takes much longer for the visually impaired. To decrease the amount of needed reading time, visually impaired students are relying to a greater extent on "auditory reading," that is, listening to audio-recorded materials. Hence, listening skills are one of the most important aspects in the educational process of the visually impaired. The teaching of these skills should begin in infancy and receive increased emphasis as the child progresses through the school years.

The development of writing skills (braille, typing, and handwriting) require particular emphasis. For the totally blind student, all three become important aspects of his or her communication system. There is a disagreement about the proper time at which to introduce typing and handwriting. Barraga (1976) suggests that about the third or fourth grade the child is ready for these skills. Handwriting skills for the low vision child begin in the early school years and use of cursive writing is recommended from the very beginning. Block letter writing requires the pencil/pen to be relocated after each letter is formed. Accurate relocation becomes a formidable task because of the difficulties in judging the proper spacing and alignment.

4. *Introduction to prevocational and career information*, not commonly available to the visually impaired student, must begin early. Often, visually impaired students lack information on what skills are required to perform a certain job and thus set unrealistic occupational goals for themselves. Providing a variety of opportunities for participating in work experiences appears to be a greater benefit than simply reading or hearing about particular occupations. Many states and local agencies are beginning to coordinate the activities "among local schools, residential schools, and rehabilitation agencies in providing career information, vocational education and job training" (Barraga, 1976, p. 95).

The importance of programming such specialized curriculum during the school years cannot be overemphasized. It plays a vital role in the total life adjustment and functioning of visually impaired individuals. Unfortunately, the emphasis primarily on academic programming in many school districts, as well as in some residential schools, results in the need for rehabilitation for a large number of people.

The Adult Years

At this time in the lifespan, the majority of visually impaired people need some type of rehabilitation program. The extent and scope of the program and the intervention approach depend upon the severity of the impairment, age of onset, chronological age, and previous training. Consideration of these variables mandates the development and implementation of programs to meet individual needs.

An overall goal of each rehabilitation program is to enable the individual to function independently and become a contributing member of the community.

The process of aging often leads to visual impairment. The rapid increase of the elderly population in this country and a number of other causes leading to visual impairment later in life result in a dramatic increase in the visually impaired population. By far, the majority of that population is adventitiously impaired.

For the congenitally impaired, the problem is one of normal growth and development within the limitations and/or deprivations that result from lack of or reduced vision. They do not have to make an adjustment to a new way of life. The condition itself is "normal" for them. It is the way they perceive the social and physical environments. If an adjustment is to be made, it is primarily one enabling them to better function within those environments.

For the adventitiously impaired, the larger problem is one of emotional adjustment, an adjustment not only to a new way of life but also to the loss of vision. The loss of any major sense necessitates compensatory training of the other senses and acquisition of new skills to perform tasks in other than already learned ways. However, the acquisition of new skills alone does not constitute complete rehabilitation. The ability to function in a given situation is affected by one's feelings about himself/herself at that time. Thus, effective rehabilitation for the adventitiously impaired must include physical retraining and psychological reconstitution. The physical skills gained may be abandoned later if one has not resolved his or her feeling about the loss of vision. Conversely, if one is given only psychological help without physical retraining, he or she may feel as helpless and certainly will be a dependent individual. The approach to the rehabilitation process then must be a holistic one, that is, dealing with the total human being rather than the loss of vision alone.

Unfortunately, many state as well as privately supported agencies take a narrow view of the problems and provide only those services that lead to immediate and visible results. A number of reasons may account for these programs. Underlying these reasons are financial considerations. The basis for agency reimbursement is the number of individuals undergoing rehabilitation rather than the quality of rehabilitation. A comprehensive rehabilitation program requires the services of a large and diverse number of professionals. The employment of such personnel is also dependent upon the financial status of the agency. However, each rehabilitation agency should employ or secure the services of an orientation and mobility specialist, a rehabilitation teacher, a social worker, a psychologist, a vocational counselor, and a career and job development and placement specialist. Without the services of these professionals and an individually planned program, the rehabilitation process cannot be complete. Barraga (1976) suggests a program that would provide the visually impaired with an equal opportunity for productive life (Table 6.5).

The recent development in technology and its application to education and employment make it possible for the visually impaired individual to obtain and/ or keep a job, move safely through the environment, read print, and in general be competitive in the job market.

Table 6.5

Components of Rehabilitation Program

Skill Area	Components	Awareness/Knowledge/Skill	Professionals Involved
Personal/ Emotional	Understanding of self as a person	Attitude about self and others Development of self-esteem Understanding and coping with visual impairment Understanding capabilities and limitations Sexual needs and behaviors	Psychologist Social Worker Counselor
Social and Living	Personal care and management	Eating, dressing, and grooming Selection, purchase, and care of appropriate clothing Use of self-care tools	Rehabilitation Teacher
	Home management	Selection and purchase of nutritious foods Meal preparation Use and manipulation of home equipment and utensils Simple mechanical repairs Managing finances and budgeting	Rehabilitation Teacher
	Social skills	Appropriate social behaviors Use of leisure time Interaction with others	Rehabilitation Teacher Orientation and Mobility Specialist Psychologist Social Worker Counselor Recreation Specialist
Communication and Business	Information gathering	Use of available resources for study or vocational preparation Selection of appropriate communication system, reading devices, and equipment, optical aids, etc. Use of microcomputer for personal/ occupational needs	Rehabilitation Teacher Reading Specialist
	Written communication	Use of braille for labeling and organization of materials Typing skills for personal, vocational, and professional purposes Handwriting Formats for tax forms, etc.	Rehabilitation Teacher

		Table 6.5 (continued)	
Skill Area	Components	Awareness/Knowledge/Skill	Professionals Involved
Orientation and Mobility	Self-orientation to objects in space	Spatial orientation to home and work area Movement through the environment Exploration of work space and other indoor settings	Orientation and Mobility Specialist
	Independent mobility	Use of cane/dog guide for travel in various environments Use of electronic devices Travel through urban/rural areas Use of public transportation	Orientation and Mobility Specialist
Career/ Vocational Development	General work skills	Attitudes toward self and others in work setting Development of appropriate work habits Work safety Arrangement of tools, materials, and/or devices for most efficient use Maintenance of orderly work area	Career/Vocational Counselor
	Career exploration and placement	Selection of career according to interest, potential for success, and family considerations Simulation of work experience Skill development for chosen career Work experience in community Placement in on-the-job training Employment and maintenance of position	Job Placement Counselor

Source: From *Visual Handicaps and Learning* by Natalie Barraga (Belmont, CA: Wadsworth Publishing Company, 1976). Reprinted by permission of PRO-ED, Inc.

FUTURE PERSPECTIVES FOR THE TREATMENT OF VISUAL IMPAIRMENTS

Although loss of vision is of critical consequence, many visually impaired persons consider it an "inconvenience" rather than a handicap. This statement is not a disclaimer of disability; rather, it is a rejection of negative societal attitudes. The visually impaired are capable human beings, and they should be accepted in society with equal opportunities for education and employment.

Organized education for the visually impaired dates back to the eighteenth century. Throughout the years, there have been several issues that still need to be resolved. By far, the most important one is the lack of communication among the professional personnel. There is an abundant knowledge base in education, rehabilitation, and medical treatment for the visually impaired. Each area is advancing within its own confines. There appears to be no synthesizing theory, thus inhibiting effective implementation of available knowledge into practice.

Underlying this issue is the lack of meaningful definitions and various other terms describing the visually impaired. The adoption of more precise terminology, such as that proposed by Barraga (1976), undoubtedly will influence research, treatment, and service delivery.

Early intervention with visually impaired infants is relatively recent. Research indicates that early intervention, particularly during the first two years of life, is most critical in minimizing emotional and physical isolation and in promoting body manipulation, tactual exploration, and all developmental areas. For the child with some residual vision, that period is the most important one in developing visual skills.

Although PL 94–142 mandates individualized programs to meet the needs of each student, many programs do not include career and employment awareness. In the later school years, students should be prepared to meet the demands for employment. Career and employment preparation must begin during the school years rather than in rehabilitation facilities after finishing school.

Visual impairment among the elderly is becoming a growing concern for all professionals. Medical treatment, restoration of functional vision, and development of recreational skills are of greater importance at this time in the lifespan than ever before. While the majority of these services have been provided in rehabilitation facilities, the current trend is for service provision at home and in the surrounding community. There is very little change in these services, but there is a reorientation as to where, how, and to whom the services are provided.

Advances in technology have had a significant impact on the education, rehabilitation, and employment of visually impaired persons. In reading, the Optacon and Kurzweil Reading Machine have provided access to printed material. Lasers and other medical technology have greatly advanced the diagnosis and treatment of visual disorders. In orientation and mobility, the Sonicguide, Mowat Sensor, and Laser Cane have provided new aids to enhance mobility and improve spatial concept development. More recently, the proliferation of the microcomputer may provide even greater and more diverse benefits to the visually impaired. The microcomputer has the potential to significantly improve educational and employment opportunities. Depending on the skills and severity of visual impairment, the visually impaired can access microcomputers in a number of ways. These include touch (braille and Optacon), hearing (digitized and synthesized speech), and vision (hardware- and software-produced large print). Thus, we may see a future where visually impaired persons are no longer at a disadvantage with regard to printed matter. It is very likely that the floppy disk, or perhaps a more compact storage system, will replace paper and print.

The teaching of communication skills presently involves the areas of braille, handwriting, listening and recording devices, and typewriting. It is very possible that these areas will be stressed less in the future and a greater emphasis placed on computer use. Assuming that microcomputers and other electronic devices become affordable, their use in the home is limited only by one's imagination. The use of a computer to set thermostats, oven temperatures, program cooking

Converting Visual Information

The lack of direct access to printed material has been a primary problem in all areas of vocation, education, and recreation for the visually impaired. Communication between employer, employee, and consumer is generally in print. The inability of the visually impaired to read print presents an inherent difficulty in partaking of that communication, thus limiting the possibilities of obtaining and/or maintaining employment.

In common with the sighted, the visually impaired have enjoyed a continuous increase in benefits from the rapid advances in scientific knowledge and technological development. The increasing volume and variety of braille literature, available through the development of automated methods of production, appear to be insufficient to keep pace with the production of print materials. Resolution of this problem appears to be in technology, designed for the visually impaired, which can utilize existing and future information delivery systems. Numerous efforts have been made over the years to develop reading aids based on conversion of visual information for detection by hearing or touch.

The origins of the Kurzweil Reading Machine (KRM) stem from the interest in artificial intelligence, mainly print recognition, decision making, and speech output. It uses a small computer-controlled camera which automatically detects and scans lines of print on a page. The image in the camera is processed by the computer which can recognize strings of letters as separate words. The computer determines the pronunciation of the word through programmed rules and exceptions of English grammar and activates a speaker to produce synthetic speech. The only requirements the user has is to open a book, journal, or any printed material and place it over a glass plate beneath which is the computer-controlled camera, and to learn the command panel—the KRM will do the reading.

The KRM's versatility and potential are limitless, since its functions are operated through computer programs which can be updated to meet future technological developments. If the user is unable to understand a particular word or phrase, he or she can command the KRM to spell that word or repeat a phrase, a sentence, a paragraph, etc., and to announce various punctuation marks. An automatic contrast control allows for reading materials that have varying print quality. When a special program is used it can be converted into a talking calculator or interfaced with an embosser, and produce hard copy braille. The KRM is equipped with earphones, thus providing privacy for its user, as well as not disturbing other individuals working nearby.

The KRM is a remarkable technological achievement which offers an opportunity to totally blind readers to access printed materials and become more competitive in education and employment. Undoubtedly, the KRM is only a harbinger of future technological developments.

times, and perform other daily tasks will likely become common. Identification of clothing, medicines, and other unknown items may be accomplished with a laser-read label, much in the same fashion as is presently accomplished for item prices in some grocery stores. Diabetic needs, such as insulin measuring and monitoring of glucose levels, will be accomplished through computers, as well. The insulin pump, already available, is an obvious forerunner of such devices.

Optical management of low vision is undergoing major changes. Most of the optical systems currently in existence will be obsolete before they gain wide acceptance. Advances in multiple lens systems, contact telescopic systems, and automatically focusing lenses are leading the way to a new era of treatment. The technology required for such innovations is already common in photographic equipment.

Medical advances in laser technology, cataract surgery, and various transplants may drastically reduce visual impairment. The progression of visual loss due to glaucoma can be arrested through early detection and appropriate treatment. Advances in laser technology may substantially reduce the effects of diabetic retinopathy, macular degeneration, retinal detachment, etc.

Perhaps the ultimate technological device is one that addresses restoration of vision. This device will attempt to provide a substitute for vision, that is, a visual prosthesis. The ultimate goal of this type of research is to use a miniature camera that will provide "visual" information from it to the visual cortex through numerous electrodes stimulating the brain to "see" an orderly pattern of phosphemes yielding an image of the objects in the environment. Advances in technology and neuroscience have made it possible thus far for several totally blind individuals to "visually" differentiate between horizontal and vertical lines. The future is indeed promising and exciting.

SUMMARY

Visual impairments can be grouped by age of onset, visual acuity, or the degree of functional vision that the individual has; but for practical purposes three categories have proved to be the most useful. Individuals who are blind are those totally without vision or those who have light perception only. Low vision is the term used to describe individuals who have difficulty seeing objects at a distance but are able to see things a few inches or a few feet away. With aids and the right environmental conditions, they may be able to read print material. Individuals who are described as visually limited may require special lighting, optical, or other aids; but they are considered to be sighted persons. Although these definitions provide the most helpful information for education and rehabilitation, there is a legal definition of blindness which is often used as the sole eligibility criterion for qualifying for special services.

The precise number of visually impaired persons is not known, but among school-age children, visual impairments are at the low end of the incidence continuum. Visual impairments and chronological age are directly related and it has been estimated that over 50 percent of the people who have visual impairments are over the age of 65.

The causes of visual impairments are many, including infectious diseases, poisoning, accidents, tumors, prenatal influences, heredity, and aging. Among children, heredity is the major cause of visual impairments. Advances in medicine and medical technology have progressed at a rapid rate in this field resulting in prevention of some forms of blindness and reduction in the number of cases of others.

Although there is no such thing as a "typical" blind person, individuals who are blind from birth often develop more slowly. This delayed development is not related to their ability nor does it predict later performance. Instead, it is caused by fewer opportunities to interact with the environment and the inability to learn from all of the visual information that is available to sighted children.

The social and emotional development of blind individuals is influenced by their early experiences and the opportunities which they have to develop independently. Like all people, blind children who are encouraged to be independent and solve problems on their own are far less likely to become helpless, dependent adults than those who are not.

Educational goals for visually impaired children are not dissimilar to those for sighted children. The major difference is the inclusion of many skills related to daily living. In recent years, technology has played a major role in the education of visually impaired students and the rehabilitation and retraining of adults who have become visually impaired. Computers have enabled material to be produced in print or in braille very quickly; scanners with synthesized voices or electrical pulses have been used to enable blind individuals to "read" print material; and lasers that "see" obstacles have been incorporated into canes.

Improvements in legislation, medical technology, education, and vocational counseling have changed the opportunities available to many people with visual impairments. These changes, along with positive changes in society's attitudes, will continue to enable many blind people to lead the life they choose in the mainstream of society.

References

Adamson, L., Als, H., Tronick, P., & Brazelton, T.B. (1977). The development of social reciprocity between a sighted infant and the blind parents: A case study. *Journal of American Academy of Child Psychiatry, 16,* 194–207.

American Foundation for the Blind (1976). *Facts about blindness.* New York: American Foundation for the Blind.

Anderson, D. W., & Olson, M. (1981). Word meaning among congenitally blind children. *Journal of Visual Impairment and Blindness, 75,* 165–168.

Apple, M. M. (1972). Kinesic training for blind persons: A vital means of communication. *New Outlook for the Blind, 66,* 201–208.

Ashcroft, S. C. (1961). Errors of oral reading of braille at elementary grade level. *Report of Proceedings of Conference on Research Needs in Braille* (pp. 16–31). New York: American Foundation for the Blind.

Ashcroft, S. C., Halliday, C., & Barraga, N. (1965). *Study 11: Effects of experimental teaching on the visual behavior of children educated as though they had no vision.* Nashville, TN: George Peabody College.

Barraga, N. (1964). *Increased visual behavior in low vision children.* New York: American Foundation for the Blind.

Barraga, N. (1976). *Visual handicaps and learning.* Belmont, CA: Wadsworth.

Barraga, N. (1980). *Program to develop efficiency in visual functioning.* Louisville, KY: American Printing House for the Blind, Inc.

Barraga, N. C., & Collins, M. (1979). Development of efficiency in visual functioning: Rationale for a comprehensive program. *Journal of Visual Impairment and Blindness, 73,* 121–126.

Bauman, M. K. (1947). Report on a non-language learning test. *American Association of Workers for the Blind Proceedings,* 99–101.

Bauman, M. K. (1958). A manual of norms for tests used in counseling blind persons. *Crawford Small Parts Dexterity Research Series No. 6.* New York: American Foundation for the Blind.

Bauman, M. K. (1968). *A report and a reprint: Tests used in the psychological evaluation of blind and visually handicapped persons and a manual of norms for tests used in counseling blind persons.* Washington, DC: American Association of Workers for the Blind.

Bauman, M. K. (1971). Overbrook Social Competency Scale. *Education for the Visually Impaired, 3,* 82–87.

Bauman, M. K. (1980). Evaluating the rehabilitation through psychological and other diagnostic proceedings. In C. W. Hoehne, J. G. Cull, & R. E. Hardy (Eds.), *Ophthalmological considerations in the rehabilitation of the blind* (pp. 164–175). Springfield, IL: Charles C. Thomas.

Bauman, M. K., & Hayes, S. P. (1951). *A manual for the psychological examination of the adult blind.* New York: The Psychological Corporation.

Betts, G. L., & Ziegler, W. A. (1946). *Manual for the rate of manipulation test.* Chicago: Educational Test Bureau.

Boldt, W. (1969). The development of scrento for thinking in blind children and adolescents. *Education of the Visually Handicapped, 1,* 5–11.

Bookbinder, S. R. (1978). *Mainstreaming: What every child needs to know about disabilities.* Boston: Exceptional Parent Press.

Burlingham, D. (1961). Some notes on the development of the blind. *The Psychoanalytic Study of the Child, 16,* 121–145.

Burlingham, D. (1965). Some problems of ego development in blind children. *The Psychoanalytic Study of the Child, 20,* 194–208.

Campbell, L. F. (1970). Mobility for young blind children. In *Selected papers: Fiftieth biennial conference.* Philadelphia: Association for Education of the Visually Handicapped.

Carroll, T. J. (1961). *Blindness: What it is, what it does, and how to live with it.* Boston: Little, Brown.

Cholden, L. S. (1958). *A psychiatrist works with blindness.* New York: American Foundation for the Blind.

Collins, M., & Barraga, N. C. (1980). Development of efficiency in visual functioning: An evolution process. *Journal of Visual Impairment and Blindness, 74,* 93–96.

Corn, A. L., & Martinez, I. (1978). *When you have a visually handicapped child in your classroom: Suggestions for teachers.* New York: American Foundation for the Blind.

Cramer, R. F. (1973). Conservation by the congenitally blind. *British Journal of Psychology, 64,* 241–250.

Cratty, B. J. (1971). *Movement and spatial awareness in blind children and youth.* Springfield, IL: Charles C. Thomas.

Cutsforth, T. D. (1951). *The blind in school and society* (rev. ed.). New York: American Foundation for the Blind.

Davidson, O. R. (1973). The accountability of nonprofit institutions in a free society. *The New Outlook for the Blind, 67,* 389–395.

DeMott, R. (1972). Verbalism and affective meaning for blind, severely visually impaired, and normally sighted children. *New Outlook for the Blind, 66,* 1–25.

Dokecki, P. R. (1966). Verbalism and the blind, a critical view of the concepts and the literature. *Exceptional Children, 32,* 525–530.

Efron, M., & Duboff, B. R. (1976). *A vision guide for teachers of deaf-blind children.* Raleigh, NC: South Atlantic Regional Center for Services to Deaf/Blind Children.

Farrell, G. (1956). *The story of blindness.* Cambridge, MA: Harvard University Press.

Ficociello-Gates, C. (1979). *Manual for visual assessment kit* (revised). Dallas, TX: South Central Regional Center for Services to Deaf/Blind Children.

Fraiberg, S. (1977). *Insights from the blind.* New York: Basic Books.

Freedman, D. A., & Cannady, C. (1971). Delayed emergence of prone locomotion. *Journal of Nervous and Mental Diseases, 153,* 108–117.

Friedman, J., & Pasnak, R. (1973). Attainment of classification and sighted children. *Education of the Visually Handicapped, 5,* 55–62.

Gearhart, B. R., & Weishahn, M. M. (1976). *The handicapped child in the regular classroom.* St. Louis: The C. V. Mosby Co.

Gottesman, M. (1973). Conservation development in blind children. *Child Development, 44,* 824–827.

Gottesman, M. (1976). Stage development of blind children: A Piagetian view. *New Outlook for the Blind, 70,* 94–100.

Harley, R. K., Jr. (1963). *Verbalism among blind children.* New York: American Foundation for the Blind.

Hatfield, E. M. (1975). Why are they blind? *Sight Saving Review, 45,* 3–22.

Hatwell, Y. (1966). *Privation sensorelle et intelligence.* Paris, France: Presses Universitaires de France.

Higgins, L. C. (1973). Classification in congenitally blind children. *Research Series No. 25.* New York: American Foundation for the Blind.

Hill, E., & Ponder, P. (1976). *Orientations and mobility techniques.* New York: American Foundation for the Blind.

Hull, W. (1983). Social development of preschool visually handicapped children. In M. E. Mulholland & M. V. Wurster (Eds.), *Help me become everything I can be* (pp. 47–50). New York: American Foundation for the Blind.

Jackson, R. M. (1983). The importance of perceptional activity in the development of visually handicapped infants and preschoolers. In M. E. Mulholland & M. V. Wurster (Eds.), *Help me become everything I can be* (pp. 63–72). New York: American Foundation for the Blind.

Johnston, S. C. (1978). Teaching science to the mainstreamed partially sighted child at the junior high level. In M. Hofman (Ed.), *A working conference on science education for handicapped students: Proceedings* (pp. 102–107). Washington, DC: National Science Teachers Association.

Jones, J. W. (1961). *Blind children—degree of vision, mode of reading.* Washington, DC: U.S. Government Printing Office.

Jose, R. T. (1983). *Understanding low vision.* New York: American Foundation for the Blind.

Langley, B., & DuBose, R. (1976). Functional vision screening for severely handicapped children. *New Outlook for the Blind, 10,* 346–350.

Lowenfeld, B. (1971). *Our blind children: Growing and learning with them* (3rd ed.). Springfield, IL: Charles C. Thomas.

Lowenfeld, B. (Ed.) (1973). *The visually handicapped child in the school*. New York: John Day.

Lowenfeld, B. (1975). *The changing status of the blind*. Springfield, IL: Charles C. Thomas.

Lydon, W. T., & McGraw, M. L. (1973). *Concept development for visually handicapped children*. New York: American Foundation for the Blind.

Maxfield, K. E., & Buchholz, S. (1957). *A social maturity scale for blind preschool children*. New York: American Foundation for the Blind.

McGuinness, R. M. (1970). A descriptive study of blind children educated in the itinerant teacher, resource room, and special school settings. *Research Bulletin No. 20* (pp. 1–56). New York: American Foundation for the Blind.

Miller, C. K. (1969). Conservation in blind children. *Education of the Visually Handicapped, 1*, 101–105.

National Society for the Prevention of Blindness (1966). *Estimated statistics on blindness and vision problems*. New York: Author.

National Society for the Prevention of Blindness (1980). *Vision problems in the United States: Facts and figures*. New York: Author.

Nolan, C. Y. (1960). On the unreality of words to the blind. *New Outlook for the Blind, 54*, 100–102.

Nolan, C. Y., & Kederis, C. J. (1969). *Perceptual factors in braille word recognition*. New York: American Foundation for the Blind.

Nolan, C. Y., & Morris, J. E. (1965). Development and validation of the Roughness Discrimination Test. *International Journal for the Education of the Blind, 15*, 1–6.

Orlansky, M. D. (1977). *Mainstreaming the visually impaired child: Blind and partially sighted students in the regular classroom*. Austin, TX: Learning Concepts.

Reynolds, M. C., & Birch, J. W. (1977). *Teaching exceptional children in all America's schools*. Reston, VA: The Council for Exceptional Children.

Roberts, J. R. (1945). *Manual for the Pennsylvania bimanual work sample*. Minneapolis: Educational Test Bureau.

Rogow, S. M. (1983). Language development in blind children. In M. E. Mulholland & M. V. Wurster (Eds.), *Help me become everything I can be* (pp. 57–61). New York: American Foundation for the Blind.

Schindele, R. (1974). The social adjustment of visually handicapped children in different educational settings. *AFB Research Bulletin, 28*, 125–144.

Schloss, I. P. (1963). Implications of altering the definition of blindness. *AFB Research Bulletin, 3*, 111–116.

Scholl, G. T. (1973). Understanding and meeting developmental needs. In B. Lowenfeld (Ed.), *The visually handicapped child in school* (pp. 61–92). New York: John Day.

Schultz, W. C. (1958). *Firo: A three dimensional theory of interpersonal behavior*. New York: Rinehart.

Scott, R. S. (1969). *The making of blind men*. New York: Russell Sage Foundation.

Shurrager, H. (1961). *A haptic intelligence scale for adult blind*. Chicago: Illinois Institute of Technology.

Shurrager, H. C., & Shurrager, P. S. (1964). *Manual for the haptic intelligence scale for adult blind*. Chicago: Psychology Research.

Sommers, V. S. (1944). *The influence of parental attitudes and social environment on the personality development of the adolescent blind*. New York: American Foundation for the Blind.

Sparrow, S. S., Balla, D. A., & Cicchetti, D. V. (1984). *Vineland adaptive behavior scales*. Circle Pines, MN: American Guidance Service.

Stephens, B., & Grube, C. (1982). Development of Piagetian reasoning in congenitally blind children. *Journal of Visual Impairment and Blindness, 76,* 133–143.

Stern, D. (1974). Mother and infant at play: The dyadic interaction including facial, vocal, and gaze behaviors. In H. Lewis & L. Rosenblum (Eds.), *The effect of the infant on its caregiver* (pp. 187–214). New York: John Wiley.

Stogner, P. C. (1970). Evaluation of intelligence, academic aptitude, and achievement of the visually impaired. In *Selected papers: Fiftieth biennial conference.* Philadelphia: Association for Education of the Visually Handicapped.

Suinn, R. M., & Dauterman, W. L. (1966). *Manual for the Stanford-Kohs block design test for the blind.* Washington, DC: Vocational Rehabilitation Administration.

Swallow, R. M., & Poulsen, M. K. (1983). Cognitive development of young visually handicapped children. In M. E. Mulholland & M. V. Wurster (Eds.), *Help me become everything I can be* (pp. 36–45). New York: American Foundation for the Blind.

Tait, P. (1972). Effect of cirenstantial rejection on infant behavior. *New Outlook for the Blind, 66,* 139–149.

Valvo, A. (1971). *Sight restoration after long-term blindness: The problems and behavior patterns of visual rehabilitation.* New York: American Foundation for the Blind.

VanderKolk, C. J. (1981). *Assessment and planning with the visually impaired.* Baltimore, MD: University Park Press.

Vision problems in the United States: Facts and figures (1980). New York: Operational Research Department, National Society for the Prevention of Blindness.

Warren, D. H. (1976). Blindness and early development: What is known and what needs to be studied. *New Outlook for the Blind, 70,* 5–16.

Warren, D. H. (1981). Visual impairments. In J. M. Kauffman & D. P. Hallahan (Eds.), *Handbook of special education* (pp. 195–221). Englewood Cliffs, NJ: Prentice-Hall, Inc.

Warren, D. H., Anooshian, L. J., & Bollinger, J. G. (1973). Early vs. late blindness: The role of early vision in spatial behavior. *AFB Research Bulletin, 26,* 151–170.

Witkin, H. A., Brinbaum, J., Lomonaco, S., Lehr, S., & Herman, J. L. (1968). Cognitive patterning in congenitally totally blind children. *Child Development, 39,* 767–786.

Resources

Organizations

American Foundation for the Blind

15 West 16th Street

New York, NY 10011

> Provides direct and technical assistance services to visually impaired persons and their families, professionals in rehabilitation and education, organizations and schools; publishes books, monographs, and a journal.

American Printing House for the Blind

1839 Frankfort Avenue

Louisville, KY 40206

> National organization for the production of literature and the manufacture of educational aids and materials.

Association for the Education and Rehabilitation of the Blind and Visually Impaired

206 North Washington Street-Suite 320

Alexandria, VA 22314

> A professional organization concerned with service provision to visually impaired individuals throughout their lifespan; publishes a journal and holds annual meetings.

National Association for Parents of the Visually Impaired

P.O. Box 180806

Austin, TX 78718

> A parent organization which promotes public understanding of the needs and rights of visually impaired children and publishes a quarterly newsletter.

National Braille Association

422 Clinton Avenue, South

Rochester, NY 14620

> Provides educational materials and texts in braille, large type, and recordings for college students, visually impaired professionals, and others.

Recording for the Blind

20 Roszel Road

Princeton, NJ 08540

> Lends taped educational materials and textbooks at no charge to visually impaired individuals.

Journals

Journal of Visual Impairment and Blindness

American Foundation for the Blind

15 West 16th Street

New York, NY 10011

> Publishes research and applied articles related to visual impairment and blindness.

Education of the Visually Handicapped

Association for the Education and Rehabilitation of the Blind and Visually Impaired

206 North Washington Street-Suite 320

Alexandria, VA 22314

> Publishes articles related to all aspects of the education of visually handicapped and blind individuals.

Newsletter

Awareness

National Association for Parents of the Visually Impaired

P.O. Box 180806

Austin, TX 78718

> Publishes information about legislation, adaptive devices, and other issues of interest to individuals with visual impairment and their families.

Books

Corn, A. L. (1985). *Are you really blind?* New York: American Foundation for the Blind.

> A playground conversation between a visually impaired child and his sighted classmate.

Warren, D. H. (1984). *Blindness and early childhood development* (2nd ed.). New York: American Foundation for the Blind.

> A thorough review of the literature on the development of visually impaired children.

Chapter 7

HEARING DISORDERS

The education of individuals with hearing disorders has a long, rich, and extremely complex tradition, with the first documented educational procedures in education of the handicapped consisting of techniques developed to teach deaf children in sixteenth- and seventeenth-century Spain. The significance of such a development assumes a proper perspective when it is remembered that literate societies—and schools—existed four and five thousand years ago along the Nile and Tigris-Euphrates Rivers. Such societies developed educational systems to educate at least some of their members to provide the sophisticated skills required for record-keeping, codification of laws, and communication by written means. From the start of recorded history through classical times, the Middle Ages, and up to the beginnings of modern times, there is no evidence of any systematic effort to provide educational services to any group of handicapped individuals.

With little or no previous work to guide them, the first educators of the deaf developed their educational techniques through trial and error and through their individual considerations of the teaching of speech, reading, and writing. The results, both in terms of the attainments of their students and in the influence on regular and special education to this day, have been tremendous.

Donald F. Moores and Julia Maestas y Moores
Gallaudet University

Before considering present day educational programs for children with hearing disorders, it is necessary to provide some background information on hearing loss and its impact on functioning. Hearing loss is quite common and has been estimated at approximately 6 percent of the American population. Thus, up to 15 million people in the United States have some form of hearing loss. However, this figure and this percentage do not give an accurate picture of the educational needs of children with hearing disorders. For example, millions of individuals suffer hearing losses as they age or through industrial exposure to loud noise. Such individuals, of course, had no hearing problems as children. It is important to remember that most hearing losses occur in adulthood. Although the onset of such a disability has great implications for social and emotional functioning, the purpose of this chapter is to examine the situation for those whose hearing loss has been early and severe.

Within this context Schein and Delk (1974) reported that there were somewhat more than 400,000 Americans of all ages who were prevocationally deaf, i.e., whose hearing loss was either present at birth or by age 19. Of this number, approximately half lost their hearing before age three. This group is classified as prelingually or preverbally deaf. When educators of the deaf refer to a deaf child the reference is typically to one who is preverbally deaf, a child with a severe to profound hearing loss that was present at birth or occurred before the acquisition of language and speech skills.

Clearly, in terms of numbers, it makes a great difference when one refers to a general American hearing impaired population of 15 million and a prelingually deaf population of 200,000. A prelingually deaf person faces fundamentally and qualitatively different obstacles in the development of linguistic, cognitive, social, and academic skills. A profoundly deaf child frequently is cut off from all but the most basic conversation within the family. Prelingual deafness can be debilitating by severely limiting the normal flow of communication between parents and child. Perhaps the greatest impact can be attributed to the significantly reduced opportunities for incidental learning which exist when parents and child share a communication system.

Currently, educational services are available to these children and their families in many states from time of identification of a hearing loss or from a very early age. From preschool and throughout the elementary and secondary years the large majority of children with severe and profound hearing losses receive extensive services. The same is not true of children with mild or moderate hearing losses. Such children are not identified at early ages and much less is known about their development of linguistic, social, and academic skills. The relative lack of services may be demonstrated by a report by Sontag, Smith, and Certo (1977) estimating that there were 377,000 school-age children in the United States with educationally relevant hearing losses, with 49,000 classified as deaf and 328,000 as hard of hearing. The figure of 49,000 deaf children is consistent with a total population of more than 200,000 prelingually deaf people of all ages.

introducing

PAUL

Paul is in his mid-thirties and lives in a moderate-sized city in Connecticut. He has a profound hearing loss, with no functional response to the spoken word. Although the loss was not diagnosed until three-and-a-half years of age, it is assumed that his deafness was congenital, i.e., present at birth. Cause is unknown. His parents are hearing, as are his two older sisters and all known relatives.

Paul was enrolled in a speech and hearing clinic after his diagnosis of deafness. He received individual and small group therapy twice a week in speech, speechreading, and use of residual hearing. He was fitted with a powerful body hearing aid which he wore at home and in the clinic. His mother received training in encouraging speech and care of a hearing aid.

At six years of age Paul was enrolled in a residential school for the deaf. Like all such schools at that time, elementary grade classroom instruction was oral-only, on the belief that the use of manual communication would inhibit the development of oral language skills. Paul, with no functional hearing and poor English skills, had great difficulty in class. In the dormitory he learned a variant of American Sign Language, which was the major mode of communication for the children.

At the junior high level the school used a combined oral-manual system of instruction. For the first time Paul understood much of the content in class. Two of his six instructors were deaf, a new experience for Paul because deaf teachers were not allowed in the preschool and elementary years on the grounds that they did not provide a good speech model. When Paul returned home for vacations the family was warm, but there were difficulties. His mother was upset that he no longer wore his hearing aid, which Paul said was of no help to him. The parents had been told both by the clinic and school not to sign with Paul, because it would hurt his speech. One sister had learned on her own and functioned in a way as the family interpreter.

At school Paul was in the vocational track and was active in athletics. He played on the football and basketball teams which competed against other schools for the deaf and against small high schools with hearing students. When he graduated he was a young man of normal intelligence who encountered great difficulty with the English language.

Fortunately for Paul, he was able to attend one of the three regional vocational programs for the deaf which had been established in the late 1960s and were the prototypes for more than 100 programs since. The program offered remedial work in English and math as well as sign language interpreters and note-takers for integrated classes. Paul successfully completed training in graphic arts and returned home, where he obtained a job as a printer in a local newspaper, a traditional area of employment for deaf men.

Paul married a woman who graduated from the same residential school and is a computer programmer. They have a boy, 10, and a girl, 7, both of whom are hearing and are progressing well in school. Paul and his wife interact socially with the hearing members of their families, with hearing neighbors, and with hearing co-workers. They also interact with hearing people through their children's activities; the boy is on a soccer team and the girl is taking dance classes. Both children sign fluently with the boy typically signing without voice and the girl simultaneously speaking and signing.

Paul and his wife participate in an active deaf community through attendance at a church for the deaf and as members of the state association of the deaf. They own what is referred to as a TTY (teletype) or more accurately TDD (Telecommunication Device for the Deaf), which enables them to communicate by phone with other TDD owners. Their portable TDD has an acoustic coupler upon which a phone can be placed, a keyboard, and a display. A message typed on a TDD is sent by phone and is displayed on the receiving TDD. Although the time involved for typing makes long distance calls expensive, the advent of the TDD has made the telephone directly accessible for the deaf for the first time. They think of the $250 cost as the best investment they have ever made and are especially pleased that Paul's parents have now bought one.

Another device which has been a major factor in making entertainment and enculturation more accessible to deaf people has been a TV decoder, a device that can make accessible on the screen captions that have been written for TV programs. Paul now watches the evening news regularly as well as TV specials and some regular programs. Although many TV programs, such as the local news, are not captioned because of cost considerations, TV decoders have made TV much more accessible to the deaf. Like TDDs, decoders are expensive. Paul paid $280 for his and is aware that many deaf people cannot afford the cost of buying either a TDD or TV decoder.

Sontag, Smith, and Certo reported that more than 90 percent of the deaf children were receiving special education services as contrasted to only 20 percent of the hard of hearing. Although the report was issued prior to the implementation of Public Law 94–142, the authors are aware of no evidence that the situation has changed substantially since that time.

Sound and Hearing

Sound, although invisible, is a physical entity, and acoustics, the study of sound, is a branch of physics. In the human voice the source of sounds are vibrations produced by means of speech mechanisms which have been adapted for human speech in addition to primary biological functions related to eating and breathing. The major articulators for human speech are the lips, teeth, tongue, palate, and pharynx. Modifications in placement and manner of the articulators produce changes in human speech sounds. The lungs and various muscular and skeletal elements of the body provide the power source for speech and respiration provides the air stream. The larynx produces a vibrating air stream which provides phonation.

Sound may be thought of as the physical stimulus which triggers the hearing process. Sound undergoes three transformations from the time it stimulates the outer ear until final processing by the human brain. Sound reaches the outer ear as acoustic energy. Upon hitting the eardrum (tympanic membrane), the sound is converted to mechanical energy and carried through the middle ear. Between the middle and inner ear, mechanical energy is transformed into hydraulic energy and conducted through the fluid of the cochlear and vestibular structures. The final transformation is from hydraulic energy to neuroelectric impulses which are transmitted to the brain.

The outer and middle ear essentially serve to collect and transform sound prepatory to hearing. The outer ear consists of external flap and the ear canal leading to the eardrum. The middle ear is very small but complex; it is attached to the eardrum, eustachian tube, and the ossicular chain. The inner ear, which consists of interlocking canals within the temporal bone deep in the skull, contains both the cochlear system (sensory organs for hearing) and the vestibular system (sensory organs for balance).

Figure 7.1

The Structure of the Ear

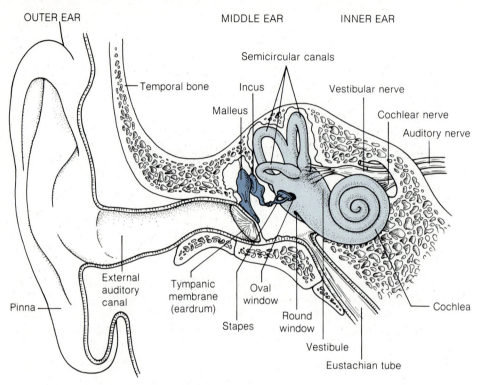

Source: From *Biosphere: The Realm of Life* by Robert A. Wallace, Jack L. King, and Gerald P. Sanders. Copyright © 1984 Scott, Foresman and Company.

The outer, middle, and inner ear make up what is known as the peripheral auditory system, which is connected to the central nervous system by the VIIIth cranial nerve, the acoustic nerve. Neurons carry acoustic energy along the nerve, which passes through a canal called the internal auditory nectus and opens into the cranial cavity.

Children who form the reference for this chapter, those with severe to profound hearing losses, typically do not suffer from losses in the outer or middle ears, what might roughly be considered conductive losses. Such losses often can be treated by surgery or by bypassing part of the conductive system. The major causes of childhood deafness, such as genetic inheritance, maternal rubella, and meningitis tend to be sensorineural in nature, i.e., they disrupt inner ear functioning and/or the inner processing of acoustic information. The prognosis for getting clear speech signals for such children whose hearing problems are more central is highly limited at present.

Educational Definitions

The most commonly cited set of definitions was developed by Frisina (1974).

1. *Level I, 35 to 54 dB hearing level (HL).* Individuals in this category routinely do not require special class/school placement; they routinely do require special speech and hearing assistance.
2. *Level II, 55 to 69 dB HL.* These individuals occasionally require special class/school placement; they routinely require special speech, hearing, and language assistance.
3. *Level III, 70 to 90 dB HL.* Those in this category of deafness occasionally require special class/school placement; they routinely require special speech, language, and educational assistance.
4. *Level IV, 90 dB HL and beyond.* These individuals routinely require special class/school placement. They routinely require special speech, hearing, language, and educational assistance.

The symbol *dB* refers to a decibel (one-tenth of a Bel), a quite complex construct. Three important things to remember in dealing with the system are that it involves a ratio, it is logarithmic, and a particular decibel value is expressed in terms of a particular reference point. Thus zero dB does not refer to a lack of sound, but rather to the faintest noise that can be heard by the young normal listener. In this way, people with better than average hearing may hear sounds of -5 decibels or even fainter. As a logarithmic system, the decibel system is not linear, i.e., the increase in pressure from zero decibels is exponential. From zero to 20 decibels the increase in pressure is 10 times; from zero to 40 decibels it is 10^2 or 100 times (10×10); from zero to 60 decibels it is 10^3 or 1000 times ($10 \times 10 \times 10$), etc.

Although there is great variation due to factors such as age and sex of speakers, environmental conditions, and distance between speakers, most conversational speech may be thought of as occurring roughly between 40 to 70 dB. Table 7.1 provides examples of levels of intensity of different noises.

The term "decibel" is related to intensity, or intensity level, the power of sound per unit area. The reader will also encounter the term "frequency" in relation to hearing. Frequency is expressed in terms of cycles per second (CPS). It is common to see CPS expressed as Hz, in honor of the German physicist Heinrich Hertz (as Bel is named in honor of Alexander G. Bell). In testing hearing, levels of intensity will be tested (in terms of dB) at least at frequencies of 500, 1000, and 2000 CPS (in terms of Hz). The interested reader is referred to a comprehensive introductory treatment of audiology by Martin (1981).

Most educators have tended to classify children in Levels I and II as hard of hearing and those in III and IV as deaf. Recently, there has been a growing acceptance of the position that the term "deaf" should be limited to only those individuals with hearing losses of 90 dB and beyond. There is a certain lack of precision due to the fact that the data are one-dimensional; they deal with only audiometric information. Other factors, such as age of identification of the loss

	Table 7.1	
Scale of Intensity for Ordinary Environmental Sounds	
0 dB	Just audible sound
10 dB	Soft rustle of leaves
20 dB	A whisper at 4 feet
30 dB	A quiet street in the evening with no traffic
40 dB	Night noises in a city
50 dB	A quiet automobile 10 feet away
60 dB	Department store
70 dB	Busy traffic
60 to 70 dB	Normal conversation at 3 feet
80 dB	Heavy traffic
80 to 90 dB	Niagara Falls
90 dB	A pneumatic drill 10 feet away
100 dB	A riveter 35 feet away
110 dB	Hi-fi phonograph with a 10 watt amplifier 10 feet away
115 dB	Hammering on a steel plate 2 feet away

Source: From *Man's World of Sound* by John R. Pierce and Edward E. David, Jr. as cited in *Waves and the Ear* by Van Bergeijk, Pierce, and David. Reprinted by permission of Doubleday & Company, Inc.

and initiation of training, reaction to auditory training and presence of other handicapping conditions, and hearing status of parents can have significant influence on development.

ETIOLOGY AND PREVENTION

Moores (1973, 1982) has postulated that deaf children and their families go through four periods of extreme stress. In each period the roles played by professionals can be crucial. The periods are:

1. Identification of hearing loss
2. Entrance into school
3. Beginning adolescence
4. Early adulthood

Unless one has gone through the process or worked with parents who have, it is difficult to appreciate the trauma frequently involved in obtaining adequate diagnosis. Typically the first professional a mother interacts with concerning her worries is a pediatrician who frequently does not call for auditory examination of the child. In a study in California, Meadow (1967) found that one-third of the parents stated that the first doctor consulted assured them that the child was not deaf. More than 60 percent of the parents had four or more medical consultations before a diagnosis was made. Freeman (1977) reported in a British Columbia study that one-third of the physicians *refused* to refer the parents to a specialist and that there was an average time lag of one year from parental suspicion to professional confirmation of a hearing loss.

Once the diagnosis is made parents may receive conflicting advice from a range of professionals, who seldom integrate or coordinate their services. It is not uncommon for a young deaf child and his or her family to be in contact with a pediatrician, audiologist, speech-language therapist, and teacher, with none knowing what any of the others may be advising. If parents receive inaccurate advice at this time, the damage may never be repaired.

At the time of entry into the school setting, the major responsibility shifts to educators and classroom teachers. In some settings the teachers provide speech and hearing therapy. In others these services are provided by specialists through-out the school years. The educational program usually serves to coordinate services, with psychologists, counselors, and language therapists providing input as needed. Toward the end of the secondary school, vocational rehabilitation personnel may play an increasingly important role.

On the average, deaf children and their parents receive services from the greatest numbers of professionals during the process of identification and during the later part of the secondary school years. In the authors' subjective opinion, communication between educational and vocational agencies concerning the needs of deaf secondary students can be quite effective and efficient. The greatest breakdown in communication most often occurs in the early ages across the fields of medicine, education, and speech and hearing services.

The causes of deafness in a population are determined by a variety of factors including cyclical epidemics, advances in medical treatment, and the extent of inbreeding or consanguineous marriages. The situation is complicated by the fact that in most studies of causation of deafness 20 percent or more are listed as unknown (Moores, 1982). Still, four major causes of deafness have been re-ported consistently in the United States: heredity, rubella, prematurity, and meningitis.

Hereditary deafness may be dominant inheritance (passed through a deaf parent), recessive inheritance (passed on through both parents, who are probably hearing), or sex linked (passed to a son through the mother). Hereditary deafness may account for one-third to one-half of deafness in the United States, with fluctuation in other causes due to the impact of epidemics. Most hereditary deafness is of the recessive variety with sex linked deafness very rare. Thus most inherited deafness is the result of parents with no hearing losses but who are carriers of genes for deafness.

It is clear that several different genes may produce recessive deafness. Brown, Hopkins, and Hudgins (1967) estimate that there are from 30 to 150 recessive genes for deafness in the general population and suggest that one out of every four hearing persons in the general population is a carrier for at least one of the recessive genes causing childhood deafness. The reason that deafness is not much more common is simply that mother and father may pass on different recessive genes for deafness, making the child hearing, but also a carrier.

The cause of deafness that has received the greatest attention since 1960 has been maternal rubella, which was not identified as a cause of hearing loss until after World War II but which received great attention in the aftermath of a world-wide epidemic in 1964–65.

Rubella is a viral disease that may have little observable effect on an adult and may be difficult to diagnose. If a woman is affected by rubella during the first three months of pregnancy, there is a danger to the fetus, especially to the tissues of the eye, ear, and other organs.

Rubella vaccine can be an effective preventive measure, although not 100 percent effective since vaccination of pregnant women is dangerous to the fetus, pregnancy within two months after vaccination puts the fetus at risk, and there may be different strains of the virus which are not affected by the vaccine. Among the continuing dangers are that rubella babies may continue to excrete the virus for up to three years, putting those who work with them at risk for contacting the disease. If any of these are pregnant women, the fetus they are carrying may become infected starting the cycle again.

The rubella epidemic of 1964–65 doubled the number of deaf children born during that period. Although many of the children suffered no additional handicaps, substantial numbers have been diagnosed as also having visual impairments, urogenital disorders, cardiovascular defects, mental retardation, and endocrine disorders (Vernon & Hicks, 1980). Since the mid-1960s rubella has accounted for approximately 12 percent of the cases of childhood deafness and there has been no epidemic like the 1964–65 disaster. However, those children have now grown to adulthood and many will require services throughout their lives. This group of individuals has presented the field of education of the deaf with major challenges at every step of the educational process and the response has been for the most part successful. For example, the spread of large numbers of publicly supported preschool programs for the deaf in the middle to late 1960s was a direct response to the challenge of serving these children. Similarly, the establishment of federally funded comprehensive programs for the deaf-blind was spurred by the fact that the epidemic left an estimated 3,600 deaf-blind children in its wake. As the children progressed through school, first elementary, secondary, and then post-secondary programs expanded their services and new programs were developed. All in all, this represents a success story in education that has received little attention.

Prematurity may not technically be considered as a cause of deafness per se but prematurity (defined as a birthweight of 5 pounds, 8 ounces, or less) is common among the deaf population. As many as 45 percent of children deaf through rubella may also be premature, for example (Moores, 1982). Medical trends indicate that increasing numbers of premature children are being born and surviving, suggesting that the numbers of children with handicaps related to prematurity will increase. Premature children are particularly susceptible to intracranial bleeding and anoxia during birth. The probability is that there will be an increase of deaf children with additional handicaps related to prematurity.

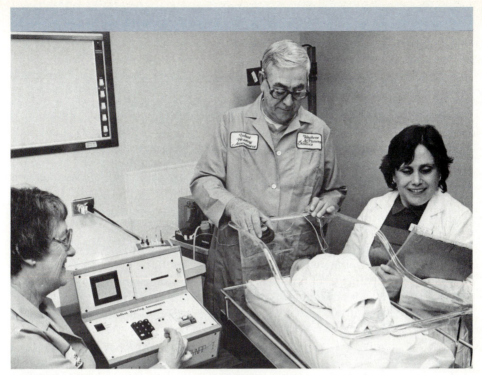

An infant hearing assessment test is conducted on a newborn, the results of which will allow for early, effective intervention if needed.

Meningitis is the only major cause that is not congenital, that is, not present at birth. The disease involves an invasion of the labyrinths through the air cell systems in the middle ear or through the meninges, a protective covering for the brain. With medical advances, the incidence of meningitic-related deafness has declined significantly, from an estimated 28 percent of all deafness in 1880 to 15 percent in 1920 to approximately 7 percent currently. It still remains the largest single source of postnatal deafness in the United States. The result of improvements in medical treatment, especially chemotherapy and antibiotics, has seen a reduction of the number of cases of deafness related to meningitis. At the same time it has produced a lowering in the age of those who have a residuum of deafness. Children who might have died a generation ago are now surviving but with deafness and, frequently, additional handicaps.

To summarize, the highest single identified course of childhood deafness is inherited recessive deafness. Because there are so many recessive genes for deafness, the condition may never have appeared in the known history of the father and mother. This probably will continue as a major cause for the foreseeable future.

Recent activity in genetic counseling is cause for guarded optimism. Much of the work in this area has focused on syndromes related to deafness, i.e., those conditions in which additional factors such as blindness, physical abnormalities,

Cochlear Implants

For some individuals who have lost their hearing as a result of disease, infections, or drug toxicity, medical science has developed a procedure which can restore hearing. The cochlear implant, an Australian product, uses the nerve fibers that transmit sound from the ear to the brain. Even following damage to the inner ear, these fibers remain healthy and able to transmit. The procedure consists of implanting a small receiver in the mastoid bone behind the ear and a platinum electrode in the inner ear. A tiny microphone, transmitter, and a pocket-size signal processor are worn outside the body. They pick up sounds, amplify and filter them, and send them to the implanted receiver. These signals are then passed along to the platinum electrode where they are turned into electrical impulses and sent along the nerve fibers to the brain. Although the technology is in its infancy with fewer than 100 such operations performed worldwide, it holds promise for some deaf individuals.

or retardation might occur. In terms of most cases of recessive deafness, diagnosis may be difficult. A child with no deaf relatives might be considered to have a rubella-related deafness, for example. An interesting sidelight is the fact that the trend toward smaller families in America increases the difficulty of identifying recessive deafness. If two hearing parents are carriers for deafness, the chances of any offspring being deaf are one in four. Since families with three children or less are now the norm, the odds are against any such family having more than one deaf child.

All of the other causes—rubella, prematurity, and meningitis—are identified with multiple handicapping conditions. There has been no reoccurrence of the 1964–65 rubella epidemic and the prognosis is favorable. Deafness through meningitis has been reduced, but the children who become deaf now run a greater risk of additional handicaps. The indications are that the numbers of deaf children with a history of prematurity will increase.

As life expectancy has increased, there has developed a concern for the status of older Americans. It has been established that with increasing age, the incidence of hearing loss increases. Part of this is due to environmental factors and part to the aging process. People who live and work in noisy environments, of course, are at more risk for hearing loss. At the present time, there is very little information on the social, psychological, and emotional impact of hearing loss in adulthood (Meadow, 1980), but recent awareness of the area suggests that significant attention will be devoted to it in the near future.

There is always the possibility that the incidence of deafness in the future may be influenced by the development or spread of any number of diseases. For example, Vernon and Hicks (1980) note that 16 different viruses are known to cause hearing losses, among these being herpes simplex. Herpes can cause deafness or other handicaps in the fetus or during passage in the birth canal. Since herpes has been considered to have reached epidemic proportions in the adult population by the early 1980s, the potential danger for causing deafness in children is real.

CHARACTERISTICS OF INDIVIDUALS
WITH HEARING DISORDERS

In considering learning, social/emotional, and medical/health characteristics, a note of caution should be raised. As previously noted, the incidence of additional handicapping conditions in the preverbally deaf population is relatively high because some of the major causes of deafness may also affect other areas of functioning. Issues related to multiple handicaps are dealt with in Chapter 5. In this chapter the focus is on the normal deaf child, i.e., the deaf child who suffers from no severe physical, social-emotional conditions.

Learning Characteristics

The range of intellectual functioning and intellectual capacity for deaf children appears to be the same as for hearing children. The major difference between a deaf and a hearing child may not be in innate ability but rather due to the fact that the deaf child as a rule just does not have the same communicative opportunities as the hearing child. Very few deaf children, less than 5 percent, have deaf parents, so most parents of deaf children have had no previous exposure to the condition and are not adept in manual communication, i.e., signs and finger-spelling. A common outcome is a child of intellectually normal potential but an experiential and informational deficit.

Deafness is unique in that the learning of a language depends to a large degree—sometimes completely—on vision rather than audition. For most children, the educational process builds on the impressive linguistic skills the child has already acquired to develop expertise in academic areas such as arithmetic, science, social studies, and reading. For deaf children the mastery of such linguistic skills cannot be used as a basis for instruction. Rather, much of the curriculum is designed to teach deaf children basic English skills and concentrates on individualized instruction in speech, English grammar, and use of residual hearing. We will treat this issue in greater detail in the section on intervention. It is mentioned here to emphasize how the importance of language and communication overrides so many aspects of the development and functioning of deaf individuals.

Research on intellectual functioning of the deaf has been conducted for generations. A review of research in the first part of the twentieth century by Pintner, Eisenson, and Stanton (1941) reported that the results were frequently confusing and even contradictory. However, Pintner noted a definite trend and concluded that the deaf scored around 10 IQ points below the hearing, placing them within the normal range, but definitely under their hearing peers.

These results were at complete variance with a later review by Vernon (1967), who analyzed 31 studies on deaf children from 1930 to 1966. This comprised all research studies Vernon could locate during the period which compared deaf children either to a control group of hearing children or to hearing norms. He reported that the deaf children had superior scores in 13 of the experiments and inferior scores in 11 of the experiments. In seven studies there were no significant differences in the scores. Vernon concluded that deaf children function as well as hearing in a wide variety of tasks that measure thinking.

The differences in the summaries of Pintner, Eisenson, and Stanton (1941) and Vernon (1967) may be explained by a number of factors. It is possible that many of the early studies did not screen out all deaf children suffering from additional handicaps, thereby depressing group scores. Also, it is highly likely that some of the early tests used had verbal components not appropriate for deaf children. Finally, the mental testing movement was in its beginning stages and there were deficiencies in materials, techniques, and scoring, especially when dealing with special populations.

An interesting and perhaps unique facet in the area of assessment of intelligence is the existence of IQ norms for deaf children. The *Wechsler Intelligence Scale for Children (WISC)* has been the most widely used scale for deaf children since the 1950s. The *WISC*, which has five verbal subscales and five performance subscales, can provide both verbal and performance IQs. Because of the English language difficulties of many deaf children, the *WISC* Performance IQ has been relied on predominantly. After 25 years a revised *WISC (WISC–R)* was published with new sets of norms and standard scores based on the testing of hearing children. Anderson and Sisco (1977) standardized the performance scale of the *WISC–R* on a national sample of 1,228 deaf children and developed norms for deaf children between the ages of 6 to 17 years. They found relatively little difference between the mean score for the hearing (100) and the deaf (96) although there was some variation across subtests. For example, the deaf children on the average scored higher than the hearing children on Object Assembly and lower on Picture Arrangement. The benefit of Anderson and Sisco's norms is that it's now possible to evaluate a deaf child's performance on the *WISC–R* relative to both deaf and hearing peers.

In addition to the mental testing or IQ testing movement, there has been a longstanding interest in the question of intellectual functioning of the deaf. In general, developments in this field have progressed from a generalized consensus that the deaf may be more "concrete" to a growing belief that deafness per se has no negative impact on intellectual development. Thus, Myklebust and Brutten (1953) concluded that deafness restricts a child functionally to a world of concrete objects and things and commented on the concreteness of the deaf child. In contrast to this, Furth (1973) has argued that the majority of deaf people make an adequate adjustment to the world and function quite successfully. Furth (1971) stated that deaf individuals develop adequately up to the beginning level of abstract thinking, but then plateau.

Other studies suggest that previous results may have as much to do with communication difficulties as with cognitive differences. For example, Rittenhouse and Spiro (1979) report on work comparing deaf and hearing children under standard testing procedures in which the hearing were superior, but when the instructions were modified there were no performance differences, suggesting that previous research showing a cognitive deficit in deaf children was likely influenced by communication problems, not intellectual differences. Rittenhouse and Spiro used an interrogation phase in their study, a procedure which Furth (1973) had concluded was unusually difficult for deaf subjects. However, the tester was proficient in both oral and manual communication and could communicate equally well with both deaf and hearing children—a surprisingly rare condition until recently. There were no differences between groups.

In an interesting review of 51 studies of cognition involving deaf subjects in North America and Europe, Ottem (1980) reported that deaf and hearing subjects performed equally well when they had to refer to one set of data. However, when the tasks required reference to two sets of data, hearing subjects were superior. In considering reasons for this apparent paradox, Ottem concluded that the difference was due not to the intellectual functioning of deaf individuals but rather to the systems of educational instruction provided the deaf. Ottem (1980) stated:

> The only reasonable explanation the author can find is that deaf people have been particularly trained or taught to communicate about single events. This may have its roots in that we, as hearing individuals, have imposed upon the deaf a requirement about simple and unambiguous communication, and that this communication is best obtained by referring to single events.   (p. 568)

In summary, the evidence that exists to date does not suggest that deafness imposes any limitation on cognitive abilities. As a group, deaf people function within the normal range of intelligence and display the same diversity as the hearing population.

On the other hand, it has been documented that the social and physical experiences of deaf children may be somewhat limited due to difficulties of communication with hearing parents, other family members, and most of the children and adults in a community. Later problems in academic achievement may not be related to intellectual potential but to limited experience and communication with significant others. Therefore, if the real intellectual potential of deaf children could be tapped effectively from the early years, there would be much greater realization of potential through school and the complete lifespan.

Academic Achievement

There is no doubt that deaf children have consistently scored lower on standardized tests of achievement than would have been predicted on the basis of their normal intellectual capacity. As measured by instruments such as the *Stanford Achievement Test*, the typical 18-year-old deaf student scores between the fourth and fifth grade level in reading and perhaps around the seventh grade in arithmetic computation. As a rule, the more that a particular subject matter depends on knowledge of English, the lower most deaf children score on standardized tests.

There are indications that tests standardized on students with normal hearing may underestimate the real achievement of deaf students. For example, most widely used tests of reading require the students to select the appropriate answer from four or five alternatives. The question may be based on reading a single paragraph or even a single sentence. A deaf student with incomplete mastery of English grammar may be penalized by such a test. It is possible that on reading a story or textbook the child can rely on context to understand a passage. In this way a child of normal intelligence but limited English grammatical skills may read quite adequately for meaning. Consistently, regular classroom teachers who have integrated students judge the students as capable of dealing with the subject matter and competing against hearing students. This is true even when the achievement test scores of deaf students are lower, suggesting that the tests in question are not always valid for the deaf.

Social/Emotional Development

One of the major themes of this chapter is that the development and functioning of deaf individuals must be perceived within a family concentration. The early experiences of any child may have limiting implications. In relation to deafness, Stein, Merrill, and Dahlberg (1974) discussed a mental health program for the adult deaf as follows:

> Many of the mental health problems of the adult deaf can be traced to inadequacies of early parent-child relationships, unrealistic expectations on the parts of parents, and the inability of parents to ever accept the fact that their growing child is different and to some extent always will be different. Basically we were interested in developing programs to prevent or at least moderate the occurrence of mental health problems in the adult deaf population by fostering a more healthy, early parent-child relationship. (p. 3)

The development of a healthy, early parent-child relationship faces many difficulties in families with hearing parents and deaf children. As we have established, the process of identification of a hearing loss can be a long, emotionally draining, traumatic experience. Parents may go through identifiable stages of denial and grief before adjusting to deafness in a child. At the same time they are expected to become knowledgeable about deafness in children and are urged to develop skills to interact with their child as rapidly as possible.

Meadow (1968, 1980) and Moores (1982) have discussed two common reactions of parents. First is the difficulty of accepting the permanency of deafness and second is the search for "normality" as indicated by intelligible speech. For most of the children we deal with there are no cures for deafness and none are foreseen in the near future. However, many parents, thinking of deafness as a disease, find it difficult to believe that their deaf child will grow up to be a deaf adult. They are convinced that some day an antidote will be developed either in a form of a medicine or surgical technique. It is a painful adjustment for parents to accept that they—the child and the family—must be prepared for a lifetime of deafness. The second common reaction, which is closely related to the search for a cure, is tied to parents' perception of children as idealized extensions of themselves. When parents express their goals of "normality" in a child, they frequently express their desire not in terms of deafness but in terms of speech. This is a natural reaction for parents who have never been exposed to deafness. The most notable thing about a deaf individual to a naive observer is not the lack of hearing; a deaf person doesn't look different from a hearing person. It is when the deaf person speaks that the deafness is noted. Therefore, many parents at first think of the child's major problem as a lack of speech when in reality it is a lack of hearing.

Schlesinger and Meadow (1972) have described the developmental issues as follows:

> Does the absence of early auditory stimulation, feedback and communication in itself create a tendency toward a particular adaptive pattern? Or, alternatively, does early profound deafness elicit particular responses from parents, teachers, siblings and peers? . . . Rather than belaboring the nature/nurture controversy, it is more fruitful to look at the entire life cycle.   (pp. 2–3)

Meadow and Schlesinger based much of their work on the developmental approach of Erikson (1969), who identified the following eight stages in the life cycle of the individual:

1. Basic trust versus mistrust: infancy
2. Autonomy versus shame and doubt: early childhood
3. Initiative versus guilt: childhood
4. Industry versus inferiority: school age
5. Identity versus identity confusion: adolescence
6. Intimacy versus isolation: young adulthood
7. Generativity versus stagnation: parenthood
8. Integrity versus despair: old age

Schlesinger (1978) has devoted particular attention to the resolution of the first three stages. She found that deaf children of hearing parents faced difficulty in moving through each of these stages. Deaf children of deaf parents displayed better overall functioning. This may be explained both by the easier acceptance of deafness by deaf parents and by the availability of a sign communication system. Now that many hearing parents are learning to use signs, Schlesinger has noted improvements in the development of deaf children of hearing parents. She reported that hearing parents who have communicated with their children through a combination of speech and signs develop a communication that is more meaningful, joyful, and reciprocal than hearing parents who rely completely on speech.

Maestas y Moores and Moores (1980) have suggested that the manner in which deaf parents interact with both deaf and hearing children might provide some guidance for hearing parents of deaf children. In a study of nine families with deaf parents and both deaf and hearing children up to 18 months of age, Maestas y Moores (1979) reported a number of characteristics of parental communication styles:

A small boy who is almost completely deaf communicates with his hearing
father through the use of sign language.

Mode of Communication.

Neither parents nor children were restricted to one
mode of communication. Signing, fingerspelling,* and voice were commonly
observed with all children. Sometimes each was used in isolation and sometimes
in combination. Although the intelligibility of parental speech varied, all vocal-
ized to some extent. The single most common mode of expression by parents
was simultaneous speech plus signs.

Signing on Child's Body.

Most parent-infant interaction involved a high de-
gree of physical contact. A unique feature of the communication between deaf
parents and their children is the use of the child's body to make signs. For
example, in normal conversation a person would make a sign for "cute," "hun-

---

*Signing and fingerspelling are different aspects of manual communication. In fingerspell-
ing, every letter of a word would be spelled through the American Manual Alphabet. Thus,
any word in the English language may be spelled. A sign does not have a one-to-one
correspondence with written English but rather consists of elements of placement in space,
hand shapes, and hand movements. Thus words such as *psychology, mother, process, environment, happy,* etc., may be either fingerspelled or signed.

gry," or "eat" through contact with his or her own chin, body, or lips. Deaf mothers were observed to make these signs on the baby's body.

Fingerspelling.   There are differences of opinion among educators of the deaf as to when children can understand fingerspelling and as to when it should be introduced. It is interesting to note parental fingerspelling of a child's name at the day of birth and fingerspelling of words such as "knockwurst" and "raspberry" before one month.

Signing Style.   Signing uses a smaller space when addressed to infants. When holding, feeding, or bathing a baby, mothers tend to use one-handed signs in substitution for two-handed signs. Also, in some ways, babies may be exposed to signs when they are not watching or are even napping. Just as a hearing parent might talk to a friend, spouse, or child while holding a baby, a deaf parent will do the same, carrying on a complete conversation using signs. The child may be exposed to tactile kinesthetic information and perhaps the rhythms of communication even when napping.

In an intensive analysis of the communication between three deaf mothers and their children from birth through six months (i.e., before the hearing status of the children had been ascertained), Maestas y Moores (1980) reported that deaf mothers used the same pragmatic functions as those reported for hearing parents interacting with their children, with a mixture of affective and cognitive components to the process. One important finding was that affective communication tended to involve voice alone, although there was individual variation. When the mothers expressed more complex cognitive functions such as reports, questions, and directions they would rely more frequently on signs plus voice.

This easy natural flow of communication unfortunately has not been found typically with hearing parents of deaf children. In comparison to hearing mothers of hearing children, Schlesinger and Meadow (1972) reported that hearing mothers of deaf children were more controlling, intrusive, and deductive, and less flexible, approving, and encouraging. Collins (1969) reported that 13 of 16 mothers he studied could communicate with their children only about things or events that were present. Gregory (1976) found that deaf children's siblings reported more feelings of jealousy than hearing children's siblings and that mothers of deaf children made more concessions to them than mothers of hearing children.

Schlesinger and Meadow (1972) stated that hearing parents of deaf children were frequently unsure of themselves, especially whether they were overprotective or underprotective. They used a more narrow range of discipline techniques, probably due to communication limitations. There was more reliance on spanking and the parents exhibited more frustration than parents of hearing children. Meadow (1980) has concluded that the overprotectiveness found in most families with hearing parents and a deaf child probably retards social development.

Meadow has claimed that, because many educators see deafness as basically an educational problem, mothers often are expected to function in the home with the child as a teacher, thus adding pressure for teaching to the existing strains of communicative frustration. Meadow (1969) cautioned:

introducing

MARIA

Maria is an 18-year-old high school senior who lives in a large city in Texas. She has a severe hearing loss and with her hearing aid can follow part of a conversation in a one-to-one situation in a quiet environment. In a group situation or in the classroom she has much more difficulty. Her hearing loss was diagnosed at 30 months, with a suspected etiology of rubella, and is assumed to be congenital. Both parents, an older brother, a younger sister, and all relatives are hearing.

Maria was enrolled in a speech and hearing center at three years of age. She went five mornings a week and received training in communication skills (speech, speechreading, use of residual hearing, Signed English) and in preacademic skills (premath and prereading training). She was fitted with a body hearing aid and her mother received training in encouraging speech, care of a hearing aid, facilitating cognitive growth, and Signed English.

At six years of age, Maria entered a local elementary program for the deaf. It consisted of 12 classes for deaf students contained in an elementary school along with 600 hearing students. It was a cooperative program for the deaf, serving 10 school districts. Like most deaf children, Maria was transported by a van paid for by the district. Her parents had hoped she could attend the neighborhood school like her brother and sister but realized that the services available were not adequate for someone with her hearing loss. Instruction at the elementary school was in Total Communication as it is in the high school Maria currently attends. The high school has 2,000 students, of whom 125 are deaf. There are 20 teachers of the deaf and eight interpreters. Maria takes all of her courses in classes for the deaf except for mathematics, where she takes second year algebra in an integrated class with an interpreter. Maria's relationships with hearing students are good but her best friends are her fellow deaf students. . . .

Maria's mother and siblings use speech and sign with her, although the siblings seem to be more proficient. The father communicates mostly by speech with some gestures. The family is close but Maria feels she is not allowed the independence of her brother and sister. Both were allowed to drive, to date, and to work at younger ages. Maria's mother acknowledges that she may be somewhat overprotective.

Maria is not sure of what she will do upon graduation. Her options clearly are much greater than Paul in the other case study who is almost 20 years her senior. She is interested in applying to Gallaudet University or the National Technical Institute for the Deaf. She is an above average student but has been told the competition for acceptance is stiff. Her family would like her to consider some options within her home state. For now, Maria is exploring various possibilities with her high school guidance counselor, a trained professional who is deaf herself.

This encourages in some mothers a didactive, intrusive overanxious surveillance of the deaf child's oral progress, with accompanying reduction in the relapsed playful creative happy interaction that may be necessary for normal growth and development. (p. 432)

As might be expected, there is great variation in the estimates of emotionally disturbed individuals in the deaf population. Craig and Craig (1983) report an estimated 3 percent of the deaf school-age population were classified as emotionally disturbed as compared to an estimated 8 percent reported by Jensema and Trybus (1975).

Some investigators have reported findings reflecting difficulties in social-emotional functioning of deaf individuals, but have gone on to question the implications of the results. R. Harris (1978) has argued that what he considers the side effects of deafness may be more important than deafness itself. Among these side effects he lists negative parental attitudes toward deafness, poor parental coping with unexpected crises, and inability of many hearing parents to communicate manually to meet the needs of the child. A. Harris (1978) has stated that parent-child interaction may be impaired long before an appropriate diagnosis is made and that the deaf child may be a limited or atypical participant in the family.

Levine (1956) reported that deaf subjects were egocentric, irritable, impulsive, and suggestable. However, in a later summary of research on social-emotional adjustment of the deaf (1960), she cautioned:

1. *Many of the instruments used assume a level of communicative interaction that may not exist between hearing testers and some deaf testers.*
2. *Adequate development of a deaf individual may be inhibited not by deafness itself but by inadequate coping behaviors of significant others in the environment.*
3. *The residua and sequelae of some of the major etiologies of deafness may involve impairments in addition to hearing loss.* (pp. 151–152)

Along the same lines Altshuler (1974) concluded that, after considering all of the obstacles faced by deaf individuals, it is clear that they develop along predictable lines. He concluded, "It is nothing short of miraculous that the majority of deaf children develop to be normal neurotics like the rest of us" (p. 370).

Recently there has been growing interest, but little information, concerning social-emotional adjustment of deaf students in mainstreamed settings and of acceptance by hearing peers. One of the authors (Moores) currently is involved in a study of students in public schools in self-contained and integrated classes. Very preliminary results suggest a somewhat lower self-image among the integrated students. However, this can not be considered as caused by class placement. It has been extensively documented that there are clear demographic differences between children in differing placements. They are not comparable in terms of several salient factors including extent of hearing loss and family income. Unless children with similar characteristics were to be assigned randomly to different placements, which is highly unlikely in the American educational system, the attribution of causality to any single factor should be considered with considerable caution.

The present situation is one in which only too often inappropriate tests are administered by unqualified personnel under unsatisfactory conditions. The lack of adequately trained personnel presents grave problems both for diagnosis and treatment. Levine (1974) found that less than 20 of 172 school psychologists working with deaf children had sign language communication skills and that 83 percent had no special training to work with the hearing impaired. Sullivan and Vernon (1979) have offered supporting information that most school psychologists in school programs are not prepared to teach deaf children; most rely on spoken English alone in their assessment; and many frequently administer tests which are appropriate only for children with standard language skills. Unfortunately, there is no way of knowing how many deaf children have been inappropriately diagnosed as emotionally disturbed or learning disabled because of limited communication skills of the testers. We also do not know how many deaf children who really do have additional handicaps have been missed by the same psychologists. The situation should be improved with the mandate of Public Law 94–142 that all children be tested through appropriate systems of communication, but conditions have been poor.

The impact of a lack of professionals trained to serve deaf individuals can be even greater when considering potential difficulties faced by deaf adults with treatment needs. In an evaluation of services for deaf patients in New York State Mental Hospitals, Rainer, Altshuler, and Kallman (1963) found they were frequently isolated, misdiagnosed, poorly evaluated, and virtually untreated. The lack of treatment tended to produce overly high estimates of emotional problems in deaf adults. As an example, original figures suggested a higher incidence of schizophrenia among the deaf. Further investigation indicated that deaf patients often were admitted, received little or no treatment, and frequently became custodial cases. Hearing patients to a larger extent received treatment and were released. In a later summary, Rainer and Altshuler (1970) concluded that mental illness and emotional difficulty are no more prevalent among the deaf than among the hearing, but diagnosis and treatment are more difficult and take longer.

In the ensuing years there have been significant developments in the provision of mental health services to deaf individuals, with many programs developed based on recommendations made by Rainer and Altshuler (1970). Progress has been inconsistent, however, with many of the improvements limited to larger states such as New York, Illinois, Texas, and California. There are still too many parts of the United States where there is a serious lack of appropriate services for the deaf.

Medical/Health Characteristics

Deafness, per se, does not affect individuals' general health status. Physical development and the acquisition of motor skills appear to follow the same patterns as for the hearing. There are no restrictions on activities and deaf children and adults participate in a typical range of physical endeavors. Deaf students compete with and against deaf and hearing peers in all sports including swimming, basketball, soccer, and track and field. There have been deaf professional athletes in football, baseball, and boxing and there is a deaf Olympics every four years (Gannon, 1980). There are deaf dancers at the high school, college, and professional level. In physical recreation activities, deaf individuals participate in the same activities as other Americans—probably to the same extent—as their interests dictate, ranging from aerobics to jogging to bowling to white-water canoeing.

Despite this impressive record of activity, it should be remembered that some of the major causes of deafness are related to other handicapping conditions, suggesting that a somewhat higher proportion of deaf individuals might have to restrict their physical activities or suffer from limiting conditions. Related to this, Freeman (1977) has provided evidence that deaf children have a higher rate of illness and hospitalization than hearing children, with the difference being most pronounced during the first two years of life. Hospitalization may be due somewhat to a heightened sensitivity on the part of parents and physicians toward children diagnosed as deaf, but it probably also reflects for some children health problems related to the cause of deafness.

Hearing Aid Usage

Although the use of hearing aids and training in the use of residual hearing have been parts of education of the deaf for generations, the major impetus for these developments grew out of work during and shortly after World War II. Pioneering work in Europe demonstrated that with early fitting of aids many children who would have previously been considered deaf were able to function in classes for the hard of hearing or could be integrated into regular classes. The widespread use of powerful hearing aids was established by the 1960s and has been a major factor in programs for the deaf since that time.

A report of hearing aid usage by 997 students in the United States (Karchmer & Kerwin, 1977) provides some interesting background information. It was found that 82 percent of the sample used group and/or personal hearing aids at least part of the time. The authors noted in this context that the term "hearing aid" refers to a wide range of amplification devices. A monaural aid is a single instrument containing a microphone, amplifier, and batteries that is either head-mounted or worn in the clothing, with the receiver in one ear. A binaural aid consists of two separate instruments—one for each ear—which may be mounted separately on the chest or head. A third type is a Y-Cord, which may be thought of as a pseudobinaural aid which consists of one instrument on the chest with receivers in each ear.

As might be expected, one factor closely related to hearing aid usage was extent of hearing loss. However the pattern was not a straight linear one. The nonwearers were found in greatest proportion at either extreme. More than 90 percent of children with losses from 41 to 90 dB wore hearing aids. For hearing losses greater than 90 dB, 77 percent of the sample wore aids. Included within the nonwearers would be individuals with little or no measurable residual hearing who would not benefit from amplification. Of the small number at the other extreme of the sample, students with hearing losses of 40 dB or less, only 44 percent wore aids.

Hearing aid usage was also related to family income and ethnic status. The percentage of children wearing aids was greater in families with higher incomes. There seemed to be complex interactions, however, across family income, ethnic

These children are wearing body-type hearing aids with receivers in each ear which help in enhancing their classroom performance.

status, and hearing aid usage. Although family income for whites was much greater than for Hispanics and blacks, 85 percent of Hispanic children wore hearing aids as compared to 82 percent of whites and 75 percent of blacks.

DETECTION OF HEARING DISORDERS

In considering detection of hearing impairment, it is helpful to make a distinction among the terms "impairment," "disability," and "handicap." For our purposes a hearing impairment refers to a physical condition of the auditory mechanism. The disability caused by the impairment is expressed in speech reception as measured by speech or other sounds calibrated for frequency and intensity. The testing usually is done by a trained audiologist and the basic testing instrument is an audiometer. A handicap represents the extent to which a person's functioning is limited by a particular disability. Thus a deaf person may have an educational handicap but deafness itself is not a handicap. The terms "deafness" and "hearing impairment" are restricted to describing disabilities.

Identification and Screening

Identification of hearing loss in school age children is a relatively straightforward process. The process of diagnosis leading to remediation is not as complex as that found in dealing with learning disabilities, mental retardation, or emotional disturbance. The issue is the identification of children at the earliest possible age in order to initiate training programs. Several countries in Western Europe, especially in Scandinavia, have established effective procedures for early identification. In the United States, where there is more of an emphasis on local and state responsibility, the existence and comprehensiveness of such programs varies greatly in different locations. It should be stressed that the identification of hearing loss in very young children and in hard-to-test school-age children, e.g., those with additional handicaps, can be quite difficult.

In many states a high-risk register is combined with neonatal screening to identify newborn children with hearing losses. Neonatal screening involves systematically exposing young children to high levels of sound (around 90 dB) to determine if there is a response. If there is no response, the infant may be retested within a matter of weeks and at three-month intervals. However, screening to date has not been found to be completely successful because some children with normal hearing may not respond and some children with hearing losses may respond (Schow & Watkins, 1978). The false negatives—where children who have normal hearing but do not respond—may cause difficulties by concerning parents needlessly. Also, the screening fails to identify children with mild to moderate losses.

Procedures have been developed for testing children as young as three months, after involving various conditioning techniques while the child is sitting in a parent's lap, sometimes involving the use of loudspeakers and testing for conditioned orienting responses (COR). With somewhat older children, usually by the age of two, play audiometry may be utilized. By school age, most children are able to partake in a formal testing situation by making a response such as raising a finger when they hear a sound.

For some difficult-to-test children, a Tangible Reinforcement Operant Conditioning Assessment (TROCA) procedure has been utilized. The procedure conditions a subject to press a button when hearing a sound, using food such as M&Ms as reinforcers. This technique is not useful for infants (Wilber, 1979) but has benefit with older subjects who might have additional handicaps.

One area of promise, and one in which there have been conflicting reports, involves the use of electrophysiological techniques, including evoked potential audiometry and brain stem evoked response. Electrodes are attached directly to the subject and hearing is measured directly without requiring a physical response. Such techniques can even be applied during sleep and cause no discomfort. Again, there are some difficulties associated with electrophysiological testing. First it is expensive and time-consuming. Second, it is sometimes difficult to interpret the responses of a very young child or of a subject with additional handicaps.

Stanford Achievement Test, Hearing Impaired Edition (SAT–HI)

The development of the *SAT–HI* represents a unique activity in standardized tests of achievement. Traditionally, although educators of the deaf have used standardized achievement tests, there has been an awareness of problems of validity in evaluating results. Primarily this is due to patterns of achievement which are different for deaf and hearing students. Most achievement tests have several different forms for children across the 12 grades of elementary and high school. For each form, there are norms with a particular age range and grade range, based on curricula appropriate for those grades. Thus a third grade math subtest would be paired with a third grade English subtest. The difficulty level for subtests in each content area should be matched to a student's general level of functioning.

Unfortunately, tests standardized on hearing children may not be appropriate for deaf children because the academic progress of deaf children may have different patterns. As noted elsewhere in this chapter, deaf children tend to achieve better in math than in reading. It would not be unusual for a deaf child to be at the third or fourth grade level in reading and the seventh grade level in math. If such a child were to receive a test relative to reading achievement, the math subtest would be too easy. If the level of test were related to math achievement, the reading subtest would be too difficult. In either case, one or more subtest scores would not be valid.

In 1983 the Center for Assessment and Demographic Studies (CADS) at Gallaudet College produced a special edition for hearing impaired students of the *Stanford Achievement Test (SAT–HI)*. The *SAT–HI '83* is an update of the *SAT–HI '73*, which appeared in 1973 (Allen, White, & Karchmer, 1983). The *SAT–HI '83* has separate reading and math booklets at each of six levels of difficulty to allow all students to be placed in an appropriate test level. There are also separate reading and math screening tests. Test items for the *SAT–HI '83* have not been altered from the regular *SAT*. Thus for any particular subtest there are hearing based norms as well as hearing-impaired based norms. CADS developed a scoring system for the *SAT–HI '83* that emphasizes flexibility in grouping at all phases in the scoring process.

Probably the most successful state program, known as SKI-HI, was established in Utah in 1972 (Clark & Watkins, 1978) through federal funding from the Bureau of Education of the Handicapped (now the Office of Special Education and Rehabilitation). The model depends on a high-risk register at hospitals throughout the state and there is follow-up of all children suspected of having a hearing loss.

The SKI-HI program has been successful in identifying many children, with a wide range of hearing losses, before the age of one and is tied in with a statewide early intervention program. The SKI-HI program has served as a model for several other programs throughout the United States. However, it must be acknowledged that we remain far behind most other industrialized nations in the early diagnosis of hearing loss. All too often, children are not diagnosed until later and parents go through the traumas of uncertainty and misdiagnosis which were discussed in an earlier section of this chapter. As might be expected, the gap in identification often is greater for children from poor and/or minority backgrounds. This means also that fewer poor and minority hearing impaired children are enrolled in early education programs, thereby starting their education at older ages and at a decided disadvantage to other hearing impaired children.

CONSIDERATIONS IN INTERVENTION

In one way, education of the deaf has undergone tremendous changes involving widespread use of manual communication, spread of preschool programs, greater educational integration, the development of a variety of options at the post-secondary level, and more effective services to the multiply handicapped. Impetus for such changes has come from a number of sources, including the challenge of the rubella epidemic of the middle 1960s, breakthroughs in the development of powerful wearable hearing aids for children, research on American Sign Language and other systems of manual communication, the impact of Public Law 94–142, and changing cultural attitudes.

Paradoxically, some basic issues and questions come down to us almost unchanged over hundreds of years. The place of manual communication still remains a matter of bitter and acrimonious debate in some areas and the arguments used are essentially the same as those employed by the pro-signing Abbé de l'Epee and the anti-signing Samuel Heinicke in their exchange of correspondence in the eighteenth century (Garnett, 1968). Issues of the relative benefits of separate versus integrated school placement received strong consideration in France and Germany in the first half of the nineteenth century (Moores, 1982) and techniques of "natural" language instruction were opposed to more structural approaches by the end of the seventeenth century (Moores, 1982). In some ways then, education of the deaf has undergone revolutionary changes in recent years. In other ways, the basic issues continue to be with us in only somewhat modified form. It is helpful for the reader to bear this paradox in mind.

The Preschool Years

Although early intervention programs for the hearing impaired have existed for a limited number of children since the eighteenth century, they have been available to the public only since the 1960s. The first schools for the deaf in the United States educated children primarily on a residential basis. Although the first schools were established in communities such as Hartford, New York, and Philadelphia, the American population was predominantly rural and even the larger cities would not be considered as such under contemporary standards. Nineteenth and early twentieth century educators of the deaf, balancing the familial needs of the young child against educational needs, recommended that the child stay at home until a certain level of maturity was developed, with many schools providing materials and advice for parents to follow at home (Moores, 1982).

Even following World War II, there was no discernible movement for public support of preschool education for deaf children. The programs that were developed were typically under the sponsorship of private schools, speech and hearing centers, and university clinics. The Tracy Clinic in Los Angeles, California, provided a major service by developing a number of correspondence courses for parents of young hearing impaired children and by providing a resource for parents with questions. Clinic materials were translated into several languages and have been used by parents around the world.

Following the rubella epidemic of 1964–65, educators of the deaf were faced with the fact that over a period of approximately two years twice as many deaf children were born as might be expected, many of them with additional handicaps. This so-called "rubella bulge" would move through the preschool years in the late 1960s, the school years throughout the 1970s and early 1980s, and into post-secondary years and adulthood from that period on. At each step of the way the presence of this population would present new challenges and demands to educators and other professionals. It is to the credit of the profession that the response was immediate—beginning with rapid expansion of preschool programs—and has continued. In some cases, the programs that have been developed have been of more benefit to deaf children who came after them. This is probably most true of preschool programs which had to be developed immediately. Educators at the elementary, secondary, and post-secondary levels had more time to prepare for the increased numbers.

The number of preschool programs for the deaf expanded drastically in the late 1960s, especially in large metropolitan areas and in residential schools for the deaf. They were established roughly within the same period as the Head Start and other early intervention programs.

The early intervention programs for the deaf faced severe obstacles. Most importantly, there was no real core of well-trained preschool teachers of the deaf. Consequently, there were very few teacher trainers qualified to prepare people to work with very young deaf children. The experience of most people with personnel preparation responsibility was restricted to elementary and, sometimes, secondary ages. In addition, there were no documented successful preschool programs which could serve as models for those springing up across the country and there were no tested curricula available which could be incorporated or used with moderate adaptation.

As might be expected, most of the newly developed programs were influenced heavily by techniques then prevailing in elementary level programs for the deaf. It was common for teachers of first and second grade children to be assigned to work with preschoolers. Because of a lack of curricular materials specifically designed for very young deaf children, many teachers inappropriately used watered-down curricula originally developed for older children. Also the programs were almost exclusively oral-only, i.e., they did not allow the use of signs or fingerspelling. In addition, the authors have no knowledge of, or can find no evidence of, the employment of deaf teachers in preschool programs prior to 1970. The emphasis was on the development of speech, with secondary importance given to English, communication, and academic subjects. It was believed that deaf teachers would not provide good speech models for the children and therefore should not be allowed to teach at preschool levels. This assumption was later challenged with evidence that deaf children of deaf parents developed equivalent speech skills to deaf children of hearing parents and were superior in English, academic achievement, and social-emotional development (Meadow, 1980).

Preliminary evaluations of preschool programs indicated that most children realized little or no lasting benefit in terms of speech, English language skills, or academic achievement, with a resultant press for change and improvement. See Moores (1985) for an extended review of research and issues in preschool education for the deaf. Very quickly, existing programs were changed and new ones developed representing wide variation in modes of communication used, amount of program structure, and extent of interaction with hearing peers. Moores and associates (Moores, Weiss, & Goodman, 1978; Moores, 1984) conducted a longitudinal evaluation of preschool programs in seven states (Connecticut, Maryland, Minnesota, New Mexico, New York, Tennessee, and Texas). Among the major findings were the following:

1. Children in programs with both cognitive/academic and socialization components were more successful than those in programs with a primarily socialization concentration.
2. Children in programs using both manual and oral communication achieved better in English and academic achievement than those in oral-only programs. There appeared to be no influence—either positive or negative—from manual communication on the development of speech and use of residual hearing.
3. Functioning of the deaf children in visual-motor tests of the *Illinois Test of Psycholinguistic Abilities* and on measures of intellectual capacity (*Wechsler Intelligence Scale for Children, Leiter Scale*) was equivalent to hearing norms.
4. Even as young as ages four and five, hearing impaired children spend less time than hearing children on academic and preacademic tasks, with substantial parts of the school day devoted to speech, speechreading, and auditory training. By age seven there is a significant difference in favor of hearing children in academic achievement.
5. Children who were integrated, or mainstreamed, tended to be those with superior expressive and receptive oral communication skills, with no differences in academic achievement. The existence of oral communication skills was usually the basis for the decision to integrate.
6. In general, the academic achievement and communication skills found in the study were superior to those reported in early research investigations of preschool programs for the deaf.

Despite the improvements noted, ample cause for concern remained, especially concerning problems in the development of effective communication skills. The evidence suggested that the children were most intelligible and understood their teachers best when simultaneous oral and manual communication was used. A child might understand approximately 50 percent of simple messages when relying on speechreading and residual hearing, for example, and 80 to 90 percent when able to read signs and fingerspelling in addition to speechreading and listening. The improvement in communication scores is impressive. However, it was found that reception of complex grammatical structures such as passives, negatives, and verb tenses was inefficient regardless of mode of communication. Analysis of information on tapes suggested that when teachers spoke and signed to the children they frequently omitted signs or fingerspelled equivalents for bound morphemes such as *-ED, -MENT, -LY, -S* and for function words such as *OF, FOR, THE*, etc. In most cases, teachers had not been trained to use simultaneous oral-manual communication in the classroom and were developing these skills on the job. In such situations, the children were exposed to content words (nouns, verbs, adjectives) consistently through signs and speech but bound morphemes and function words often were spoken but not signed. The result was an apparent increase in the reception of content in which English word order was clear, but which expressed English syntax through speech alone.

Another important issue that has surfaced is the allocation of time during the school day, an issue that has great implications throughout the school years. Simply put, deaf children have special educational needs and may receive special training in areas such as speech, use of residual hearing, manual communication, English grammar, etc. If they are in school the same length of time as hearing children, they cannot receive the same amount of general instruction as hearing children and still receive special training. Educators of the deaf have been reluctant to address this difficult choice and have hesitated to state the issue in terms of the tradeoffs involved. Traditionally, the issue has been decided in favor of special training, with speech and language taking precedence over academic subject matter. However, the implications of this emphasis have never been discussed in an open forum. Given the clear trends in American education toward demands for higher academic achievement, this should be a topic of debate for educators of the deaf in the years ahead.

The School Years

In the United States the post-World War II baby boom lasted until the early 1960s, when the number of births started to decrease. The decrease began to have an effect on elementary school enrollment in the late 1960s and the secondary schools some time after that. The pattern was somewhat different in education of the deaf. Enrollment in programs for the deaf remained fairly consistent from the mid-1960s to the beginning of the 1980s. First, when the beginning school-age population was declining, educators of the deaf were gearing up to serve children affected by the rubella epidemic. Also, the field was serving hearing impaired children with minority status to a much greater extent than in the past. Data provided by the Gallaudet Center for Assessment and Demographic Studies indicate that almost one-third of children enrolled in programs for the hearing impaired in the country in 1982–83 were minority status, with over 20 percent being black and almost 10 percent Hispanic. This representation is greater than that found in the regular school-age population. Moores and Oden (1978) reported that the numbers of black deaf individuals had been underestimated throughout American history and their needs had never been addressed. As recently as the last census of the deaf in the United States (Schein & Delk, 1974), it was stated that deafness was less common in blacks than in other groups. Current school enrollment data show that this is not the case. The 1974 census did not attempt an enumeration of Hispanic American deaf but enrollment trends for the deaf document rapidly increasing Hispanic enrollment in all parts of the country, with heavy concentrations in the Southwest (Texas, New Mexico, Colorado, Arizona, California), Midwest (Illinois, Michigan), Northeast (New York, New Jersey), and Florida. Maestas y Moores (1984) has discussed the issues of Hispanics in education of the deaf.

Information on enrollment for almost 50,000 students in 643 schools and classes in the United States (Craig & Craig, 1983) reveals that in the 1982–83 academic year approximately 50 percent attended public school classes for the hearing impaired. Of this number, half were in self-contained classes for all the academic day and half spent at least some time in classes with hearing students. The second major enrollment consisted of almost 18,000 students in 73 public residential schools for the deaf. Roughly 12,000 were residential students at the schools and 6,000 commuted on a daily basis. The only other major placement was in public day schools which enrolled approximately 3,500 students. Public day schools are considered separately from public day classes. A day school serves only deaf children, who commute on a regular basis, and usually is located within a large population area. Day classes contain one or more classes for deaf students within schools where the majority of students are hearing.

Students then are found in three general settings; approximately half are in day classes (with or without mainstreaming) in public schools, 40 percent are in public residential schools, and somewhat less than 10 percent are in public day schools. In the past private residential schools and private day schools enrolled significant numbers of deaf children. Over the years private school attendance has declined with the impact of PL 94–142 apparently speeding up the process. By 1982–83 only 475 students attended private residential schools for the deaf in the United States and 818 attended private day schools (Craig & Craig, 1983).

Perhaps the most drastic change in the field has been in the widespread acceptance of manual communication in the classroom. Until the late 1960s almost all programs, both day and residential, were oral-only throughout the elementary years. The belief was that the use of signs and fingerspelling would prevent the development of oral skills. Most day programs and all private day and residential programs continued oral-only instruction through high school. In the public residential schools there was more of a mixture for high school programs; some continued oral-only instruction, some had oral-only and combined oral-manual tracks, and some taught all high school classes through combined oral-manual communication.

A drastic shift occurred in a very short period of time. Jordan, Gustason, and Rosen (1976) reported that from 1968 to 1975 education of the deaf changed from being predominantly oral-only to total communication, which they defined as the use of residual hearing, speech, speechreading, fingerspelling, and signs. During that period 302 programs reported abandoning oral-only instruction and 333 changed to total communication. In a follow-up, Jordan, Gustason, and Rosen (1979) found a continuation of the trend. For the 10-year period 1968–1978, 481 programs discontinued oral-only instruction and 538 initiated instruction in total communication. A majority of public day and residential programs had changed to total communication and the change had occurred at every level—preschool, elementary, junior high, and senior high.

Two significant developments related to the spread of mainstream practices and the use of manual communication should be noted. Before the acceptance of total communication, deaf teachers were very rare in public day school and day class programs and usually were restricted in residential schools to teaching at the high school level. Increasing numbers are now beginning to teach in public day schools and classes and more are now employed in all settings as teachers across all age ranges (Jensema & Corbett, 1981). Deaf teachers still are underrepresented in day schools and day classes and in classes with younger children. It will be years before the effects of past discrimination are overcome, but the situation is improving.

The second development, unique to the field of education of the deaf, has been the growing utilization of manual interpreters for hearing impaired children in regular classrooms. Jordan, Gustason, and Rosen (1979) found that over 50 percent of programs with partial or full mainstreaming components provide manual interpreters in the regular classrooms. Although the effectiveness of manual interpreters has been documented with college level students, there is little or no information regarding its benefit with school-age children. The widespread acceptance of the practice in a short period of time suggests that students, teachers, and administrators find the use of interpreters to be effective, but empirical data are lacking.

At this point it is advisable to bear in mind that when we talk about the use of manual communication in the classroom, the reference is not to American Sign Language (ASL) but to manual codes on English. Stokoe (1975) has argued that the instructional communication systems are not fully developed languages but are codes developed to represent English. Because most of the vocabulary in such systems has been drawn from ASL, there has been a tendency to incorrectly equate ASL and the classroom systems.

American Sign Language has its roots in French Sign Language and, probably, in indigenous American Sign Languages in existence in America prior to establishment of schools for the deaf. Laurent Clerc, a deaf teacher of the deaf in Paris, came to the United States as the first teacher of the deaf in America in 1817. He modified the instructional sign system used in Paris to reflect English word order, morphology, and vocabulary. This invented sign system apparently interacted with one or more existing sign languages outside of class to form American Sign Language, which is heavily influenced by English but which also has unique linguistic characteristics. The manual codes on English, or signed English systems, have been developed to reflect English in a manual mode. Although heavily based on ASL, they are consciously designed to reflect English.

ASL and the codes on English do share the American Manual Alphabet, which is based on the French Manual Alphabet, brought to this country by Clerc. The French alphabet, in turn, can be traced back to a Spanish Alphabet used with a deaf child as long ago as 1620. Figure 7.2 presents the American Manual Alphabet and the numeral system.

ASL has structures that are different from standard English and it has not been used formally in the classroom, although Stokoe (1975) has developed a

Figure 7.2

American Manual Alphabet

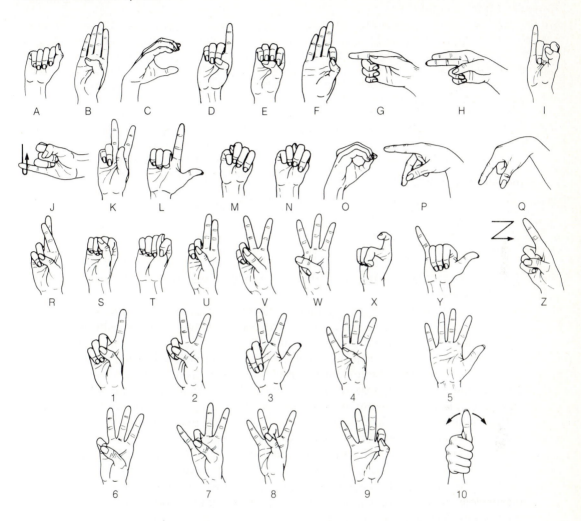

rationale for first teaching ASL to deaf children and then developing English skills on the basis of ASL competency. The major thrust, however, has been to develop English in a "bimodal" vocal and manual manner (Meadow, 1980). To accomplish this, signs are presented along with speech in English word order. New signs have been developed to represent English morphemes such as -ED, -S, -MENT, -NESS, -LY, etc. Several manual codes on English have been developed and to date there are no comparative data. In a review, Jordan, Gustason, and Rosen (1979) reported the most commonly used system was Signing Exact English, which was developed by Gustason, Pfetzing, and Zawolkow (1972). For those interested in a complete treatment of ASL and instructional systems, a

Leadership Training for Deaf Youth

The National Association of the Deaf (NAD) has been in existence for more than 100 years and is the largest organization of deaf people in the United States and Canada. The NAD is a sponsor of the Junior National Association of the Deaf (Jr. NAD) which has chapters in school programs throughout the United States and Canada. In 1969 the Jr. NAD established a Deaf Youth Leadership Development Camp at East Stroudsberg State College in Pennsylvania. Since 1970, Deaf Youth Development Camp programs are held at Swan Lake Lodge in Pengilly, Minnesota.

Each year between 50 and 60 deaf high school students are selected to attend the month-long lead-ership camp. Participants are chosen by fellow students in their school programs on criteria of scholarship and leadership. The goal is to identify and provide leadership training to young deaf people with the potential to make significant contributions as adults. Activities consist of self-directed pro-grams of learning and development, including partic-ipation in a wilderness survival program. The empha-sis is on teamwork, problem solving, analytical skills, and time management. A special feature is partici-pation by deaf professionals who visit the camp and share their personal experiences as well as provide advice and guidance to the students.

book by Wilbur (1979), *American Sign Language and Sign Systems*, provides in-depth analysis.

The ability of teachers, especially hearing teachers, to use a sign system effectively in coordination with speech has been a matter of discussion, with Kluwin providing leadership in research in the area. In a comparison of deaf teachers, inexperienced hearing teachers, and experienced hearing teachers (1981a), he found that inexperienced hearing teachers deleted more signs, but fluency increased with experience. Kluwin (1981b) argued that the invented systems include some inefficient elements which tend to detract from the com-munication of content. Kluwin stated that the primary reason for the switch to manual communication in classrooms was that teachers find it the most efficient form of communicating with their students. In his view the goal of teachers is the communication of content, but that many of the elements of the invented systems concentrate completely on rigid English structure rather than ease of communication. In actual practice teachers and children modify the invented systems to fit their needs.

The Adult Years

The development of post-secondary educational and vocational training options for the deaf in recent years represents a significant breakthrough, one of revolu-tionary proportions.

Around 1960, Gallaudet College, the only liberal arts college for the deaf in the world, enrolled less than 400 students. A study (Quigley, Joune, & Phillips, 1968) involving the cooperation of the Alexander Graham Bell Association, the

Using sign language, a college tutor communicates with hearing impaired students who are learning how to operate microcomputers.

National Association of the Deaf, Gallaudet College, and various state agencies was able to identify a total of only 113 prelingually deaf graduates of regular colleges in the 45-year period from 1910 to 1955. Even this might have been an overcount since their definition of deafness was a loss of 65 dB or more. It appeared then that Gallaudet College provided the only opportunity for post-secondary training for deaf students with the exception of a handful of students in regular colleges. Related to this, the economic status of deaf adults was low. In a study of graduates of programs for the deaf in New England, Boatner, Stuckless, and Moores (1964) found that the majority of young deaf adults were underemployed, with a majority in semiskilled or unskilled positions. Wages were relatively low and unemployment was much higher than for hearing peers in the region. Deaf students received insufficient vocational training, counseling, and placement services. Deaf employees were rated good or superior workers by their supervisors and would have been qualified for higher positions if they had received training. Kronenberg and Blake (1966) replicated the New England study in seven southern and southwestern states and reported similar results. Rates of unemployment, occupational level, wages, and opportunities for advancement were inferior for deaf workers.

The situation began to change with the establishment of the National Technical Institute for the Deaf (NTID), which opened in 1968 as part of the Rochester (New York) Institute of Technology, and with the establishment of three regional federally funded vocational technical programs for the deaf in 1968 and 1969. The programs, established within existing programs for hearing students, were located at Delgado Vocational Technical Junior College in New Orleans (Louisiana), at Seattle (Washington) Community College, and at St. Paul (Minnesota) Technical Vocational Institute.

Federal legislation which stipulated that significant portions of federal money to states in support of vocational education had to be spent for handicapped students provided support for the development of additional programs. Also, the stipulations of Section 504 caused many institutions of higher education to establish procedures to facilitate the matriculation of deaf students and to provide support services such as counseling, notetaking, and interpreting.

In an evaluation of the effectiveness of the three regional vocational-technical programs, Moores, Fisher, and Harlow (1974) found that the training provided deaf adults facilitated upward movement in the job market and that graduates of the programs reported more job satisfaction than in previous studies. Deaf workers were rated as high job performers; because there remained a tendency toward underemployment, a deaf person more often than not is the intellectual superior of hearing people working in the same kind of job. When problems arose they were not because of the cognitive demands of a job but more typically because of difficulties in communication, especially insufficient command of the English language. Communication problems were a factor in limiting possibilities of advancement. An issue of concern was the finding that training, placement opportunities, salaries, and chances for advancement of deaf females were much more restrictive than for deaf males. Overall, the investigators concluded that the effectiveness of well-run post-secondary vocational-technical training programs for the deaf had been documented. It was recommended that they be continued and specific recommendations for the training programs were made. The growth of post-secondary options for deaf students, in retrospect, has been truly remarkable. Rawlings, Karchmer, and Decaro (1983) identified 5,567 students attending 102 separate programs in 1982–83, with 1,142 at Gallaudet College and 993 at NTID. Most of the programs are in facilities for students with normal hearing and over 90 percent offer interpreting, notetaking, and vocational counseling services. Armstrong and Schneidmiller (1983) have estimated that 40 percent of graduates from high school programs for the hearing impaired now enroll in some type of post-secondary training institution, a percentage equivalent to the hearing population. This represents a significant change in a short period of time.

Adult education and adult basic education programs for the deaf exist in many large cities. The National Academy of Gallaudet College serves in an advocacy function for the deaf. It contains the National Center of Law and the Deaf and provides seminars and training programs for professionals working with the deaf, including physicians, nurses, law enforcement personnel, and government workers. It also provides seminars across the country to deaf audiences. There is a wide range of seminar topics including: You and the Law; To Your Good Health; Careers: Past, Present, and Future; How to Make the Best of the Best Years of Your Life; Understanding the Political Process; and Everything You Wanted to Know About Museums.

FUTURE PERSPECTIVES FOR THE TREATMENT OF HEARING DISORDERS

To some extent in the future there will be concentration on the gains recently achieved by deaf individuals with attention to improving administration of the programs and procedures that are in place. However, it would be too optimistic to claim that all is well in the field. Many parents do not receive adequate counseling and are not helped to develop appropriate coping skills. Communication between parents and deaf children often is limited to concrete situations. Unacceptably large numbers of deaf children enter, attend, and graduate from school programs with little or no mastery over written or oral language skills. Difficult as it may be to believe, the techniques used to teach deaf children to speak, read, and write are based on procedures developed by the first teachers of the deaf in Spain more than 350 years ago (Moores, 1982). Despite all of the organizational improvements and technical advances in hearing aids and teaching technology there have been no breakthroughs in developing effective ways of facilitating the development of English skills in deaf children.

There has been growing interest in the efficiency of cochlear implants—surgically implanted electronic devices designed to stimulate the cochlear directly—which can bypass much of the hearing mechanism. Results suggest that the implants may be beneficial for adults who have lost their hearing but probably not for children or adults whose deafness has been present from birth.

The use of microcomputers as instructional devices also clearly is of potential benefit and it is possible that some of the current research on artificial intelligence may be applied to the teaching of deaf children. At present it is still too early to identify trends in these areas. Still, we must come back again to the issue of time on task; we must look at student involvement in various activities in relation to time allocated to learning. The priorities—whether implicit or explicit—established by educators of the deaf will dictate whether or not we change the emphasis of our efforts.

It is the authors' prediction—and hope—that the focus of attention will shift to the teaching-learning process itself and that greater resources will be brought to bear on the development of communication skills and academic achievement appropriate to the intellectual capacity of deaf individuals. The administrative and support structures developed over the past generation are in place and, to a large extent, are adequate, but we still face the same fundamental challenges as the educators Pedro Ponce de Leon in 1550 and Juan Pablo Bonet in 1620. The time has come to build upon their work rather than to continue to merely copy it.

SUMMARY

Hearing disorders include a wide range of hearing loss from a mild loss which may have little if any impact on learning and achievement to total deafness. It has been estimated that approximately 15 million people in the United States have some form of hearing loss; and, like visual impairments, hearing disorders are directly related to aging. Mild to severe hearing loss is part of the aging process. This chapter, however, focused on the group of individuals with severe hearing losses which were present before the child had learned language, i.e., those who were preverbally or prelingually deaf.

Heredity and infections such as maternal rubella, childhood meningitis, and herpes simplex are common causes of deafness in young children. Losses which result from these causes are usually sensorineural, meaning that they interrupt the functioning of the inner ear and/or the processing of acoustic information. Unlike conductive losses which affect the inner and middle ear and can often be treated, the prognosis for sensorineural losses is severely limited at present.

Hearing is measured in units called decibels, and losses are categorized into four levels with the mildest loss from 35 to 54 decibels and the greatest loss 90 decibels or more. Zero decibels (dB) refers to a sound that is just audible; normal conversation where the listener and speaker are three feet apart varies from 60 to 70 dB; and a phonograph with a 10 watt amplifier 10 feet away is approximately 110 dB.

Since preverbal deafness is often caused by genetic disorders which produce multiple handicaps, many preverbally deaf individuals have more than one handicapping condition. This chapter, however, focuses on preverbally deaf children of normal cognitive ability and without additional physical or sensory handicaps. Within this group, the intellectual functioning and capacity does not differ from that of hearing children. The major difference between the two groups is in the deaf child's lack of communicative opportunities which may result in deficits in experience and information.

The social and emotional development of deaf children cannot be separated from their family's attitudes, coping skills, and ability to adapt their communication to the child. Although many studies have reported negative personality characteristics among deaf individuals, this interpretation must be viewed with caution. Some of the instruments used may not have been appropriate for people with deafness, and the significant others in the lives of deaf individuals may have lacked the skill and understanding to support healthy emotional growth.

Education for deaf students emphasizes instruction in basic English skills, speech, English grammar, and the use of residual hearing. Amplification devices such as hearing aids and the combination of oral and manual instruction are prominent features of current programs for deaf children. Although opportunities for deaf students to enroll in college, university, and vocational training programs have increased, many deaf adults continue to be underemployed. Increased acceptance and opportunities at all age levels coupled with quality instructional training for deaf individuals should perpetuate the gains that have been made.

References

Allen, T., White, C., & Karchmer, M. (1983). Issues in the development of a special edition for hearing impaired students of the seventh edition of the Stanford Achievement Test. *American Annals of the Deaf, 128,* 34–39.

Altshuler, K. (1974). The social and psychological development of the deaf child: Problems and treatment. In P. Fine (Ed.), *Deafness in infancy and early childhood.* New York: Medcom Press.

Anderson, R., & Sisco, F. (1977). *Standardization of the WISC-R performance scale for deaf children.* Washington, DC: Gallaudet College Office of Demographic Studies, Ser. T, No. 1.

Armstrong, D., & Schneidmiller, K. (1983). *Hearing impaired students enrolled in U.S. higher education institutions.* Washington, DC: Gallaudet College Office of Planning.

Boatner, E., Stuckless, E., & Moores, D. (1964). *Occupational status of the young adult deaf of New England and the need and demand for a regional vocational-technical training center.* West Hartford, CT: American School for the Deaf.

Brown, K., Hopkins, S., & Hudgins, M. (1967). Causes of childhood deafness. *Proceedings of the International Conference on Oral Education of the Deaf* (pp. 77–107). Washington, DC: A. G. Bell Association.

Clark, T., & Watkins, S. (1978). *Programming for hearing impaired infants through amplification and home intervention.* Logan: Utah State University.

Collins, J. (1969). *Communication between deaf children of preschool age and their mothers.* Unpublished doctoral dissertation, University of Pittsburgh.

Craig, W., & Craig, H. (Eds.) (1983). Directory of services. *American Annals of the Deaf, 127.*

Erikson, E. (1969). *Identity, youth and the life cycle.* New York: International University Press.

Freeman, R. (1977). Psychiatric aspects of sensory disorders and intervention. In P. Graham (Ed.), *Epidemiological approaches in child psychiatry* (pp. 275–304). New York: Academic Press.

Frisina, R. (1974). *Report of the Committee to Redefine Deaf and Hard of Hearing for Educational Purposes* (mimeo).

Furth, H. (1971). Education for thinking. *Journal of Rehabilitation of the Deaf, 5,* 7–71.

Furth, H. (1973). *Deafness and learning.* Belmont, CA: Wadsworth.

Gannon, J. (1980). *Deaf heritage.* Silver Spring, MD: National Association of the Deaf.

Garnett, C. (1968). *The exchange of letters between Samuel Heinicke and Abbé Charles Michel de l'Epée.* New York: Vantage.

Gregory, S. (1976). *The deaf child and his family.* London: George Allen.

Gustason, G., Pfetzing, D., & Zawolkow, E. (1972). *Signing exact English.* Rossmoor, CA: Modern Signs Press.

Harris, A. (1978). The development of the deaf individual and the deaf community. In L. Liben (Ed.), *Deaf children: Developmental perspectives* (pp. 217–233). New York: Academic Press.

Harris, R. (1978). Impulse control in deaf children. In L. Liben (Ed.), *Deaf children: Developmental perspectives* (pp. 137–156). New York: Academic Press.

Jensema, C., & Corbett, E. (1981). *A descriptive study of teachers of the hearing impaired in the United States.* Washington, DC: Gallaudet College Press.

Jensema, C., & Trybus, R. (1975). *Reported emotional/behavioral problems among hearing impaired students in special educational programs.* Washington, DC: Gallaudet College Office of Demographic Studies, Ser. R, No. 1.

Jordan, I., Gustason, G., & Rosen, R. (1976). Current communication trends in programs for the deaf. *American Annals of the Deaf, 121,* 527–531.

Jordan, I., Gustason, G., & Rosen, R. (1979). An update on communication trends in programs for the deaf. *American Annals of the Deaf, 124,* 350–357.

Karchmer, M., & Kerwin, L. (1977). *The use of hearing aids by hearing impaired students in the United States.* Washington, DC: Gallaudet College Office of Demographic Studies, Ser. S, No. 2.

Kluwin, T. (1981a). The grammaticality of manual representations of English in classroom settings. *American Annals of the Deaf, 126,* 417–421.

Kluwin, T. (1981b). A rationale for modifying classroom signing systems. *Sign Language Studies, 31,* 179–188.

Kronenberg, H., & Blake, G. (1966). *Young deaf adults: An occupational survey.* Hot Springs, AR: Arkansas Rehabilitation Services.

Levine, E. (1956). *Youth in a soundless world.* New York: New York University Press.

Levine, E. (1960). *The psychology of deafness.* New York: Columbia University Press.

Levine, L. (1974). Psychological tests and practices with the deaf. *The Volta Review, 76,* 298–319.

Maestas y Moores, J. (1979). *Language acquisition: Mother-child interaction.* Paper presented at NATO Advanced Institute on Sign Language Cognition. Copenhagen, Denmark.

Maestas y Moores, J. (1980). *A descriptive study of the communication modes and pragmatic functions used by three prelinguistically profoundly deaf mothers with their infants one to six months of age in their homes.* Unpublished doctoral dissertation, University of Minnesota.

Maestas y Moores, J., & Moores, D. (1980). Language training with the young deaf child. *New Directions for Exceptional Children, 1,* 49–61.

Maestas y Moores, J., & Moores, D. (1984). The status of Hispanics in special education. In G. Delgado (Ed.), *The Hispanic deaf: Issues and challenges in bilingual special education* (pp. 14–27). Washington, DC: Gallaudet College Press.

Martin, F. (1981). *Introduction to audiology.* Englewood Cliffs, NJ: Prentice-Hall.

Meadow, K. (1967). *The effect of early manual communication and family climate on the deaf child's development.* Unpublished doctoral dissertation, University of California, Berkeley.

Meadow, K. (1968). Parental response to the medical ambiguities of deafness. *Journal of Health and Social Behavior, 9,* 299–309.

Meadow, K. (1969). Self-image, family climate and deafness. *Social Forces, 47,* 428–438.

Meadow, K. (1980). *Deafness and child development.* Berkeley: University of California Press.

Moores, D. (1973). Families and deafness. In A. Norris (Ed.), *Deafness annual* (pp. 115–130). Silver Spring, MD: Professional Rehabilitation Workers with the Adult Deaf.

Moores, D. (1982). *Educating the deaf: Psychology, principles and practices* (2nd ed.). Boston: Houghton-Mifflin.

Moores, D. (1984). A longitudinal evaluation of preschool programs for the deaf. In K. Nelson (Ed.), *Children's language: Volume 5.* Hillsdale, NJ: Lawrence Erlbaum.

Moores, D., & Oden, C. (1978). Educational needs of black deaf children. *American Annals of the Deaf, 122,* 313–318.

Moores, D., Fisher, S., & Harlow, M. (1974). *Post-secondary programs for the deaf: Monograph VI: Summary and overview.* University of Minnesota Research, Development, and Demonstration Center in Education of Handicapped Children, Research Report No. 60.

Moores, D., Weiss, K., & Goodman, M. (1978). Early intervention programs for hearing impaired children. *American Annals of the Deaf, 123*, 925–936.

Myklebust, H., & Brutten, M. (1953). A study of visual perception in deaf children. *Acta Oto-Laryngolugica*, Supplementum 105.

Ottem, E. (1980). An analysis of cognitive studies with deaf subjects. *American Annals of the Deaf, 125*, 564–575.

Pintner, R., Eisenson, J., & Stanton, M. B. (1941). *The psychology of the physically handicapped.* New York: Crofts & Co.

Quigley, S., Joune, W., & Phillips, S. (1968). *Deaf students in colleges and universities.* Washington, DC: Council for Exceptional Children.

Rainer, J., & Altshuler, K. (1970). *Expanded mental health for the deaf.* Washington, DC: U.S. Department of Health, Education, and Welfare, Social and Rehabilitation Services.

Rainer, J., Altshuler, K., & Kallman, F. (1963). *Family and mental health problems in a deaf population.* New York: Columbia University Press.

Rawlings, B., Karchmer, M., & Decaro, J. (1983). *College and career programs for deaf students: 1983 Edition.* Washington, DC: Gallaudet College and Rochester, NY: National Technical Institute for the Deaf.

Rittenhouse, R., & Spiro, R. (1979). Conservation-interrogation of deaf and normal hearing children. *Journal of Childhood Communication Disorders, 3*, 120–127.

Schein, J., & Delk, M. (1974). *The deaf population of the United States.* Silver Spring, MD: National Association of the Deaf.

Schlesinger, H. (1978). The effects of deafness on childhood development. In L. Liben (Ed.), *Deaf children: Developmental perspectives* (pp. 157–172). New York: Academic Press.

Schlesinger, H., & Meadow, K. (1972). *Sound and sign: Childhood deafness and mental health.* Berkeley: University of California Press.

Schow, R., & Watkins, S. (1978). Aural rehabilitation for children. In R. Schow & M. Nerbone (Eds.), *Aural rehabilitation* (pp. 224–274). Baltimore: University Park Press.

Sontag, E., Smith, J., & Certo, N. (1977). *Educational programming for the severely and profoundly handicapped.* Reston, VA: Council for Exceptional Children.

Stein, M., Merrill, N., & Dahlberg, P. (1974). *Counseling parents of hearing impaired children.* Paper presented at American Speech and Hearing Association National Conference, Las Vegas.

Stokoe, W. (1975). The use of sign language in teaching English. In J. Maestas y Moores (Ed.), *Proceedings of the Minnesota special study institute in education of the deaf* (pp. 62–85). Minneapolis: University of Minnesota.

Sullivan, P., & Vernon, M. (1979). Psychological assessment of hearing impaired children. *School Psychologist, 8*, 271–290.

Vernon, M. (1967). Relationship of language to the thinking process. *Archives of Genetic Psychiatry, 16*, 325–333.

Vernon, M., & Hicks, D. (1980). Relationship of rubella, herpes simplex, cytomegalovirus, and certain viral disabilities. *American Annals of the Deaf, 125*, 529–534.

Wilber, L. (1979). Threshold measurement measures and special considerations. In W. Rintelmann (Ed.), *Hearing assessment* (pp. 1–28). Baltimore: University Park Press.

Wilbur, R. (1979). *American sign language and sign systems.* Baltimore: University Park Press.

Resources

Organizations

Alexander Graham Bell Association for the Deaf, Inc.
3417 Volta Place, N.W.
Washington, DC 20007
> Provides information, maintains an extensive library, and publishes books, pamphlets, and a journal about issues of interest to parents and professionals.

Convention of American Instructors of the Deaf
5034 Wisconsin Avenue, N.W.
Washington, DC 20016
> An organization of teachers of deaf students which provides information about best practices.

International Parents Organization
Alexander Graham Bell Association for the Deaf, Inc.
3417 Volta Place, N.W.
Washington, DC 20007
> Provides information, support, and opportunities for parents of deaf children to share ideas and expertise.

National Association of the Deaf
814 Thayer Avenue
Silver Spring, MD 20910
> Provides information, technical assistance, and lobbying on issues of interest to deaf individuals.

National Association of Parents of the Deaf
814 Thayer Avenue
Silver Spring, MD 20910
> Organization of parents which provides information, support, and opportunities to share experience and expertise.

National Registry of Interpreters for the Deaf
814 Thayer Avenue
Silver Spring, MD 20910
> A list of individuals who have been trained and qualify as interpreters for deaf individuals.

Professional Rehabilitation Workers with the Adult Deaf
814 Thayer Avenue
Silver Spring, MD 20910
> A professional organization which provides information, publishes a journal, and holds national meetings which focus on issues related to rehabilitation of deaf adults.

Journals

American Annals of the Deaf
5034 Wisconsin Avenue, N.W.
Washington, DC 20016
> The official publication of the Convention of American Instructors of the Deaf and of the Conference of Educational Administrators Serving the Deaf which includes articles on educational research and practice as it relates to deaf individuals.

The Deaf American
5125 Radnor Road
Indianapolis, IN 46226
> First published in 1892 under the title *Silent Worker,* this journal provides information of interest to deaf individuals.

Journal of Rehabilitation of the Deaf
814 Thayer Avenue
Silver Spring, MD 20910

The official journal of the Professional Rehabilitation Workers with Deaf Adults, this publication deals primarily with vocational and independent living issues.

The Volta Review
3417 Volta Place, N.W.
Washington, DC 20007

Publishes research, reviews, and descriptions of innovative and effective interventions with deaf individuals.

Chapter 8

COMMUNICATION DISORDERS

In our society, the ability to communicate effectively is a highly valued skill. Communication in one form or another is an integral part of the various aspects of our waking lives, and a deficit in this area may have anywhere from minimal to profound effects. Disordered communication:

> . . . *prevents the individual from realizing fulfillment, from becoming all he or she is capable of being. It dooms some to maladjustment, some to educational isolationism, and many to more subtle forms of disability: from minor inconvenience to disaster, and all the graduations along the continuum. . . . Communication is a powerful tool, an eloquent weapon, a manipulative agent, a distinctive attribute and as recognizable for each individual as is appearance.* (Van Hattum, 1983, p. 47)

As Van Hattum states so eloquently, the importance of communication should not be underestimated. But what is communication? In its most basic form, it is an exchange of information, and this information may be either verbal or nonverbal. What then, is a communication disorder? Van Riper (1978) suggests: "Speech is abnormal when it deviates so far from the speech of other people that it calls attention to itself, interferes with communication, or causes the speaker or his listeners to be distressed" (p. 43). This practical definition considers the impact of a disorder on the listener as well as the speaker.

Carol A. Swift
Oakland University

A more formal definition, supported by the American Speech-Language-Hearing Association (ASHA, 1982) states: "A *COMMUNICATIVE DISORDER* is an impairment in the ability to (1) receive and/or process a symbol system; (2) represent concepts or symbol systems; and/or (3) transmit and use symbol systems" (p. 949). Thus, communication disorders may involve difficulty in comprehension, or understanding the communication of others, and difficulty in expression, or speaking so that the person may be readily understood by others. Important to school personnel is the definition contained in Public Law 94–142 which describes a communication disorder by listing its types: stuttering, articulation, voice, and language. This law further stipulates that, in order to be considered a handicap, the disorder must adversely affect a student's educational performance (U.S. Office of Education, 1977). Educational performance has been expanded to include both academics and oral communication as it occurs in the school setting (Bennett & Runyan, 1982).

The primary professionals concerned with the assessment and treatment of communication disorders are speech-language pathologists. They are trained to serve in both public school and clinical settings. Although some clinicians may specialize, most school-based professionals deal with all types of communication disorders. Medical specialists, including the neurologist and the otolaryngologist (a physician who specializes in diseases of the ear and throat), are essential in the diagnosis and often the treatment of organically based disorders. Other disciplines which contribute include special education, audiology, and mental health.

TYPES OF COMMUNICATION DISORDERS

Communication disorders have been traditionally divided into two major categories: disorders of speech, and disorders of language. Recently, the American Speech-Language-Hearing Association has designated two additional categories, hearing disorders and communicative differences, as separate categories.

Speech may be defined as the oral production of the meaningful sounds of language. A disorder in this area involves a deficit in the "transmission and use of the oral symbol system" (ASHA, 1982, p. 949). As transmission includes the articulation of specific sounds, the production of voice, as well as rate and rhythm, speech disorders may involve any or all of these characteristics. These divisions—articulation, voice, and speech—define the major element involved in a disorder. However, an assortment of labels may be applied to deviations in each of these areas which serve to further identify the particular disorder. In some cases, these labels reflect the cause of the disorder; in others, they describe specific symtomology of the disordered speaker.

Disorders of articulation involve the abnormal production of phonemes or individual speech sounds. One sound may be substituted for another, omitted, added, or distorted. An example is the frontal lisp, in which "th" is substituted for "s." *Disorders of voice* involve faulty sound production (phonation) or the improper modification of sound in the oral cavities (resonance). Voice may be judged deviant on the basis of quality, intensity, or pitch. *Disorders of fluency* affect the rate and rhythm of speech to the extent that the forward flow of verbal expression becomes abnormal. Sounds, syllables, or words may be repeated or prolonged as in stuttering, or words phrased in abnormal patterns as in cluttering.

Language may be defined as an arbitrary symbol system used for the purpose of communication. Any language system consists of five major components:

1. Phonology, the sound system of a language and the rules which determine their combinations;
2. Morphology, the smallest meaningful units of a language and the rules which determine the structure of words and their various forms;
3. Syntax, word order and the rules which determine the relationship among the elements in a sentence;
4. Semantics, the content or meaning;
5. Pragmatics, the use of language in a sociolinguistic context.

A disorder in language is characterized by difficulty in the understanding or use of language in either its spoken or written form and involves one or more of the five components listed above. Disorders may be grouped according to three major types: developmental delay, those associated with learning disabilities, and those resulting from known neurological involvement.

Due to the special nature of the communicative problems of hearing disordered persons, this population is now classified as a separate type of communication disorder. The characteristics and impact of a hearing disorder, including its effects on communication, are discussed in Chapter 7.

Individuals who do not have speech and language disorders in the traditional sense, but nonetheless may require or benefit from the services of the speech-language professional, are classified as "communicatively different." Persons with dialect differences or bilingual backgrounds and those who require the use of communication enhancement devices due to an inability to speak fall within this category.

Communication disorders are likely to have the most impact in the social-emotional domain, although learning and physical health may also be affected depending upon the nature of the particular disorder. In general, disorders range from mild articulation difficulties which have minimal effect on the speaker to global aphasia, a language disorder which severely limits both the comprehension and expression of speech and language. However, the severity of a communication disorder is dependent upon more than the extent of deviation from the norm. Cultural, environmental, and personal factors all interact to determine the impact of the disorder on a particular individual. When the demand for communication is high and the individual has few positive traits to offset the effects of the communication deficit, the disordered speaker is likely to be more disadvantaged (Van Riper, 1978). The attitudes of both the disordered speaker and the listeners are critical, not only in establishing the severity of the disorder, but for successful treatment as well.

BOB

Bob S., a 34-year-old engineer, has a lateral lisp which has defied complete correction since childhood. The distortion of the sibilant sounds ("s," "z," "sh," "zh") give an overall "slushy" impression to his speech. Although Bob had several years of speech therapy as a child which was successful in correcting most of his articulation difficulties, his lateral lisp remains. At age 24, unhappy with his personal life and blaming all his social failures on his speech, Bob once again sought speech therapy. After about seven months, Bob withdrew from the clinic and has not been back since.

Bob admits that the therapy sessions as an adult helped in two ways: he began to feel better about himself as a person and did learn techniques to lesson the distortion effect. He admits that had he remained in therapy, the difficulty might have disappeared; however, he feels that this is unlikely. Now, happily married and successful in his engineering career, Bob only occasionally feels "different" because of his speech difficulty. He reported: "I went car shopping a few months ago and was really interested in a particular model. I chose this dealer because of the good reputation for maintenance as well as convenience to my office. When the salesman approached me, I barely had a chance to tell him what I was interested in before he began drilling me with questions like, 'Are you sure you can drive? Do you have a driver's license?' and the kicker was, 'Are you sure you have enough money to buy a car?' He would never have asked those questions of anyone else."

Exact determination of the prevalence of communication disorders is difficult. Estimates in the general population range from 2.3 million persons, or 1.1 percent of the population (National Health Interview Survey of the National Center for Health Statistics, 1982, cited in Fein, 1983) to ASHA's claim of 10 million persons (Cleland & Swartz, 1982). Figures appear to vary considerably depending upon where, how, by whom, and for what purpose the data were collected. For example, the U.S. Department of Education (1982) reported that, in the 1980–81 school year, approximately 1.1 million students age 3 to 21 years were served in programs where communication disorders was identified as the primary handicap. Children labeled as primary mental retardation or hearing disordered were not included. Other studies have been similarly limited by excluding some portion of the population, such as preschool children, prison inmates, or residents of long-term care facilities.

Communication disorders may manifest themselves at any age, but they are more frequent in the school years and at the upper ends of the age continuum. The rate for the 5-to-14 age group is twice that of the under-5 population (HIS, 1977, cited in Fein, 1983). Approximately 75 percent of communication disordered school-age children have articulation difficulties, while another 17 percent demonstrate language deficiencies. Less frequent are voice disorders (5 percent) and disruptions in fluency (3 percent) (Weiss & Lillywhite, 1981). At age 15, the rate drops dramatically and remains fairly constant until age 55 when the trend is a steady upward increase through the 75+ age range. This variation among age groups is influenced by such factors as successful treatment, unreported cases in preschool and adult populations, and increased medical problems in the aged, such as strokes resulting in aphasia, which can disrupt communication. In addition to age, other variables affect prevalence figures. For example, approximately twice as many males as females and individuals of non-Anglo ethnicity in comparison to Anglos are identified as communicatively disordered (NCHS, 1981, cited in Fein, 1983).

ETIOLOGY AND PREVENTION

Communication disorders may have either organic or nonorganic causes. Organic etiologies assume a physical or physiological disruption to one or more of the systems involved in the production or comprehension of speech and language. Nonorganic causes may be environmental or psychological, but, in the majority of cases, specific causative agents cannot be identified and conditions are typically referred to as functional or developmental. The organic-nonorganic dichotomy is useful at one level of diagnosis and, as such, will be one of the organizing principles for this chapter. However, it is important to note that the two are not mutually exclusive. Most communication disorders, regardless of initial etiology, have both organic and functional components (Weiss & Lillywhite, 1981). For example, a child's hoarseness may be attributed to nodules on the vocal folds, certainly a pathological condition; however, nodules are primarily a result of excessive screaming or yelling or some other form of vocal abuse, and this is behavioral. The reverse may also be true: a condition which originated in pathology may be maintained for psychological reasons.

Organic Disorders

Structural deviations in the oral mechanism may cause a variety of speech difficulties. Tongue-tie, in which the lingual frenulum (the skin which connects the tongue to the lower jaw) is too short to allow adequate movement during speech, may cause mild articulation difficulties.

Other types of abnormalities will affect voice quality. An obstruction in the nasal passages will cause denasality, a condition in which the speaker sounds as though he or she has a bad cold. In the opposite condition, when too much air passes through the nasal cavities, the speaker will sound hypernasal, or have a whining quality to the voice. Hypernasality is associated with cleft palate, a severe congenital disorder in which the individual is born with an opening in the palate (the roof of the mouth) which sometimes extends through the lip. Children with a cleft palate typically exhibit articulation difficulties with sibilant sounds (e.g., "s" and "z") in addition to their voice deviations. Even after surgical correction, problems such as nasal emission (excessive air flow) during speech may continue (Peterson, 1975).

Structural deviations of the vocal folds, such as paralysis, missing pharyngeal tissue (surgically removed due to cancer), or the presence of a large mass (e.g., a tumor), all interfere with the movement of the vocal folds. This restriction of movement causes problems in voice production. Severe pathology may result in aphonia (no voice) or spastic dysphonia (intermittent voice). Vocal nodules (hard growths on the vocal folds) and polyps (pockets or swellings engorged with blood), typically the result of vocal abuse or misuse, are associated with breathiness or hoarseness (Moore, 1971; Perkins, 1978).

An example of muscular imbalance is tongue thrust (sometimes called reverse swallowing), in which the tongue is pushed too far forward in the mouth during swallowing and during speech. This abnormal protrusion may interfere with articulation, causing some distortion of sounds or a frontal lisp (substitution of "th" for "s").

Damage to the nervous system can have particularly severe and long-lasting effects on the communication ability of an individual. External head injuries due to falls or other accidents, infectious or degenerative diseases which affect brain tissue, tumors, and vascular disturbances (strokes) can all cause a disruption in one or more aspects of communication. Generally, the site and the extent of the neurological involvement will determine the nature of the communication disorder. When motor areas of the brain are affected, incoordination of the musculature involved in speech production may result, thus creating the condition known as dysarthria. Predominantly an articulation disorder, dysarthria may involve voice and prosody (rate and rhythm) deviations as well (Darley, Aronson, & Brown, 1975). Stuttering may also result from brain damage, but this tends to be less frequent (Canter, 1971; Rosenbek, Messert, Collins & Wertz, 1978). Left hemisphere damage frequently results in a loss of language functioning called aphasia which may be temporary or permanent, mild or global, depending on the site and the extent of the damage. Dysarticulation may also occur as a result of left hemisphere damage (apraxia), but the difficulty is one of impaired purposeful movement rather than incoordination. Both dysarthria and apraxia, along with voice and fluency disturbances, may be associated with a variety of conditions which affect the nervous system. Examples are cerebral palsy, Parkinson's disease, and multiple sclerosis.

Nonorganic Disorders

Communication disorders may also be psychologically or environmentally caused. Lack of stimulation in the home environment or an emotional trauma can bring about a variety of symptoms, from a severe delay in the development of speech and language to a falsetto (unusually high-pitched) voice in males. In addition, poor vocal habits can result in physiological changes to the system which, in turn, create deviations in some aspect of communication. For example, children who yell excessively may develop nodules on their vocal folds, thus creating a voice disorder. Repeated exposure to loud noise or music (such as in a factory or rock band) may cause a loss in hearing which, in time, will affect both voice quality and articulation. However, the majority of communication disorders have no identifiable etiology. Developmental dysarticulation, the most frequently occurring disorder in children, cannot be attributed to any particular cause in 60 to 80 percent of the cases (Powers, 1971b). The absence of known etiology is also true in many cases of delayed language and stuttering. Many children simply fail to talk and do not gain articulatory proficiency or fluency at the expected time.

Prevention

The likelihood that certain communication disorders will occur can be decreased with preventive measures. The negative impact of an existing disorder can also be diminished, thus preventing the occurrence of concomitant psychological or emotional problems. One of the most critical factors, both in the prevention of functional disorders and in the facilitation of communicative skills in the presence of known organicity, is a positive communicative atmosphere. Parents begin by becoming aware of the stages in speech and language development. This awareness provides for realistic expectations of the child. The home environment is the critical element during the preschool years. Good speech and language modeling and active listening, along with attention to the overall physical and mental health of the child, are basic to the development of communicative competency.

Early medical treatment may also be seen in terms of its preventive aspects. Even if a disorder itself cannot be prevented, medical intervention in the form of medication or surgery can lessen the severity of the disorder. An example of this is cleft palate, in which early reconstructive surgery creates a better structural environment for the development of speech; even if deviations occur, which they often do, they tend not to be as severe.

Preventive programs have also been suggested for school-age children. A focus on good general health, vocal hygiene, knowledge of the causes of vocal abuse and ear pollution (prolonged exposure to loud noise), along with disability awareness, are all important elements (Flynn, 1983; Nilson & Schneiderman, 1983). When the speech-language professional handles preventive programs through the regular classroom environment, teachers also become more aware of causative factors and are better able to monitor newly developing difficulties, thereby facilitating both prevention and early intervention (Nilson & Schneiderman, 1983).

CHARACTERISTICS OF INDIVIDUALS WITH COMMUNICATION DISORDERS

The characteristics of a communication disordered person will vary considerably according to the type of disorder, etiology, and age of onset, as well as personal and environmental factors. The symptomology, by definition, will vary according to the disorder, although there is overlap in many situations, particularly when there is organicity.

Articulation Disorders.

Mastery of the phonemes of the language does not come all at once. Infants are not born speaking intelligibly, although they do have the capacity for producing virtually all phonemes. However, as sounds become associated with meaning, the early reflexive production of the more difficult ones disappears for a time (Weiss & Lillywhite, 1981). Sounds are not learned in isolation, but rather in context with one another (Bloom & Lahey, 1978). However, in spite of some individual differences, the order of phoneme acquisition is predictable. Vowels appear first and consonants follow according to position of the articulators used to produce the sound and frequency of occurrence in the language. Sounds which are easier to produce, such as "p," "b," and "m" (bilabials) appear earliest, while sounds such as "s," "r," and "l" which require more complex coordination of the musculature develop later. By 6½ years, single consonant sounds are typically present; consonant clusters, or blends, appear about six months later (Weiss & Lillywhite, 1981). Even with the wide variation in normal development, all phonemes should be acquired by eight years of age (Winitz, 1969); in fact, there is evidence that children are incorporating many phonemes into their speech at younger ages than indicated by earlier studies (Arlt & Goodban, 1976).

A disorder in articulation, then, involves errors in the production of the sounds of the language. These errors may be of four types: substitutions, omissions, distortions, and/or additions of phonemes. In functional or developmental articulation difficulties, the most common error is the substitution of one sound, usually one which is developmentally easier to produce, for another. Frequent substitutions in developmental articulation problems include "th" for "s" and "z" (called a frontal or interdental lisp); "w" for "r," "l," or "th"; and "t" for "k." For example, a child may say "wabbit" meaning "rabbit" or "tite" meaning "kite." Common omission errors involve the "s" sound, in which the child might say "baketball" instead of "basketball," "boat" instead of "boats," or "oap" instead of "soap." Distortions, or the near approximation of a sound, are a third type of error. Two common distortion patterns involve the "r" or "er" sound and sibilant sounds such as "s," "z," "sh," and "zh." In the latter the air stream is misdirected during phonation resulting in "slushy" sounding speech; this distortion is referred to as a lateral lisp. The fourth type of error, which occurs more rarely, involves the addition of extra sounds in words. For example, the child might say "stoap" instead of "soap."

Intelligibility of speech, which should be considered in the context of normal development, will vary depending on the number of incorrectly produced phonemes and the frequency of occurrence of those phonemes in the language. Speech is usually not 100 percent intelligible (which does not mean error-free) until about age four (Weiss & Lillywhite, 1981).

Normally developing dysarticulate children may be distinguished from unintelligible speech disordered children by their lack of consistency in errors. The errors of the latter tend to form patterns, with a single sound taking the place of

A speech therapist uses a communication board with a child who exhibits a severe language disorder.

a whole class of sounds (Weiner, 1981). For example, "t" may be substituted for "s," "z," "th," "f," and "v."

Children with functional or developmental articulation disorders do not seem to differ from nondisordered children in cognitive development, understanding of language (Smit & Bernthal, 1983), or motor skills outside the area of speech. They can imitate rhythm and intonation patterns equally as well as their non-disordered peers (Shadden, Asp, Tonkovich, & Mason, 1980). However, there is some support for differences in auditory perception (Smit & Bernthal, 1983).

Although functional articulation difficulties may persist into adulthood, articulation difficulties in adults are more commonly associated with organic impairment. The impairment may be developmental, such as cerebral palsy, or acquired, such as Parkinson's disease.

Voice Disorders.   The characteristics of the human voice are extremely varied and, in turn, have a wider range of acceptability than some other aspects of communication. However, there are certain expectancies surrounding voice characteristics that are integrally related to age, sex, and body build. For example, we expect a young child to have a higher-pitched voice than an adult and we expect women to have higher-pitched voices than men. In addition, the appropriateness of certain aspects of voice, such as intensity, vary according to context. A whisper in church is not only acceptable, but expected; a whisper in the classroom in response to the teacher's question is not.

Tonality—which involves the integration of vocal quality, intensity, and pitch—develops quite early in the young child. Infants differentiate their cries and utterances according to communicative intent, and caregivers are readily able to determine whether the message in the utterance is "I'm hungry!" or "I'm scared!" In addition, young children respond to tonality and intensity of voice in others before they respond to semantic content (Bloom & Lahey, 1978). Generally, children learn to control their voices by seven years of age, if they have not already done so (Curran & Cratty, 1978).

Voice disordered individuals do not differ from the general population in either intelligence, physical development (motor), or learning capacity. The major effect of a voice disorder on an individual is emotional or psychological, as in the majority of communication disorders. An individual's voice is so closely associated with personality that, if it is inconsistent with expectations (either the person's own expectations or those of others), it is likely to create problems for the disordered speaker.

Fluency Disorders.   As adults we are all dysfluent from time to time. We hesitate when we are formulating our next thought, interject nonwords such as "uh" and "ah," and repeat occasional words and phrases; however, all of these behaviors are acceptable in the majority of people. Likewise, children are not born with perfect fluency. As they develop proficiency with language, most will exhibit some form of dysfluency. The amount and type are extremely variable from child to child, but particular patterns of dysfluency appear to be consistent within individuals (Colburn & Mysak, 1982b; Weiss & Lillywhite, 1981). The type of dysfluency changes systematically as utterances become longer (Colburn & Mysak, 1982a), but disappears as a noticeable deviation in most children by about age six or seven. Between three and five years of age, speech is fluent about 90 percent of the time, and the rate ranges from about 50 to 130 words per minute. Between five and seven years, fluency increases by about 5 percent, while the rate range changes slightly to about 60 to 130 words per minute (Weiss & Lillywhite, 1981). If noticeable dysfluency continues beyond this age, or is severely discrepant from that expected, the behavior can be considered stuttering or cluttering.

Stuttering, the major disorder of fluency, is characterized by repetitions and prolongations of words, syllables, or sounds which result in an abnormal rate of rhythm during speech production. The characteristics of stuttering, as with normal dysfluency, vary with age. Young stutterers more frequently repeat vowels and monosyllabic function words such as "the" and "a" while adults tend to block on consonant sounds, multisyllabic words, and content words (those with more meaning) (Bloodstein & Grossman, 1981).

The incidence of stuttering in very young children is equally distributed between the sexes (Yairi, 1983); however, in older children and adults, two to ten times as many males as females are identified as stutterers. Although stuttering is not usually associated with any specific cognitive deficiencies, a review of the

introducing

SALLY

Sally R., an eight-year-old second grader, exhibits moderate to severe dysfluency when she speaks. Her parents first noticed the difficulty at age two and a half. Understanding that some dysfluency is to be expected in young children, the parents were not immediately concerned. However, when Sally's speech was still noticeably dysfluent at age four, with repetitions of sounds at the beginnings of words and prolongations of other sounds, Mr. and Mrs. R. decided to seek help from professionals. The initial intervention involved a play setting in which no mention was made of Sally's dysfluent speech. She continued in this situation for about two years; while her dysfluency did not noticeably decrease, it did not get any worse either.

During first grade, Sally's first year in public school, the R. family moved. The clinic Sally had attended was no longer convenient. However, the parents realized that their daughter needed some kind of help and decided to explore those services provided in school. Sally was subsequently identified as communication disordered and began seeing the speech therapist in her school twice a week.

The school speech therapist took the opposite approach with Sally than had her first therapist, acknowledging her stuttering. He forced her to attend to all the bad habits she had acquired associated with speaking, such as biting her lip and refusing eye contact. He also introduced her to relaxation techniques, which she is now using spontaneously. In spite of the initial increase in dysfluency in the new setting, Sally's speech has gradually become more fluent. Although she still stutters, she does so less frequently and appears more confident. While still somewhat shy, Sally has made friends and participates readily in classroom activities.

literature indicates that as a group, stutterers tend to score half a standard deviation below their nonstuttering peers on standardized intelligence tests (Andrews, Craig, Feyer, Hoddinott, Howie, & Neilson, 1983). In addition, concomitant speech, language, and learning problems are often present in the school-age population.

Certain phenomena, such as increased fluency while singing, reading, or role-playing, are characteristic of some individuals who stutter. While this may seem to support the neurotic nature of stuttering, current research offers an alternative explanation. Colcord and Adams (1979) suggest that during singing, for example, the patterns of phonation, pitch, and rhythm differ from those employed in conversation. It may be these physiological variables which facilitate fluency, rather than the personal detachment provided by these situations, as suggested by the proponents of a psychological etiology.

Aside from the symptom of stuttering itself, individuals who stutter do not appear to be any more neurotic than nonstuttering persons (Andrews et al., 1983). However, the most devastating effects of severe dysfluency are still in the social/emotional domain. That these individuals frequently have adjustment problems (Prins, 1972) is not surprising, as listener attitudes toward stuttering are often severely penalizing.

Cluttering, another fluency disturbance, is characterized by rapid speech, erratic rhythm, excessive repetitions (Perkins, 1978), and phonological or articulatory errors (Weiss & Lillywhite, 1981). The frequent addition and omission of sounds, along with inappropriate syllabication and phrasing, make the clutterer difficult to understand. Since they often appear unaware of their difficulty, calling attention to it will increase intelligibility. In fact, speech will improve under stressful conditions and deteriorate in relaxed situations, the opposite of the reactions in both stutterers and most normal speakers (Weiss & Lillywhite, 1981).

Language Disorders

In the normal development of language, comprehension generally precedes expression. Infants have been found to discriminate phonemes as early as one month of age (Eimas, Siqueland, Jusczyk, & Vigorito, 1971), certain elements of syntax are understood prior to the child's ability to combine words into sentences (Bloom & Lahey, 1978), and labels are comprehended before the child can effectively produce them. Although the age of acquisition and subsequent mastery of the elements of language production is extremely variable from one child to another, the sequence of acquisition, especially within systems (Muma, 1978), is predictable (Cazden, 1968). For example, with verb tense markers, the present perfect ("-ing") is acquired earlier than the past tense ("-ed") (deVilliers & deVilliers, 1978). Nouns and verbs predominate in child language during the first four years (Weiss & Lillywhite, 1981) and single words and two-word phrases are used holophrastically. For example, "ball" might mean "my ball" or "Give me the ball"; likewise, the two-word utterance "throw ball" might be used to mean "I threw the ball," "I am throwing the ball," or "You throw the ball" depending upon the context of the situation. That the child uses the same combination of words to convey different meanings is clear, especially when the listener fails to respond appropriately! This stage of development, often called telegraphic speech, is characterized by omission of articles such as "the" and inaccurate subject-verb agreement (Smith, 1978). Although by 2½ years half of the child's utterances may be sentences, the type of errors just described continue through age three or four.

The development of sentence types is also predictable; simple sentences appear first, followed by compound then complex constructions (Pflaum-Connor, 1978). Declarative sentences are the most frequent through about age eight, and their frequency increases while other types, such as the interrogative form, decrease (Weiss & Lillywhite, 1981). The acquisition of vocabulary is particularly variable, with interests playing a crucial role in determining the categories or classes of words which will be acquired first (Rosenblatt, 1975, cited in Bryan & Bryan, 1979). However, for many children, words which represent action or movement in some capacity, expressing dynamic rather than static relationships or concepts, will be acquired earlier than more abstract words (Nelson, 1974; Weiss & Lillywhite, 1981). The majority of linguistic development takes place by age five, but the process does not suddenly stop at this time. Rather, development continues into the teen years (Loban, 1963, 1966; Palermo & Molfese, 1972), with semantic and syntactic skills becoming increasingly more sophisticated.

Language disorders may be developmental or acquired. When the problem is developmental, there is usually a delay in the onset of speech and language; due to the interrelated nature of language components, most will be affected. When a young child fails to talk at the expected time, the delay may be due to any of the variety of factors including mental retardation or emotional disturbance. In addition, causation cannot be determined in many cases. Although there are linguistic similarities in most language-delayed children (Bloom & Lahey, 1978), cognitive, motoric, and behavioral characteristics will vary.

The most severe of the childhood language disorders is due to central nervous system involvement and, although there is disagreement as to the appropriateness of the term, it is often labeled childhood or developmental aphasia. Much of the research in language delay and language disorders in children has been done with this population.

The question most often asked regarding the characteristics of language disordered children is whether the language difficulty seems more typical of younger children, i.e., a delay, or whether there is actually a deviance in linguistic performance. Although the evidence is inconclusive, Carrow-Woolfolk and Lynch (1982) suggest that, as a rule of thumb, if all elements of language are discrepant to a similar degree, then the disorder might be classified as delayed; if, on the other hand, only one or two elements are discrepant, the difficulty can be considered deviant.

The intellectual performance of language disordered children on standardized tests is below average. This is not unexpected, considering the heavy loading of verbal items on such measures. These children perform better in performance-oriented tests (Weiner, 1969); however, there is some evidence that even this type of cognition is affected (Johnston & Weismer, 1983). This depression in nonverbal cognitive functioning may be due to a more general problem of representational skills, or the inability to imagine or internalize external objects or events (Johnston & Weismer, 1983; Morehead & Ingram, 1973).

The primary acquired organic disturbance of language in adults is aphasia. Language may be deficient in expression, comprehension, or both. Although some may be affected more than others, depending upon the site and the extent of the cerebral injury, usually more than one element will be involved. Dysarthria or apraxia represents a deficit in the phonological system; speech may be telegraphic, representing a deficit in the morphemic and syntactical systems; word-finding difficulties indicate a disruption in the semantic system; and finally, the inability to manipulate language to the extent of nonaphasic individuals illustrates the involvement of the pragmatic aspects of language.

Eisenson, in his 1973 classic text on adult aphasia, describes several characteristics associated with this condition: (1) extreme variability of response, especially immediately following the cerebral injury; (2) emotional liability, in which the individual exhibits extremes of emotion, such as crying easily or showing violent reactions to minor disruptions; (3) perseveration, or continuing to talk about a subject beyond its appropriateness; (4) mood swings, from extreme euphoria to depression; and (5) concretism, an increase in literal thinking and a concomitant decrease in abstracting ability.

As with other communication disorders, the social-emotional functioning of the individual is likely to be affected the most. Extreme frustration at being unable to communicate effectively can increase depression and reinforce the negative aspects of the personality. There is likely to be a degree of reduced intellectual functioning, usually in the form of more rigidity and egocentricity in behavior and less flexibility in thinking. New learning may be slower with a lower level of attainment although the general pattern is the same as for nonaphasic individuals (Eisenson, 1973). In addition to problems with oral language, an aphasic may also have difficulty with reading and written expression, the latter often complicated by motor involvement. Comprehension of written material is the skill most severely affected (Webb & Love, 1983).

Social/Emotional, Health, and Cognitive Characteristics

Emotional or affective development is the area most affected in the majority of communication disorders. The extent of the negative effects depends not only upon the severity of the disorder itself but on the interaction of a complex set of factors. If the individual has enough positive personal characteristics to offset the communication disorder, as well as the support of significant others, that individual may suffer minimal interference with emotional development. However, if the circumstances surrounding the disorder are predominantly negative, the effects are likely to be devastating.

There is a high incidence of psychological and behavioral problems associated with communication disordered children; furthermore, those who have both speech and language disorders seem to have more adjustment problems than those who have only speech impairments (Baker, Cantwell, & Mattison, 1980).

Adjustment problems do not disappear with age. Most adults replace school with a job or career, and the adjustment problems present in school may transfer to the new setting. Adults are no more accepting of communicative differences than are children. Occupational choices are likely to be limited, as some rely heavily upon communicative skills. Even if adequate speech and language are not a requirement for the job itself, the communication disordered person may be discriminated against by the prospective employer in favor of one who is not so handicapped, in spite of comparable ability in other respects (Love, 1981). Many in the general population mistakenly associate impaired communication with incompetence and even mental retardation. Some individuals may react to this kind of pressure by resorting to crime and, indeed, there is a higher incidence (10–15 percent) of communication disorders reported among prisoners than in the general population (Bountress & Richards, 1979); furthermore, this figure does not include those who might have had a communication disorder as a child. The overt symptoms of the original disorder may have been removed but not the emotional trauma associated with it. Weiss & Lillywhite (1981) claim: "The cumulative effects of moderate and severe communicative disorders on psychological development may be among the major etiological factors in adult psychological problems" (p. 7).

When a communication disorder is organically based, there are medical considerations. However, the overall health of the individual may or may not be affected, depending upon the nature of the problem. If the communication difficulty is a part of another condition such as cerebral palsy or muscular dystrophy, then concomitant health problems will exist. Most children who have communication disorders develop normally in the physical and motor domain unless the disorder is associated with some other condition that contraindicates this.

Cognitive ability, or the range of intelligence, of the communicatively disordered is comparable to the general population although this too may vary according to the particular disorder. For example, due to the high incidence of hearing loss in cleft palate youngsters, this population tends to score up to an average of 10 points lower than the general population on standardized intelligence tests (Richman, 1980). However, even normal potential does not ensure average academic performance. We know that a variety of factors other than measured intelligence influence a child's performance in school. A child who is severely penalized for a communication disorder through teasing, criticism, or ostracism may suffer such a severe blow to self-esteem that normal achievement is impossible.

Although it seems obvious that communicative competence and academic performance are closely related, very little actual research exists as to the relationship between communication disorders and either educational capacity or performance. However, Bennett and Runyan (1982) reported on a survey of educators in which 66 percent indicated that communication disorders adversely affected educational performance in some way. Although the bases for these judgments were not clear, the fact that the teachers perceived a problem is important.

DETECTION OF COMMUNICATION DISORDERS

The first step in the identification of a communication disorder is to determine whether a problem may exist. Many school districts screen for communication disorders along with other handicapping conditions at the time of readiness screening prior to school entry. Others screen selected grades, particularly kindergarten and lower elementary, after the school year begins. Screening can take various forms, such as completion of communication skills checklists by classroom teachers or both formal and informal measures administered by the speech and language pathologist.

Screening determines whether a child is sufficiently different from the peer group in some aspect of communicative development to warrant further evaluation. Screening procedures, whatever the methodology, are generally successful in identifying severe problems; however, more subtle difficulties, such as those language deficits associated with learning disability, may only surface after the child is observed over time in the classroom. Screening procedures may also fail to identify those children whose disorders are episodic, such as voice problems related to vocal abuse. For these reasons it is important that classroom teachers be aware of both normal and abnormal communicative development so that they may feel comfortable referring children who "passed" an earlier screening procedure.

Once the screening procedure establishes the potential for a significant discrepancy between the student's communicative performance and that expected for his or her age and background, the speech pathologist will continue the assessment process to determine if there is indeed a significant deviance from normal in one or more areas of speech and language. Depending upon the nature and history of the presenting difficulty, at this point the clinician may make referrals to specialists such as the otolaryngologist, the audiologist, or the psychologist. If the clinician continues the evaluation, the diagnostic methods and materials will vary somewhat from this point, depending upon the age of the speaker and the nature of the disorder. The younger the child, the more indirect the assessment procedures are likely to be, with the emphasis on informal observation rather than standardized tests.

The screening procedure identifies the area or areas of concern. The diagnostic evaluation focuses on those particular aspects of communicative behavior identified and attempts to further define the problem: both quantitatively by determining if there is a significant discrepancy, and qualitatively by describing the disorder. There are some commonalities in procedures regardless of the type of disorder. For example, the initial step is to confirm the presence or absence of a disorder. In order to do this, the speech and language pathologist may administer a norm-referenced test, examine the oral speech mechanism for any structural abnormalities or muscular incoordination which may be contributing to the problem, and gather a detailed case history regarding the onset, duration, and characteristics of the disorder. In addition, informal measures, including systematic observation and collection of language samples, will be included.

Speech Disorders

Articulation. Many standardized articulation tests consist of pictures designed to elicit single-word responses from the child. The words represented by the pictures are carefully chosen to incorporate the phonemes of the language in the initial, medial, and final positions of words. Although many tests focus on the production of isolated words, some instruments include sounds in the context of sentences. The *Goldman-Fristoe Test of Articulation* (Goldman & Fristoe, 1972) is an example. Others focus on the phonological system by attempting to identify patterns of errors through "distinctive features" analysis. Examples of distinctive features are placement of the tongue and the voiced or unvoiced nature of sounds.

If the child's phonemic development is found discrepant, additional diagnostic assessment may include standardized measures such as *A Deep Test of Articulation* (McDonald, 1964) which assesses sound production in various phonemic contexts. As sound production will vary according to contextual influences, i.e., the sounds directly preceding and following the target sound, this information is helpful in determining both the starting point and the focus of therapy.

In addition to the production of sounds, the ability to perceive phonemes may be of interest. Several tests, such as the *Goldman-Fristoe-Woodcock Test of Auditory Discrimination* (Goldman, Fristoe, & Woodcock, 1970), are available for this purpose.

The child's spontaneous speech may be recorded and analyzed not only for the presence of error sounds but intelligibility. Sometimes errors appear in conversational speech that are not present in isolated words. Also, intelligibility may be situational. If the child is talking about a familiar object, the listener gains much from contextual clues. If the subject matter is unfamiliar, or removed from the immediate environment, intelligibility may decrease significantly.

Voice.   Voice characteristics are always evaluated in terms of appropriateness for age, sex, and physical build. If any aspect of the child's voice is sufficiently deviant, the speech and language pathologist will usually refer the child to an otolaryngologist at this time. A determination as to the presence or absence of laryngeal pathology must be made before proceeding further.

The clinician will then gather supplemental information concerning family history, the onset and progression of the disorder, conditions which affect its severity, and description of daily vocal use. Once this information is obtained, voice production under varying conditions, along with breathing patterns, will be observed. For example, if pitch is varied, does quality or intensity change? Unlike other areas in communication, voice disorders are not typically evaluated by standardized test instruments. The major tool of the speech and language pathologist is observation.

Dysfluency.   As fluency disturbances develop between two and four years of age, these conditions are frequently identified prior to school entry, often through parent referral to a clinic or community agency. A case history, in addition to observation under a variety of conditions, will be the major tools of assessment at this age. A determination of the stage of the disorder, that is, how far it has progressed in terms of severity, dictates the course of treatment.

Standardized instruments are not typically used with young children in the assessment of dysfluency. However, normative comparisons are made according to the percentage and type of dysfluency present, as well as the rate of speech.

In adults, there is very little question as to whether the condition exists. The purpose of assessment with this age group is to determine the severity of the stuttering behavior and identify patterns in the dysfluencies for a particular individual. Observation, along with questionnaires and rating scales, provide information concerning the conditions that precipitate dysfluency, the type of dysfluencies present, the amount of tension and struggle behavior, and the methods used by the speaker to reduce the dysfluency. The attitudes of the person who stutters toward the dysfluencies are critical; although these may be determined informally, they may also be evaluated with a standardized instrument such as Ammons and Johnson's *Iowa Scale of Attitude Toward Stuttering* (printed in Johnson, Darley, & Spriestersbach, 1963).

Of the communicative skills, language is the most complex and yet the least well defined. It is not surprising that procedures for diagnosing language disturbances vary widely. Typically, however, a combination of standardized tests, language sampling, and informal observation is used. Standardized measures, as they provide normative data, are perhaps the most useful in establishing the presence or absence of a disorder (Carrow-Woolfolk & Lynch, 1982; Schery, 1981; Swisher & Aten, 1981). Established normative criteria are particularly important in a public school setting where eligibility requirements for special services are more rigorous than in clinical settings.

The child's language functioning may be sampled indirectly through administration of developmental schedules or directly through the recording of language samples and administration of standardized tests. The *Vineland Adaptive Behavior Scales* (Sparrow, Balla, & Cicchetti, 1984) and the *Verbal Language Scale* (Mecham, 1971) are instruments designed to sample the child's language behavior indirectly through parental interviews. Developmental schedules are often used as screening devices when the child is difficult to test (Mecham, 1971) or when the language disability is a part of another condition such as mental retardation.

Instruments which directly sample the child's language behavior may be classified according to the aspect of language evaluated. First it is necessary to determine how the child functions both receptively and expressively, that is, to find out how well language is understood and how well it is communicated to others. Some instruments, such as the *Northwestern Syntax Screening Test* (NSST) (Lee, 1971), assess both dimensions. Tests that assess only one dimension include *The Test of Auditory Comprehension of Language* (TACL) (Carrow, 1973) and *The Peabody Picture Vocabulary Test–Revised* (PPVT) (Dunn & Dunn, 1981) which address only comprehension, and the *Carrow Elicited Language Inventory* (CELI) (Carrow, 1974) which assesses only expression.

In addition to the receptive-expressive dimension of language, the elements of phonology, morphology, syntax, semantics, and pragmatics need to be considered. Phonology will only need to be assessed if dysarticulation is present. Morphology and syntax (grammar) can be evaluated with tests such as the *NSST* or the *CELI*, as well as through systematic analysis of a language sample. Although there are several systems available for evaluating syntactical development through spontaneous language, one which is commonly used is Lee's *Developmental Sentence Analysis* (1974).

Tests which cover both receptive and expressive dimensions, as well as two or more of the five major elements of language, include The *Clinical Evaluation of Language Functions* (CELF) (Semel & Wiig, 1980), *The Carrow Auditory and Visual Abilities Test,* (CAVAT) (Carrow-Woolfolk, 1981), and the *Illinois Test of Psycholinguistic Abilities* (ITPA) (Kirk, McCarthy, & Kirk, 1968). Systematic procedures for evaluating pragmatic functioning, or the child's use of language in a social context, do exist (Leonard, Perozzi, Prutting, & Berkley, 1978; Miller, 1978). However, no standardized test really evaluates this aspect of language adequately.

The Illinois Test of Psycholinguistic Abilities is one instrument that assesses the receptive-expressive dimension of language.

This is understandable, given that this particular function is idiosyncratic by definition.

Naturalistic observation and the collection of language samples through informal means should be a part of every language assessment. In fact, some speech and language professionals recommend that this type of evaluation be used exclusively. Although certain aspects of language develop sequentially in all children, the rate of development varies considerably from one child to another (Muma, 1978). In addition, standardized instruments are removed from context and therefore do not give an adequate picture of language competency (Rees, 1978).

In adults, the primary language disorder is aphasia. A detailed case history (including etiology and the progression of the disorder), informal measures of language functioning, and standardized tests are as appropriate with the aphasic adult as with the young child. There are a variety of standardized instruments on the market, and the selection will depend on the theoretical background and training of the speech and language pathologist. Examples are *Examining for Aphasia* (Eisenson, 1954) and the *Porch Index of Communicative Ability* (Porch, 1971) which include evaluation of both verbal and nonverbal reception and expression of language.

In addition to standardized tests specifically designed for use with aphasic individuals, the clinician may wish to use tests of reading ability, tests of cog-

Eliciting a Language Sample

In many types of communication disorders, eliciting a language sample, that is, obtaining a sample of the person's spontaneous speech and language, is part of the assessment process. However, when a language disorder is suspected, this procedure is critical. The setting, stimuli, and the specific procedures of the speech and language pathologist will vary, as there is no one best way to elicit talking. The way in which it is evaluated will also vary. However, each of these variables has an effect on the response of the child, and should be considered when making decisions about communicative competency. Hubbell (1981) suggests focusing on real events outside the clinic setting, such as mealtime, in order to get a more representative sample of the child's language. He further suggests that the sample be taken in a situation similar to the one in which intervention will take place, as language is highly contextual. This means that a child's language activity in one situation may not be the same as in another, and, as a result, language skills may be over- or underestimated.

The actual procedure typically involves the tape recording of the child's language, while the examiner also records utterances, noting the context in which they occur. Once a sufficient number of utterances (usually about 50) have been elicited, they are then analyzed. Mean length of response, the presence or absence of various syntactical structures, and vocabulary are elements which may be evaluated in comparison to development norms. In addition, the clinician will want to determine how the child uses language in a social context.

nitive functioning, and tests of auditory and visual perception. Informal procedures such as engaging the person in conversation are frequently utilized. As with the language disordered child, if the language disturbances are evaluated in relationship to the total individual, assessment will be more meaningful in terms of intervention.

CONSIDERATIONS IN INTERVENTION

School services for the communication disordered student range from indirect consultation of a speech professional to placement in a self-contained classroom. Several factors influence the type of service a student receives, including the size of the district, the number of students allowed in a case load (as determined by state legislation), other conditions accompanying the communication disorder, and the severity of the disorder. Generally, a student with a mild disorder will leave the regular classroom for two or three half-hour sessions per week with the speech and language professional. This may be done on an individual basis or with a small group of students who have similar disabilities. Students with severe language deficits may be enrolled in a self-contained classroom, with a speech and language pathologist as their primary teacher. Programming for the communication disordered may begin in the preprimary population in some school systems, and continue into the vocational years, depending upon the ages provided for in special education legislation.

In addition to the public schools, other agencies provide services to the communication disordered. Clinics which specialize in this area are located in most cities. A clinic may operate independently or be associated with a university,

This child is using a mirror to watch his mouth and lips as he produces a target sound.

social service agency, or hospital. In addition, many long-term care facilities for the disabled or elderly now provide their own services in the identification and treatment of communication-related difficulties. While a particular agency may limit the age range it serves, generally there is something available for any age group.

The goal for treatment of any communication disorder is to increase the effectiveness of communication, and that may involve improving intelligibility or fluency, altering voice characteristics, or increasing language production or comprehension. However, the specific objectives and the methods employed to meet those objectives will vary according to the age of the speaker as well as the nature and type of the disorder.

Speech Disorders

Articulation.   The focus of articulation therapy is the phonological system, and the major goal is to improve the production of speech sounds. Although accuracy in connected discourse (conversational speech) is certainly desirable as a final goal, this may be unrealistic for some individuals. Closer approximation of the correct phonemes, along with increased intelligibility, may be all that is possible for those with severe neuromuscular involvement.

Traditionally, intervention in developmental dysarticulation has focused on the correction of single sounds from either an analytical (Van Riper, 1978) or synthetic (Backus & Beasley, 1951) perspective. Analytic methods begin by teaching a sound in isolation and progress toward inclusion in words, and finally, connected speech. Imitation, placement of the articulators, and drill and practice through games are common techniques. When the child is successful in producing the sound in isolation, the sequence is repeated at the syllable, word, and sentence levels. The synthetic approach begins remediation with conversation in appropriate contexts.

Another approach, used with preschool children, suggests engaging the child in play interactions which are thought to aid in the development of the phonological system (Kupperman, Bligh & Goodban, 1980). The activities—such as cooing, babbling, counting, rhyming, singing songs, and playing peek-a-boo—are those thought to be important in parent-child interactions for developing knowledge about the phonological system. The clinician plays a nurturing parenting role and selects target sounds for inclusion in the play; however, no demands are made upon the child to produce the sounds.

There are a number of factors which influence both the type and the sequence of intervention techniques: auditory discrimination skill, the developmental levels of the error sounds, the type of errors, the frequency of occurrence of the errors, the consistency of the errors, and the ability to imitate. If a child has difficulty discriminating one sound from another or is unable to imitate the sounds modeled by the speech and language pathologist, treatment will involve more elaborate visual and tactile stimulation in addition to the auditory. The clinician may use mirrors, a tongue depressor, or drops of flavored water on the tongue to facilitate accuracy in placement of the articulators. More traditional approaches target one sound at a time for correction, requiring some mastery before focusing on a second sound. Current phonological approaches select a group or category of sounds for correction and point out the importance of the interaction of other linguistic factors, such as syntax or semantics, on the phonological errors (Dunn & Barron, 1982).

In order to facilitate carryover outside the treatment setting, children should be actively involved in their own treatment programs; self-assessment of progress can lead to more rapid improvement (Ruscello & Shelton, 1979). By reinforcing newly learned responses, teachers and family can also help in the transition from the controlled treatment setting to spontaneous use in the everyday world.

Regardless of the methods used to improve articulatory proficiency, in practice a combination of approaches is more typical; therapy includes feedback and the opportunity to practice. Correct responses are reinforced while incorrect ones are not. Careful attention must be given to psychological influences as well as the child's attitudes toward communication. Although the success rate for correcting functional articulation problems in children is high, the most gains are made when treatment is a cooperative venture between the disordered speaker, the speech professional, and significant others in the speaker's environment (Powers, 1971a).

The treatment of organic speech disorders is determined mainly by the etiology. For example, in dysarthria, the difficulty lies in the innervation of the musculature, or the muscles not receiving the message from the brain to move. Therefore, the focus is on the movements that are necessary to make the speech sounds. The approach to remediation with the apraxic individual is somewhat different because the problem is not with the musculature but at a higher processing level.

Voice Disorders.   Regardless of age, the majority of voice disorders stem from vocal abuse; thus treatment may be prescribed jointly by the laryngologist and the speech and language pathologist, or prescribed by the former and carried out by the latter. In extreme cases surgery may be necessary; however, altering destructive vocal habits to more productive ones is usually sufficient for the majority of individuals. Rules of vocal hygiene are taught to prevent future abuse while altering either the response or the conditions under which the abuse occurs most frequently. For example, a child whose activity on the playground is accompanied by excessive yelling and screaming may be guided into quieter activities or provided with a whistle to get the attention of teammates during sports activities.

Whether the voice disorder is due to vocal abuse or some other pathological condition, initial treatment is medical. Subsequent intervention will vary not only according to the type of disorder, but the differences within each disordered speaker. Boone (1979) points out that our voices change according to mood and environmental demands, thus indicating a different and highly individualized program for each disordered speaker.

Initial treatment of voice disorders is often done individually. Adaptation of poor vocal production utilizes self-awareness activities which may focus on either the effective (Boone, 1977) or the ineffective practices of the individual. Imitation, relaxation, pitch alteration, and operant conditioning are examples of techniques which are used to improve voice production (Boone, 1977; Perkins, 1978). In special cases, either prosthetic devices or compensatory measures must be used. For example, laryngectomized patients no longer have an intact speech mechanism. Some learn to speak on expelled air (called esophageal speech), and others use a mechanical device called an artificial larynx.

Fluency Disorders.   There are as many techniques for the treatment of stuttering as there are theories of causation; the theoretical bent and training of the clinician, as well as the age of the disordered speaker, will determine the nature of the intervention.

If a preschool child shows symptoms beyond those of normal developmental dysfluency, intervention often begins with environmental manipulation. Parents are counseled as to good listening behavior and shown ways to facilitate fluency. This may be all that is necessary for some children. If the dysfluency is severe, however, or the parents are particularly anxious or unable to make the changes suggested, intervention by a speech and language pathologist is recommended.

The goal of therapy with the very young stuttering child is spontaneous fluency. However, there are two opposing views on how to approach the young dysfluent child: the more traditional one suggests an indirect approach and avoidance of calling any undue attention to speech behavior; the other suggests confronting the child, but in a positive manner.

A nondirective play therapy approach which utilizes role-playing and games provides a comfortable setting for reinforcing fluency. There is usually no need to teach control of speech behavior in this age group as fluency is easily generalized outside the treatment setting (Guitar & Peters, 1980).

Usually young children do not avoid speech and, although they may express frustration, they do not associate all the negative emotions with the dysfluent behavior that are typical with older children and adults. However, if negative feelings or attitudes toward speech are evident, more direct intervention may be necessary.

Methods will vary considerably with elementary-age children, depending upon the characteristics of the individual child. Younger children are likely to be in the early stages of stuttering and, if this is the case, the indirect approach may be appropriate. However, older children require more direct methods similar to those used with adults.

Williams (1971) suggests a program for elementary-age stutterers which includes learning about talking, talking in informal situations, and talking in formal situations. Students are provided information about the nature of stuttering, the various functions of communication, and learning in general. Arts and crafts or academic tasks provide an informal setting for relaxed communication, as well as nonspeech learning experiences which can be directly compared to the learning of speech behaviors. Public speaking classes, in which the size and scope of the audience is gradually increased, provide a more formal setting for practice of speech under pressure. Interaction with the audience is encouraged so that nonstuttering students may share their own anxieties about speaking or performing, along with individual ways of coping.

Intervention approaches used with adults, also appropriate for older children in the secondary stages of stuttering, reflect the theoretical beliefs of the speech and language pathologist. Learning theory suggests modification of the stuttering symptoms. Overt behavior may be modified without conscious awareness; however, in the case of stuttering, change is more likely to occur when the stutterer accepts the dysfluency and is aware of the behaviors that occur at the time of the stuttering (Guitar & Peters, 1980). The goal is to make stuttering easier when it does occur, not to eliminate it. Deliberate stuttering in an easier, more controlled fashion immediately following a bad block (cancellation) and prolonging a syllable smoothly (pull-out) are two frequently used techniques which enable the stutterer to control the dysfluency at the time of occurrence (Dell, n.d.; Van Riper, 1971). In addition, the elimination of secondary characteristics such as facial tics or grimaces, finger tapping, and tensing of the mouth will make the actual dysfluency seem less abnormal.

Easing Stuttering

The technique labeled "pull-outs" involves teaching the student to change hard stuttering into an easier form during the moment of occurrence. This means that the student has to be aware of his stuttering and be willing to confront it, rather than try to avoid it. Dell (n.d.) suggests the following scenario as an introduction to the method:

(C) *"Let me show you something. See this pencil? Watch what happens to it. (The clinician closes her hand around the pencil and tries unsuccessfully to push it up through her clenched fist.) Why can't I push the pencil out?"*

(S) *"Because you have your fist too tight."*

(C) *"That's right. I am squeezing my fist so hard that I cannot push the pencil through. That is very much like a word that you get stuck on. The word is like the pencil and your mouth is like the fist. Sometimes when you squeeze up your mouth too hard the word just cannot come out. Now watch what happens to my fist when I try to say a word. This is my wa . . . (The clinician tries to push the pencil through her clenched fist as she is having some hard stuttering. As she gradually begins to loosen both her mouth and fist the pencil and word come out slow.) WaWaWatch. Can you tell me what happened?"*

(S) *"Well, when you loosened your fist the pencil could come through."*

(C) *"And what about the word* watch *that I was stuck on?"*

(S) *"Well, it started to come out when you loosened your fist too."*

(C) *"That's right, it was like my mouth was doing what my fist was doing. Watch again. When I squeeze up my fist I am going to squeeze up my mouth, and then when I start to slowly loosen up my fist, I will loosen my mouth at the same time. See the wa . . . (The clinician blocks the airflow and clenches her fist.) wawawatch. (As her fist loosened so did her mouth and the word started to come out slow and easy. She continues to do this for several words until he is getting the idea.) "Now I am going to squeeze up my mouth and start doing some hard stuttering. When I do, you make a fist. Then when you loosen your fist I will loosen my mouth and let the word come out nice and easy. Are you ready? Let's try it."*

"Here's an elephant and it has a long tr . . . (blocks the airflow). Hey, you are forgetting to clench your fist. Let's try it again. Here's a ka . . . KANGAROO. (The word explodes out because he has sprung open his fist too quickly.) You see, you opened your fist too fast and the word really popped out. Now remember to make your fist loosen up slowly so that I can make my mouth loosen up slowly too. Let's try it again."

"The hippo is bi . . . bibig. Say, that was more like it. Did you hear how nice the word came out? I got stuck real hard but I changed it into a nice, slow and easy one. Let's do it some more." (pp. 71–72).

Intervention approaches for cluttering tend to be very different from those used with stutterers. As individuals who clutter are often unaware of their arhythmic speech, the first step in therapy is to call the irregularities to their attention. If they can be taught to speak more slowly, intelligibility greatly improves. Articulation therapy is often indicated as well. Vocabulary enhancement, along with drills to make syntactical choices more automatic, may also improve speech

(Perkins, 1978; Weiss & Lillywhite, 1981). Unfortunately, the success rate in totally eliminating the cluttering behavior is low. But fortunately the syndrome is rare.

Language Disorders

A variety of interventions have been used successfully with language-delayed children, including operant procedures (Cottrell, Montague, Farb, & Throne, 1980; Harris, 1975; Ruder, Smith, & Hermann, 1974), modeling (Seitz & Hoekenga, 1974), imitation (Courtright & Courtright, 1979), conversation (MacDonald & Blott, 1974), and play. Although the focus of intervention is often on increasing both the quantity and quality of language production, comprehension is also an important element in increasing language functioning. Other approaches also realize the importance of the pragmatic aspect of language (Rees, 1972), viewing it both as a system and as an element of the child's behavior system. Language in context is critical to this approach. In addition, the focus is at least partly shifted to the language environment (Mahoney, 1975) rather than the deviance of the child.

Creating a facilitating environment for speech and language requires a knowledge of those behaviors or events which inhibit speech as well as those which facilitate it. For example, any interruption of ongoing behavior, including praise and positive reinforcement, tends to decrease subsequent speech output just as much as punishment (Patterson & Cobb, 1973). Language may be facilitated by verbalizing what the child is doing while playing (parallel talk) and verbalizing the adult's ongoing activity (self-talk). Most parents use these techniques automatically during their interaction with normal infants and toddlers. In fact, mother-child interactions have been found to be very closely related to the child's level of linguistic maturity. Although mothers of language-disordered children seem to interact with their children in the same ways as do mothers of nonlanguage-disordered children, the interactions are not as closely related to their children's level of linguistic maturity (Lasky & Klopp, 1982).

Creative art and other play activities provide good opportunities for increasing vocabulary. In addition, following the child's lead will result in increased language production (Hubbell, 1977, 1981). When specific vocabulary is selected for teaching, it should reflect normal language development; the same principle applies to the other elements of language such as syntax (Holland, 1975). Many commercially available language programs, although carefully designed and appropriate developmentally, are not appropriate in the context of the child's world, thus ignoring the pragmatic aspect of language. The best program reflects the child's interests and needs, something that cannot be guaranteed in any readily available program. However, the latter can be extremely beneficial in providing guidelines, especially in regard to developmental expectancies.

When a child's language problem is severe enough to be labeled aphasia, intervention may incorporate some or all of the above mentioned techniques, but the general tendency is to provide more structure. The success rate is often low with children who are severely language disordered, and some experts have suggested redirecting the focus of intervention to communication rather than oral language. Sign language and nonverbal symbol systems (Carrier, 1976) have been tried with some success.

Usually by the time the functionally delayed child enters school, language is fairly well established. The focus of intervention at this level is likely to be on residual articulation difficulties, improving syntax, or enhancing semantic development. If the language delay is associated with severe retardation, the emphasis may be on the development of functional language, the pragmatic aspects of language which will enable the individual to become as independent as possible. If the disorder is a more subtle difficulty associated with a learning disability, intervention might focus on the language demands of the classroom (Staab, 1983).

Intervention for adult aphasics typically begins in the hospital. The first two months post-trauma are critical in re-establishing communicative functioning (Eisenson, 1973) and, although there is considerable spontaneous recovery where the individual regains temporarily lost communication skills without the benefit of specific treatment (Culton, 1969), early intervention is recommended as a preventative measure. A combination of both individual and group therapy is typical practice; the former allows concentration on individual difficulties and the latter allows guided practice. In addition, groups provide the primary social outlet for many aphasic individuals.

FUTURE PERSPECTIVES FOR THE TREATMENT OF COMMUNICATION DISORDERS

Students in speech and language pathology have been traditionally trained as generalists; they graduate from their training programs with both coursework and clinical experience in a variety of communication disorders. This approach makes sense, especially for public school personnel. Although specialization is common and even the norm in a clinical setting, the public school speech and language pathologist is typically assigned to one or more buildings to serve whatever problems, exist in those locations. There is a current trend to encourage specialization at this level to better serve the different needs of communicatively disordered students. Although this may be desirable, it is not yet a reality.

Interestingly enough, there is a shift in perspective in other aspects of the field from the specific to the general. For example, although assessment still includes standardized tests and normative data, at least in part, more value is assigned to informal measures. Child language research makes it clear that, although children acquire communication skills in approximately the same sequence, the rate is so variable as to make normative data relatively useless in identifying some disorders. This is particularly true in the area of language. In addition, standardized tests are, by their very nature, unrelated to context and thus ignore the pragmatic aspects of communication.

Another shift in perspective can be seen in the goals of intervention. The focus is now on more effective communication rather than better oral speech and

Communication Aids

The area of augmentative/alternative communication has been advanced tremendously by current technology. Noncomputerized communications boards for the nonoral individual have been in use for years; however, advances in computer technology have allowed these low-tech devices to become increasingly more sophisticated in their potential, while also becoming more flexible and more functional for the communication disordered individual. An example is ALLTALK (Adaptive Communications Systems, Inc.), a portable communications aid which features human voice quality output, and touch-sensitive overlays which can be adapted to the student's needs.

Some individuals who require augmentative/alternative communication are severely physically disabled as well, such as some cerebral palsied children and adult stroke victims; their range of motion is restricted, thus limiting the usefulness of aids which require pointing. The EyeTyper (Sentient Systems Technology, Inc.) is a device operated exclusively by eye movement and has interchangeable keyboards, including pictures. It is compatible with many personal computers, thus increasing both the flexibility and sophistication of its use.

language. Augmentative communication devices and nonoral means of communication are now more acceptable alternatives for severely disordered speakers. Technological advances in this area allow increasingly higher sophistication in their application.

There has also been a shift from treatment of an isolated element to affecting change in a system. A good example of this is the changing view that children's articulation errors are a part of a phonological system. Errors are not seen as random occurrences, but are compared to the application of an inappropriate algorithm which affects a whole class of sounds. Another even broader application of the shift from element to system, or part to whole, is the view that the child and his or her communication are a part of an even larger social structure and a change in one element, for example, the child's communicative competency, affects the entire system.

The role of the speech and language pathologist has also changed from one that is clearly defined to one that is considerably more complex. The clinician used to be the one who made people talk better; now, the boundaries between language and cognition or communication and academics are not as obvious as they once appeared.

A final trend is for the speech and language pathologist to play a more active role in the prevention of communication disorders. More and more schools are promoting programs in vocal hygiene and assisting students in becoming more effective communicators.

SUMMARY

Communication disorders have traditionally been divided into two major categories: disorders of speech and disorders of language. Speech disorders, such as articulation problems, stuttering, and voice problems, make it difficult to understand the individual's speech production. Disorders of language are characterized by difficulty in understanding or using language in either its written or spoken form.

Estimates of the number of individuals with communication disorders vary from 2.3 million to as high as 10 million. Among those with disorders, the problems range from mild to severe. Although these disorders can become apparent at any age, they are most frequent among school-age children and elderly people.

The causes of communication disorders can be described as organic or nonorganic. Organic causes are physical or physiological in nature whereas nonorganic causes are environmental, psychological, or unknown. Although many communication disorders cannot be prevented, their impact can be lessened through surgery, therapy, and/or a positive, nonthreatening atmosphere which encourages speech production.

The type of disorder, the age at which it occurs, and the environmental response to the problem all interact to determine the impact that a communication disorder has. Because there are so many variables, it is impossible to isolate specific learning and personality characteristics of individuals with communication disorders. Just as the disorders and their impact vary, so too does the treatment. Treatment techniques range from structured, behavioral procedures to guided play strategies to the use of augmentative or alternative communication devices, depending upon the age of the individual and the type of disorder.

Like all of the handicapping conditions discussed in this book, effective programs for individuals with communication disorders involve many professionals. Speech and language teachers and therapists, audiologists, and otolaryngologists work together to diagnose and treat communication disorders. And, like all handicapping conditions, the impact of a communication disorder can be lessened by improved public attitudes, acceptance, and opportunities for these individuals to participate in the life of the community.

References

Andrews, G., Craig, A., Feyer, A. M., Hoddinott, S., Howie, P., & Neilson, M. (1983). Stuttering: A review of research findings and theories, circa 1982. *Journal of Speech and Hearing Disorders, 48,* 226–246.

Arlt, P., & Goodban, M. (1976). A comparative study of articulation acquisition as based on a study of 240 normals, aged three to six. *Language, Speech, and Hearing Services in Schools, 7,* 173–180.

ASHA. (1982). Definitions: Communicative disorders and variations. *ASHA, 24,* 949–950.

Backus, O., & Beasley, J. (1951). *Speech therapy with children.* Boston: Houghton Mifflin.

Baker, L., Cantwell, D. P., & Mattison, R. E. (1980). Behavior problems in children with pure speech disorders and in children with combined speech and language disorders. *Journal of Abnormal Child Psychology, 8*, 245–256.

Bennett, C. W., & Runyan, C. M. (1982). Educators' perceptions of the effects of communication disorders upon educational performance. *Language, Speech, and Hearing Services in the Schools, 13*, 260–263.

Bloodstein, O., & Grossman, M. (1981). Early stutterings: Some aspects of their form and distribution. *Journal of Speech and Hearing Research, 24*, 298–302.

Bloom, L., & Lahey, M. (1978). *Language development and language disorders.* New York: John Wiley & Sons.

Boone, D. R. (1977). *The voice and voice therapy* (2nd ed.). Englewood Cliffs, NJ: Prentice-Hall.

Boone, D. R. (1979). Voice remediation: An eclectic approach. *ASHA, 21*, 912–914.

Bountress, N., & Richards, J. (1979). Speech, language, and hearing disorders in an adult penal institution. *Journal of Speech and Hearing Disorders, 44*, 293–300.

Bryan, J. H., & Bryan, T. H. (1979). *Exceptional children.* Sherman Oaks, CA: Alfred Publishing Co., Inc.

Canter, G. J. (1971). Observations on neurogenic stuttering: A contribution to differential diagnosis. *British Journal of Disorders of Communication, 6*, 139–143.

Carrier, J. K. (1976). Application of a nonspeech language system with the severely language handicapped. In L. L. Lloyd (Ed.), *Communication assessment and intervention strategies* (pp. 523–547). Baltimore: University Park Press.

Carrow, E. (1973). *Test of auditory comprehension of language.* Hingham, MA: Teaching Resources Corp.

Carrow, E. (1974). *Carrow elicited language inventory.* Hingham, MA: Teaching Resources Corp.

Carrow-Woolfolk, E. (1981). *The Carrow auditory and visual abilities test.* Hingham, MA: Teaching Resources Corp.

Carrow-Woolfolk, E., & Lynch, J. I. (1982). *An integrative approach to language disorders in children.* New York: Grune & Stratton.

Cazden, C. (1968). The acquisition of noun and verb inflections. *Child Development, 39*, 433–438.

Cleland, C. C., & Swartz, J. D. (1982). *Exceptionalities through the lifespan.* New York: Macmillan Publishing.

Colburn, N., & Mysak, E. D. (1982a). Developmental dysfluency and emerging grammar; I. Disfluency characteristics in early syntactic utterances. *Journal of Speech and Hearing Research, 25*, 414–420.

Colburn, N., & Mysak, E. D. (1982b). Developmental dysfluency and emerging grammar: II. Co-occurrence of dysfluency with specified semantic-syntactic structures. *Journal of Speech and Hearing Research, 25*, 421–427.

Colcord, R. D., & Adams, M. R. (1979). Voicing duration and vocal SPL changes associated with stuttering reduction. *Journal of Speech and Hearing Research, 22*, 468–479.

Cottrell, A. W., Montague, J., Farb, J., & Throne, J. M. (1980). An operant procedure for improving vocabulary definition performances in developmentally delayed children. *Journal of Speech and Hearing Disorders, 45*, 90–102.

Courtright, J. A., & Courtright, I. C. (1979). Imitative modeling as a language intervention strategy: The effects of two mediating variables. *Journal of Speech and Hearing Research, 22*, 389–402.

Culton, G. L. (1969). Spontaneous recovery from aphasia. *Journal of Speech and Hearing Research, 12*, 825–832.

Curran, J. S., & Cratty, B. J. (1978). *Speech and language problems in children.* Denver: Love Publishing.

Darley, F. L., Aronson, A. E., & Brown, J. R. (1975). *Motor speech disorders.* Philadelphia: W. B. Saunders.

Dell, C. W. Jr. (n.d.) *Treating the school age stutterer: A guide for clinicians.* Memphis, TN: Speech Foundation of America (Publication 14).

de Villiers, J. G., & de Villiers, P. A. (1978). A cross-sectional study of the acquisition of grammatical morphemes in child speech. In L. Bloom (Ed.), *Readings in language development* (pp. 74–84). New York: John Wiley & Sons.

Dunn, C., & Barron, C. (1982). A treatment program for disordered phonology: Phonetic and linguistic considerations. *Language, Speech, and Hearing Services in Schools, 13,* 100–109.

Dunn, L. M. (1981). *Peabody picture vocabulary test–revised.* Circle Pines, MN: American Guidance Service, Inc.

Eimas, P. D., Siqueland, E. R., Jusczyk, P., & Vigorito, J. (1971). Speech perception in infants. *Science, 171,* 303–306.

Eisenson, J. (1954). *Examining for aphasia.* Cleveland, OH: Psychological Corporation.

Eisenson, J. (1973) *Adult aphasia: Assessment and treatment.* Englewood Cliffs, NJ: Prentice-Hall.

Fein, D. J. (1983). The prevalence of speech and language impairments. *ASHA, 25,* 2, 37.

Flynn, P. T. (1983). Speech-language pathologists and primary prevention: From ideas to action. *Language, Speech, and Hearing Services in Schools, 14,* 99–104.

Goldman, R., & Fristoe, M. (1972). *Goldman-Fristoe test of articulation.* Circle Pines, MN: American Guidance Service, Inc.

Goldman, R., Fristoe, M., & Woodcock, R. W. (1970). *Goldman-Fristoe-Woodcock test of auditory discrimination.* Circle Pines, MN: American Guidance Service, Inc.

Guitar, B., & Peters, T. J. (1980). *Stuttering: An integration of contemporary therapies.* Memphis, TN: Speech Foundation of America.

Harris, S. L. (1975). Teaching language to non-verbal children—with emphasis on problems of generalization. *Psychological Bulletin, 82,* 565–580.

Holland, A. L. (1975). Language therapy for children: Some thoughts on context and content. *Journal of Speech and Hearing Disorders, 40,* 514–523.

Hubbell, R. D. (1977). On facilitating spontaneous talking in young children. *Journal of Speech and Hearing Disorders, 42,* 216–231.

Hubbell, R. D. (1981). *Children's language disorders: An integrated approach.* Englewood Cliffs, NJ: Prentice-Hall, Inc.

Johnson, W., Darley, F. L., & Spriestersbach, D. C. (1963). *Diagnostic methods in speech pathology.* New York: Harper & Row.

Johnston, J. R., & Weismer, S. E. (1983). Mental rotation abilities in language-disordered children. *Journal of Speech and Hearing Research, 26,* 397–403.

Kirk, S. A., McCarthy, J. J., & Kirk, W. D. (1968). *Illinois test of psycholinguistic abilities* (rev. ed.). Urbana: University of Illinois Press.

Kupperman, P., Bligh, S., & Goodban, M. (1980). Activating articulation skills through theraplay. *Journal of Speech and Hearing Disorders, 45,* 540–545.

Lasky, E. Z., & Klopp, K. (1982). Parent-child interactions in normal and language-disordered children. *Journal of Speech and Hearing Disorders, 47,* 7–18.

Lee, L. L. (1971). *Northwestern syntax screening test.* Evanston, IL: Northwestern Univ. Press.

Lee, L. L. (1974). *Developmental sentence analysis.* Evanston, IL: Northwestern Univ. Press.

Leonard, L. B., Perozzi, J. A., Prutting, C. A., & Berkley, R. K. (1978). Nonstandard approaches to the assessment of language behaviors. *ASHA, 20,* 371–377.

Loban, W. D. (1963). *The language of elementary school children* (Research Report No. 1). Champaign, IL: National Council of Teachers of English.

Loban, W. D. (1966). *Problems in oral English* (Research Report No. 5). Champaign, IL: National Council of Teachers of English.

Love, R. J. (1981). A forgotten minority: The communicatively disabled. *ASHA, 23,* 485–489.

MacDonald, J. D., & Blott, J. P. (1974). Environmental language intervention: The rationale for a diagnostic and training strategy through rules, context, and generalization. *Journal of Speech and Hearing Disorders, 39,* 244–256.

Mahoney, G. J. (1975). Ethological approach to delayed language acquisition. *American Journal of Mental Deficiency, 80,* 139–148.

McDonald, E. T. (1964). *A deep test of articulation, picture form.* Stanwix House, Inc.

Mecham, M. J. (1971). *Verbal language development scale.* Circle Pines, MN: American Guidance Service, Inc.

Miller, L. (1978). Pragmatics and early childhood language disorders: Communicative interactions in a half-hour sample. *Journal of Speech and Hearing Disorders, 43,* 419–436.

Moore G. P. (1971). Voice disorders organically based. In L. E. Travis (Ed.), *Handbook of speech pathology and audiology* (pp. 535–570). Englewood Cliffs, NJ: Prentice-Hall.

Morehead, D. M., & Ingram, D. (1973). The development of base syntax in normal and linguistically deviant children. *Journal of Speech and Hearing Research, 16,* 330–352.

Muma, J. R. (1978). *Language handbook: Concepts, assessment, intervention.* Englewood Cliffs, NJ: Prentice-Hall, Inc.

Nelson, K. (1974). Concept, word, and sentence: Interrelations in acquisition and development. *Psychological Review, 81,* 267–285.

Nilson, H., & Schneiderman, C. R. (1983). Classroom program for the prevention of vocal abuse and hoarseness in elementary school children. *Language, Speech, and Hearing Services in Schools, 14,* 121–127.

Palermo, D. S., & Molfese, D. L. (1972). Language acquisition from age five onward. *Psychological Bulletin, 78,* 409–428.

Patterson, G., & Cobb, J. (1973). Stimulus control for classes of noxious behaviors. In J. Knutson (Ed.), *The control of aggression: Implications from basic research.* Chicago, Aldine Press.

Perkins, W. H. (1978). *Human perspectives in speech and language disorders.* St. Louis: The C. V. Mosby Company.

Peterson, S. J. (1975). Nasal emission as a component of the misarticulation of sibilants and affricates. *Journal of Speech and Hearing Disorders, 40,* 106–114.

Pflaum-Connor, S. W. (1978). *The development of language and reading in the young child* (2nd ed.). Columbus, OH: Merrill Publishing.

Porch, B. E. (1971). *Porch index of communicative ability* (rev. ed.). Palo Alto, CA: Consulting Psychologists Press.

Powers, M. H. (1971a). Clinical and educational procedures in functional disorders of articulation. In L. E. Travis (Ed.), *Handbook of speech pathology and audiology* (pp. 877–910). Englewood Cliffs, NJ: Prentice-Hall.

Powers, M. H. (1971b). Functional disorders of articulation: Symptomology and etiology. In L. E. Travis (Ed.), *Handbook of speech pathology and audiology* (pp. 837–876). Englewood Cliffs, NJ: Prentice-Hall.

Prins, D. (1972). Personality, stuttering severity, and age. *Journal of Speech and Hearing Research, 15,* 148–154.

Rees, N. S. (1972). Bases of decision in language training. *Journal of Speech and Hearing Disorders, 37,* 283–304.

Rees, N. S. (1978). Pragmatics of language: Application to normal and disordered language development. In R. L. Schiefelbusch (Ed.), *Basis of language intervention* (pp. 196–268). Baltimore: University Park Press.

Richman, L. C. (1980). Cognitive patterns and learning disabilities in cleft palate children with verbal deficits. *Journal of Speech and Hearing Research, 23*, 447–456.

Rosenbek, J., Messert, B., Collins, M., & Wertz, R. T. (1978). Stuttering following brain damage. *Brain and Language, 6*, 89–96.

Ruder, K. F., Smith, M. D., & Hermann, P. (1974). Effect of verbal imitation and comprehension on verbal production of lexical items. In L. V. McReynolds (Ed.), *Developing systematic procedures for training children's language*, ASHA Monographs Number 18 (pp. 15–29). Washington, DC: American Speech and Hearing Association.

Ruscello, D. M., & Shelton, R. L. (1979). Planning and self-assessment in articulatory training. *Journal of Speech and Hearing Disorders, 44*, 504–512.

Schery, T. K. (1981). Selecting assessment strategies for language-disordered children. *Topics in Language Disorders, 1* (3), 59–74.

Seitz, S., & Hoekenga, R. (1974). Modeling as a training tool for retarded children and their parents. *Mental Retardation, 12*, 28–31.

Semel, E. M., & Wiig, E. H. (1980). *Clinical evaluation of language functions.* Columbus, OH: Merrill Publishing.

Shadden, B. B., Asp, C. W., Tonkovich, J. D., & Mason, D. (1980). Imitation of suprasegmental patterns by five-year-old children with adequate and inadequate articulation. *Journal of Speech and Hearing Disorders, 45*, 390–400.

Smit, A. B., & Bernthal, J. E. (1983). Performance of articulation-disordered children on language and perception measures. *Journal of Speech and Hearing Research, 26*, 124–136.

Smith, M. E. (1978). Grammatical errors in the speech of preschool children. In L. Bloom (Ed.), *Readings in language development* (pp. 31–38). New York: John Wiley & Sons.

Sparrow, S. S., Balla, D. A., & Cicchetti, D. V. (1984). *Vineland adaptive behavior scales.* Circle Pines, MN: American Guidance Service, Inc.

Staab, C. F. (1983). Language functions elicited by meaningful activities: A new dimension in language programs. *Language, Speech, and Hearing Services in Schools, 14*, 164–170.

Swisher, L., & Aten, J. (1981). Assessing comprehension of spoken language: A multi-faceted task. *Topics in Language Disorders, 1* (3), 75–86.

U.S. Department of Education (1986). *Eighth annual report to Congress on the implementation of The Education of the Handicapped Act.* Washington, DC: Author.

U.S. Office of Education (1977). Education of handicapped children. *Federal Register, 42*, 163.

Van Hattum, R. (1983). More is not enough. *ASHA, 25*, 2, 47–49.

Van Riper, C. (1971). *The nature of stuttering.* Englewood Cliffs, NJ: Prentice-Hall.

Van Riper, C. (1978). *Speech correction: Principles and methods* (6th ed.). Englewood Cliffs, NJ: Prentice-Hall.

Webb, W. G., & Love, R. J. (1983). Reading problems in chronic aphasia. *Journal of Speech and Hearing Research, 48*, 164–171.

Weiner, F. F. (1981). Systematic sound preference as a characteristic of phonological disability. *Journal of Speech and Hearing Disorders, 46*, 281–285.

Weiner, P. (1969). The perceptual level functioning of dysphasic children. *Cortex, 5*, 440–457.

Weiss, C. E., & Lillywhite, H. S. (1981). *Communicative disorders: Prevention and early intervention* (2nd ed.). St. Louis: The C. V. Mosby Company.

Williams, D. E. (1971). Stuttering therapy for children. In L. E. Travis (Ed.), *Handbook of speech pathology and audiology* (pp. 1073–1094). Englewood Cliffs, NJ: Prentice-Hall.

Winitz, H. (1969). *Articulatory acquisition and behavior.* New York: Appleton-Century-Crofts.

Yairi, E. (1983). The onset of stuttering in two- and three-year-old children: A preliminary report. *Journal of Speech and Hearing Disorders, 48,* 171–177.

Resources

Organizations

American Cleft Palate Educational Foundation—Parent Liaison Committee
Louisiana State University Medical Center
Department of Audiology & Speech Pathology
P.O. Box 33932
Shreveport, LA 71130

Parent organization offering information and assistance to families of children with cleft palates.

American Speech, Language, & Hearing Association
10801 Rockville Pike
Rockville, MD 20852

Professional organization which accredits individuals providing speech, language, and hearing services; publishes journals which focus on research and practice; provides information; and lobbies for services for individuals with speech, language, and hearing disorders.

Division on Communication Disorders
Council for Exceptional Children
1920 Association Drive
Reston, VA 22091

Professional organization which focuses on the education of students with communication disorders.

Journals

ASHA
American Speech, Language, and Hearing Association
10801 Rockville Pike
Rockville, MD 20852

Monthly publication of topics of interest to those working in the field of communication disorders.

Journal of Speech and Hearing Disorders
10801 Rockville Pike
Rockville, MD 20852

Professional journal which focuses on a variety of issues and topics related to communication disorders.

Journal of Speech and Hearing Research
10801 Rockville Pike
Rockville, MD 20852

Professional journal which publishes research on communication disorders.

Language, Speech, and Hearing Services in the Schools
10801 Rockville Pike
Rockville, MD 20852

Professional journal which publishes articles related to educational services for students with communication disorders with emphasis on best practices.

Chapter 9

LEARNING DISABILITIES

Learning disabilities are subtle handicaps. In most important respects, learning disabled individuals look and act like other persons. Their handicap does not become apparent until they are asked to read, write, calculate, or demonstrate some other academic skill. Learning disabilities are considered mild handicaps, at least in relation to other exceptionalities like mental retardation, because they do not affect all areas of functioning. Learning disabled persons are able to do some things quite well. What they do not do well is meet the academic demands of the typical school classroom.

Teachers often describe learning disabled children as "puzzling." These children seem intelligent, but they perform poorly in school. They do not learn as quickly and as easily as their peers, and they soon fall behind their agemates in academic pursuits. Reading is the major problem area for many learning disabled students. For others, it is writing or spelling or math, or a combination of several skills. Learning disabled persons share the characteristic of underachievement; they achieve poorly, despite average intelligence. There is a serious discrepancy between the achievement expected from such persons and their actual performance in school.

Learning disabled persons are not the only ones marked by underachievement. What distinguishes learning disabled persons from other underachievers is the reason for their poor performance, the learning disability itself. Learning disa-

Rena B. Lewis
San Diego State University

bilities are disorders in cognitive development, thinking and learning, and communication. These disorders have been given many names through the years: perceptual handicaps, minimal brain dysfunction, psychological processing deficits, dyslexia, and so forth. Today, at least in the educational world, they are called learning disabilities or, to differentiate them from more global handicaps, specific learning disabilities.

There are many types of learning disabilities. Among the traditional areas of concern are disorders of perception, attention, and memory. These disorders, and other conceptualizations of learning disabilities, are discussed in this chapter. Several disciplines have influenced the study of learning disabilities, and each discipline explains the handicap in a somewhat different way. The fields of education, psychology, and medicine each offer an important perspective of the nature of learning disabilities.

Individuals with learning disabilities experience learning needs at some time in their lives. Most often, this happens during the school years, when learning disabilities interfere with the acquisition of basic academic skills. However, if learning disabilities are severe, they may be detected before children begin formal schooling. Learning needs are usually associated with basic school subjects such as reading, writing, and mathematics. But poor achievement in these tool subjects can affect performance in other areas. For example, poor reading skills may have an impact on an individual's ability to participate in a wide range of activities, from reading a science textbook to reading a menu in a restaurant.

Some learning disabled persons experience social-emotional needs. Learning problems may affect self-concept, lowering the individual's perception of self-worth. It is also possible for learning disabilities to inhibit a person's acquisition of social and interpersonal skills, just as they inhibit the acquisition of academic skills. Social-emotional needs are most common during the school years, but they can persist into adulthood. In the adult years, continuing academic and social difficulties can affect community and vocational adjustment. In addition, some learning disabled persons show physical-health needs. These are of special interest when the learning disability is associated with neurological impairment or hyperactivity.

Some learning disabled persons experience only learning needs. Others will require assistance in learning and also have social-emotional needs, physical-health needs, or both. Learning disabled persons, like the members of other groups of exceptional people, are first and foremost individuals.

INDIVIDUALS WITH LEARNING DISABILITIES

Individuals with learning disabilities have lived in all periods of history. In fact, it is believed that Leonardo da Vinci, Thomas Edison, Albert Einstein, and Woodrow Wilson were learning disabled. Until quite recently, however, the learning problems of persons with learning disabilities were attributed to some other handicapping condition or called by some other name. It was not until the 1960s that the term "learning disabilities" became widely accepted. But, whatever

introducing

LOUIS

Louis is eight years old. He's a lively child, with red hair, freckles, and a wide grin. Like most eight-year-old boys, Louis likes video games, baseball, and riding his bike with his friends. This year, Louis is in third grade, and, last year, he was identified as learning disabled.

Louis began second grade with few academic skills and his teacher, Ms. Fischer, soon became concerned. At the start of school, Louis knew the sounds of some of the letters and a few sight words; he was able to read only the beginning first grade reader. His spelling skills were also poor, although his printing was better than that of most of his classmates. In math, Louis's performance was average. He was able to work in the same math book as the rest of the class with little difficulty.

Ms. Fischer was puzzled by Louis. He seemed bright and willing to learn, but in some subjects he was struggling to do first grade work. In others, he was a successful second grader. Ms. Fischer shared her concerns with Louis's parents. They agreed that school seemed hard for Louis this year, but they felt he was trying to do his best and that he was an intelligent child. Louis's parents were worried about the changes they were seeing in Louis at home. He'd liked school in first grade, eager to start to school each morning and to tell his mom and dad about what he'd been learning. Lately, however, his attitude had changed. He said he didn't like school and many mornings he complained of a headache or a stomachache, saying that he'd better stay home. Louis stopped talking about his school activities, and, when asked what he was learning, he would reply "nothing."

Louis's parents and Ms. Fischer agreed that something was wrong, and they decided to refer Louis for special education assessment. At the same time, Louis's parents made an appointment for him with the pediatrician for a complete physical examination. The physical exam showed Louis to be in good health, with no physical problems. The results of the educational assessment pointed to a learning disability.

The school assessment team included Louis's teacher, Ms. Fischer, as well as the school psychologist, school nurse, the special education resource teacher, and the principal. Ms. Fischer shared her observations of Louis's current classroom performance, and the school nurse reviewed Louis's health history and reported the results of the recent physical examination. The school psychologist met with Louis and administered several tests, including an individual test of intellectual performance. Ms. Carroll, the resource teacher, observed Louis in his classroom. She also met with Louis to administer standardized tests of achievement in reading, spelling, and math.

The results of these assessments indicated a discrepancy between expected achievement and actual achievement. Louis scored well on the intelligence test, showing at least average intellectual performance. On spelling and reading measures, however, his achievement was poor, just as it was in the classroom. The school psychologist and the resource teacher both noticed that, when Louis was given a task that was difficult for him, he appeared distractible and unable to focus his attention. This was particularly true of memory tasks. Louis would begin to look at or listen to the material he was supposed to remember, and then start to talk about something else. As a consequence, Louis performed poorly on the memory tests he took.

When Louis was observed in the classroom, he sat quietly while the teacher was talking. Although he caused no disturbance, his attention seemed to shift as he looked first at the teacher, then at his desk, then out the window, and so forth. Later, he seemed absorbed in the spelling worksheet he was working on, but he hadn't finished it when it was time to hand it in. Instead of filling in the answers to the questions, Louis had underlined all of the words on the worksheet and drawn circles around the numbers preceding each question.

After a careful review of these findings, the assessment team concluded that learning disabilities in memory and attention were contributing to Louis's poor school performance. Louis's parents met with the school team to discuss these results, and they agreed with the team's recommendation for part-time special education services.

So, at the end of second grade, Louis began visiting Ms. Carroll, the resource teacher, for 30 minutes each day. Ms. Carroll discussed the assessment results with Louis, explaining that he was smart and able to learn but that he needed some extra help with reading and spelling. Ms. Carroll set up an instructional program for Louis, based on the goals agreed upon by Louis's parents and his second grade teacher. That program focused on reading and spelling skills, with special emphasis on teaching Louis to attend to the task at hand and to use systematic strategies for memorizing information.

Louis began to make progress last year, and he's continuing that progress this year. He's still far behind his classmates in reading and spelling, but is beginning to catch up. Louis now likes school again. As he tells his mom and dad, flashing his wide grin, "I need some extra help but I'm not dumb."

name was given to this handicap, learning disabled individuals in earlier times experienced the same struggles as their contemporary counterparts. For example, Hinshelwood, writing in 1907 about a condition he called "word-blindness," could have been describing a schoolboy of today:

> H., aged 14 years has been at school for nine years. The greatest difficulty has been experienced all through those nine years in teaching him to read. . . . It has been this difficulty in learning to read which has kept him back, as otherwise he is a smart and intelligent boy. . . he can learn by heart easily what is imparted to him by word of mouth. He writes well, and no difficulty was experienced in teaching him either arithmetic or writing.   (p. 1230)

The study of learning disabilities began in the 1800s with the work of physicians such as Gall and Broca who studied the performance problems of adults who had sustained brain injuries (Wiederholt, 1974). Many of these adults had lost their ability to read, write, calculate, or speak as a result of damage to the central nervous system, or these functions were severely impaired. Soon, other professionals began to investigate children who showed performance problems similar to those of brain-injured adults. The children had not yet acquired academic skills but experienced great difficulty in their first attempts to learn to read, write, or calculate.

In the first half of the twentieth century, psychologists and educators built upon the findings about brain-injured adults to develop educational interventions for children who were presumed to be brain injured. At this time, the label used to describe this population was "brain-injured children" or "children with minimal brain dysfunction." Active during this period were the persons now considered to be the founders of the field of learning disabilities: Fernald, Monroe, Kirk, Myklebust, Kephart, Wepman, Cruickshank, Getman, Frostig, and Barsch.

In the 1960s, "learning disabilities" became the accepted term for individuals who had been called brain injured, neurologically impaired, and perceptually handicapped. Wiederholt (1974) describes this time as a period of great activity:

Professional and parent organizations were founded; legislation and funding mechanisms were established; textbooks, reports, and articles were made available; programs for providing educational support were set up in the schools; teacher-training programs were instituted to prepare professionals; and theories, research, and instructional materials and methods were generated. (p. 46)

Activity continued through the 1970s and into the 1980s. With the passage of the Education for All Handicapped Children Act in 1975, public school services became available for learning disabled children across the United States. Parent and professional organizations remained active, and a new multidisciplinary group was formed: the National Joint Committee on Learning Disabilities, composed of representatives from several of the major organizations interested in learning disabilities. Research and study continued and five large-scale university research institutes were funded by the federal government to study the condition of learning disabilities and develop successful intervention strategies (Kneedler & Hallahan, 1983).

Today, the field of learning disabilities remains a dynamic one, as public schools provide services to hundreds of thousands of learning disabled students. However, many questions remain unanswered about the condition of learning disabilities, its identification, and its treatment. That is not surprising considering that recognition of learning disabilities as a major handicapping condition is a relatively recent phenomenon (Cruickshank, 1977).

Definitions of Learning Disabilities

Many attempts have been made to define and describe this handicapping condition, but no proposed definition has escaped criticism. However, as Wallace and McLoughlin (1979) point out, definitions of learning disabilities are similar in the basic dimensions they address:

1. *Discrepancy between expected and actual performance.* Most definitions state or at least imply that the performance of learning disabled persons falls short of expectations. Because their intelligence is at least at the average level, learning disabled persons are presumed to have the potential for average achievement. Despite this expectation, learning disabled persons achieve poorly, at least in some area. Their underachievement is a cause for concern, so much so it is considered a handicap. Another part of the discrepancy notion is uneven development. Poor performance in one realm contrasts with at least adequate performance in another. Unlike more global conditions such as mental retardation, learning disabilities tend to affect specific areas of functioning.

2. *Behavioral manifestations of learning disabilities.* Behavioral manifestations are the outward signs of the disability. The most common manifestations of learning disabilities are poor achievement in the academic skills of reading, writing, and mathematics. Many definitions also include poor performance in listening and speaking, the basic skills of oral communication. Some add disorders of thinking and reasoning. Future definitions may also list deficits in social

and interpersonal skills because current research findings point to a relationship between learning disabilities and socialization disorders.

3. *Integrities (or exclusion of other learning problems)*. To separate the learning disabled population out from the total population of underachievers, definitions attempt to exclude learning problems which are due to other factors. Usually excluded are difficulties which are primarily the result of other handicapping conditions, of cultural or economic factors, or of poor instruction. Thus, in Wallace and McLoughlin's view, learning disabilities are defined in part by the integrities of the individual: normal intelligence (because mental retardation is excluded), adequate vision and hearing (because sensory impairments are excluded), and so forth. However, learning problems are denied consideration as learning disabilities only if they are due *primarily* to other causes. It is certainly possible for one individual to be both hearing impaired and learning disabled, with one set of difficulties attributable to a hearing loss and another set to a learning disability.

4. *Focus or explanation of the learning problem*. Definitions also attempt to delimit the learning disabled population by inclusionary clauses that explain the nature of the learning problem. The focus of the definition may be medical, psychological, educational, or a combination of these. Medical definitions typically explain the discrepancy between actual and expected achievement in terms of neurological impairment. Psychological definitions speak to cognitive functioning and disorders which might occur in the processing of information; typical concerns are the cognitive processes of memory, attention, and perception. With educational definitions, the focus is the behavioral manifestations of the learning disability, particularly deficits in basic school skills.

In 1968, the National Advisory Committee on Handicapped Children framed the definition that would be incorporated into federal law as the standard national definition of learning disabilities:

> *Children with special learning disabilities exhibit a disorder in one or more of the basic psychological processes involved in understanding or in using spoken or written language. These may be manifested in disorders of listening, thinking, talking, reading, writing, spelling, or arithmetic. They include conditions which have been referred to as perceptual handicaps, brain injury, minimal brain dysfunction, dyslexia, developmental aphasia, etc. They do not include learning problems which are due primarily to visual, hearing, or motor handicaps, to mental retardation, to emotional disturbance, or to environmental disadvantage.*

This definition is a psychological one because the learning disability is explained as a cognitive disorder. It also has an educational focus because it lists the academic and language areas in which learning disabled students typically experience difficulty. With slight modifications, this definition appears in the federal law mandating special education services to handicapped children and youth, PL 94–142, and in its regulations (*Federal Register*, Dec. 29, 1977). Two changes were made. First, the term "specific learning disabilities" was substi-

Word attack skills remain a problem area for many learning disabled high school students.

tuted for "special learning disabilities." Second, learning problems due primarily to cultural or economic disadvantage were added to the list of conditions excluded from consideration as learning disabilities.

The National Advisory Committee definition has been criticized for its vagueness, lack of specificity, and its reliance on exclusion clauses for description of the population. A major concern is that it is not an operational definition. It is not possible to set forth a set of identification criteria from so general a statement. Another concern is its exclusion of learning problems due primarily to environmental, cultural, or economic disadvantage. Poor learning environments could be a cause of learning disabilities just as poor medical care could contribute to neurological dysfunction. Although culturally and linguistically different students are not barred from special educational services, it is a difficult diagnostic task to separate out the effects of language and culture from those of a learning disability (Lynch & Lewis, 1982).

One of the more recent definitions is that of the National Joint Committee for Learning Disabilities (NJCLD) (1981):

Learning disabilities is a generic term that refers to a heterogeneous group of disorders manifested by significant difficulties in the acquisition and use of listening, speaking, reading, writing, reasoning, or mathematical abilities. These disorders are intrinsic to the individual and presumed to be due to central nervous system dysfunction. Even though a learning disability may occur concomitantly with other handicapping conditions (e.g., sensory impairment, mental retardation, social and emotional disturbance) or environmental influences (e.g., cultural differences, insufficient/inappropriate instruction, psychogenic factors), it is not the direct result of those conditions or influences.

This definition emphasizes the heterogeneity of the condition and explains it as a group of disorders, rather than a single disorder. The disorders are within the individual (intrinsic) and they are presumed to be due to neurological causes. This represents a movement toward a neurological perspective and away from the psychological focus of the National Advisory Committee definition. However, an educational perspective is maintained in the NJCLD definition by its identification of language, thinking, and academic skill deficits as the manifestations of learning disabilities. In addition, it mentions not only the acquisition of these skills but also their application. The definition clarifies that a learning disability can occur in conjunction with other handicaps and with environmental disadvantage, as long as it is not the direct result of these factors.

More so than many handicaps, the condition of learning disabilities is difficult to define. This may be because it is not a visible handicap but one whose presence must be inferred (Lynch & Lewis, 1982). The heterogeneity of the condition also complicates its description. As the National Joint Committee definition suggests, it is more a collection of disorders than a single disability. And just as diverse are the explanations offered for these learning problems.

General Nature of the Exceptionality

Learning disabilities are not necessarily mild handicaps. Contrary to the popular view, learning disabilities can be mild, moderate, or even severe (Weller, 1980). Mild achievement problems may require only remedial education whereas severe learning disabilities necessitate special education (Poplin, 1981). In a recent study of public school programs, learning disability teachers identified 20 percent of their students as severely learning disabled (De Loach, Earl, Brown, Poplin, & Warner, 1981). These students showed extreme underachievement and the need for intensive, specially designed instruction.

It is also possible to categorize learning disabilities by type of disorder. One common system sets up subgroups on the basis of cognitive disorders: learning disabilities in perception, in attention, in memory, and so forth. Another commonly used classification system is based upon the academic skill areas that learning disabilities affect. This is an educational system with subgroups such as reading disabilities, writing disabilities, math disabilities, and so forth.

Learning disabilities are a high incidence handicap, at least among children and youth. Empirical studies usually find that learning disabled children make up more than 3 percent of the school-age population (e.g., Meier, 1971; Myklebust

SARA

Sara just graduated from high school. She's 19 and she'll be attending the local community college in the fall. Sara is learning disabled. When Sara was growing up, her school didn't offer any special services for learning disabled students. She began to fall behind her classmates in first grade, but it wasn't until third grade that her teacher referred her for evaluation. The tests Sara took showed that her school achievement was poor, especially in reading. But, because her intelligence test performance was not below average, she did not qualify for the one special education service in her school, a class for mentally retarded students.

In elementary school, Sara did receive some help in reading from the school's reading teacher. This assistance was only a few minutes of instruction three times a week, and it was not enough to prevent Sara from failing sixth grade. She repeated sixth grade, finishing elementary school with third grade reading skills.

Sara entered junior high the year that her district began a learning disabilities program. She was one of the first students identified for this program, and she began junior high as a member of a special class for learning disabled students. The assessment team found her eligible for this service because of her severe achievement problems and learning disabilities in auditory discrimination and memory. When evaluating Sara for placement, the team found out that she had great difficulty telling if sounds were the same or different and in remembering things that she'd heard. Her former teachers confirmed that Sara often confused similar sounding words and that even at age 13 she still did not know all of the letter sounds. Sara also was unable to remember a sequence of oral directions, a problem that contributed to her failure in the regular classroom.

Sara made excellent progress in the junior high learning disabilities class, increasing her reading skills to the sixth grade level. She began high school, again in a special class, but transferred to a resource program in her sophomore year. At that time, she began taking college prep courses with support from the resource teacher. In her resource class, she worked hard to learn effective study strategies and ways to compensate for her persisting reading problem.

Today, Sara can read almost anything, but the reading process is still difficult for her and she reads very slowly. Her writing skills are also affected by her learning disabilities. Her thoughts are good, and she can organize her thoughts, but her handwriting is slow and spelling is a major problem. To succeed in college, Sara will need some help. To get that help, Sara has decided to attend the community college in her city that offers support services for learning disabled adults.

The first semester, Sara will enroll in only three courses, and she has arranged for two types of assistance in those courses: notetakers to record the lecture information for her, and readers to tape-record the required readings for each class. In addition, Sara has learned how to do word processing on her home computer, and she feels this will really help her to produce good term papers. As the semester goes on, Sara may need to take advantage of some of the other services offered by the college. For example, she may need a special proctor for examinations, if she isn't able to complete them within the time limits set down by her course instructors.

Sara is optimistic about her future. She's not sure yet what career path she will follow, but she's aware of her limitations and she feels she can cope with them. She knows that it won't be easy. School has never been easy for her. But she's bright, determined to work hard, and very excited about becoming a college student.

& Boshes, 1969). At present, learning disabilities are the most commonly identified handicap among school-age individuals. In the 1983–84 school year, 41.7 percent of the handicapped students served in special education programs were identified as learning disabled. These 1,811,489 students represented approximately 4.6 percent of the total school population (U.S. Department of Education, 1985). Not only are learning disabled students the largest group of handicapped persons of school age, their numbers are growing. In 1980–81, approximately 3 percent of the school-aged population in the United States was identified as learning disabled (U.S. Department of Education, 1982). In 1983–84, that percentage rose to 4.6 percent.

Males outnumber females in the learning disabled population. Lerner (1981) estimates that learning disabled children are "four to six times more likely to be boys than girls" (p. 17). Although empirical studies typically do not report ratios this high, males appear to make up much more than half of those identified as learning disabled. Kirk and Elkins (1975), in a study of 3,000 school-identified learning disabled children, found a 3 to 1 male-to-female ratio; for every girl with learning disabilities, there were three boys. In a similar study of nearly 2,000 learning disabled students, Norman and Zigmond (1980) reported a ratio of 3.7 males to every female. The reasons for this discrepancy are not known but several tentative explanations have been offered. These include the possibility of greater vulnerability to brain damage in males, boys' slower maturation rates, and society's higher achievement expectancies for males (Smith, 1983).

The relationship between socioeconomic status, cultural group, and learning disabilities is less clear. Norman and Zigmond (1980) described their school population as similar in ethnic proportions to national census data. However, Leinhardt, Seewald, and Zigmond (1982) reported that whites and males were overrepresented in elementary classes for learning disabled students. Some experts argue that learning disabilities programs tend to serve white students of middle and upper socioeconomic status, ignoring students from minority groups and less affluent students (Hobbs, 1975; Kavale, 1980). This is not to say that learning disabilities are less common among these groups. Some maintain they are more common (Hallahan & Kauffman, 1976).

Concerned Disciplines

Throughout its history, the field of learning disabilities has been influenced by the contributions of many professions, most notably medicine, psychology, and education. Today, this multidisciplinary perspective is evident in the range of professions that collaborate in the study and treatment of individuals with learning disabilities.

Disciplines Concerned with Learning Needs.   During the school years, many learning disabled students are unable to succeed without some modification of standard educational practice. The primary profession concerned with their learning needs is special education. Learning disability specialists and other special educators provide specially designed instruction to learning disabled students, most typically in academic skill areas such as reading, math, and written language. Special teachers also assist in assessment of learning disabilities, planning and evaluation of instruction, communication with parents and family, and coordination of the overall intervention plan.

Other education specialists who often make up part of the service team for students with learning disabilities are school psychologists, speech-language pathologists, and adaptive physical education teachers. School psychologists' contributions include diagnostic services, counseling, and consultation with classroom teachers and other professionals. Specialists in speech and language serve learning disabled students with communication disorders, and adaptive physical education teachers assist students with psychomotor disorders. In addition, the regular classroom teacher plays an important role because the majority of these students spend at least part of their school day in a mainstream classroom.

An important educational service newly available to the learning disabled population is vocational rehabilitation. As Gerber (1981) notes, in the past, individuals with learning disabilities were excluded from such services because their handicap was not recognized as a mental or physical disability. However, learning disabilities are now recognized as a legitimate concern of vocational rehabilitation counselors, as long as the disorder is a substantial impediment to employment and there is reasonable expectation that services will increase employability. Typical rehabilitation services include vocational assessment and counseling, assistance in job training, and job placement and followup.

Disciplines Concerned with Social/Emotional Needs.

Education professionals such as learning disability specialists, school psychologists, and vocational rehabilitation counselors address the affective needs of their students as well as their learning needs. Goals for the improvement of socialization skills, self-concept, and interpersonal relations are often part of the individualized education program or rehabilitation plan.

Counselors and social workers also assist, both with learning disabled persons and with their families. Counseling and social services continue to be important in the adult years for individuals with severe learning disabilities who require aid in developing the social skills necessary for success in the workplace and community.

Disciplines Concerned with Physical/Health Needs.

Medical personnel attend to physical and health needs. Although many persons with learning disabilities have no special needs in these areas, it is important for all individuals with suspected achievement problems to be screened for vision and hearing impairments.

In addition, pediatricians may be the professionals to whom parents first bring their concerns about their child's learning problems. Levine (1982) says, "When a child is underachieving or failing to adapt in school, it is not uncommon for a parent to consult a pediatrician or family physician" (p. 296). Physicians contribute to the multidisciplinary effort by assisting in diagnosis of the medical aspects of the learning problem and by providing medical treatment when appropriate. Learning disabled individuals with diagnosed neurological dysfunction may require the services of a neurologist. Physicians may also treat children who are both learning disabled and hyperactive in an attempt to reduce their activity level and increase their ability to concentrate in school.

ETIOLOGY AND PREVENTION

Study of the causes of learning disabilities has a long, rich history. Professionals have been interested in the etiology of the handicapping condition since its symptoms were first described by early physicians. One way of thinking about hypothesized causes is to look at three different viewpoints: medical explanations, genetic explanations, and environmental explanations.

Causes of Learning Disabilities

Medical Explanations of Learning Disabilities.   Since nineteenth-century physicians began their pioneering work with brain-injured adults, there has been interest in the relationship between brain damage and impairments in learning and performance. The study of brain-injured adults resulted in a set of terms to describe the different disabilities associated with damage to the central nervous system. For example, the term aphasia refers to a loss of function in oral communication skills. In relation to academic skills, dyslexia refers to a loss of function in reading skills, dysgraphia to an impairment in writing skills, and dyscalculia to an impairment in arithmetic computation skills.

These terms have also been used to describe children with disabilities similar to those of brain-injured adults. However, the terminology is modified by adding the word "developmental": developmental aphasia, developmental dyslexia, and so forth. The addition of the qualifier "developmental" indicates that children with these disabilities do not lose acquired skills but instead are hampered in their original attempts to acquire them.

Through the 1960s, the neurological basis of learning disabilities was generally accepted. Children with this disability were called brain-injured or brain-damaged. Another neurological term, minimal brain dysfunction (MBD), was introduced to differentiate between learning disabled persons and those with major, comprehensive neurological dysfunctions such as cerebral palsy or some forms of mental retardation. Clements (1966) explained that MBD refers to "children whose neurological impairment is 'minimal' (as on a continuum), subtly affecting learning and behavior, *without* evident lowering of general intellectual capacity" (pp. 8–9).

For many of these children, however, there was no medical record of neurological impairment. Brain injury was inferred on the basis of their performance, not on the basis of a diagnosed injury, disease, or condition. It was assumed that damage to the central nervous system had occurred because of the difficulties these individuals experienced in the acquisition of school skills.

Research on the link between brain injury and learning disabilities shows that the relationship between these conditions is not a clear one. In one important study, Myklebust and Boshes (1969) attempted to differentiate learning disabled children from normal children on the basis of electroencephalogram (EEG) results. In an EEG examination, the electrical activity of the brain is measured and recorded on a graph that can be used for diagnostic purposes. The EEG readings of 35 percent of the children with severe learning disabilities in this study were found to be abnormal. But, abnormal EEG patterns were also shown by 26 percent of the normal control group children. Myklebust and Boshes reported similar findings when groups were compared on hard and soft signs of neurological impairment. These general findings have since been substantiated by other researchers (e.g., Gottesman, Croen, & Rotkin, 1982; Meier, 1971).

It appears that some portion of the learning disabled population exhibits symptoms of brain injury, but so does a sizable portion of the normal population. As Reid and Hresko (1981) explain, "Although these signs [of neurological impairment] are prevalent among the learning disabled, they do not constitute a discriminating characteristic" (p. 9). Although neurological impairment is not a definitive symptom of learning disabilities, the association between learning disabilities and neurological dysfunction remains strong. For example, in the definition proposed by the National Joint Committee for Learning Disabilities (1981), learning disabilities are "presumed to be due to central nervous system dysfunction."

There are several other medical explanations of learning disabilities. Learning disabilities, like mental retardation, may follow any one of a number of assaults to the unborn fetus, newborn infant, or young child. Prenatal factors that may result in learning problems are Rh incompatibility, infections such as rubella, exposure to radiation, effects of drugs, maternal endocrine disorders, and maternal age (Pasamanick & Knoblock, 1973). Other factors that may produce learning disabilities as sequelae are prematurity and low birth weight, complications during delivery or the prenatal period, maternal or child malnutrition, childhood illnesses such as meningitis, and traumatic head injuries producing central nervous system damage. Studies of the medical histories of learning disabled children indicate a higher incidence of complications during pregnancy and birth than in the normal population (Colletti, 1979).

Genetic Explanations of Learning Disabilities. The idea that heredity may play a role in learning disabilities was first introduced in the late nineteenth and early twentieth centuries. For example, Hinshelwood (1907) described several members of the same family who showed severe reading problems despite apparent normal intelligence. Subsequent research has confirmed that reading problems tend to cluster in families. As an example, in the Colorado Family

Reading Study (Decker & DeFries, 1980), the families of reading disabled children showed poorer reading skills than the families of normal readers.

Twin studies have also been used to investigate the hypothesis that learning disabilities are transmitted genetically. In such studies, the number of learning problems among identical twins is compared to that among fraternal twins. More frequent appearance of a trait among identical twins is seen as support for the heritability theory because identical twins share the same genes. In general, results indicate that identical twins are more similar in reading abilities than fraternal twins. Also, academic problems are more likely to affect both members of the twin pair when twins are identical (e.g., Hermann, 1959; Matheny & Dolan, 1974).

There is substantial support for a familial factor in learning disabilities. However, genetic inheritance is only one possible explanation of the similarities among family members and between twin pairs. Another explanation is the environment shared by these persons. Coles (1980) criticizes family studies for their failure to attend to important environmental factors. Environmental influences such as educational experiences and family relationships must also be considered as possible contributors to school performance problems.

Environmental Explanations of Learning Disabilities.   There are two major sets of considerations in environmental theories of learning disabilities: home and family factors, and school influences. A poor home environment—one that is impoverished socially, emotionally, and intellectually—can accentuate the effects of a learning disability. Economic disadvantage may also be a factor. According to Kavale (1980), poverty increases the likelihood of learning problems because poverty is associated with prematurity, malnutrition, disease and accidents, and adverse childrearing conditions. Cultural and linguistic factors may be just as important as socioeconomic status (Argulewicz, 1983). This view is supported by the results of the nationwide High School and Beyond Study (Plisko & Owings, 1982). As part of this study, high school students were asked to report about participation in special education programs and other indicators of handicapping conditions. Minority students were most likely to identify themselves as handicapped as were students of low socioeconomic status.

The school environment may also contribute to learning disabilities. It has been suggested that poor or inadequate instruction plays a major role in the development of school learning problems. It appears obvious that learning disabled students will not benefit from poorly managed instruction, inappropriate learning activities, and unrealistic performance expectations. Some experts believe that inadequate instruction may precipitate some learning disabilities just as excellent instruction may prevent them. For example, Reynolds and Birch (1977) say that "most pupil behaviors called learning disabilities and behavior disorders are best acknowledged as the consequence of failure to provide enough high quality individualized instruction" (p. 351). In this extreme environmentalist viewpoint, learning disabilities are seen as the result of inadequate instruction.

Prevention of Learning Disabilities

Many different causes of learning disabilities have been suggested, and etiological research continues today. However, it is not possible to point to one major cause of this handicapping condition. It is likely that several causative factors are responsible for learning disabilities, and these factors may interact with each other. For instance, poor environmental conditions at home and poor instructional conditions in school could worsen the effects of a neurologically based learning disorder. At present, it is rarely possible to determine the cause or causes of the learning disabilities of any one individual. As Hallahan and Kauffman (1976) comment, "For the great majority of children identified as learning disabled, emotionally disturbed, and educable mentally retarded there is no known cause of the condition" (p. 31).

What is possible today is identification of a range of factors that may contribute to the presence or to the severity of learning disabilities. This information provides direction for prevention. Preventive efforts center around the provision of as optimal an environment as possible. Central to these efforts are assurances of adequate medical care during pregnancy, prevention of complications during delivery and the perinatal period, adequate maternal and child nutrition, and the provision of a safe, supportive, and cognitively stimulating home environment. In addition, the effects of the handicap may be lessened by early detection and treatment of learning disabilities, before the child has accumulated a history of school failure.

CHARACTERISTICS OF INDIVIDUALS WITH LEARNING DISABILITIES

The young kindergarten child, unable to count from one to ten or recite the alphabet, the fifth grader whose handwriting is virtually illegible, the college student who relies upon tape-recorded texts because of an inability to read quickly and with ease—these individuals all share the primary characteristic of learning disabilities, poor achievement despite adequate intelligence.

In the study of learning disabilities, much attention has been paid to describing the condition and its effects upon cognitive, social-emotional, and physical development. Because learning disabilities are cognitive disorders, learning characteristics have been a major research focus. Until recently, school-age individuals were the primary population of interest, particularly elementary school students. At present, new emphases are emerging: study of the characteristics of learning disabled adolescents and adults, and investigation of the social-emotional concomitants of learning disabilities.

Learning Characteristics

Learning disabilities affect the rate of learning, the ease with which learning takes place, or both. Despite average intelligence, a person with learning disabilities may learn some things more slowly than peers do. Or, learning may be more laborious, requiring great effort. Learning disabilities do not affect all spheres of performance. Learning disabled persons may achieve quite well in some areas of school performance while failing in others. For example, a young learning disabled child may acquire computational skills with ease while struggling to learn the rudiments of reading. Or, a disabled high school student may succeed in mastering the content of a history course but be unable to express his or her ideas on written tests and examinations.

Why do learning disabled persons encounter these learning problems? How do they learn, and how much do they learn? These questions have spurred research since the beginning of interest in this puzzling handicap. At present, there are three main bodies of research on the learning characteristics of individuals with learning disabilities. The first describes the academic skills and intellectual performance of this population. The second is concerned with specific cognitive disabilities; it focuses on deficits in perception, attention, memory, and other psychological processes. The third and newest strand is an attempt to describe the interaction between the abilities and disabilities of disabled learners and the tasks they must perform. Emphasized in this strand are the strategies used by learning disabled individuals as they attempt to acquire new skills and learn new information.

Academic Achievement and Intellectual Performance. Most studies of the academic achievement of learning disabled persons have concentrated on the basic school skills of reading, mathematics, and written language. These studies confirm that learning disabled children and adolescents show poor academic achievement, when compared to nonhandicapped students (e.g., Bryan, Pearl, Donahue, Bryan, & Pflaum, 1983; Schumaker, Deshler, Alley, & Warner, 1983). Also, the achievement gap between learning disabled students and their nondisabled peers widens with age (Shepard, Smith, & Vojir, 1983).

In the elementary school grades, the underachievement of learning disabled children is mild or moderate (Lewis, 1983). For example, one study found learning disabled students in grades 4 through 6 to score approximately 1.5 years below grade level (Shepard et al., 1983). In a study of more than 3,000 elementary grade students with learning disabilities, the average discrepancy between actual and expected achievement was 1.7 grade levels in reading, 1.2 grade levels in arithmetic, and 1.8 grade levels in spelling (Kirk & Elkins, 1975). Norman and Zigmond (1980) noted, in an investigation of approximately 2,000 learning disabled students, "discrepancies of two or more grade levels were not evident until 12 years of age" (p. 546).

In adolescence, the achievement problems of learning disabled students become severe. There is comprehensive underachievement in all basic skill subjects, rather than isolated skill deficits. Learning disabled adolescents have been described as "the lowest of low achievers, typically scoring below the tenth percentile in achievement in reading, written language, and mathematics" (Schumaker et al., 1983, p. 47). In one study of secondary level learning disabled students, all were at least three years below grade level in spelling, 83 percent showed this degree of underachievement in mathematics, 81 percent in reading, and 55 percent in language (Shepard et al., 1983).

In senior high school, learning disabled students show little progress in acquisition of basic skills. They appear to reach a plateau in skill development of approximately the fifth grade level in reading and written language and approximately the sixth grade level in mathematics (Schumaker et al., 1983). Academic achievement problems may continue into the adult years. One follow-up study of men diagnosed as dyslexic in childhood found persisting basic skills deficits (Frauenheim, 1978). These learning disabled adults showed an average performance of grade 3.6 in reading, grade 2.9 in spelling, and grade 4.6 in arithmetic.

The intellectual performance of learning disabled students has also been studied extensively. Most often, studies have used measures of general intelligence such as the *Wechsler Intelligence Scale for Children–Revised* (Wechsler, 1974) or other popular intelligence tests (Terman & Merrill, 1973; Wechsler, 1967, 1981). In general, learning disabled students score within the average range on intelligence measures. However, their performance falls somewhat below IQ 100, the general population's average score on such tests. The average IQ score of learning disabled students is typically in the low 90s (Kirk & Elkins, 1975; Norman & Zigmond, 1980) both for elementary and for secondary grade students (Warner, Schumaker, Alley, & Deshler, 1980).

Cognitive Deficits.   Underachievement is not the sole characteristic of learning disabilities. What differentiates learning disabled individuals from other poor achievers is a deficit in one or more of the cognitive functions important for learning. From the very beginnings of the study of brain-injured children, there have been attempts to find out what sets this group of learners apart from their normally achieving peers. In the early years, clinicians carefully observed learning disabled individuals and reported their findings in case studies. Strauss, for example, described a set of characteristics that would come to be called the Strauss Syndrome (Strauss & Lehtinen, 1947). These characteristics included perceptual impairments, distractibility, and hyperactivity.

In 1966, Clements published a review of the literature on minimal brain dysfunction in children. In that review, the ten characteristics most often associated with minimal brain dysfunction were identified:

1. *Hyperactivity*
2. *Perceptual-motor impairments*
3. *Emotional lability*
4. *General coordination deficits*
5. *Disorders of attention (short attention span, distractibility, perseveration)*
6. *Impulsivity*
7. *Disorders of memory and thinking*
8. *Specific learning disabilities:*
   a. Reading
   b. Arithmetic

    c. *Writing*

    d. *Spelling*

 9. *Disorders of speech and hearing*

10. *Equivocal neurological signs and electroencephalographic irregularities.* (p. 13)

Several of these characteristics relate directly to cognitive functioning: perceptual-motor impairments, disorders of attention, impulsivity, and disorders of memory and thinking. Others are concerned with emotional and medical aspects of the disability, as well as its effects upon academic skill development.

The 1968 National Advisory Committee definition used the term "psychological process disorders" to describe the cognitive deficits associated with learning disabilities. Psychological processes are the set of abilities individuals use to receive and to respond to incoming information. The three major components of psychological processing are the reception of information, the association of incoming information with previously stored information, and the expression of information. Because psychological processing is concerned with the comprehension and transmission of information, it is also called information processing. Lerner (1981) defines psychological processes as "the ways in which human beings organize and interpret data or stimuli in the world" (p. 170). Examples of psychological processes are auditory processes, visual processes, kinesthetic and tactile processes, memory abilities, and language abilities (Lerner, 1981). Attention is another important example.

In the 1950s and 1960s, several theories of learning disabilities were proposed and each reflected an orientation toward a specific type of psychological processing disorder. Many were concerned with disorders of perception. Perception is the psychological ability to process or to use the information received through the senses. Persons with perceptual disorders are able to receive sensory information through their eyes or ears or other sensory modality, but they have difficulty extracting meaning from that information.

Visual perception was the focus of many of the perceptual theories of learning disabilities. In the work of Frostig (Frostig & Horne, 1964) and Getman (1961; Getman & Kane, 1968), visual perception deficits were linked to children's reading disorders. Others such as Wepman (1967) were interested in the relationship of auditory perception deficits to the development of oral language skills. Another area of interest was the relationship between perceptual development and motor development. Kephart (1960, 1963) and Barsch (1965, 1967) were among the theorists working with perceptual-motor impairments. Poor perceptual-motor skills were thought to contribute to problems in handwriting and other eye-hand coordination tasks and to difficulties with gross motor functions such as balance and coordination.

At about the same time, other theorists stressed the link between cognition and language. Johnson and Mykelbust (1967), for example, described several types of language disabilities, including disorders of receptive language and disorders of expressive language. Building upon the work of Osgood (1957a,

The teacher in a learning disabilities class works with her students as they practice counting change.

1957b), Kirk proposed a psycholinguistic model of information processing (Kirk & Kirk, 1971; Kirk, McCarthy, & Kirk, 1968). This model attempted to describe the relationships between the psychological processes (*psycho-*) and language (*-linguistic*). It highlighted three major components of psycholinguistics: (a) the processes of communication (reception, association, and expression); (b) the sensory channels used for communication (auditory-vocal and visual-motor); and (c) the levels of language (meaningful discourse and automatic communication).

Many early theories of learning disabilities offered strategies for diagnosis and remediation of cognitive deficits. Tests of perception and other psychological processes were available, and many tests were accompanied by remedial programs designed to ameliorate the deficits identified in testing. For example, children were assessed with Kirk's *Illinois Test of Psycholinguistic Abilities* (Kirk et al., 1968), Frostig's *Developmental Test of Visual Perception* (Frostig, Lefever, & Whittlesey, 1966), or Kephart's *Purdue Perceptual-Motor Survey* (Roach & Kephart, 1966). Test results were then used to select instructional activities from the remediation programs accompanying these tests.

Tests of perception, perceptual-motor skills, and psychological processing were also used to gather information about the cognitive characteristics of children with learning disabilities. This line of research did not prove fruitful. A major reason for this were the measurement problems associated with tests of perception and psycholinguistic functioning (Coles, 1978; McLoughlin & Lewis, 1986; Salvia & Ysseldyke, 1981). Many of these tests proved to be unreliable or their validity was in question. Potentially inaccurate measures could not be used to describe the cognitive abilities of the learning disabled population.

However, it is possible to draw conclusions about other areas of cognition, notably memory, attention, and language. According to Weener and Senf (1982), "attention and memory are the two most commonly measured variables showing consistent deficits in the learning-disabled group" (p. 1062). In language, young learning disabled children may experience delays in the development of listening and speaking skills and in the acquisition of knowledge about linguistic structures. Communication problems may result from disorders of language processing and language production (Wiig & Semel, 1976).

Disorders of attention were one of the first characteristics of learning disabilities to be identified. Individuals with learning disabilities may fail to pay attention. Or, they may attend, but direct their attention to the unimportant aspects of the situation rather than to its most relevant features. Ross (1976) suggests that learning disabled children show a delay in the development of selective attention abilities. These children are slower to learn how to focus their attention upon relevant dimensions of the learning task.

Attention disorders are sometimes associated with the characteristics of distractibility, impulsivity, and hyperactivity. Some learning disabled persons are easily distracted from the task at hand, and they have difficulty sustaining their attention. Impulsivity is another concern. Impulsive persons act quickly, without careful thought and reflection. In contrast, reflective persons think before acting; they pay attention to the situation before committing themselves to action. Learning disabled children tend to be impulsive rather than reflective. They develop reflective thinking skills more slowly than normal children do (Cullinan, Epstein, Lloyd, & Noel, 1980). Hyperactivity is excessive activity. A child's activity level is considered excessive when it is inappropriate for the child's age or for the situation in which it occurs. Some children with learning disabilities are also hyperactive. Their constant activity may interfere with their ability to direct and to maintain attention.

Problems in memory are another characteristic of many learning disabled individuals. One of the most frequent observations of teachers is that students with learning disabilities have difficulty remembering what they learn. For example, a student may learn new spelling words or math facts on one day, but forget them by the next. Individuals may have poor short-term memory, poor long-term memory, or both. In school learning, long-term memory is the major concern, but information must pass through short-term memory before it can be stored for long-term retrieval.

Strategies for Learning.   Recently, research in learning disabilities has moved away from looking at learner characteristics in isolation. Instead, the goal is investigation of how learning disabled persons use the cognitive abilities they have when confronted with learning tasks. Learning strategies, rather than learning deficits, are of interest. Learning strategies are the methods persons use when they attempt to acquire new skills or learn new information. Strategies are active ways of interacting with the demands of the learning task.

Learning strategies have been studied in relation to two important cognitive deficits of the learning disabled population: memory and attention. In memory tasks, normal learners adopt a strategy that will help them in remembering the material that is presented. They may organize the material in some way, deduce or create associations between the items to be remembered, and actively practice the act of recall. Learning disabled students do not appear to use these strategies. Persons with learning disabilities recall less information than their nonhandicapped peers, and they approach the memory task in a different way. They are less likely to interact with the material to be learned and less likely to actively rehearse it (Torgesen, 1977a, 1979, 1980). These findings have led Torgesen (1977b) to conclude that learning disabled students are inactive learners.

Attention disorders may also be related to learning strategies. Learning disabled individuals may fail to attend to school tasks because they do not have strategies for beginning and carrying out these tasks. When faced with an activity, they do not know how to approach it and their attention may wander. Or, they may attend to an unimportant part of the task. In a review of the research on selective attention and learning disabilities, Hallahan and Reeve (1980) conclude:

> At this time, it appears that the most parsimonious explanation for the learning disabled child's tendency to have problems in attending to relevant cues and ignoring irrelevant cues is his inability to bring to the task a specific learning strategy. (p. 156)

Learning strategies have been studied in relation to academic tasks. In most cases, this research has focused on the study skills of students with learning disabilities. For example, Deshler and others at the University of Kansas have conducted a series of investigations of the learning strategies of learning disabled adolescents (Alley, Deshler, Clark, Schumaker, & Warner, 1983; Deshler, Schumaker, Alley, Warner, & Clark, 1982; Schumaker et al., 1983). Findings suggest that these students have difficulty in note-taking, listening comprehension, attending to teachers' statements, scanning textbook passages, monitoring writing errors, test-taking skills, and other important study strategies (Deshler et al., 1982).

Deficits in the strategies for learning may be related to metacognition. Metacognition is thinking about thinking. Normal learners are able to remove themselves from the learning situation and think about the strategies that they use. They can talk about whether a particular task is easy or difficult for them, what strategies they have used successfully and unsuccessfully in the past, and how they make decisions about choosing an appropriate learning strategy. Learning disabled students may be less adept at metacognition than their nonhandicapped peers. Or, they may fail to consider the metacognitive information they possess when selecting strategies for learning (Hallahan et al., 1983).

Studies on
Learning Disabled Students
as Inactive Learners

Do learning disabled persons have deficits in memory? Or, is their poor memory performance due to a poor choice of strategies for memory tasks? Torgesen (1977b) suggests that learning disabled students fail to select appropriate learning strategies. They are inactive learners who do not become actively involved in the learning task.

Torgesen and his colleagues have conducted a series of studies of the memory performance of learning disabled students. Some of their most interesting results have been obtained in studies where they have attempted to improve memory functioning.

For example, Torgesen, Murphy, and Ivey (1979) set up an experiment in which a memory task was presented to students in two different ways. Two groups of fourth grade students were chosen to participate in this study, reading disabled children and normal readers.

In the first part of the experiment, the students were shown 24 pictures of common objects. The pictures were arranged in a circle, and they represented sets of objects that belonged to four conceptual categories. Attention was not drawn to these categories. The students were simply asked to name each picture and then told to study the pictures so that they could remember them later. The experimenters emphasized that students could move the pictures around or do anything else that would help them remember better. After a three-minute study period, the pictures were removed and students were asked to name the pictures in any order. Their recall was tested again later after a 10-minute reading activity.

On this task, poor readers recalled fewer pictures than good readers. This was true both for immediate recall (directly following the study period) and delayed recall (after the 10-minute activity). In addition, observations of students' study strategies showed that good readers were much more likely to cluster the pictures into categories as a study aid. Sixty-eight percent of the good readers used a clustering strategy in comparison to only 31 percent of the disabled readers.

In the second part of the experiment, a similar memory task was used, but the students were forced to use a clustering strategy. Again, they were presented with 24 pictures representing objects in four conceptual categories. However, students were instructed to sort the pictures into four groups of objects that somehow go together. The sorting activity continued for three minutes, and then the students were asked to recall as many of the pictures as they could. Delayed recall was tested after a 10-minute activity period.

On this second task, reading disabled students performed as well as normal readers. They remembered an equal number of pictures on both the immediate and delayed recall tests. The difference in memory performance disappeared when disabled readers were forced to adopt the effective learning strategies of normal readers. The researchers concluded:

> This study suggests that, at least for some kinds of memory problems, it may be inaccurate to speak of "specific disabilities" in memory per se and more accurate to think in terms of the reading disabled child's failure to approach certain kinds of cognitive tasks in an efficient manner. (p. 401)

This study improved the memory performance of learning disabled students by teaching a clustering strategy. However, clustering is not the only possible memory strategy. Other strategies in which learning disabled students appear to be deficient are verbal labelling and rehearsal (Haines & Torgesen, 1979; Torgesen, 1977a). These strategies, like clustering, appear to respond to training. For example, Torgesen and Goldman (1977) found that requiring verbal rehearsal in a memory activity eliminated the performance differences between reading disabled and achieving children.

Several other explanations of learning disabilities are currently under consideration in addition to the learning strategies hypothesis. For example, it has been suggested that learning disabled persons fail to overlearn tasks to the extent that performance becomes automatic (Sternberg & Warner, 1982). When skills are automatic, they can be performed without conscious thought. However, learning disabled individuals must continue to think about the mechanics of reading and spelling and writing, long after these skills should have become habits. Another explanation is the developmental lag hypothesis. In this view, learning disabled students develop cognitive abilities in the same sequence as normal learners but development is delayed. Thus, children with learning disabilities perform in some ways like younger children with average learning abilities. For example, there may be a delay in the development of selective attention (Ross, 1976) and of reflective thinking skills (Cullinan et al., 1980; Tarver & Maggiore, 1979).

At present, the study of learning strategies appears to be one of the most promising approaches to describing individuals with learning disabilities. It also has implications for treatment because learning strategies appear to be susceptible to training (Connor, 1983; Hallahan et al., 1983; Schumaker et al., 1983). Preliminary studies indicate that learning disabled youngsters can learn to use appropriate strategies, and these strategies increase the probability of classroom success.

Social/Emotional Characteristics

There is a growing body of research suggesting that learning disabled individuals experience difficulty in social interactions as well as in academic achievement. In general, handicapped children are not well accepted by their nonhandicapped peers (Gresham, 1982). In mainstreamed classrooms, there is little interaction between nonhandicapped and handicapped students. These general findings appear to accurately describe the social status of school-age individuals with learning disabilities.

As a group, learning disabled students are less popular than their nondisabled peers (Bruininks, 1978; Bryan, 1974, 1976; Garrett & Crump, 1980; Horowitz, 1981; Siperstein & Goding, 1983). Teachers tend to prefer normally achieving children to those with learning disabilities (Garrett & Crump, 1980). Even naive observers form negative first impressions of learning disabled children (Bryan et al., 1983). However, not all learning disabled students are unpopular. Some are among the most popular students in their class (Perlmutter, Crocker, Cordray, & Garstecki, 1983; Siperstein & Goding, 1983).

As a group, learning disabled persons show a poorer self-concept and lower self-esteem than nonhandicapped persons (Bruininks, 1978; Hiebert, Wong, & Hunter, 1982; Winne, Woodlands, & Wong, 1982). Self-esteem appears to be related to school achievement (Patten, 1983). The less learning disabled students achieve in school, the lower their self-esteem.

Several studies have investigated learning disabled students' attributions of success and failure. Success and failure can be attributed to internal causes such as effort and ability or to external causes such as luck, other people, or the

Attention and praise from his teacher will help give a learning disabled child confidence and raise his level of self-esteem.

characteristics of the task. In a series of studies by Bryan and others (1983) at the University of Illinois at Chicago, learning disabled children were less likely than achieving children to believe that task success or failure was due to internal causes such as effort and ability. They were less likely to show an internal locus of control. Because they attributed their task performance to luck and other external factors, they did not believe that failure could be overcome by effort. However, not all researchers have found this attribution pattern (Tollefson, Tracy, Johnsen, Buenning, Farmer, & Barke, 1982).

In the classroom, some learning disabled students display inappropriate behaviors. In one study, children with learning disabilities were less task-oriented, more distractible, and less extroverted than their nonhandicapped peers (McKinney, McClure, & Feagans, 1982). Behavior disorders are more prevalent in the learning disabled population than in the general school population (Cullinan, Epstein, & Lloyd, 1981). Examples of problem behaviors are self-consciousness, lack of self-confidence, withdrawal, anxiety, and tension.

Teachers interact frequently with learning disabled students. However, these interactions focus on the management of behavior (McKinney & Feagans, 1983). Teachers praise learning disabled students as often as other students, but they criticize them more often (Bryan, 1974). In interactions with peers, learning disabled students may have difficulty interpreting social cues (Axelrod, 1982; Pearl & Cosden, 1982). In some studies, the social interactions of learning disabled students are described as negative and aggressive (Bryan & Bryan, 1977, 1978). In others, their communication style is described as passive (Bryan et al., 1983). They appear to be inactive listeners who are reluctant to request clarification and likely to agree with others.

In secondary classrooms, learning disabled adolescents interact with their peers as frequently as nonhandicapped students do (Alley et al., 1983). Out of the classroom, that picture changes. Adolescents with learning disabilities do not participate in social activities as often as their achieving peers. Social needs may continue into adulthood (Alley et al., 1983). In one follow-up study, young adults with learning disabilities were found to be dependent upon family support in social activities (Fafard & Haubrich, 1981). Both social and vocational needs were identified in a series of studies comparing learning disabled young adults to normal achievers (Alley et al., 1983). The learning disabled adults held jobs with lower social status and they were less satisfied with their employment situations. In the interpersonal realm, they participated less often in social and recreational activities, they reported more dating problems, and they were less satisfied with their relationships with parents and relatives.

Physical/Health Characteristics

In general, the health status of the learning disabled population is unexceptional, and physical development is normal. For some learning disabled persons, however, there is a medical diagnosis of brain injury. These persons may show perceptual-motor disorders, coordination deficits, and other symptoms associated with neurological impairment. Another medical condition associated with learning disabilities is hyperactivity, sometimes called hyperkinesis. To educators, hyperactivity is a behavior disorder and it is treated instructionally. It can also be considered a physical condition to be treated medically.

Hyperactivity may be accompanied by distractibility, impulsivity, and disorders of attention and concentration. In analyzing the physician's role in relation to children with school problems, Levine (1982) observes that "problems with sustained selective attention may constitute the most common form of dysfunction in the school-age child" (p. 300). However, hyperactivity does not appear to be a typical characteristic of learning disabilities. In a study of school-age individuals identified as learning disabled, physicians and classroom teachers classified only 4.5 percent of the students as hyperactive (Shepard et al., 1983).

DETECTION OF LEARNING DISABILITIES

Most learning disabilities are identified in the school years. Sometime during the early elementary grades, students with learning disabilities begin to fall behind in one or more academic subjects. Some children with severe problems may be identified before they enter school because of serious delays in the acquisition of preacademic skills. For example, they may show severe disorders of attention and concentration or marked delays in the development of listening and speaking skills.

At present, the vast majority of persons identified as learning disabled are of school age. In school special education programs, 95 percent of the learning disabled students served are ages 6 to 17 (U.S. Department of Education, 1984). Only 1 percent are younger than 6 years old, and 4 percent are 18 to 21 years old.

Identification and Screening

There is much interest in the early identification of children "at risk" for school learning problems. If young children can be identified and provided treatment early in their school careers, it may be possible to avert later academic problems, or at least minimize them.

Many schools conduct programs to screen incoming kindergarteners or first graders for school readiness. Like vision and hearing screening programs, the purpose of readiness screening is to survey large groups of children and identify those with possible learning problems. School readiness tests may be used as screening devices. Such tests usually assess preacademic skills such as auditory memory, listening, visual discrimination, language, and quantitative concepts.

The goal in early identification is the prediction of school learning problems. A kindergarten child's performance on a test of school readiness is used to predict how well that child will achieve in the academic curriculum of the early elementary grades. Reid and Hresko (1981) observe that screening tests are best at predicting the performance of children who are gifted and those with severe impairments. They are least effective with learning disabled children. Another strategy for early identification is the use of teacher observations and reports. Mercer, Algozzine, and Trifiletti (1979) suggest that "teacher perceptions are good predictors of school problems, especially if teachers are provided checklists which include items (preacademic) that are related to the criterion performance (academic learning)" (p. 22).

Identification of children with possible learning disabilities becomes an easier task in the elementary grades when academic achievement problems become evident. In most schools, elementary grade students are identified through a referral process. Teachers, parents, or others who are concerned about a child's performance initiate a referral for special education assessment.

There are several warning signs of learning disabilities in addition to poor school performance. These include student behaviors such as the following:

- *Speaks well but reads poorly;*
- *Confuses similar letters and words such as b and d, was and saw;*
- *Guesses constantly when reading;*
- *Has extreme difficulty with math;*
- *Is clumsy; has difficulty with laces, buttons, ball-catching;*
- *Has trouble understanding or following directions;*
- *Has difficulty expressing thoughts;*

- *Has trouble understanding time and distance;*
- *Confuses up/down, left/right, and front/back;*
- *Has a short attention span; is easily distracted;*
- *Is overactive; or inactive, listless;*
- *Is impulsive; cannot wait; cannot foresee consequences.*
  (California Association for Neurologically Handicapped Children, 1980, p. 3)

Most elementary-age students with learning disabilities will show one or more of these behaviors.

Criteria for the Determination of Learning Disabilities

It is an easy task to determine when students are failing in school. However, it has not proven easy to differentiate between individuals with learning disabilities and others with school achievement problems. Definitions of learning disabilities do not translate directly into program eligibility criteria. First, definitions must be analyzed to determine the critical characteristics of the handicap. Then, each of these characteristics must be operationalized so that they can be observed and measured. Table 9.1 outlines the ways that most educational programs operationalize the critical characteristics of learning disabilities. Kirk and Chalfant (1984) add another consideration: demonstration that the individual has failed to learn with ordinary instructional methods and therefore is in need of special educational services.

It is also necessary to set criteria for determining when results document a learning disability and when they do not. Setting these criteria is not an easy task.

An example is discrepancy analysis. To document an aptitude-achievement discrepancy, it is necessary to determine how large a difference between expected and current performance indicates an important difference, that is, a substantial discrepancy. The standard used most commonly is two years below grade level. The student's scores on achievement tests are compared to his or her present grade in school. Those that fall more than two years below the student's current grade placement are presumed to indicate a major discrepancy.

Although much used, this method is an inappropriate and inaccurate one. First, it fails to consider the student's ability. Current achievement is compared to grade in school, not expected achievement. Also, grade scores are not appropriate measures for comparing expected and actual performance. It is impossible for a first grader to score two years below grade level. And, grade scores do not accurately reflect the school curriculum. Progress from grade 1.0 in reading to grade 1.5 indicates a much larger step than progress from grade 12.0 to 12.5.

There are several other ways to analyze discrepancies, and some overcome the weaknesses of the years-below-grade-level method (Beck, 1982). However, each

Table 9.1	
Determination of Learning Disabilities	
Characteristic	*Operationalized as*
A discrepancy between expected and actual performance	A difference between current performance on a test of intelligence and current performance on measures of academic achievement (or other important age-appropriate skills)
Exclusion of other conditions, characteristics, or handicaps as the reason for the discrepancy	Negative findings for mental retardation, emotional disturbance, and so forth
Inadequate cognitive functioning in some specific ability or strategy associated with learning disabilities	Poor performance on measures of attention, memory, perception, or other psychological processes; documentation of ineffective strategies for learning

method utilizes a different set of standards, so that each identifies a different group of students. One study compared eight common techniques for discrepancy analysis and found a wide variation in the numbers of students identified by the different methods, from 11 percent to 39 percent of a clinic population (Forness, Sinclair, & Guthrie, 1983).

Another concern is the availability of adequate measurement tools. Attempts to develop valid and reliable measures of cognitive functioning have met with little success. The early tests of perception and psychological processing have been soundly criticized for their lack of psychometric quality (Arter & Jenkins, 1979; Coles, 1978; Salvia & Ysseldyke, 1981). New tests have been developed, but their effectiveness with the learning disabled population is still under study (Hallahan et al., 1983).

One trend that is apparent is the development of tests that assess several aspects of performance. For example, the *Woodcock-Johnson Psycho-Educational Battery* (Woodcock & Johnson, 1977) includes measures of general intellectual performance, specific cognitive abilities, academic achievement, and interests. Test batteries such as this may take the place of tests of visual perception, auditory discrimination, psycholinguistic processing, and other specific abilities. Another trend is the growing interest in learning strategies and their role in the performance of learning disabled individuals. As research progresses in this area, it is likely that techniques for the assessment of learning strategies will be developed for school use.

Common Methods for
Diagnosis and Assessment

In school programs, the usual approach to assessment of learning disabilities is administration of a battery of psychological and educational tests. The first goal is to determine whether students meet eligibility criteria for special learning disability services. In order to make this decision, the multidisciplinary team relies heavily upon the results of norm-referenced tests of intelligence and academic achievement. Classroom and home observations, interviews with parents and regular educators, and informal measures such as inventories and criterion-referenced tests may also supply information about the student's present levels of performance.

Although assessment of learning disabilities takes place less frequently in the preschool and adult years, the same general procedures are followed. What is different are the skills considered in determining a discrepancy between expected and actual performance. With young children, the concern is the child's developmental status in speech and language, cognition, interpersonal relationships, and other preacademic skill areas. Vocational and social skills are usually the major concerns in the assessment of learning disabilities in adult populations.

Determining eligibility for special services is only the first step in assessment. What comes next is the collection of specific information about the person's current ability to perform important skills. This information is used to plan the intervention program and, later, to evaluate the effectiveness of this program. For example, if a fourth grader with learning disabilities is failing in math, it's important to find out exactly which math skills that student has mastered and which he or she has not yet mastered. Informal assessment strategies are preferred for this purpose, particularly those that are direct measures of the skills under study (Deno, Marston, & Mirkin, 1982; Deno, Mirkin, & Chiang, 1982). To find out about a child's math skills, for example, several informal strategies could be used: direct observation of the student performing math tasks, analysis of the student's math errors on worksheets and other written assignments, administration of criterion-referenced tests of specific math skills (e.g., addition of one-digit numbers, addition of two-digit numbers, addition with regrouping), and so forth.

There have been several studies of current school practices in the assessment of learning disabilities (Davis & Shepard, 1983; Mardell-Czudnowski, 1980; Perlmutter & Parus, 1983; Thurlow & Ysseldyke, 1979). Schools tend to use three types of tests in evaluating students for learning disabilities programs: intelligence tests, achievement tests, and tests of perception and other psychological processes. Tests of language abilities are sometimes included in the assessment battery, but measures of the social and emotional concomitants of learning disabilities are rarely administered.

One of the most commonly used tests is the *Wechsler Intelligence Scale for Children–Revised* (Wechsler, 1974), an individually administered test of intellectual performance. The *WISC–R* provides information about current intellectual functioning, and its results may be used to estimate expected achievement levels. The *WISC–R* is composed of several subtests, and some of these are of particular interest in the assessment of learning disabilities.

The Wechsler Intelligence Scale for Children–Revised

The *Wechsler Intelligence Scale for Children–Revised* (Wechsler, 1974) is one of the tests most frequently used in the assessment of learning disabilities. It is an individual test of intellectual performance, and it is divided into two scales, the Verbal Scale and the Performance Scale. Each of these scales contains several subtests.

Verbal subtests emphasize language abilities. On these subtests, children listen to questions and answer orally. There are six subtests on the *WISC–R* Verbal Scale, one of which is supplementary:

Information—The child is asked general information questions such as "How many eyes do you have?"

Similarities—Two items are named (e.g., a car and an airplane) and the child must tell how these items are alike.

Arithmetic—The child listens to arithmetic problems and then attempts to solve them without pencil and paper.

Vocabulary—The child must tell the meaning of several words.

Comprehension—Questions requiring social reasoning are presented, such as, "What are some reasons why we need firemen?"

Digit Span (Supplementary)—The child listens to a series of numbers read at the rate of one per second. On the first part of the subtest, the child repeats the numbers in the order they were presented. On the second part, the child repeats the numbers in backwards order.

Performance subtests deemphasize verbal skills. On these subtests, children look at pictures or objects and respond motorically—by pointing, by moving objects around, or by writing.

Picture Completion—The child is shown an incomplete drawing and must point to (or tell) what important part is missing.

Picture Arrangement—Several cards with pictures on them must be arranged in an order that tell a story.

Block Design—The child is given several colored blocks and shown a picture of a design. The blocks must be arranged in this design.

Object Assembly—The child is provided with several puzzle pieces to put together.

Coding—A code is presented in which each digit stands for a geometric shape. The child is shown a series of digits and must fill in the correct geometric shapes.

Mazes (Supplementary)—The child attempts to solve paper-and-pencil mazes.

The *WISC–R* produces several scores. There is a scaled score for each subtest, and three IQ scores. The Verbal IQ reflects the child's performance on the Verbal Scale subtests, and the Performance IQ the child's Performance Scale functioning. The Full Scale IQ takes both Verbal and Performance Scale subtests into account. It is an indicator of general intellectual functioning.

Much research has been done on the *WISC–R* performance characteristics of learning disabled students. It appears that students with learning disabilities have particular difficulty with one subset of the Wechsler scale subtests: Arithmetic, Coding, Information, and Digit Span (Kaufman, 1981). With the exception of Information, these subtests are considered measures of freedom from distractibility (Dudley-Marley, Kaufman, & Tarver, 1981; Kaufman, 1981). Thus, this *WISC–R* performance pattern may point to the disorders of attention and concentration associated with learning disabilities. It is important to note that these subtests represent areas of *relative* weakness for most learning disabled students. While students may show their lowest scores on these subtests, the scores they earn typically remain within the average range of performance (Kavale & Forness, 1984).

Another area of *WISC–R* research has been the investigation of discrepancies between Verbal IQ and Performance IQ. Learning disabled students often perform quite differently on these *WISC–R* scales, but so do other groups of students including nonhandicapped students (Kaufman, 1981). In one study of the *WISC–R* profiles of more than 450 learning disabled children, verbal-performance discrepancies were found in only 10 percent more of the students than would be expected in a nonhandicapped population (Shepard et al., 1983). Learning disabled students may show discrepancies between Verbal and Performance IQ scores, but this is not a definitive sign of learning disabilities.

Individually administered tests of achievement are also a standard component of the learning disabilities assessment battery. These tests focus on basic school skills such as reading and math. They usually do not include measures of content subjects like science, social studies, and history. Some school achievement tests survey several skill areas.

For example, the *Peabody Individual Achievement Test* (Dunn & Markwardt, 1970) is made up of five subtests: Reading Recognition, Reading Comprehension, Mathematics, Spelling, and General Information. Other tests are designed to evaluate one skill area in depth. The *Key Math Diagnostic Arithmetic Test* (Connolly, Nachtman, & Pritchett, 1976), for instance, contains 14 different measures of mathematics performance.

A disturbing finding of the studies of school assessment practices is that early tests of perception and psychological processing are still in use today, despite heavy criticism of their technical adequacy. Unreliable tests have no place in any assessment battery, and tests with questionable validity provide meaningless and potentially harmful information. One explanation for the continued use of these instruments is that few new measures have been developed to take their place. The scarcity of appropriate measures explains the practice of using inappropriate tests, but it does not excuse it. If a technically adequate test is not available, no test should be administered.

There has been much criticism in recent years of assessment practices in learning disabilities. One concern is misidentification. In one large-scale study, over 50 percent of the students identified as learning disabled in school assessments failed to meet definitional criteria for this handicap (Shepard & Smith, 1983). Another difficulty in assessment is the lack of standards for evaluating assessment results. Because of this, school assessment personnel have been forced to rely upon professional judgment in deciding whether a particular student satisfies the eligibility requirements for learning disabilities services (Perlmutter & Parus, 1983). This has resulted in inconsistent educational decisions and, at times, inappropriate ones (Ysseldyke, Thurlow, Graden, Wesson, Algozzine, & Deno, 1983).

CONSIDERATIONS IN INTERVENTION

Most learning disabled individuals require some type of intervention at one time or another during their lifespan. Most typically, this intervention is a special educational program designed to improve academic performance during the elementary and secondary grades.

The following sections describe the range of interventions available, first for school-age students and then for preschool children and adults. Educational interventions are emphasized, because special education is the most usual treatment approach to the learning and social-emotional needs of the learning disabled population.

From the beginning of kindergarten to graduation from high school, learning disabled children and youth are entitled to special educational services if their handicap interferes with school performance. Most students with learning disabilities continue in regular educational programs while they are receiving special education services. In the 1981–82 school year, 80 percent of the learning disabled students in the United States received part-time special education services in a resource room or other setting (U.S. Department of Education, 1984) while spending the rest of their school day in regular classes. Separate special classes were provided to only 18 percent of the learning disabled population, and less than 2 percent attended separate schools or other segregated educational environments.

Mainstreaming is one of the major trends affecting the education of learning disabled students. In a true mainstreaming program, handicapped and nonhandicapped students are integrated socially and instructionally, not just physically (Kaufman, Gottlieb, Agard, & Kukic, 1975). Many learning disabled students who are members of regular classes are not integrated socially. They tend to be isolated from and rejected by their nonhandicapped peers (Siperstein & Goding, 1983).

There has been much research comparing the effects of regular class placement versus special class placement for mildly handicapped students, and the findings are conflicting. One review of the literature found few advantages for full-time special classes, except perhaps for students with IQs near the retardation range (Madden & Slavin, 1983). In contrast, another analysis concluded that, although special classes were generally inferior, they were least effective for lower IQ students (Carlberg & Kavale, 1980, as reported in Kavale & Glass, 1982). For learning disabled pupils and others with average intelligence, special classes were more beneficial than regular classes. Kavale and Glass (1982) noted that "the average learning disabled (LD) or behaviorally/emotionally disturbed (BD/ED) pupil in a special class was better off than 61 percent of those placed in a regular class" (pp. 5–6).

One explanation for these conflicting results is that efficacy studies are considering the wrong variable. The critical determinant of student success is not the setting in which education takes place (Leinhardt & Pallay, 1982). It is the educational practices that take place in that setting. According to Leinhardt and Pallay (1982), because effective instruction can occur in most settings, handicapped students should be placed in the least restrictive educational environment.

The mainstreaming movement has led to changes in the role of learning disability specialists. With more handicapped students moving into regular classes and remaining in the mainstream, special education resource teachers are expected to act as consultants to regular educators. Where once the learning disability teacher's major role was the delivery of instruction, now he or she is viewed both as an instructor and as a consultant (Davis, 1983; Freeman & Becker, 1979). The consultant role is a new one for many special educators, and in many programs teachers continue to spend most of their time in instructional activities.

However, in one study, regular classroom teachers, resource teachers, and principals agreed that more of the special educator's time should be devoted to consultation (Evans, 1981).

Noncategorical programming in special education is another important trend. This approach integrates students with various handicapping conditions within the same special education resource room or special class. The most usual arrangement is to combine mildly handicapped students—those with learning disabilities, behavior disorders, and mild mental retardation—into one group for instruction. As yet, there are few empirical studies of the effects of noncategorical programming. However, one study reported that learning disabled students achieved positive academic gains in a noncategorical special education program (Idol-Maestas, Lloyd, & Lilly, 1981).

Although noncategorical approach to service delivery appears to be gaining popularity (Blackhurst, 1981; Sparks & Richardson, 1981), professionals do not seem to favor this practice. In a survey of school personnel, special educators advised against merging the categories of learning disabilities and mental retardation in the delivery of services (Gaar & Plue, 1983). Over 90 percent of the teachers in learning disabilities programs favored the continuation of a separate category system.

Educational Interventions.

The goal of educational services for students with learning disabilities is to decrease the discrepancy between ability and achievement. Most educational programs, past and present, have approached this task by providing remedial instruction in the basic skills of reading, mathematics, and language arts. Interest in the development of remedial programs for learning disabled individuals dates back to the work of early clinicians such as Fernald (1943) and Monroe (1932). Today, basic skills training continues to take precedence over other educational goals in public school programs for students with learning disabilities.

Learning disability teachers see the teaching of basic skills as one of the most important professional competencies for special educators (Davis, 1983; Freeman & Becker, 1979). In addition, teachers report that the majority of the school day is devoted to basic skills instruction (Houck & Given, 1981). Reading and math instruction are allocated the most instructional time, but language arts are also part of the curriculum. The National Joint Committee on Learning Disabilities (1982) endorsed this practice in a recent position paper on educational services:

> For individuals with learning disabilities, the primary instructional or remedial focus should be on activities directly related to the enhancement of functioning in the areas of manifested disabilities, i.e., listening, speaking, reading, writing, reasoning, and mathematics.

The findings of several recent observational studies confirm the basic skills emphasis in current learning disabilities programs (Leinhardt, Zigmond, & Cooley, 1981; Thurlow, Graden, Greener, & Ysseldyke, 1983; Thurlow, Ysseldyke, Graden, & Algozzine, 1983; Zigmond, Vallecorsa, & Leinhardt, 1980). Special education programs for the learning disabled concentrate on academic instruction, particularly in reading, and instruction is delivered individually or to small groups of learners. However, both in special education and regular education, there is a discrepancy between the time scheduled for academic activities and the time students actually spend actively participating in academic activities.

Another emphasis in educational programs is the improvement of student behavior (Davis, 1983; Freeman & Becker, 1979). Many students with learning disabilities have classroom conduct problems that are related to their handicap. For example, they may act impulsively, fail to attend, or be highly distractible. The social and interpersonal skills of learning disabled students may also be poor, resulting in their lack of acceptance by nonhandicapped peers. Thus, the management of behavior and the improvement of interpersonal skills are important components of the educational program for learning disabled students.

In secondary level programs for learning disabled students, there appears to be some concern with career awareness and vocational preparation. In one survey of school programs for learning disabled adolescents, the most commonly identified need was to provide appropriate vocational and career education services (McNutt & Heller, 1978). Secondary special educators view skill in teaching career and vocationally related subjects as important (Freeman & Becker, 1979). However, it is not clear to what extent career education is systematically included in school programs for learning disabled students.

One study of educational programs for adolescents with learning disabilities found that five different curricular approaches were in use (Deshler, Lowrey, & Alley, 1979). The most common was basic skills training. This approach, reported by 45 percent of the programs surveyed, emphasizes remedial instruction in basic skills such as reading and mathematics. A tutorial approach was reported by 24 percent of the programs. In the tutorial approach, teachers focus on content area subjects, not basic skills, and the goal is to maintain the learning disabled student in the regular secondary curriculum. Seventeen percent of the schools surveyed provided a functional curriculum to learning disabled adolescents. Programs with a functional curriculum emphasize career counseling, skills of independent living, and survival academic skills such as money management and completing job applications. Only 5 percent of the programs said that they had adopted a work-study approach. In work-study programs, students learn job skills and practice those skills in on-the-job training experiences. The least common curricular approach for educating learning disabled adolescents was learning strategies training.

Thus, basic skills appear to be the major focus of the curriculum for learning disabled students both at the elementary and secondary levels. However, at the secondary level, there are other options available. Tutoring in regular class content area subjects is one of these options, and it seems an appropriate one for mildly learning disabled students who are able to succeed in mainstream classes. At the other extreme are the functional skills curriculum and the work-study option. These may be most appropriate for students who are severely learning disabled (Deshler et al., 1979). It is unlikely that any one curriculum will meet the needs of all learning disabled students.

Instructional Approaches.

For most learning disabled students, the ultimate goal of the special education program is preparation for successful integration into the mainstream of the school and into the mainstream of adult society. Because it is believed that the skills taught to normal learners are also important for learning disabled students, there is considerable overlap between the regular school curriculum and the curriculum offered in the special class or resource room.

At the elementary level, both the regular and the special curriculum focus on the acquisition of basic academic skills. What differentiates regular and special education for learning disabled students in the elementary grades is not the skills that are taught but the methods used to teach them. At the secondary level, special educators continue to use different instructional strategies, and differences begin to appear between the regular curriculum and that provided to learning disabled adolescents. While many secondary special education programs continue to emphasize basic skills, regular education programs progress to the teaching of content subjects such as English, history, and science.

There are a variety of special instructional methods and techniques available to teach basic skills, social skills, and other content to students with learning disabilities. Some of these methods date from the early years of learning disability programming. Since that time, there have been major changes in professional thinking about the best way to educate learning disabled students. As a result, many of the traditional instructional methods in learning disabilities have fallen into disfavor.

An example is the deficit remediation model. In the 1960s and early 1970s, the major instructional approach in learning disabilities was the remediation of psychological processing deficits. First, students were tested with one or more of the popular perception or processing tests in an attempt to identify their strengths and weaknesses. Then, instruction focused on the weaknesses. It was thought that, if disorders of perception and other psychological processes could be remediated (that is, remedied), students would then be able to learn to read, write, and calculate. For instance, if a student with reading problems also showed a disorder in visual perception, the instructional program would emphasize improving the student's perceptual abilities.

Studies of the deficit remediation approach have provided little support for its effectiveness. Perceptual-motor training appears to produce few positive effects (Kavale & Glass, 1982), and only minimal gains result from training psycholinguistic processes (Hammill & Larsen, 1974, 1978; Kavale, 1981; Larsen, Parker, & Hammill, 1982). The results are quite clear: training deficit psychological processes does not result in substantial improvements in psychological processing, nor does it lead to significant improvement in academic performance (Arter & Jenkins, 1979).

Another instructional method that did not prove successful was the preferred modality approach. In this method, students were classified according to their strongest sensory channel (or modality). Some were considered visual learners, others auditory learners, and still others kinesthetic learners. Then, academic instruction was geared to the student's strength, his or her preferred modality. For example, in the teaching of reading, instruction for auditory learners might stress phonetic analysis whereas instruction for visual learners would emphasize sight word recognition. Teaching to the student's strength or preferred modality has not turned out to be a useful approach. As Larrivee (1981) concluded in a review of the research on modality preference and reading instruction: "Differentiating instruction according to modality preference apparently does not facilitate learning to read" (p. 180).

At about the same time that professionals were beginning to question the effectiveness of modality preference, the behavioral approach to instruction began to gain support. This approach deemphasizes learner characteristics and concentrates instead upon the skill to be taught and the procedures the teacher should follow in teaching. It incorporates the technique of task analysis with the applied behavior analysis technology for managing student behaviors. The first step is task analysis. The skill to be taught is analyzed into component subskills. Second, the sequence of instruction is determined, and instructional objectives are specified for each step in the sequence. Objectives describe the behavior of interest precisely, so that it can be observed and measured. Then, instruction is delivered with careful attention to reinforcement and other techniques for managing academic behaviors. Finally, the effects of instruction are carefully monitored and instructional strategies are modified as necessary.

Today, most instructional programs for learning disabled students incorporate the principles of the behavioral approach. For example, Kirk and Chalfant (1984) describe a series of steps for remedial teaching that reflect many of the major components of the behavioral approach: task analysis, specification of objectives, the provision of feedback to learners, reinforcement of appropriate responses, and continual monitoring of the effectiveness of instruction.

One of the current trends in academic instruction for learning disabled students is direct instruction (Lloyd & Carnine, 1981; Reith, Polsgrove, & Semmel, 1981; Stevens & Rosenshine, 1981). This approach has developed from the research on teacher effectiveness, and it addresses the teacher behaviors associated with student achievement. It is related to the behavioral approach in that it stresses teacher behaviors, not learner characteristics.

In direct instruction, academics are the major focus (Stevens & Rosenshine, 1981; Weil & Murphy, 1982). Teachers, not students, direct classroom learning activities, and teachers hold high expectations for the academic progress of their students (Weil & Murphy, 1982). Instruction is systematic (Stevens & Rosenhine, 1981). The teacher demonstrates the skill to be learned, and students practice that skill. In the first stages of learning, students practice under the direct supervision of the teacher who provides prompts and corrections. Later, students practice independently. One of the primary goals of direct instruction is to increase the amount of time in which students are actively engaged in academic learning.

As yet, most of the research on direct instruction has studied regular class populations, not special learners. However, Lewis (1983) suggests that direct

Providing short, specific instructions on how to complete a task is one instructional technique practiced with learning disabled students.

instruction may also be an appropriate instructional strategy for learning disabled students because it attempts to activate learners and ensure that they are engaged in the learning task.

Not all of the instructional approaches used with learning disabled students are directed toward the mastery of basic academic skills. For example, compensation may be the goal for some older students who have not achieved basic skills proficiency. In the compensatory approach, students are trained to bypass their academic deficiencies by using other skills. Instead of reading textbooks, for instance, the student may listen to a tape recording of the textbook material (Deshler & Graham, 1980). The compensatory approach is most often used at the secondary and college levels to allow learning disabled students with poor basic skills to participate in regular classes.

A new area of interest is the training of learning strategies. Learning disabled students appear to be characterized by inefficient cognitive strategies, and there is some evidence that strategy performance can be improved by training. Preliminary efforts to train learning strategies have met with success, and it is interesting to note that these efforts have used direct instruction teaching methodologies.

Most of the research on cognitive strategy training has concentrated on the improvement of memory and attention. As described earlier in this chapter,

Torgesen (1980) and his colleagues have used strategy training to eliminate differences in memory performance between learning disabled and normal students. When learning disabled students were required to rehearse or to use mnemonic strategies such as chunking, their ability to recall improved dramatically. Other researchers have also reported success in training memorization strategies. Connor (1983) improved the recall of learning disabled children by providing direct instruction in the use of study strategies. Memory performance improved, and students were able to transfer the strategies they had learned to other memory tasks.

Attentional disorders have responded to strategy training. In this line of research, the most common treatment approach has been the use of cognitive behavior modification. In cognitive behavior modification or cognitive training, students learn how to manage their own learning in some way. They may learn to monitor their own behavior, to present themselves with task instructions, or to correct their own errors. In one group of studies, the use of self-monitoring by learning disabled students improved their attention to task and increased academic productivity (Hallahan et al., 1983; Hallahan & Sapona, 1983; Kneedler & Hallahan, 1981). Other cognitive behavior modification techniques such as self-instruction and self-correction have also been found effective in improving academic performance (Kosiewicz, Hallahan, Lloyd, & Graves, 1982).

Researchers at the University of Kansas have developed and tested a learning strategies curriculum for adolescents with learning disabilities (Alley et al., 1983; Deshler et al., 1982; Schumaker et al., 1983). This instructional program is designed to train academic learning and study strategies identified as important for school success at the secondary level. Evaluation results indicate that the program is effective in improving learning disabled students' ability to use appropriate strategies for academic tasks such as reading comprehension, theme writing, listening, and notetaking. Other researchers have successfully trained academic learning strategies in elementary grade populations (Hallahan et al., 1983). For example, in one study, training in strategies for multiplication and division improved the math performance of young learning disabled boys (Lloyd, Saltzman, & Kauffman, 1981).

Another area of concern is the improvement of social skills. Strategy training may be of value here too. Learning disabled students may be able to acquire social skills through cognitively-based methods such as modeling, coaching, and self-control training (Gresham, 1981). Zigmond and her colleagues recommend that social skills be taught directly to learning disabled students (Silverman, Zigmond, & Sansone, 1981; Zigmond & Brownlee, 1980). They propose a school survival skills curriculum which includes instruction in behavior control, teacher-pleasing behaviors, and study skills.

In social skills training and in other kinds of instruction, it is important to consider the transfer or generalization of skills. If academic and social skills are to be of value to learning disabled students, students must be able to apply them in new settings and new situations. Skills do not always transfer automatically. Often, it is necessary to train learning disabled students to generalize what they have learned. For example, in a set of studies, learning disabled adolescents were

Learning Strategy Training

The learning strategies curriculum developed by researchers at the University of Kansas (Alley et al., 1983; Deshler et al., 1982; Schumaker et al., 1983) holds real promise for secondary grade students with learning disabilities. The goal of this curriculum is the development of effective strategies for academic learning, and research results indicate that this approach does improve academic performance (Deshler et al., 1982).

Learning strategy training is organized around two skill areas necessary for success at the secondary level: gaining information from written and oral materials, and expressing information in writing. According to Schumaker and others (1983), the learning strategies included in the curriculum are:

Strand 1: Strategies for Gaining Information
- Word Identification
- Visual Imagery
- Self-Questioning
- Paraphrasing
- Interpreting Visual Aids
- Multipass (a strategy for studying textbook chapters)
- S.O.S. (an adaptation of Multipass for students with severe reading problems)
- Listening-Notetaking

Strand 2: Strategies for Expressing Information
- Sentence Writing
- Paragraph Writing
- Theme Writing
- Error Monitoring
- Test Preparation
- Memorization
- Test-Taking
- Assignment Completion

The Multipass strategy for studying textbook chapters has been described by Schumaker, Deshler, Alley, Warner, and Denton (1982). This strategy is made up of three substrategies, each of which is trained separately. First, students learn to "pass" through a chapter using the Survey substrategy. The purpose here is to preview the chapter and become familiar with its main ideas and organization. Students are taught to use specific techniques for previewing, such as reading the chapter title, reading the introductory and summary paragraphs, and reading major subtitles within the chapter. When students have mastered this strategy, they learn how to make a second pass through the chapter using the Size-Up substrategy. The goal here is to gain specific facts and information without reading the entire chapter from start to finish. Sort-Out is the third substrategy and, in this pass, students test themselves on the chapter's material by answering the questions at the end of the chapter.

One instructional method is used to train students to use appropriate learning strategies (Deshler, Alley, Warner, & Schumaker, 1981). In this method, the first step is analysis of the student's current learning strategies. The student is asked to perform a task requiring the strategy to be trained, in order to make the student aware that his or her current strategy is ineffective. Then, the teacher describes the new strategy and models it. Before practice begins, the student verbally rehearses the steps in the strategy. This helps students commit the steps to memory, so that later they can provide themselves with prompts, without having to rely upon the teacher. Practice takes place first in controlled materials such as high-interest low-vocabulary texts. Then, students practice with regular classroom materials. During each of the steps in strategy acquisition, the teacher monitors the student's performance and provides corrective feedback.

Instruction does not end when students have learned the strategies. It is not sufficient to train students within a special education setting and assume that they will transfer what they have learned to the regular education classroom. Deshler and others (1981) maintain that the real measure of instruction is "the degree to which the student can generalize the acquired strategy to the *regular classroom when using regular class materials* and then maintain the strategy over time" (p. 418).

There are many ways to promote the generalization of skills, and Deshler and others (1981) adopt several of the techniques suggested by Stokes and Baer (1977). When training students to use a strategy, teachers should provide several types of tasks in which the strategy can be practiced, and these tasks should be as diverse as possible. Once students have initial mastery of a strategy, training for generalization can begin. At this point, the teacher should "train loosely" by varying the format of lessons, the instructions given to students, and the examples used. If possible, students should practice in a variety of settings, under different instructional conditions, and with different teachers and tutors. Reinforcement should now be intermittent and delayed, not immediate and continuous as in the initial stages of learning. And, students should be trained to ask for feedback and reinforcement from their regular classroom teachers and others.

The last technique for generalization training that Deshler and others (1981) suggest is a very simple but powerful one:

Perhaps the least expensive and certainly the most straightforward technique for promoting generalization of behaviors is simply to tell students to generalize what they have learned. . . . Too frequently, we assume that students will see the connection between what is taught in the resource room and what is demanded of them in the regular classroom. It should never be assumed that a student will realize that skills taught and practiced in the resource room are to be applied in other settings. Frequent reminders to "try out" and "practice" what was taught in the resource room in different settings and with different contents can be very effective. (p. 420)

taught several types of social skills (Alley et al., 1983; Schumaker et al., 1983). Although students were able to demonstrate their newly learned skills in role-playing situations, these did not necessarily transfer to the natural environment.

Medical Interventions.   Although the primary way of treating learning disabilities is through educational interventions, some learning disabled students are also treated medically. Information about a student's physical condition and health status may not assist educators in planning the instructional program (Johnston, 1982; Reed, 1979), but teachers and other school professionals should be aware of the more common medical treatments, particularly those that may affect students' classroom performance.

One medical intervention often associated with learning disabilities is the use of drug therapy to treat hyperactivity. Stimulant medications such as dextroamphetamine (dexedrine) and methylphenidate (ritalin) are prescribed in an attempt to reduce hyperactive behavior and the accompanying symptoms of poor attention and distractibility. This type of medical intervention appears to be quite common. According to Gadow (1983b), approximately 1 to 2 percent of all elementary school students receive drug therapy for hyperactivity.

Much research has been conducted in an attempt to determine the effects of stimulant drugs on hyperactivity and other problem behaviors. As yet, results are inconclusive. It appears that stimulant medication may increase on-task behavior and academic productivity (Gadow, 1981, 1983a, 1983b). There are positive effects for behavioral and cognitive outcomes such as activity level, attention, concentration, and achievement (Kavale, 1982). However, the educational gains are short-term gains, not long-term gains (Aman, 1980). Childhood improvements in academic performance do not persist into adolescence and adulthood (Gadow, 1983a). Another serious concern are the negative effects of drug therapy upon the child's physical condition (Kavale, 1982).

Other, more controversial medical interventions have also been proposed for the treatment of hyperactivity. Levine (1982) warns that "unsubstantiated treatments frequently become popularized and acclaimed in the media, the press, in communities and schools" (p. 301). Some of the more controversial treatments suggested for the treatment of learning disabilities are neurophysiologic training regimes such as the Doman-Delacato patterning program (Delacato, 1963), megavitamin therapy, dietary treatments for hypoglycemia, and the Feingold diet (Feingold, 1975, 1976). None of these controversial treatments has been established as effective (Sieben, 1977). However, several continue to enjoy popularity.

An example is the dietary treatment proposed by Feingold (1975, 1976). According to Feingold, hyperactivity is caused by an allergic reaction to food additives, particularly artificial colors and flavors. To treat hyperactivity, children are placed on a special diet which excludes all foods containing artificial additives, dyes, and natural salicylates. This diet is very restrictive because additives are found in many foods. And, many foods are natural sources of salicylates (e.g., almonds, apples, cherries, cucumbers, grapes, oranges, many types of berries, tea, tomatoes, and others). The Feingold diet also prohibits aspirin, any medications with artificial colors or flavors, and toothpastes and toothpowders.

There have been several studies of the effects of the Feingold diet upon hyperactivity. Research results indicate that this treatment is not an effective method of reducing hyperactivity (Kavale & Forness, 1983; Mattes, 1983). Despite the lack of research support, interest in the Feingold diet continues, and some professionals urge continued study of this approach (Rimland, 1983). However, many professionals caution against the use of the Feingold treatment, both because its effectiveness is unsupported and because of the stress it places upon the child and the family.

Many controversial medical (and pseudomedical) treatments have been proposed for learning disabilities in the past, and it is likely that this will continue in the future. Fads and "cures" seem to appear more often for learning disabilities than for other exceptionalities. Parents and professionals should proceed cautiously when new treatments are described as panaceas. Physicians can offer valuable assistance in the evaluation of new medical interventions. In fact, Levine (1982) suggests that one of the physician's key roles in the treatment of learning disabilities is to help parents and schools evaluate controversial medical treatments.

The Preschool and Adult Years

Preschool children are usually not identified as learning disabled. There are several reasons for this. Most important, many young learning disabled children do not begin to experience learning problems until they enter school. For those that do show disorders of learning, differential diagnosis is often difficult. Also, special education programs for this age group are not mandated in many states (O'Connell, 1983), and professionals may be reluctant to stigmatize young children by labeling them as handicapped (Leigh & Riley, 1982).

Intervention at the preschool level is typically a noncategorical educational program that emphasizes important developmental skills. Lerner (1981) says that preschool programs for young learning disabled children "generally include instruction in four areas: cognitive development, perceptual-motor development, language development, and preacademic skills development" (p. 454). For example, one early intervention program for young handicapped children stresses the curriculum areas of body management, self-care, communication, preacademics, and socialization (McCarthy, Lund, & Bos, 1983).

Preschool educational services may be delivered in the child's home, in a school-based program, or in a combination of these settings. Whatever the location, an important factor in the success of any early intervention program is the active involvement of the family of the young learning disabled child. That involvement may take the form of a warm and supportive home environment, or family members may choose to participate in the handicapped child's educational program by providing opportunities for the practice of new skills at home.

Intervention in the adult years is relatively new, but there are a growing number of postsecondary settings that offer services to learning disabled adults (Vogel, 1982). Most typically, services for this population are educational in nature and they are provided in conjunction with regular educational programs at community colleges and four-year colleges and universities. In addition, vocational rehabilitation services have recently become available to adults with learning disabilities (Gerber, 1981).

Adults with learning disabilities may be characterized by academic underachievement, poor social perception and peer relationships, problems in attention and impulsivity, and below average career success (Patton & Polloway, 1982). To meet these needs, most postsecondary educational programs offer a wide range of services.

Counseling services may be available (Gray, 1981), and these can take several forms: academic counseling, vocational and career counseling, and counseling to assist adults with interpersonal problems. College programs may also offer special instructional services to learning disabled adults. These could include remedial basic skills programs, study skills training, and academic tutoring in regular college courses (Blalock & Dixon, 1982; Gray, 1981).

Perhaps the most common strategy for assisting learning disabled college students is to provide support within the regular education program. This occurs in two ways. In the first method, the goal is to assist students to meet the requirements of the institution (Blalock & Dixon, 1982). For example, to help students succeed in regular college classes, compensatory aids such as taped textbooks, readers, and notetakers may be provided. In the second approach, course instructors and the institution itself make reasonable modifications in academic requirements (Vogel, 1982). For example, the institution may allow reduced course loads, substitution or waiver of required courses, and differential admissions standards (Blalock & Dixon, 1982). Or, course instructors may permit the use of alternative procedures for exams. Possible modifications are untimed examinations, the use of a reader for objective tests, and the acceptance of oral or taped responses to exam questions in lieu of handwritten answers (Vogel, 1982).

In a recent survey of over 100 community colleges within the state of California, more than 75 percent provided formal programs for learning disabled adults and an additional 12 percent offered informal programs (Ostertag, Baker, Howard, & Best, 1982). Among the most common services for learning disabled college students were tutorial support, availability of learning centers for remediation, auxiliary services such as readers and notetakers, modification of class scheduling, and counseling.

FUTURE PERSPECTIVES FOR THE TREATMENT OF LEARNING DISABILITIES

Many of the challenges facing the field of learning disabilities today are not new ones. Definitional problems persist, and the search continues for appropriate operational criteria for the identification of learning disabilities in young children, school-age students, and adults. Research on characteristics is just beginning to describe the ways in which learning disabled individuals interact with the learning tasks they are required to perform. In intervention, ineffective instructional strategies have been identified, and research continues in an attempt to develop and validate educational and medical treatments that consistently produce positive results for individuals with learning disabilities.

One major concern today is the increasing number of children and youth being identified as learning disabled. As Kirk and Chalfant (1984) have noted, the percentage of the school-age population receiving learning disabilities services has increased while, in the same period, the numbers of speech impaired and mentally retarded students have declined. Learning disabilities is the most commonly identified learning problem in schools today. It is probable that this is due at least in part to the difficulty in distinguishing between underachievement due to learning disabilities and underachievement due to other causes. If the learning disabled segment of the school population continues its growth, professionals may be forced to seriously address the problem of misidentification.

Another important area of concern is the effectiveness of integration, not only the integration of handicapped and nonhandicapped peers in mainstreamed settings but also the mix of students with different exceptionalities in special education settings. The merits of regular class placement for learning disabled students are still under investigation, and systematic study of the effects of noncategorical programming on child achievement is just beginning. What may result, dependent upon the outcome of these empirical investigations, is a realignment of the educational service delivery system for individuals with learning disabilities.

The late 1970s and early 1980s was a period of tremendous growth for the field of learning disabilities. School programs for children and youth expanded, services for learning disabled adults were begun, and the research base forming the foundation for educational practice increased dramatically. Changes will continue to occur in the coming years, and it is hoped they will produce the following results:

Computer Technologies and Learning Disabilities

Microcomputer technology has the potential for improving the way in which schools prepare learning disabled students for their roles in adult society. At present, the major use of computers in the classroom is the delivery of computer-assisted instruction. In most cases, instructional software programs offer the opportunity for drill and practice. Few are tutorial programs, attempting to present new information.

Drill and practice may be one of the least creative applications of computer technology, but it is an excellent one for students with learning disabilities. These students do not learn academic skills easily and effortlessly. They need drill, they need unlimited practice opportunities, and they need to receive feedback about the accuracy of their responses. Instructional software provides this type of learning environment. The computer can act as a tireless tutor that offers continual, nonjudgmental feedback.

Word processing is another important computer application for learning disabled persons. Writing is one of the most difficult skills for learning disabled students to master, and word processing programs take much of the drudgery out of writing. With word processors, mistakes are easy to correct. A letter, word, or an entire paragraph can be erased and then replaced with another. Any type of text—letters, words, phrases, sentences, paragraphs, even pages—can be deleted, inserted, or moved from one place to another. What has been written can be stored and retrieved later to use again.

And, there are programs that help students to proofread their writing and check their spelling and grammar. Spelling programs contain a dictionary, and they work by trying to match every word that the student has written with a dictionary entry. When the program encounters a word that cannot be matched, the student is informed. Some programs even offer to "guess" at the correct spelling of the word.

At present, learning disabled individuals face some barriers in their attempts to use microcomputers and computer software. Most current computer applications rely heavily on the ability to read and the ability to type, skills that learning disabled persons may not possess. However, already we are seeing new ways of interacting with computers that may alleviate these problems. Today's computers can present information not only in words but also in pictures, speech, and music. People can respond by typing or by touching the screen, manipulating a joystick, moving a mouse, or speaking using a voice input device.

One of the most exciting prospects for classrooms of the future is interactive videodisc technology. Videodiscs are devices that store moving or still visual images and auditory information. These devices can be used with microcomputers so that students can view and listen to dynamic video displays similar to videotapes or movies. This capability has enormous potential for instruction. Using videodisc technology, students can interact with a limitless variety of subject matters, situations, and people.

Think, for example, about a videodisc program to teach social skills. Such a program could present a rule for interacting with others and then pose a problem situation in which the student has to apply the rule. The problem situation would be acted out for the student. He or she would watch other persons interacting, not merely read or hear about it. The solution the student chooses would also be portrayed in video. And, if the solution was not the correct one, the student could choose again and watch that selection come to life.

- Better understanding of the condition of learning disabilities, its characteristics, and its effects upon learning and performance.
- Increased knowledge about the causes of this disability and improved techniques for its prevention.
- More effective methods for the detection of learning disabilities, particularly in young children and in individuals with diverse linguistic and cultural backgrounds.

- Improved educational interventions which are effective, efficient, and humane.
- Better utilization of modern technologies to promote true individualization of instruction.
- A broadened conceptualization of the nature of education for learning disabled individuals, to include lifelong learning and increased concern for content other than basic skills.

SUMMARY

The handicap of learning disabilities is a cognitive disorder which affects learning and social-emotional development. Its primary impact is felt during the school years when learning disabled children and youth experience extreme difficulty in the acquisition and use of basic academic skills. Learning disabilities are defined as a significant discrepancy between actual and expected achievement in important life skills. Underachievement that can be explained by other handicaps, cultural factors, or environmental disadvantage is excluded from this category. Learning disabilities are the most commonly identified handicap among the school-age population, and they are of concern to the disciplines of education, psychology, and medicine.

Many possible causes of learning disabilities have been identified. Among these are neurological damage and other medical factors, heredity, and environmental influences. Individuals with learning disabilities are characterized by the difficulties they encounter in learning. Attention and memory disorders are common, school achievement is poor, and learning disabled individuals may fail to produce or to apply appropriate strategies for learning. Learning disabilities also affect social-emotional development. In general, learning disabled students are less popular than peers, show lower self-esteem, and are less adept in social interactions.

Differentiation between achievement problems due to learning disabilities and those due to other factors has not proved to be an easy task. Definitions of learning disabilities are not easily transformed into specific identification criteria. In school programs, learning disabilities are assessed with a battery of psychological and educational tests including measures of intellectual performance and academic achievement. Tests of perception and psychological processes continue to be used, despite criticism of their measurement qualities.

The most common intervention for individuals with learning disabilities is the provision of educational services during the school years. Most learning disabled students are mainstreamed into regular education programs while also receiving part-time special education services. The primary goal of educational services is the improvement of basic skills deficiencies. Strategy training is one of the most promising instructional approaches in current research. Attempts to train learning disabled students in strategies for academic task performance, attention to task, and memorization have met with success. Attention disorders, impulsivity, and hyperactivity are treated medically with drug therapy, but research results are less conclusive. For the small number of preschool children identified as learning disabled, educational interventions focus on developmental skills. As adults, learning disabled persons may participate in educational and counseling services at institutions of higher education.

References

Alley, G. R., Deshler, D. D., Clark, F. L., Schumaker, J. B., & Warner, M. M. (1983). Learning disabilities in adolescent and adult populations: Research implications (Part II). *Focus on Exceptional Children, 15* (9), 1–14.

Aman, M. G. (1980). Psychotropic drugs and learning problems—A selective review. *Journal of Learning Disabilities, 13,* 87–97.

Argulewicz, E. N. (1983). Effects of ethnic membership, socioeconomic status, and home language on LD, EMR, and EH placements. *Learning Disability Quarterly, 6,* 195–200.

Arter, J. A., & Jenkins, J. R. (1979). Differential diagnosis-prescriptive teaching: A critical appraisal. *Review of Educational Research, 49,* 517–555.

Axelrod, L. (1982). Social perception in learning disabled adolescents. *Journal of Learning Disabilities, 15,* 610–613.

Barsch, R. H. (1965). *A movigenic curriculum* (Bulletin No. 25). Madison, WI: Department of Public Instruction, Bureau for the Handicapped.

Barsch, R. H. (1967). *Achieving perceptual-motor efficiency* (Vol. 1). Seattle: Special Child Publications.

Beck, R. A. (1982). Effectiveness of discrepancy score methods for screening children with learning disabilities. *Learning Disabilities, 1,* 11–24.

Blackhurst, A. E. (1981). Noncategorical teacher preparation: Problems and promises. *Exceptional Children, 48,* 197–205.

Blalock, G., & Dixon, N. (1982). Improving prospects for the college-bound learning disabled. *Topics in Learning & Learning Disabilities, 2* (3), 69–78.

Bruininks, V. L. (1978). Peer status and personality characteristics of learning disabled and nondisabled students. *Journal of Learning Disabilities, 11,* 484–489.

Bryan, T. H. (1974). Peer popularity of learning disabled children. *Journal of Learning Disabilities, 7,* 621–625.

Bryan, T. H. (1976). Peer popularity of learning disabled children: A replication. *Journal of Learning Disabilities, 9,* 307–311.

Bryan, T. H., & Bryan, J. H. (1977). The social-emotional side of learning disabilities. *Behavioral Disorders, 2,* 141–145.

Bryan, T. H., & Bryan, J. H. (1978). Social interactions of learning disabled children. *Learning Disability Quarterly, 1* (1), 33–38.

Bryan, T., Pearl, R., Donahue, M., Bryan, J., & Pflaum, S. (1983). The Chicago institute for the study of learning disabilities. *Exceptional Educational Quarterly, 4* (1), 1–22.

California Association for Neurologically Handicapped Children. (1980). *If they aren't learning, don't write them off.* Sacramento, CA: Author.

Carlberg, C., & Kavale, K. (1980). The efficacy of special versus regular class placement for exceptional children: A meta-analysis. *Journal of Special Education, 14,* 295–309.

Clements, S. D. (1966). *Minimal brain dysfunction in children, Terminology and identification.* Washington, DC: U.S. Department of Health, Education, and Welfare.

Coles, G. S. (1978). The learning disabilities test battery: Empirical and social issues. *Harvard Educational Review, 48,* 313–340.

Coles, G. S. (1980). Evaluation of genetic explanations of reading and learning problems. *Journal of Special Education, 14,* 365–383.

Colletti, L. F. (1979). Relationship between pregnancy and birth complications and the later development of learning disabilities. *Journal of Learning Disabilities, 12,* 659–663.

Connolly, A. J., Nachtman, W., & Pritchett, E. M. (1976). *KeyMath diagnostic arithmetic test.* Circle Pines, MN: American Guidance Service.

Connor, F. P. (1983). Improving school instruction for learning disabled children: The Teachers College Institute. *Exceptional Education Quarterly, 4* (1), 23–44.

Cruickshank, W. M. (1977). Myths and realities in learning disabilities. *Journal of Learning Disabilities, 10,* 51–58.

Cullinan, D., Epstein, M. H., & Lloyd, J. (1981). School behavior problems of learning disabled and normal girls and boys. *Learning Disability Quarterly, 4,* 163–169.

Cullinan, D., Epstein, M. H., Lloyd, J., & Noel, M. (1980). Development of cognitive tempo in learning disabled and normal children. *Learning Disability Quarterly, 3* (2), 46–53.

Davis, W. E. (1983). Competencies and skills required to be an effective resource teacher. *Journal of Learning Disabilities, 16,* 596–598.

Davis, W. A., & Shepard, L. A. (1983). Specialists' use of tests and clinical judgment in the diagnosis of learning disabilities. *Learning Disability Quarterly, 6,* 128–138.

Decker, S. N., & DeFries, J. C. (1980). Cognitive abilities in families of reading-disabled children. *Journal of Learning Disabilities, 13,* 517–522.

Delacato, C. H. (1963). *The diagnosis and treatment of speech and reading problems.* Springfield, IL: Charles C. Thomas.

DeLoach, T. F., Earl, J. M., Brown, B. S., Poplin, M. S., & Warner, M. M. (1981). LD teachers' perceptions of severely learning disabled students. *Learning Disability Quarterly, 4,* 343–358.

Deno, S. L., Marston, D., & Mirkin, P. (1982). Valid measurement procedures for continuous evaluation of written expression. *Exceptional Children, 48,* 368–371.

Deno, S. L., Mirkin, P. K., & Chiang, B. (1982). Identifying valid measures of reading. *Exceptional Children, 49,* 36–45.

Deshler, D. D., Alley, G. R., Warner, M. M., & Schumaker, J. B. (1981). Instructional practices for promoting skill acquisition and generalization in severely learning disabled adolescents. *Learning Disability Quarterly, 4,* 415–421.

Deshler, D. D., & Graham, S. (1980). Tape recording educational materials for secondary handicapped students. *Teaching Exceptional Children, 12,* 52–54.

Deshler, D. D., Lowrey, N., & Alley, G. R. (1979). Programing alternatives for LD adolescents: A nationwide survey. *Academic Therapy, 14,* 389–397.

Deshler, D. D., Schumaker, J. B., Alley, G. R., Warner, M. M., & Clark, F. L. (1982). Learning disabilities in adolescent and young adult populations: Research implications. *Focus on Exceptional Children, 15* (1), 1–12.

Dudley-Marling, C. C., Kaufman, N. J., & Tarver, S. G. (1981). WISC and WISC-R profiles of learning disabled children: A review. *Learning Disability Quarterly, 4,* 307–319.

Dunn, L. M., & Markwardt, F. C. (1970). *Peabody individual achievement test.* Circle Pines, MN: American Guidance Service.

Evans, S. (1981). Classroom teachers', principals', and resource room teachers' peceptions of the actual and desired roles of the resource teacher. *Journal of Learning Disabilities, 14,* 600–603.

Fafard, M. B., & Haubrich, P. A. (1981). Vocational and social adjustment of learning disabled young adults: A followup study. *Learning Disability Quarterly, 4,* 122–130.

Federal Register. (1977, December 29). Washington, DC, pp. 65082–65085.

Feingold, B. F. (1975). *Why your child is hyperactive.* New York: Random House.

Feingold, B. F. (1976). Hyperkinesis and learning disabilities linked to the ingestion of artificial food colors and flavors. *Journal of Learning Disabilities, 9,* 551–559.

Fernald, G. M. (1943). *Remedial techniques in basic school subjects.* New York: McGraw-Hill.

Forness, S. R., Sinclair, E., & Guthrie, D. (1983). Learning disability discrepancy formulas: Their use in actual practice. *Learning Disability Quarterly, 6,* 107–114.

Frauenheim, J. G. (1978). Academic achievement characteristics of adult males who were diagnosed as dyslexic in childhood. *Journal of Learning Disabilities, 11,* 476–483.

Freeman, M. A., & Becker, R. L. (1979). Competencies for professionals in LD: An analysis of teacher perceptions. *Learning Disability Quarterly, 2* (1), 70–79.

Frostig, M., & Horne, D. (1964). *The Frostig program for the development of visual perception.* Chicago: Follett.

Frostig, M., Lefever, W., & Whittlesey, J. R. B. (1966). *Marianne Frostig developmental test of visual perception* (Rev. 1966). Palo Alto, CA: Consulting Psychologists Press.

Gaar, B. L., & Plue, W. V. (1983). Separate vs. combined categories for mental retardation and specific learning disabilities? *Learning Disability Quarterly, 6,* 77–79.

Gadow, K. D. (1981). Effects of stimulant drugs on attention and cognitive deficits. *Exceptional Education Quarterly, 2* (3), 83–93.

Gadow, K. D. (1983a). Effects of stimulant drugs on academic performance in hyperactive and LD children. *Journal of Learning Disabilities, 16,* 290–299.

Gadow, K. D. (1983b). Pharmacotherapy for learning disabilities. *Learning Disabilities, 2,* 127–140.

Garrett, M. K., & Crump, W. D. (1980). Peer acceptance, teacher preference, and self-appraisal of social status of learning disabled students. *Learning Disability Quarterly, 3* (3), 42–48.

Gerber, P. J. (1981). Learning disabilities and eligibility for vocational rehabilitation: A chronology of events. *Learning Disability Quarterly, 4,* 422–425.

Getman, G. N. (1961). Visual success in reading success. *Journal of the California Optometric Association, 29,* 1–4.

Getman, G. N., & Kane, E. R. (1968). *The physiology of readiness: An action program for the development of perception for children.* Minneapolis, MN: Programs to Accelerate School Success.

Gottesman, R. L., Croen, L. G., & Rotkin, L. G. (1982). Urban second grade children: A profile of good and poor readers. *Journal of Learning Disabilities, 15,* 268–272.

Gray, R. A. (1981). Services for the LD adult: A working paper. *Learning Disability Quarterly, 4,* 426–434.

Gresham, F. M. (1981). Social skills training with handicapped children: A review. *Review of Educational Research, 51,* 139–176.

Gresham, F. M. (1982). Misguided mainstreaming: The case for social skills training with handicapped children. *Exceptional Children, 48,* 422–433.

Haines, D. J., & Torgesen, J. K. (1979). The effects of incentives on rehearsal and short-term memory in children with reading problems. *Learning Disability Quarterly, 2* (2), 48–55.

Hallahan, D. P., Hall, R. J., Ianna, S. O., Kneedler, R. D., Lloyd, J. W., Loper, A. B., & Reeve, R. E. (1983). Summary of research findings at the University of Virginia learning disabilities research institute. *Exceptional Education Quarterly, 4* (1), 95–114.

Hallahan, D. P., & Kauffman, J. M. (1976). *Introduction to learning disabilities: A psycho-behavioral approach.* Englewood Cliffs, NJ: Prentice-Hall.

Hallahan, D. P., & Reeve, R. E. (1980). Selective attention and distractibility. In B. K. Keogh (Ed.), *Advances in special education* (Vol. 1). Greenwich, CT: J.A.I. Press.

Hallahan, D. R., & Sapona, R. (1983). Self-monitoring of attention with learning-disabled children: Past research and current issues. *Journal of Learning Disabilities, 16,* 616–620.

Hammill, D. D., & Larsen, S. C. (1974). The effectiveness of psycholinguistic training. *Exceptional Children, 41,* 5–15.

Hammill, D. D., & Larsen, S. C. (1978). The effectiveness of psycholinguistic training: A reaffirmation of position. *Exceptional Children, 44,* 402–414.

Hermann, K. (1959). *Reading disability: A medical study of word-blindness and related handicaps.* Springfield, IL: Charles C. Thomas.

Hiebert, B., Wong, B., & Hunter, M. (1982). Affective influences on learning disabled adolescents. *Learning Disability Quarterly, 5,* 334–343.

Hinshelwood, J. (1907). Four cases of congenital word-blindness occurring in the same family. *The British Medical Journal, 2,* 1229–1232.

Hobbs, N. (1975). *The futures of children.* San Francisco: Jossey-Bass.

Horowitz, E. C. (1981). Popularity, decentering ability, and role-taking skills in learning disabled and normal children. *Learning Disability Quarterly, 4,* 23–30.

Houck, C., & Given, B. (1981). Status of SLD programs: Indications from a teacher survey. *Learning Disability Quarterly, 4,* 320–325.

Idol-Maestas, L., Lloyd, S., & Lilly, M. S. (1981). A noncategorical approach to direct service and teacher education. *Exceptional Children, 48,* 213–220.

Johnson, D., & Myklebust, H. (1967). *Learning disabilities: Educational principles and practices.* New York: Grune & Stratton.

Johnston, R. B. (1982). Neurological assessment of the learning-disabled child. *Learning Disabilities, 1,* 137–149.

Kaufman, A. S. (1981). The WISC-R and learning disabilities assessment: State of the art. *Journal of Learning Disabilities, 14,* 520–526.

Kaufman, M. J., Gottlieb, J., Agard, J. A., & Kukic, M. D. (1975). Mainstreaming: Toward an explication of the construct. In E. L. Meyen, G. A. Vergason, & R. J. Whelan (Eds.), *Alternatives for teaching exceptional children.* Denver: Love Publishing.

Kavale, K. A. (1980). Learning disability and cultural-economic disadvantage: The case for a relationship. *Learning Disability Quarterly, 3* (3), 97–112.

Kavale, K. A. (1981). Functions of the Illinois Test of Psycholinguistic Abilities (ITPA): Are they trainable? *Exceptional Children, 47,* 496–510.

Kavale, K. A. (1982). The efficacy of stimulant drug treatment for hyperactivity: A meta-analysis. *Journal of Learning Disabilities, 15,* 280–289.

Kavale, K. A., & Forness, S. R. (1983). Hyperactivity and diet treatment: A meta-analysis of the Feingold hypothesis. *Journal of Learning Disabilities, 16,* 324–330.

Kavale, K. A., & Forness, S. R. (1984). A meta-analysis of the validity of Wechsler scale profiles and recategorizations: Patterns or parodies? *Learning Disability Quarterly, 17,* 136–156.

Kavale, K. A., & Glass, G. V. (1982). The efficacy of special education interventions and practices: A compendium of meta-analysis findings. *Focus on Exceptional Children, 15* (4), 1–14.

Kephart, N. C. (1960). *The slow learner in the classroom.* Columbus, OH: Merrill Publishing.

Kephart, N. C. (1963). *The brain injured child in the classroom.* Chicago: National Society for Crippled Children and Adults.

Kirk, S. A., & Chalfant, J. C. (1984). *Academic and developmental learning disabilities.* Denver: Love Publishing.

Kirk, S. A., & Elkins, J. (1975). Characteristics of children enrolled in the Child Service Demonstration Centers. *Journal of Learning Disabilities, 8,* 630–637.

Kirk, S. A., & Kirk, W. D. (1971). *Psycholinguistic learning disabilities: Diagnosis and re-mediation.* Urbana: University of Illinois Press.

Kirk, S. A., McCarthy, J. J., & Kirk, W. D. (1968). *Illinois test of psycholinguistic abilities* (Rev. ed.). Urbana: University of Illinois Press.

Kneedler, R. D., & Hallahan, D. P. (1981). Self-monitoring of on-task behavior with learning-disabled children: Current studies and directions. *Exceptional Education Quarterly, 2* (3), 73–82.

Kneedler, R. D., & Hallahan, D. P. (Eds.) (1983). Research in learning disabilities: Summaries of the institutes. *Exceptional Education Quarterly, 4* (11), entire issue.

Kosiewicz, M. M., Hallahan, D. P., Lloyd, J., & Graves, A. W. (1982). Effects of self-instruction and self-correction procedures on handwriting performance. *Learning Disability Quarterly, 5,* 71–78.

Larrivee, B. (1981). Modality preference as a model for differentiating beginning reading instruction: A review of the issues. *Learning Disability Quarterly, 4,* 180–188.

Larsen, S. C., Parker, R. M., & Hammill, D. D. (1982). Effectiveness of psycholinguistic training: A response to Kavale. *Exceptional Children, 49,* 60–66.

Leigh, J. E., & Riley, N. (1982). Learning disabilities in the early years: Characteristics, assessment, and intervention. *Topics in Learning & Learning Disabilities, 2* (3), 1–15.

Leinhardt, G., & Pallay, A. (1982). Restrictive educational settings: Exile or haven? *Review of Educational Research, 52,* 557–578.

Leinhardt, G., Seewald, A. M., & Zigmond, N. (1982). Sex and race differences in learning disabilities classrooms. *Journal of Educational Psychology, 74,* 835–843.

Leinhardt, G., Zigmond, N., & Cooley, W. (1981). Reading instruction and its effects. *American Educational Research Journal, 18,* 343–361.

Lerner, J. (1981). *Learning disabilities: Theories, diagnosis, and teaching strategies* (3rd ed.). Boston: Houghton Mifflin.

Levine, M. D. (1982). The child with school problems: An analysis of physician participation. *Exceptional Children, 48,* 296–304.

Lewis, R. B. (1983). Learning disabilities and reading: Instructional recommendations from current research. *Exceptional Children, 50,* 230–240.

Lloyd, J., & Carnine, D. W. (1981). Foreword. *Exceptional Education Quarterly, 2* (1), viii–ix.

Lloyd, J., Saltzman, J., & Kauffman, J. (1981). Predictable generalization in academic learning as a result of preskills and strategy training. *Learning Disability Quarterly, 4,* 203–216.

Lynch, E. W., & Lewis, R. B. (1982). Multicultural considerations in assessment and treatment of learning disabilities. *Learning Disabilities, 1,* 93–103.

Madden, N. A., & Slavin, R. E. (1983). Mainstreaming students with mild handicaps: Academic and social outcomes. *Review of Educational Research, 53,* 519–569.

Mardell-Czudnowski, C. D. (1980). The four Ws of current testing practices: Who; what; why; and to whom—An exploratory survey. *Learning Disability Quarterly, 3* (1), 73–83.

Matheny, A. P., & Dolan, A. B. (1974). A twin study of genetic influences in reading achievement. *Journal of Learning Disabilities, 7,* 99–102.

Mattes, J. A. (1983). The Feingold diet: A current reappraisal. *Journal of Learning Disabilities, 16,* 319–323.

McCarthy, J. M., Lund, K. A., & Bos, C. S. (1983). Assessment of young children with special needs. *Focus on Exceptional Children, 15* (5), 1–11.

McKinney, J. D., & Feagans, L. (1983). Adaptive classroom behavior of learning disabled students. *Journal of Learning Disabilities, 16,* 360–367.

McKinney, J. D., McClure, S., & Feagans, L. (1982). Classroom behavior of learning disabled children. *Learning Disability Quarterly, 5,* 45–52.

McLoughlin, J. A., & Lewis, R. B. (1986). *Assessing special students* (2nd ed.). Columbus, OH: Merrill Publishing.

McNutt, G., & Heller, G. (1978). Services for learning disabled adolescents: A survey. *Learning Disability Quarterly, 1* (4), 101–103.

Meier, J. H. (1971). Prevalence and characteristics of learning disabilities found in second grade children. *Journal of Learning Disabilities, 4,* 1–16.

Mercer, C. D., Algozzine, B., & Trifiletti, J. (1979). Early identification—An analysis of the research. *Learning Disability Quarterly, 2* (2), 12–24.

Monroe, M. (1932). *Children who cannot read.* Chicago: University of Chicago Press.

Myklebust, H. R., & Boshes, B. (1969). *Minimal brain damage in children.* Washington, DC: Neurological and Sensory Disease Control Program, Department of Health, Education, and Welfare.

National Advisory Committee on Handicapped Children. (1968). *Special education for handicapping children.* First Annual Report. Washington, DC: U.S. Department of Health, Education, and Welfare.

The National Joint Committee on Learning Disabilities. (1981). *Learning disabilities: Issues on definition.* A position paper of the National Joint Committee on Learning Disabilities, January 30, 1981.

The National Joint Committee on Learning Disabilities. (1982). *Issues in the delivery of educational services to individuals with learning disabilities.* A position paper of the National Joint Committee on Learning Disabilities, February 21, 1982.

Norman, C. A., & Zigmond, N. (1980). Characteristics of children labeled and served as learning disabled in school systems affiliated with Child Service Demonstration Centers. *Journal of Learning Disabilities, 13,* 542–547.

O'Connell, J. C. (1983). Education of handicapped preschoolers: A national survey of services and personnel requirements. *Exceptional Children, 49,* 538–540.

Osgood, C. E. (1957a). A behavioristic analysis. In *Contemporary approaches to cognition.* Cambridge, MA: Harvard University Press.

Osgood, C. E. (1957b). Motivational dynamics of language behavior. In *Nebraska Symposium on Motivation.* Lincoln: University of Nebraska Press.

Ostertag, B. A., Baker, R. E., Howard, R. F., & Best, L. (1982). Learning disabled programs in California community colleges. *Journal of Learning Disabilities, 15,* 535–538.

Pasamanick, B., & Knoblock, H. (1973). The epidemiology of reproductive casualty. In S. Sapir & A. Nitzburg (Eds.), *Children with learning problems.* New York: Brunner/Mazel.

Patten, M. D. (1983). Relationships between self-esteem, anxiety, and achievement in young learning disabled students. *Journal of Learning Disabilities, 16,* 43–45.

Patton, J. R., & Polloway, E. A. (1982). The learning disabled: The adult years. *Topics in Learning & Learning Disabilities, 2* (3), 79–88.

Pearl, R., & Cosden, M. (1982). Sizing up a situation: LD children's understanding of social interactions. *Learning Disability Quarterly, 5,* 371–378.

Perlmutter, B. F., Crocker, J., Cordray, D., & Garstecki, D. (1983). Sociometric status and related personality characteristics of mainstreamed learning disabled adolescents. *Learning Disability Quarterly, 6,* 20–30.

Perlmutter, B. F., & Parus, M. V. (1983). Identifying children with learning disabilities: A comparison of diagnostic procedures across school districts. *Learning Disability Quarterly, 6,* 321–328.

Plisko, V. W., & Owings, J. (1982). *Defining, counting, and characterizing handicapped students in the nation's high schools.* Paper presented at the annual meeting of the AERA Annual Convention, New York. (ERIC Document Reproduction Service No. ED 223 036)

Poplin, M. S. (1981). The severely learning disabled: Neglected or forgotten? *Learning Disability Quarterly, 4,* 330–335.

Reed, H. B. C. (1979). Biological defects and special education—An issue in personnel preparation. *Journal of Special Education, 13*, 9–33.

Reid, D. K., & Hresko, W. P. (1981). *A cognitive approach to learning disabilities.* New York: McGraw-Hill.

Reith, H. J., Polsgrove, L., & Semmel, M. I. (1981). Instructional variables that make a difference: Attention to task and beyond. *Exceptional Education Quarterly, 2* (3), 61–71.

Reynolds, M. C., & Birch, J. W. (1977). *Teaching exceptional children in all America's schools.* Reston, VA: Council for Exceptional Children.

Rimland, B. (1983). The Feingold diet: An assessment of the reviews. *Journal of Learning Disabilities, 16*, 331–333.

Roach, E. G., & Kephart, N. D. (1966). *The Purdue perceptual-motor survey.* Columbus, OH: Merrill Publishing.

Ross, A. O. (1976). *Psychological aspects of learning disabilities and reading disorders.* New York: McGraw-Hill.

Salvia, J., & Ysseldyke, J. E. (1981). *Assessment in special and remedial education* (2nd ed.). Boston: Houghton Mifflin.

Schumaker, J. B., Deshler, D. D., Alley, G. R., & Warner, M. M. (1983). Toward the development of an intervention model for learning disabled adolescents: The University of Kansas institute. *Exceptional Education Quarterly, 4* (1), 45–74.

Schumaker, J. B., Deshler, D. D., Alley, G. R., Warner, M. M., & Denton, P. H. (1982). Multipass: A learning strategy for improving reading comprehension. *Learning Disability Quarterly, 5*, 295–304.

Shepard, L. A., & Smith, M. L. (1983). An evaluation of the identification of learning disabled students in Colorado. *Learning Disability Quarterly, 6*, 115–127.

Shepard, L. A., Smith, M. L., & Vojir, C. P. (1983). Characteristics of pupils identified as learning disabled. *American Educational Research Journal, 20*, 309–331.

Sieben, R. L. (1977). Controversial medical treatments of learning disabilities. *Academic Therapy, 13*, 133–147.

Silverman, R., Zigmond, N., & Sansone, J. (1981). Teaching coping skills to adolescents with learning problems. *Focus on Exceptional Children, 13* (6), 1–20.

Siperstein, G. N., & Goding, M. J. (1983). Social integration of learning disabled children in regular classrooms. *Advances in Learning and Behavioral Disabilities, 2*, 227–263.

Smith, C. R. (1983). *Learning disabilities: The interaction of learner, task, and setting.* Boston: Little, Brown.

Sparks, R., & Richardson, S. O. (1981). Multicategorical/cross-categorical classrooms for learning disabled students. *Journal of Learning Disabilities, 14*, 60–61.

Sternberg, R. J., & Warner, R. K. (1982). Automatization failure in learning disabilities. *Topics in Learning & Learning Disabilities, 2* (2), 1–11.

Stevens, R., & Rosenshine, B. (1981). Advances in research on teaching. *Exceptional Education Quarterly, 2* (1), 1–9.

Stokes, T. F., & Baer, D. M. (1977). An implicit technology of generalization. *Journal of Applied Behavior Analysis, 10*, 349–367.

Strauss, A. A., & Lehtinen, L. (1947). *Psychopathology and education of the brain-injured child* (Vol. I). New York: Grune & Stratton.

Tarver, S., & Maggiore, R. (1979). Cognitive development in learning disabled boys. *Learning Disability Quarterly, 2* (3), 78–84.

Terman, L. M., & Merrill, M. A. (1973). *Stanford-Binet intelligence scale, 1972 norms edition.* Boston: Houghton Mifflin.

Thurlow, M., Graden, J., Greener, J., & Ysseldyke, J. (1983). LD and non-LD students' opportunities to learn. *Learning Disability Quarterly, 6*, 172–183.

Thurlow, M. L., & Ysseldyke, J. E. (1979). Current assessment and decision-making practices in model LD programs. *Learning Disability Quarterly, 2* (4), 15–24.

Thurlow, M. L., Ysseldyke, J. E., Graden, J. L., & Algozzine, B. (1983). What's "special" about the special education resource room for learning disabled students? *Learning Disability Quarterly, 6,* 283–288.

Tollefson, N., Tracy, D. B., Johnsen, E. P., Buenning, M., Farmer, A., & Barke, C. R. (1982). Attribution patterns of learning disabled adolescents. *Learning Disability Quarterly, 5,* 14–20.

Torgesen, J. K. (1977a). Factors related to poor performance on memory tasks in reading disabled children. *Learning Disability Quarterly, 2* (3), 17–23.

Torgesen, J. K. (1977b). The role of nonspecific factors in task performance of learning disabled children: A theoretical assessment. *Journal of Learning Disabilities, 10,* 27–34.

Torgesen, J. K. (1979). What shall we do with psychological processes? *Journal of Learning Disabilities, 12,* 514–521.

Torgesen, J. K. (1980). Conceptual and educational implications of the use of efficient task strategies by learning disabled children. *Journal of Learning Disabilities, 13,* 364–371.

Torgesen, J. K., & Goldman, T. (1977). Rehearsal and short-term memory in reading disabled children. *Child Development, 48,* 56–61.

Torgesen, J. K., Murphy, H. A., & Ivey, C. (1979). The influence of an orienting task on the memory performance of children with reading problems. *Journal of Learning Disabilities, 12,* 396–401.

U.S. Department of Education, Office of Special Education and Rehabilitative Services (1982). *Fourth annual report to Congress on the implementation of Public Law 94–142: The Education for All Handicapped Children Act.* Washington, DC: Author.

U.S. Department of Education, Office of Special Education and Rehabilitative Services (1984). *Sixth annual report to Congress on the implementation of Public Law 94–142: The Education for All Handicapped Children Act.* Washington, DC: Author.

Vogel, S. A. (1982). On developing LD college programs. *Journal of Learning Disabilities, 15,* 518–528.

Wallace, G., & McLoughlin, J. A. (1979). *Learning disabilities: Concepts and characteristics* (2nd ed.). Columbus: Merrill Publishing.

Warner, M. M., Schumaker, J. B., Alley, G. R., & Deshler, D. D. (1980). Learning disabled adolescents in the public schools: Are they different from other low achievers? *Exceptional Education Quarterly, 1* (2), 27–36.

Wechsler, D. (1967). *Manual for the Wechsler preschool and primary scale of intelligence.* Cleveland, OH: Psychological Corporation.

Wechsler, D. (1974). *Manual for the Wechsler intelligence scale for children–revised.* Cleveland, OH: Psychological Corporation.

Wechsler, D. (1981). *Manual for the Wechsler adult intelligence scale–revised.* Cleveland, OH: Psychological Corporation.

Weener, R. D., & Senf, G. M. (1982). Learning disabilities. In H. E. Mitzel (Ed.), *Encyclopedia of educational research* (5th ed.) (pp. 1059–1068). New York: The Free Press.

Weil, M. L., & Murphy, J. (1982). Instruction processes. In H. E. Mitzel (Ed.), *Encyclopedia of educational research* (5th ed.). New York: The Free Press.

Weller, C. (1980). Discrepancy and severity in the learning disabled: A consolidated perspective. *Learning Disability Quarterly, 3* (1), 84–90.

Wepman, J. (1967). The perceptual basis for learning. In C. Frierson & W. Barbe (Eds.), *Educating children with learning disabilities.* New York: Appleton-Century-Crofts.

Wiederholt, J. L. (1974). Historical perspectives on the education of the learning disabled. In L. Mann & D. Sabatino (Eds.), *The second review of special education* (pp. 103–152). Philadelphia: Journal of Special Education Press.

Wiig, E. H., & Semel, E. M. (1976). *Language disabilities in children and adolescents*. Columbus, OH: Merrill Publishing.

Winne, P. H., Woodlands, M. J., & Wong, B. Y. L. (1982). Comparability of self-concept among learning disabled, normal, and gifted students. *Journal of Learning Disabilities, 15*, 470–475.

Woodcock, R. W., & Johnson, M. B. (1977). *Woodcock-Johnson psycho-educational battery.* Boston: Teaching Resources.

Ysseldyke, J. E., Thurlow, M., Graden, J., Wesson, C., Algozzine, B., & Deno, S. (1983). Generalizations from five years of research on assessment and decision making: The University of Minnesota Institute. *Exceptional Education Quarterly, 4* (1), 75–93.

Zigmond, N., & Brownlee, J. (1980). Social skills training for adolescents with learning disabilities. *Exceptional Education Quarterly, 1* (2), 77–83.

Zigmond, N., Vallecorsa, A., & Leinhardt, G. (1980). Reading instruction for students with learning disabilities. *Topics in Language Disorders, 1* (1), 89–98.

Resources

Organizations

Association for Children and Adults with Learning Disabilities

4156 Library Road
Pittsburgh, PA 15234

A group composed of parents and professionals provides and disseminates information, conducts annual national meeting, and has active, local chapters throughout the United States.

Council for Learning Disabilities

P.O. Box 40303
Overland Park, KS 66204

Professional organization which publishes a journal, meets annually, and disseminates information about research and best practices in the education of students with learning disabilities.

Division of Learning Disabilities

Council for Exceptional Children
1920 Association Drive
Reston, VA 22091

An organization of professionals that publishes journals related to learning disabilities and advocates for the improvement of educational services.

Journals

Journal of Learning Disabilities

PRO-ED
5341 Industrial Oaks Blvd.
Austin, TX 78735

A professional journal that disseminates research findings as well as information about the best practices in the treatment of learning disabilities.

Learning Disability Quarterly

P.O. Box 40303

Overland Park, KS 66204

Publishes articles with an applied emphasis which focus on learning disabilities including interpretation of research literature, issues of assessment, identification, placement, remediation, and discussion of pertinent issues.

Remedial and Special Education

PRO-ED

5341 Industrial Oaks Blvd.

Austin, TX 78735

Focuses on issues related to educating students for whom traditional instruction is ineffective with emphasis on interpretation of research literature and recommendations for practice.

Chapter 10

BEHAVIOR DISORDERS

We are all aware of a few individuals who encounter problems because they behave in ways which are considered to be very unusual or inappropriate. A student may be aggressive in the classroom; a co-worker may fear meeting with new clients; a person on the street may mumble epithets at passersby; a friend may no longer be able to hold a job; or an elderly aunt may forget recent events and disregard her own personal care. Problem behaviors are not confined to any single age group and the nature of the behaviors can be quite varied. They may range from extremely aggressive, or bizarre, to exceedingly withdrawn. While many labels have been used for those with problem behaviors, terms such as behavior disorders, maladjusted, mental disorders, or emotionally disturbed are most frequently used by professionals to describe individuals whose problem behaviors interfere with their performance.

Individuals with mild problems may be accepted as unusual or peculiar and their behavior may have little effect on their accomplishments. Those with moderate and severe problems often experience difficulty with their academic achievement, job performance, personal satisfaction, or social interactions with others. Even the casual observer of individuals with moderate to severe problems has little difficulty determining that their acquaintances, or others around them, may not care to associate with them and that they themselves never appear to be content. Evidence of the dramatic effect of their behavioral problems may be observed when they are in school, at home, or in the community.

Donald H. Doorlag
San Diego State University

The attitudes of society toward this group have improved somewhat over the past two decades; the need for services is accepted, yet funds are often not provided for these services and many of these people are rejected by those whom they contact in the community. Many individuals with behavior disorders are served by a variety of counselors, clinics, and mental health or law enforcement agencies because of the problems created by their inappropriate behaviors; others, whose behaviors are not threatening to society, may receive very little attention. As a group they are typically considered to be functioning in the average range of intelligence; but individuals identified as learning disabled, gifted, mentally retarded, physically handicapped, or health impaired may also have behavior disorders.

Although "emotional disturbance" was the term used in the earlier special education literature, the use of this term is declining. The term "seriously emotionally disturbed" is used in PL 94–142 to describe all students with emotional or behavioral problems, but many professionals consider "behavior disorders" to be a more appropriate term for covering a broad range of mild, moderate, and severe behaviors. This term does not convey the sense of uniform severity communicated by "seriously emotionally disturbed" (Grosenick & Huntze, 1980). Additionally, the concept of behavior disorders suggests that it is more appropriate to deal with the person's observable behaviors than to attempt to evaluate disturbance in underlying emotions or thought processes. The lack of adequate instruments to objectively measure emotions and the increased use of behavioral approaches directed at assessing and modifying observable behaviors support the use of the term "behavior disorders" for both children and adults. Consequently, this term will be used throughout this chapter to describe individuals with varying degrees of behavior problems.

INDIVIDUALS WITH BEHAVIOR DISORDERS

The problems exhibited by those with behavior disorders may range from mild to severe. These may include extremely aggressive or acting-out behavior, psychosis or schizophrenia (incoherent thinking or loss of touch with reality and an inability to perform expected responsibilities, sometimes associated with delusions or hallucinations), social deviance, extreme anxiety, social withdrawal, or depression. Others may exhibit autism (extreme withdrawal and lack of language or communication skills) or eating disorders such as anorexia nervosa or bulimia.

Behavior disorders may be transitory in nature, appearing at one point in the lifespan and disappearing later for no apparent reason or without any apparent relationship to treatment. The source of the problem behaviors, and their seriousness, may be related to the individual's experiential background or biological make-up, the setting in which the problem occurs, the quality of the educational program being provided, the access to appropriate interventions, the amount of observer discomfort that they create, or other factors. The effects of these various factors will be discussed later in the chapter.

Behavior disorders may also be situational in nature. The problem behaviors may occur in some settings while not in others; or a behavior considered to be "normal" in one setting may be interpreted as disordered in another. For example, the behaviors of children from various ethnic backgrounds which are encouraged at home may be unacceptable at school. Since the behavioral expectations of the school are usually based on the typical behaviors of the middle-class white student, "normal" behavior of the students from other ethnic backgrounds may be viewed as aberrant in the school setting. Examples of behaviors which may be inaccurately considered as disordered could be the "withdrawn" behavior of the Indian child who has learned to withdraw socially when he or she is unfamiliar with the expected or acceptable behavior (Pepper, 1976); the aggressive, assertive behavior of some young black males which is often interpreted as hostile and quite threatening to authority figures (Dent, 1976); or the Mexican-American child who has learned to avoid competition and therefore is considered to lack motivation (Castaneda, 1976).

The lack of universal acceptance of a specific definition for behavior disorders makes it difficult to determine exactly how many behavior disordered individuals are present in any group. Although typical prevalence figures project that 2 percent of the school-age population can be expected to be identified as behavior disordered and in need of specialized services, research cited by Grosenick and Huntze (1980) and Kauffman (1981) indicates that 3 to 12 percent of the school-age population exhibits behavior disorders with approximately 20 percent of the individuals considered severely behavior disordered.

The Joint Commission for Mental Illness and Health in Children surveyed the incidence of emotional dysfunction in children (Glidewell & Swallow, 1969) and found that 10 percent of the elementary students are sufficiently maladjusted to require professional assistance and 30 percent suffer identifiable difficulties in school adjustment. A severe disorder, autism, is estimated to occur in approximately one of every 2,500 children (Wing, 1966). The longitudinal study conducted by Rubin and Balow (1978) found that during the elementary school years over 50 percent of all students were considered to have behavior problems by at least one of their teachers. In addition, 7.4 percent of all the students included were rated as having a behavior problem by every teacher rating them over a three-year period. These findings are consistent with others in this area for they found that boys are identified much more frequently than girls as having behavior disorders; the representation of boys in special programs for these students is often as high as 10 to 1 (Nelson, 1981a). An exception to the prevalence of boys is found with anorexia nervosa. Approximately 95 percent of the cases of anorexia nervosa are females, with the disorder occurring in approximately .5 percent of the females between the ages of 12 and 18 (Crisp, Palmer, & Kalucy, 1976).

The prevalence of behavior disorders in adult populations is similar to that found in children and adolescents. A careful examination of the presence of psychological disorders in an entire community (Srole, Langner, Michael, Opler, & Rennie, 1962) found that 2.7 percent of the people in the community were totally disabled; 7.5 percent had problems which made it difficult for them to function; and 13.2 percent had marked symptoms which interfered in their func-

introducing

JOE

Joe is a 16-year-old tenth grader who is currently in his first year of attendance at a program operated at a special school for students with behavior disorders; his story is typical of many of the students often referred to these special programs. During the time he has attended public school, he has experienced many of the special education services offered by his school district. He never has been one of the favorite students of his regular teachers or the adults and children living in his neighborhood. He has few friends and he has been differentially tolerated by those around him. Joe has been served by teacher consultants working with the teachers in regular classes, resource programs, and special day classes; he's also received services from psychologists, social workers, counselors, and has spent many hours in the offices and waiting rooms of various school principals.

When Joe first entered school he experienced trouble with reading readiness and writing activities and he was quite active in the classroom, especially during the periods devoted to academic tasks. As he advanced through school (he was retained for one year in first grade), he continued to have difficulties with reading (also spelling and math) and he fell further behind; his active classroom behaviors continued and their occurrence often led to aggressive incidents and intense arguments which took place in the classroom and on the playground. Last school year he spent his third consecutive year in the junior high special class program and his behavior had become increasingly difficult to deal with. He refused to complete most of the academic tasks assigned to him by the teacher and given to him in a folder at the start of each period, calling them "baby work," and he constantly interrupted the teacher and other students in the class with yelling, singing, excess movement, teasing, and profanity. Fighting and verbal abuse got him into trouble with students and other teachers in the lunch area and

on the playground. The teachers in the junior high program became very relieved when he began to miss a great deal of school because of truancy.

Because he lived with his mother, who worked weekday evenings, Joe received very little after-school supervision or encouragement to complete his homework or to get up and off to school in the morning. Joe has had little contact with his father for the last few years: their meetings usually ended with loud arguments. He has created a great deal of trouble at home and his mother has been reluctant to demand that he attend school each day because she wished to avoid the possible arguments and conflicts. Seldom did he help with the household chores and his own room was always a mess. Recently there was some concern that he was experimenting with drugs and alcohol. Joe has had difficulties with the police on several occasions; he has been cited for loitering and curfew violations and recently they have questioned him regarding the use of drugs in his neighborhood. As he has grown physically larger and more physically aggressive, he became more defiant of attempts to have him follow directions at school or at home; this aggression has led to many arguments and fights with others at home, school, and in the neighborhood. Teachers and peers are less likely to "get in his way" at this point in his life.

Joe was placed in the special school partially because of the need for additional supervision and because of his need for their highly structured program which established systematic instruction in both academic and social skills for the entire day. In addition, the instructional program offered at the school emphasized instruction in group settings which attempted to increase student responses and the opportunities for teachers to provide immediate feedback to the students. This type of instructional program had assisted many other students in acquiring the academic and social skills they had not developed when they were working "out of a folder" in their previous special education placements. In this program specific data were kept on the progress of each student and they were provided specific feedback (through the use of praise and points) throughout the instructional period and at the end of each period; these points could be redeemed daily (or accumulated for a longer period of time) for a wide variety of activities and reinforcers such as movie tickets, rentals of tapes, and additional snacks during the school day. The staff of the school assisted Joe's mother in establishing a comparable program at home which was directed at increasing his completion of homework and chores and improving his school attendance.

By the end of the third month in the program Joe is showing progress in improving both his academic and social skills. Directions are followed much more frequently because he is fully aware that there will be positive consequences for complying with requests and penalties for refusing. He is experiencing much less trouble with peers and regularly provides help to his mother at home. His counselor is considering returning him to a regular class for at least one period each day and he may have an after-school job by the semester break.

tioning. While 58.1 percent of the population were found to have mild or moderate symptoms which did not appear to interfere with their adjustment, only 18.5 percent of those in the study were symptom-free. In other research, 10 to 15 percent of the adult population has been shown to have mental disorders (Regier, Goldberg, & Taube, 1978). Estimates of schizophrenia, often considered to be the most severe psychological disorder, range from a conservative 1 percent (Dohrenwend & Dohrenwend, 1974) to as high as 3 to 4 percent (Heston, 1970). The initial occurrence of schizophrenia usually takes place with those under the age of 45; men are considered to be more at risk before age 25 and women more at risk after this age (Lewine, 1981; Zigler & Levine, 1981).

Those over age 65 are considered to be "increasingly at risk for physical and psychological disorders" (Eisdorfer, 1983, p. 198). Lowenthal and Berkman (1967) indicate that 30 percent of the population over 65 may suffer from moderate to severe psychiatric problems with 10 percent requiring hospitalization. Terry and Davies (1980) suggest that approximately 15 percent of this population suffers from dementia, a progressive loss of higher mental functions such as the ability to store information maintained in short-term memory into long-term memory. About half of those with dementia are considered to have Alzheimer's disease, which involves a deterioration of brain cells and neurons and a biochemical deficit which affects the neural transmissions in the brain. Nearly one-third of those with dementia are considered severely handicapped.

Certain characteristics of those with behavior disorders are easily recognizable while others are much less obvious. Aggressive or acting-out behaviors are generally obvious, but anxiety and self-concept problems may not be as noticeable to the casual observer. Determining the effect of the behavior disorder on the person's overall performance is often difficult. The individual's behavior problems may be considered to contribute to symptoms of physical illness or to the lack of academic performance. Verbal or physical aggression or social withdrawal may contribute to the inability to initiate or sustain appropriate social interactions. Problems related to hyperactivity (excessive activity), distractibility (lack of attention to the task), or impulsivity (acting without thinking) may influence the individual's performance in academic tasks, job-related tasks, or in social interactions. As a group, persons considered to have behavior disorders are remarkably heterogeneous. They do not display a consistent array of specific characteristics which can be readily identified to place them in this group.

Definitional Issues

As was noted earlier, there is no single definition of behavior disorders or emotional disturbance which is universally accepted by professionals. Examples of current definitions are presented in Table 10.1 for the review of the reader. School districts use the definition provided by PL 94–142. Although this definition is based primarily on the earlier work of Bower (1969) and has been accepted for some time, it lacks the specificity which is necessary to establish reliable identification procedures across the many individuals who may be involved in the identification process. The other definitions are examples of ones which have attempted to operationally define behavior disorders (specify behaviors which are observable and measurable; e.g., frequency of hitting or biting rather than "aggressive") in a way which can increase the consistency needed for accurate and reliable identification of individuals in need of special intervention services.

A system which involves symptomatic diagnosis of abnormal behavior is included in the third version of the *Diagnostic and Statistical Manual of Mental Disorders (DSM-III)* developed by the American Psychiatric Association (1980). Although this system is used by many clinicians to diagnose or categorize disorders in individuals of all ages with varying types of abnormal behaviors, it is seldom used in public school programs.

Common factors which consistently appear in definitions of behavior disorders are as follows:

1. Inappropriateness of the individual's behavior when compared to the expected behavior (e.g., age or situation appropriateness).
2. Degree of severity or intensity of the behavior disorder.
3. Frequency of occurrence of the behavior.
4. Duration of time that the disorder exists (i.e., the problem has existed for a long period rather than being transient).
5. Individual has not responded positively to normally available intervention.
6. Elimination of potential contributions of physical, sensory, or intellectual deficits to the behavior.
7. Effect of the behavior on the individual's (a) employment or academic performance, (b) learning, (c) personal satisfaction, or (d) interactions with others.

A major portion of the lack of agreement in the various definitions is generated by the differences in the theoretical orientations of the professionals who develop and/or implement the definitions. For example, those who believe that the major consideration in behavior disorders involves identifying the biological factors which contribute to the behavior problem will have a somewhat different opinion of an acceptable definition than those who have a psychodynamic perspective

Table 10.1

Definitions of Behavior Disorders/Emotional Disturbance

The following are definitions which are frequently used to define or describe individuals who have been, or may be, identified as having behavior disorders or emotional disturbance.

The Federal regulations associated with PL 94–142 indicate that:
"Seriously emotionally disturbed" is defined as follows:

(i) *The term means a condition exhibiting one or more of the following characteristics over a long period of time and to a marked degree, which adversely affects educational performance:*
   (a) *An inability to learn which cannot be explained by intellectual, sensory or health factors;*
   (b) *An inability to build or maintain satisfactory relationships with peers and teachers;*
   (c) *Inappropriate types of behaviors or feelings under normal circumstances;*
   (d) *A general pervasive mood of unhappiness or depression; or*
   (e) *A tendency to develop physical symptoms or fears associated with personal or school problems.*

(ii) *The term includes children who are schizophrenic. The term does not include children who are socially maladjusted, unless it is determined that they are seriously emotionally disturbed. (Federal Register, 1977, 42, 42,474, as amended in Federal Register, 1981, 46, 3866)*

Nelson (1981a) indicates that a student's behavior "may be judged disordered (1) if it deviates from the range of behaviors for the child's age and sex which significant adults perceive as 'normal'; (2) if it occurs very frequently or too intensely; or (3) if it occurs over an extended period of time" (p. 394).

Kauffman (1977) states: "Children with behavior disorders are those who chronically and markedly respond to their environment in socially unacceptable and/or personally unsatisfying ways but who can be taught more socially acceptable and personally gratifying behavior" (p. 23).

Algozzine, Schmid, and Mercer (1981) suggest: "The emotionally disturbed child is one who, after receiving supportive educational services and counseling assistance available to all students, still exhibits persistent and consistent severe to very severe behavioral disabilities that consequently *interfere* with productive learning processes. This is the student whose inability to achieve adequate progress and satisfactory interpersonal relationships cannot be attributed primarily to physical, sensory, or intellectual deficits" (p. 4).

Cullinan, Epstein, and Lloyd (1983) propose the following definition: "Behavior disorders of a pupil are behavior characteristics that (1) deviate from educators' standards of normality and (2) impair the functioning of that pupil and/or others. These behavior characteristics are manifested as environmental conflicts and/or personal disturbances, and are typically accompanied by learning disorders" (p. 149).

The American Psychiatric Association (1980) in its *Diagnostic and Statistical Manual of Mental Disorders*, Third Edition *(DSM-III)* uses the term "mental disorder" and defines this as a disorder which is: *conceptualized as a clinically significant behavioral or psychological syndrome or pattern that occurs in an individual and that is typically associated with either a painful symptom (distress) or impairment in one or more important areas of functioning (disability). In addition, there is an inference that there is a behavioral, psychological, or biological dysfunction, and that the disturbance is not only in the relationship between the individual and society. (When the disturbance is limited to a conflict between an individual and society, this may represent social deviance, which may or may not be commendable, but is not by itself a mental disorder)* (p. 6).

which relates behavioral disorders to underlying emotional or psychological causes. Those with a behavioral perspective consider the problem behavior a learned response to a specific situation and are concerned with a different set of environmental factors. Attempting to develop a definition which meets the needs

introducing

MARIA

Maria never creates problems for the students in her class; yet the teacher is concerned about her behavior. She is 10 years old and attends a regular fifth grade class in her neighborhood school. During both independent and group work times, and during activity and recess periods, she is very quiet and avoids others for she is reluctant to interact with either her teacher or other students; she openly avoids visual, physical, and verbal contact with anyone. She misses out on the benefits of many instructional activities because she carefully avoids participation in all group activities and will not respond when called upon. Her academic performance has been falling further behind because she will not seek help when she encounters a problem or an area in which she has a question.

Maria's parents have been concerned about her behavior for some time because she always talks very quietly, seldom has friends over to her house, and never mingles with the neighborhood children after she arrives home from school. She has no real friends at school and tends to play by herself on the playground or at lunchtime. At home she spends much of her time playing with dolls or toys in her room and doesn't talk much with her parents during meals or when they are in the same area of the house.

Concerned about Maria's lack of social interactions, the fifth-grade teacher worked closely with a teacher-consultant and developed an observation system to evaluate the current level of the behavior. They developed a system in which she recorded the number of Maria's interactions with peers and adults and the amount of time she interacted with members of either group each day. This information was collected for five school days before the teacher attempted any interventions. Once the teacher designed an intervention which was to be implemented in separate phases, she monitored the effectiveness of the intervention by continuing to collect the same type of information.

The initial phase of the intervention involved the teacher using a great deal of social reinforcement (e.g., praise and physical touch) each time that Maria approached, made visual contact, or interacted verbally with her or with students. Next, the teacher added the use of small group role-playing activities which dealt with skills related to social interactions (e.g., greeting a stranger, introducing a friend to an adult) which were designed to allow other students to model appropriate behaviors associated with these skills and then involve Maria after others had demonstrated how the activity could be completed successfully. Later, Maria's participation, and that of the group, was further encouraged by the teacher's providing special reinforcers (e.g., one minute of free time) for Maria and each member of the group each time Maria participated appropriately in the activity. Finally, the teacher provided opportunities for the "real life" implementation of the newly developed skills, initially with persons in the class who were not involved in the group activity and then with individuals outside the classroom.

The frequency and duration of Maria's interactions with others increased gradually with the introduction of each new phase of the intervention and the quality of her academic work continued to improve.

of all these viewpoints has been a difficult, if not impossible, task.

A large part of the definitional problem is related to the different perceptions of professionals involved in identifying and serving these individuals as to which behaviors are appropriate, or normal, and which are disordered. The decision regarding the presence of behavior disorders is ordinarily made by individual professionals such as psychologists or by an interdisciplinary team in public school settings. In schools, teachers may be the first to identify students who appear to have behavior disorders, but teachers' personal differences in behavioral expectations may produce the identification of vastly different candidates from teacher to teacher. In other instances, professionals (e.g., psychologists, psychiatrists, psychiatric social workers) may interpret the appropriateness of the behaviors of the client quite differently. This dilemma is created because many of the available definitions do not specifically and clearly state the characteristics or behaviors which are expected to be present for an individual to be identified as having behavior disorders or emotional disturbance. These definitions lack the specificity necessary for different observers to consistently identify the same persons who are in need of special services.

Once a diagnosis has been made, categorical designations or labels generally lack utility in indicating an appropriate intervention program. This occurs because there has been a lack of agreement (or empirical evidence) supporting the use of specific interventions for particular categories of disorders. Professionals who design and implement interventions which follow a medical model usually expect that the provision of a particular diagnostic category or label will indicate a specific treatment or intervention, but this has not been the case with behavior disorders. While several of the interventions discussed later in the chapter have research support which demonstrates them to be more effective than others, these interventions have not been universally accepted or implemented by different types of professionals in the field. Therefore the information provided by the diagnostic category cannot regularly be used to determine the specific intervention procedure which is most appropriate for that individual.

Definitions for behavior disorders continue to maintain varying degrees of subjectivity and leave a great deal of interpretation up to the observer or "beholder." Professionals who must implement these definitions need to establish clearly stated operational criteria and to identify specific critical behaviors and/or characteristics which reduce the subjectivity in diagnosing, placing, educating, and treating individuals with behavior disorders.

Concerned Professionals

Many different professionals may work with people with behavior disorders. The specific needs of the individual, the orientation of the professional(s) involved in the initial contacts, and the types of services available in the community generally govern the professional services provided. Young preschool children with more severe behavior disorders may be served initially by a physician who works with the child and the parents or refers them to other services. Many of these children may be served by public school preschool programs. Regular classroom teachers are generally the first professionals to have regular contact with behavior disordered students and in the majority of cases the regular teacher will continue to work with them throughout the students' days in school. Many of these students will also benefit from the services of their school counselor. If the individual is a candidate for special education services he or she will have contact with special education teachers or consultants, school psychologists and possibly special school counselors or school social workers. Frequently, because of disciplinary actions, the student with behavior disorders has a great deal of contact with the school administrator who becomes aware of the student whether he or she is in regular or special education classes. School nurses may be involved in administering medication or in arranging for other medical services for these students.

In the community, individuals may receive services from physicians, mental health workers, social workers, psychologists, psychiatrists, psychiatric nurses, or vocational rehabilitation counselors. Their services may be provided to the individual at home, in a clinic, at the hospital or in a residential or institutional setting. Often the parents, or other significant persons in the life of the behavior disordered individual, also participate when services are provided by these professionals.

ETIOLOGY AND PREVENTION

Many factors can contribute to the development of a behavior disorder, but it is extremely difficult to isolate the exact extent to which a specific factor or event contribute to a particular disorder. Children may have a predisposition to a certain type of temperament which affects their interactions with others; their temperament has a specific negative impact on the behavior of others and on the interactions which take place in the family setting (Thomas & Chess, 1977). Individuals may have a genetic or biochemical disorder or a disease which influences their behavior to an extent which is not readily measurable. Events which occur in school frequently influence the development of behavior disorders. For example, poorly designed and/or delivered instruction, unrealistic expectations, and inconsistent classroom management can all contribute to initiating or sustaining behavior disorders. Any of these or other factors, alone or in combination, may contribute to the initiation or continuation of a behavior disorder, but it is extremely difficult to determine the extent of the contribution of any one factor.

Causes of Behavior Disorders

The relative importance of causative factors is generally related to the theoretical perspective of the individual making the judgment. Consider for a moment a child who has great difficulty getting along with others. In a social setting he has problems playing games with his friends. Problems occur because he disregards the rules, doesn't attend to the game's progress, interferes with the play of others, and is in constant conflict over the score. Because similar problems have occurred during many other activities, he is no longer invited by his friends to participate in social activities, therefore missing many opportunities for positive social interactions. Later, comparable problems will occur in his work experience and will result in the loss of several jobs. In this section we will examine the etiological factors considered by those with different perspectives when they review such a case.

A professional with a psychodynamic viewpoint is concerned with how the individual's behavior is influenced by the effect of unconscious psychological forces on his or her mind. Sigmund Freud, regarded as the original developer of this perspective, developed a set of theories which suggest that the mind's inner forces often conflict causing the individual to defend him/herself against the resulting anxiety and unhappiness. Therapists with this perspective attempt to improve the individual's behavior by resolving these intrapsychic conflicts. Before the behavior problems can be resolved, early developmental history and family interactions will be explored to determine how they have contributed to the individual's current behaviors.

The professional with an ecological perspective is concerned with the reciprocal influences of the person with behavior disorders with his or her environment. Close examination would be given to the individual's interactions with persons in the environment and the disturbing impact they may have on this system. Intervention plans would include modifications in the individual's environment.

Professionals with a behavioral orientation are most interested in examining the conditions present when the behavior occurs (antecedents) and the consequences since these events are assumed to influence the occurrence of the behavior. The behaviorist gives little consideration to intrapsychic causes or prior events on the individual's experience; instead, historical information is only used to determine whether the individual is capable of learning the behavior or to ascertain if specific events have continued to provoke or reinforce the occurrence of the behavior.

Unlike behaviorists, cognitive psychologists consider that behavior is influenced by more than the direct relationship between the environment and the response. This perspective assumes that the behavioral reaction to a stimulus is moderated by the individual's thought process. In other words, behavior is influenced by what one attends to, thinks, or believes; mental events can cause behavior. If the cognitive processes are disordered, they may cause psychological disorders. Interventions developed under this approach assume that disorders can be cured, or at least alleviated, by changing the individual's disordered thoughts.

Professionals with a biomedical orientation would be much more interested in the medical status and health history of the troubled individual. They would examine his or her genetic history, pattern of medication, dietary habits, neurological functioning, related illnesses, allergies, or other factors, carefully considering any possible medical problems which might contribute to or cause such problem behaviors.

Many behavior disorders are frequently related to organic or biogenic factors such as central nervous system dysfunction which are thought to cause, or contribute to, their presence. On the other hand, several physical illnesses or disorders such as asthma and peptic ulcers are often considered to have a psychological base (Van Evra, 1983). Research regarding one of the areas related to severe behavior disorders has found that "most professionals . . . do believe that autism is caused by organic factors, and that the disorder is probably present from birth" (Schreibman, Koegel, Charlop, & Egel, 1982, p. 891). Although the specific contributions of biological factors, especially those related to heredity and postconception physical development, have not yet been determined, their potential effects must be considered when studying the etiology of behavior disorders.

Genetic factors have been found to have a strong influence on the differences between individuals in intelligence. Although the behaviors of the mildly and moderately behavior disordered are less likely to have a genetic base, research indicates that genetic factors affect those individuals who exhibit psychotic behavior after puberty and that there is a relationship between the likelihood of schizophrenia in individuals with schizophrenic relatives (Rosenthal, 1970a; Rosenthal, 1970b). Twin studies have supported the influence of inheritance in criminality and sociopathy (e.g., Hutchings & Mednick, 1977) and in schizophrenia (e.g., Gottesman & Shields, 1972). Chromosome abnormalities, such as possessing an additional male or female chromosome (XYY and XXY chromosomal abnormalities), are frequently considered to be associated with criminal behavior (e.g., Witkin et al., 1976). Generally it is assumed that genetic factors contribute to the individual's vulnerability to the disorder rather than completely explaining its presence.

The genetic makeup of individuals can also influence their temperament or behavioral style. Temperament, in turn, influences the way they react to environmental events and the way others react to them. Researchers (Chess & Thomas, 1977; Thomas, 1971; Thomas & Chess, 1977) describe these temperamental characteristics in nine different categories (e.g., activity level, adaptability, intensity of reaction, quality of mood). Although they found that individuals with all types of temperaments might develop behavior disorders, those who were slow in adapting to environmental changes, negative in responding to new stimuli, and had a prevalence of intense reactions were most likely to develop inappropriate behavioral patterns. These innate patterns of behavior cannot be considered to be the sole cause of behavior disorders, but persons with more difficult temperaments are more likely to elicit negative responses from those with whom they associate. The presence of these negative reactions increases the likelihood that behavioral problems will occur in the future.

Brain damage occurring before, after, or during birth is frequently considered to be a contributing factor to behavior disorders. When the damage is not gross, its presence and influences are often difficult to verify. Although brain disorders are usually assessed using medical histories, neurological examinations, electroencephalogram analysis, or psychological testing, it is often difficult to obtain reliable and valid assessment. Results are frequently not consistent across administrations and the information gathered from different procedures is often contradictory. Current research evidence does not support using brain damage as a viable explanation for the presence of behavior disorders, except possibly when gross damage exists. Care should be taken in using information relating to the presence of brain damage as a basis for selecting or designing intervention procedures since this type of information has been demonstrated to be of minimal value in this process (Cullinan, Epstein, & Lloyd, 1983; Kauffman, 1981; Nelson & Polsgrove, 1981).

Biochemical imbalances in an individual are often related to the etiology of specific disorders. One of the explanations for schizophrenia is the presence of an excessive amount of the chemical dopamine in the brain which is believed to affect the transfer of signals from one neuron to another. Medical treatment has not been able to cure the disorder, but the use of drugs which block the dopamine have been found to reduce the schizophrenic symptoms such as bizarre behavior, delusions, and hallucinations (Matthysse, 1973). The symptoms of manic-depressive disorders have been effectively prevented or alleviated through the use of lithium carbonate. Approximately 80 percent of this population are positively affected by the administration of lithium, but its use and potential side effects must be monitored continually (Depue, 1979; Depue & Monroe, 1978). Stimulant medications have been used to reduce hyperactivity in children. An analysis of studies related to this practice (Kavale, 1982) demonstrated it to be effective in improving behavior and educational performance, yet others question its efficacy (Axelrod & Bailey, 1979). A similar analysis has determined that stimulants, major tranquilizers, and antidepressants have been used relatively successfully in the treatment of severe behavior disorders, especially with persons over 16 years of age (Kavale & Nye, 1984).

One's behavior can be affected by nutritional factors. Mental development and performance are negatively affected by malnutrition which retards neurological development and contributes to social withdrawal, apathy, and school failure. Feingold (1975) has proposed that food additives contribute to hyperactivity in children, and others feel that certain foods damage the body or produce allergic reactions which cause behavior disorders. However, research summarized by Kavale and Forness (1983), Mattes (1983), and Waksman (1983) indicates that a definite relationship between the foods ingested and behavioral disorders can be found in only a small number of individuals.

Physical stature and appearance can influence the development of behavioral patterns. Researchers (Glueck & Glueck, 1950; Sheldon, 1967) have examined the relationship between the various body types and the presence of behavioral disorders. While no evidence exists indicating that certain body types cause behavioral disorders, there is evidence to indicate that juvenile delinquents are more likely to have well-developed, muscular builds. The appearance of these individuals also influences their perceptions of themselves and tempers the initial reactions of others toward them.

Psychosomatic or psychophysiological disorders describe physical disorders and illnesses which are believed to be caused by psychological problems which the individual is experiencing. Kauffman (1981) groups these disorders into breathing, eating, gastric, elimination, movement, and skin disorders. Many consider that evidence is lacking to substantiate that psychological problems cause these disorders, yet physical problems such as high blood pressure and peptic ulcers are generally associated with stress or other psychological factors (Rosenhan & Seligman, 1984).

Relationships may exist between the medical and health characteristics of individuals and the presence of behavior disorders, but there is little evidence to indicate that one causes disorders in the other. Genetic or biogenic factors may affect emotional development by influencing the individual's reaction to environmental stimuli and others' reactions to them. The quality of these interactions can have a definite effect on the emotional development of individuals and their behavior.

Information regarding causative factors must be carefully interpreted by the professional. Realizing that it is impossible to go back to change those events which have occurred previously, we are left with the task of dealing with the individual's present behavior. In many cases, extended periods of time spent on determining causes could be more productively spent on modifying the behavior as it currently exists. For most professionals, determination of the specific events which "caused" the behavior disorder are of little value in determining an appropriate intervention. However, determining events which are presently contributing to the behavior's occurrence assists in targeting factors to change in the intervention.

Prevention of Behavior Disorders

Since prevention requires that factors identified as contributing to or causing disorders be controlled or modified, the current state-of-the-art makes prevention difficult. In addition, factors which contribute to the development of these disorders may not be controlled to any appreciable extent by outside influences. However, there are many possible improvements which may help to prevent, or at least reduce, the possibility of individuals developing behavior disorders. The school's contributions to creating or sustaining problem behaviors can be reduced by providing quality inservice programs for regular and special educators. These programs should be directed toward improving the quality of educational programs in meeting the specific needs of individual students. Early identification and intervention for primary-grade students at high risk of developing learning or behavior problems can be effective in preventing behavior disorders. Such a program has been successfully implemented by Emory Cowen (Cowen, 1980; Cowen et al., 1975) in Rochester, New York. This program involves the identification of high-risk students by teachers or others, collection of information on their performance, making a team decision regarding the need for services, and the assignment of a nonprofessional aide to those needing services. The students receive tutoring, ongoing support, and other services from the aides who have been trained by psychologists and educational specialists. The professionals recruit and train aides, consult, and supervise but do not provide direct services to the students. This program has been successful and has been adopted by a number of other school systems.

An autistic child in a special program may respond to direct communication strategies by teachers and counselors.

The quality of the school's instructional program for students with behavior disorders is a critical factor in a preventive program. Academic activities should include clearly stated initial instruction, repeated opportunities for practice of the new skill or concept being taught, specific feedback on performance from the teacher, and opportunities for the student to practice independently once the skill is initially mastered. Many of these students benefit from the provision of specific instruction in social and study skills which follow the same principles cited for academic skills. Such a program provides individuals with the opportunity to learn skills which they have not acquired through their regular contacts in the classroom or through incidental learning. Cooperation of the schools and other agencies in the community in providing support and instruction for parents or other family members on how to deal with an individual who begins exhibiting behavioral disorders can reduce the possibility of negative experiences which contribute to the problem behavior (Sulzer-Azaroff & Pollack, 1982).

Community efforts may be implemented to prevent the occurrence of behavior disorders. Childcare and preschool programs can do much to alleviate the tension created when parents work and also have responsibilities for care of their children; these programs can also provide excellent experiences to promote the cognitive and social growth of the student. The availability of job training in the community can help to reduce the psychological stress of poverty and unemployment by facilitating the development of job skills and employment opportunities. The availability of services such as "hotlines" and crisis treatment centers provide ways to deal immediately with psychological crises and contain, or limit the consequences of, these crises (Rosenhan & Seligman, 1984).

Preventive efforts to reduce or eliminate behavior disorders have demonstrated some promise to this point. Medical interventions, such as drugs and genetic counseling, provide some evidence of effectiveness, especially for the more severe psychotic disorders. Teaching specific social skills and adaptive behaviors to those who appear to be "at risk" may also be a practice which holds promise for reducing future problems. Regardless of the specific nature of the proposed preventive measure, it is important that research be conducted on programs which have good prospects for assisting in preventing behavior disorders. This research should be carefully designed and conducted systematically to enable other professionals to review the findings and determine their applicability to a broader range of individuals. Because of the longitudinal nature of the problem to be examined, it will be important that individuals are followed to determine the long-term effects of specific interventions.

CHARACTERISTICS OF INDIVIDUALS WITH BEHAVIOR DISORDERS

Learning Characteristics

Learning problems are often considered to precede the development of behavioral and emotional problems. This assumption is frequently based on the premise that individuals experiencing difficulty in learning at home, in academic areas at school, or in acquiring new job skills frequently become frustrated and express their frustration by displaying a variety of behaviors which are not appropriate for the setting. Others might consider that the problem behaviors are displayed in these settings because they require less effort or they result in greater amounts of attention or recognition. Often the behaviors displayed lead to additional rejection and a decreased opportunity to obtain the necessary prerequisite skills needed to assure appropriate performance at a later time.

Although the intellectual ability of those with behavior disorders is usually not the primary area of concern related to the learning problems, their measured intellectual ability deserves consideration because it can provide a prediction of their future performance. For example, individuals with behavior disorders and intellectual limitations are more likely to have difficulty achieving in the school or employment setting and will be less likely to receive positive attention. In addition, their behavior problems may lead to exclusion from classes and deprive them of involvement in class activities which contribute to their cognitive development.

Individuals with behavior disorders display a wide range of cognitive abilities. The majority of this group are considered to function intellectually in the "average" range of measured intellectual functioning, yet researchers have consistently found their actual level of performance to be in the lower portion of the average range for individuals of the same age (Kauffman, 1981; Stainback & Stainback, 1980). Performance on intellectual measures is generally reported to average 5 to 10 points lower than expected with a broad range of scores from extremely low to exceptionally high. Individuals with more severe behavior disorders have typically scored in the retarded range of intellectual functioning.

It appears that a relationship exists between the combination of low intelligence, school failure, and severe acting-out behaviors in students and poor adjustment as an adult (Kauffman, 1977). When these conditions exist, it is important to consider them as indicators of problems later in life. Hobbs (1977) indicated that academic underachievement is the most common characteristic of these individuals as students. In school settings, students with behavior disorders consistently display low achievement in the important academic areas of reading, spelling, and especially arithmetic (e.g., Edwards & Simpson, 1982; Kauffman, 1981), a problem which persists as they grow older (Cullinan et al., 1983; Robins, 1972; Werner & Smith, 1977) and after they leave school (Leone, 1984). A large percentage of elementary school boys with behavior disorders have been found to have reading achievement problems (81%) and arithmetic deficits (73%) (Glavin & Annesley, 1972). Cawley and Webster (1981) report the results of functional literacy tests for "emotionally disturbed" high school students in which 50 percent of the students' reading scores and 85 percent of their math scores failed to reach the levels required to receive a high school diploma. Many of the problems experienced by students in school are similar in nature to those experienced by adults in an employment or community setting, and the characteristics and behaviors which contribute to these problems may be comparable.

Many factors contribute to the lack of achievement by persons with behavior disorders, and several of these are characteristics of students with other handicapping conditions such as learning disabilities. Individuals with behavior disorders are frequently distractible, impairing their ability to establish and maintain appropriate attention to the task, which interferes with school or job performance. Others have difficulty responding to appropriate academic stimuli or become overdependent on teachers or individuals in positions of authority. Many are found to be low in verbal and interpersonal skills (Bryan & Bryan, 1977). The lack of success in academic achievement helps to create a negative attitude, poor self-concept, and lack of motivation to achieve, contributing to poor performance and a continued lack of motivation.

Social/Emotional Characteristics

Many of the difficulties encountered by individuals with behavior disorders are associated with their inappropriate social behaviors. These behaviors are usually the primary concern of their associates and the professionals who work with

Table 10.2

Quay's (1979) Empirically-Derived Characteristics of Children and Adolescents with Behavior Disorders

Problem Area	Common Characteristics of the Disorder (Listed in descending order)
Conduct Disorder	Fighting, hitting, assaultive behaviors Temper tantrums Disobedient, defiant Destructiveness of own or other's property Impertinent, "smart," impudent Uncooperative, resistive, inconsiderate Disruptive, interrupts, disturbs Negative, refuses direction; restless; boisterous, noisy; irritable, "blows up" easily Attention-seeking, "show-off"; dominates, bullies, threatens others Hyperactive; untrustworthy, dishonest, lies Profanity, abusive language; jealousy; quarrelsome Irresponsible, undependable Inattentive; steals Distractibility
Personality Problem or Anxiety-Withdrawal	Anxious, fearful, tense Shy, timid, bashful; withdrawn, seclusive, friendless Depressed, sad, disturbed Hypersensitive, easily hurt Self-conscious, easily embarrassed Feels inferior, worthless Lacks self-confidence; easily flustered Aloof Cries frequently; reticent, secretive
Immaturity or Inadequacy-Immaturity	Short attention span, poor concentration Daydreaming Clumsy, poor coordination Preoccupied, stares into space, absent-minded Passive, lacks initiative, easily led; sluggish Inattentive; drowsy Lack of interest; bored, lack of perseverence; fails to finish things
Socialized Aggression	Has "bad" companions; steals in company with others Loyal to delinquent friends; belongs to a gang; stays out late at night; truant from school Truant from home

Source: From *Psychopathological Disorders of Childhood,* 2nd ed. by H. C. Quay. Copyright © 1979 by John Wiley & Sons, Inc. Reprinted by permission.

them. The extent of the problem can be noted in dropout rates of high school students which are reported to be as high as 30 percent with one-half of this population found to exhibit serious social maladjustment (Ahlstrom & Havighurst, 1971).

The behavioral patterns of these individuals typically include either behavioral excesses or deficiencies in areas which are critical for appropriate social interaction and emotional development. Students may be excessively verbally or physically aggressive or deficient in their ability to relate to others or complete tasks. These inappropriate behavioral patterns contribute to rejection and lack of development of appropriate social skills. Quay (1979) has established an empirically based system which identifies characteristics associated with the dimensions of behavior disorders for children and adolescents. These characteristics are listed in Table 10.2 and grouped according to the four major problem areas associated with those with behavior disorders.

Behavior disorders are closely related to the person's lack of adequate social skills and appropriate emotional development. Individuals normally develop appropriate social skills and a sense of emotional stability through positive experiences in their everyday performance and in their interactions with others. Positive experiences in these areas lead to positive feedback which indicates that their behaviors are appropriate and they are accepted by others they consider to be significant. Deficits in these areas may lead to the development of behaviors which are considered inappropriate or disordered by others.

It was noted earlier in the chapter that the designation of an individual's behavior as disordered is generally made by an individual or team by comparing the person's behavior with their perceptions of the behavioral expectations for some normative or comparison group. Individuals may have several norm groups in their lives which each have different sets of behavioral expectations. For example, a student may have completely different sets of expectations in the classroom, at home, when playing in the neighborhood, at church, on a date, or with a group of peers or a gang. It is the responsibility of the individual to determine the expectations for the present setting and to act accordingly. This may require dramatic adjustments in behavior or the adjustments may be very subtle, but it is important that the individual perceives these required adjustments and is able to compensate for the difference in expectations. Many people with behavior disorders are not proficient at making these adjustments. They may have difficulty making initial distinctions between the expectations, may not be able to demonstrate the appropriate behaviors required for each of the situations, or may not have learned the behaviors required because of lack of experience, models, or instruction. Because the acceptance of others is dependent on appropriate performance, it is essential that individuals develop appropriate behaviors to gain the acceptance they desire.

Often there are questions relating to the relationship between behavior disorders and juvenile delinquency or crime at other age levels. Those who have been identified as having conduct disorders, which consist mainly of antisocial or aggressive behaviors, are much more likely to be involved with delinquency and encounter problems with the law. Robins (1966) reported the results of a follow-

A chart listing expectations or appropriate behavior goals is one example of a technique used with behavior disordered youngsters.

up of clients of a child guidance clinic who had received services before age 18 and found that those who had exhibited antisocial behavior were 3 to 10 times more likely than a normal control group to be involved in crime. A distinction is frequently made between the socialized delinquent (the individual who relates well to others such as those in his own group or gang) and the unsocialized delinquent (a person who does not relate well to others, sometimes a "loner"); the unsocialized delinquent is generally considered to have behavior disorders. Although it is difficult to obtain exact figures in this area, Yule (1978) suggests that five predictive factors can be used to distinguish potential delinquent from nondelinquent boys: low family income, large family size, parental criminality, low intelligence, and poor child-rearing practices. Boys were found to be six times more likely to make repeated appearances before a court if they were exposed to three or more of these adverse factors.

The affective development of the individual can be disordered at any stage in the lifespan. Different titles may be used for disorders which have similar characteristics yet are exhibited at different points in the person's life. For example, the *DSM-III* system mentioned earlier in the chapter has a set of classification categories used primarily for children and youth and another set used primarily with adults. Conceivably, the same individuals could progress from being described by a label used for youth to a different label used for adults with little change in their observed characteristics or behaviors.

DETECTION OF BEHAVIOR DISORDERS

Identification and Screening

Identification of individuals with behavior disorders involves determining whether a problem exists and establishing if the problem is serious enough to require additional evaluation to determine the need for intervention. Identification of those who may need services may be initiated by referrals from the individuals themselves, parents, physicians, teachers, social agency workers, psychologists, employers, police, or others interested in the welfare of the individuals or concerned about the effects of their behavior. The identification of those with behavior disorders may also result from a systematic screening process which attempts to identify members of a group who require specialized preventive help before their problem becomes serious enough to necessitate the introduction of a much more intensive intervention.

The majority of those with behavior disorders are identified during their years in school. Because of their constant contact with students, teachers are often responsible for the initial identification of these individuals. The use of teacher ratings in this process has been found to be valid and reliable, especially if ratings are provided by several teachers over a period of time (Epanchin, 1982; Kauffman, 1981). There appears, however, to be some bias in the identification practices of teachers since they are more likely to identify students with learning and overt behavior problems and to overlook moody, withdrawn students as needing special services. While parents are frequently involved in the referral and identification process, both Epanchin (1982) and Kauffman (1981) report that parents have been found to be less reliable than teachers in their ratings because of a wide variability in their tolerance for the behavioral differences in children.

Screening programs attempt to detect individuals who may have behavior disorders which are not yet immediately obvious. Following screening, potential candidates are provided with more intensive evaluation and are considered for services which are of a preventive nature. When considering the implementation of a screening program, careful planning requires that questions regarding the following should be considered (Hobbs, 1975): Who is to conduct the actual screening? What instruments are to be used and what is the accuracy of these instruments? Will the process identify individuals with problems which are not already obvious? Will the system identify persons as disordered when they are not and overlook those who are in need of services? Can the services needed by those identified be provided? Is screening more cost-effective than comprehensively assessing those currently receiving services? It is essential that these areas be considered since screening programs are effective only if they use valid and reliable measures which lead to the provision of available services for those who are actually in need. Negative effects can occur if services are not provided following an indication to the individuals, their parents, their teachers, or others that their behavior is disordered.

Screening programs use sources of information such as behavior rating scales, sociometric techniques, interviews, medical and school histories, measures of intellectual potential, academic or job performance assessments, attitudinal measures, or direct observation of behavior to collect data on the actual or predicted behavior of individuals. The results are interpreted/evaluated by individuals or groups who use definitions provided by professional organizations or state or federal agencies to guide their determination of whether those being evaluated are potential candidates for intervention.

Social functioning of students may be assessed using instruments such as the *Walker Problem Behavior Identification Checklist (WPBIC)*; (Walker, 1983), which is a behavior rating scale completed by teachers. This instrument provides a total score and five subtest scores: Acting Out, Withdrawal, Distractibility, Disturbed Peer Relations, and Immaturity. The instrument has been found to discriminate between behavior problem and "normal" children and has been shown to have at least moderate correlation between the observed behavior and sociometric ratings of students (Greenwood, Walker, Todd, & Hops, 1976; Walker, 1983).

Systems relying on referrals are more prevalent than those which screen large groups to detect a few persons with behavior disorders. There are several reasons this occurs. Screening programs for children not yet in school and adult populations are difficult to administer because no single source has consistent opportunities to collect appropriate data on these individuals. Additionally, funds are often not available to cover the cost of conducting a large-scale screening or to provide the additional evaluation or preventive services needed by those identified in a screening program. This area's lack of norm-referenced screening instruments and procedures which possess high validity and reliability raise questions regarding the possibility of inaccurate labeling of those with or without behavior disorders. Other deterrents to screening programs exist, but as a result of the lack of screening programs the individuals who are currently provided with services are generally those who have immediate needs. Little is done to screen those with less obvious needs or to provide services which are of a preventive nature.

Criteria for Determination of Behavior Disorders

The problems of interpreting current definitions affect the development of specific criteria for determining the presence of behavior disorders. Because definitions lack specificity, the criteria used are often subjective and leave much to the interpretation of individuals or groups determining the existence of a behavior disorder. Subjective definitions increase the difficulty of consistently making accurate decisions regarding the need for services; they also increase the difficulty of communicating with potential referral agents (e.g., physicians, teachers, parents) regarding who would be appropriate candidates for referral and consideration for services. In addition, many identification systems currently used are based on a medical model which stresses the etiology of and label for the disorder, information which may have little relevance when designing an appropriate intervention.

Schools, agencies, and individual professionals are often required to develop their own interpretations of criteria for determining if the behavior problems of individuals are of sufficient magnitude to warrant further investigation or possible intervention. The criteria may have a basis in the professional training or experience of the individual, or members of the group, or they may relate closely to the behavioral expectations of the situation in which the individual is functioning. They may also relate to the types of services actually offered and the ability of these services to provide appropriate interventions for individuals with specific types of disorders. For example, different therapists may use quite diverse criteria for evaluating problem behaviors and the need for services: the therapist who deals well with withdrawn individuals may not readily identify those with acting-out behaviors. In other cases, the therapist, or team, may not feel that they have the time to deal with the withdrawn student because the acting-out individuals are creating more problems in the school. These strategies make it difficult to compare the current identification practices for those with behavior disorders who are served by different schools, districts, agencies, or states.

Methods for Diagnosis and Assessment

Once it is determined that these individuals have behavior problems which are serious enough to interfere with their performance, they are generally referred for consideration for treatment or intervention. The referral agent (e.g., the parent, teacher, or the individual) often serves as a primary source of information regarding the need for services. Their information may be obtained in a variety of ways and it often serves to assist in the diagnostic process and in the assessment needed to develop an appropriate intervention plan for the individual.

Interviews, either informal or structured, can provide information regarding the nature and extent of the problem. They may also help to identify factors which are contributing to the perceived problem or those which should be considered in developing an appropriate intervention. Interviews may be conducted by school psychologists, special teachers, social workers, counselors, or others involved in the diagnostic process. They may be conducted with the person being considered, with others knowledgeable of the candidate's behavior, or with groups such as those composed of teachers or parents, family members, and the individual. Depending on who is involved in the interview, the process may allow the interviewer to establish rapport with the individual and to collect basic introductory information, background information to establish the context of the problem, developmental history, and strengths and weaknesses (Van Evra, 1983). The individual's medical and school records may also be reviewed.

Behavior rating scales provide an excellent method to systematically collect data about an individual's behavior. They are composed of a standard group of items which describe a behavior or behavior problem, and the respondents are

Parent Interviews:
An Important Assessment
Technique

The assessment of behavior problems in children and adolescents and planning of appropriate interventions can be facilitated by obtaining information from their parents. Information can be acquired most systematically in a semistructured interview with one or both parents. While some may question the reliability of the information obtained from parents, other professionals (e.g., Rutter, Tizard, & Whitmore, 1970) have found it to be the best single indicator of behavior disorders. Others (Achenbach & Edelbrock, 1978) suggest that parents are able to report behaviors which are not seen in clinical settings and may be the most reliable source of information concerning the child.

The primary purpose of the interview is to identify the behaviors that are to be the focus of a treatment or intervention plan. During the process of obtaining this information it is also important to identify factors which may occur both before and after the problem behavior and possibly contribute to its reoccurrence. The interview can also serve other essential purposes. The interactions which take place during the interview can assist in establishing rapport with the parent(s) and possibly initiate a relationship which will help to actively involve them in assisting to implement interventions which will be developed after the assessment is completed. It may also help to assess the parent's ability and interest in executing the interventions once they are developed. Historical information on the pattern of the development of problem behaviors may also be gained from the parents. Finally, the interview process may promote parents' understanding of the factors which contribute to the occurrence of the behavior and the role their actions may have in the promoting the problem behavior; yet the interview should not attempt to place the blame for the behaviors on the parents (Barkley, 1981; Forehand & McMahon, 1981).

The parental interview should review the interactions of the parent and child in common situations, both those which occur at home and out in public. The parent should be asked about whether problem behaviors occur in a variety of situations such as: when the child plays with other children, when playing alone, at bedtime, at mealtimes, when preparing for school, while watching television, when there are guests in the home, when the parents are occupied (e.g., doing chores, talking on the telephone, talking to others in the store), while the child is at the store, when only the mother is present, when the father is present, when both are present, or in a variety of other possible situations. To facilitate this process the interviewer should prepare a list of possible situations, such as those noted above, which can be followed during the interview. The interviewer should pursue a questioning process somewhat like the following suggested by Barkley (1981):

1. Ask about each situation on the list and determine if the problem occurs in that situation. If a problem does not occur in the situation, the interviewer should proceed to inquire about the next situation, and if a problem does occur in the situation, then the interviewer should proceed with the following questions.

2. Exactly what is the behavior in this situation which is seen as a problem?

3. How do the parents respond to this behavior?

4. What does the child do after the parent responds?

5. What do the parents do next if the problem continues?

6. What is generally the result of this interaction?

7. With what frequency do these problems occur in this situation?

8. What are the parent's reactions or feeling about these problems?

9. Have the parents provide their rating of the severity of the behavior on a scale between 0 and 10 (10 being a severe problem and 0 being no problem).

The same list of questions is used for each situation in which a problem behavior is identified. Such a questioning process permits the interviewer to establish the pattern of behavioral controls used by the parent(s) and it also provides information relating to their effectiveness in modifying the behavior. Information gained from the interview can prove useful in designing and implementing interventions for the child because it can help to identify specific behaviors which are to be the target of the interventions. It also reveals the types of situations under which the problem behaviors occur and may provide clues as to what may "set-off" the behavior and what activities may maintain its continuation.

expected to rate the individual on each item. For example, the rater may be asked to rate the person's behavior on a scale from very acceptable to highly unacceptable on items such as "the student follows classroom rules" or "the student uses physical contact in an appropriate way." These rating scales are completed by persons who have had the opportunity to observe the individuals and are aware of how they react in various settings.

Parents may be asked to complete a rating scale such as the *Louisville Behavior Checklist* (Miller, 1977) which has been normed on parent ratings and provides 164 items, including both desirable and inappropriate behaviors. Besides providing a measure of adaptive and deviant behavior, it also provides a scale which gauges the parent's tolerance for troublesome behavior. Self-ratings may be completed on self-concept scales such as the *Piers-Harris Children's Self-Concept Scale* (Piers & Harris, 1969) which is appropriate for students in grades 3 through 12. It is composed of 80 declarative statements (e.g., "My classmates make fun of me"; "I am smart") with scores clustered into six dimensions of self-concept such as behavior, happiness-satisfaction, anxiety, and popularity. Physicians and psychiatrists may use the *DSM-III* as a rating scale for it lists criteria and symptomatic behaviors which are used to develop a psychiatric diagnosis or classification for children, adolescents, or adults.

Teachers may complete instruments such as the *Behavior Rating Profile* or *BRP* (Brown & Hammill, 1983) for grades 1 through 12 or the *Hahnemann High School* Behavior Rating Scale (Spivack & Swift, 1972) for grades 7 through 12. The *BRP* includes ratings to be completed by teachers, parents, peers, and the students themselves; scaled scores from each of these ratings are compared and a sociogram is also provided. The Hahnemann scale is completed by the teacher and consists of 45 items relating to 13 academic and behavioral areas (e.g., reasoning ability, general anxiety, withdrawal, rigidity) with major attention given to academic areas.

Direct observation of behavior involves the identification of specific behaviors to be observed, selecting an observation system, collecting the data, recording/graphing the data, and analyzing the results. This technique for evaluating the behavior of individuals of all ages is being used increasingly for both diagnosis and assessment of behavior disorders. Information obtained from direct observation can supplement or validate data obtained from rating scales, interviews, or other evaluation techniques. Direct observation, such as that described in

Table 10.3

Observational Data Example

Johnny

Johnny was an 8-year-old third grader whose teacher (Ms. Mack) felt was creating a great deal of "strife" in the classroom. When this was reported to the resource teacher in the school, she scheduled a meeting with Johnny's teacher to review the problem. Ms. Mack agreed to complete a behavior rating scale on Johnny before the meeting. The rating scale showed that there were two areas of Johnny's behavior which were of most concern to Ms. Mack: loud talking during quiet or work times and interfering with the work of others by being out of his seat during the same period of time. It was decided that in order to determine the type of intervention needed, and to determine the exact extent of the problem, observation of Johnny's behavior would take place during the class time devoted to quiet and independent work sessions for the next five days. This information could be used in designing an intervention and to evaluate the intervention once it was implemented. The teachers agreed on the behaviors to be observed and completed the observation form as follows:

Student ___*Johnny*___   Observer ___*Ms. Mack*___

Description of Behaviors to be Observed:

1. Talking-out: Each time during the quiet or independent work sessions that Johnny talked loud enough to be heard by the teacher was considered to be a "talk-out" and it was counted as one occurrence.

2. Out-of-seat: Johnny was considered to be out-of-seat when during the quiet or independent work sessions he no longer had physical contact with the seat of his chair.

Recording Procedure:

1. Talk-outs: An event recording system records each time this behavior occurs each day.

2. Out-of-seat: A duration recording system was to be used to record the actual number of minutes per day that he was away from his seat.

Observation Day:	1	2	3	4	5	6	7	8	9	10	11	12
# of talk-outs												
Time out-of-seat												

Table 10.3, facilitates the collection of reliable data to describe the behavior of concern, determines whether the behavior is serious enough to require intervention, and serves as the basis for establishing and evaluating an intervention plan. Observation systems are most productive if they are conducted in the actual situation in which the problem behavior is occurring. A carefully designed observation system can be implemented by an individual who has limited training or experience (e.g., a parent or classroom aide) or by a highly trained observer. The data obtained are most reliable if the behaviors to be observed are clearly

Biofeedback: The Use of Technology with Behavior Disorders

Using biofeedback to assist in treating various types of medical and psychological disorders is a technology which has been evolving recently. This practice has been one which has received somewhat mixed reviews regarding its effectiveness in modifying the effects of psychological factors on the individual's functioning. Basically, biofeedback attempts to use specialized and highly sensitive electronic equipment to monitor the responses of the body to various types of stimuli and situations which are impossible to monitor with any conventional observational techniques. The electronic equipment may be designed to monitor one of a number of bodily systems such as blood pressure, heart rate, stomach secretions, body temperature, the movement of small muscles, brain waves, or penile erection. The equipment is designed to monitor the very tiny electrical signals emitted by the system being monitored and those signals are amplified and then converted to an auditory or visual signal. This auditory or visual signal provides the individual being monitored with a form of immediate feedback on changes in the system. It is proposed that the subject can improve the ability to gain voluntary control over the system of concern because he or she is able to monitor the effects of various activities on that system.

The technique has frequently been used with disorders which are considered to be psychosomatic in nature. Biofeedback has been successful in the alleviation of tension-caused headaches, muscular pain, some types of seizures, hypertension, asthma, peptic ulcers, and certain types of sexual disorders (Doleys & Bruno, 1982; Rosenhan & Seligman, 1984). In a few cases, it has been effective in reducing muscular activity and tension with young students (e.g., Braud, Lupin, & Braud, 1975). In a review of research related to the use of biofeedback with anxiety-related disorders, Emmelkamp (1982) found that there was no substantial evidence that the technique was of any value to anxious or phobic individuals.

Frequently the use of biofeedback is combined with some form of relaxation therapy or with the use of cognitive strategies or self-control techniques to assist in modifying the desired system. For example, the subjects may undertake to reduce tension headaches by attempting to decrease the contractions of muscles in the forehead by relaxing when the monitoring device indicates that the tension is present; in some cases they may be provided with a reinforcer (such as music) when they are successful in reducing the level of tension. While biofeedback is considered by some to hold a great deal of promise, additional research is required to support or reject the early claims for its effectiveness before it can obtain any widespread acceptance. Research using biofeedback with many types of disorders, especially those with children, has been sparse.

stated in a way that leaves little room for the subjective interpretation of the observer and if the data are collected during several observations.

Older students and adults can be taught to use self-monitoring systems in which they observe and record their own problematic behaviors as they occur in their own environment. For example, someone concerned about not feeling well can be assigned the task of recording exactly what he or she is thinking and doing, as well as the environmental circumstances, when these "feelings" occur. Another person experiencing an eating and weight problem may be expected to keep daily records of food intake and weight. Students having difficulty completing assignments can use a stopwatch to measure the actual amount of time they are working on the assignments during the class period or the amount of time they are not sitting in their seat. The accuracy of these data should be checked periodically by another observer and those monitoring their own performance should receive positive attention for keeping accurate records. This technique provides data which are collected with the actual occurrence of the target behavior as well as information on responses which are only accessible to the persons experiencing them. Biofeedback may also demonstrate its effectiveness in monitoring human reactions which are difficult to observe.

Sociometric measures are used to gather information regarding the perceptions of group members toward particular individuals in that group. These measures attempt to identify the level of acceptance of particular individuals and to note individuals who are isolates or group leaders. The procedures may involve nomination (e.g., "Name two people you would like to work with on a project"), rating scales (i.e., rating each individual in the group on a particular factor such as interest in working with that person), or paired-comparisons (i.e., choosing a preferred person from two choices). Under some conditions it is neither permissible nor appropriate to use these measures because it places individuals in the position of making judgments of others (Lewis & Doorlag, 1987). While they have been shown to be reliable over time, they should not be used in isolation. Though they can effectively supplement the results of other assessment data collected regarding the individual (Asher & Taylor, 1981), professionals should be cautious in their use of the results.

Additional assessment data customarily obtained for individuals with behavior disorders are similar to that required in other areas of exceptionality. Their academic achievement and intellectual potential is assessed using instruments such as those described for the learning disabled. For example, in a school setting, the student identified as a potential candidate for services for those with behavior disorders is likely to be administered an individual intelligence test and one or more formal or informal measures of reading, math, spelling, or other school skills.

Special Considerations with Preschool Children and Adults

Diagnosis and assessment of preschool children and adults often requires the use of other measures or assessment techniques. Careful observation of the child's behavior, interviews with family members, preschool teachers, or baby-sitters supplemented by formal measures of intelligence and assessments in playroom settings provide diagnostic information. With very young children a central concern is often differential diagnosis. When a preschooler does not relate well to others, uses little appropriate language, and performs at a very low level, the diagnostic team tries to determine whether the child is mentally retarded or autistic. In instances in which a very young child is consistently aggressive, out-of-control, or withdrawn, the team may focus on the way that the child has been managed. They would want to determine whether the child was behavior disordered or had simply learned to behave in inappropriate ways because of the family's poor management techniques. With preschoolers, the diagnosis may lead to different treatment strategies.

Adults may be evaluated in a variety of areas. For example, individuals with job performance problems may be evaluated using rating scales such as the *Job Site Evaluation Rating Form* (Brolin, 1982, p. 162) which provides a checklist for rating the individual's work habits and his or her ability to acquire new job skills. Other instruments such as the *Alcohol Questionnaire, Drug Questionnaire,* and *Eating Questionnaire* (Cautela & Upper, 1976) are also available to assist in the identification of target behaviors requiring further study.

Adults are often assessed using psychological inventories which are very structured psychological tests requiring the examinee to respond to an assortment of true/false statements. They generally can be administered individually or in groups and provide normative comparisons of the individual's performance. The most widely used and studied of these inventories for adults is the *Minnesota Multiphasic Personality Inventory (MMPI)* (Hathaway & McKinley, 1943). Inquiries are made into a wide variety of behaviors, feelings, and thoughts through the use of 550 test items, with scores provided in 10 categories such as depression, hysteria, paranoia, social introversion-extroversion, and mania. The results of the test are recorded in a profile which is more useful than the scores alone for it can be compared to sources containing the profiles of individuals whose history is well known (Gilberstadt & Duker, 1965) and this analysis can be considered with other assessment information when interventions are planned.

Occasionally other types of instruments or procedures are used to collect data on adult behavior disorders. Projective personality tests such as the *Rorschach Test* (Rorschach, 1942) which examines the client's response to a series of abstract inkblots or the *Thematic Apperception Test (TAT)* (Murray, 1943) which requires responses to somewhat vague pictures are also used diagnostically. These tests focus on the person's unconscious motivations and conflicts and are used primarily by therapists with a psychodynamic orientation to assist them in assessing the personality make-up and underlying psychodynamics of the individual. Information obtained from instruments such as these is difficult to interpret because the analysis involves formulating conclusions which are based on inferences drawn from client responses. Projective instruments are frequently questioned regarding the reliability of both their scoring and protocol interpretation, and studies regarding their validity have often not supported their usefulness (Mischel, 1968, 1976; Murstein, 1965; Peterson, 1968; Zubin, Eron, & Schumer, 1965).

CONSIDERATIONS IN INTERVENTION

Interventions for individuals with behavior disorders are normally developed following a thorough assessment conducted by professionals. Information obtained during this process is used to evaluate factors which may be affecting performance and to identify relative strengths and weaknesses to determine the nature of an appropriate intervention. The design of this intervention will be affected by the needs of the individual; the theoretical perspective, training, and experience of those designing the intervention; the availability of services by those offering the intervention; and funding limitations.

It is important to note that earlier research indicates that many persons with behavior disorders improve without the introduction of any intervention. Ross (1974) reports that approximately two-thirds of the children with behavior disorders improve within two years even without intervention. Others (Clarizio & McCoy, 1983) indicate that 70 percent of children who are maladjusted appear to "outgrow" their problems. Two-thirds to three-fourths of those individuals who receive formal professional treatment at school or elsewhere improve, regardless of the age of the children, the treatment setting, or the discipline of the therapist (Lewis, 1965). While recent research indicates that several treatment approaches currently being used demonstrate effectiveness in improving behavior, particularly behaviorally-oriented programs, there is a need to conduct additional research regarding the generalization of behaviors learned in the treatment setting.

The Preschool Years

The social-emotional behavior of young children is considered to be highly pliable and consequently program goals for these children are usually geared to early identification and prevention. In addition, evaluation of young children's behaviors is easier because the expectations for normal behavior are much simpler than those for older children or adults. The effect of early behavior patterns is illustrated by children who are unusually irritable, have irregular behavior patterns (e.g., eating or sleeping), or do not adapt well to new social situations; they may develop serious behavior problems if the parents are not unusually adept at handling these children.

Unless the child's behavior disorders are severe and bring that child into frequent conflicts with adults or other children, there is a good possibility that the potential disorder will not be identified. If the child is not working with a teacher in a preschool program, the parents or the physician are the most likely referral agents for students at this age level. Assessment tools designed for young children seek to measure their development in the following areas: cognitive development, motor development, language development, self-help skills, play skills, and personal-social skills. Those with severe behavior disorders (i.e., autistic or psychotic) will often exhibit deficits in all six of the areas, while those with mild behavior disorders will be more likely to exhibit deficits in the self-help, play, and personal-social skills areas.

Intervention programs for young children attempt to provide for their early involvement in a home-based, center-based, or a combined home-center program. Other types of programs may be offered for the children and/or the parents by psychiatrists, physicians, social workers, community mental health workers or others at their offices, clinics, or in the home. Children with severe behavior disorders may require the intensive medical, instructional, and counseling services provided in a residential institution.

Preschool programs assist children in developing appropriate social skills and improve their performance in areas related to school readiness. Behaviorally-

Programs that are successful in modifying problem behaviors may include modeling, self-instruction, self-reinforcement, and problem solving.

oriented programs which define and measure the behavior and then rearrange environmental events to teach and nurture more appropriate behavior are frequently used with this population. Besides improving the skills of the child, many of the behaviorally-oriented programs attempt to improve the skills of the parents in working with their child in the home setting by teaching the parents specific management techniques and monitoring their progress. There is significant evidence to indicate that behavioral approaches are effective for improving the behaviors of preschool and school-age children (Sulzer-Azaroff & Pollack, 1982). These children are often served in settings which include children with other types of handicaps and an increasing number of programs afford the opportunity for them to be integrated regularly with their "normal" age peers.

The School Years

Students may enter school with behavior disorders or these disorders may develop during their time in school. The ability of the school program to provide adequately for the particular needs of these students may be a primary determining factor in their level of performance while at school. Many students enter school lacking the prerequisite academic or social skills which would permit them to adapt easily to the demands of the classroom. Others have a temperament which brings them rapidly into conflict with their teachers or fellow students. While academic underachievement is considered the most common characteristic of behaviorally disordered students and is the primary criterion used for defining and identifying these students, it is the disturbing behaviors of these students which are the major concern of the educator. Meeting the need for students with behavior disorders to develop adequate classroom skills and social skills is increasingly emphasized in educational programs designed for these students (Gresham, 1981, 1982; Michelson, Sugai, Wood, & Kazdin, 1983).

Conduct-disordered and anxious-withdrawn students are those most frequently found in special education programs serving behavior disordered students. In contrast, children with severe behavior disorders, especially those with childhood psychoses, demonstrate much lower functional capabilities, and their inappropriate behaviors make up a much higher percentage of their total behaviors. Those students may function as if they are retarded, avoid interactions with others, lack touch with reality, lack functional language, have ritualistic behaviors, or exhibit other types of highly inappropriate behaviors. If their inappropriate behavioral patterns are evident before they are 30 months old they are designated as autistic, and if the patterns are evident after 30 months old their condition is labeled as childhood schizophrenia or atypical psychosis (Dunlap, Koegel, & Egel, 1979; Kauffman, 1981). Autistic students are no longer included under the heading of seriously emotionally disturbed by the regulations associated with PL 94–142; instead they are grouped under the category of other health impaired because of the suspected biogenic nature of their disorders and the effect of their developmental delays on their progress.

School programs may contribute to the development of behavior disorders in students in a variety of ways. Teachers may not provide the consistent classroom management which is needed by many students. Classroom rules and behavioral expectations for students often are not reasonable, possibly being overly strict or nonexistent. Realistic performance expectations may not be held for students and they may be frustrated by those which are too high or not challenged by those which are too low. Frequent reinforcement may not be provided for appropriate behaviors while inappropriate student behaviors receive a great deal of teacher attention (Kauffman, 1981). An increasing body of research (e.g., Reith, Polsgrove & Semmel, 1979, 1981; Stevens & Rosenshine, 1981; Thompson, White, & Morgan, 1982) indicates that the effectiveness of educational programs in developing academic and social skills is related to the teacher's skills in effectively conducting instruction and managing the classroom. The teacher's ability to provide instruction which includes components such as the use of data to place students in instructional sequences, ensuring that they achieve a high percentage of correct responses and appropriate feedback and correction for these responses, and maximizing the amount of time that students are engaged in instruction, increase the probability that students will achieve both academic and social skill gains in the program for behavior disordered students (Doorlag, 1982; Ruggles & LeBlanc, 1982). Kauffman (1981) indicates:

A behavioral analysis of the academic performance of children shows many inadequacies assumed to be inherent in the child actually are instructional deficiencies in teachers. Thus, what is most needed by special educators who are confronted with academic failure in a disturbed child is careful examination of instructional tactics, not a probe of the child's psyche. (p. 261)

Educational programs which follow different theoretical approaches have typically been offered for students with behavior disorders. For example, psychodynamic programs are concerned with unconscious motivations and have relied upon individual psychotherapy for the student and often for the parents; such programs are generally quite permissive and give slight attention to academic instruction. Psychoeducational approaches are based upon similar beliefs regarding the cause of the problems and add some stress on working on surface behaviors and an individual approach to academics. Humanistic approaches encourage trying to help the individual achieve self-fulfillment in a nonthreatening, nondirective atmosphere. Behavioral approaches stress that behaviors have been learned and education involves instruction which manipulates the antecedents and consequences for the behavior. Ecological approaches are based upon tenets similar to those of the behavioral approach, yet they attempt to modify those factors which influence the individual's behavior in their entire social system (e.g., school, neighborhood, family).

Current practices which have gained increasing support as a result of research include cognitive behavior modification (CBM), which considers that behavior change is affected by factors such as self-perceptions and self-dialogue, and social learning theory, which extends the analysis of behavior to include observational learning and internal states (e.g., thoughts, feelings). These approaches, which stress procedures such as modeling, self-instruction, self-reinforcement, and problem solving, have demonstrated effectiveness in modifying problem behaviors (Karoly & Kanfer, 1982; Kneedler, 1980; Meichenbaum, 1977, 1980). For example, an implementation of CBM may involve teaching the student a self-instructional training program which involves a step-by-step strategy to attack a problem using specific verbalizations, with components such as defining the problem, focusing attention, developing statements to cope with errors, and establishing a method for self-reinforcement (Lewis & Doorlag, 1987).

Currently available empirical evidence indicates that behaviorally-oriented strategies have been documented to be the most effective in reducing anxieties and fears and in improving the academic and social behaviors of students with behavior disorders (Kauffman, 1981; Kauffman & Kneedler, 1981; Morris & Kratochwill, 1983; Nelson, 1981a, 1981b; Ruggles & LeBlanc, 1982). Programs with a behavioral orientation have also been demonstrated to be very successful in improving the behaviors of autistic children (Dunlap, Koegel, & Egel, 1979; Schreibman et al., 1982) and delinquents (Burchard & Lane, 1982). The Promising Practices Section provides an example of one behavioral program that is very effective in working with adolescents with behavior disorders. There continues to be a need to enhance the effectiveness of approaches that work in the classroom or clinic to provide students with skills which generalize to other settings.

Many students with behavior disorders are served in regular classrooms by consultants who assist the regular teacher in working with these students. Those who require more direct assistance are served by resource room programs, yet

Achievement Place: A Model Program for Adolescents with Behavior Disorders

Achievement Place is a residential treatment program which is designed to teach prosocial behaviors to predelinquent adolescent boys. The program, which is an outstanding example of the application of behavioral principles to problem behaviors, was initially begun in 1967 by the students and faculty of the University of Kansas Department of Human Development and is now operated in several other places around the country (Fixen, Wolf, & Phillips, 1973; Phillips, 1968).

The program is operated by two professionally trained "teaching parents" who live together in a house with six to eight boys in a family-style arrangement. The boys are placed in the program by the court because they have legally been declared as delinquent or dependent-neglect cases; many of the boys' homes are in the same community, and while in the program they continue to attend their home school and visit occasionally in their homes. Each of the boys is responsible for regular work tasks and he is expected to attend school daily. The program uses instruction, practice, modeling, and feedback combined with a token economy providing points and praise for appropriate behavior such as doing chores, achieving in school, watching the news on television, and being neat in appearance. Points are lost for inappropriate behaviors like stealing, lying, being verbally aggressive, or cheating. Points or checkmarks are recorded (or subtracted) on a 3-by-5 card carried by the student. The teaching parents play a critical role in the success of the program as they are expected to establish a mutually reinforcing working relationship with the boys and to serve as role models, reinforcers, and instructors who provide for the development of appropriate social skills. Examples of skills emphasized in the program are responding appropriately to criticism and academic skills which are important to success in school and in later obtaining a job.

Achievement Place emphasizes self-government; the boys are expected to take increasing responsibilities for their own behavior and for helping others living in the house. This emphasis has increased over the years the program has operated because the empirical evidence collected by the program evaluators has demonstrated that the program is more effective if this component is in place. This research has also identified the importance of the houseparents' use of social reinforcement and social interaction with the boys in maintaining the program's success.

The boys are able to exchange their points for a variety of privileges of the type which are naturally available in a home setting (e.g., after-school snacks, time watching television, late bedtimes) but available to them only by earning the appropriate number of points. Once the boys have achieved a certain level of performance they can purchase the right to no longer use the point system and to transfer to a merit system. This step attempts to assist in the transfer of the individual to a system of more natural reinforcers and methods of feedback which are readily available in his own environment, such as social praise, status, and personal satisfaction. If the boy is able to perform appropriately on the merit system, he is then considered for return to his home. The boy's parents are provided with assistance and instruction in establishing a similar management system in their own home in order to maximize the carryover of the gains accomplished at Achievement Place. This process is also helpful in improving the skills of the parent in managing the boy at home.

The most important aspect of the Achievement Place program is the success it has achieved since its inception. The rate at which individuals got into serious enough trouble to be returned to an institution after their initial release was much lower for those who had been at Achievement Place when compared with boys who had been treated at a traditional institutional program (approximately 19% compared to 45% for a two-year period); similar results were obtained when the Achievement Place boys were compared to similar boys who had received no institutional care and had received only probation (54% return rate). In addition, comparison of the relative costs of the programs indicated that the per person cost for providing the Achievement Place program was approximately one-third of that incurred for operating the traditional institutional program (Kirgin, Wolf, Braukmann, Fixsen, & Phillips, 1979; Phillips, Phillips, Fixsen, & Wolf, 1973).

The program's effectiveness and monetary efficiency help to explain its acceptance in other parts of the country and the promise it may hold for treating this population. The Achievement Place program is currently being disseminated in several states under its new name, Teaching-Family Program (Nelson & Polsgrove, 1984).

they still spend the majority of their school day in the regular class. Others, especially those students with more severe conduct disorders, are frequently educated in the more restrictive settings provided by special class programs. Approximately 20 percent of this population is considered to be severely behavior disordered and served primarily in special schools or institutional programs (Grosenick & Huntze, 1980).

Because of the similarity of the academic problems experienced by students with behavior disorders to those of the learning disabled, the instructional programs in academic areas commonly follow the same guidelines and are based on the same premises. When developing educational programs it is important to consider that students with behavior disorders are consistently found to be academic underachievers. School programs for these students have often provided a general emphasis (as opposed to specific skill training) on the development of appropriate social behaviors and a relatively minor emphasis on improving the academic performance of the students. This has placed the students at a disadvantage when they return to the regular classroom program without adequate academic skills to maintain an acceptable level of performance.

The degree of classroom behavior and social skill problems displayed by behavior disordered students requires that their educational program include specific instruction in these areas. In order to exhibit appropriate social behaviors, these students must be able to evaluate a social situation when they encounter it and they must have learned the possible outcomes from using a repertoire of strategies appropriate for each situation (Trower, 1979). This need has been stressed in recent reports of research (e.g., Cartledge & Milburn, 1978; Gresham, 1981), and this research has served as the basis for the development of several programs which assist teachers in providing instruction in this area. The ACCEPTS (A Curriculum for Children's Effective Peer and Teacher Skills) Social Skills Curriculum (Walker et al., 1983), and Social Skills in the Classroom (Stephens, 1979) are programs which are designed primarily for use with elementary level students. Another available program directed toward adolescents is Skillstreaming the Adolescent (Goldstein, Sprafkin, Gershaw, & Klein, 1980). These programs all provide instructional activities for each of the skill areas and recommend specific teacher practices to be used during instruction. Each of the programs assumes that students have not learned the social skills required as a result of incidental learning and that effective instruction in this area will occur only when it is teacher directed. As students' skills increase through social skills training, their level of acceptance and ability to relate to their peers, teachers, and other adults will improve (Foster & Ritchey, 1979; Gresham, 1981, 1982; Michelson & Wood, 1980; Van Hasselt, Hersen, Whitehill, & Bellack, 1979).

Schools and community agencies often seek out the parents or other family members to participate in the intervention activities provided. The families may receive actual skill training involving enhancing their ability to deal effectively with the student or the service may assist the family in coping with the student's problems.

The Adult Years

As is the case with children and adolescents, adults may exhibit a wide range of behavior disorders. It is difficult to predict the extent to which children who have had behavior problems will also experience problems as adults (Lewis, 1965). Although it is possible to predict the approximate percentage of children with behavior disorders who will improve, it is not possible to determine which individuals will improve. Abnormal behaviors of adults may be judged on a continuum extending from effective functioning on one end to personality disorganization on the other. The severity of the behavior problem is usually judged by: (a) the bizarreness of the behavior, (b) the persistence of the behavior pattern, and (c) the effect of the problem on the individual's social functioning. Behavior disorders exhibited by adults may be categorized generally as: (a) extreme social deviance, i.e., inappropriate or disorganized social behaviors which disturb others around them; (b) subjective distress, i.e., excessive fearfulness, depression, agitation, etc. perceived by the individuals themselves; and (c) psychological handicaps, i.e., the problem impairs the person's ability to function adequately in daily social and occupational roles (Goldstein, Baker, & Jamison, 1980).

DSM-III provides an extensive and elaborate categorization system for the disorders of adults which is used by many professionals in the field in their diagnosis of these disorders. These disorders may be more simply grouped into schizophrenia, mood disorders, organic disorders, anxiety and psychophysiological disorders, and social deviance (Goldstein et al., 1980). In reviewing behavioral problems which are noted in aged populations (i.e., individuals over 65 years of age), Burnside (1980) indicates that problems experienced by the aged can be categorized in the following groups: aggression, confusion and disorientation, loneliness, incontinence, insomnia, and wandering.

Schizophrenia is a form of psychosis which has no specific identifiable cause and is usually accompanied by very inappropriate social behaviors, hallucination, and delusions. It is the most common diagnosis for individuals between 18 and 34 years old who are admitted to public mental hospitals, and there are purportedly two million diagnosed schizophrenics in the United States. Mood or affective disorders may involve depression or manic behaviors which may be characterized by extreme elation, high activity levels, irritability, or feelings of grandiosity. Organic disorders involve a dysfunction of the brain which may result from disease, injury, degeneration resulting from aging, or drug or toxic conditions. The disorder may result in impaired orientation, memory, intellectual functioning, judgment, affect, attention, perception, or thinking. Anxiety or neurotic disorders are expressions of fear which are disproportionate to the actual external danger which exists. The behaviors and/or physiological problems (i.e., actual or perceived physical ailments) which may interfere with daily performance and social interactions are often associated with the individual's ability to cope with stress. Social deviance involves the problems associated with substance abuse or dependence, illegal activities and crimes of violence, and sexual deviance (Goldstein et al., 1980).

Traditional interventions conducted with adults with behavior disorders by psychiatrists and clinical psychologists have used a disease model similar to that used in medicine. Implementation of this model involves seeking the underlying pathological, or diseased, processes which will account for the disordered behavior. Interventions conducted under this model involve the use of psychotherapy, or other counseling techniques, and medical treatments to reduce the causes of the disorders. Psychotherapy attempts to resolve intrapsychic conflicts which are considered to be causing the behavior disorder and medical treatments involve the use of drugs, surgery, or other medical interventions to diminish the effect of the biological causes of the disorder. Behavioral approaches consider that behavior is learned and they deal with the current level of specific observable problem behaviors which are measurable rather than being concerned with the historical determinants of the behavior. The underlying causes of the disorder are not of primary concern to the professionals providing behavioral treatment for they believe that new behaviors can be learned to replace the disordered behavior. The interventions designed are based on findings from research in psychology and generally attempt to teach behavior disordered individuals new skills (e.g., teaching assertiveness, communication, or social interaction skills) or strategies for coping with their behavioral problems. The successful use of behavioral approaches has increased in recent years (Kazdin, 1982; Spiegler, 1983). Other approaches such as group therapy and family therapy have gained recent attention. Each of these approaches, or combinations of them, is used in attempting to modify the adult's behavior disorders.

Interventions used with schizophrenic patients have changed since the 1950s. There has been a change in emphasis from custodial care to the use of hospital settings to provide for their rehabilitation. Halfway houses or group homes are currently being used to prepare patients for their reentry into society and the use of drug therapy with antipsychotic drugs (e.g., major tranquilizers such as the phenothiazines and butyrophenones) help to control schizophrenic behaviors. Psychotherapy, behavioral therapy, and family therapy during aftercare are also used with this population. In some treatment programs several approaches are used effectively together. The effectiveness of drug therapy and psychotherapy with this population has not been clearly established and behavioral research has indicated that schizophrenic symptomatology can be modified but the maintenance and generalization of these changes has not been clearly documented (Curran, Monti, & Corriveau, 1982; Goldstein et al., 1980; Hersen, 1979).

Mood disorders have been treated with a variety of interventions. Medical interventions include the use of medications such as lithium to reduce manic and depressive episodes; other treatments use antidepressants, electroconvulsive therapy, and sleep deprivation. Psychological approaches include cognitive therapy which attempts to help individuals to identify and control factors which are supporting negative thinking and contributing to maintaining their depressive moods. Behavioral approaches attempt to decrease unpleasant events and to increase pleasant events. In addition, the interventions attempt to teach skills which will improve the individual's patterns of interactions with the environment. A special area of consideration for this group of individuals is the prevention of suicide (which is the most disastrous result of depression) among persons with this type of behavior disorder. Prevention of suicide is most often attempted through the use of telephone hotlines which are available for individuals considering suicide; volunteers or professionals then attempt to initiate immediate crisis intervention to prevent the suicide and this is frequently followed by the use of one of the more traditional therapeutic approaches (Goldstein et al., 1980; Lewinsohn & Hoberman, 1982).

Organic disorders are frequently treated with surgery or medications which attempt to correct the problem or to resolve the problem to such a degree that people can function in their current environment. Surgery may attempt to remove tumors or restrictions which affect the blood flow to the brain. Medications may be used to reduce the effects of infection in cases such as those with encephalitis or to balance endocrine levels in disorders such as epilepsy. Often these treatments are accompanied by counseling or more directive techniques which attempt to help the individuals resolve their behavior problems.

Drug interventions with anxiety disorders have been shown to demonstrate short-term effectiveness, but there is little evidence to indicate that they will have long-term effects on behavior. Both psychotherapy and behavioral approaches are being used in treating individuals with anxiety disorders and social deviance. Those with anxiety problems appear to respond well to a variety of approaches, while behavioral approaches have been most effective in treating persons with simple fears or phobias (Emmelkamp, 1982; Goldstein et al., 1980). Social deviants have not responded well to psychotherapy because of their lack of concern with their problem or unwillingness to participate in treatment. Behavioral approaches such as aversive conditioning (i.e., pairing an aversive consequence such as electric shock or a noxious circumstance with the problem behavior) or the use of specific procedures for teaching appropriate adaptive skills have been used with increasing effectiveness with alcohol and drug abuse and dependence (Hersen, 1979; Miller, 1981; Sobell, Sobell, Ersner-Hershfield, & Nirenberg, 1982), sexual deviance (Friedman, Weiler, LoPiccolo, & Hogan, 1982), and criminal behavior (Burchard & Lane, 1982).

Problems with drug and alcohol abuse have increased in recent years. Many individuals enter adulthood with a familiarity with the use of these substances; it is reported that, in 1983, 93 percent of high school students had tried alcohol and 60 percent had tried marijuana. Treatment for chronic drug use is difficult for it requires breaking habits which have been established over many years. The most effective treatment programs help the persons to find jobs, change life-styles, and find different places to live. Residential programs with aftercare treatment tend to be superior to outpatient programs. It is reported that treatment programs usually result in great improvements in 20 percent of the persons, somewhat of an improvement in 60 percent, and no improvement in the remaining 20 percent of the individuals (Rosenhan & Seligman, 1984). Many who have become addicted to alcohol, narcotics, smoking, or overeating possibly suppress the practice without the aid of formal treatment (Schacter, 1982).

Various aspects of the interventions used with adults may be implemented by a variety of professionals. Physicians, psychologists, psychiatrists, counselors, social workers, or nurses may direct or assist in the implementation of the various types of interventions used with this group. Educators may not be directly involved in the treatment, but they often serve as a source of information regarding the past performance level of individuals with behavior disorders. These persons may receive services at a clinic, the professional's private practice office, halfway houses or group homes, community-based institutions, psychiatric wards of hospitals, state or regional institutions, convalescent homes, or in their home or the home of a friend or family member. An intervention may involve only the professional and the person with behavior disorders or it may be conducted in a group composed of family members or friends or others with similar problems. The services may be funded by local mental health agencies, insurance plans, governmental agencies (e.g., a state social service department or the Veterans Administration) or it may be the direct responsibility of the patients themselves.

FUTURE PERSPECTIVES FOR THE TREATMENT OF BEHAVIOR DISORDERS

Programs designed to treat individuals with behavior disorders have attempted to serve a much broader clientele in recent years. Such programs are currently available for those from preschool age to the aged. There is no longer the heavy reliance on a few treatment options, such as psychotherapy or custodial care in an institution, which may have been the only ones available in the past. Legislative mandates are identifying the responsibility of states and communities for providing appropriate services, with local services being provided to replace the need to send the majority of individuals with behavior disorders to far-off institutions. Professionals are being trained to use a much wider variety of treatment approaches, with many new approaches based on empirical research, not solely on theories. School-age students are receiving services which were not available a few years ago and many of them are being served by teachers who have received specialized training in newly developed teacher training programs. Public and private community agencies are providing a wider range of services which allow the behavior disordered individuals to remain in, or return to, their home community. This practice is promising for it permits them to remain in a more normalized environment and reduces the chances of "warehousing" them in large institutions. Problems such as alcohol and drug abuse have continued to grow in size and increase the need for new resources to respond to the needs they, or other new or growing problems, create. In addition, research is currently being conducted in many areas to identify factors which contribute to the development of behavior disorders and to isolate the critical variables essential for effective treatment programs.

While recent developments in behavioral and medical research may hold much promise for this area, there are still many issues of concern to professionals and other interested individuals. The actual extent to which behavioral or emotional disorders exist continues to be a major question; incidence and prevalence figures vary greatly in reports from different studies and various agencies. Accurate information here would assist in predicting the need for services and determining the extent to which these services are being provided. The lack of a clearly stated definition of what constitutes behavior disorders or emotional disturbance contributes to many problems in this area. Current definitions vary between agencies and professions (e.g., mental health agencies, educational institutions, social work, medicine, and psychiatry) creating a variety of problems in prediction, communication, and treatment.

There are several problems in critically evaluating and comparing the effectiveness of the different interventions used with behavior disordered individuals. The lack of clear definitions for the diverse categories of behavior disorders makes it difficult to compare research on various interventions. In addition, the perceptions of what is a behavior disorder may change as our knowledge of the disorders increases or simply with the passage of time. It is difficult to replicate or to generalize the findings of research conducted on a particular intervention to other settings if it is not possible to determine that the population of subjects receiving the proposed intervention are the same as those who were involved in the original research.

A major issue not yet resolved relates to the effectiveness of the interventions used with this population to develop skills or adaptive behaviors which can be transferred to settings other than those in which they received the treatment. Individuals who develop skills in clinics, schools, correctional institutions, or group homes are frequently not able to exhibit the skills outside these settings. Additional research is needed to examine this phenomenon and to use this information to develop strategies which facilitate the development of skills which can be exhibited in the normal environment.

Research on medical interventions has led to the use of chemotherapy approaches which have assisted in resolving certain types of behavioral problems (e.g., the use of lithium with manic-depressive disorders), yet the promise held for the use of drugs may be somewhat misleading in others (e.g., hyperactivity in children). Other medical research continues to examine the possible contributions of biochemical imbalances to various types of disorders. At this time we are not able to rely totally on the medical approach for resolving a large percentage of the disorders and should continue to use other approaches with these individuals which will assist in improving their social skills and adaptive behaviors. Current research on the chemical make-up of the brain may also lead to developments to identify specific drugs which can be used to assist in modifying the behaviors of an individual with disorders.

The rapid expansion of current research on behaviorally-oriented social skills training has been especially promising. Interventions are being developed for persons of all ages and the research cited in this chapter indicates that there is a strong basis to indicate that social skills can be taught and developed by using specific training procedures.

The information currently available is not definitive in identifying those who will have behavior disorders at some time in the future. We may have gross indicators (e.g., psychotic and conduct-disordered children have a high probability of exhibiting disorders as adults), but we are not able to specifically predict which types of problems will become more severe as the individual grows older. Research directed at identifying critical prediction variables would assist in focusing both screening and preventive programs.

Future programs should concentrate on training individuals in specific social, academic, and vocational skill areas. Interventions should be based on principles and procedures which have an empirical basis for indicating their effectiveness. The design of a specific intervention should be based on assessment information which is used to evaluate the extent of the individual's behavior problems and also serves as a basis for evaluating change when using the ongoing collection of data to gauge the effect of the intervention on the problem behaviors. The emphasis of programs should continue to be the provision of skills which will permit the person to function effectively in as normalized a setting as possible. Professionals should be well trained in current empirically-based techniques as accountability will be a key in assuring the appropriateness and effectiveness of interventions. Those responsible for their implementation should be responsible for being aware of options which must be considered if the individual is not developing new skills as a result of the current intervention and should be able to recommend appropriate modifications to improve their effectiveness. Finally, information on the effectiveness of current practices will be accurate only to the extent that practitioners carefully evaluate their work and share the results of their work with others in the field.

SUMMARY

Individuals with behavioral problems exhibit behaviors which interfere with their academic achievement, job performance, personal satisfaction, or their social interactions with others while they are in school, at home, and/or in the community. These individuals are frequently described as behavior disordered, maladjusted, or emotionally disturbed. They may display a variety of problem behaviors which can range from extremely aggressive or bizarre to exceedingly withdrawn. Persons with other handicaps may also display behavior disorders.

There is no one single definition for behavior disorders which is accepted by all professionals who work with this group. The definitions used are quite subjective and most of the responsibility for determining who is behavior disordered is left to those responsible for determining the individual's need for services.

Current definitions do not permit a reliable comparison of the effectiveness of various interventions with individuals with similar problems and the labels provided in the definitions do not provide an exact indication of the specific treatment needs.

Professionals with different theoretical perspectives do not agree on the causes of behavior disorders, and some believe that etiological information is of limited help in selecting interventions or in predicting their success. The causes of behavior disorders are typically related to biogenic or organic factors, intrapsychic conflicts, lack of self-fulfillment, poor interactions with the environment, or the presence of inappropriate learned responses. There are not adequate data to indicate that an individual who exhibits a disorder at one point in his or her life will always have the same, or more severe, problems. Many behavior disorders are very transient and improvement occurs even without treatment.

Individuals with behavior disorders are usually identified by referrals from others, but identification may result from the use of screening programs in schools or self-referral by adolescents or adults. Following identification, the subject is assessed using observation procedures, academic achievement measures, personality measures, or other appropriate techniques which concentrate on gathering accurate information which will be used to determine the need for professional help and the nature of the most appropriate interventions. Assessment practices will vary depending upon the age of the person, the nature of the problem, the orientation of the assessors, and the types of interventions which are available.

Typically, interventions used with individuals with behavior disorders follow theoretical models which are either psychodynamic, psychoeducational, humanistic, ecological, or behavioral. The empirical evidence available on the effectiveness of approaches used with each of these models most strongly supports the effectiveness of a behavioral model in improving the behaviors of those involved in treatment. This model has demonstrated effectiveness in improving the academic, social, job-related, and interpersonal skills of those with behavior disorders. There continues to be a need to validate the effectiveness of current interventions in generalizing the behavioral improvements to settings other than those in which the treatment occurred.

References

Achenbach, T. M., & Edelbrock, C. S. (1978). The classification of child psychopathology: A review and analysis of empirical efforts. *Psychological Bulletin, 85,* 1275–1301.

Ahlstrom, W. M., & Havighurst, R. J. (1971). *400 losers.* San Francisco: Jossey-Bass.

Algozzine, R., Schmid, R., & Mercer, C. D. (1981). *Childhood behavior disorders.* Rockville, MD: Aspen Systems.

American Psychiatric Association. (1980). *Diagnostic and statistical manual of mental disorders* (3rd ed.). Washington, DC: Author.

Asher, S. R., & Taylor, A. R. (1981). Social outcomes of mainstreaming: Sociometric assessment and beyond. *Exceptional Education Quarterly, 1* (4), 13–30.

Axelrod, S., & Bailey, S. L. (1979). Drug treatment for hyperactivity: Controversies, alternatives, and guidelines. *Exceptional Children, 45,* 544–550.

Barkley, R. A. (1981). Hyperactivity. In E. J. Mash & L. G. Terdal (Eds.), *Behavioral assessment of childhood disorders* (pp. 127–184). New York: Guilford Press.

Bower, E. M. (1969). *The early identification of emotionally handicapped children in school* (2nd ed.). Springfield, IL: Charles C. Thomas.

Braud, L., Lupin, M. N., & Braud, W. G. (1975). The use of electromyographic biofeedback in the control of hyperactivity. *Journal of Learning Disabilities, 8,* 420–425.

Brolin, D. E. (1982). *Vocational preparation of persons with handicaps.* Columbus, OH: Merrill Publishing.

Brown, L. L., & Hammill, D. D. (1983). *Behavior rating profile.* Austin, TX: Pro-Ed.

Bryan, T. H., & Bryan, J. H. (1977). The social-emotional side of learning disabilities. *Behavioral Disorders, 2,* 141–145.

Burchard, J. D., & Lane, T. W. (1982). Crime and delinquency. In A. S. Bellack, M. Hersen, & A. E. Kazdin (Eds.), *International handbook of behavior modification and therapy.* New York: Plenum Press.

Burnside, I. M. (1980). Symptomatic behaviors in the elderly. In J. E. Birren & R. B. Sloane (Eds.), *Handbook of mental health and aging.* Englewood Cliffs, NJ: Prentice-Hall.

Cartledge, G., & Milburn, J. F. (1978). The case for teaching social skills in the classroom: A review. *Review of Educational Research, 1,* 133–156.

Castaneda, A. (1976). Cultural democracy and the educational needs of Mexican American children. In R. L. Jones (Ed.), *Mainstreaming and the minority child* (pp. 181–194). Reston, VA: Council for Exceptional Children.

Cautela, J. R., & Upper, D. (1976). The behavioral inventory battery: The use of self-report measures in behavioral analysis and therapy. In M. Hersen & A. S. Bellack (Eds.), *Behavioral assessment: A practical handbook.* New York: Pergamon Press.

Cawley, J. F., & Webster, R. E. (1981). Reading and behavior disorders. In G. Brown, R. L. McDowell, & J. Smith (Eds.), *Educating adolescents with behavior disorders.* Columbus, OH: Merrill Publishing.

Chess, S., & Thomas, A. (1977). Temperamental individuality from childhood to adolescence. *Journal of the American Academy of Child Psychiatry, 16,* 218–226.

Clarizio, H. F., & McCoy, G. F. (1983). *Behavior disorders in children.* New York: Harper & Row.

Cowen, E. L. (1980). The Primary Mental Health Project: Yesterday, today and tomorrow. *Journal of Special Education, 14,* 133–154.

Cowen, E. L., Trost, M. A., Lorion, R. P., Dorr, D., Izzo, L. D., & Isaacson, R. V. (1975). *New ways in school mental health: Early detection and prevention of school maladaption.* New York: Human Sciences Press.

Crisp, A. H., Palmer, R. L., & Kalucy, R. S. (1976). How common is anorexia nervosa: A prevalence study. *British Journal of Psychiatry, 128,* 549–555.

Cullinan, D., Epstein, M. H., & Lloyd, J. W. (1983). *Behavior disorders of children and adolescents.* Englewood Cliffs, NJ: Prentice-Hall.

Curran, J. P., Monti, P. M., & Corriveau, D. P. (1982). Treatment of schizophrenia. In A. S. Bellack, M. Hersen, & A. E. Kazdin (Eds.), *International handbook of behavior modification and therapy.* New York: Plenum Press.

Dent, H. E. (1976). Assessing Black children for mainstream placement. In R. L. Jones (Ed.), *Mainstreaming and the minority child* (pp. 77–92). Reston, VA: Council for Exceptional Children.

Depue, R. (1979). *The psychobiology of the depressive disorders: Implications for the effect of stress.* New York: Academic Press.

Depue, R. H., & Monroe, S. (1978). The unipolar-bipolar distinction in depressive disorders. *Psychological Bulletin, 85,* 1001–1029.

Dohrenwend, B. S., & Dohrenwend, B. P. (Eds.). (1974). *Stressful life events: Their nature and effects.* New York: John Wiley.

Doleys, D. M., & Bruno, J. (1982). Treatment of childhood medical disorders. In A. S. Bellack, M. Hersen, & A. E. Kazdin (Eds.), *International handbook of behavior modification and therapy.* New York: Plenum Press.

Doorlag, D. H. (1982, December). *The relationship of teacher behaviors to the performance of behaviorally disordered students: Implications of research on teacher effectiveness for teacher training and teacher practice.* Paper presented at the 6th annual Conference on Severe Behavior Disorders of Children and Youth, Arizona State University, Tempe, AZ.

Dunlap, G., Koegel, R. L., & Egel, A. L. (1979). Autistic children in school. *Exceptional Children, 45,* 522–558.

Edwards, L., & Simpson, J. (1982). Emotional disturbance. In E. L. Meyen & D. H. Lehr (Eds.), *Exceptional children in today's schools: An alternative resource book.* Denver: Love Publishing.

Eisdorfer, C. (1983). Conceptual models of aging. *American Psychologist, 38,* 197–202.

Emmelkamp, P. M. G. (1982). Anxiety and fear. In A. S. Bellack, M. Hersen, & A. E. Kazdin (Eds.), *International handbook of behavior modification and therapy.* New York: Plenum Press.

Epanchin, B. C. (1982). Screening, identification and diagnosis. In J. L. Paul & B. C. Epanchin (Eds.), *Emotional disturbance in children.* Columbus, OH: Merrill Publishing.

Feingold, B. F. (1975). *Why your child is hyperactive.* New York: Random House.

Fixen, D. L., Wolf, M. M., & Phillips, E. L. (1973). Achievement Place: A teaching-family model of community-based group homes for youth in trouble. In L. Hammerlynck, L. Handy, & E. Mash (Eds.), *Behavior change: Methodology, concepts, and practice.* Champaign, IL: Research Press.

Forehand, R. L., & McMahon, R. J. (1981). *Helping the noncompliant child.* New York: Guilford Press.

Foster, S. L., & Ritchey, W. L. (1979). Issues in the assessment of social competence in children. *Journal of Applied Behavior Analysis, 43,* 625–638.

Friedman, J. M., Weiler, S. J., LoPiccolo, J., & Hogan, D. R. (1982). Sexual dysfunctions and their treatment: Current status. In A. S. Bellack, M. Hersen, & A. E. Kazdin (Eds.), *International handbook of behavior modification and therapy.* New York: Plenum Press.

Gilberstadt, H., & Duker, J. (1965). *A handbook for clinical and actuarial MMPI interpretations.* Philadelphia: W. B. Saunders.

Glavin, J. P., & Annesley, F. R. (1972). Reading and arithmetic correlates of conduct problem and withdrawn children. *Journal of Special Education, 5,* 213–219.

Glidewell, J., & Swallow, C. (1969). *The prevalence of maladjustment in elementary schools.* Chicago: University of Chicago Press.

Glueck, S., & Glueck, E. (1950). *Unraveling juvenile delinquency.* Cambridge, MA: Harvard University Press.

Goldstein, A. P., Sprafkin, R. P., Gershaw, N. J., & Klein, P. (1980). *Skillstreaming the adolescent.* Champaign, IL: Research Press.

Goldstein, M. J., Baker, B. L., & Jamison, K. R. (1980). *Abnormal psychology.* Boston: Little, Brown.

Gottesman, I. I., & Shields, J. (1972). *Schizophrenia and genetics: A twin study advantage point.* New York: Academic Press.

Greenwood, C. R., Walker, H. M., Todd, N. M., & Hops, H. (1976). *Preschool teachers' assessments of social interaction: Predictive success and normative data* (Report No. 26). Eugene: University of Oregon Press.

Gresham, F. M. (1981). Social skills training with the handicapped: A review. *Review of Educational Research, 51,* 139–176.

Gresham, F. M. (1982). Misguided mainstreaming: The case for social skills training with handicapped students. *Exceptional Children, 48,* 422–433.

Grosenick, J. K., & Huntze, S. L. (1980). *National needs analysis in behavior disorders: Severe behavior disorders.* Columbia, MO: University of Missouri–Columbia.

Hathaway, S. R., & McKinley, J. C. (1943). *MMPI manual.* Cleveland, OH: Psychological Corporation.

Hersen, M. (1979). Modification of skill deficits in psychiatric patients. In A. S. Bellack & M. Hersen (Eds.), *Research and practice in social skills training.* New York: Plenum Press.

Heston, L. L. (1970). The genetics of schizophrenia and schizoid disease. *Science, 167,* 249–256.

Hobbs, N. (1966). Helping disturbed children: Psychological and ecological strategies. *American Psychologist, 21,* 1105–1115.

Hobbs, N. (1975). *The futures of children.* San Francisco: Jossey-Bass.

Hutchings, B., & Mednick, S. A. (1977). Criminality in adoptees and their adoptive and biological parents: A pilot study. In S. A. Mednick & K. O. Christiansen (Eds.), *Biosocial bases of criminal behavior* (pp. 127–141). New York: Gardner Press.

Karoly, P., & Kanfer, F. H. (1982). *Self-management and behavior change: From theory to practice.* New York: Pergamon Press.

Kauffman, J. M. (1977). *Characteristics of children's behavior disorders.* Columbus, OH: Merrill Publishing.

Kauffman, J. M. (1981). *Characteristics of children's behavior disorders* (2nd ed.). Columbus, OH: Merrill Publishing.

Kauffman, J. M., & Kneedler, R. D. (1981). Behavior disorders. In J. M. Kauffman & D. P. Hallahan (Eds.), *Handbook of special education.* Englewood Cliffs, NJ: Prentice-Hall.

Kavale, K. A. (1982). The efficacy of stimulant drug treatment for hyperactivity: A meta-analysis. *Journal of Learning Disabilities, 14,* 531–538.

Kavale, K. A., & Forness, S. R. (1983). Hyperactivity and diet treatment: A meta-analysis of the Feingold hypothesis. *Journal of Learning Disabilites, 16,* 324–330.

Kavale, K. A., & Nye, C. (1984). The effectiveness of drug treatment for severe behavior disorders: A meta-analysis. *Behavioral Disorders, 9,* 117–130.

Kazdin, A. E. (1982). History of behavior modification. In A. S. Bellack, M. Hersen, & A. E. Kazdin (Eds.), *International handbook of behavior modification and therapy.* New York: Plenum Press.

Kirgin, K., Wolf, M. M., Braukman, C. J., Fixsen, D. L., & Phillips, E. L. (1979). Achievement Place: A preliminary outcome evaluation. In J. S. Stumphauzer (Ed.), *Progress in behavior therapy with delinquents.* Springfield, IL: Charles C. Thomas.

Kneedler, R. D. (1980). The use of cognitive training to change social behaviors. *Exceptional Education Quarterly 1* (1), 65–74.

Leone, P. (1984). A descriptive follow-up of behaviorally disordered adolescents. *Behavioral Disorders, 9,* 207–214.

Lewine, R. R. J. (1981). Sex differences in schizophrenia: Timing or subtypes. *Psychological Bulletin, 90,* 432–434.

Lewinsohn, P. M., & Hoberman, H. M. (1982). Depression. In A. S. Bellack, M. Hersen, & A. E. Kazdin (Eds.), *International handbook of behavior modification and therapy.* New York: Plenum Press.

Lewis, R. B., & Doorlag, D. H. (1987). *Teaching special students in the mainstream* (2nd ed.). Columbus, OH: Merrill Publishing.

Lewis, W. W. (1965). Continuity and intervention in emotional disturbance: A review. *Exceptional Children, 31,* 465–474.

Lowenthal, M. F., & Berkman, P. L. (1967). *Aging and mental disorders in San Francisco: A social psychiatric study.* San Francisco: Jossey-Bass.

Mattes, J. A. (1983). The Feingold diet: A current reappraisal. *Journal of Learning Disabilities, 16,* 319–323.

Matthysse, S. (1973). Antipsychotic drug actions: A clue to the neuropathology of the schizophrenias. *Federation Proceedings, 32,* 200–205.

Meichenbaum, D. (1977). *Cognitive-behavior modification: An integrative approach.* New York: Plenum Press.

Meichenbaum, D. (1980). Cognitive behavior modification with exceptional children: A promise yet unfulfilled. *Exceptional Education Quarterly, 1* (1), 83–88.

Michelson, L., Sugai, D. P., Wood, R. P., & Kazdin, A. E. (Eds.) (1983). *Social skills assessment and training with children.* New York: Plenum Press.

Michelson, L., & Wood, R. (1980). Behavioral assessment and training of children's social skills. *Progress in Behavior Modification, 9,* 241–291.

Miller, L. C. (1977). *Louisville behavior checklist.* Los Angeles: Western Psychological Services.

Miller, P. M. (1981). Assessment of alcohol abuse. In D. H. Barlow (Ed.). *Behavioral assessment of adult disorders.* New York: Guilford Press.

Mischel, W. (1968). *Personality and assessment.* New York: John Wiley.

Mischel, W. (1976). *Introduction to personality* (2nd ed.). New York: Holt, Rinehart & Winston.

Morris, R. J., & Kratochwill, T. R. (1983). *Treating children's fears and phobias.* New York: Pergamon Press.

Murray, H. A. (1943). *Thematic apperception test.* Cambridge, MA: Harvard University Press.

Murstein, B. I. (1965). New thoughts about ambiguity and the TAT. *Journal of Projective Techniques and Personality Assessment, 29,* 219–225.

Nelson, C. M. (1981a). Behavior disorders. In A. E. Blackhurst & W. H. Berdine (Eds.), *An introduction to special education* (pp. 391–429). Boston: Little, Brown.

Nelson, C. M. (1981b). Classroom management. In J. M. Kauffman & D. P. Hallahan (Eds.), *Handbook of special education.* Englewood Cliffs, NJ: Prentice-Hall.

Nelson, C. M., & Polsgrove, L. (1981). The etiology of adolescent behavior disorders. In G. Brown, R. L. McDowell, & J. Smith (Eds.), *Educating adolescents with behavior disorders.* Columbus, OH: Merrill Publishing.

Nelson, C. M., & Polsgrove, L. (1984). Behavior analysis in special education: White rabbit or white elephant? *Remedial and Special Education, 5* (4), 6–17.

Pepper, F. C. (1976). Teaching the American Indian child in mainstream settings. In R. L. Jones (Ed.), *Mainstreaming and the minority child* (pp. 133–158). Reston, VA: Council for Exceptional Children.

Peterson, D. R. (1968). *The clinical study of social behavior.* New York: Appleton.

Phillips, E. L. (1968). Achievement Place: Token reinforcement procedures in a home-style rehabilitation setting for pre-delinquent boys. *Journal of Applied Behavior Analysis, 1,* 213–223.

Phillips, E. L., Phillips, E. A., Fixsen, D. L., & Wolf, M. M. (1973). Behavior shaping for delinquents. *Psychology Today, 1,* 74–79.

Piers, E. V., & Harris, D. B. (1969). *The Piers-Harris self-concept scale.* Nashville, TN: Counselor Recordings and Tests.

Quay, H. C. (1979). Classification. In H. C. Quay & J. S. Werry (Eds.), *Psychopathological disorders of childhood* (2nd ed.). New York: John Wiley.

Quay, H. C., & Peterson, D. R. (1967). *Behavior problem checklist and manual.* Champaign: University of Illinois Press.

Regier, D. A., Goldberg, I. D., & Taube, C. A. (1978). The defacto U.S. mental health services system. *Archives of General Psychiatry, 35,* 685–693.

Reith, H. J., Polsgrove, L., & Semmel, M. I. (1979). Relationship between instructional time and academic achievement: Implications for research and practice. *Education Unlimited, 1* (6), 53–56.

Reith, H. J., Polsgrove, L., & Semmel, M. I. (1981). Instructional variables that make a difference: Attention to task and beyond. *Exceptional Education Quarterly, 2* (3), 61–71.

Robins, L. N. (1966). *Deviant children grow up.* Baltimore: Williams & Wilkins.

Robins, L. N. (1972). Follow-up studies of behavior disorders in children. In H. C. Quay and J. S. Werry (Eds.), *Psychopathological disorders of childhood.* New York: John Wiley.

Rorschach, H. (1942). *Psychodiagnostics.* New York: Grune & Stratton.

Rosenhan, D. L., & Seligman, M. P. (1984). *Abnormal psychology.* New York: W. W. Norton.

Rosenthal, D. (1970a). Genetic research in the schizophrenic syndrome. In R. Cancro (Ed.), *The schizophrenic reactions* (pp. 245–258). New York: Brunner/Mazel.

Rosenthal, D. (1970b). *Genetic theory and abnormal behavior.* New York: McGraw-Hill.

Ross, A. O. (1974). *Psychological disorders of children.* New York: McGraw-Hill.

Rubin, R., & Balow, B. (1978). Prevalence of teacher identified behavior problems: A longitudinal study. *Exceptional Children, 45,* 102–111.

Ruggles, T. R., & LeBlanc, J. M. (1982). Behavior analysis procedures in classroom teaching. In A. S. Bellack, M. Hersen, & A. E. Kazdin (Eds.), *International handbook of behavior modification and therapy.* New York: Plenum Press.

Rutter, M., Tizard, J., & Whitmore, K. (Eds.) (1970). *Education, health, and behavior.* London: Longmans.

Schacter, S. (1982). Recidivism and self-cure of smoking and obesity. *American Psychologist, 37,* 436–444.

Schreibman, L., Koegel, R. L., Charlop, M. H., & Egel, A. L. (1982). In A. S. Bellack, M. Hersen, & A. E. Kazdin (Eds.), *International handbook of behavior modification and therapy.* New York: Plenum Press.

Sheldon, W. H. (1967). Constitutional psychiatry. In T. Millon (Ed.), *Theories of psychopathology.* Philadelphia: W. B. Saunders.

Sobell, M. B., Sobell, L. C., Ersner-Hershfield, S., & Nirenberg, T. D. (1982). Alcohol and drug problems. In A. S. Bellack, M. Hersen, & A. E. Kazdin (Eds.), *International handbook of behavior modification and therapy.* New York: Plenum Press.

Spiegler, M. D. (1983). *Contemporary behavioral therapy.* Palo Alto, CA: Mayfield.

Spivack, G., & Swift, M. (1972). *Hahnemann high school behavior rating scale manual.* Philadelphia: Departmental Health Sciences, Hahnemann Medical College and Hospital.

Srole, L., Langner, T. S., Michael, S. T., Opler, M. K., & Rennie, T. A. C. (1962). *Mental health in the metropolis: The midtown Manhattan study.* New York: McGraw-Hill.

Stainback, S., & Stainback, W. (1980). *Educating children with severe maladaptive behaviors.* New York: Grune & Stratton.

Stephens, T. M. (1979). *Social skills in the classroom.* Columbus, OH: Cedars Press.

Stevens, R., & Rosenshine, B. (1981). Advances in research on teaching. *Exceptional Education Quarterly, 2* (1), 1–10.

Sulzer-Azaroff, B., & Pollack, M. J. (1982). The modification of child behavior problems in the home. In A. S. Bellack, M. Hersen, & A. E. Kazdin (Eds.), *International handbook of behavior modification and therapy.* New York: Plenum Press.

Terry, R. D., & Davies, P. (1980). Dementia of the Alzheimer type. *Annual Review of Neuroscience, 3,* 77–95.

Thomas, A. (1971). Impact of interest in early individual differences. In H. E. Rie (Ed.) *Perspectives in child psychopathology.* Chicago: Aldine Press.

Thomas, A., & Chess, S. (1977). *Temperament and development.* New York: Brunner/Mazel.

Thompson, R. H., White, K. R., & Morgan, D. P. (1982). Teacher-student interaction patterns with mainstreamed mildly handicapped students. *American Educational Research Journal, 19,* 220–236.

Trower, P. (1979). Fundamentals of interpersonal behavior: A social-psychological perspective. In A. S. Bellack & M. Hersen (Eds.), *Research and practice in social skills training.* New York: Plenum Press.

Van Evra, J. P. (1983). *Psychological disorders of children and adolescents.* Boston: Little, Brown.

Van Hasselt, V. B., Hersen, M., Whitehill, M. D., & Bellack, A. S. (1979). Social skills assessment and training for children: An evaluative review. *Behavior Research and Therapy, 17,* 413–437.

Waksman, S. A. (1983). Diet and children's behavior disorders: A review of the research. *Clinical Psychology Review, 3,* 201–213.

Walker, H. M. (1983). *Walker problem behavior identification checklist* (Rev. 1983). Los Angeles: Western Psychological Services.

Walker, H. M., McConnell, S., Bolmes, D., Todis, B., Walker, J., & Golden, N. (1983). *The Walker social skills curriculum: The ACCEPTS program.* Austin, TX: PRO-ED.

Werner, E. E., & Smith, R. S. (1977). *Kauai's children come of age.* Honolulu: University of Hawaii Press.

Wing, J. K. (1966). Diagnosis, epidemiology, actiology. In J. K. Wing (Ed.), *Early childhood autism.* London: Pergamon Press.

Witkin, H. A., Mednick, S. A., Schulsinger, F., Bakkestrom, E., Christiansen, K. O., Goodenough, D. R., Hirschhorn, K., Lundsteen, C., Owen, D. R., Philip, J., Rubin, D. B., & Stocking, M. (1976). Criminality in XYY and XXY men: The elevated crime rate of XYY males is not related to aggression. *Science, 193,* 547–555.

Yule, W. (1978). Behavioral treatment of children and adolescents with conduct disorders. In L. Hersov, M. Berger, & D. Shaffer (Eds.), *Aggression and anti-social behaviour in childhood and adolescence.* Oxford: Pergamon.

Zigler, E., & Levine, J. (1981). Age on first hospitalization of schizophrenics; A developmental approach. *Journal of Abnormal Psychology, 90,* 458–467.

Zubin, J., Eron, L. D., & Schumer, F. (1965). *An experimental approach to projective techniques.* New York: John Wiley.

Resources

Organization

Council for Children with Behavior Disorders
Council for Exceptional Children
1920 Association Drive
Reston, VA 22091
> Organization of teachers, teacher educators, and others interested in the education of students with behavior disorders.

Journals

Behavioral Disorders
Council for Exceptional Children
1920 Association Drive
Reston, VA 22091
> Publishes articles on current issues, research, and theory related to behavior disorders.

Behavior Therapy
Academic Press
111 Fifth Avenue
New York, NY 10003
> Professional journal that publishes results of research with individuals and groups of behavior disordered children and adults.

Books

Kerr, M. M., & Nelson, C. M. (1983). *Strategies for managing behavior problems in the classroom.* Columbus, OH: Merrill Publishing.
> Discusses issues in identification, assessment, implementation, and evaluation of behavior management procedures including specific strategies for working with a variety of problem behaviors within and outside the classroom.

Rosenhan, D. L., & Seligman, M. P. (1984). *Abnormal psychology.* New York: W. W. Norton.
> Includes information on emotional and behavioral problems with comparative data on various treatment approaches, and information on etiology, assessment, and interventions with various disorders.

Chapter 11

GIFTEDNESS AND TALENT

The abilities of gifted and talented individuals embody the ultimate levels of human learning. Highly able individuals may manifest their potential at any point in their lives, from childhood through their later years. Their gifts can be shared in one or more fields of endeavor: art, science, leadership, literature, architecture, mathematics, or any other discipline in which a culture is willing to recognize an outstanding achievement or contribution. High levels of learning take place in the early years; however, most extraordinary attainments occur in the years following formal schooling. School experiences may provide crucial opportunities to explore and develop areas of potential giftedness in an environment which facilitates the pursuit of new knowledge for the simple satisfaction of knowing.

Precocity is not universal across developmental domains. A four-year-old child may demonstrate advanced verbal abilities with sophisticated language and yet be "immature" in play activities. The apparent lag in social skills is no more than the normal behavior of a four-year-old, yet the expectation is to find affective development commensurate with intellectual development. Discrepancies in skills and abilities are the rule rather than the exception throughout the lives of the gifted.

Sanford J. Cohn and Catherine M. G. Cohn
Arizona State University

Lannie S. Kanevsky
McGill University

Individuals of extraordinary talent have always inspired humankind. The history of interest in such persons is distinguished, however, by an intensely dualistic relationship. Attitudes toward the ablest members of society have often fluctuated from the heights of acclaim and adulation to the depths of fear and resentment. In moments of dour threat, those of great talent have been expected to contribute to civilization's tasks of survival and cultural advancement; in moments of fervent egalitarianism, those attributes that speak to individual differences in capabilities have been ignored and obscured (Stanley, 1976a).

Lewis Madison Terman, acknowledged as the father of the gifted child movement in this country, observed that "it is the prevailing *Zeitgeist* that will decide, by the rewards it gives or withholds, what talents will come to flower" (1954, p. 227). Indeed, each epoch throughout history has evidenced its own particular characteristics of exceptional ability by which individuals have been recognized as gifted as well as those rules by which limited resources have been allotted to them.

In ancient times, gifted individuals were thought to be the instruments of benevolent gods or even themselves demigods possessed by geniuses (synonymous with muses and demons at that time). Material goods, creature comforts, and other resources were made abundantly available to them. When organized religion in turn dominated the contest for humankind's spiritual need, such individuals were considered possessed by devils and were often hunted down and killed as witches. As knowledge led to scientific advances in our understanding about the nature of our world, the highly able were viewed less as supernatural than as merely neurotic deviants from the normal.

During the nineteenth century, systematic theories emerged to explain the origin and evolution of species. These theories promoted the notion that gifted individuals offer civilization its primary hope for cultural survival and advancement. It was out of this concern for the improvement of our species that early interest in the science of individual differences, including the gifted, arose. The growth of mental measurement brought forth a multitude of assessment tools that focused initially on global indicators of inlligence and later on more specific abilities, such as mathematical, verbal, spatial, and abstract reasoning. Aptitude and achievement tests abounded, their development stimulated by two world wars and the personnel needs of mechanized society.

Intelligence had been assumed to be synonymous with convergent thinking ability but, in the 1950s, attention shifted to the creative aspects of cognitive ability. J. P. Guilford (1956) suggested a three-dimensional model, the Structure of Intellect (SOI), originally composed of 120 separate abilities. The SOI had a great impact on education as it included divergent production, or creative production, as one of the legitimate mental processes. The willingness of educators to accept this trend encouraged the work of others, such as E. Paul Torrance, who had also felt creativity to be a neglected issue.

Support for gifted programs rose dramatically in the late 1950s following the launch of Sputnik in 1957. Concern for American advancement in science motivated radical changes in public education. Human intellect became a valuable natural resource worthy of nurturance and educational support.

The civil rights movements of the 1960s forced educators to recognize the bias in existing assessment instruments and procedures which had limited the participation of minority and disadvantaged youth in gifted education opportunities. Multidisciplinary identification strategies which considered biographical and creative aspects of a child's background were developed. This interest in more accurate assessment of talent continued into the 1970s. Legislation supported the development of appropriate educational assistance programs for the most able learners.

The 1950s and 1960s, however, initiated an era of social concern that focused on diminishing prejudice and equalizing opportunity for all individuals, regardless of race, religion, or gender. Characteristics common to all were emphasized and exalted, while those ideas that underscore differences among individuals, such as intelligence, were largely overlooked and sometimes even suppressed. This social movement has accomplished much that continues to be important, necessary, and appropriate for our society; however, it also introduced an unfortunate skepticism/cynicism toward intelligence as a psychological construct and instruments that purport to measure it.

Now in the 1980s, American education is said to be in a crisis (*A Nation at Risk*, 1983). Expectations for academic performance of schoolchildren have fallen lower than can ever be remembered, and attention is riveted on ways to enhance achievement (Resnick & Resnick, 1985). The ablest students have been especially affected by these circumstances in the most adverse of ways (Lerner, 1982). As a result, parents of these children have instigated a re-examination of the ways by which we are encouraging our best and brightest young people to realize their outstanding potential and become productive citizens.

A consequence of this renewed interest in education of the gifted has been the proliferation of a wide variety of programs intended to address their educational needs. Gone is the well-worn myth that gifted children simply "make it on their own." In its place is the recognition that such seemingly benign indifference not only inhibits the pace and level of our ablest children's ultimate development, but also undermines their motivation to achieve in all spheres of endeavor beyond their school years. The set of principles and procedures for evaluating and educating gifted and talented children can, therefore, no longer be considered the stepchild of special education. Support for them has become an educational imperative and a national priority. Inclusion of this population and descriptions of its nature and nurture in a work concerning exceptional individuals is thus both timely and appropriate.

Definitions of Giftedness

The terms "gifted" and "talented" have been used in two distinct ways in the literature. They may describe either the quantity or quality of abilities or talents. Quantity refers to the degree to which an individual is endowed with certain abilities or skills. An exceptionally gifted sculptor would have a greater amount

Figure 11.1

Normal Distribution of Intelligence Test Scores

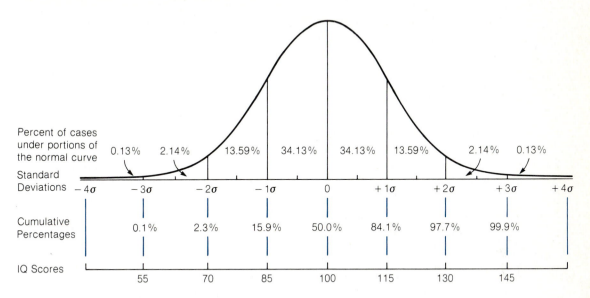

Percent of cases under portions of the normal curve: 0.13%   2.14%   13.59%   34.13%   34.13%   13.59%   2.14%   0.13%

Standard Deviations: -4σ -3σ -2σ -1σ 0 $+1\sigma$ $+2\sigma$ $+3\sigma$ $+4\sigma$

Cumulative Percentages: 0.1%   2.3%   15.9%   50.0%   84.1%   97.7%   99.9%

IQ Scores: 55   70   85   100   115   130   145

of ability than a talented sculptor. Quality distinguishes an individual's ability based on the area of endeavor, such as academic gifts versus artistic talents.

Psychometric (or measurement-based) definitions of giftedness which resulted from the testing movement linger in many locations. Although dependence on a single test score is discouraged, operational definitions of giftedness commonly focus on standardized evaluation of abilities and achievement. In many cases, the same tests are administered to highly able learners as are used in the assessment of other exceptional students; however, their scores will reflect outstanding, rather than limited, performance. Individuals identified as gifted on the basis of tests perform in the top percentiles of a range of possible scores.

Scores on two of the most common tests of mental ability—the *Wechsler Intelligence Scale for Children–Revised (WISC–R)* and the *Stanford Binet Intelligence Scale*—are normally distributed with the average, or most frequently earned score, IQ 100 (see Figure 11.1). In practice, this means the further above or below 100 a score occurs, the fewer individuals we can expect to earn that score. Setting a criterion, or cutoff, score of IQ 130 on the *WISC–R* for identification of giftedness would statistically limit the number of students eligible to approximately 2 to 3 percent of the population. A criterion of IQ 148 limits it to approximately .05 percent. Liberal estimates include the top 5 to 8 percent of the population, while more conservative estimates limit themselves to the top 1 percent.

The release of the Marland Report by the United States Office of Education, Office of Gifted and Talented (USDE/OGT) (Marland, 1972) provided one popularly recognized attempt to address the issue of definition. Individuals were deemed "gifted and talented" if they were judged capable of outstanding performance in any of the following six areas:

1. General intellectual ability
2. Specific academic aptitude
3. Creative or productive thinking
4. Leadership ability
5. Visual and performing arts aptitude
6. Psychomotor ability

Within a few years of the release of the Marland definition, however, the community of educators of the gifted succeeded in having the psychomotor category removed from the list on the grounds that athletic talent is both highly recognized and well-funded in this country. They felt that offering additional funds to the already well-funded athletic programs in schools was tantamount to providing welfare to the wealthy. Therefore the definition included in Public Law 97–35, The Education Consolidation and Improvement Act, passed by Congress in 1981, offered a refined description of children to be considered gifted and talented:

> Children who give evidence of high performance capability in areas such as intellectual, creative, artistic, leadership capacity or specific academic fields and who require services or activities not ordinarily provided by the school in order to fully develop such capabilities. (Sec. 582)

Both federal definitions are a great departure from the psychometric, or IQ, orientation of the past. They offer educators a broad range of program options which attempt to address the diversity of strengths individuals may demonstrate when provided appropriate opportunities to do so. States commonly fund programs based on a percentage of enrollment. School districts may receive funding and therefore develop programs for the top 1, 2, 3, 5, or 10 percent of their student population in one or more categories depending on the legislation governing their programs.

The IQ-based definition reflects an academic orientation toward giftedness as IQ tests are recognized as effective predictors of academic achievement. Gifts in nonacademic disciplines, such as art, music, or leadership, cannot be assessed on these measures.

Incidence and prevalence statistics for this exceptionality are difficult to locate. The variety of definitions, strategies, and instruments which could be used to identify or select students to be served in a state, district, or school seems infinite. This diversity contributes to the confusion one meets in attempting to estimate the number of truly gifted individuals. In 1973, an estimated 4 percent of approximately two million gifted in the United States were being served. By 1977, this proportion had climbed to 14 percent (Zettel, 1982). As in other areas of exceptionality, interest in the identification and development of appropriate

ROSA

Rosa enters every room with an artist's flourish. For a 14-year-old, her sophistication and composure often startle adults. She participates on a local board which selects themes and artwork for displays in the State gallery. Her own pottery and sculptures have been included regularly since she was nine when her family moved to the United States from Mexico. Rosa sought out the Community Gallery within her first week in her new town.

The state of Rosa's locker and bedroom are a source of jokes among her peers. Her parents see no humor in it. Rosa's reply is, "Ah, but a creative mess is much more fulfilling than idle tidiness." She has a difficult time finding moments to housekeep between her commitments to a modern dance troupe, children's arts workshop, a job four afternoons a week in a local photography studio, ballet lessons, early morning aerobics classes, the future

problem-solving team, and as arts representative on the student government board. Last year she organized a student art show and sale to raise money for low income children to attend a summer arts camp. Rosa's goal in life is to open a Community Artists Workshop supported by local businesses.

Academically Rosa is a B+ student. She is equally comfortable expressing herself in either English or Spanish. Her teachers enjoy her creative input to discussions. Her academic grades have been consistently high in the last two years but seldom outstanding. This may be due to Rosa's recent acquisition of English as her second language. The results of tests administered by the school psychologist show that Rosa is bright; however, she may be limited by her verbal skills even though this may not be apparent in daily conversation and class activities.

educational opportunities for the gifted has fluctuated dramatically depending upon the current societal orientation toward intellect. Unlike other exceptionalities, service is not mandated by federal legislation. The gifted were not included in Public Law 94–142. As a result, states are not required to provide educational opportunities for their highly able learners.

One of an educator's most important decisions in gifted education is to define who is to be served by a program. A variety of perspectives are apparent when one examines the range of talent development options available through school systems, after school, on weekends, or during the summer. If one has in mind identifying young people who would benefit by special educational opportunities and then proceeding to provide them, specific operational definitions of the gifted are required (Cohn, 1981).

Renzulli (1978) feels his three-ring conceptualization operationalizes giftedness as it is based on research which investigated the characteristics of gifted and talented individuals. It also has implications for identification and programming strategies. Three overlapping clusters of traits provide the necessary ingredients for the creative/productive achievements which differentiate the gifted

Figure 11.2

A Graphic Definition of Giftedness

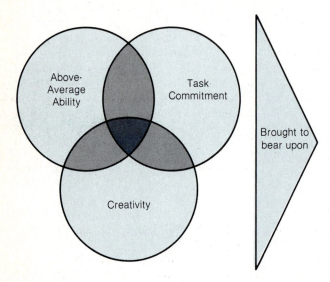

GENERAL PERFORMANCE AREAS

Mathematics • Visual Arts • Physical Sciences • Philosophy • Social Sciences • Law • Religion • Language Arts • Music • Life Sciences • Movement Arts

SPECIFIC PERFORMANCE AREAS

Cartooning • Astronomy • Public Opinion Polling • Jewelry Design • Map Making • Choreography • Biography • Film Making • Statistics • Local History • Electronics • Musical Composition • Landscape Architecture • Chemistry • Demography • Microphotography • City Planning • Pollution Control • Poetry • Fashion Design • Weaving • Play Writing • Advertising • Costume Design • Meteorology • Puppetry • Marketing • Game Design • Journalism • Electronic Music • Child Care • Consumer Protection • Cooking • Ornithology • Furniture Design • Navigation • Genealogy • Sculpture • Wildlife Management • Set Design • Agricultural Research • Animal Learning • Film Criticism • Etc. • Etc. • Etc.

Source: From "What Makes Giftedness? Reexamining a Definition" by Joseph S. Renzulli, *Phi Delta Kappan,* November 1978, Vol. 60, No. 3, p. 184. Reprinted by permission of the author.

from their less able peers (see Figure 11.2). These are above average ability, task commitment, and creativity. Each is considered equally important in the actualization of gifted potential in a performance area and therefore must be considered in identification procedures and program development. Above average ability means a student may be in the top 5 to 10, or even 20 percent of his or her class in order to meet this criterion. Task commitment is composed of traits that produce a "refined or focused form of motivation . . . which is brought to bear on a particular problem (task) or specific performance area" (p. 182). Creativity includes traits which allow an individual to think of unique or original versions of situations or problems and enables the development of novel solutions or interpretations.

A psychosocial definition, developed by Tannenbaum (1983), proposes the interrelationship of five factors which "mesh" to produce excellence (see Figure 11.3). He prefaces the description of the factors with this comment:

Keeping in mind that developed talent exists only in adults, a proposed definition of giftedness in children is that it denotes their potential for becoming

Figure 11.3

The Five Factors That "Mesh" into Excellence

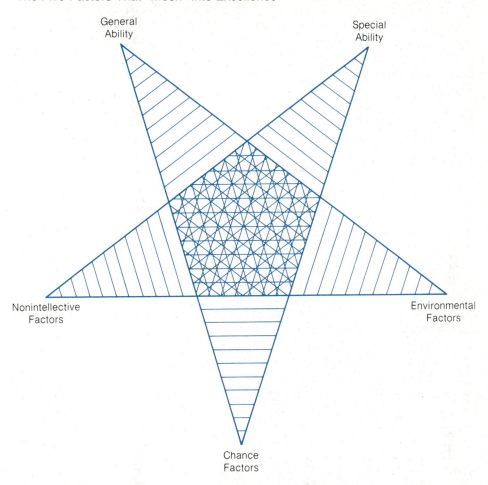

General
Ability

Special
Ability

Nonintellective
Factors

Environmental
Factors

Chance
Factors

Source: Reprinted with permission of Macmillan Publishing Company from *Gifted Children: Psychological and Education Perspectives* by A. J. Tannenbaum. Copyright © 1983 by Abraham J. Tannenbaum.

critically acclaimed performers or exemplary producers of ideas in spheres of activity that enhances the moral, physical, emotional, social, intellectual, or aesthetic life of humanity. (p. 86)

Therefore the young are considered potentially gifted until they have made a contribution to humanity. He also distinguishes between "producers" and "consumers." Producers contribute to the expansion of knowledge whereas consumers merely learn what is known.

General ability (or tested intelligence) is of varying importance in different talent areas. It plays a larger role in academic excellence than in musical achievements. Special abilities become apparent in particular areas in which an individual demonstrates outstanding talent and interest. Nonintellective factors represent personality traits which facilitate the manifestation of ability in performances or products. These include ego strength, dedication to a field of knowledge, and many more. Environmental factors are those external pressures which encourage the development of ability, such as role models, peer attitudes, and stimulating home, school, or community settings. Tannenbaum's model is novel in its consideration of chance factors in the development of gifts and talents. These include unforeseen circumstances and opportunities which arise at critical moments. These unpredictable factors facilitate the realization of promise which might otherwise not have become apparent.

Concerned Professionals

Formal recognition of talented young people usually occurs in the schools, although parents are often aware of their child's potential before school officials make a formal identification. Educators, then, are the singularly most important group of professionals upon whom responsibility rests for helping the gifted or talented child. School psychologists and counselors can play an especially valuable role in screening and diagnosing a youth's outstanding special abilities. Their roles in the identification and placement process include participation in the decisions of the identification team and selection of appropriate instrumentation. Professionals outside the education field may be invited to act as mentors and role models for highly able youngsters. Educators of eager learners often find the "extended classroom," which involves community resources, a more challenging and least restrictive learning environment.

ETIOLOGY

Unlike other areas of exceptionality, the study of giftedness has yielded no specific etiology, nor have modes of prevention been sought. Few topics have caused greater controversy, however, than discussions of the origins of outstanding abilities in individuals and the environmental influences that might enhance their development (Jensen, 1980).

Interest in the gifted, and the study of individual differences, originated out of an obsession with the idea of improving the human species through knowledge about the genetic transmission of genius. Concerned by what he saw as a steady deterioration in the human condition *circa* 1860, Sir Francis Galton, father of differential psychology (the study of individual differences), and cousin to Charles Darwin, set out to examine the degree to which, if any, intellectual ability was inherited. Galton speculated that "[e]ach generation has enormous power over the natural gifts of those that follow" (1869, p. 1).

Reasoning that reputation or eminence of men over the age of 50 would be an adequate index of high ability, Galton set out to study the relationship between eminence and kinship across several generations. Galton reported his results in *Hereditary Genius,* published in 1869. His methods introduced statistics to the social sciences and established psychometrics, the science of mental measurement, as the leading method by which to assess individual differences in intellect.

When Galton analyzed the heritability of genius, he also recorded information about the physical characteristics and personality traits of the eminent men he chose to study and their descendants whom he also classified on the basis of their reputations. His findings were contrary to the then already well established notion that men of genius were sickly and generally of poor constitution. Some 20 years later, however, Cesare Lombroso, an Italian criminologist and professor of forensic medicine, published *The Man of Genius,* in which he strongly asserted that genius was in and of itself a degenerative psychosis (Lombroso, 1891). Although Lombroso's work was a collection of illustrative case studies, and therefore failed to offer the conditions upon which sound conclusions could be drawn, the influence it exerted was profound. Even Galton (1892) himself eventually succumbed to its postulates.

This question of the degree to which giftedness accompanied psychic aberration came to fascinate Lewis Terman, a young psychologist of the time. As a student of mental measurement and individual differences, Terman had become disenchanted with the measures of differential ability that had come out of the laboratories of the great psychophysicists, Wundt and Cattell. Rather than using simple behaviors such as reaction times and finger tapping (characteristic of the psychophysical methods) to predict the complex behaviors expressing intelligence, Terman turned to the complex thought processes, following the work of French psychologists, Binet and Simon, to yield a global indicator of mental adaptation (Terman, 1916). Translating the *Binet Scales of Intelligence* into the American idiom, Terman picked those test items that tapped more complex mental processes. He and his colleagues at Stanford speculated that these items would differentiate most effectively varying levels of intellectual behavior. They were the first to apply the precision of the experimental laboratory to the observation of human intellectual behavior under standard conditions.

Modern science has established both heredity and environment as significant influences upon the development of outstanding intellectual ability (Jensen, 1980, 1981). Indeed, tearing apart the separate influence of one without the other in some conclusive way has eluded researchers to date. Extraordinary verbal reasoning ability does seem more subject to environmental influence than does either mathematical or abstract reasoning ability, the latter appearing from among a wide variety of cultural and socioeconomic strata in this country (Keating, 1976; Stanley, Keating, & Fox, 1974). Sex differences in mathematical reasoning ability and their origins, both biological and environmental, have also received considerable attention (Benbow & Stanley, 1980; Fox, Brody, & Tobin, 1980) but remain embedded in controversy as well.

The home environment and parents exert a strong influence in the development of potential. Early recognition and nurturance as well as a "high degree of adult attention have been found to be common characteristics of the home environments of eminent individuals in retrospective studies" (Robinson, Roedell, & Jackson, 1981).

CHARACTERISTICS OF GIFTED
AND TALENTED INDIVIDUALS

Much time and energy has been spent attempting to explain the nature of gift-edness. The result has been an appreciation for the diversity of inter- and intra-individual differences. The gifted are not a homogeneous group. Within the gifted population, differences in ability and interest can be found which are as great as will be found between the gifted and their more average peers. This has con-founded researchers' efforts to reduce giftedness to a set of recognizable, excep-tional behaviors or personality characteristics. Educators must be sensitive to this variation in order to recognize able youngsters and to design learning op-portunities which facilitate the development of their full potential. Understand-ing giftedness requires the same sensitivity to individual differences expected in other areas of exceptionality.

Armed with a tool that could raise society's understanding of giftedness be-yond superstition, Terman (1925) launched his monumental longitudinal study, *Genetic Studies of Genius*. For the first time in history, empirical methods were used to examine the relationship between intellect and a wide variety of devel-opmental characteristics, such as physical growth, medical history, economic, ethnic, and social background, peer interactions, and social and emotional ad-justment (Terman, 1925).

Young people earning IQ scores of 140 or above were found to be neither sickly, frail, neurotic, nor socially maladapted. In fact, just the opposite emerged from Terman's studies. Children of exceptionally high general intelligence were phys-ically and emotionally robust as well as socially adept. Five volumes and nu-merous articles have been written about the 1,528 gifted children who were subjects in Terman's studies (Burks, Jensen, & Terman, 1930; Cox, 1926; Oden, 1968; Terman, 1925; Terman & Oden, 1947). Presently in their seventies and eighties, these individuals continue to take part in follow-up surveys, which afford evidence that attests to the fulfillment of their outstanding promise as children (Goleman, 1980; Sears, 1977, 1979; Sears & Barbee, 1977).

Learning Characteristics

The gifted often benefit from their ability to collect information more efficiently and effectively than average learners. This becomes apparent in preschool, the home, community, or workplace. Learning ability facilitates adaptation and prob-lem solving. Both are valuable survival skills in any age, but are particularly crucial in an era of high speed technological change.

In 1971, Julian C. Stanley launched the second major study of gifted children, the Study of Mathematically Precocious Youth (SMPY). SMPY was based in large part on the techniques used by Terman but with two important differences: it included a program of educational intervention whereas Terman's study did not; and ability in specific academic talent areas was the basis of selection rather than a global measure of intelligence. Stanley focused on mathematically talented young people because he determined through early studies (Stanley, Keating, & Fox, 1974) that they held the promise of great scientific advancement for our culture. He concentrated primarily on junior high school age students because by that age their mathematical reasoning ability was sufficiently mature and because they faced a school curriculum that he termed "an educational wasteland."

Using the College Board's *Scholastic Aptitude Test (SAT)* as the screening tool, SMPY began its Talent Search for seventh and eighth graders who reasoned extremely well mathematically. The successes are well documented (Benbow & Stanley, 1983a; Fox, Brody, & Tobin, 1980; George, Cohn, & Stanley, 1979; Keating, 1976; Stanley, George, & Solano, 1977, 1978; Stanley, Keating, & Fox, 1974). Stanley and his associates continue to follow many of the over 12,000 Talent Search participants, many of whom are presently entering adulthood (Benbow & Stanley, 1983a, 1983b; Cohn, 1980).

The one characteristic both Terman's and Stanley's subjects share is the ability to learn extremely well. Outside of this common attribute, these individuals exhibit a broad range of cognitive and affective possibilities.

As a result of a review of the literature related to behavior characteristics of highly able learners, Renzulli, Smith, White, Callahan, and Hartman (1976) have developed 10 sets of characteristics which represent behaviors most likely to differentiate the gifted from their less able peers. The characteristics for learning and creativity are provided in Table 11.1. They are bordered on either side by positive and negative indicator behaviors which might result in school environments. Gifted individuals may or may not choose to manifest their abilities in socially acceptable ways. Therefore educators need to be sensitive to the desirable, as well as the undesirable, behavioral outcomes of extremely high levels of ability.

Lists of characteristics of the gifted can offer a starting point for recognizing potentially gifted individuals. They must be used with the understanding that not all gifted will embody all characteristics, and not all behaviors will appear in socially desirable forms.

Exceptionally gifted individuals have a passion for learning, absorbing knowledge from all of their experiences. In their early years, gifted children learn to speak and develop sophisticated language patterns well in advance of their age-mates. They may teach themselves to read by age three or four without direct instruction. Their verbal and reading fluency and comprehension improve rapidly. These abilities contribute to a large storehouse of information, facts, concepts, and principles which they are capable of processing at an extraordinary rate. The level of complexity and abstraction found in their probes and responses reflects phenomenal perceptiveness and sensitivity to relationships and patterns in knowledge and in the environment.

Martinson (1961) encouraged kindergarten teachers to watch for an usually good memory, long attention span, advanced and abstract reasoning abilities, curiosity about relationships, specific talents (rhythm, drama, music, art), and other indications of high ability. The performance of intellectually precocious preschoolers is therefore qualitatively different from their less able agemates. Whether this is the result of a qualitative difference in thinking, advanced development, or a combination of both, has not been resolved.

Table 11.1

Characteristics of Superior Students

Negative Indicator Behaviors	Learning Characteristics	Positive Indicator Behaviors
Talks in terms peers don't understand	Has unusually advanced vocabulary for age or grade level; uses terms in a meaningful way; has verbal behavior characterized by richness of expression, elaboration, and fluency.	Speaks eloquently on issues related to world peace
Is a "know-it-all"	Possesses a large storehouse of information about a variety of topics (beyond the usual interests of youngsters his age).	Knows *everything* about the New York Yankees since the team played its first game
Is *always* first to have hand up with correct answer—alienates peers	Has quick mastery and recall of factual information.	*Always* wins trivia games
Understands how to infuriate peers and teachers better than agemates	Has rapid insight into cause-effect relationships; tries to discover the how and why of things; asks many provocative questions (as distinct from informational or factual questions); wants to know what makes things (or people) "tick."	Enjoys designing complex experiments to see what influences plant growth
Reinterprets school rules in defense of disobedience	Has a ready grasp of underlying principles and can quickly make valid generalizations about events, people, or things; looks for similarities and differences in events, people, and things.	Loves exploring scientific notation while the rest of the class is learning place value in math
Is first to notice any inconsistency in teacher's application of discipline—what goes for one *must* go for all	Is a keen and alert observer; usually "sees more" or "gets more" out of a story, film, etc., than others.	Is able to play a piece of music after hearing it once

Table 11.1 (continued)

Negative Indicator Behaviors	Creativity Characteristics	Positive Indicator Behaviors
Hides "Diary of Anne Frank" inside Social Studies text during class	Reads a great deal on his own; usually prefers adult level books; does not avoid difficult material; may show a preference for biography, autobiography, encyclopedias, and atlases.	Independently studies and enthusiastically demonstrates and explains Napoleon's strategies at Waterloo to 5th grade classmates
Is arrested for finding a way into a large, private computer system	Tries to understand complicated material by separating it into its respective parts; reasons things out for himself; sees logical and common sense answers.	Enjoys "reasoning out" complex, intricate problems by working backwards
Asks endless WHY questions	Displays a great deal of curiosity about many things; is constantly asking questions about anything and everything.	Wants to know what *really* makes tides rise and fall at age 4
Always has just a few more ideas for the brainstorming list that *must* be included	Generates a large number of ideas or solutions to problems and questions; often offers unusual ("way out"), unique, clever responses.	Thinks of new and successful fund-raising plan for school projects
Starts arguments in class over religious issues	Is uninhibited in expressions of opinion; is sometimes radical and spirited in disagreement; is tenacious.	Will stick to a well thought-out opinion in an argument
Is caught with drugs in school locker	Is a high risk taker; is adventurous and speculative.	At age 9, wants to invest in the stock market
Enjoys playing "devil's advocate" at inappropriate moments	Displays a good deal of intellectual playfulness; fantasizes; imagines ("I wonder what would happen if . . ."); manipulates ideas (i.e., changes, elaborates upon them); is often concerned with adapting, improving, and modifying institutions, objects, and systems.	Loves designing homework machines, bedroom cleaning machines . . .

Table 11.1 (continued)

Negative Indicator Behaviors	Learning Characteristics	Positive Indicator Behaviors
Sarcastic	Displays a keen sense of humor and sees humor in situations that may not appear to be humorous to others.	Uses humor to lighten tense moments between classmates
During current events discussion wants to discuss a recent strange dream	Is unusually aware of his impulses and more open to the irrational in himself (freer expression of feminine interest for boys, greater than usual amount of independence for girls); shows emotional sensitivity.	Is willing to be the only girl in Law class or only boy in modern dance troupe
Becomes jealous of a classmate's extraordinary artistic talent	Is sensitive to beauty; attends to aesthetic characteristics of things.	Is truly and deeply touched by a classmate's sculpture
Has the world's messiest bedroom despite parents' threats and rationalizations	Nonconforming; accepts disorder; is not interested in details; is individualistic; does not fear being different.	Has own sense of color and fashion independent of current trends in clothing
Offers criticism to principal regarding her choice of clothing at Open House	Criticizes constructively; is unwilling to accept authoritarian pronouncements without critical examination.	Wants to help peers improve their poor study skills while preparing for a test.

Source: From Scales for Rating Behavior Characteristics of Superior Students by Joseph S. Renzulli et al. Copyright © 1976 by Creative Learning Press. Reprinted by permission.

Social and Emotional Characteristics

A number of nonintellective attributes have been found common to gifted individuals. Some are distinctive and some are shared with the rest of the population but to a different degree. Terman's findings longitudinally described a population of well adjusted, emotionally stable individuals. Although some of the gifted are bound to experience social and emotional difficulties, Milgram and Milgram (1976) found intellectual giftedness to be an asset in coping with life's challenges.

Galton (1869) was the first to draw attention to the "zeal" with which his eminent subjects approached their area of expertise, and their "power of doing a great deal of laborious work." More recent authors have called this high degree of self-motivation "persistence" (Terman & Oden, 1947) or task commitment (Renzulli, 1978). Regardless of its label, this willingness to devote great amounts of time and energy to the pursuit of a solution often differentiates the gifted and talented from the rest.

introducing

TOMMY

Tommy arrived for the first day of first grade with a ninth grade chemistry text under his arm and a vivacious grin on his freckled, six-year-old face. He has been the subject of numerous TV and newspaper features as a result of his precocious interest in science. He has been working with a professor at a local college for the past few months on various chemistry problems.

Recently his first grade teacher expressed concern over Tommy's refusal to complete written assignments. He has no doubt Tommy is cognitively able to do the work as he earned an IQ score of 194 on the *Stanford–Binet*. However, Tommy is unable or unwilling to write. Through discussions with Tommy and his mother, it was discovered that until arriving

at school Tommy had dazzled those around him with his advanced cognitive development and wizardry with words. His motor skills had not kept pace with his mental ability. His fine-motor coordination was amazingly average. This discrepancy became a source of stress for Tommy. He had seldom, if ever, experienced failure and for all of his six years had succeeded in pursuing only those activities in which he was successful. Tommy, his parents, and teacher were provided a quick lesson on intraindividual differences in abilities and rates of development. Tommy's frustration was relieved somewhat and he agreed to try harder. He was encouraged to broaden his interests into other fields where he is not the "star."

Peer Relations. The enthusiasm and flexibility of gifted students' thinking contributes to their popularity as they are chosen more often as friends by their less able peers. However, from the perspective of the gifted child, Hollingworth (1929) found their friendship choices were reduced as their IQs rose. Students with IQs above 150 experienced extreme difficulty finding friends and teachers also perceived the gifted as having few friends. Following her study of a sample of 180 + IQ children, Hollingworth (1942) commented, "Isolation is the refuge of genius, not its goal."

Bright individuals may prefer a small number of close friends who are their intellectual peers rather than being popular in a large group (O'Shea, 1960). In their work with two- to five-year-old children, Kline and Meckstroth (1985) observed the interaction of average playmates with gifted children. The less able peer often became physical and, as a result, the gifted child withdrew. They also reported the gifted to be more internally focused. Many create an imaginary playmate. In their investigation of friendship patterns, Janos, Kristi, and Robinson (1985) found 28 percent of the gifted children sampled had fewer friends than they would like. These high IQ children felt that being smart made it harder to make friends.

A distinct sex difference in perceptions of the desirability of intellectual ability appears during adolescence. Girls view high achievement as a threat to their popularity with the opposite sex, while boys feel scholarship does not affect

Characteristics of Gifted and Talented Individuals

their popularity with peers of the same or opposite sex. The career and academic interest of gifted girls are more similar to gifted boys than to those of their average female agemates. However, social pressures attempt to diminish their career aspirations and reinforce compliant behaviors and acceptance of less aggressive, less dynamic careers than might have been their original goal (Kerr, 1985).

Self-Concept.   It is not surprising that gifted and talented youngsters have consistently been found to have significantly more positive social and academic self-concepts than their intellectually average peers (Kelly & Colangelo, 1984; Lehman & Erdwins, 1981) as well as higher levels of self-confidence (Davis & Rimm, 1985), self-sufficiency, and independence (Lehman & Erdwins, 1981). The perceived internal locus of control is the psychological construct frequently identified as the source of the gifted individual's self-esteem. They accept responsibility for their successes and failures and feel in control of their destinies. Failures are considered constructive learning experiences or momentary setbacks. In contrast, individuals having an external locus of control attribute positive experiences to luck or chance factors and poor achievement to unfair evaluations and bad luck. They feel their destiny is controlled by external forces. They have no personal power over the direction their life will take (Milgram & Milgram, 1976).

Attempts to meet their own high standards and the expectations of teachers and parents can create stress. High achieving students can be unrealistically self-critical as a result of the extremely high internal standards they have set for themselves. They are frustrated by their desire for perfection in all endeavors. Intraindividual discrepancies in abilities can create internal stress as they are not able to achieve with the same level of success across all performance areas.

Personality.   The flexibility of perspective common to the gifted enables them to view circumstances and situations from another person's point of view. For example, a young gifted girl may feel frustrated by the realization that she understands her peers better than her peers understand her (Kline & Meckstroth, 1985).

The heightened awareness with which these children approach their environment contributes to their ability to empathize. It also leaves them vulnerable to influences which may not affect their agemates. Their response to emotional experiences may be exaggerated by their intense sensitivity. As a defense, they may become cynical or sarcastic.

A well-developed and refined system of values and justice develops early in gifted children. They enjoy discussions of controversial issues and perceive the complexities of social, ethical, and moral factors. They are likely to become outraged when their sense of fair play or justice is violated.

An appreciation for uniqueness and diversity is the key to understanding the social and emotional development of the gifted. About twice the percentage of gifted students as regular students experience social adjustment difficulties such as loneliness and isolation (Janos, Kristi, & Robinson, 1985). Heightened cognitive abilities intensify affective sensitivity. Discrepancies in achievement levels

Students at the Bronx High School of Science, a school for those gifted in science and mathematics, display some of the awards they have won.

within such children contribute to their struggles with perfectionism. Parents and teachers can encourage gifted youngsters to set realistic, attainable goals consistent with their current and desired levels of performance. Kline and Meckstroth (1985) observed that for the gifted, "normal abilities appear incongruent and deficient by comparison . . . adults are prone to focus on the relative problems of the exceptionally gifted rather than recognition of their strengths" (p. 27). Contradicting what one might expect, able youngsters may become more aware of their weaknesses than their strengths. Time should be taken to reflect positively on all achievements whether large or small, or academic, social, or physical.

Research on the strength of self-concepts and social skills should be considered in light of the following concerns. The populations evaluated in these studies have been identified by psychometrics and have been primarily white and middle class children. The socioemotional characteristics of minority, low income, underachieving gifted have not been addressed (Kitano & Kirby, 1986). Therefore, generalizations to all gifted individuals are discouraged.

As their years advance, outstanding potential manifests itself in the performances and products expected of these individuals and their actualized giftedness. Roe's (1952) study of 64 eminent scientists (biologists, physicists, and social scientists) offers insight into the life history, family background, professional and recreational interests, intelligence, achievements, and personality of her subjects.

Although there is no "typical" scientist, she offers a description of the "average" eminent scientist:

> He was the first-born child of a middle-class family, the son of a professional man. He is likely to have been a sickly child or have lost a parent at an early age. He has a very high I.Q. and in boyhood began to do a great deal of reading. He tended to feel lonely and "different" and to be shy and aloof from his classmates. He had only a moderate interest in girls and did not begin dating them until college. He married late (at 27), has two children, and finds security in family life; his marriage is more stable than the average. Not until his junior or senior year in college did he decide on his vocation as a scientist. What decided him (almost invariably) was a college project in which he had occasion to do some independent research—to find out things for himself. Once he discovered the pleasures of this kind of work, he never turned back. He is completely satisfied with his chosen vocation. . . . He works hard and devotedly in his laboratory, often seven days a week. He says his work is his life and he has few recreations . . . The movies bore him. He avoids social affairs and political activity and religion plays no part in his life or thinking. Better than any other interest or activity, scientific research seems to meet the inner need of his nature.   (p. 104)

One cannot help but notice the gender bias in this passage. Since the early 1950s, when this article was first published, many changes have taken place which have encouraged women to develop career aspirations similar to those of their male agemates. Whether or not they achieve their goals has been attributed to a number of internal and external factors (Kerr, 1985). Potentially gifted girls begin compromising their professional goals in adolescence. Career education and counseling may mediate this decline and promote greater lifelong achievements.

Physical and Health Characteristics

Since Terman's (1925) work described the gifted as healthy, vigorous, and strong, little attention has been given to their medical and health characteristics. Recently, Kelly and Colangelo (1984) found their sample of gifted seventh to ninth graders reported fewer physical complaints.

It should be remembered that the diversity apparent in cognitive and affective rates of development can also be found in motor skills. Age-appropriate motor skill development may contribute to frustration as able youngsters cannot perform physically what they are able to conceive intellectually. The rates of intellectual, physical, and motor development are not strongly related (Mussen, Conger, & Kagan, 1969). Body build and physical development are more influenced by health practices, opportunities for exercise, quality of nutrition, and genetic endowments (Biehler, 1981).

Giftedness is not limited to healthy, able-bodied individuals. Recent advances in microtechnology have opened a door to gifted individuals with physical or sensory impairments; this has provided new means of expression which allow them to communicate their ideas and potential for contribution in all realms of knowledge. This was not available in the past due to their physical limitations.

DETECTION

Two strategies for the identification of the gifted will be presented. The first is an abbreviated specific application of some of the alternatives suggested in The Optimal Match Strategy; this approach is used in efforts to find students in need of additional services in specific academic ability areas such as mathematical reasoning. The second, the Generic Gifted Identification Strategy, suggests a broad, flexible approach and is appropriate in efforts to locate all types of ability in students from a variety of cultural and socioeconomic backgrounds. Educators of the gifted must remember that, although the right to due process is not mandated for the gifted, it is wise to keep its elements in mind when developing and implementing assessment procedures.

The Optimal Match Strategy

The general principles that provide the foundation for this approach center on the appraisal of the youngster's characteristics (both cognitive and affective) and on the manipulation of significant educational variables (Stanley, 1980). Originating with the work of H. B. Robinson, this process has as its ultimate goal the formulation of a match between a youngster's assessed academic needs and a variety of alternatives for appropriate educational facilitation. For this reason the method has been named "The Optimal Match Strategy."

In order to exercise the Optimal Match Strategy, the assessment and facilitation process should address the following set of broad-range goals:

1. Assessment for identification should provide a profile of a child's abilities in specific areas as accurately and precisely as possible.
2. Assessment for identification should diagnose the status of the youngster's developed skills in curricula related to areas of outstanding ability.
3. Assessment for identification should also include some survey of the youth's attitudes toward school in general, specific subjects, career aspirations, values, and interests.
4. Following the assessment procedure, the youngster (whenever suitable) and his or her family should be informed about the profile of abilities and developed skills; they should also be assisted in the process of exploring educational alternatives that are appropriate to the child's assessed educational needs and helped to determine which of those alternatives are feasible for them to pursue.
5. Documentation concerning the child's abilities, skills, and the family's desired educational options should be provided to the family and to specified agencies in which these alternatives are to be implemented.
6. Opportunities for follow-up assessment and counseling should be provided.
7. Families in need of special services (such as psychological counseling) should be referred to appropriate sources of information and services.

A two-step identification strategy is used. This process has its roots in the earlier work of Leta Hollingworth (1929, 1942) and has been applied extensively in the Study of Mathematically Precocious Youth (George, 1979; George & Solano, 1976; Solano, 1979; Stanley, 1976b, 1977).

Step One: Eligibility. The first step involves selecting a group of students who, based upon past performance, are likely to be eligible for advanced educational alternatives. In this phase of the identification process it is important to avoid leaving out any possible candidate (i.e., minimize false negatives). To do this, students might be chosen based upon past performance on age-appropriate tests of virtually any kind or recommendations from teachers and parents that relate a youngster's specific accomplishments. The goal is to establish the broadest possible talent pool. This minimizes the problem of the poor reliability of age-appropriate tests.

Step Two: The Out-of-Level Test. The second step in the process is presented to youths who have qualified via step one and have *chosen* to take a difficult test of mathematical and verbal reasoning ability designed for older students. This is called an "out-of-level" testing procedure because tests designed for more advanced students are given to younger children. The use of a test in this manner adds a great deal of ceiling to the assessment process by providing many items that are more difficult than those typically found on age-appropriate instruments.

Instruments that have been found particularly useful in mapping a child's profile of specific abilities are typically difficult tests that yield separate scores for verbal and mathematical reasoning in addition to whatever else is being measured.

In order to map a child's profile of developed skills in relevant curricula, tests are used that have relatively wide grade level ranges. These tests provide an appropriate degree of specificity for diagnosing those aspects of particular subjects that the highly able student already knows well and determine where and at what level instruction should begin.

The assessment of a highly able child's abilities in specific talent areas related to academic performance presents several assessment problems to the professional that must be overcome:

1. *The Need for Educationally Relevant Information.* In our society, intellectual giftedness has become virtually synonymous with high IQ scores. A recent national survey of identification practices for finding gifted youngsters indicates that tests of general intelligence are used for such purposes more frequently than any other selection tool (Alvino, McDonnel, & Richert, 1981). Although the psychological construct that we have come to know as "intelligence" is recognized as one of the most valuable contributions that psychology has provided us, measures of global intellectual ability like IQ fail to provide information relevant to planning appropriate educational experiences for highly able youths. For Optimal Match intervention, a child's profile of specific abilities must include measures of both mathematical and verbal reasoning ability, since all courses at the elementary, secondary, and post-secondary levels relate to some degree to one or both of these ability dimensions.

2. *Poor Reliability at the Extremes.* For the ablest youngsters in an age group, tests will yield scores that show diminished reliability compared with those earned by more typical youths. Because a small number of items actually discriminate individual differences at the upper levels of ability, random influences

or error can account for more variation among the scores earned by members of the highly able group than among the more typical group. The problem of poor reliability at the upper "tail" has been increased by the relatively recent development of minimal competency curricula and instruments to measure performance at minimal levels. In some of the worst cases, only five test items are available to discriminate among the top 25 percentile ranks of the norm group. Missing even one item on such a test might result in a highly able youth's failing to qualify for special educational services that are, in fact, appropriate for the child's learning needs.

3. *The Ceiling Effect*. The problem of poor reliability at the upper end of the test-score continuum is inextricably entangled with the equally disturbing problem of "ceiling effect." This term refers to the fact that the ablest students will, almost by definition, get all or most of the test items correct on an instrument developed for youths their own age. They are quite literally bouncing against the ceiling of the test. In this circumstance, the test yields a low estimate of the youngster's actual ability or developed skills because there is no place higher to go on that particular test (Keating, 1975). On some tests currently published, the ceiling effect is so pronounced that a perfect score yields a percentile rank of less than 90. Inexperienced school personnel might incorrectly interpret the student's failure to reach a criterion of the 96th percentile as justification for refusing to consider the child gifted even though reaching such a criterion is impossible! The use of such inappropriate instruments as determinants of eligibility for special educational services represents an illustration of the worst possible consequences of the ceiling effect.

The ideal test to use in a procedure for assessing gifted children and adolescents is one that has plenty of difficult items so that individual differences at the uppermost regions of capability within specific talent areas can be assessed accurately and precisely. An out-of-level testing procedure such as that described in the second step of the Optimal Match Strategy identification process compensates for the absence of tests with adequate ceiling (Keating, 1975; Stanley, 1954).

Generic Gifted Identification Strategy

This identification process involves three phases which precede placement: nomination, screening, and selection. Each requires a decision be made based on a number of sources and types of information (see Table 11.2). The Optimal Match Strategy can be seen as a selected subset of the options provided in the Generic strategy. The goals and warnings are also entirely relevant. This multifaceted approach results in the development of a case study for each candidate which is composed of a number of educationally relevant items. These will contribute not only to appropriate selection decisions but also to placement and programming decisions. The data sources and instrumentation are flexible depending upon the type of ability one is seeking to identify and serve. Individuals who may offer valuable information regarding the subject's potential abilities may be data sources. The strategies and materials can be tailored to suit the selection needs of a program whether it focuses on computers and technology, or music. Each phase should require the collection of data from two or more sources with

Table 11.2

Generic Gifted Identification

Phase	Data Source (Individuals)	Data Collection		Decision Makers
		Instruments and Strategies	Type of Data Collected	
I. Nomination	Administrators Classroom Teachers Coaches Counselors Librarians Parents Peers Self Significant Others	Verbal Reports Questionnaires	Referrals Biographical	Coordinator of Identification Process

II. Screening	Administrators
	Classroom Teachers
	Coaches
	Counselors
	Librarians
	Parents
	Peers
	Self
	Significant Others
		Checklists
		Group tests of
		  achievement,
		  creativity, mental
		  abilities, etc.
		Detailed questionnaires
		  (biographical data)
		Interest surveys
			Attitudes
			Behavior ratings
			  (cognitive and affective)
			Biographical
			Interests
			Test scores
				Identification Team:
				Classroom Teacher
				Gifted Education
				  Specialist
				Parent
				School Psychologist
				Student

III. Selection	Student	Auditions
		Interviews
		Evaluation of pupil
		  products/portfolio
		Individual tests of
		  achievement,
		  creativity, intelligence,
		  etc.
			Biographical
			Proof of excellence and/
			  or potential
			Test scores
				Identification Team:
				Classroom Teacher
				Gifted Education
				  Specialist
				Parent
				School Psychologist
				Student

IV. Placement				

appropriate instrumentation. Each phase gradually reduces the number of students under consideration.

The entire process of data collection should be managed by an identification coordinator. This role should be filled by an educator or psychologist who has had specific training in the nature and nurture of potentially gifted students.

Nomination. The objective of the nomination phase is to develop a pool of approximately 15 to 20 percent of the student body which will be considered in the screening phase. Nominations are often collected informally in conversation with each data source; however, a more comprehensive, defensible strategy is to provide data sources with a brief questionnaire asking for a set number of names of students. This allows data sources to observe candidates in their "home" environments, situations in which the highly able student has performed well in the past. Students should be observed in situations in which they are most likely to demonstrate their extraordinary capabilities as no gifted student is gifted all the time in every environment.

The identification coordinator provides data sources with a list of characteristics similar to those in Table 11.1. A frequent benefit of participation in this phase is that the data sources attend to students who demonstrate behaviors which had not previously been considered indicators of talent. Data sources are asked to nominate individuals who demonstrate the greatest number of indicator behaviors most often. The positive and negative indicator behaviors should be revised by the identification coordinator to reflect content and contexts more representative of the age, interests, and environment of the target population. The result of this procedure is a pool of candidates to be considered in the next phase.

Screening.   Screening requires the collection of more structured, objective information regarding a candidate's abilities. Criteria are set to reduce the number of students progressing beyond this phase by half, to approximately 10 percent of the original student body. Past performance and products are evaluated, students complete interest surveys, teachers may be asked to complete checklists (such as the *Scales for Rating Behavior Characteristics of Superior Students*, Renzulli et al., 1976) and, when appropriate, group tests of achievement, mental ability, and creativity may be administered. Cutoff scores on tests should be based on local or site needs, not national norms. High test scores, in the top 3 to 5 percent, would be useful when screening students for specific academic programs. A broader range, including students in the top 5 to 8 percent or more, may be appropriate when screening for nonacademic ability (i.e., musical, artistic, etc.) is the goal. Examination of anecdotal records and student files may provide further insights. All information contributes to the decision regarding the students to be considered for more intensive individual consideration. A team, similar to an IEP committee, composed of a specialist in gifted education, a school psychologist or counselor, and the classroom teacher meet to consider the case studies and to identify those that are to be recommended for further assessment. Parents are advised of the results of the screening phase and asked for permission to administer any individual tests used in the final phase.

Selection.   Selection requires the collection of scores, performances, and products which demonstrate or provide specific, convincing evidence of extraordinary capabilities. These sources of information should be evaluated by the team which gathered to evaluate the case studies in the screening phase. An expert in the learner's area of expertise should be asked to evaluate the performance or product, especially in areas of creative production or the visual and performing arts where test scores may not accurately reflect potential.

Students selected by the team for gifted programs should participate, with their parents and the team, in the placement decision which concludes the process. Members of the identification committee should discuss placement alternatives with the parents and the student before assigning the child to a particular program. Ongoing evaluation must be maintained in order to ensure appropriate decisions have been made.

Issues in the Identification of the Gifted

Special Needs Populations. Special identification procedures need to be followed to determine a child's areas of strength when assessing non-English-speaking children and youngsters who come from backgrounds that might lead one to suspect inhibited verbal functioning. The latter may be due to the low social value placed on education by the family or because of other social or economic pressures that create more pressing survival priorities.

If verbal reasoning tests are available in the youth's native language, they should be administered in exactly the same way they would be for English-speaking children. The *Comprehensive Tests of Basic Skills (CTBS)* and the *Wechsler Adult Intelligence Scale (WAIS)* are available in Spanish editions. If such tests are not available, a nonverbal reasoning test, such as Raven's (1938) *Standard Progressive Matrices* or *Advanced Progressive Matrices* or the *Differential Aptitude Test (DAT)* Abstract Reasoning Subtest can be used.

Checklists. In the nomination phase, checklists can provide a structured observation tool for educators and other data sources unfamiliar with gifted behavior. In this role, as one aspect of one phase of a multifaceted identification procedure, a checklist may be a useful data collection tool.

Criticism of tests based on alleged bias against minority youngsters has aroused interest in the use of checklists such as the *Scales for Rating Behavior Characteristics of Superior Students* (Renzulli et al., 1976) to identify gifted students. Although they have become popular, checklists lack a standardized frame of reference. Besides lacking evidence of their reliability and validity, they frequently distill ratings over several presumed different categories of behavior into a single score. In so doing, they present the same problem that global measures of intelligence do; they fail to provide sufficiently detailed information for realistic educational planning. Complete reliance on checklists as the sole means of identification is indefensible. The time taken by the identification coordinator to operationalize characteristics and to provide teachers with locally relevant indicator behaviors for each item on a checklist will improve the accuracy of referrals.

Assessing Creativity. Much of the controversy over the concept of creativity involves the question of the extent to which it is a personality trait, a specific cognitive ability, or a type of problem-solving strategy that might be learned (Michael, 1977). If it is the latter, there is less need to search for those who know the process than to teach the process to everyone.

Recent and longstanding critiques of methods for assessing creativity and the effectiveness of creativity training programs suggest that evaluation of children in this area be postponed until more evidence supports its use (Cohn, 1984; Mansfield, Busse, & Krepelka, 1978). As previously mentioned, evaluation of creative products (dance, art, music) should be left to experts in those fields. Their judgment may be subjective but its reliability and validity will be much greater than a pencil and paper assessment of talents expressed in other media.

Early Identification.   In the preschool years, parents may be the most reliable source of information regarding a child's ability because they have had greater opportunity to observe the child in a variety of environments. Robinson, Roedell, and Jackson (1981) have reported the results of their longitudinal work with young children undertaken at the Child Development Research Group at the University of Washington. They found inconsistent test performance over time and poor predictions of test performance based on the achievement of developmental milestones. The test battery they have developed to be used in conjunction with information provided by parents and teachers include the *Peabody Individual Achievement Test*, the short form of the *Stanford-Binet Intelligence Scale*, subtests of the *Wechsler Preschool Primary Scale of Intelligence*, the numerical memory subtest from the *McCarthy Scales of Children's Abilities*, and an informal test of reading.

CONSIDERATIONS IN INTERVENTION

Regardless of the cause of giftedness, failure to nurture its development will surely frustrate its potential fulfillment of promise.

The Preschool Years

Early identification of potential allows parents to learn to support their child's curiosity and enthusiasm for learning while encouraging independence, creativity, leadership, cooperation, and social skills. Parents must often become advocates for their child's learning and emotional needs in many institutions and situations.

The number of formal intervention programs is growing with interest in this age group at all levels of ability. Kitano and Kirby (1986) describe five exemplary programs developed to meet the needs of gifted preschoolers: The Seattle Child Development Preschool, The Hunter College Elementary School, The Astor Program, the New Mexico State University Preschool for the Gifted, and the University of Illinois (Champaign-Urbana) Program. All offer an academic component and some include affective, creative thinking and/or psychomotor components. Elements of model gifted preschools were identified by Karnes (1980): a conceptual model, clearly defined program goals with appropriate instructional methods, a well-defined identification procedure, a conducive learning environment, competent teachers, parent involvement, program evaluation, ample materials, flexible administrative arrangements, continuity after moving into regular schooling, inservice training, program advocates, and a specialist consultant.

As these elements are repeatedly combined in order to provide more opportunities for young, highly able learners to participate in structured educational experiences before entering the general education system, more refinements can be made in our understanding of development in the early years and the means for encouraging optimal learning for these children.

The School Years

Stanley (1980) and Cohn (1981) stress the importance of addressing the core aspects of the educational process if effective educational intervention is to be achieved for highly able youngsters. Five factors are identified as important manipulable education variables:

1. *Onset.* As the term implies, onset refers to the point in a student's educational development at which a desired educational alternative should be implemented. Typically, questions regarding the student's maturity and his or her profile of developed skills are crucial when making decisions involving questions of onset. Concerns about a youth's readiness for advanced-level coursework in specific subject areas, early entrance to school or college, or a well-planned strategy of grade skips would fall under this category.

2. *Content.* Content is the actual scope and sequence of educational objectives that characterize the curricula in subjects related to a student's area(s) of outstanding capability. Difficulty of the coursework, levels of advancement, suggested avenues for exploration and application, and concern about articulation across educational levels within institutions (e.g., elementary and secondary) and across institutions (e.g., secondary and post-secondary), and the awarding of credit for accomplishments—all are issues that fall under the heading of content.

3. *Style.* Style refers to the manner in which instruction is provided to the student. Formal lectures, casual inquiry or discovery methods, and individualized diagnostic and prescriptive instruction represent several examples of style that can be implemented to achieve an appropriate match for individual students.

4. *Pacing.* Pacing refers to the speed with which a student passes through curriculum in subject matter. Pacing has been demonstrated as a crucial variable in the successful educational facilitation of highly able students, particularly in mathematics (e.g., Stanley, Keating, & Fox, 1974) but also in the humanities (Durden, 1979, 1980). The key to appropriate pacing centers on teacher supervision which is based upon continued monitoring of the student's acquisition of important skills as he or she advances through the scope and sequence of educational objectives comprising the curriculum.

5. *Context.* The term "context" refers to the setting in which instruction is to occur, as well as the level of administrative organization (e.g., classroom, school, district, region) from which students are to be drawn and then to be served. Context can embrace a single classroom setting, in which the concern might be to individualize the student's progress in some fashion. Context might also mean that students are invited to a special classroom from different classrooms within a particular school or from different schools within a school district. When educational alternatives are offered at a college or university, or by a regional educational service center or a state department of education, students might be invited from across several school systems, counties, regions, states, and even from different countries. In some circumstances, educational options might be

provided by institutions such as museums or academies of arts and sciences. Thus, educational alternatives can extend beyond the limits of the school system. School is viewed as one environment, not the only environment, in which learning can occur.

The Smorgasbord of Educational Alternatives.

There is no one special way in which the educational needs of all students identified as gifted can be met. Instead, a smorgasbord of educational alternatives is suggested so that students and their families can select options which are most appropriate to their needs, resources, and constraints. Educational facilitation of gifted children and youths needs to involve all components of the fundamental educational structure in a comprehensive, integrated, and well-planned fashion.

The options included as educational alternatives for highly able students range from mild deviations from typical educational procedures to rather radical ones, such as leap-frogging as many as four or five grades or entering college full-time as much as three or five years earlier than usual. The central issue is the determination of a match between the appropriate educational alternatives and a youngster's assessed educational needs.

Some options can be integrated into the regular classroom. Enrichment traditionally refers to experiences which broaden or deepen an individual's knowledge or skills in a particular discipline or across a number of disciplines. Other options involve having a youngster move ahead of his or her more typical age-mates to attend a specific subject at a higher grade level, or even to skip one or more grades entirely. These two types of options are identified as "enrichment" and "accelerative" strategies. They are not mutually exclusive; programs often reveal a blend of the two.

Enrichment Strategies.

There are a variety of options available to enrich or augment the standard curriculum:

- *More complex problem solving in the regular classroom.* Students of above average ability can benefit from coursework designed for their age level that includes more complex ideas and problems to solve. Such mild modification of the school curriculum creates a class that is much more challenging to gifted learners.
- *Exploration.* This involves exposing youngsters to opportunities that enable them to understand the nature of a variety of disciplines which they might ultimately be interested in pursuing at an advanced level. For example, seventh graders might enjoy and benefit from an introductory college-level psychology course or anthropology course. The problem for these students is that without these opportunities they do not know what psychology or anthropology is nor what psychologists or anthropologists do. An appropriate enrichment experience might focus on a "guided tour" through such advanced level possibilities so that wise selections can be made in the future. For students who are in the junior high school years and beyond, and in some cases for younger students, career exploration is an extremely important enrichment strategy.

- *Role modeling.* Particularly for students in groups that are underrepresented in certain talent areas (e.g., verbally gifted minority students or mathematically gifted girls), role models can be tremendously important. Seeing a successful female mathematician or scientist who also has a family might help a young gifted girl overcome the persistent advice from virtually all corners of her life (friends, parents, teachers, counselors, etc.) to avoid developing her outstanding abilities (Fox, 1977).
- *Study skills training.* Students who have never been asked to complete substantial amounts of meaningful homework often find themselves under-skilled when suddenly faced with the demand for good study skills and homework behaviors. It is important to remember, however, that for direct instruction in these academic survival skills to succeed, there must be homework assigned that is both challenging and possible to accomplish. Study skills have been identified by the College Board's Education Equality Project (College Board, 1981) as an extremely important area of emphasis for preparing youths to do well in their advanced studies.
- *Communication skills training.* A communication skills program focuses upon learned behaviors that tend to stimulate social effectiveness (Cohn & Finlay, 1982). Emphasis is placed on developing interpersonal skills, understanding small groups (including the family), and developing large group skills. "Immaturity" is most often cited as a reason for refusing to allow a child to move ahead of his or her agemates. In some instances, immaturity means that the youngster is not as gregarious as his or her contemporaries. Ironically, some highly able young people are characteristically stable introverts. That is, they tend to form close bonds with a few individuals and appear shy or withdrawn in large group activities. Evidence suggests that allowing such youngsters the prerogative to move ahead may help them academically as well as socially (Benbow & Stanley, 1983a; George, Cohn, & Stanley, 1979).
- *Counseling for educational planning.* For many highly able young people, passage through the educational system is a mysterious journey through a labyrinth of unknowns. A systematic presentation of the structure of the elementary, secondary, and post-secondary curricula that shows key prerequisites for additional advanced educational opportunities serves these youngsters well. It is virtually never too early for a family and a gifted youngster to assume increased responsibility for educational planning. Gathering data (self-evaluations, teacher evaluations, peer evaluations, test scores, etc.) about one's self, learning how to interpret such information, and locating appropriate learning opportunities are all valuable activities for the able student.
- *Community opportunities.* Schools are not the only places for students to find challenging learning experiences. Many outstanding multidisciplinary offerings are provided by local universities and colleges, museums, libraries, and local interest groups after school, during the summer, and on the weekends.

Current Enrichment Models. Once a program is in place, the responsibility rests with the teacher for the development of appropriate, differentiated learning experiences for the gifted student. A number of instructional models or strategies have been developed to assist educators in this task. Three of the more popular models are introduced briefly here. Additional models relevant for the gifted are described more fully in Maker (1982).

1. *Creative problem solving.* Based on the work of Osborn (1963), Sidney Parnes expanded the concept of applied imagination into the Creative Problem Solving (CPS) Process in order to offer teachers a means to stimulate the development of successful strategies to solve practical problems in all students (Parnes, Noller, & Biondi, 1967). Gifted students are assumed able to gain greater benefits from experience with this model than average learners (Maker, 1982). Brainstorming is a key activity in this versatile model. Educators must use caution when basing a gifted program on Creative Problem Solving as it requires careful selection of appropriate problems to maintain a defensible level of curriculum differentiation. Its application is common in enrichment programs.

2. *The Enrichment Triad.* Joseph Renzulli's (1977) Triad (see Figure 11.4) is developed specifically for gifted learners. Of the three interactive components, Type I, General Exploratory Activities, and Type II, Group Training Activities, are intended for all learners; Type III, Investigations of Real Problems, is most appropriate for the interests, learning style, and needs of gifted students. With Type I, the teacher plans experiences which allow students to explore an area of personal interest. Type II promotes the development of the thinking and feeling processes associated with the student's area of interest. Type III requires learners to develop and investigate a "real problem" with methods of inquiry appropriate to the discipline from which it is derived. The resulting product is to be shared with a real audience. This model has been widely implemented. Although its flexibility makes it attractive, it must be supported with other strategies. The Creative Problem Solving Process would nest comfortably in Type II activities. Also "real problems" are often difficult for a classroom teacher to manage within existing administrative structures and school resources. The guiding principles of curriculum differentiation (Passow, 1982) must be met within each "real problem" in order for this approach to maintain its integrity in gifted programs.

3. *Structure of Intellect.* This three-dimensional model (see Figure 11.5) developed by J. P. Guilford (1956) represents intellect in terms of three facets: content, mental process, and mental product. Each of the 120 mental abilities (150 if one splits figural content into auditory and visual as Guilford later suggested) is represented by one block in the cube. Meeker (1969) is responsible for the development of a large number of the instructional materials based on this model. These have taken the form of assessment materials, student workbooks, and teacher guidebooks. Although the materials promote individualization, the diagnostic materials lack research support for their reliability and validity. According to Maker (1982), it "does not provide a total framework for curriculum development, although it does provide for curricular modifications in several areas" (p. 133).

Figure 11.4

The Enrichment Triad Model

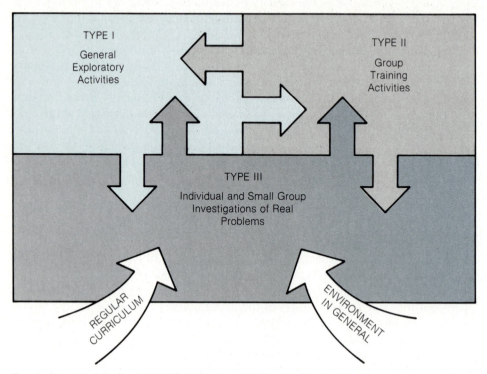

TYPE I

General
Exploratory
Activities

TYPE II

Group
Training
Activities

TYPE III

Individual and Small Group
Investigations of Real
Problems

REGULAR
CURRICULUM

ENVIRONMENT
IN GENERAL

Source: From *The Enrichment Triad Model* by Joseph S. Renzulli. Copyright © 1977 by Creative Learning Press. Reprinted by permission.

Accelerative Strategies. This approach is used to increase the speed with which students pass through the curriculum. One method of acceleration is grade advancement. Options include:

- *Entering kindergarten or first grade early.* In many states, students who demonstrate the prerequisite skills are allowed to enter kindergarten or first grade earlier than usual. Typically, the waiver of the usual age criterion requires documented evidence of the child's advanced abilities and developed skills. Performance on standardized tests and systematic information about the child's behaviors from the parents appear equally important (Roedell, Jackson, & Robinson, 1980).
- *Grade skipping.* Skipping one or more grades is perhaps the most controversial alternative among the smorgasbord's options. It occurs most often at the elementary level. A grade-skip is not appropriate for all gifted youngsters, and there are many important factors to consider. The four most important considerations are the student's level of achievement in both mathematical

Figure 11.5

Structure of Intellect Model

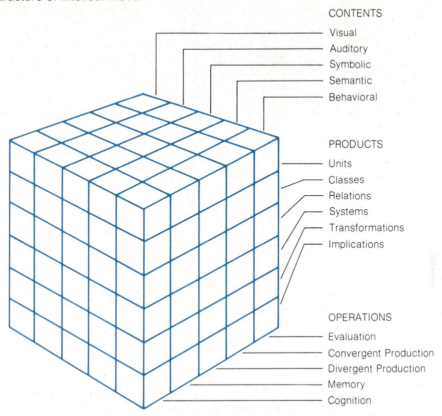

CONTENTS
- Visual
- Auditory
- Symbolic
- Semantic
- Behavioral

PRODUCTS
- Units
- Classes
- Relations
- Systems
- Transformations
- Implications

OPERATIONS
- Evaluation
- Convergent Production
- Divergent Production
- Memory
- Cognition

Source: From *Way Beyond the IQ* by J. P. Guilford. Copyright © 1977 Creative Education Foundation, Inc. Reprinted by permission of the author.

and verbal reasoning, the level of skill development in curricula, the youngster's eagerness to move ahead more rapidly than usual, and the parents' support. Often it is necessary to educate both parents and the child as to why this option might be an appropriate one to consider.

Those students with abilities and skills two to five grade-levels above their grade placement would be good candidates to skip a grade if they are eager to move into more challenging material in all areas. The student with either mathematical or verbal ability and skills significantly above grade level might be better advised to seek advanced coursework in the area of strength while remaining in the typical grade level.

Grade-skips need to be planned strategically to avoid possible pitfalls. There are ways to take advantage of natural breaks in the schooling process when a grade-skip is being considered. One such break involves moving to a new school or school district; another is moving into a new phase of schooling (such as from elementary to middle school). In each of these cases a youngster enters a new situation in which there will be a need to make new friends regardless of the fact that a grade has been skipped. Often this type of strategic grade-skipping lessens the potential for negative social impact by not drawing attention to the atypical advancement.

Educators and others have been hesitant to use this technique to meet the needs of academically talented youths. Arguments that are used against grade-skipping often pertain to the presumed social and emotional maladjustment that is imagined to accompany it. Studies have shown that skipping a grade (or entering kindergarten, first grade, or college early) is not socially or emotionally harmful. It appears that the support of the family plays an extremely important role in fostering a youngster's social and emotional adjustment whether or not a grade is skipped. Youngsters who were advanced were at least as well adjusted as those at the typical age-grade placement (Daurio, 1979).

- *Entering college early.* An increasing number of colleges and universities recognize the role that they might play in facilitating the development of highly able minds and its value as a recruiting strategy. Besides allowing underage students to take one or two courses per semester on their campuses, some institutions permit highly able and well-prepared underage students to enter as full-time college students. In some circumstances, the student's high school automatically awards a high school diploma upon the successful completion of the first year of college.

- *Entering multiple concurrent degree programs.* Several institutions across the country offer undergraduate students the opportunity to earn master's degrees or other advanced degrees while they are earning their baccalaureate degree. In most cases, the time period required to complete both degrees is less than it would be if each degree program were pursued sequentially.

In addition to grade advancement, students can participate in subject matter acceleration. Among the options are the following:

- *Starting course sequences early.* If a student's ability level in a specific talent area is highly developed, starting a course sequence related to that talent area might be a stimulating alternative. Mathematically talented youths might wish to complete the computation sequence as rapidly as possible and enter the precalculus mathematics sequence as soon as they have garnered the requisite skills. Similarly, verbally talented youngsters might want to start foreign language sequences or social studies earlier than usual. Artistically able children might become involved in courses at a multimedia studio allowing them training in perspective and sculpture.

- *Compacting course sequences.* Gifted individuals differ in their rate of learning new material well. The usual school curriculum is paced so that a person of average ability can comprehend, remember, and use the skills being taught. Students whose ability is highly developed and who are very motivated and interested in a related subject area may want to investigate the possibility of compacting, or telescoping, a sequence of relevant courses. Examples of this option that have been accomplished by very able students include completing a year or more of a foreign language during a special

These middle school students, gifted in science, are allowed to take enrichment classes at a local community college.

three-week summer program or completing more than one full year science course in an academic year.

- *Working individually or in small groups with a mentor.* Sometimes schools are not able to provide options such as starting course sequences early or compacting coursework into less time. Under such circumstances, a mentor might be able to work with one or several students to cover the material as expeditiously as possible. Negotiations with the school should be pursued so that the students can be excused from their regular class period in that subject to work on the more advanced homework assigned by the mentor. It is important to arrange credit for the material covered by the mentor and to encourage frequent communication between the mentor and school personnel.

This alternative is popular in the arts, as well as academics, because it allows youngsters to explore a discipline of their interest while developing the techniques of an expert. Materials and environments not common in the regular school system add to the value of a mentorship experience. Choosing an appropriate mentor is crucial. One should look for an individual with great enthusiasm, depth, and breadth in the subject as well as interest and skill in working with highly able youths. Often such individuals can be found at nearby colleges and universities. Many advanced undergraduate and graduate students have the necessary training and interest, as do retired teachers, professors, engineers, and the like.

- *Taking a course at a nearby college or university.* One solution to the problem of finding appropriately challenging subject matter may be to have the student take a course at a nearby college or university while still in high school (or junior high school). Many institutions of higher learning have established a special student status for able and ambitious youths who are younger than the typical college entrant. Starting a course sequence early or compacting a course sequence may be an even more feasible option at a college or university. Some of the courses that have been taken by junior high school students in the past with much success include astronomy, chemistry, German, precalculus, computer science, expository writing, and psychology.
- *Taking challenging coursework in other areas.* Highly able and eager students should also be encouraged to seek out challenging high-level courses in all areas of study. They should not limit their exploration to those subjects generally taught in school or their particular area of talent. They may wish to consider languages in the elementary grades, or Eastern religions and cultures in the high school years.
- *Taking Advanced Placement courses.* Advanced Placement (AP) courses, which prepare a student for AP examinations in specific subjects, are usually the highest level courses offered in a high school. In an AP course, students have the opportunity to study college level material while still in high school, and, if they take the respective AP exam and do well on it, they can earn advanced standing college credits for this work. By earning college credits, a student can save substantially in college tuition and time. AP examinations are currently offered in more than 22 different subjects, including computer science, music theory, and studio art. High schools vary greatly in the number of AP courses they offer.

Two Caveats. These warnings involve two possible solutions commonly considered by parents and counselors: private schools and self-paced study.

- *Private schools.* Although many private schools are noted for their high-level academic curricula (Howley, Howley, & Pendarvis, 1986), they may not allow enough flexibility for very able individuals. It clearly depends upon the specific school. One possible advantage of some private institutions might be increased individual attention within the classroom setting if the teacher/student ratio is close to one-to-ten. Another possible advantage might be increased ease in arranging a curriculum specifically keyed to the student's assessed abilities and developed skills. If the school is willing to place a youth in specific subject-matter classes, regardless of age, it may be a good educational investment. All options should be investigated, however. The money that would be spent in sending a child to a private school might in fact be better invested in piecing together a patchwork of several different kinds of options in several different settings.
- *Self-paced study.* That self-paced instruction is especially desirable for the ablest students is a common misimpression, seldom borne out in fact. Ap-

propriate pacing by a teacher, involving interaction with other students at or near the same ability level, seems preferable. Students who have participated in various fast-paced mathematics classes have found that their actual competition is with national norms on standardized achievement tests, but they find motivation in knowing that they are completing as much material as another person in their class who they perceive to be at the same ability level as they are.

Individually paced instruction that has been successful usually has involved a mentor or teacher who set the pace on the basis of careful diagnosis. In the most typical case, the student meets regularly with the mentor, once a week or more, in order to ask questions that come up between meetings. The instructor goes over homework outside of class, carefully annotating feedback on important points or misunderstood items. Instructional time is spent on going over new material and in dialogue.

It is not very often that secondary-age (and in many cases even college-age) students have the self-discipline to pace themselves through an entire course without regular encouragement and feedback from an outside source. For this reason, even highly able young people usually fail to complete correspondence courses, although in some extremely rural settings such options might be the only context for appropriate educational facilitation of such youngsters.

Issues in Intervention

Controversy has always surrounded the design and content of special learning opportunities for the gifted. Four issues deserve attention: the question of "programs" as opposed to "provisions," curriculum differentiation, the effects of ability grouping, and least restrictive environments for the gifted and talented.

Programs versus Provisions.
Tannenbaum (1983) makes a critical distinction between "provisions" and "programs" for the gifted. A program is an educational imperative founded securely on a comprehensive, well-articulated scope and sequence of cognitive and affective objectives across all disciplines and grade levels. Provisions, on the other hand, are "fragmentary learning experiences lacking in complex form, long-range purpose, or clear directionality" (p. 423). These haphazard collections of units, brainteasers, and extra worksheets have no underlying theme or design. They may be based predominantly on what the teacher has at hand or knows best rather than student interest or skill. In contrast, programs are complex, thoroughly planned, district-wide reflections of a local commitment to excellence in the education of potentially productive, highly able learners.

Curriculum Differentiation.
This refers to the degree to which the learning experiences in a gifted program are appropriate to meet the specific needs of the gifted which differentiate them from their less able peers. The Curriculum Council of the National/State Leadership Training Institute on the Gifted/Talented has developed seven guiding principles of curriculum differentiation (Passow, 1982):

1. The content of curricula for the gifted/talented should focus and be organized to include more elaborate, complex, and in-depth study of major ideas, problems, and themes that integrate knowledge with and across systems of thought.
2. Curricula for the gifted/talented should allow for the development and application of productive thinking skills to enable students to reconceptualize existing knowledge and/or generate new knowledge.
3. Curricula for the gifted/talented should enable them to explore constantly changing knowledge and information and develop the attitude that knowledge is worth pursuing in an open world.
4. Curricula for the gifted/talented should encourage exposure to, selection of, and use of appropriate and specialized resources.
5. Curricula for the gifted/talented should promote self-initiated and self-directed learning and growth.
6. Curricula for the gifted/talented should provide for the development of self-understanding and the understanding of one's relationship to persons, societal institutions, nature, and culture.
7. Evaluations of curricula for the gifted/talented should be conducted in accordance with prior stated principles, stressing higher-level thinking skills, creativity, and excellence in performance and products.

In order to determine whether or not a program is solely appropriate for the gifted or whether it is equally appropriate for all, one must answer three questions: (1) *Would* all children want to be involved in such learning experiences? (2) *Could* all children participate in such learning experiences? (3) *Should* all children be expected to succeed in such learning experiences? (Passow, 1983). "Yes" answers to these questions should lead to reconsideration of the opportunities in mind. What is appropriate for all does not provide the desired differentiation in learning opportunities required to challenge the gifted. "No" responses ensure a differentiated curriculum, but not a program. Educators must deal with these two issues independently.

The National State Leadership Training Institute raised concern over the proliferation of "provisions" for the gifted being billed as "programs." The lack of defensible services and reliable evaluation resulted in public concern over the necessity for such programs in a time of financial restraint. The popularity of "thinking skills" programs in gifted education brought public criticism and doubt. Why should the gifted be the only students provided opportunities to develop cognitive skills? Many educators and parents felt all students could benefit from this type of instruction. They were right. Therefore, the principles of curriculum differentiation were developed to guide the design of legitimate learning programs for the gifted from the outset.

Ability Grouping Strategies.   To group or not to group? The question of social and academic outcomes has been addressed repeatedly in the literature (Coleman & Fults, 1982, 1985; Maddux, Scheiber, & Bass, 1982). A continuum of grouping alternatives can be made available within a school system depending on the flexibility of the administration and support services.

Ability grouping strategies for gifted students include attending magnet schools which offer accelerated programs in one or more subject areas.

- **Full-Time Homogeneous Classes**
  Magnet Schools
  Special Schools for the Gifted
  Private Schools
  School within a School
  Special Gifted/Talented Classes in the Elementary School

- **Full-Time Heterogeneous Classes**
  Combined Grades in a Regular Class
  High-ability Cluster Groups of Gifted Students Placed with "Regular" Students
  Mainstreaming in the Regular Class

- **Part-Time or Temporary Groups**
  Pullout Programs
  Resource-room Plans
  Special Classes
  Activity Clubs
  Honors Programs
  Special or Accelerated Classes in the Secondary School

(Davis & Rimm, 1985, p. 111)

Many of these organizational structures are inherent in the alternatives previously suggested and in the discussion of context as a factor in gifted education. However, the full range of possibilities must be stated for educators to realize the variety of service models available. A careful mix-and-match of student needs, desired outcomes, local resources, and service delivery alternatives (enrichment, acceleration, and grouping) will result in a program to serve gifted students well.

The effects of grouping structures have been investigated in order to understand their academic and nonacademic results. Segregated or integrated special programming has provided conflicting data regarding self-concept and peer acceptance. Coleman and Fults (1982, 1985) report lower self-concepts may result as gifted children in special programs make comparisons between themselves and their classmates. Students in these studies were involved in pullout programs. Retesting eight months after returning to the regular classroom revealed no difference between self-concepts of the students who had participated in the pullout and those who had not. Maddux, Scheiber, and Bass (1982) studied fifth and sixth graders in segregated and integrated special programming. Their results indicated no decrease in self-concept and peer acceptance as a result of homogeneous, separate programs.

Least Restrictive Environments for the Gifted and Talented. Based on her review of the literature, Whitmore (1980) suggests: "research could prove that the regular classroom is the most restrictive environment for the gifted child, in contrast to the expected effects of 'mainstream' education on handicapped children" (p. 68). Ability grouping appears to have little or no lasting negative effects on social and emotional development while encouraging the greatest academic gains. In school or out, throughout the life of any individual, the need for interaction with intellectual peers is a relevant issue. Providing gifted individuals these opportunities may challenge and stimulate them to create and contribute at the extreme of their potential.

The Adult Years

Willings (1985) found that highly able children carry their extraordinary abilities and expectations into adulthood. Their capacity for hard work may result in employment opportunities in which they are "overworked and underpaid." Gifted adults will frequently change jobs as they "can get as much out of a job in a few years as a more normally endowed person would get in a lifetime" (p. 37). Their reasons for job change are frequently a lack of intellectual stimulation and boredom. Their career aspirations may be frustrated as business tends to neglect the independent thinker in favor of those who think as the management does (Willings, 1983).

Many adults are able to find sufficient intellectual stimulation through their professional and leisure activities. However, highly intelligent adults may join community organizations, such as Mensa, which make membership dependent upon superior performance on an intelligence test. Willings (1985) also describes a club in Canada, "The Tuesday Club," for gifted adults in need of interaction with like-minded people.

FUTURE PERSPECTIVES FOR GIFTED
AND TALENTED INDIVIDUALS

Identification and programming for the atypical gifted continue to haunt education as unresolved issues. Groups who are currently underrepresented in gifted education include the very young, minorities, culturally diverse (including non-English speaking), underachievers, and students with physical or learning disabilities or sensory impairments. Appropriate procedures for recognition of their talents and abilities which provide information relevant to the design of differentiated challenging learning experiences must be developed. Enrichment, acceleration, and grouping alternatives can be explored in new and flexible combinations to meet the needs of this increasingly diverse group.

The technological advances offered by the development of microprocessors hold new alternatives for the field of educating the gifted and talented. At present, administering the many tests necessary to offer meaningful advice for educational planning, scoring the tests, charting profiles of existing knowledge, and determining appropriate steps to take requires enormous amounts of time. The use of "expert systems" to administer, score, profile, and help interpret test results will reduce the time required to a mere fraction of current practice. Moreover, as programmed instruction takes advantage of the tremendous capacity for information storage offered by the compact interactive video disc, opportunities to see and hear the most brilliant scholars discuss their areas of expertise will be extended across time and geography (when coupled with telecommunications networks).

Microcomputers offer gifted learners of all ages a challenging interactive environment in which they can apply and develop their skills in a discipline of their choosing, be it music, art, science, languages, literature, or game technology. Computer applications are developing in all disciplines. The effects that the social structure of learning environments based on computer or human interaction have on the achievement and emotional development of the gifted need to be explored (Kanevsky, 1985).

Renewed interest in theories which account for differences in learning ability and intelligence is encouraging gifted educators to examine the assumptions on which programs have been developed in the past. The analysis of the development of observable characteristics of gifted young people and adults in order to establish useful theories and investigate their underlying cognitive mechanisms and neurophysiological correlates appears promising (Eysenck, 1979; Sternberg, 1984). It has been suggested (Eysenck, 1979) that a theory of neurophysiological processes offers a promising path of research for understanding individual differences in mental capabilities. It is the development of increasingly sophisticated techniques for watching specific areas of the brain function as an individual performs various tasks, that offer spectacular possibilities to localize even at the cellular level different behaviors within the nervous system with extraordinary precision.

In contrast to Eysenck's preoccupation with physiological correlates, Sternberg (1984) has suggested an information processing model, which he argues provides an explanation for individual differences in cognitive functioning. He has focused on the role of "insight" in giftedness, interpreting that function as well-developed strategies for encoding information and solving problems. Sternberg asserts that the level of intelligence is a function of identifiable components of human information processing.

The speculation of these modern scholars is appealing. They have yet, however, to apply their hypotheses to empirical investigations of persons who have been identified and described as gifted.

SUMMARY

Giftedness and talent are the only two fields of exceptionality which are not handicapping conditions. Instead, they are characterized by extremely high abilities in one or more areas. An individual may be intellectually gifted and excel in science, mathematics, literature, or other fields; or he or she may have special talents in leadership, or in the creative or performing arts. Although giftedness and special talents are often apparent early in one's life, they may be recognized at any time.

Educators are usually the most involved professionals in the identification and encouragement of gifted and talented students; but school psychologists and counselors also work with gifted children in assessing their abilities and helping them achieve their potential. Often, professionals from other fields and disciplines are invited to serve as mentors for gifted students to extend their learning and experience outside the classroom.

The etiology of giftedness is unknown, but modern science has established that both heredity and environment have significant influences upon the development of outstanding intellectual ability. Although researchers have been interested in determining the relative contributions of each, there are no data which provide an answer to the question.

The characteristics of gifted and talented people have been studied extensively. Unlike the early beliefs that these individuals were frail, sickly, and emotionally unstable, results of long-term studies indicate that the opposite is true. The single most important characteristic that these individuals share is their ability to learn, absorb, and utilize knowledge efficiently and creatively. The enthusiasm and flexibility which characterizes their approach to thinking serves them well in peer relations. Gifted students are chosen more often as friends than their less able peers. However, as intelligence increases above IQ scores of 150, peer relationships sometimes become more difficult because of dramatic differences in interests and abilities between gifted students and their age peers.

Special educational programs are not mandated for gifted and talented students as they are for handicapped students, so educational opportunities vary considerably throughout the country. Where programs do exist they differ in type from special classes or schools exclusively designed for gifted and/or talented students, to enrichment programs which supplement regular classes, to acceleration by skipping grades. Some universities have developed early entrance programs for highly gifted students.

Much remains to be learned about the nature of giftedness and talent and the most effective ways to encourage and develop the unique abilities of these individuals. Improved methods of identification, especially for members of minority groups, more opportunities to use their abilities, and school and community programs which promote and value superior achievement need to be developed.

References

A nation at risk (1983). Government report by the Congressional Commission on the Study of Excellence in Education. Washington, DC: U.S. Government Printing Office.

Alvino, J., McDonnel, R. C., & Richert, S. (1981). National survey of identification practices in gifted and talented education. *Exceptional Children, 48,* 124–132.

Benbow, C. P., & Stanley, J. C. (1980). Sex differences in mathematical reasoning ability: Fact or artifact? *Science, 210,* 4475.

Benbow, C. P., & Stanley, J. C. (Eds.) (1983a). *Academic precocity.* Baltimore: Johns Hopkins University Press.

Benbow, C. P., & Stanley, J. C. (1983b). Differential course taking behavior revisited. *American Educational Research Journal, 4,* 469–473.

Biehler, R. F. (1981). *Child development: An introduction* (2nd ed.). Boston: Houghton Mifflin.

Burks, B. S., Jensen, D. W., & Terman, L. M. (1930). The promise of youth. *Genetic studies of genius. Vol. 3.* Stanford: Stanford University Press.

Cohn, C. M. G. (1984). *Effectiveness of creativity training: A research synthesis.* Unpublished doctoral dissertation, Arizona State University.

Cohn, S. J. (1980). *Two components of the Study of Mathematically Precocious Youth's (SMPY) intervention studies of educational acceleration.* Unpublished doctoral dissertation, Johns Hopkins University.

Cohn, S. J. (1981). What is giftedness? A multidimensional approach. In A. H. Kramer (Ed.), *Gifted children: Challenging their potential (New perspectives and alternatives)* (pp. 33–45). New York: Trillium Press.

Cohn, S. J., & Finlay, P. M. (1982). *Preventive and interventive strategies for counseling intellectually gifted students.* Paper presented at the 6th Annual Conference on Severe Behavior Disorders sponsored by Teacher Educators of Children with Severe Behavior Disorders, Tempe, Arizona.

Coleman, J. M., & Fults, B. A. (1982). Self-concept and the gifted classroom: The role of social comparisons. *Gifted Child Quarterly, 26,* 116–120.

Coleman, J. M., & Fults, B. A. (1985). Special class placement, level of intelligence, and the self-concepts of gifted children: A social comparison perspective. *Remedial and Special Education, 6* (1), 7–12.

College Board (1981). *Project equality.* Princeton: The College Board.

Cox, C. M. (1926). The early mental traits of three hundred geniuses. *Genetic studies of genius, Vol. 2.* Stanford: Stanford University Press.

Daurio, S. P. (1979). Educational enrichment versus acceleration: A review of the literature. In W. C. George, S. J. Cohn, & J. C. Stanley (Eds.), *Educating the gifted: Acceleration and enrichment.* Baltimore: Johns Hopkins University Press.

Davis, G. A., & Rimm, S. B. (1985). *Education of the gifted and talented.* Englewood Cliffs, NJ: Prentice-Hall.

Durden, W. G. (1979). The Johns Hopkins Program for Verbally Gifted Youths: Summer Humanities Institute. *ITYB (Intellectually Talented Youth Bulletin), 5* (10), 4.

Durden, W. G. (1980). Gifted programs: The Johns Hopkins Program for Verbally Gifted Youth. *Roeper Review, 2,* 34–37.

Eysenck, H. J. (1979). *The structure and measurement of intelligence.* New York: Springer-Verlag.

Fox, L. H. (1977). Changing behaviors and attitudes of gifted girls. *Talents and Gifts, 19* (4), 13–15, 21–22.

Fox, L. H., Brody, L. E., & Tobin, D. H. (Eds.) (1980). *Women and the mathematical mystique.* Baltimore: Johns Hopkins University Press.

Galton, F. (1869). *Hereditary genius.* New York: St. Martin's Press.

Galton, F. (1892). *Hereditary genius.* New York: St. Martin's Press.

George, W. C. (1979). The talent-search concept: An identification strategy for the intellectually gifted. *Journal of Special Education, 13,* 221–237.

George, W. C., Cohn, S. J., & Stanley, J. C. (Eds.) (1979). *Educating the gifted: Acceleration and enrichment.* Baltimore: Johns Hopkins University Press.

George, W. C., & Solano, C. H. (1976). Identifying mathematical talent on a statewide basis. In D. P. Keating (Ed.), *Intellectual talent: Research and development* (pp. 55–89). Baltimore: Johns Hopkins University Press.

Goleman, D. (1980). 1528 little peppers and how they grew. *Psychology Today, 13* (9), 28–53.

Guilford, J. P. (1956). The structure of the intellect. *American Psychologist, 53,* 267–293.

Hollingworth, L. S. (1929). *Gifted children: Their nature and nurture.* New York: Macmillan.

Hollingworth, L. S. (1942). *Children above 180 IQ, Stanford-Binet: Origin and development.* New York: World Book Company.

Howley, A., Howley, C. B., & Pendarvis, E. D. (1986). *Teaching gifted children.* Boston: Little, Brown.

Janos, P. M., Kristi, A. M., & Robinson, N. M. (1985). Friendship patterns in highly intelligent children. *Roeper Review, 8* (1), 46–49.

Jensen, A. R. (1980). *Bias in mental testing.* New York: The Free Press.

Jensen, A. R. (1981). *Straight talk about mental tests.* New York: The Free Press.

Kanevsky, L. (1985). Computer-based math for gifted students: Comparison of cooperative and competitive strategies. *Journal for the Education of the Gifted, 4,* 239–255.

Karnes, M. B. (1980). Elements of an exemplary preschool/primary program for the gifted and talented. In *Educating the preschool/primary gifted and talented.* Ventura, CA: Ventura County Superintendent of Schools.

Keating, D. P. (1975). Testing those in the top percentiles. *Exceptional Children, 41,* 435–436.

Keating, D. P. (Ed.) (1976). *Intellectual talent: Research and development.* Baltimore: Johns Hopkins University Press.

Kelly, K. R., & Colangelo, N. (1984). Academic and social self-concepts of gifted, general, and special students. *Exceptional Children, 50,* 551–554.

Kerr, B. A. (1985). Smart girls, gifted women: Special guidance concerns. *Roeper Review, 8,* 30–32.

Kitano, M. K., & Kirby, D. R. (1986). *Gifted education: A comprehensive view.* Boston: Little, Brown.

Kline, B. E., & Meckstroth, E. A. (1985). Understanding and encouraging the exceptionally gifted. *Roeper Review, 8* (1), 24–30.

Lehman, E. B., & Erdwins, D. J. (1981). The social and emotional adjustment of young intellectually gifted children. *Gifted Child Quarterly, 25,* 134–137.

Lerner, B. (1982). American education: How are we doing? *Public Interest, 69,* Fall, 59–82.

Lombroso, C. (1891). *Man of genius.* London: Walter Scott.

Maddux, C. D., Scheiber, L. M., & Bass, J. E. (1982). Self-concept and social distance in gifted children. *Gifted Child Quarterly, 26,* 77–81.

Maker, C. J. (1982). *Teaching models in education of the gifted.* Rockville, MD: Aspen.

Mansfield, R. S., Busse, T. V., & Krepelka, E. J. (1978). The effectiveness of creativity training. *Review of Educational Research, 48,* 517–536.

Marland, S. P. (1972). *Education of the gifted and talented: Report to the Congress of the United States by the Commissioner of Education.* Washington, DC: U.S. Government Printing Office.

Martinson, R. A. (1961). *Educational programs for gifted pupils.* Sacramento, CA: California State Department of Education.

Meeker, M. (1969). *The structure of intellect: Its interpretation and uses.* Columbus, OH: Merrill Publishing.

Michael, W. B. (1977). Cognitive and affective components of creativity in mathematics and the physical sciences. In J. C. Stanley, W. C. George, & C. H. Solano (Eds.), *The gifted and creative: A fifty-year perspective* (pp. 141–172). Baltimore: Johns Hopkins University Press.

Milgram, R. M., & Milgram, N. A. (1976). Personality characteristics of gifted Israeli children. *Journal of Genetic Psychology, 129,* 185–192.

Mussen, P. H., Conger, J. J., and Kagan, J. (1969). *Child development and personality* (3rd ed.). New York: Harper & Row.

Oden, M. H. (1968). The fulfillment of promise: 40-year follow-up of the Terman gifted group. *Genetic Psychology Monographs, 77,* 3–93.

Osborn, A. (1963). *Applied imagination.* New York: Scribner's.

O'Shea, H. (1960). Friendships and the intellectually gifted child. *Exceptional Children, 26,* 327–335.

Parnes, S. J., Noller, R., & Biondi, A. (1967). *Guide to creative action.* New York: Scribner's.

Passow, A. H. (1982). Curricula for the gifted. *Selected proceedings of the first national conference on curriculum for the gifted/talented.* Ventura, CA: Ventura County Superintendent of Schools.

Passow, A. H. (1983). *Differentiated curricula for the gifted/talented: Some further reflections.* Unpublished manuscript.

Raven, J. C. (1938). *Standard progressive matrices.* London: H. K. Lewis.

Renzulli, J. S. (1977). *The enrichment triad: A guide for developing defensible programs for the gifted and talented.* Mansfield Center, CT: Creative Learning Press.

Renzulli, J. (1978). What makes giftedness? Re-examining a definition. *Phi Delta Kappan, 60,* 180–184; 216.

Renzulli, J. S., Smith, L. H., White, A. J., Callahan, C. M., & Hartman, R. K. (1976). *Scales for rating the behavior characteristics of superior students.* Mansfield Center, CT: Creative Learning Press.

Resnick, D. P., & Resnick, L. B. (1985). Standards, curriculum, and performance: A historical and comparative perspective. *Educational Researcher, 14* (4), 5–20.

Robinson, H. B., Roedell, W. C., & Jackson, N. E. (1981). Early identification and intervention. In W. Barbe & J. Renzulli (Eds.), *Psychology and education of the gifted* (3rd ed.). New York: Irvington.

Roe, A. (1952). A psychologist examines 64 eminent scientists. *Scientific American, 187* (5), 21–25.

Roedell, W. C., Jackson, N. E., & Robinson, H. B. (1980). *Gifted young children.* New York: Teachers College Press.

Sears, R. R. (1977). Sources of life satisfactions of the Terman gifted men. *American Psychologist, 32,* 119–128.

Sears, P. S. (1979). The Terman genetic studies of genius, 1922–1972. In A. H. Passow (Ed.), *The gifted and the talented: Their education and development: Seventy-eighth yearbook of the National Society for the Study of Education (NSSE), Part I* (pp. 75–96). Chicago: University of Chicago Press.

Sears, P. S., & Barbee, A. H. (1977). Career and life satisfactions among Terman's gifted women. In J. C. Stanley, W. C. George, & C. H. Solano (Eds.), *The gifted and creative: A fifty-year perspective* (pp. 28–65). Baltimore: Johns Hopkins University Press.

Solano, C. H. (1979). The first D: Discovery of talent, or needles in a haystack: Identifying the mathematically gifted child. In N. R. Colangelo & R. T. Zaffrann (Eds.), *New voices in counseling the gifted* (pp. 89–106). Dubuque: Kendall/Hunt.

Stanley, J. C. (1954). Identification of superior learners in grades ten through fourteen. *Supplementary Educational Monographs, 81,* 31–34.

Stanley, J. C. (1976a). Concern for intellectually talented youths: How it originated and fluctuated. *Journal of Clinical Child Psychology, 5* (3), 38–42.

Stanley, J. C. (1976b). Test better finder of great math talent than teachers are. *American Psychologist, 31,* 313–314.

Stanley, J. C. (1977). The predictive value of the SAT for brilliant seventh and eighth graders. *The College Board Review, 106,* 2–7.

Stanley, J. C. (1980). Manipulate important educational variables. *Educational Psychologist, 15,* 164–171.

Stanley, J. C., George, W. C., & Solano, C. (Eds.) (1977). *The gifted and the creative: A fifty-year perspective.* Baltimore: Johns Hopkins University Press.

Stanley, J. C., George, W. C., & Solano, C. H. (Eds.) (1978). *Educational programs and intellectual prodigies.* Baltimore: The Study of Mathematically Precocious Youth, Johns Hopkins University.

Stanley, J. C., Keating, D. P., & Fox, L. H. (Eds.) (1974). *Mathematical talent: Discovery, description, and development.* Baltimore: Johns Hopkins University Press.

Sternberg, R. (1984). What should intelligence tests test? Implications of a triarchic theory of intelligence for intelligence testing. *Educational Researcher, 13,* 5–15.

Tannenbaum, A. J. (1983). *Gifted children: Psychological and educational perspectives.* New York: Macmillan.

Terman, L. M. (1916). *The measurement of intelligence.* Boston: Houghton Mifflin.

Terman, L. M. (1925). Mental and physical traits of a thousand gifted children. *Genetic Studies of Genius, Vol. 1.* Stanford: Stanford University Press.

Terman, L. M. (1954). The discovery and encouragement of exceptional talent. *American Psychologist, 9,* 221–230.

Terman, L. M., & Oden, M. H. (1947). The gifted child grows up. *Genetic studies of genius, Vol. 4.* Stanford: Stanford University Press.

Terman, L. M., & Oden, M. H. (1959). The gifted group at mid-life. *Genetic studies of genius, Vol. 5.* Stanford: Stanford University Press.

Whitmore, J. R. (1980). *Giftedness, conflict, and underachievement.* Boston: Allyn & Bacon.

Willings, D. (1983). The gifted at work. In B. M. Shore (Ed.), *Face to face with giftedness.* New York: Trillium Press.

Willings, D. (1985). The specific needs of adults who are gifted. *Roeper Review, 8* (1), 35–38.

Zettel, J. J. (1982). The education of gifted and talented children from a federal perspective. In J. Ballard, B. A. Ramirez, & F. J. Weintraub (Eds.), *Special education in America: Its legal and governmental foundations.* Reston, VA: Council for Exceptional Children.

Resources

Organizations

The Association for the Gifted
Council for Exceptional Children
1920 Association Drive
Reston, VA 22091

Professional organization which is primarily concerned with the education of gifted and talented students.

National Association for Gifted Children
5100 North Edgewood Drive
St. Paul, MN 55111

Disseminates information, lobbies for programs and services, and provides a network for those interested in all aspects of giftedness in children.

Mensa
5304 First Place North
Arlington, VA 22203

Organization for individuals with high IQs.

Journals

The Gifted Child Quarterly
Purdue University, SCC-G
West Lafayette, IN 47907

Publishes articles related to all aspects of giftedness in children and youth.

Journal for the Education of the Gifted
College of Education
Wayne State University
Detroit, MI 48202

Professional journal which focuses on issues related to educating gifted and talented students.

The Roeper Review
Roeper City and Country School
2190 N. Woodward
Bloomfield Hills, MI 48013

Publishes articles on a wide range of topics related to the gifted and talented.

Books

Maker, J. (1982). *Teaching models in the education of the gifted.* Rockville, MD: Aspen.

Tannenbaum, A. J. (1983). *Gifted children: Psychological and educational perspectives.* New York: Macmillan.

Part Three

ISSUES IN THE PROVISION
OF SERVICES

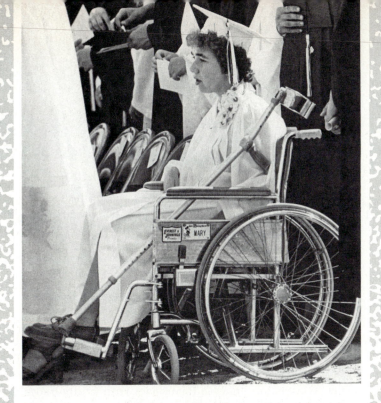

Many issues and influences affect the provision of services to exceptional people, and Part Three is devoted to exploring these factors.

Chapter 12, "The Impact of Handicapped Children on Families," considers the effect of exceptionality on the family constellation as well as the impact of the family on the types of services required and the ultimate success of these services.

In Chapter 13, "Multicultural Considerations," the issue is cultural diversity as it relates to exceptionality; past practices in the education of culturally diverse, handicapped individuals are described and recommendations are provided for improving the interventions that are available to this special group.

Chapter 14, "Preparation for Adulthood," focuses on a number of issues in career education and vocational preparation for adolescents and young adults who are handicapped as they prepare to leave school.

In the last chapter, "Adulthood and Maturity," the problems of middle and old age are considered in relationship to lifelong exceptionalities.

Chapter 12

THE IMPACT OF HANDICAPPED CHILDREN ON FAMILIES

Why should special educators concern themselves with family issues? What are the responsibilities of the school to the home? Teachers are, after all, concerned primarily with achieving certain instructional objectives with their students.

The fact is that schools in general, and special education programs in particular, have always had a very important relationship to families. In earlier years, however, that connection was often adversarial. Some of the earliest "special education" classes were established for non-English-speaking children of immigrants; the school was seen as a way to "Americanize" these children and wean them away from the culture of their parents (Sarason & Doris, 1979). The development of IQ measurement and the strong belief in hereditary influences in the first decades of this century added to the view that parents were the "cause" of the child's problems. In the 1940s, '50s, and '60s the emphasis shifted from heredity to environment—but once again, parents were essentially to "blame" for a failure to provide adequate emotional or intellectual stimulation (Paul & Porter, 1981).

Jean Ann Summers
University of Kansas

Mary Jane Brotherson
University of Minnesota–Duluth

Ann P. Turnbull
University of Kansas

Special education today is largely a product of parental influence. Parents began in the 1930s and 1940s by establishing private classes for children who had been excluded from school (President's Committee on Mental Retardation, 1977). Parents brought pressure to bear on schools to include their children in the 1950s and 1960s, and turned to the courts in the early 1970s to force inclusion of handicapped children (see for example, *Pennsylvania Association for Retarded Children vs. Pennsylvania*, 1972). All this influence culminated in the passage in 1975 of the Education for All Handicapped Children Act (PL 94–142), which has had a revolutionary impact on special education.

Not surprisingly, PL 94–142 includes parent participation as one of its major principles. Parental approval of individualized education programs (IEPs) is intended to be a primary format for allowing families to participate actively in their child's education. Due process procedures are part of the enforcement mechanisms built into the act, allowing parents in effect to assure their child's appropriate education in the schools (Turnbull & Turnbull, 1982).

In addition to involvement in educational decision making, special educators have gradually come to realize the importance of sharing information with families so they can best help their child to develop independence. Especially in early childhood programs, parents are often taught how to interact successfully with their child in teaching daily living skills. Some programs have even been designed for siblings to serve as teachers of their handicapped brothers and sisters (Cicirelli, 1976; Weinrott, 1974).

All in all, parent pressure on the one hand, and professional judgment on the other, have led to the realization that families are, and ought to be, intimately involved in the educational process. But nagging questions remain. Why do some parents participate fully and cooperate diligently with home programs, while others have to be prodded to attend an educational planning meeting once a year? Why do some families seem to be overprotective while others push their child to achieve—perhaps too much? Why are some families strengthened by the presence of a handicapped member and other families negatively influenced?

The answers lie in the nature of the family. A full understanding of a student's family will provide important clues to help teachers work more effectively with him or her. The goal of this chapter is to provide an understanding of the impact of handicap on families in order to place the family-school partnership on a solid foundation. The approach utilizes family systems theory to explore that impact.

Family systems theory has long been used in the fields of psychology and social work as a therapeutic technique. But family systems theory has uses beyond therapy; it provides an explanation of behavior that looks beyond the individual to the interactions of the individual with others in the environment. The basic rationale is that all parts of the family are interrelated; further, the family has properties of its own beyond the collective characteristics of its members. The family systems framework used in this chapter (Turnbull, Summers, & Brotherson, 1983) contains four major components, as shown in Figure 12.1.

1. *Family structure* describes the family. The number of people in the family, individual characteristics of its members, its cultural background, and its values and beliefs are all elements that shape the way the family interacts.

Figure 12.1

Family Systems Framework

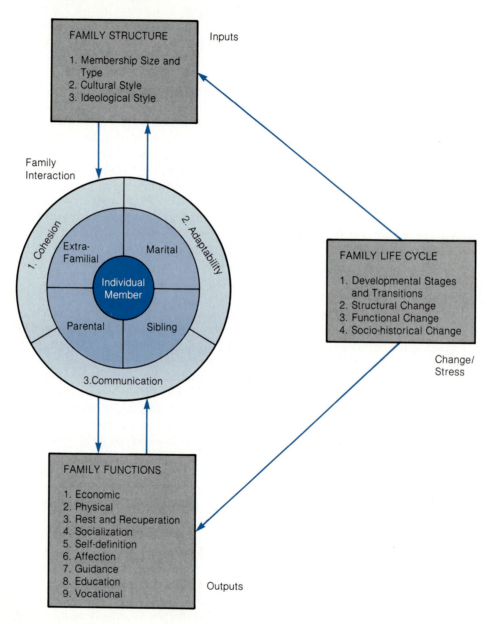

Figure by Ann Turnbull from *Education of Learners With Severe Handicaps* by Robert H. Horner, L. H. Meyer, and H. D. Fredericks. Copyright © 1986 by Paul H. Brookes Publishing Co., Inc. Reprinted by permission of Paul H. Brookes Publishing Co., Inc., and Ann Turnbull.

2. *Family interaction* is the day-to-day process of living together as a family. Family members interact with each other in different roles—e.g., as husband and wife, parent and child, brother and sister. These interactions are governed by rules that dictate family members' degree of closeness with or distance from each other, their flexibility, and their style of communication.
3. *Family functions* are the result of these interactions. Family members have a number of tangible and intangible needs, and it is the purpose, or function, of the family to fulfill those needs.
4. *Family life cycle* introduces the element of change into the family system. As the family members are born, grow older, and die, or as people's needs change for some other reason, the family must alter the way it interacts in order to continue functioning effectively.

All four of these major components have important implications for the way educators should interact with families, not only for the benefit of the child, but for all of the people who are affected by the exceptionality. The sections that follow describe the special impacts of handicap on each of the four components of the family system, and explain the implications of those impacts for educators working with families.

FAMILY INTERACTION

Because family interaction is the essential focus of the family system, it should be discussed first. Family interaction describes the way in which family members or subgroups within the family interact with each other on a day-to-day basis.

Two basic concepts are necessary for an understanding of family interaction. First, the family consists of definable subsystems, within each of which a given family member has a different role (Minuchin, 1974). Second, these subsystems interact according to rules governed by the family's level of cohesion, its adaptability, and its communication style. Each of these concepts require further discussion.

Family Subsystems

The four major subsystems within the family system are: (1) the marital (husband/wife interactions); (2) the parental (child/parent interactions); (3) the sibling (child/child interactions); and (4) the extrafamilial (whole family or individual member interactions with extended family, friends, neighbors, community, and professionals). Of course, depending on the makeup of the family, families may vary tremendously in the size or even the existence of these subsystems. In single-parent families, for example, there is no marital subsystem. Neither is there a sibling subsystem in a family with an only child.

Individual family members play different roles in each subsystem. For example, a man will behave differently when he is being a "husband" than he behaves when he is being a "father." Children behave differently toward each other than they behave toward their parents. And the whole family behaves differently toward one another than it behaves toward the grandparents, the neighbors, or a teacher. The unspoken rules which let people know how to behave within each subsystem define the subsystem boundaries. Clearly defined boundaries which still allow flexibility are a hallmark of well-functioning families.

The presence of a handicapped child has implications for all four subsystems. For example, if the family isolates itself as a reaction to stigma, the extrafamilial system is reduced. Siblings—especially older female daughters—may be pulled into the parental subsystem when they are asked to help care for a disabled brother or sister (Farber & Ryckman, 1965; Gath, 1974; Trevino, 1979). A mother may neglect her role as wife in order to cope with the demands of a handicapped child. Or, out of fear they might produce another handicapped child, the parents may decide not to have more children, thus curtailing or eliminating the sibling subsystem.

Even in families where the boundaries are rigidly drawn, anything that happens in one subsystem has effects in all the others. Hoffman (1980) uses the metaphor of a kaleidoscope to describe this phenomenon: " . . . when one small particle shifts, the whole pattern changes" (p. 56). This has important implications for intervention. All too often, interventions have been fashioned with only the handicapped child in mind, with no consideration of the effect of that intervention on the rest of the family.

Cohesion, Adaptability, and Communication

Cohesion (the degree of closeness or distance among family members), adaptability (the degree of family stability and its reaction to change), and communication (the degree of openness among family members) are the dynamic elements of family interaction. They are the rules by which individuals and subsystems within the family interact. There are two key concepts these dynamic elements share.

First, cohesion, adaptability, and communication are constantly changing in response to life cycle and other stressors impinging on the family. Returning to Hoffman's (1980) metaphor of the kaleidoscope, one can think of the outer "rim" of family interaction (see Figure 12.1) as constantly readjusting over time as the needs or structure of the family change. As they shift, they impact on the subsystems in the inner circle, causing changes in roles the family members play.

A second key concept is that well-functioning families are those who are able to maintain a balance in their levels of cohesion, adaptability, and communication (Olson, Russell, & Sprenkle, 1980). Families can be too cohesive or too distant; too rigid or too chaotic in the face of change; and too open or too closed in their communication. Each dimension, then, is like a continuum whose extremes on either end make it difficult for the family to function successfully. This does not mean, however, that successful families are always balanced; they may "flip" to extremes on one or another dimension as the situation demands (Beavers & Voeller, 1983). But they will not typically remain at those extremes for long

introducing

THE CORCORAN FAMILY

Jim and Pat Corcoran are a middle-class couple living in a quiet suburb of a midwestern city. They have two children: Connie, age 13, and Mark, age 8. Jim is an attorney in a small law firm, and Pat sells real estate on a part-time basis. Both are college educated. Connie is in the gifted program in her junior high school. Mark has severe autism.

The Corcorans have had a difficult time coping with Mark's condition. Jim suffers from bouts of depression—he had always dreamed of having a son with whom he could share his love of sports, but he realizes that Mark will never fill that need. He has turned more and more of his attention to Connie, taking her to ball games and centering his fatherly pride on Connie's academic achievements. He doesn't know any other fathers of handicapped children and feels there must be something wrong with him to harbor this secret resentment for Mark for his failure to live up to Jim's expectations.

Pat's stress arises from the day-to-day burden of caring for Mark. Mark has unpredictable episodes of violence or self-destruction. His need for order and structure in his environment is also a problem. Pat never did place a very high priority on a spic-and-span house, but now finds the best way to keep peace is to have everything in the home neatly picked up and put away. Also, she occasionally needs to show real estate to clients in the evenings or on weekends, which causes unpredictable changes in Mark's schedule that are difficult for him to tolerate. Pat turns to Connie for help with the care of Mark. She depends on Connie to pick up around the house and to be with Mark when she needs to leave. Otherwise, she has a very difficult time finding (and keeping) qualified sitters. Pat also worries about how to cope with Mark's violent episodes as he gets older and stronger.

Connie is a very mature young person. She is bright, energetic, and eager to please both her parents. She adores her father and often puts in late hours on homework or special projects to please him. Though she occasionally complains about her housekeeping duties, she has learned to be fairly efficient about her task. She has ambivalent feelings about her little brother. On the one hand, she loves him very much, and often can coax him to do things or settle him down when neither Pat nor Jim can make any headway. She defends him stoutly to her parents and thinks him capable of doing more than they do. On the other hand, however, she feels a little resentment that her responsibilities to Mark keep her out of some after-school activities, and also is embarrassed when her friends visit while Mark is having one of his "spells." She feels a lot of pressure from her parents: pushed by her father to achieve, pulled by her mother to help care for Mark.

periods of time. For example, when a handicapped child is born, the family members might pull very close together for awhile in order to comfort and nurture each other through the initial shock. But after a time, the family will return to its more usual pattern of interacting. The family's ability to cope with stress becomes an active process of achieving a balance in the family system. A closer examination of the three dynamic elements of family interaction (Table 12.1) provides a breakdown within each of the components of cohesion, adaptability, and communication.

Table 12.1

Family Interactional System

Subsystem	Cohesion	Adaptability	Communication
Marital subsystem	Closeness	Power structure	Closed
Parental subsystem	Support	Role relationships	Open
Sibling subsystem	Decision making	Relationship rules	Random
Extrafamilial subsystem	Commonality		

Cohesion

low ← → high

disengaged   separated   connected   enmeshed

Adaptability

low ← → high

rigid   structured   flexible   chaotic

Communication

closed ← open → random

Cohesion. Family cohesion is defined as the emotional bonding members have toward one another, balanced against the individual autonomy or independence a person has within the family system (Olson, Sprenkle, & Russell, 1979). It can be thought of as the family's ability to maintain unity and at the same time allow for individuation (Whittaker, 1977). On the cohesion continuum, families with little or no individual autonomy are considered enmeshed, while families with little or no unity are termed disengaged.

Only in very severely dysfunctional families is the entire family enmeshed or disengaged. More often, these situations occur within or across subsystems. For example, a mother may be completely absorbed in the care of her handicapped son or daughter, so that her life revolves around that child. Her social and recreational needs (e.g., participation in a mother's support group), and her self-identity ("I am a good mother") are centered on her child. Meanwhile, her husband may be disengaged—unable (or unwilling) to enter the tightly knit circle. He may look for fulfillment of his needs outside the family—on the job, with his male friends. As he becomes increasingly distanced from his wife, she becomes even more closely tied to her child. From the perspective of some special educators who focus only on the child's needs, this family may appear to be "successful"; the mother is actively involved in the program, participating in mothers' groups, diligently following through with suggestions for home interventions. But once again, anything that happens to one person in the family has an impact on everyone. It is important to consider the impact of such involvement on the family as a whole. Is the mother overidentifying with her child? What about her husband and the nonhandicapped children? Are their needs being met? What are the long-term consequences of this enmeshment for the independence of the handicapped child? It makes little sense to encourage maximum development for the child if, in the process, his or her family falls apart.

The four major elements of cohesion shown in Table 12.1 are indicators of the level of cohesion in a given family (Carnes, 1981). Closeness is the feeling of warmth and care among family members; in other words, where family members give their emotional energy—internally or externally. In contrast, support asks where families receive their emotional support—from inside or outside the family? Decision making is an indicator of whether decisions are made collectively or individually. Are decisions always made on the basis of whole-family concerns, or are family members always out for themselves? Finally, commonality is the time, space, interests, activities, and friends family members share. Do family members have no lives of their own, always working and playing together? Or, conversely, do they seem to lead parallel lives with nothing in common except the home where they live? All these elements, taken together, define the family's level of cohesion. Again, a balance between the two extremes on all four measures is best for healthy functioning.

Adaptability. Family adaptability is the ability of the family to change in response to stress (Olson, Sprenkle, & Russell, 1979). Adaptability in successful families is a balance between stability and change. Without stability, the family would have no identity as a definable unit; but, without flexibility, it cannot withstand change. On one end of the adaptability continuum, rigid families are unable to change when they should. At the other end, chaotic families are continually unstable; relationship rules are in flux, and nobody seems to be in charge.

For example, in families with a handicapped child, a rigid family might not be able to recognize that the child is now an adult and perhaps should move to a residential setting outside the home. On the other hand, the story of a chaotic family was told by the sister of a severely handicapped woman (Ackerman, 1985). The mother had previously made all the decisions and provided all the emotional support for her daughter. When the mother died unexpectedly, the family was thrown into chaos. No one had authority to make decisions about the disabled member's care; responsibility fell randomly on various brothers, sisters, and stepmother—none of whom felt any authority for decision making.

We responded to calls from the school in haphazard fashion. Family visits were sporadic. Six months would pass without anyone arranging to see Beckie, and then suddenly, everyone would show up at the school's Christmas play. Or one of us would mention to a staff member that we thought Beckie should come home for Christmas, and then never follow up on the suggestion, leaving the staff to wonder at our commitment. (p. 153)

As shown in Table 12.1, the family's adaptability is shaped by three indicators. Power structure is the relative authority assigned to members. Does one person in the family make all the decisions, or is decision making shared? Do the children feel free to negotiate? Role relationships define how family members participate in carrying out family functions. Are tasks assigned according to traditional sex-role stereotypes, or do people share such functions as expressing affection, doing household chores, and so forth? Finally, relationship rules are the explicit and/or implicit rules that guide the family's power structure and role relationships. In a rigid family there will be many rules and they will be strictly enforced; in a chaotic family, rules are seldom enforced or always changing, so that no one knows what is expected.

It is important for special educators to have a general idea of these elements. For example, the family member who is the decision maker is the obvious person to approach for educational decisions. Families with a traditional sex-role orientation may feel more stress when the handicapped child is a boy, because the son may not be able to participate in "men's roles," such as playing team sports (Farber, 1959). Helping a traditional family develop realistic expectations for a handicapped child may involve helping them see alternative roles outside the traditional sex stereotype that the child can fulfill. Finally, a family with rigid relationship rules might find it especially difficult to encourage their handicapped adolescent toward greater independence; such families might require smaller, more incremental steps toward any educational objectives designed to increase independent functioning.

Communication.   Communication is the process by which information is exchanged and transmitted in families. Some theorists consider communication to be the most important element in the family dynamic (Kantor & Lehr, 1975). It is the vehicle through which the family members transmit rules, establish roles, and express closeness. Open and honest communication promotes the resolution of conflict and problems, and has been characterized as the single most important factor affecting a person's health and his or her relationship to others.

Some families or individuals adopt predominantly "rational" or "emotional" modes of communication. Rational communicators tend to intellectualize most issues and to communicate them as ideas. Emotional communicators, on the other hand, see issues as primarily emotional and tend to communicate in terms of feelings. Again, a balance between the two is optimal (Kantor & Lehr, 1975).

Some families with handicapped children seem to avoid immediate stress by avoiding communication. While it is impossible to say whether these families might have been characterized as closed with or without a disabled member, it is possible to say that closing off communication is one way to cope with stress. For example, one mother, who was asked how she felt about strangers staring at her child in public, said, "Well, I don't like it, but it's not something we talk about in this family" (Turnbull, Brotherson, & Summers, 1982). It is important, therefore, for special educators to realize that an unwillingness to discuss problems may be due to several reasons. Is it a coping strategy to avoid stress? Or is it the family's style of communication? Or both?

Family interaction is a complex interplay of individuals and subsystems within the family, and understanding family's responses and reactions requires attention to this interplay.

FAMILY STRUCTURE

One of the dominant impressions to arise from the previous discussion of family interaction is that the system is so complex and filled with so many variables that families can interact in a seemingly endless variety of ways. Indeed, the ways in which families arrange themselves into subsystems, their variable levels of cohesion and adaptability, and the wide range of communication styles renders every family unique. But the question is, why? How does a given family acquire its particular interactional "fingerprint"? The answer is that the elements that go into the system—the family structure—shape the pattern. Each member of the family brings his or her own individual characteristics, cultural background, and beliefs to the family. It may be helpful to view structural characteristics (input) as the ingredients, or possible variations, and family interaction as the process by which those ingredients are melded—sometimes harmoniously, sometimes decidedly not—into a recognizable unit.

Family structure is composed of three major categories of variations: membership characteristics, cultural style, and ideological style. These are interrelated and influence each other to a certain extent. But taken together, they describe the family and identify its place in the infinite range of family structures. Table 12.2 lists the components of these structural elements.

Membership Characteristics

Membership characteristics have a bearing on how the family defines itself. Some families include a wide variety of people in their boundaries, for example, a neighbor, a live-in boyfriend, a babysitter, a deceased family member whose views still influence family thinking. In the end, the best way to define a family is simply to ask them: "Who is in your family?" As shown in Table 12.2, the answer to this question involves three elements: individual characteristics, size of the family, and the nature of the extrafamilial system.

Individual Characteristics. Every member brings a set of personal idiosyncrasies, characteristics, and problems to the family. Some of these might be related to interactional preferences, e.g., the need for more privacy. Others are related to special problems an individual might have, including alcoholism, mental illness, and disability.

It goes without saying that a handicapped child has an enormous impact on his or her family. But not all handicaps are the same, and the impact on the

Table 12.2		
Family Structure		
Membership Characteristics	*Cultural Style*	*Ideological Style*
Individual characteristics	Ethnicity	Beliefs and values
Family size	Religion	Coping styles
Nature of extrafamilial system	Socioeconomic status	
	Geographic location	

Table by Ann Turnbull from *Families of Handicapped Persons,* edited by James Gallagher and Peter Vietze. Copyright © 1986 by Paul H. Brookes Publishing Co., Inc. Reprinted by permission of Paul H. Brookes Publishing Co., Inc., and Ann Turnbull.

family varies with the nature of the condition. For example, the more visible the handicap, the more stress the family is likely to feel as a result of stares, rude comments, and general rejection from both strangers and (perhaps) from extended family and friends. On the other hand, when the child's handicap is highly visible, his or her siblings are less likely to overidentify with him or her (Grossman, 1972). With invisible disabilities, such as learning disabilities, non-handicapped brothers and sisters worry that maybe something is wrong with them, too, and parents may have trouble establishing realistic expectations about their handicapped child's performance (Willner & Crane, 1979).

Mild handicaps do not necessarily mean less stress for families. Indeed, one study found a more positive attitude toward their child's handicap among parents of trainably mentally retarded children than among parents of educably mentally retarded children (Nihira, Meyers, & Mink, 1980). Families may have difficulty accepting their mildly handicapped child (Wadsworth & Wadsworth, 1971). Very severe handicaps are often apparent at birth; with mild disabilities, the parents may have established bonds with an image of a "normal" child. The stress of having their dreams dashed is worsened by the fact that mild handicaps are often difficult for professionals to pinpoint—and the delayed or ambiguous diagnoses may provoke the parents to anger and mistrust of professionals in general (Willner & Crane, 1979). Finally, people with mild handicaps may go through periods of gain, only to slip back. The family thus rides an emotional roller coaster of expectations, with hopes alternately raised and dashed.

Undoubtedly, some specific handicapping conditions place greater stress on families than others. For example, Holroyd and McArthur (1976) found that families with autistic children experienced much more stress than families with Down Syndrome children. One mother of an autistic child, when told that parents with mentally retarded children often commented they were living life only one day at a time, angrily responded: "That would be great for me. I have to take it an hour at a time" (Turnbull et al., 1982). Aside from the fact that autism is a more ambiguous problem, the bizarre and unpredictable behaviors of autistic children put a heavy strain on families. Indeed, in almost every handicap complicated by a behavior problem—hyperactivity, self-injury, aggression—the family experiences difficulty in coping with the day-to-day demands for care, and further, finds less support from others who might otherwise be willing to provide respite care.

Family Size.   Family size has important implications for family interaction simply because the sheer number of possible interactions increases geometrically with size. Interactions can occur between any two people in the family, between one person and any subsystem, between subsystems, and so on, ad infinitum. Nuclear families vary not only in the number of children, but also in the number of parents.

Concerning the number of parents, there are a wide range of possibilities beyond the traditional nuclear family mother-father pair. The growing number of single parent families has been a topic of increasing research. Families with more than two parent figures are also common as, for example, in families where extended family members either live in the household or are heavily involved in the family system. This arrangement is especially common in black families (Williams & Stockton, 1973). Finally, the number of parents can increase with each divorce and remarriage of an original couple. Here a bewildering array of subsystem configurations is possible, with children "belonging" to two or more families, interacting with biological parents and stepparents, biological siblings and stepsiblings, and so on (Sager, Brown, Crohn, Engel, Rodstein, & Walker, 1983). Special educators may find themselves faced with delicate problems in working with a reconstituted family. Should both divorced parents be included in conferences? Should the stepparents? These questions must be answered on an individual family basis.

The number of children also has implications for family interaction. In larger families, one or more of the older children—especially daughters—may be pulled into the parental subsystem and expected to help raise the younger children (Bossard & Boll, 1956). Because there is a similar tendency in families with handicapped children for older sisters to take on a parental role (Cleveland & Miller, 1977; Grossman, 1972), the likelihood of this phenomenon is even greater in large families with a handicapped child. Gath (1974) found that older daughters in large families with Down Syndrome children were at greater risk for emotional disturbance; Gath speculates that a contributing factor may be that they bear "more than their fair share of community care" (p. 197).

On the other hand, a large family with a handicapped member may have an advantage due to a greater atmosphere of normalcy (Trevino, 1979). In two-child families where one is handicapped, parents place greater expectations on the nonhandicapped sibling to live out their dreams of achievement through their children (Farber & Jenne, 1963). When the only nonhandicapped child is a daughter, she may be caught in a double-bind: expected to help care for the handicapped sibling and also expected to fulfill expectations for achievement (Cleveland & Miller, 1977).

Support to the family of a handicapped infant is offered by an early interventionist who pays periodic visits to their home.

Nature of the Extrafamilial System. Both the size of the extrafamilial system and its availability as a resource for the family are crucial indicators of a family's ability to cope with a handicapped child. In regard to size, it seems likely that, in the case of an extrafamilial system, more is better. Isolated families are at risk for almost any kind of problem, including divorce, alcoholism, child or spouse abuse, and mental illness. This is especially true in the case of single parent families. Wahler (1980) found that isolated mothers were less able to maintain gains made in a parent training program, but they were more often able to use their training in the presence of a supportive friend. Educators need to be aware of families that seem more isolated, and to refer them to groups or programs that can lend support.

The second factor, availability, dictates the extent to which a family with a handicapped child is at risk of becoming isolated. Acceptance by the extrafamilial system is crucial to most families. Compare the experiences of two families with handicapped children (Turnbull et al., 1982): First, a mother of a 45-year-old woman with a mental handicap:

There was only one other family that I could talk to. One of my friends was put off by our taking Carol everywhere because she thought such things should be hidden. . . . *One of the teachers at Carol's school—not her own teacher, just a busybody—told me we should put her in an institution because it wasn't fair to Patsy. That was when we took her out of school.*

Second, a sister of a 30-year-old man with cerebral palsy:

My parents were well-known in (our home town) and I remember a tremendous amount of support from neighbors close by. I don't recall any rejection by anyone. I do remember suggestions, constructive ideas about "Why don't you try this or that," but nobody said, "Don't tell anybody we are related," nobody ever suggested putting Jeremy in an institution.

Cultural Style

In addition to the influences of membership characteristics, a family is also influenced by its membership in larger social groups. Cultural style refers to the background or heritage that gives the family a sense of belonging or identity. There are four major components of cultural style: ethnicity, religion, socioeconomic status, and geographic location. Compared to other elements of family structure, cultural style is relatively static; it is the background or foundation that shapes the way the family absorbs everything that happens to it. But even cultural style is subject to change. For example, one family member might marry someone from another ethnic group. A wife might go to work and suddenly change the family's socioeconomic standing. Thus, while cultural style is certainly the background against which the family plays out its interactions, it is more like the background of a movie than the background of a stage play—it too is in motion.

Ethnicity.
Ethnicity involves more than one's race, religion, and country of national origin. It is a sense of "we-ness" handed down across generations. As McGoldrick (1982a) noted:

Ethnicity patterns our thinking, feeling, and behavior in both obvious and subtle ways. It plays a major role in determining what we eat, how we work, how we relax, how we celebrate holidays and rituals, and how we feel about life, death, and illness. (p. 4)

In the United States, with its myth of the "melting pot," ethnic influences are often overlooked. Yet research has shown that traditional values and attitudes are still influencing families who are in their third generation of living in a "modern" culture (McGoldrick, 1982a). Ethnicity shapes every aspect of a family's interaction: the importance it places on closeness or cohesion, its power structure or adaptability, and its predisposition toward open or closed communication.

Unfortunately, very little research has been conducted on reactions of different ethnic groups to the presence of a handicapped child. It is only possible at this point to understand characteristics of ethnic groups and draw inferences as to the possible strengths and weaknesses different groups may have as they cope with handicap.

For example, Jewish families tend to value intellectual ability and scholastic achievement highly (Herz & Rosen, 1982); this may mean that the birth of a retarded child may be particularly tragic for them. Irish families tend to internalize suffering and consider tragedy to be no more than they deserve (McGoldrick, 1982b); they may be especially susceptible to feelings of guilt at the birth of a handicapped child. On the other hand, Italian families value family solidarity above individual achievement, and marshall their resources to care for disabled or elderly members within the family circle; yet their suspicion of outsiders (Rotunno & McGoldrick, 1982) might make it difficult for Italians to accept help from professionals—especially those who want to come into the home. Mexican-American families tend to be relaxed about developmental milestones and to encourage dependence longer (Falicov, 1982); they may not see a value in working with their handicapped child on goals designed to improve the child's level of independent functioning.

Some ethnic groups may have access to important resources to help them cope with a handicapped child. Black families, for example, often have extensive extended family networks, with children living for varying periods of time with friends or relatives other than their parents (Stack, 1975). Educators should take a flexible view in such families as to exactly who should take an active part in the educational process—perhaps the real "parent" is an aunt or grandmother. Also, the black extended family network involves an elaborate system of sharing or exchanging resources, in which people may participate only so long as they both give and receive. Social workers and teachers from the school may be regarded with suspicion if they do not make an effort to become a part of this reciprocal system (Pinderhughes, 1982).

In the midst of discussing some of these characteristics, however, it is important to avoid stereotyping. There is no such thing as the "typical" German or Italian or black family. Nevertheless, special educators should make an effort to understand the values and family structures of the ethnic groups they serve. It provides not only an insight on the particular interpretation the family makes of the handicap, but it also provides clues as to resources which might be marshalled to help the family.

Religion. A family's religious affiliation also shapes its values and its perspective of the world. In addition to the specific religious affiliation, another factor to consider is the family's degree of emphasis on religion, or the degree to which it relies on religious interpretation and spiritual support. But even in families with very little emphasis on religion, basic perspectives of the world may remain—for example, whether human beings are seen as basically good or evil.

Some early research was conducted in the late 1950s and early 1960s on the reactions of families of different religious denominations to handicaps. These studies focused on the effect of religion on acceptance or attitudes toward the handicapped child, and often showed conflicting results (Farber, 1959; Stubblefield, 1965; Zuk, Miller, Bartram, & Kling, 1961). More recent studies have found that the particular denomination was less important than the family's personal religious interpretations of the handicap. Bristol and Schopler (1983) found that churches were consistently ranked low by parents of autistic children as a source of support, even though they often noted their personal religious beliefs as an important factor in coping. Because private beliefs fall into the realm of ideological style in the framework discussed here, they will be explored further in a later section.

Socioeconomic Status.

The amount of money people make, their level of education, and the kinds of jobs they hold have an enormous impact on their perception of the world. Of the many differences among families of higher and lower socioeconomic status (SES), two differences that have particular relevance for families with handicapped children are the degree of feeling "in control" of the environment and the degree of future orientation. Rubin (1976) points out that working class families often perceive—quite realistically—that they have very little control over what happens to them. Keeping one's job in a factory assembly line, for example, depends much less on skill and competence than it does on the vagaries of the economy; in a recession there will be layoffs. Such families may be more passive about participation in educational decision making. In contrast, middle and upper-middle class white Americans place a strong emphasis on self-determination: nature is to be tamed and dominated; problems are to be "faced" with "responsibility"; science and rationality are the keys (McGill & Pearce, 1982). Thus, these families might be much more active participants in educational planning. On the other hand, upper-middle-class families may not know how to accept (implying submission to) such an uncontrollable phenomenon as handicap. They may respond with denial, scapegoating, or disengagement (McGill & Pearce, 1982).

Related to these observations is the research of Bernard Farber and his colleagues on families with handicapped children in the early 1960s. These studies found that families tend to experience one or the other of two types of stress associated with a handicapped child: the "tragic crisis" and the "role organization crisis" (Farber & Ryckman, 1965). In the tragic crisis, the family views the handicap as a frustration of future aspirations for achievement and a happy life; this crisis is more often experienced by higher SES families. Lower SES families, on the other hand, are more likely to experience a role organization crisis—stress centering around the problem of marshalling the family's resources to cope with a lifelong burden of care (Farber, 1960).

Geographic Location.

Of all the elements of cultural style, geographic location may be one of declining importance. Even 20 years ago, there were important regional differences in attitudes and values among Southern, Northern, and Western families. But increased mobility and electronic media have chipped away at those differences in recent years. Some vestiges remain, however. For example, the pace or rhythm of daily life might be slower for Southerners than for Northeasterners (McGill & Pearce, 1982).

Rural-urban differences are other elements of geographic location that have received attention. Most of the literature makes the assumption that the lack of availability of services and transportation problems hamper rural families with handicapped children. In addition, the assumption is made that family values in rural areas are more traditional in such areas as sex roles and beliefs in family independence (e.g., "we take care of our own"). A recent study of rural, urban, and suburban special education programs, however, raises questions about these assumptions as well. Very little difference was found between rural and inner-city programs in terms of availability of services, but these both differed from suburban schools. The differences may more likely be due to other cultural variables such as social class and ethnicity. These variables are so intricately bound up in geographic location—middle class families tend to live in suburban areas—that they give an appearance of the importance of geographic location which may actually be an artifact of socioeconomic status.

Ideological Style

Whereas cultural style is the result of a family's identification with a group larger than itself, ideological style is unique to the individual family. Falicov (1982) helps to make the distinction clear:

> [B]road cultural generalizations do not do justice to regional, generational, socioeconomic, and idiosyncratic variations in lifestyle . . . descriptions and analyses of values and norms that may be valid at the macrosocial level need refinement and qualification at the microsocial level. . . . Cultural norms tend to refer to the public reality of how relationships or behaviors "ought" to be. These internalized behavioral prescriptions sometimes do not coincide with private realities . . . Both public (cultural) and private (idiosyncratic) norms govern family relationships and combine to make every family unique. (p. 137)

In short, the family combines the elements of its membership characteristics and cultural style to produce its own unique ideological style. The two major components of ideological style are (1) beliefs and values, and (2) coping styles. Both of these elements are extremely important in determining family interaction processes in general, and a family's reaction to a disabled member in particular.

Beliefs and Values.   Beliefs are convictions about the truth of some matter or perceptions of a state of reality. Values are perceptions of the importance of those beliefs (Kahn, 1969). Finally, those beliefs and values are played out in action. Beliefs may be highly subjective, and as a result the whole chain of belief-value-action may vary widely from family to family. For example, one person's "clean" room may look "dirty" to someone else, and if "cleanliness" is valued, the perception may lead to different actions. Or, two people may value religion highly, but one may express this value by going to church while the other seeks solitude for meditation and prayer. The chain of belief-value-action permeates family life.

Beliefs abound concerning "proper" roles for men and women, the degree to which families should do things together, the kinds of things one should or shouldn't talk about.

The impact of a handicapped child on the family may also vary with the family's belief-value-action structure. This is another area where very little research has been done. Most relevant are anthropological studies of cultural beliefs about childrearing practices. The degree to which autonomy and self-reliance are valued over conformity and obedience to authority depends on the family's perceptions and experiences. For example, in the experience of working class families, a successful adult is one who is a steady worker and who does what he is told on the job—which leads to a high value on conformity and obedience. In contrast, middle and upper-middle class white collar workers are expected to take initiative, to be competitive, and to be self-starters (Lee, 1982). These values result in different childrearing practices. Working class families tend to be more concerned with teaching children to do as they are told, while middle-class families may tolerate children questioning their authority to a point that might be considered "talking back" in working-class families. Further, middle-class families may control their children more indirectly (for example, avoiding physical punishment) as they teach them internalized self-control.

For families with handicapped children, these value differences may affect their reaction to the child. A family placing a high value on conformity and obedience may find it particularly trying to cope with a child with a behavior disorder such as hyperactivity or autism. It might be wise in such cases to give a higher priority to instructional objectives designed to improve the child's behavior.

A more general issue is the extent to which the family's values conflict with those of educators and other helping professionals. Do educators have the right to impose their own values on the family as they select educational objectives or instructional methods? Do they have the child's "best interests" any more at heart than the child's parents? Exactly what is "best" is a subjective perception. Educators must respect the family's belief-value-action system as equally valid as their own, and forge educational decisions that truly reflect the family's perception of needs.

Coping Patterns.   The second major element of a family's ideological style is its coping pattern. Coping patterns or strategies are defined as anything the family does to reduce stress (McCubbin, Joy, Cauble, Comeau, Patterson, & Needle, 1980; Pearlin & Schooler, 1978). Stress may result from a number of sources. The family may not only respond to these stresses with a variety of coping strategies, but also may feel more stressed (and therefore respond more quickly) to some stressors than to others. Another important concept is the fact that coping strategies may, while reducing stress in some areas, actually produce stress in some other area (McCubbin et al., 1980). For example, feeling guilty about a child's handicap may serve as a coping strategy for some parents because their guilt "explains" the disability and makes the world seem more controllable (Gardner, 1971). Yet guilt feelings are themselves stressors. It is important for educators to realize that

introducing

THE RILEY FAMILY

Clarise Riley is a black, single woman living with her parents in one of the poorer areas of a large city in the Southeast. She gave birth to Angelica, a child with Down Syndrome, when she was only 15. Her mother, Jessica, has had most of the responsibility for raising Angelica and Clarise's four other children from a marriage that ended in divorce. Angelica is now 19 and attends a special class for trainable mentally handicapped students. Clarise's father, Joel, is a city sanitation worker, and Jessica takes in laundry. Clarise works as a waitress in the evenings.

The Riley home is a large, ramshackle old house with big trees festooned with tire swings and numerous homemade toys (built by Joel) in the yard. The home is always full of people, with neighborhood children in the yard and adults dropping by to sit on the porch. Jessica shares her good nature and motherly advice with anyone who needs it. She has a special place in her heart for Angelica, and often has her by her side on the porch swing, snapping beans or sharing some other little task. Angelica, on

her part, will do anything for Grandma. Joel and Jessica accept and love Angelica the same as they do all their other children and grandchildren. In fact, they find her to be less of a trial than one or two of their children who have had brushes with the law or trouble with alcohol. As far as they are concerned, Angelica has a home with them for as long as they live. She is, according to Jessica, "a blessing from the Lord and a balm for my soul."

Joel is an elder in the local church and both he and his wife are deeply religious. They have worked hard all their lives to provide for their family, and are proud that they have never been on welfare. Lately, however, Joel's arthritis has been acting up, and Jessica learned last winter that she has diabetes. Clarise worries about what to do when her parents die—she has neither the resources nor the patience of her mother. She has no idea where to turn for advice. Jessica knows her daughter worries, but she pats her hand and tells her the Lord will provide when the time comes.

seemingly counterproductive actions may well be serving a real purpose in reducing a family's stress in some area, and that the stresses addressed by that action must be the ones that are (currently) most important to the family. It follows that the family must be helped to find a new coping strategy that addresses those stresses without the counterproductive effects.

McCubbin and Patterson (1981) consider coping strategies to be either internal—using resources within the family; or external—using resources outside the family. They developed five major classifications of strategies within these two broad categories. Internal strategies include passive appraisal (avoiding or denying a problem in the hope it will "go away") and reframing (analyzing or redefining a problem so that it may be solved or at least viewed in a less stressful way). External strategies include the use of social, spiritual, or formal (professional) support.

Passive appraisal in families with handicapped children may take the form of denial, anger, and withdrawal. These are the strategies often employed in the period immediately following the diagnosis or identification of the disability and are considered a normal response to tragedy (Vernon, 1979). Another passive appraisal strategy is a refusal to think about the future. Problems in the future (e.g., Where will the handicapped child live? What happens when the parents die?) seem much more overwhelming than day-to-day worries such as scheduling and physical care. A family's refusal to plan for the future may be a barrier to teaching the handicapped child more independent living skills. For example, it is easier in the short-run to continue to dress a handicapped child than to teach him or her to dress alone. The long-term benefits of greater independence and elimination of a time-consuming chore for other family members is ignored if the family cannot think about the future.

In contrast to passive appraisal, reframing is an active approach. An important reframing strategy is rational problem solving. For example, one disabled adult described his family's approach to problems this way:

> We never looked at a situation as something we couldn't handle. Whenever somebody had a problem, we always talked it out, considered the pros and cons of all the alternatives. We always knew we could count on each other for help. (Turnbull et al., 1982)

Another reframing technique involves making attitude adjustments, which may take the form of positive comparisons of the child with other handicapped children. For example, one mother of a moderately retarded adult commented:

> We're lucky because Carol isn't aware she's different. I know lots of others who are very hurt because they know they're retarded. But Carol is too handicapped to be hurt by her limitations. (Turnbull et al., 1982)

Other families may use selective attention, that is, they may focus on positive attributes in stressful situations or on strengths of the handicapped child. A father of a young woman with mild cerebral palsy said:

> We're lucky Denise has been healthy—she's never been sickly. The only real expense has been the electric wheelchair—otherwise she's been no more expensive than any other child. (Turnbull et al., 1982)

Finally, some families learn to recognize their successes and use them to build confidence and self-esteem. This strategy seems particularly important in view of research findings that self-esteem is perhaps the key resource that families can bring to bear on a stressful situation (Pearlin & Schooler, 1978). It is important to help families recognize their successes in order to give them the strength to tackle new problems.

Social support as a coping strategy involves reliance on friends and extended family for emotional and practical help in stressful situations. As noted in the discussion of the extrafamilial system, such support is crucial. Although the availability of a social support network varies, families also vary in their ability to use support effectively. Not everyone knows how to accept help from their friends. Also, as exemplified by black families, one of the most important characteristics of their elaborate support network is reciprocity—social support extinguishes for people who are only "takers."

The use of spiritual support is an often-used coping strategy (Olson, McCubbin, Barnes, Larsen, Muxen, & Wilson, 1983). Personal interpretations of religious teaching seem to be more helpful to families with handicapped members than formal church participation (Bristol & Schopler, 1983; Turnbull, Brotherson, & Summers, 1985). These personal interpretations can take a wide variety of forms. Here are some of the interpretations families used (Turnbull et al., 1983):

> God must think I'm a pretty strong person to trust me with all these problems.

> We just tried to do our best and trusted in the Good Lord to look after us.

> I think God has a plan for that boy.

> I thought I would be helped (by God) if I helped others.

> The most important support for me was a book by Alan Watts on Zen. It taught me to accept what I can't change with serenity.

Educators should recognize and encourage the use of spiritual support as a coping strategy with families who are so inclined. This may involve enlisting the aid of local clergy and providing them with more information about handicapping conditions, so they can be an effective resource.

Effective use of formal support—i.e., professionals and public services—involves both the ability and the willingness to seek out and use them. Families with a strong distrust of outsiders or a strong belief in "making it on our own" may find this difficult to do. Also negative experiences with professionals who are insensitive or incompetent may curtail the family's willingness to seek out other help. Finally, effective use of formal support requires skill in advocating for one's needs. Families need to learn assertiveness as well as more information about the services available in their locality.

There are many more specific coping strategies than the ones highlighted here. Every family utilizes its membership characteristics and its cultural style to develop its own unique patterns of coping.

FAMILY FUNCTIONS

The enormous complexity of the family unit, the structural inputs and its interactional processes, leads to the question: What is the purpose of all this activity? The answer is that the family's purpose is the same as that of any social organization—to serve the needs of its individual members. Serving the individual and collective needs of the family is the function of the family system. Functions are the product, or output of family interactions. The family exists in the first place

Table 12.3

Family Functions

Economic	Physical	Rest and Recuperation
Generating income Paying bills and banking Handling investments Overseeing insurance and benefit programs Earning allowance Dispensing allowance	Food purchasing and food preparation Clothes purchasing and preparation Health care and maintenance Safety and protection Transportation Home maintenance	Individual and family-oriented recreation Setting aside demands Developing and enjoying hobbies
Socialization	**Self-Definition**	**Affection**
Interpersonal relationships Developing social skills	Establishing self-identity and self-image Recognizing strengths and weaknesses Sense of belonging	Nurturing and love Companionship Intimacy Expressing emotions
Guidance	**Education**	**Vocational**
Problem solving Advice and feedback Shaping basic beliefs and values Transmitting religious beliefs	Continuing education for parents Schoolwork Homework Cultural appreciation	Career choice Development of work ethic Support of career interests and problems

Table by Ann Turnbull from *Families of Handicapped Persons*, edited by James Gallagher and Peter Vietze. Copyright © 1986 by Paul H. Brookes Publishing Co., Inc. Reprinted by permission of Paul H. Brookes Publishing Co., Inc., and Ann Turnbull.

to serve the economic, physical, and emotional needs of its members. And it is toward this goal that the system is ultimately bent.

Family functions may be classified in nine basic areas (Turnbull, Summers, & Brotherson, 1983): economic, physical, rest and recuperation, socialization, self-definition, affection, guidance, education, and vocational. Table 12.3 provides examples of functions or activities under each of these broad areas.

A review of the table gives some idea of the wide variety of tasks a family must somehow accomplish. These tasks range from such everyday and tangible chores as carrying out the trash, to intangible functions like establishing a sense of self-identity. Family members may or may not do all of these tasks themselves. For example, parents may send their disabled child to summer camp where camp counselors help the child fill many needs: physical (exercise), socialization (meeting friends), recreation (learning new art and crafts), and self-definitional

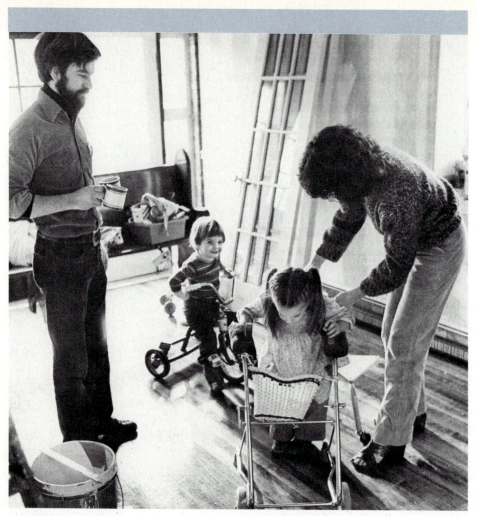

In addition to the parents of handicapped children, the siblings are instrumental in providing support in the sharing of family activities and the meeting of family goals.

("I *can* be away from home," "I *can* accomplish things on my own"). But the family still is the orchestrator of these functions, even when they are done by someone else. The family is the center for arranging, prioritizing, encouraging, or doing all the tasks that are required to meet individual members' needs.

The presence of a handicapped child increases the number of needs a family must meet; at the same time, it decreases the family's capacity to meet those needs. In the economic area, for example, a disabled child with medical needs can place a heavy financial strain on a family. At the same time, the family's earning power may be reduced because one parent must stay home to care for the child or because a parent must turn down a job opportunity that requires moving the family to a place where services are unavailable (McAndrew, 1976). Similarly, parents' needs for rest and recuperation may be increased by the exhausting demands of an autistic child, but their opportunity to get away for an evening may be limited because they can find no one who is qualified—or willing—to care for the child.

The effect of increased demand coupled with reduced resources has two implications for educators. First, educators must be careful not to add unnecessarily to the family's list of things to do. All families are busy, but families with a handicapped child are more so. Nobody is sitting idly at home waiting for helpful suggestions about activities they might do at home. Participating in education, at home or at school, requires time, energy, and emotional investment. Educators need to be absolutely certain that the family's participation is worth the effort.

Second, educators should help families develop strategies to meet their needs. One useful strategy might be time management training, which involves setting priorities and eliminating less important tasks. It may also involve taking inventory of who accomplishes what tasks, and perhaps renegotiating some of the assignments. Another strategy is to help the family determine what tasks might be accomplished outside the family. What resources are available, both formal and informal, and how might these resources be mobilized to serve their needs? The scope of this intervention with families might range from helping them more often enlist friends and relatives, to more extensive training to prepare families to serve as case managers and advocates as they locate and access services in the community. But at any level, using outside resources requires that families realize they are not expected to do everything on their own, and that organizing services and/or helping the handicapped child to be more independent is just as fulfilling—perhaps more—than carrying the load alone.

Because many family functions are intangible, it is sometimes difficult to recognize the need or to decide who is filling it. Families do not, of course, consciously tell themselves "now we are engaging in rest and recreation" or "now it's time for a little guidance." A mother may hug her child once or twice as they stand together by the sink washing dishes. Cuddling up to read a bedtime story accomplishes affectional, educational, and recreational functions. Because of the integrated way that functions are accomplished, family members may not be consciously aware of the more intangible contributions they make to each other. This may be especially true of the contributions of the handicapped family member. Often researchers and educators focus on the negative aspects of having a handicapped child, e.g., stress, dysfunctional interactions, financial hardship. Yet many families are consistently able to provide an answer when asked about the benefits of having a handicapped child. Most often those answers showed that he or she was an active contributor to affectional, self-definitional, and guidance functions. As one sister of a retarded woman said:

> She just gives me a better perspective on life. The eggs could be burning, the baby could be crying, and I'll be in a perfectly rotten mood. But then she says, "Isn't it a pretty day?" She helps me see what's really important in life. (Turnbull et al., 1982)

As noted earlier, focusing on positive characteristics is an active coping strategy for many families. For families who do not naturally use this strategy, educators might help them do so by pointing out the many intangible functions the member with a handicap provides.

Some families emphasize some functions more than others. In a family placing a low value on education, for example, there is likely to be less emphasis on this function—fewer books in the home, less encouragement to do homework, and so on. Families may also serve needs for some members more than others. For example, a husband and wife may "sacrifice" their need to be alone together in order to care for their children. These variances depend on both family structure and interaction. Cultural style, membership characteristics, and ideological style determine needs and the priorities given them. Family interaction determines the way those needs are met.

Both functional priorities and the way functions are accomplished also vary over the life cycle. Families with young children may be more preoccupied with physical care, while families with adolescents may be more concerned with guidance and vocational choice. Expression of affection with young children usually takes the form of physical contact, such as being tucked into bed at night. But with adolescents, such expressions would be considered inappropriate, and expressions of affection must take other forms.

The changing priorities and modes of expression for family functions through the life cycle may pose problems for families with a handicapped child. Such a child may have some needs that are age-appropriate and some that are not. For example, a 15-year-old retarded adolescent with a mental age of seven does not physiologically need the same bedtime hour as a seven-year-old. But parents may have difficulty perceiving this fact because in many other ways they relate to him or her as a seven-year-old. The emerging sexuality of a disabled teenager is an often-cited problem parents confront (or fail to confront). Continuing physical care needs of a physically disabled young adult is another area of dissonance. The family must cope with age-appropriate needs in some functions and age-discrepant needs in others.

One important point that must not be overlooked is the fact that all family members have needs. In the past, professionals have advocated neglecting the handicapped person's needs in favor of the rest of the family by institutionalizing him or her. Now, they are more likely to demand that families organize their lives to accommodate the handicapped child. Neither perspective is valid. The least restrictive environment for the handicapped person may be the most restrictive environment for the rest of the family. Families need to learn (1) that everyone's needs are legitimate, and (2) how to balance those needs so that some equitable arrangement can be reached.

Interventions with family functions are perhaps easier to achieve than interventions targeted directly at the interactional system. First, functions are more visible and therefore more measurable—more amenable to change. Second, suggestions about changes in family functions (e.g., time management, finding outside support) may be less threatening than suggestions that the family should readjust its pattern of cohesion or that the marital relationship is poor. But third, and perhaps most importantly, the vast majority of families with handicapped children are no more dysfunctional in their interactional system than any other family. Therapy is needed less often than practical, concrete suggestions on handling the day-to-day problems associated with living with, caring for, and loving a handicapped child.

FAMILY LIFE CYCLE

A description of a family's structure; an enumeration of its subsystems and identification of its levels of cohesion, adaptability, and communication; and an evaluation of the way it meets its individual and collective needs provide a good description of that family at a given point in time. But such a description would probably not be accurate for long. Families are continually adding and losing new members, changing their beliefs, shifting roles, moving closer or farther apart, changing in their needs, and even dissolving and forming new families. Change sets the family system into motion. And that change occurs through the family life cycle. Among family theorists, the concept of a family life cycle has been around for a long time (e.g., Duvall, 1957; Hill, 1949). A family life cycle encompasses more than the sum of individual family members' life cycles; it also describes the way interactions among the members change through time.

Change is a natural part of life, and yet change means stress. People seem constantly to be on a search for stability, for routine, for calm. But change intrudes from both inside and outside the family, and the new rules and roles it demands can be uncomfortable. Change thus means stress, even for the most adaptive families (Terkelsen, 1980). Yet families with handicapped children face an additional stress of not enough change. The prospect that changes will occur off-schedule or not at all can be even more stressful than change itself (Neugarten, 1976). Families with handicapped children face the stress of chronicity: perpetual caretaking responsibilities, long-term dependency, problems that will never go away or get better. The dual stresses of change and chronicity take their toll (Turnbull, Summers, & Brotherson, 1983).

The types of change families experience through the life cycle include developmental stages and transitions, structural change, functional change, and sociohistorical change. Table 12.4 provides an overview of these components. Each of these has implications for stress—from change and failure to change—for families with handicapped children.

Developmental Stages and Transitions

The basic premise of life cycle change is that human beings, from infancy to death, are always growing and developing. Such growth involves responsibility for developmental tasks (Duvall, 1957). In infancy, for example, the baby learns how to use his or her body and begin the process of exploring the world. The period of time required to learn a related set of tasks is called a developmental stage.

Table 12.4			
Family Life Cycle			
Developmental Stages and Transitions	*Structural Change*	*Functional Change*	*Socio-Historical Change*
Couple	Membership	Economic	Cultural trends
Childbearing	Cultural style	Physical	Economy
School age	Ideological style	Rest and recuperation	Political trends
Adolescence			Formative events
Launching		Socialization	
Post-parental		Self-definition	
Aging		Affection	
		Guidance	
		Education	
		Vocational	

Table by Ann Turnbull from *Families of Handicapped Persons*, edited by James Gallagher and Peter Vietze. Copyright © 1986 by Paul H. Brookes Publishing Co., Inc. Reprinted by permission of Paul H. Brookes Publishing Co., Inc., and Ann Turnbull.

A family developmental stage is characterized by a set of tasks related both to the growth of individual members, and to the interactions required by that growth (Carter & McGoldrick, 1980). The tasks involved at each stage are distinct enough to allow identification as a discrete stage, and yet they build on the accomplishments of the preceding stages. Family developmental stages are thus sequential periods of time during which the family is engaged in a discrete set of tasks. These stages are grounded in age-role expectations and are usually defined in terms of the oldest child (Hill & Rodgers, 1969).

It is important to remember, however, that these identified stages are generalizations. The number of stages, the nature of tasks within each stage, and the duration of stages vary with differences in family structure. For example, adolescence might be attenuated in a lower socioeconomic status family because the children might go to work or begin establishing their own families at an early age—in short, they may be required to "grow up fast." A reconstituted family may be faced with tasks in more than one developmental stage at once; for example, a remarried couple may be establishing their new relationship at the same time they are coping with the emerging independence of adolescent children (Sager et al., 1983). Family structure dictates the nature of developmental stages.

In turn, the specific developmental stage dictates the nature of family functions. Needs are different at each stage because the tasks are different. As noted in the discussion of family functions, priorities for functions vary across stages as well as the way specific tasks, e.g., affection, are carried out. Shifts also occur in the responsibility for functions. When children are younger, responsibility for most functions usually falls to the parents, but as the family progresses through its life cycle stages responsibility gradually shifts to the children and the extra-familial system.

Developmental tasks are learning requirements within the established roles of a stage. In contrast, transitions to a new stage involve a major shift in family interactional patterns. Other major changes—such as wars, moving, or divorce—can also cause shifts in family interaction. But developmental transitions are normal changes experienced by most families. McCubbin and Patterson (1983) consider transitions as normative when they are "ubiquitous (they occur to most families), expectable (families could anticipate their occurrence at certain scheduled points in the family life cycle), and short-term (not chronic)" (p. 8).

Transition to a new developmental stage is usually recognized by the family and marked by some form of ritual (Friedman, 1980). Weddings, funerals, christenings, and graduations are all examples of these. Of course, the number and form of the rituals vary widely with the family's cultural and ideological style. But even when there is no ceremony per se, there is often some event that marks the passage, e.g., moving from elementary to junior high school. These traditions and events serve a very real purpose as "punctuation marks along the life cycle" (Neugarten, 1976, p. 18), which signal the need for interactional shifts.

Transitions are a major point of stress for most families. Change may result in brief periods of confusion and conflict over social and emotional roles (Neugarten, 1976; Weeks & Wright, 1979). The consequence is stress even in the smoothest of transitions, and families failing to adapt to the transitions are at risk for dysfunction (Haley, 1973; Hughes, Berger, & Wright, 1978). Variations in family structure and interaction will influence the amount of stress a family feels. For example, a more rigid family may experience more stress as the children enter adolescence and begin to demand new roles and freedoms.

One factor that mitigates the stress of transitions somewhat is the knowledge that these changes are a normal part of life. Expected times to marry, to raise children, to retire, and so forth are prescribed by each culture. Thus, life cycle transitions are much more traumatic and stressful when they occur at other than the expected times (Neugarten, 1976). The concepts of developmental tasks, stage transitions, and the stress of off-time transitions have major implications for families with handicapped children.

These families have additional developmental tasks related to their adjustment to the fact of handicap and their efforts to meet the needs of the child. The process of adjustment to the handicap is not time-bound within the relatively brief period following the diagnosis. Some researchers have postulated specific "stages of adjustment," for example, shock, despair, guilt, withdrawal, acceptance, and finally adjustment (Parks, 1977; Vernon, 1979). Increasingly, however, researchers and practitioners have come to recognize that there are many points along the life cycle when feelings of grief and stress are reactivated. Olshansky

As a handicapped child grows older, the family may face additional problems related to the child's leaving home and uncertainties about the future.

(1962) first characterized this reaction as "chronic sorrow." Wikler (1981) hypothesized 10 major crisis points for families with a handicapped child. In a related study, Wikler, Wasow, and Hatfield (1981) compared the perceptions of social workers and parents concerning the stressful impact of particular life events. The professionals tended to overestimate the stress of early events, and to underestimate the impact of later events, for example, the child's twenty-first birthday.

These findings are only part of the accumulating evidence of need to attend to the problems of families with older handicapped children. For example, families with older children tend to be less supported and more isolated than families with young children (Suelzle & Keenan, 1981). Yet as the handicapped child grows older, it becomes increasingly difficult to maintain the image of "normalcy" in routines of everyday life as well as the life cycle (Birenbaum, 1971). Community acceptance and services decrease (Bristol & Schopler, 1983). Finally, there is some evidence that the emphasis on intensive parent involvement in early intervention may result in "parent burn-out" (Bristol & Schopler, 1983; Morton, 1985). Educators should help families see that their responsibility for a handicapped child is like a marathon race: if they sprint the first mile, they may never make it to the finish line.

Transitions are also more problematic for families with handicapped children for several reasons. First, the transition is likely to be delayed or nonexistent. Parents may face the prospects of continued dependency at a time when their peers are launching their children and enjoying a newly rediscovered freedom to travel, socialize, and otherwise relate as a couple without the responsibilities of child care. Second, events or ceremonies marking the transition to a new stage may be different or missing altogether. What marks the passage to adulthood of a handicapped individual who is not leaving home, not marrying, not finding a job? Third, when transitions do occur, they may be more abrupt than usual. For example, most children typically move from grade to grade each year, requiring that they (and their parents) adjust to new teachers and classrooms; thus the stress of adjustment to junior high school may be eased somewhat. But disabled children who are not mainstreamed may stay in the same special education classroom with the same teacher for several years, making the transition from elementary to secondary placement especially traumatic.

Perhaps the biggest life cycle stresses families with handicapped members face, however, is their awareness of change and fear of what the future might bring. The lack of community services for disabled adults and the uncertainties of funding and guardianship laws make this fear quite realistic. The strategy chosen to cope with this fear may be one of passive appraisal: a refusal to think about the future. Educators must help families overcome this barrier, because planning for the handicapped child's future needs (as well as those of other family members) is vital to the development of appropriate instructional objectives.

Structural Change

Passage through developmental stages usually involves changes in family structure, primarily in the area of membership characteristics. But family structure can also change in ways that are unrelated to developmental progression through the life cycle. These changes (e.g., alcoholism, divorce) are stressful when they are of sufficient magnitude to require a shift in family interactional patterns. In addition, some unchanging structural elements can put chronic stresses on the family—e.g., poverty, racial discrimination.

Moving is an example of a structural change that can exacerbate the stress of the disability. Moving means the family must adjust to a new school system, going through evaluations and assessments, and so forth. On the other hand, families may relocate in order to be near services. For example, one family moved three times in two years in their search for a school district with an appropriate program for their hearing impaired daughter. Another family moved across the state to find services for their disabled son. The father said:

> We just picked up and moved. We didn't have a house and I didn't have a job here. But we knew we had to be here for Jeremy to get what he needed. We just had to trust that the Good Lord would provide. (Turnbull et al., 1982)

Future Planning in Families with Adolescents Having Mental Retardation

Many parents of sons and daughters who are mentally retarded have reported that the uncertainty of the future has caused the family deep concern and stress. There are a variety of stressors that all families face over the life cycle, but one of the most difficult is the transition of children from adolescence into adulthood. This transition is difficult for most families, but it becomes increasingly stressful when the son or daughter is mentally retarded. Research indicates that parents at this life cycle transition experience greater parent burnout, less support, less community acceptance, fewer services, and more isolation than parents at earlier life cycle stages.

Currently in process at the University of Kansas is a research and demonstration program funded by the United States Department of Education. One of the research studies has investigated the relationship between future planning and family functioning. Future planning encompasses what adult needs parents are planning for, and whom they are contacting to plan for those future needs. The study has included interviews with 48 mothers and fathers of sons and daughters with mental retardation and physical disabilities over the age of 18.

Parents are asked about future planning in 10 areas of adult needs, and how social supports help them.

Social Support

Family Members	Clergy/Church
Friends and Neighbors	Members
Other Parents	Other Disabled
Professionals	Persons

Adult Needs

Financial	Self-Concept
Residential	Affection/
Health and Safety	Companionship
Leisure/Recreation	Education
Socialization	Vocation
Self-Direction	

Data from this study are being used to develop a model demonstration program to assist 30 families of adolescents with severe mental retardation to plan for the future. The goals of this program include:

1. Preparation of families and special educators to identify and consider the preferences and choices of adolescents with severe mental retardation concerning their adult lifestyle.

2. Preparation of families and special educators in the identification of skills individuals with severe mental retardation will need to function as independently as possible in adult environments.

3. Preparation of families and special educators to form an effective partnership in planning and implementing individualized education programs during secondary school to teach critical adult skills.

4. Preparation of families to make legal, ethical, and effective lifelong planning decisions (e.g., estate planning, guardianship) that will enhance the individual's quality of life.

Another structural stressor that has received attention in the literature is the process of institutionalizing or deinstitutionalizing a handicapped child. Researchers have found that removing a handicapped family member from the home does not generally reduce the overall stress a family is experiencing (Fotheringham, Shelton, & Hoddinott, 1972). Institutionalization may produce feelings of separation and loss as well as feelings of guilt and inadequacy ("I don't have what it takes to cope," or "I'm abandoning my child"). One mother described the stress of institutionalizing her child:

> *Giving her up at three years of age was the hardest thing I've ever done, other than my husband's death. They were both like deaths.*   (Turnbull et al., 1982)

Deinstitutionalization is also stressful for families. No matter how bad an institution is, it represents a haven of security and permanence to many parents. This fact may be behind the widely reported parental resistance to deinstitutionalization (Keating, Conroy, & Walker, 1980; Meyer, 1980; Payne, 1976). Families may prefer the known problems of the institution to the unknown problems of community placement.

Functional Change

Like structural change, functional change is nondevelopmental in nature. It involves shifts in family members' needs which may be gradual or which may be sudden and temporary. For example, a father's hospitalization following an automobile accident requires the other family members to shift their roles temporarily, both to "cover for" the role he ordinarily fulfills, and to attend to tasks surrounding the injury. Naturally, these changes produce stress. Also, stress can arise from chronic failure to meet some or all of the family members' needs. These problems can build over time to a crisis point, or they can simmer under the surface and exacerbate other stresses and changes the family experiences. Many of these stressors involve everyday, practical problems of living. They are the stressors most often reported by families (Dunlap & Hollingsworth, 1977).

The time demands for care and the problem of maladaptive behavior are examples of functional stressors. Another stress that seems almost universal for families is public reaction to the obvious "differentness" of the handicapped family member. One man with cerebral palsy recalled that, as a child, he often endured stares from other children in church:

> *Once I totally lost it and started to cry, so Dad took me out to the car. After that they decided not to take me to church during that period.*   (Turnbull et al., 1982)

A mother of a disabled adult felt saddened by her daughter's restricted social opportunities and angered when acquaintances did not follow through on promises to visit:

> *People tell Sheila they will come out and see her and then they never come. She stays home and won't go places with us because she thinks they might come by. So she sits here waiting and waiting. It would be better if they wouldn't even say "I'm coming." It's very distressing to watch her.*   (Turnbull et al., 1982)

On the positive side, the fact that functional stressors are often practical problems means that they often have practical solutions. For example, an extreme time demand for care is an often-cited stressor. But this issue can be addressed through training in time management, providing attendant care, and/or respite care services. Similarly, the stress of maladaptive or inappropriate behavior might be reduced through a good parent training program.

It is important to realize, however, that these interventions involve tradeoffs in stress. The act of reorganizing involved in time management requires a time investment that may initially take up more time, not less. The same is true of behavior management training, and if the program includes home visits and observations it also means a loss of privacy. Using respite care involves coping with possible feelings of guilt about leaving the handicapped child behind as well as anxiety about the quality of the care. A family's acceptance of interventions depends on whether it perceives the benefits as having higher priority than the drawbacks. This in turn depends on the family's values; if privacy is important, for example, a behavior problem may reach severe proportions before the family will allow a service provider into the home. Values not only dictate family coping patterns, they also dictate which stressors the family will attend to and which they will continue to endure. Interventions should minimize the stress that serves as a barrier to the family's use of them. Also, the family needs help to look to the future consequences of an intervention so they can realize that a short-term increase in stress associated with tackling a problem can mean a long-term reduction of stress after the problem is eliminated.

Socio-Historical Change

Most of the influences discussed to this point are internally derived stressors; but stressors obviously impinge on the family from outside its boundaries as well. Socio-historical change involves all the trends and events going on in the larger world over which families have little or no control, but which nevertheless produce stress and corresponding change in families. Socio-historical change includes cultural trends, such as the women's movement; economic trends, such as inflation or recession; and political trends, such as war. It also includes formative events, which are less global than trends, such as natural catastrophes (fire, floods, tornadoes), or idiosyncratic events related to personal involvement with social movements, e.g., participation in civil rights protests, being a prisoner of war, growing up in the Depression.

These trends and events affect families because they produce structural or functional change, and because they have a profound effect on family members' perspective of the world. Unemployment, wars, and hurricanes have a direct and immediate effect on the families involved, requiring them to regroup, change functional priorities (at least temporarily), and activate their coping strategies to deal with the problem. Cultural trends and formative events may have a more subtle but no less profound impact on families by shaping the members' perspectives and expectations—that is, their needs. A veteran whose experiences in a war have profoundly altered his image of himself and the world may return to his family with a whole new set of needs and values. Less dramatically, an inspiring teacher or mentor can influence one family member's values or expectations, and the result may be shifts in the whole family's interactional patterns.

In one sense the birth of a handicapped child or the onset of a disability can in itself be a formative event that shapes the family's perspective of itself and the world. The fortuitous presence of an exceptionally understanding professional during the diagnosis (or, conversely, a callous and inept professional) will have a large impact on how the family subsequently perceives the disability (Sarason & Doris, 1979).

A political climate denying or reducing services to handicapped people is stressful to families. During an effort by the Reagan Administration to deregulate PL 94–142, one mother said:

> I thought that was all behind us. I thought I'd never have to worry about Tim's getting served again, or go to the school and beg and plead for them to serve him. But now I realize that it's never going to be over. We always have to be on guard or we lose the ground we've gained. . . . I'm so tired of fighting but I don't have any other choice.   (Turnbull et al., 1982)

Another potentially stressful socio-historical change is the trend toward normalization in services for handicapped people. This is especially a problem for older families. Avis (1985) terms it "deinstitutionalization jet lag." She describes the dissonance experienced by families who were told their child would need lifelong protection, and who are now told their child (now an adult) should be moved into the community and allowed to make his or her own choices. This point touches directly on that family's belief-value-action system. If the family has learned over the years to believe the handicapped child had no potential for independence, it is unreasonable to expect that belief to change overnight.

FUTURE PERSPECTIVES FOR FAMILIES WITH HANDICAPPED CHILDREN

In recent years, professionals have begun to acknowledge the importance of the family's role in the lives of handicapped members. Perhaps even more important, professionals have begun to learn from parents and use their experience and expertise in planning, policy-making, and programming. The future in this area is extremely positive as parents and professionals begin to work collaboratively, sort out their roles, and begin to trust and respect each other's judgment and needs.

It is probable that the combined efforts of parents and professionals will assist in the development of programs and services that more closely match the needs of the individuals with handicaps. The parental perspective of dealing with a handicapped child over his or her lifetime can help provide continuity of services assuring that each program is a building block toward the future. The professional perspective which is grounded in sound practice and experience with many handicapped individuals can provide the framework for service delivery. Although the perspectives of parents and professionals will always differ, each can enhance the effectiveness of the other.

SUMMARY

The purpose of education is to prepare students for a functional role in the adult world. This also is one of the purposes of families. There is no way for educators to avoid interaction with the families of students. But interaction can either be positive or negative—educators can work against families, or work with them. An effective partnership, however, requires an understanding of families: how they function, how they interact, and how they change.

Many concepts that are relatively new in the special education literature were introduced in this chapter including family interaction, family structure, and family life cycle. Family interaction is a complex interplay among individuals and subsystems within the family. Everyone has different roles within each subsystem. The rules of interaction are governed by the family's particular level of cohesion, adaptability, and communication style. A family may be balanced on all of these dimensions, at one extreme or another on all of them, or balanced in some and extreme in others.

Truly dysfunctional families occupy only a small portion of the extreme at each end of the continua. Families may vary along a wide swath in the center and still be successful—that is, meet each member's needs. Professionals should not label a family as dysfunctional simply because it does not fit their own preferred level of cohesion, adaptability, or communication style. In the vast majority of families with handicapped children, the dynamics will be reasonably comfortable to the members. But there are several reasons why it is important to understand family interaction. First, it provides a clue to the possible impact of proposed interventions with a handicapped child. Second, an understanding of the family's communication style is useful in working with the family. Finally, eliciting cooperation with programs is often a matter of understanding family adaptability. These and many other questions can best be answered only through an understanding of family interaction.

Understanding a family's structure can help professionals develop an inventory of resources available to a given family. Most simply put, structure describes the family. Membership characteristics, including individual characteristics, size of family, and the nature of the extrafamilial system give the family its shape. Cultural style—ethnic background, religion, socioeconomic status, and geographic location—provides the family with its identity with past and present groups. Finally, ideological style—beliefs and values, coping patterns—gives the family its sense of direction. These factors provide valuable information about the types of interventions which might be best for a particular family. For example, a strong sense of family solidarity might mean that grandparents or other extended family members should also be included in educational programs. A family with strong religious beliefs should be encouraged to channel those beliefs to serve as effective coping strategies. If the interventions fit in with the family's overall structure, they are much more likely to be of benefit both to the child and to the family as a whole.

The changes in a family over time are described by the family life cycle. Changes occur in response to the development of family members, changing structures and needs, and outside influences. For families with handicapped children, both change and failure to change produce stress. Ideally, the service system—including schools—should be designed to minimize these stressors. Unfortunately, however, services are more often another source of stress. Participation in educational decision making, for example, can be an extremely stressful event for families. Educators should be aware of this and alert for ways to make families more comfortable. Further, teachers should be sensitive to the changes families are experiencing, and adjust expectations accordingly. For example, if the family is passing into adolescence with its nonhandicapped siblings, educators might help parents plan ways to reduce requirements for care of the handicapped child in order to free both themselves and their nonhandicapped teenagers to attend to other needs. Also, transitions to new placements should be planned in advance and discussed thoroughly, so that the family has an opportunity to prepare for the change. Finally, families should be encouraged to strengthen the strategies they use to cope with stress. Professionals should make every effort to point out family successes in order to build confidence and restore a sense of control. No one can hope to eliminate the stress that accompanies change, but careful planning and sensitive professionals can at least minimize it.

To be successful with handicapped children and families, it is necessary to understand the impact of a handicapped child on the family. A handicap affects more than the child. It has a profound effect on everyone whose life is in contact with that child, especially his or her family.

References

Ackerman, J. (1985). Preparation for separation. In A. P. Turnbull & H. R. Turnbull (Eds.), *Parents speak out: Then and now* (pp. 149–158). Columbus, OH: Merrill Publishing.

Avis, D. W. (1985). Deinstitutionalization jet lag. In A. P. Turnbull & H. R. Turnbull (Eds.), *Parents speak out: Then and now* (pp. 185–192). Columbus, OH: Merrill Publishing.

Beavers, W. R., & Voeller, M. N. (1983). Family models: Comparing and contrasting the Olson circumplex model with the Beavers systems model. *Family Process, 22,* 85–97.

Birenbaum, A. (1971). The mentally retarded child in the home and the family cycle. *Journal of Health and Social Behavior, 12,* 55–65.

Bossard, J. H. S., & Boll, E. S. (1956). *The large family system.* Philadelphia: University of Pennsylvania Press.

Bristol, M. M., & Schopler, E. (1983). Stress and coping in families of autistic adolescents. In E. Schopler & G. B. Mesibov (Eds.), *Autism in adolescents and adults* (pp. 251–258). New York: Plenum Press.

Carnes, P. J. (1981). *Family development I: Understanding us.* Minneapolis: Interpersonal Communication Programs, Inc.

Carter, E., & McGoldrick, M. (1980). The family life cycle and family therapy: An overview. In E. Carter & M. McGoldrick (Eds.), *The family life cycle: A framework for family therapy* (pp. 3–20). New York: Gardner Press.

Cicirelli, V. G. (1976). Siblings teaching siblings. In V. L. Allen (Ed.), *Children as teachers*. New York: Academic Press.

Cleveland, D. W., & Miller, N. (1977). Attitudes and life commitments of older siblings of mentally retarded adults: An exploratory study. *Mental Retardation, 15*(3), 38–41.

Dunlap, W. R., & Hollingsworth, J. S. (1977). How does a handicapped child affect the family? Implications for practitioners. *The Family Coordinator, 26*(3), 286–293.

Duvall, E. (1957). *Family development*. Philadelphia: Lippincott.

Falicov, C. J. (1982). Mexican families. In M. McGoldrick, J. K. Pearce, & J. Giordano (Eds.), *Ethnicity in family therapy* (pp. 134–163). New York: The Guilford Press.

Farber, B. (1959). Effects of a severely mentally retarded child on family integration. *Monograph of the Society for Research in Child Development*.

Farber, B. (1960). Family organization and crisis: Maintenance of integration in families with a severely retarded child. *Monograph of the Society for Research in Child Development, 25*(1).

Farber, B., & Jenne, W. C. (1963). Family organization and parent-child communication: Parents and siblings of a retarded child. *Monograph of the Society for Research in Child Development, 7*(28).

Farber, B., & Ryckman, D. B. (1965). Effects of severely mentally retarded children on family relationships. *Mental Retardation Abstracts, 2*, 1–17.

Fotheringham, J. B., Shelton, M., & Hoddinott, B. A. (1972). The effects on the family of the presence of a mentally retarded child. *Canadian Psychiatric Association Journal, 17*, 283–290.

Friedman, E. H. (1980). Systems and ceremonies: A family view of rites of passage. In E. A. Carter & M. McGoldrick (Eds.), *The family life cycle* (pp. 429–460). New York: Gardner Press.

Gardner, R. A. (1971). The guilt reactions of parents of children with severe physical disease. In R. L. Noland (Ed.), *Counseling parents of the ill and the handicapped* (pp. 27–43). Springfield, IL: Charles C. Thomas.

Gath, A. (1974). Sibling reactions to mental handicap: A comparison of the brothers and sisters of mongol children. *Journal of Child Psychology and Psychiatry and Allied Disciplines, 15*(3), 838–843.

Grossman, F. K. (1972). *Brothers and sisters of retarded children: An exploratory study*. Syracuse, NY: Syracuse University Press.

Haley, J. (1973). *Uncommon therapy*. New York: W. W. Norton.

Herz, F. M., & Rosen, E. J. (1982). Jewish families. In M. McGoldrick, J. K. Pearce, & J. Giordano (Eds.), *Ethnicity in family therapy* (pp. 364–392). New York: The Guilford Press.

Hill, R., & Rodgers, R. H. (1969). The developmental approach. In H. T. Christensen (Ed.), *Handbook of marriage and the family* (pp. 171–211). Chicago: Rand McNally.

Hoffman, L. (1980). The family life cycle and discontinuous change. In E. A. Carter & M. McGoldrick (Eds.), *The family life cycle: A framework for family therapy* (pp. 53–68). New York: Gardner Press.

Holroyd, J., & McArthur, D. (1976). Mental retardation and stress on the parents: A contrast between Down's syndrome and childhood autism. *American Journal of Mental Deficiency, 80*, 431–436.

Hughes, S. F., Berger, M., & Wright, L. (1978). The family life cycle and clinical interventions. *Journal of Marriage and Family Counseling, 4*(4), 33–40.

Kahn, A. J. (1969). *Theory and practice of social planning.* New York: Russell Sage Foundation.

Kantor, D., & Lehr, W. (1975). *Inside the family.* San Francisco: Jossey-Bass.

Keating, D. J., Conroy, J. W., & Walker, S. (1980). *Longitudinal study of the court-ordered deinstitutionalization of Pennhurst: Family impacts of residents of Pennhurst.* (Contract #130–79–3). Unpublished paper, Temple University, Developmental Disabilities Program/UAF, Philadelphia.

Lee, G. R. (1982). *Family structure and interaction: A comparative analysis.* Minneapolis: University of Minnesota Press.

McAndrew, I. (1976). Children with a handicap and their families. *Child Care, Health and Development, 2,* 213–237.

McCubbin, H. I., Joy, C. B., Cauble, A. E., Comeau, J. K., Patterson, J. M., & Needle, R. H. (1980). Family stress and coping: A decade review. *Journal of Marriage and the Family, 42*(4), 855–871.

McCubbin, H. I., & Patterson, J. M. (1981). *Systematic assessment of family stress, resources and coping: Tools for research, education and clinical intervention.* St. Paul: University of Minnesota, Family Stress and Coping Project, Department of Family Social Science.

McCubbin, H. I., & Patterson, J. M. (1983). Family transitions: Adaptation to stress. In H. I. McCubbin & C. R. Figley (Eds.), *Stress and the family. Vol. I: Coping with normative transitions* (pp. 5–25). New York: Brunner/Mazel.

McGill, D., & Pearce, J. K. (1982). British families. In M. McGoldrick, J. K. Pearce, & J. Giordano (Eds.), *Ethnicity in family therapy* (pp. 457–482). New York: The Guilford Press.

McGoldrick, M. (1982a). Ethnicity and family therapy: An overview. In M. McGoldrick, J. K. Pearce, & J. Giordano (Eds.), *Ethnicity in family therapy* (pp. 3–30). New York: The Guilford Press.

McGoldrick, M. (1982b). Irish families. In M. McGoldrick, J. K. Pearce, & J. Giordano (Eds.), *Ethnicity in family therapy* (pp. 310–339). New York: The Guilford Press.

Meyer, R. J. (1980). Attitudes of parents of institutionalized mentally retarded individuals toward deinstitutionalization. *American Journal of Mental Deficiency, 85*(2), 184–187.

Minuchin, S. (1974). *Families and family therapy.* Cambridge, MA: Harvard University Press.

Morton, K. (1985). Identifying the enemy—A parent's complaint. In A. P. Turnbull & H. R. Turnbull (Eds.), *Parents speak out: Then and now* (pp. 143–148). Columbus, OH: Merrill Publishing.

Neugarten, B. (1976). Adaptations and the life cycle. *The Counseling Psychologist, 6*(1), 16–20.

Nihira, K., Meyers, C. E., & Mink, I. (1980). Home environment, family adjustment, and the development of mentally retarded children. *Applied Research in Mental Retardation, 1,* 5–24.

Olshansky, S. (1962). Chronic sorrow: A response to having a mentally defective child. *Social Casework, 43,* 191–194.

Olson, D. H., McCubbin, H. I., Barnes, H., Larsen, A., Muxen, M., & Wilson, M. (1983). *Families: What makes them work.* Beverly Hills, CA: Sage Publishing.

Olson, D. H., Russell, C. S., & Sprenkle, D. H. (1980). Circumplex model of marital and family systems II: Empirical studies and clinical intervention. In J. P. Vincent (Ed.),

Advances in family intervention assessment and therapy (Vol. 1) (pp. 129–179). Green-wich, CT: JAI Press.

Olson, D. H., Sprenkle, D. H., & Russell, C. S. (1979). Circumplex model of marital and family systems I: Cohesion and adaptability dimension, family types and clinical applications. *Family Process, 18,* 3–28.

Parks, R. (1977). Parental reactions to the birth of a handicapped child. *Health Social Work, 2,* 52–66.

Paul, J. A., & Porter, P. B. (1981). Parents of handicapped children. In J. Paul (Ed.), *Understanding and working with parents of children with special needs.* New York: Holt, Rinehart and Winston.

Payne, J. E. (1976). The deinstitutional backlash. *Mental Retardation, 3,* 43–45.

Pearlin, L. I., & Schooler, C. (1978). The structure of coping. *Journal of Health and Social Behavior, 19,* 2–21.

Pennsylvania Association for Retarded Children (PARC) v. Pennsylvania, 344 F. Supp. 1257 (E. D. Pa. 1971) and 343 F. Supp. 279 (E.D. Pa. 1972).

President's Committee on Mental Retardation (1977). *Mental retardation: Past and present.* Washington, DC: U.S. Government Printing Office.

Pinderhughes, E. (1982). Afro-American families and the victim system. In M. McGoldrick, J. K. Pearce, & J. Giordano (Eds.), *Ethnicity in family therapy* (pp. 108–122). New York: The Guilford Press.

Rotunno, M., & McGoldrick, M. (1982). Italian families. In M. McGoldrick, J. K. Pearce, & J. Giordano (Eds.), *Ethnicity in family therapy* (pp. 340–362). New York: The Guilford Press.

Rubin, L. B. (1976). *Worlds of pain: Life in the working-class family.* New York: Basic Books, Inc.

Sager, C. J., Brown, H. S., Crohn, H., Engel, T., Rodstein, E., & Walker, L. (1983). *Treating the remarried family.* New York: Brunner/Mazel.

Sarason, S. B., & Doris, J. (1979). *Educational handicap, public policy, and social history.* New York: The Free Press.

Stack, C. (1975). *All our kin.* New York: Harper & Row.

Stubblefield, H. (1965). Religion, parents and mental retardation. *Mental Retardation.*

Suelzle, M., & Keenan, V. (1981). Changes in family support networks over the life cycle of mentally retarded persons. *American Journal of Mental Deficiency, 86,* 267–274.

Terkelsen, K. G. (1980). Toward a theory of the family life cycle. In E. A. Carter & M. McGoldrick (Eds.), *The family life cycle: A framework of family therapy* (pp. 21–52). New York: Gardner Press.

Trevino, F. (1979). Siblings of handicapped children: Identifying those at risk. *Social Casework: The Journal of Contemporary Social Work, 60*(8), 488–492.

Turnbull, A. P., Brotherson, M. J., & Summers, J. A. (1982). [Raw data from unpublished study.]

Turnbull, A. P., Brotherson, M. J., & Summers, J. A. (1985). The impact of deinstitutionalization on families: A family systems approach. In R. H. Bruininks (Ed.), *Living and learning in the least restrictive environment* (pp. 115–140). Baltimore, MD: Paul H. Brookes Publishers.

Turnbull, A. P., Summers, J. A., & Brotherson, M. J. (1983). *Family life cycle: Theoretical and empirical implications and future directions for families with mentally retarded members.* Paper presented at the NICHD Conference on "Families with Retarded Children."

Turnbull, H. R., & Turnbull, A. P. (1982). *Free appropriate public education* (3rd ed). Denver: Love Publishing.

Vernon, M. (1979). Parental reactions to birth-defective children. *Postgraduate Medicine, 65*, 183–189.

Wadsworth, H. G., & Wadsworth, J. B. (1971). A problem of involvement with parents of mildly retarded children. *The Family Coordinator, 28*, 141–147.

Wahler, R. G. (1980). The insular mother: Her problems in parent-child treatment. *Journal of Applied Behavior Analysis, 13*, 207–219.

Weeks, G. R., & Wright, L. (1979). Dialectics of the family life cycle. *American Journal of Family Therapy, 1*(7).

Weinrott, M. R. (1974). A training program in behavior modification for siblings of the retarded. *American Journal of Orthopsychiatry, 44*, 362–375.

Whittaker, C. A. (1977). Process techniques of family therapy. *Interactions, 1*, 4–19.

Wikler, L. (1981). Chronic stresses of families of mentally retarded children. *Family Relations, 30*(2), 281–288.

Wikler, L., Wasow, M., & Hatfield, E. (1981). Chronic sorrow revisited: Attitude of parents and professionals about adjustment to mental retardation. *American Journal of Orthopsychiatry, 51*, 63–70.

Williams, J. A., Jr., & Stockton, P. (1973). Black family structures and functions: An empirical examination of some suggestions made by Billingsley. *Journal of Marriage and the Family, 35*(1), 39–49.

Willner, S. K., & Crane, R. (1979). A parental dilemma: The child with a marginal handicap. *Social Casework, 60*, 30–35.

Zuk, G. H., Miller, R. I., Bartram, J. B., & Kling, F. (1961). Maternal acceptance of retarded children: A questionnaire study of attitudes and religious background. *Child Development, 32*, 515–540.

Resources

Organizations for Parents (Also see listings in all other chapters)

National Information Center for Handicapped Children and Youth
P.O. Box 1492
Washington, DC 20013

Provides information, publishes a newsletter, and provides technical assistance to parents and professionals about handicapping conditions, legislation, and available programs and services.

National Network of Parent Centers
9451 Broadview Drive
Bay Harbor, FL 33154

Provides information, training, support, and technical assistance to parents of handicapped individuals through centers located throughout the United States and Puerto Rico.

Periodical

Exceptional Parent Magazine
296 Boylston St. (Third Floor)
Boston, MA 02116

A magazine which deals with the kinds of problems faced by all parents of handicapped children with practical information and an exchange of parents' ideas and experiences.

Books

Featherstone, H. (1981). *A difference in the family: Living with a disabled child.* New York: Penguin Books.

Goldfarb, L., Brotherson, M. J., Summers, J. A., & Turnbull, A. P. (1986). *Meeting the challenge of disability or chronic illness: A family guide.* Baltimore, MD: Paul H. Brookes.

Lynch, E. W., Murphy, D. S., & Lewis, R. B. (1986). *Making things better for chronically ill children: A guide for schools and families.* San Diego, CA: San Diego State University.

Turnbull, A. P., & Turnbull, H. R. (1985). *Parents speak out: Then and now.* Columbus, OH: Merrill Publishing.

Winton, P. J., Turnbull, A. P., & Blacher, J. (1984). *Selecting a preschool: A guide for parents of handicapped children.* Austin, TX: Pro-Ed.

Chapter 13

MULTICULTURAL CONSIDERATIONS

The cultural and linguistic diversity of the population of this nation is increasing dramatically. Since the early 1970s there has been a heightened awareness of the implications of this diversity to the education of American children. Attempts to facilitate the academic and social development of students from minority group backgrounds have resulted in a variety of innovative educational approaches. Some of these have involved various forms of bilingual education for children who do not speak English well; others have focused primarily on incorporating multicultural concepts into the education of all students; still others have combined aspects of both.

More recently, it has become clear that special educators cannot meet the individual needs of culturally diverse, handicapped students without addressing the unique characteristics deriving from their ethnolinguistic backgrounds. If appropriate educational services are to be provided these students, their linguistic, learning, and affective needs must be taken into account in the design and delivery of their individual educational programs. Until quite recently, efforts to accomplish this have been attenuated and experimental, incorporating selected theories and practices from the fields of both bilingual/bicultural education and special education. The validity of these amalgamations has not been established and few attempts have been made to systematically develop and evaluate new approaches.

Patricia T. Cegelka

San Diego State University

Any attempt to understand what is happening—and what should be happening—relative to educational programs for these students requires a familiarity with basic concerns and tenets of both special education and bilingual education. This chapter discusses key concepts and underlying considerations in bilingual/ bicultural education, details their implications for the education of handicapped children, and describes their application to special education processes.

CULTURAL DIVERSITY

The United States is characterized by its cultural and linguistic diversity. It is estimated that by 1990 there will be approximately 35 million persons in the United States whose language background is other than English, with this number rising to approximately 39 million by the year 2000 (Oxford, Pol, Lopez, Stupp, Peng, & Gendell, 1980). Included here are individuals from Hispanic and Asian origins, individuals who are American Indians, and individuals from such diverse linguistic and cultural background as the Middle East, South Africa, Portugal, Finland, Poland, and many others. There are 2.7 million LEP (limited English proficient) students in the U.S. with California accounting for 525,000 of these (a number greater than the total school population of 25 other states combined). California projects that 52 percent of its school population will be of minority background by the year 2000; at present 90 languages are spoken by students in this state. The educational implications of this diversity become apparent when one California elementary school serves students from 25 different language groups (*Newsweek*, 1982) and Hollywood High School has a total of 38 different language groups (*Time*, 1984).

Despite this range of ethnolinguistic diversity, four groups have emerged as the ones most typically recognized as having unique educational needs. These are groups which have (1) a history of either cultural or language differences, or (2) a history of imposed educational deprivation, and (3) are of sufficient size to attract attention. They include the following:

1. American Indian or Alaska Native or a person having origins in any of the original peoples of North America.
2. Asian or Pacific Islander, or a person having origins in any of the original peoples of the Far East, Southeast Asia, or the Pacific Islands.
3. Black/Negro, or a person having origins in any of the black racial groups of Africa.
4. Hispanic, or a person of Mexican, Puerto Rican, Cuban, Central or South American, or other Spanish culture or origin, regardless of race. (Cartwright, Cartwright, & Ward, 1981)

The Afro-American or black population comprises the largest single subgroup, accounting for approximately 9 percent of the total U.S. population. Ethnolinguistic minorities make up nearly 20 percent of the national population and, by the year 2000, are estimated to increase to 32 percent. Of this total, Spanish background or Hispanic individuals represent the largest subgroup, approxi-

introducing

CHAU

Chau became an honor student this year. Seventeen years old and a tenth grader, she is enrolled in a college prep curriculum with plans for becoming a counseling psychologist. She is a bright, dynamic girl with a beautiful complexion. Somewhat shy at first, she displays a good sense of humor with the people she knows well. She also is exceptionally hard working, in part, she explains, to keep her from thinking about those things that make her sad.

Born to a privileged Vietnamese family, Chau was six years old when the North Vietnamese entered Saigon as victors. She remembers hiding for hours with relatives in a cellar until the shooting stopped and then walking home over, and on, the bodies of those massacred. She remembers the government troops replacing a picture of her grandparents with one of Ho Chi Minh and then removing all furniture, clothes, and other belongings from her home. She remembers her family subsisting on grain, eaten off the floor. And she remembers her first attempt to flee Vietnam with two brothers. Discovered by roving government troops, one brother escaped, one was killed, and Chau was shot and left for dead. Other government troops found her to be alive the next day, and took her to a hospital where she spent several months. When she emerged, blind and disfigured around the eyes from her wounds, she was sent to a political reeducation camp before being returned to her family. Finally, three years after the first attempt, Chau and other relatives successfully fled Vietnam by boat.

After a year in a relocation camp in the Phillipines, she acquired USA sponsorship of a Roman Catholic priest and a physician. Living with the family of the physician for two years, she boarded at a nearby residential school for the blind. There she received excellent mobility training and learned to use a computer brailler. She also learned to speak, read, and write English fluently.

At the beginning of the last school year, she moved to another city to join members of her family.

They include the brother who had been successful in the first escape attempt, his Vietnamese wife and child, and another brother who recently fled Vietnam. This extended family lives in a small apartment over a store in a Vietnamese section of the city. The husband and wife hold full-time jobs, the other brother attends the local university, and each day Chau boards the bus at her doorstep to be transported to the high school where a teacher of the visually handicapped is available full time to provide support services for blind and partially sighted students. The school is some 15 miles from Chau's home; the first on and last off the bus, Chau spends over an hour a day traveling to and from her doorstep.

She is enrolled in college prep classes and spends approximately an hour a day in the VH resource room. This teacher provides braille materials (texts, tests, worksheets) for her classes; in addition, Chau receives continuing instruction in using the computer braille systems. She uses a modified Perkins brailler interfaced with an Apple computer to transcribe print into braille; given an assignment sheet in one of her classes, for instance, a teacher or a student will read it aloud as Chau types it into the system for her braille copy. She prepares her homework on the VersaBrailler which, when interfaced with the Apple and with the Braille Edit program, transcribes the braille into print. Chau has developed considerable skill with these systems, with her only errors being infrequently used braille contractions. Similarly, she is quite proficient in her English language skills, making few errors and, once corrected, never repeating them. During the fall semester, Chau earned grades of B and C, but by the end of the year she had become a straight A student.

The focus of her special education support services has been academic so far. For the following year, however, her IEP reflects additional mobility training and socialization objectives. Because Chau lives in an urban neighborhood several miles from the affluent suburban school she attends, she has had little social contact with her peers and she has acquired few skills in moving about her neighborhood independently. Her teachers hope to build on her proficiency with her cane to teach her to shop with a grocery cart and to perform other errands for herself and her family. Despite the transportation barriers, they also hope to devise ways of extending her social participation with her classmates. Their long-range goal is to facilitate this extraordinary girl in meeting the challenges presented by the circumstances of her life.

mately 40 percent of the total ethnolinguistic population and 75 percent of those who have been designated as limited in English proficiency (LEP). This is the fastest growing minority and, within the foreseeable future, it may replace the black population as the largest minority group in this country (Cannon, 1978). Asian groups account for approximately 7 percent of individuals with non-English language backgrounds (NELBs), with a variety of other cultural/language minorities—American Indian, Farsi, Urdu, Hindi, Arabic, Portuguese, Haitian, Acadian French, Greek, to name but a few—constituting the remaining subgroups. The states of California, Texas, and New York rank the highest in numbers for individuals who are not native-speakers of English, as well as for those who are limited in English proficiency. These states also show the highest growth rates for both groups.

The rights of culturally and linguistically diverse children to equality of educational opportunity has been established through litigation and legislation in much the same manner as have the rights of handicapped children. The landmark *Brown v. Board of Education* case of 1954, brought on behalf of a black child relegated to a racially segregated school, laid the foundation for much of the equal opportunity litigation in both special education and bilingual education. The unanimous decision of the United States Supreme Court held that:

> *Today education is perhaps the important function of state and local government. . . . It is the very foundation of good citizenship. Today it is a principal instrument of awakening the child to cultural values, in helping him to adjust normally to his environment. In these days, it is doubtful that any child may reasonably expect to succeed in life if he is denied the opportunity of an education. Such an opportunity, where the state has undertaken to provide it, is a right which must be available to all on equal terms.* (Brown v. Board of Education, 1954)

The nondiscrimination principles implicit in this decision became the basis for federal mandates prohibiting educational discrimination against minority children, as well as against handicapped children. The overlap between multicultural/bilingual education and special education goes beyond that of a shared litigative/legislative history and a similar philosophical orientation, however. Within the recent past it was common to find dramatically disproportionate numbers of ethnic and linguistic minorities placed in special education classrooms for the handicapped, particularly for the educable (or mildly) mentally retarded. The most widely endorsed viewpoint is that exceptionality, both hand-

An ethnic festival representing many cultures is shared by a mainstreamed handicapped child along with her nondisabled peers.

icapping conditions and giftedness, should occur at approximately equal rates across all populations and ethnic/racial subgroups. Higher rates of linguistic and academic delays among some groups of children have typically been attributed to differences in the nature and quality of experiences provided by the environment. A decidedly different interpretation was proposed by Jensen (1969), a Berkeley educational psychologist. He concluded from his studies and analyses that, at least with blacks, lower IQ test scores were due to a generally deficient ability to abstract. His position created considerable controversy and even outrage, but the prevailing view still holds that functioning differences among groups are primarily a result of environmental differences, not genetic deficiencies. This is clearly the position endorsed by PL 94–142, whose requirements for nonbiased assessment, parental participation, and due process procedures attempt to address, in part, the ethnolinguistic imbalances in special education.

While overrepresentation of minority children is still a problem, particularly with some categories of handicapping conditions, at the same time there is increasing concern that some minority children are being denied needed special education services. In situations where language minority children evidence learning difficulties, for example, there may be reluctance on the part of educators, sensitive to the discriminatory nature of past practices, to refer them for special education assessment. At the other end of the spectrum, minority children who are gifted and talented also may not be identified for placement in programs designed to meet their unique needs.

Pluralistic Education

Several factors have contributed to the development of a more pluralistic approach to education. Increases in the numbers of nonmajority groups have precluded their being overlooked or ignored. Social and political forces have also been a factor. The civil rights activities of the 1960s and since then created a political climate which promoted self-definition on a number of socio-cultural fronts. This has been particularly true of Hispanic groups, most notably Puerto Ricans in the northeastern states and Mexican-Americans in the Southwest. These groups tend to maintain cultural and family ties with relatives in their homelands and may return to their native homes for family celebrations, holidays, and/or various periods of residence. Many Hispanics in the Southwest, for whom geographic proximity to Mexico facilitates the maintenance of these ties, retain Spanish as the primary language of the home. In some cities in this region, it is possible to find neighborhoods in which most social, educational, and commercial endeavors are conducted in Spanish. In other words, in the day-to-day lives of the people, English is not essential.

A better understanding of the fundamental interrelationships of culture and learning has also contributed to the development of a more pluralistic approach to education. Research studies and observational reports have documented differences among cultural groups for such characteristics as personality style, cognitive style, values, and belief systems, variables that all relate to the acquisition of new knowledge and skills (Lynch & Lewis, 1982). Multicultural and bilingual approaches to education attempt to accommodate these characteristics, as opposed to ignoring or eradicating them. It is widely held today that culturally sensitive instruction can result in greater educational achievement for nonmajority students and, at the same time, benefit majority students by providing them a more comprehensive world view.

This pluralistic approach is in sharp contrast to the traditional "melting pot" view of the schools as a major vehicle for acculturation and assimilation. Indeed, a major motivation for compulsory education in this country was to facilitate the cultural assimilation of immigrant children and to prepare them to fulfill economic roles in an industrialized nation. The goal was to "melt away" cultural differences, to encourage diverse groups to abandon their unique characteristics and to practice the traditions of the majority society. This Anglo conformity model (Gonzales, 1979) was geared toward perpetuating a monocultural and monolingual society. Ethnicity was frequently viewed as un-American and strongly discouraged through a variety of social sanctions. Not only did schools offer instruction only in English, but some, in their zeal to eradicate differences, went so far as to forbid the use of any language other than standard English, punishing children for transgressions of this rule on the playground as well as in the classroom.

Educational Status

Nationwide educational data collected by the National Center for Education Statistics (Oxford et al., 1980) found that persons with language-minority backgrounds in grades 5 through 12 were more than three times as likely to perform below grade level than those with English language backgrounds. For students whose primary language was Spanish, the percentages of those falling two or more years below grade level were as follows: 15 percent for grades 1–4, 25 percent for grades 5–8, and 18 percent for grades 9–12. Ten percent of black students ages 16 and 17 were reported to be at least two years behind academically. According to Chinn (1979b), 800,000 minority students drop out of school each year. Compared to a total school dropout of 23 percent, Hispanics leave secondary school at a rate of 45 percent, blacks at a rate of 35 percent, and American Indians at a rate of 55 percent (Carnegie Council, 1979; Garcia, 1976). Constituting 25 percent of the national school population, minority students account for 90 percent of those suspended from school (National Coalition of Advocates for Students, 1985). In addition, the historical pattern has been for minority students to be overrepresented in classes for handicapped students and underrepresented in classes designed for gifted and talented students. Identification practices that are not sensitive to the influences of cultural and linguistic differences have contributed to this phenomenon. Disproportionate representation of minority children, particularly blacks and Hispanics, in classes for the mentally retarded was the basis for much of the educational critique and class-action litigation that eventuated in an extensive reconceptualization of special education service delivery. Many of the provisions of PL 94–142 were explicitly designed to address the problems of overidentification and misclassification of minority children as handicapped and their unnecessary removal from mainstream educational environments.

Socioeconomic Influences

Because disproportionate numbers of minority group children are also poor, it is difficult to make clear distinctions between the influences of poverty and of culture. Little of the research on the cognitive, social, and emotional development of ethnic minority children has successfully separated the potential effects of poverty from those of cultural diversity. Hence, we must exercise caution in our interpretations of this research as indicative of cultural as opposed to socioeconomic variables, or vice versa. Existing data do suggest that poverty in itself is predictive of low academic achievement. During the 1960s and 1970s, federally funded programs for the "culturally deprived," such as Head Start, the Job Corps, and others, were initiated in attempts to prevent and/or compensate for the effects of poverty. The benefits of these programs have been variable, with low socioeconomic status continuing to be associated statistically with poor academic achievement.

Understanding of the interrelationships between minority group status, poverty, and school achievement is further complicated by the fact that discriminatory practices against ethnic minorities, more than low SES, may account for the poorer academic achievement. Kagan and Buriel (1977) point out that "the life experiences of middle-class Chicanos are different from those of middle-class Anglos and equating groups on economic class does not equate them on numerous other variables, including exposure to prejudice and realistic perceptions of limited economic or educational opportunities" (p. 281).

For this variable, as for all others, it is important to keep in mind that while generalized statements may hold true for an identifiable group as a whole, they are not descriptive of all of the individuals within that group. Many children from poverty backgrounds achieve very well in schools, with some being identified as gifted and talented. The same is true for children from ethnically/racially diverse backgrounds. In the same vein, many other characteristics (e.g., learning styles, personality traits) found to be descriptive of a group are not descriptive of every individual member of that group. There is every reason to believe that there is as much intracultural variation on a given trait as there is cross-cultural variation. Therefore, while descriptive information about the characteristics of different groups can be of value, we must be careful to avoid stereotyping all members of that group.

It is particularly important to keep this in mind when dealing with exceptional children from culturally diverse backgrounds. For this group, inferences can only be extrapolated from research with nonexceptional populations for "there is currently a significant lack of research on crosscultural differences with exceptional populations" (Rueda & Prieto, 1979, p. 51). As with nonexceptional populations, we must also remember that cultural differences are just that—differences, not deficiencies.

EFFECTS ON SCHOOLING

A variety of social, cultural, and linguistic factors interact in ways that reduce the probability that schools, as presently constituted, will meet the cognitive and emotional needs of children from culturally diverse backgrounds (Garwood, 1979; Henderson, 1980). The manner in which schools operate is frequently alien to the child. Further, many school practices and expectations are predicted on a background of experiences not always available in the child's preschool environment. At the same time, educators tacitly assume that most, if not all, of the early experiences and later development of the racially or ethnically diverse child are negative and deprived (Johnson, 1969). The National Coalition of Advocates for Students noted that the operating assumption in many schools "is that different backgrounds and languages constitute deficits to be corrected, rather than strengths upon which to build" (p. 16).

The development of much of the school curriculum has proceeded as though cultural distinctions were irrelevant to the learning process, with instructional materials and strategies designed to facilitate the learning styles of the dominant Euro-American culture. Minority groups tend to be both underrepresented and misrepresented in curriculum materials, which may provide distorted and denigrating portrayals of the contributions and characteristics of various groups. The

National Coalition reported instances "of Native American children sitting through lessons about 'taming the frontier' and of Columbus 'discovering America,' of world history texts which devote no more than a few paragraphs to Africa; of Asian history courses that treat all Japanese, Chinese, and Filipino people as if they were one; and of schools in the Southwest which teach the history of their region with little more than a cursory look at its rich pre-Anglo culture" (p. 17). In short, curriculum practices, language usage, instructional strategies, and organizational features of the classroom all tend to be geared toward children with particular cognitive and perceptual styles, movement repertoires, language proficiencies, and backgrounds of experience and preparation.

It comes as no surprise, then, that the behaviors of teachers reflect many of the same biases. In a study sponsored by the U.S. Commission on Civil Rights (1974), the classroom interactions of teachers with Anglo-American and Mexican-American children were observed in nearly 500 classrooms in the Southwest. Systematic differences that emerged included the following:

1. *Teachers praised Anglo-Americans 36 percent more often than they praised Mexican-Americans;*
2. *Teachers used or built upon the ideas of Anglo-American students 40 percent more frequently than they used or built upon the ideas of Mexican-American students;*
3. *Teachers responded 40 percent more positively to Anglo-American than to Mexican-American students;*
4. *Teachers directed questions to Anglo-Americans 21 percent more often than to Mexican-Americans;*
5. *Teachers spent 23 percent more time in all in non-disapproving talk with Anglo-American than with Mexican-American students;*
6. *The average Anglo-American spent approximately 27 percent more time speaking in the classroom than did the average Mexican-American student.* (Smith, 1979, pp. 40–41)

These findings are not unique to this study. Other research has revealed a fairly consistent pattern of differential treatment of students by teachers as a function of the sex, academic achievement, and socioeconomic status of the student (Good & Brophy, 1974). An important instance of this differential treatment is that, with children from low SES or minority backgrounds, teacher communications are likely to focus on the managing or controlling of classroom behavior, while with majority, middle-class children, teacher communications are likely to be relevant to the content or skills of instruction (Henderson, 1980; Laosa, 1977). This is important because research has consistently demonstrated that student achievement is related to the nature of teacher-student interactions (Hoge & Luce, 1979). In one particularly dramatic instance, the achievement levels of high-achieving Mexican-Americans dropped significantly when these students were taught by teachers identified as high in discrimination (Johnson, Gerard, & Miller, 1975). Negative teacher attitudes and expectations have also been cited as a problem relative to the educational attainment of American Indian children. Ramirez and Tippeconnic (1979) identified low expectations of Anglo teachers in reservation schools as an important contributor to the underachievement and high dropout rates of Indian students. The National Coalition of Advocates for Students (1985) also found multiple forms of discrimination:

> Some counselors have discouraged Indian children from either staying in school or returning to school after dropping out ... some teachers are not sensitive enough in dealing with and understanding the Indian culture and values, and convey the message, either knowingly or unknowingly, that Indian children do not belong in the classrooms ... some teachers simply ignore Indian children in the classroom and have little concern over their attendance and schoolwork. (p. 18)

Thus, there are a variety of ways that teachers can negatively affect the academic achievement of culturally diverse children. Biases toward the adequacy of the child's background and language, racial and ethnic prejudices, the nature of teacher communications with children, teacher expectations for student success, and the extent to which they devalue and/or discriminate against their students are all potentially strong deterrents to the academic success of these children.

Changing School Practice

Another deterrent to school success for language minority students has been the failure to provide instruction in a language that they understood. In the 1974 *Lau v. Nichols* case, the Supreme Court ruled that the mere provision of the same facilities, books, teachers, and curriculum did not constitute equality of educational opportunity. It stated that "students who do not understand English are effectively foreclosed from any meaningful education." This ruling was in response to a class-action suit which argued that nearly 1,800 Chinese students in the San Francisco schools were being denied educational opportunity because instruction was provided only in English, a language that they did not understand and were not being helped to learn.

While this ruling did not specify bilingual education as the remedy, it did mandate that the district take affirmative action so that non-English-speaking children would have equal access to the educational opportunities offered to all other children. The Court did not specify how this was to be accomplished, stating that there were several alternatives, of which bilingual education was one. Concerning the impact of this ruling, Pifer (1979) observed:

> The import of Lau was enormous. The Bilingual Education Act (passed in 1968 as the Title VII amendment to the 1965 Elementary and Secondary Education Act) had already given federal validation to the voluntary use of native languages in the classroom. Now, for the first time, language rights were recognized as a civil right. Federally aided schools henceforth were legally obligated to provide special assistance to students with limited English-speak-

ing ability in overcoming their language difficulties. Furthermore, schools were told that children must not be denied full participation in the educational process while they were learning English. (p. 7)

Following the *Lau* ruling, a federal task force was appointed to develop guidelines, known as the *Lau Remedies*. These recommended that school districts establish bilingual education programs whenever there were 20 or more students of the same language group, with individual assessments of language proficiency determining students' eligibility for bilingual education assistance. The five *Lau* categories of language proficiency are:

1. Monolingual speaker of a language other than English; speaks this language exclusively.
2. Predominantly speaks the language other than English, although some English is spoken.
3. Bilingual, speaks both English and primary language with equal ease.
4. Predominantly speaks English, although not exclusively.
5. Monolingual speaker of English; speaks this language exclusively.

Designated program features included requirements that students be provided academic instruction in their native language, be provided instruction in their native culture, and that the design of these programs not result in segregated environments or "permanent tracks" for language-minority students. Further, instruction was to be responsive to the "different types of cognitive learning styles and incentive motivational styles—e.g., competitive v. cooperative learning patterns" (Office for Civil Rights, 1975, pp. 1–27).

While requiring structured instruction for the acquisition of English language skills, the *Lau Remedies* rejected the use of ESL (English as a Second Language) as the sole instructional technique. ESL is an approach that provides for isolated second-language acquisition training in a setting that removes children from the academic classroom; in itself it does not provide for academic instruction in a language other than English and does not address affective or cultural dimensions.

Although intended only as guidelines, the *Lau Remedies* had the effect of mandating that bilingual-bicultural education programs be established. Concerns over the extent to which instruction must be provided bilingually led, in 1980, to an attempt to revise and clarify the *Lau Remedies* in a set of proposed government regulations. If passed, these would have replaced the existing guidelines with legal requirements. This factor, in combination with concerns over the potential costs of implementation, led to considerable opposition, and the proposed regulations were withdrawn in 1981 leaving the *Lau Remedies* in effect. However, some of the specificity of the *Lau Remedies* was diluted by the 1981 Federal Court ruling in the *Castaneda v. Pickard* case involving a school district in Texas. Under this ruling, the determination that a school district is meeting its obligations under *Lau* is based on three concerns: the pedagogical soundness of the program, the adequacy of the resources, and the effectiveness of the program. As a consequence, the OCR has shifted its emphasis in reviewing school district plans to a consideration of "evidence that they are likely to work, rather than on their consistency with the specified educational methods described in the *Lau Remedies*" (Rotberg, 1982).

Bilingual Education

The focus of federal legislation relative to bilingual education has been on transition programs as opposed to maintenance programs. In the transition approach, the child's primary language is used for instructional purposes only until such time as English becomes a functional language for that child; in other words, bilingual instruction serves a purely transitional role. The alternate approach provides for maintenance and further development of the primary language simultaneously with the development of English language skills. The rationale for this can be found in Cummins's (1981) theory of Common Underlying Proficiency, which holds that concepts developed in either language promote overall cognitive development and linguistic competence. Therefore, continued development of the primary language not only promotes academic learning in that language, it facilitates later linguistic and academic proficiency in the second language. This interpretation is in contradiction to earlier interpretations that viewed the continuation of a primary language as harmful to the development of the new or secondary language. This Separate Underlying Proficiency model of bilingual proficiency viewed the two sets of linguistic abilities as separate entities, wherein the speaking of one language led to the decline of the other. The two balloon model in Figure 13.1a suggests that each entity must be developed separately. Hence, time spent on one language is time not spent on the other, with anything learned in the first language having to be relearned in the second. In contrast, the Common Underlying Proficiency model of Cummins is depicted in Figure 13.1b as a single balloon, with experience in either language promoting the development of the proficiency underlying both languages.

According to this theory, continued development of the primary language not only does not interfere with the development of the second language, but facilitates the development of the concepts and understandings required for the cognitive-academic learning proficiency required for most academic tasks. A major criticism of transitional approaches has been that the academic development of students is curtailed when they are switched into English-only instruction before developing adequate English-language skills. Their second language proficiency may be at the level required for interpersonal communications, where there are many context clues (e.g., expressions, gestures, illustrations, concreteness of situation, interpersonal feedback), but not at the level required for the cognitive-academic learning of literacy skills. If they are not permitted to continue learning in their primary language, their development of a sound conceptual and information base suffers.

Although much of Cummins's work is based on bilingual education studies performed in Canada and other countries, other recent reports also provide data

Figure 13.1

Bilingual Proficiency

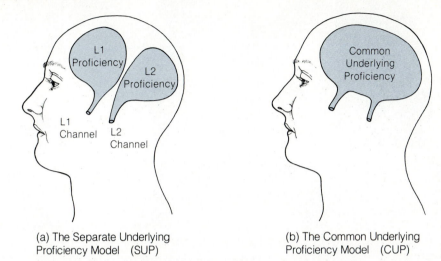

(a) The Separate Underlying
Proficiency Model   (SUP)

(b) The Common Underlying
Proficiency Model   (CUP)

Source: From "The role of primary language development in promoting educational success for language minority students" in *Schooling and Language Minority Students: A Theoretical Framework* by J. Cummins (Sacramento: California State Department of Education, 1981). Reprinted by permission.

supportive of the benefits of bilingual instruction. A meta-analysis of bilingual education effectiveness studies reported that, although bilingual education has been badly served by poorly designed research, in every instance of well designed studies the data demonstrated that children in bilingual programs averaged higher than the comparison children on criterion measures. Tempes (1984) reported that school districts are demonstrating that Spanish-speaking children who receive initial academic instruction in the primary language demonstrate grade-level academic achievement in English by the middle elementary grades. Benefits for initial primary language development and instruction may also accrue for handicapped students. Bilingual instruction has been reported as at least equally effective as instruction delivered in the primary language with low-IQ students (Genesee, 1976) and with learning disabled students (Bruck, 1978) in the Canadian French-immersion programs. Similar benefits have been reported for Spanish-speaking children provided bilingual education programs at elementary school levels (Sanua, 1975; Sirota, 1976) and in preschool programs (Askins et al., 1978; Evans, 1974). To date, reports and opinions relative to the benefits of bilingual education approaches for handicapped students have been limited to the milder levels of intellectually handicapping conditions.

Hispanic children enjoy books in Spanish as well as in English as part of their school's bilingual education program.

Many theorists and researchers maintain that there are inherent advantages to bilingualism itself. These include a more analytic orientation to linguistic input, greater sensitivity to linguistic feedback cues, enhanced ability to analyze ambiguities in sentence structure, and greater cognitive and verbal flexibility and originality (Ben-Zeev, 1977; Cummins, 1978; Cummins & Gulutsen, 1974; Cummins & Mulcahy, 1978; Feldman & Shen, 1971). In other words, bilingual approaches are supported both because they facilitate continued academic learning and because they may improve overall cognitive functioning. In addition, some authorities have stressed the affective benefits of continued primary language instruction for students with limited English proficiency. Benefits for nonhandicapped students have been reported in regard to low anxiety (Stevick, 1976), positive motivation (Gardner & Lambert, 1972), and self-confidence (Krashen, 1981; Wong-Fillmore, 1979). It has been suggested that similar results might accrue for handicapped students (Kiraithe, 1982; Langdon & Parker, 1982).

The push for bilingual education has been motivated by sociopolitical considerations as well as educational ones. The major impetus for bilingual education has come from citizens of Mexican-American and Puerto Rican backgrounds, not immigrants from Europe, Asia, or other continents. Bilingual education is viewed by Hispanic groups as both an avenue to educational equality and as a means of maintaining their cultural identities. Similarly, the spread of bilingualism to reservation schools is closely linked to Indian interests in establishing and strengthening their political sovereignty. Changes in the political climate of this nation are reflected by changes in public policy. By 1981, changes in presidential administrations resulted in the downplaying of bilingual education. At the present time, bilingual/bicultural education appears to be characterized by political and financial confusion, with local school district policies ambivalent and indecisive (King, 1981). The renewed national interest in academic achievement, coupled with the apparent decline in governmental interest in civil rights and equity issues, may signal that we are at a juncture where data demonstrating the academic advantages of bilingual education would have unprecedented potential for influencing public policy in this area.

SPECIAL EDUCATION FOR THE CULTURALLY DIVERSE

A large number of issues and considerations impinge on the provision of special education to ethnic minority group children. These include (1) the extent to which representation in special education is proportional; (2) the appropriateness of the identification, assessment, and placement procedures; (3) the lack of a sufficient database upon which to select placement configurations that will best serve the educational needs of culturally diverse handicapped children; (4) deficiencies in curriculum practices; and (5) the availability of culturally sensitive and/or bilingual special education teachers.

Past Practices

Within the recent past, it was common to find dramatic overrepresentation of minority children in special education programs for the handicapped, particularly those designated as being for educable mentally retarded (EMR) children. The 1950s and 1960s was a period of remarkable growth and expansion for special education programs for the handicapped. In its zeal to serve those children who did not function well in regular educational settings, special education let itself become a dumping ground for culturally different and minority children. The failure of these children to perform well on English-language intelligence tests, in combination with classroom behaviors that did not meet the standards of the middle-class Anglo culture, resulted in their being identified as handicapped.

The civil rights movement of the 1960s led to an increased awareness of the inappropriateness of these practices. In what was to become one of the most influential single articles ever published in special education, Dunn (1968) called for a reexamination of special education. He wrote:

> A better education than special class placement is needed for socioculturally deprived children with mild learning problems who have been labeled educ-

able mentally retarded. . . . In my best judgment about 60–80% of the pupils taught by these teachers are from low status backgrounds, including Afro-American, American Indians, Mexicans, and Puerto Rican Americans; those from nonstandard English speaking, broken, disorganized, and inadequate homes; and children from other nonmiddle-class environments. It is my thesis that we must stop labeling these deprived children as mentally retarded. Furthermore, we must stop segregating them by placing them into our allegedly special programs. (pp. 5–6)

The following year, Johnson (1969) published an indictment against the educational system for its failure to provide meaningful programming for inner-city black students. He charged:

Special education is implicated for it has cheerfully accepted the charge with little or no scrutiny of either the faulty conception upon which the IQ is grounded or the sociocultural environment of its clientele. Special education has continued blithely initiating special classes, work study programs, resource rooms, and other stigmatizing innovations which blame the poor, black child for the failure of the dominant educational system. (p. 244)

That same year, a publication of the President's Committee on Mental Retardation (1969), entitled *The Six Hour Retarded Child,* documented that many minority group children were labeled as mentally retarded solely on the basis of school-related difficulties. Within their families and neighborhoods, these children frequently demonstrated very acceptable adaptive behavior. In other words, their behavior was "retarded" for only the six hours a day that they were in school. Adaptive behavior, defined as the "effectiveness or degree with which individuals meet the standards of personal independence and social responsibility expected for age and cultural group" (Grossman, 1983, p. 1), became an increasingly important consideration in the labeling process. It is assumed that the use of dual criteria—adaptive behavior measures and intelligence test scores—result in a more valid diagnosis. The National Association for Retarded Citizens (1971) recommended that a child's adaptive behavior be assessed within the home, neighborhood, and school environments before applying the label of mental retardation.

Overrepresentation in special education typically has been reported for two groups, blacks and Hispanics. Mercer's (1973) study in Riverside, California, found the enrollment of blacks to be three times greater than their numbers in the general population and the enrollment of Hispanics four times that which would be predicted statistically. In Tempe, Arizona, enrollment figures suggested that, while 17.8 percent of the total school population was Mexican-American, 67.7 percent of the enrollments in EMR classes and 46.3 percent of the enrollments in classes for the trainable mentally retarded (TMR) were Mexican-American (Kirp, 1973).

Within California, one response to concerns over inappropriate placement was the shift from traditional categorization of handicapped children (educable mentally retarded, learning disabled, and behaviorally disordered) to the more generic, cross-categorical designation of "learning handicapped." Later data in that state, however, suggested that black and Hispanic children continued to be overrepresented in classes for EMR students (California State Board of Education, 1979). Although the overall number of children placed in EMR classrooms in California decreased substantially, the proportion of Hispanic to non-Hispanic remained the same (Lambert, 1981).

It is estimated that somewhere between 8 and 10 percent of all school-age children require special education, but data collected by the Office of Civil Rights found that approximately one-third of minority group children are placed in special education (Killalea Associates, 1980). Black children, who comprised 15.7 percent of the study population, were reported as being overrepresented in classes for the EMR (38%), TMR (27%), and seriously emotionally disturbed (24%). There were notable regional differences as well. In southern states, where black children comprised 26.8 percent of the total school population, they accounted for 60 percent of the EMR population. Hispanic students appeared to be proportionately represented in special education classes nationally, but were overrepresented in some states, namely California, New Mexico, Texas, Arizona, and Colorado. This overrepresentation was found in EMR, TMR, severe learning disability, and speech impaired categories. Nationwide, both blacks and Hispanics were underrepresented in programs for gifted and talented students. Asian-American children presented quite a different picture. Constituting approximately 1 percent of the total school population, they were found also to comprise 1 percent of the enrollment in programs for the handicapped, but 3 percent of the enrollment in gifted and talented programs.

In many regions throughout the country, it appears that school personnel are achieving proportional representation of ethnic and racial minorities in classes for the EMR (Tucker, 1980). However, as Tucker has noted, this may result in increasing the proportion of minorities being placed in classes for the learning disabled. Possible explanations for this include the vague LD eligibility requirements and the greater social acceptability of the learning disabilities label. In a large school district in the Southwest, for example, blacks and Hispanics were less likely to be diagnosed as EMR than were Anglos (Argulewicz, 1983). However, Hispanics were most likely to be found in LD classroom placements and least likely to be placed in EH (or behaviorally disordered/emotionally disturbed) placements. Mid-SES blacks had the lowest placement probabilities of all, possibly a function of black resistance to special education placements in general.

Within the past few years, there has been growing concern that there may be underrepresentation in other categorical programs (Bergin, 1980; Sedo, 1978). Sensitivity to past practices of overidentification and inappropriate placement into special education has led to a reluctance on the part of many educators, administrators as well as teachers, to refer culturally different children for special education placement. The lack of bilingual special education programs, teachers, and curricula are additional factors that may contribute to this reluctance. These teachers and administrators may opt to leave limited English proficient (LEP) children with learning difficulties in bilingual education classes where they at

JUANITA

Juanita, an only child, was born in Los Angeles seven years ago, a few months after her mother emigrated to this country from Mexico. The school has no information about Juanita's natural father, but her stepfather adopted Juanita shortly after her birth and, despite a separation from Juanita's mother, maintains an active interest in the child. Juanita's mother, educated in Mexico and essentially monolingual in Spanish, now works as a waitress. The financial strains of single parenthood led her to hold as many as three jobs at one time, a situation that resulted in Juanita's alternating her time between living in Mexico with her grandmother and in Los Angeles with her mother. Both parents as well as the grandmother speak to Juanita primarily in Spanish, although her stepfather has taught the child some English vocabulary.

Juanita began her schooling in Mexico while living with her grandmother. Her disruptive behavior resulted in the decision to return Juanita to her mother for the last two months of that school year, at which time she was placed in a bilingual kindergarten. Early the next fall, her teacher referred the girl to special education primarily because of the extremely disruptive classroom behavior she evidenced. Before assessment procedures could be completed, however, Juanita once again went to Mexico. When she returned to L.A. toward the end of February that year, special education assessment proceedings were reinitiated, with her teacher again noting both academic and social difficulties. At school Juanita yelled in the classroom, refused to follow directions, and occasionally hit other children.

In addition to the school concerns, at this time Juanita's mother requested assistance in managing her child's behavior at home. She reported that Juanita regularly grabbed her mother's keys when they got into the car, refusing to give them back. She also released the emergency brake in the car, stole from her mother's purse, failed to respond to direc-

tion, yelled and screamed at her mother and other adults, wet her bed, and ate from strangers' plates in restaurants. The mother identified the stealing, the noncompliance, and the bedwetting as the most troublesome behaviors.

During assessment, Juanita was found to speak a garbled, almost incomprehensible babytalk in which she mixed English and Spanish. She was not proficient in English or in her primary language, Spanish. She could pantomine responses more adeptly than give expressive verbal labels. She attained a *Leiter* IQ score of 68 and demonstrated few academic readiness skills. The IEP team agreed that the most appropriate placement for Juanita was in a special day class where the teacher was prepared to implement a highly structured behavior management system and provide an experiential enrichment program. Although the teacher was not bilingual (no bilingual special education teachers were available at that level), she does have some proficiency in Spanish and has a half-time classroom aide who is fully proficient in Spanish. In addition, Juanita attends the bilingual kindergarten part of each day for development of preacademic concepts in her primary language. She also receives some ESL training each week. While prereading skills are provided in Spanish in the bilingual education program, the special education teacher is teaching Juanita survival reading skills (e.g., stop signs, etc.) in English. The focus of the special education instruction is on broadening Juanita's experiences, utilizing the classroom aide to provide Spanish labels for these experiences. The development of basic concepts in Spanish should facilitate her later acquisition of English language skills.

One of the first tasks of the special education teacher, of course, was to decelerate Juanita's disruptive and noncompliant behaviors. The teacher adapted her classroom token economy to address Juanita's specific behaviors, utilizing behavior charts, "smiley faces," praise, and the opportunity to watch selected videotapes. The high level of interest shown by Juanita's mother facilitated effective home-school communication and the establishment of similar behavior management procedures in the home. Recognizing the seriousness of her daughter's problems, the mother was able to find a single job so that she could spend more time with her daughter. With counseling from the teacher, the mother became more consistent and firm in her expectations relative to Juanita's behavior. Not only did Juanita earn special treats at home for acceptable behavior, but acceptable home behavior was reinforced at school by permitting Juanita to participate in selected favorite activities.

At the end of the school year, the IEP team determined that Juanita should remain in essentially the same placement for the following year. They anticipate that, after this additional year of special day class placement, she may be ready for a less restrictive placement into a bilingual first grade with resource teacher support.

least understand the language. Inadequacies in assessment procedures have made it difficult to differentiate cultural/language differences from mild learning handicaps. A 1978 survey of Massachusetts school districts found that only 4.5 percent of the bilingual population had been placed in special education or identified as needing special education services and these typically were served in the most restrictive, least mainstreamed settings (Landurand, 1980). Baca and Chinn (1982) refer to several cases in the state of New York as further evidence of a shift of emphasis from overinclusion of minorities in special education to underinclusion.

A comprehensive study of service delivery patterns for bilingual handicapped children in California suggests that, at least for language minority children, disproportionate representation may be a regional, not a national, phenomenon (Cegelka, Rodriguez, Lewis, & Pacheco, 1984). This survey found that students identified for bilingual education were generally proportionately represented in special education. A comparison of special education prevalence rates for the various language groups (Spanish, Vietnamese, Cantonese, Korean, Filipino/Tagalog, and others) among the total limited English proficient (LEP) population also revealed no significant differences. For only one analysis were any significant differences found: when specific handicapping conditions were examined, underrepresentation of LEP students was found in the categories of seriously emotionally disturbed and other health impaired. There were no significant differences among LEP representation and that of the general school population for any other category of handicap served in special education.

The extent to which similar data might be found in other states and regions, or the reasons for representational equity in California are not known. As the defendant in much of the class-action litigation concerning biases in special education assessment, identification, and placement, it may be that California has taken particular care to deal with these issues. The disparity between the California data, the data reported for Massachusetts, national data, and practices alleged in court cases in New York suggests that caution must be exercised in generalizing from one region to another, from one ethnic or minority group to another, from one special education category to another, and from one time period to another.

Identification

Concerns over identification problems have most typically focused on the instrumentation and procedures utilized in the assessment of culturally diverse children. Tests for determining the level of language proficiency and language dominance of LEP children have been criticized as being inadequate and unreliable. Critics have alleged that many of the IQ tests and other measures utilized for determining eligibility for special education placement are invalid and biased for use with this group. Bias can be said to occur in the schools whenever educational decisions are inappropriately influenced by the race, culture, economic background, or disability of a child (Bailey & Harbin, 1980).

Since about 1970, a large number of class-action cases have focused on the extent to which such biases have resulted in overrepresentation of minority group children in special education. Judicial decisions in these cases have found that the rights of children were abridged both by the use of biased tests and by failure to provide for adequate parental representation in the decision-making process. Table 13.1 summarizes the major court cases and their findings.

In education, assessment is the process of collecting data to assist professionals in making decisions concerning the appropriate delivery of services to students. Assessment is but one step in the multifaceted decision-making process. The potential for bias and error exists at each step and decision point, from referral to testing and test interpretation, to program placement, instructional delivery, and program evaluation (Oakland, 1980). Table 13.2 summarizes bias in assessment. Formal testing is but one part of the assessment procedure, albeit an important one. While there is widespread agreement that "assessment instruments should be nondiscriminatory in terms of ethnicity and culture, administered in the language of the child, and validated for the purpose for which they are used, the available technology does not always permit this" (Lynch & Lewis, 1982, p. 96). Many frequently used tests have been criticized as being technically inadequate for use with culturally diverse populations. Concerns have focused on the normative groups used for standardizing some tests, the culturally specific content, the language prerequisites, and the limited sociocultural context (e.g., only school behavior) of assessment procedures. Some critics have called for a moratorium on all standardized testing until identified problems can be corrected. Less extreme strategies to reduce bias include utilization of translators as well as the formal translation and/or renorming of existing English language tests; the development of new tests; the creation of culture-free tests, culture-fair tests, and culture-specific tests; the use of criterion-referenced tests as well as adaptive behavior measures; the use of Piagetian tasks; training children to take tests; and the development of pluralistic norms.

One widely employed strategy involves the oral translation of English-language tests as they are administered. If a bilingual examiner is not available, a translator may assist during the testing process. While such translations are better than nothing, there are many problems with them. These include the lack of word equivalencies among languages, differences in relative frequency of word usage from one language to another, regional variations in the meanings of some words,

Table 13.1

Court Cases

Year	Court Cases	Issue	Resolution
1970	Diana v. Board of Education of California	Class-action suit on behalf of Mexican-American children (Spanish speaking) placed in classes for EMR on basis of English language tests.	Out-of-court stipulated agreement requiring testing in primary language, retesting and re-evaluation of those already placed in special education, review of proportional representation in special ecation, and cultural-fair testing procedures.
1971	Covarubias v. San Diego Unified School District	Class-action suit on behalf of all minorities (focused on black and Mexican-American groups) wrongfully placed in special education.	Parental notification in home language required with right to challenge placement.
1972	Guadalupe Organization v. Tempe Elementary School	Yaqui Indian and Mexican-American children placed in EMR classes on basis of English language IQ tests.	Out-of-court agreement stipulated that children must score at least two standard deviations below norm on IQ tests to be placed in EMR classes, nontest evaluations required, re-evaluation in primary language, and parental notification prior to special education placement.
1975	Larry P. v. Wilson Riles	Six black students in San Francisco public schools placed on basis of intelligence test scores.	Ruling that IQ tests were culturally biased; moratorium placed on use of IQ tests; re-evaluation of students relative to eligibility and placement required; mandate for employment of minority group school psychologists.

the lack of equivalence of some concepts, and syntax difficulties. Fluent translators are difficult to come by, and even then the dialect of the translator may not be the dialect of the student. Further, translation of a test does not change the extent to which the standardization sample is or is not reflective of an individual

Table 13.2

Bias in Assessment

Prior to Assessment

Referral and Screening	Teacher bias and prejudice can lead to either overreferral or underreferral of members of particular groups.
Test Norms	The standardization sample upon which a test has been normed may not reflect the sociocultural characteristics of the child to be assessed.
Test Reliability	An assessment instrument may have poor reliability, with little stability in scores from one administration to the next.
Test Validity	A test may not be a valid measure of the skill for which it is designed, or it may be used for other than its intended purpose.

Bias Points During Assessment

Child's Language Abilities	For children not proficient in standard English, results of English-language tests cannot be interpreted as indicative of child characteristics.
Test Wiseness	Some children are more "test-wise" than others, having developed test-taking behaviors that tend to optimize their performance.
Motivation, Anxiety, and Expectancy	Test results are affected by the extent to which the child being assessed is motivated to perform well, but whose anxiety over the testing situation does not interfere with test performance.
Cultural Differences	The acculturation experiences of an individual child may be qualitatively different from those of children included in the test's standardization sample.
Bias in Examiner Attitudes	Prejudice on the part of the examiner or teacher toward particular racial, ethnic, or social groups, toward particular types of behavior, or toward various home backgrounds can bias the placement decision.
Examiner Competence	A lack of technical competence in administering and scoring the test as well as the absence of cross-cultural sensitivity can adversely affect a child's test performance.

Bias After Assessment

No Intervention	Failure to provide appropriate educational interventions as indicated by the assessment results.
No Reexamination	Failure to reassess children, evaluate their progress, and reexamine intervention placements and procedures following initial.

Source: Adapted from T. Oakland (1980). Nonbiased Assessment of Minority Group Children. *Exceptional Education Quarterly, 1*(3), 31–46.

student. Finally, straightforward or literal test translations ignore basic cultural and linguistic differences.

Many of these same criticisms also apply to the development of translated versions of test instruments. This notwithstanding, there has been considerable activity in this area. For example, Spanish-language versions of both the *Brigance* inventories and the *Woodcock-Johnson Psycho-Educational Battery* are now commercially available. Just as with all other assessment devices, such versions are appropriate only with the specific subgroups upon which they were normed. Hence, the *Escala de Inteligencia Wechsler para Niños* developed in Puerto Rico as a Spanish translation of the 1949 *WISC* should be used only with Puerto Rican children, and the *Zimmerman Preschool Language Scale*, Spanish version, is appropriate only for use with Mexican-Americans. Failure to recognize this important point can lead to erroneous and even ludicrous practices, such as when California spent approximately $100,000 testing Chicano children with the *Inter-American Series*, a test originally developed on a Puerto Rican population sample (DeAvila, 1976).

Another strategy for eliminating bias involves the development of local test norms. This practice appears fair in that a child is compared only with children with similar opportunities and backgrounds. However, some view this approach as too provincial, restricting the generalizability of the information, and precluding meaningful predictions about the child relative to a broader context (Bailey & Harbin, 1980).

For years test developers attempted to eliminate assessment bias by minimizing the cultural and verbal components of tests. Of primarily historical interest today was the development of culture-free tests. Initially endorsed as a reasonable approach, it soon became apparent that, because all learning occurred within environmental or cultural contexts, it is impossible to develop learning measures free of cultural content. Attempts to develop culture-fair tests which included content from many cultures and did not differentiate the performance of individuals from various racial, ethnic, and SES groups also met with little success. They proved to have poor predictive validity within the context of monocultural school systems (Duffey, Salvia, Tucker, & Ysseldyke, 1981).

Performance tests, which are free of oral and written verbal responses, attempt to bypass the cultural bias of language-based or verbal measures. Frequently, psychologists will differentially weight the scores of performance measures and verbal measures, emphasizing the former as more indicative of actual intellectual functioning levels of nonmajority children. Some psychologists do not utilize verbal measures of intellectual ability with language-minority children, employing only performance measures such as the *Leiter International Performance Scale*, the *Ravens Progressive Matrices*, and the performance scale of the *WISC–R*. These attempts to eliminate bias have not been particularly satisfactory; various studies (Costello & Dickie, 1970; Gonzales, 1981) have suggested that such measures can discriminate against minority groups as often as verbal measures. As a certain amount of verbal mediation is required for the child to label task components and select alternatives, these so-called performance measures are not altogether nonverbal. Further, Cohen (1969) has suggested that the analytical approach required to problem solve on these tests favors the logical reasoning approaches fostered by the dominant, middle-class culture as opposed to the more non-analytical or relational cognitive styles typical of many other subgroups.

Criterion-referenced tests assess specific child behaviors in terms of a given standard of mastery, instead of some normative group. While these measures can provide information essential to identification/placement procedures, they, like normative measures, can contain wording or content that is culturally biased. Further, they are frequently too narrow in scope to suggest reasons for performance patterns. Adaptive behavior scales have also been advocated for use in identifying children as mentally retarded. However, the extent to which existing scales actually provide a more meaningful index of individual abilities has been questioned (Bailey & Harbin, 1980).

DeAvila (1976) has championed the use of a neo-Piagetian approach to the assessment of children from non-English speaking homes. Equivalence of performance on these measures by samples of Mexican-American and Anglo-American children led to the conclusion that the cognitive development of the groups was similar and that "the failure of Mexican American children to achieve in schools and to perform well on capacity and achievement measures must be attributed to reasons other than a presumed lack of cognitive ability..." (DeAvila, 1976, p. 98). Another group of psychologists has proposed that bias can be reduced through the use of procedures that measure a child's ability to improve test performance as a result of practice or training sessions (Feuerstein, 1979; Kunzelman & Koenig, 1976). Feurstein's *Learning Potential Assessment Device (LPAD)* includes problem-solving tasks with little cultural interference, thus appearing to be culturally nondiscriminatory. After initial testing, the student is instructed in those cognitive strategies identified as deficient and then retested, with the change in performance interpreted as an index of the student's learning potential. To date, it appears that neither this approach nor that proposed by DeAvila has been proven to meaningfully reduce bias in labeling and placement practices.

One widely known and popularized effort to develop a pluralistic approach to assessment is the *System of Multicultural Pluralistic Assessment (SOMPA)* developed by Mercer and Lewis (1978). This system involves utilization of existing adaptive behavior, personality, and intelligence measures along with several indices of medical status. Its *Adaptive Behavior Inventory for Children (ABIC)* provides a measure of social role performance and the *WISC–R* is used as an index of academic performance. The Estimated Learning Potential score compares the performance of the student to that of individuals from a similar sociocultural background. Despite widespread endorsement and use, concerns have recently been raised over lack of conceptual clarity and empirical support for the pluralistic norms and estimated learning potential (see *School Psychology Digest*, 1979, 8, pp. 1–2).

It may be that the search for a single test or procedure for measuring general ability that is equally applicable to all groups is too simplistic a response to a complex problem (Bailey & Harbin, 1980). Completely bias-free testing may be an unrealistic goal. Tests are in themselves cultural artifacts that necessarily must reflect the environment against which they measure performance (Adler, 1968). As testing constitutes a social interaction embedded within a cultural context (DeAvila, 1976), it follows that tests will reflect the differences in achievement of children who are culturally different (Cole, 1975). It may be that bias exists more in the use of the tests than in the tests themselves. Test data can be no more valid than the professional judgments made in applying them. Not only must we keep in mind areas of potential bias in using a test, we must also remember that tests are but one source of data in the educational decision-making process. When making decisions that can involve placement of a student into bilingual education, special education, or bilingual/special education programs, professionals must utilize all of the data available from all relevant sources.

An Integrated Approach

The extent to which identified educational problems are attributable to cultural and linguistic differences and the extent to which they are the function of true learning disorders must be determined if children are to receive appropriate educational programs. At the outset, there must be a determination of whether or not the child is to be considered limited English proficient, thereby qualifying for bilingual education services. Language proficiency levels, both oral and written, should be determined for each language used by the child or by members of the child's family. This process is complicated by the low reliability and dubious value of many language proficiency tests. Frequently the obtained scores are only accurate to plus or minus one standard deviation. In practice this means that a child scoring at the 4 level in English proficiency, suggesting that bilingual education is not necessary, may actually be functioning at a 3 level and need bilingual education support. In addition, states and districts may establish arbitrary standards for exiting students from bilingual education programs, a factor that can complicate placement considerations upon reevaluation.

Bernal and Tucker (1981) have described a screening-assessment process for Hispanic students that integrates many of the bilingual and special education considerations previously discussed. This model includes three phases which are explicated in the following paragraphs.

Phase 1: Informal Language Screening: Student/Home Language Questionnaire. The informal language screening of this phase centers primarily on a home-language questionnaire, with formal language assessment indicated when the child appears to have limited English proficiency or when questionnaire data suggest that a language other than English is spoken regularly in the home, even when the child appears to be proficient in English. Whenever a non-Anglo child is referred for special education assessment, a formal language assessment should occur.

Phase 2: Formal Language Assessment. Language proficiency tests are administered to all children referred through Phase 1. For Hispanic children in grades

3 through 12, achievement test data in language arts and possibly other areas are reviewed as well. Based on these data, the child should be assigned to one of the following categories:

1. *English proficient and English dominant or English monolingual.* When a child shows at least minimal proficiency in English and lower or no proficiency in Spanish, referral is made to the regular education screening/placement system.

2. *English proficient, balanced, or Spanish dominant bilingual.* Children who demonstrate at least minimal proficiency in both English and Spanish, may get placed in either regular education or bilingual education programs, depending on the philosophy of the district. After grade three, however, if the English proficient bilingual children are not achieving well in English language arts, they should be considered limited English proficient and provided bilingual education programming. A child who scores at the highest levels of proficiency for both English and Spanish should be screened for the gifted education programs.

3. *Spanish proficient LEP.* Children who are not at least minimally proficient in oral English (i.e., who do not obtain level 4 on the oral language proficiency test) but do demonstrate normal competence in oral Spanish (i.e., either level 4 or 5) should be referred to the bilingual education program, with data from English language achievement tests providing a basis for planning the alternative educational program.

4. *LEP, not Spanish proficient.* Students who do not demonstrate at least minimal oral proficiency in either English or Spanish should be referred for special education screening and assessment, described in Phase 3.

Phase 3: Multidisciplinary Assessment. Given the legal, ethical, and professional responsibilities of this phase, a detailed 4-step process is specified.

1. *Further determination of language dominance and proficiency.* When a bilingual student has been referred for special education assessment, a bilingual psychometrist experienced in language proficiency testing should administer an additional and different language assessment instrument to determine the relative levels of language functioning. For children who do not indicate normal proficiency in English, the level of proficiency for both languages should be determined, with a decision being made as to language dominance. Whether the child mixes or switches languages during conversation should be noted. If a child scores no better than a 2 level in either language, there may not be sufficient oral proficiency for testing to be conducted in either language; the examiner will have to consider using techniques which do not require much oral production.

2. *Obtain informed consent and select appropriate team members.* Consent forms should be published bilingually and may have to be presented orally to parents who cannot read in either language. At a minimum, the team should include: (a) a specialist in first and second language development/acquisition; (b) a specialist in the area or areas of suspected disability; (c)

a classroom teacher, either referring teacher or teacher in whose room child is currently placed; and (d) someone knowledgeable about the child's culture and family background.

3. *Conduct assessment: Counterindicators.* Interviews, adaptive behavior questionnaires or observation forms, and empirically verified systems to "correct" for bias in results of standardized tests should be used. If the data are counterindicative for a suspected disability, the child should be exempted from further testing for that specific problem. If counterindicators do not rule out certain exceptionalities, the residual set of suspected exceptionalities should be specified and the remaining assessment conducted as specified in Step 4.

4. *Conduct assessment: Indicators.* At this point, assessment will almost unavoidably include the use of instruments that are at least somewhat inappropriate for the linguistically different child and for whom standardized criteria may underestimate potential. These tests, administered in the child's dominant language, constitute a collection of tasks from which the examiner can make clinical judgments. Careful examination of patterns of items passed and failed provides a basis for judging whether or not student performance is indicative of the suspected handicap. One of the following decisions will be made:

   a. *Student is not handicapped.* If the pattern of test performance fails to indicate the suspected disability, the child should not be considered handicapped and should be placed into either the bilingual education or the regular class program, depending on language dominance and school philosophy.

   b. *Mildly handicapped.* A child whose pattern of performance indicates a mildly handicapping condition should be mainstreamed into either a bilingual education classroom or the regular education program, depending on language dominance and school philosophy. Special education support and resources, such as an IEP, periodic reviews of progress, and reassessment of status, should be provided.

   c. *Severe or profound handicap.* When indicators lead to this diagnosis, the child should be placed in the appropriate special education placement, with all special education provisions (IEP, periodic reviews, reassessment). The child's dominant language should be used for at least a portion of the special intervention.

The careful delineation of multiple steps and decision points described above are indicative of the caution that must be employed if valid and fair decision making is to occur. Through the judicious selection and application of tests that probe multiple abilities, the validity of identification-placement decisions affecting language minority students can be enhanced. Periodic reviews and reassessments can minimize the effects of misclassification and inappropriate placement when they do occur.

Issues surrounding the inappropriateness of identification and special education placement procedures for culturally diverse children have been the target of professional as well as judicial concern. In contrast, only recently has attention begun to be directed toward delivery of meaningful educational services for culturally diverse and/or LEP handicapped children. Once a student has been found eligible for special education and/or bilingual education services, decisions must be made relative to educational goals and objectives, placement of the student, and services to be provided. Within special education, a multidisciplinary IEP team is responsible for developing this program plan, specifying whether the student is to be served in a self-contained, resource, or itinerant program. For children with limited English proficiency, the designated district personnel responsible for bilingual education must determine/approve placement of the student into a bilingual education program. Bilingual education options vary considerably from district to district and state to state, but they typically range from part-day to full-day classes, depending on the level of language proficiency of the individual student. Teachers for these classes not only should be bilingual themselves, but they should have special training/credentials in bilingual education if they are to adequately provide for the academic instruction and affective development of children who are in the process of acquiring proficiency in a second language. In those instances where there are too few students (usually less than 10) of a particular language group for a school district to establish a bilingual education class, an Individualized Learning Plan (ILP) may be developed for the student in the English language classroom. Typically, the ILP will include provisions for ESL instruction, for basic skills/academic subjects delivered in the primary language, and for promoting a positive self-image and crosscultural understanding. In a study of 104 school districts in California, approximately half the bilingual handicapped students were served by both special education and bilingual education, with most of the remaining students being served by one program but not the other (Cegelka et al., 1984). Table 13.3 depicts these data.

School districts may choose to modify the IEP to include the specific requirements of the ILP. To do this, the following ILP requirements would have to be added to the IEP format:

1. *The identification assessment in English.*
2. *The diagnostic assessment in the primary language.*
3. *A designation of the pupil's strongest language for basic skills/subject matter instruction.*
4. *English language development, content instruction in the primary language to sustain academic achievement, and activities to promote a positive self-image and crosscultural understanding.*
5. *Sufficient bilingual teachers and aides.*

Table 13.3	
Educational Placements of LEP Handicapped Students in California	
Placement	*Mean Percentage of Students*
Special Education (only)	26.3
Bilingual Education (only)	7.6
Bilingual Individual Learning Plan (only)	16.0
Special Education and Bilingual Education (both)	49.4
Regular Class (only)	.7

6. *Parental option to withdraw the pupil upon written request.*
7. *Provision for reclassification to FEP fluent English speaker status and English-only instruction, if and when it is appropriate.*
   (Langdon & Parker, 1982, p. 61)

The IEP committee for the limited English proficient handicapped student should have at least one member who is proficient in the primary language of the child and/or parents. While it is preferable for this to be a bilingual educator who is familiar with the student, it frequently is a translator who is not a credentialed educator. IEP forms should be available whenever possible in the primary language of the child, and the IEP itself should be developed in (or translated into) that language as well. To ensure due process and informed parental consent, all written information about special education placements and due process rights, including notifications of meetings, should be provided in the parent's primary language. The additional precaution of providing oral presentation of this same information may be necessary for those LEP parents who are not literate in their primary language. Throughout these processes, special educators should be sensitive to cultural differences that may affect parental interactions with school personnel.

A variety of placement or service delivery configurations are possible for the LEP handicapped child. The primary placement for a mildly handicapped student might be a self-contained special education program, a regular classroom with resource "pull-out" support, or a bilingual education classroom with special education resource support. Any of these options could be taught by a bilingual teacher; if this is not the case, then for all but the last option, some form of bilingual education support (partial day program, ILP, ESL, etc.) should be provided as well as special education services.

For moderately and severely handicapped individuals, a self-contained special education placement is likely. Where these programs are not taught by a bilingual special education teacher, then appropriate bilingual education services should

Educational Programs for Handicapped, Limited English Proficient Students

An ideal school program for children who are both handicapped and limited in English proficiency would feature a number of elements not frequently found in today's educational programs. Among these would be a full complement of bilingual multicultural personnel, including psychologists, administrators, clerical and janitorial staff, teachers, and teachers' aides. There would be a well articulated interface among regular education, bilingual education, and special education, with collaborative planning, staff teaming, and inservice training of teachers.

The specially trained bilingual school psychologists would utilize a variety of nonbiased assessment procedures and instruments after the bilingual teacher had already employed several alternative instructional approaches in an attempt to address the learning difficulties leading to the special education referral. Adequate numbers of bilingual regular class teachers, remedial instruction teachers, special day class teachers, resource teachers, speech and language specialists, designated instructional services personnel, and school social workers would be available at each school site. There would be school-based professional staff for all the major language groups while, for less frequently occurring languages, itinerant specialists supported by bilingual aides would facilitate educational programming.

A full range of special education, regular education, and bilingual educational placement options and support services would be available from which to choose and all would feature culturally sensitive instructional approaches and a variety of curriculum materials in English as well as in other languages. For those children whose dominant language is not English, bilingual instruction would be available at least through the primary grades and English as a second language (ESL) training would be offered from mid-primary through high school. Secondary programs would feature transitional bilingual instruction, particularly in reading and language arts.

Across the district there would be a carefully structured approach to home-school communication, with parent facilitators (parents of handicapped children who are employed by the school district to serve as liaisons with other parents of similar ethnic/linguistic backgrounds) actively involved in both home visits and school meetings. IEP team meetings would be scheduled at times that parents were most able to attend, with childcare being provided as necessary. A parent facilitator would participate, as well as other members of the community selected by the parent. Explanatory materials and IEP forms would be printed in the language of the parent and strategies would be employed to elicit meaningful input from the parents at all assessment, program planning, and child placement steps. The IEP would be developed in both English and the language of the parent, with both first and second language acquisition goals as well as cultural appreciation goals being included along with the other special educational goals and objectives. Annual evaluations of student progress would include assessment of language proficiency as well as academic progress in both the native language and English.

be provided by a qualified professional support person. While bilingual aides may be found in both special education and regular education classes to assist in this regard, the bilingual components of the program should be designed and monitored by a fully-credentialed professional educator.

The low number of bilingual special education teachers currently available requires that bilingual education and special education personnel carefully coordinate their educational service delivery efforts to meet the needs of the handicapped LEP student. While many universities are currently developing bilingual special education teacher preparation education programs, it is unlikely that in the foreseeable future it will be possible to train/retrain sufficient numbers of personnel to serve as bilingual special education teachers. At the very least, however, all preservice and inservice personnel preparation efforts in special education should be directed toward making all teachers at least multicultural in their orientations. This means that they should understand both overt and covert aspects of culture, be sensitive to subtle cultural differences, be familiar with culturally associated characteristics (perceptual, cognitive, social, affective, and learning), and understand basic precepts of bilingualism and second-language acquisition. Various listings of multicultural/special education teacher competencies have been developed in recent years (Bergin, 1980; Prieto, Rueda, & Rodriguez, 1981) and a program guide for refocusing special education teacher preparation efforts to emphasize cultural diversity is now available (Meyen, Rodriguez, & Erb, n.d.).

Educational Programming

The provision of appropriate and effective education for students who are exceptional as well as culturally/linguistically diverse is one of the greatest challenges facing special education in this decade. To date, the crucial issues of the actual design and delivery of culturally/linguistically appropriate special education have received little systematic attention. When addressed at all, the focus has been on developing an awareness of the discontinuities that may exist between home and school learning. While this may be an important step toward sensitizing teachers to cultural pluralism, it does not designate particular curricular practices as appropriate. Research on culturally related learning characteristics is somewhat contradictory, can lead to unwarranted stereotyping, and was conducted on nonexceptional populations of students—all of which make its implications for special educational instructional practices problematic. Further, even for regular class instruction, little is known about how practices should be adapted to account for documented cultural differences. In reviewing bilingual education practices in California, Berke (1982) noted that "while the state's bilingual education legislation prescribes in great detail how students are to be identified and assessed, the qualifications their teachers must have, and the proportion of students that shall exist in the classroom, etc., almost no prescriptions regarding curriculum exist in California . . . no widely held linguistic philosophy, other than the self-evident virtue of bilingualism is apparent" (p. 30). There is little assistance available, either in the professional literature or from commercial vendors of materials, that supports teachers in their attempts to deliver culturally appropriate special education.

A critical component to providing appropriate educational services is the utilization of instructional materials that are linguistically and culturally relevant. However, few such materials exist (Chinn, 1979a; Cegelka & Pacheco, 1984), possibly because curriculum developers have viewed the categories of handicaps as the basic variables for curriculum differentiation. Curricular materials appropriate for use with culturally diverse exceptional children include materials written in the primary language of the student, materials that are written bilin-

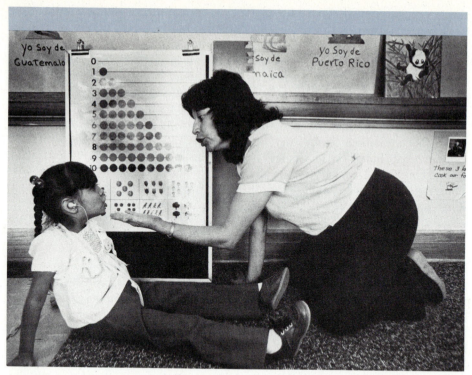

A hearing-impaired child with limited English proficiency receives instruction in a bilingual education program with a bilingual special education teacher and aide.

gually, and/or materials that, regardless of the language in which they are written, reflect the cultural values and the cultural learning styles of the student. Cegelka and Pacheco (1984) offer the following recommendations for developing and analyzing instructional materials for culturally diverse exceptional students:

1. The material should depict various dimensions of culture, including explicit culture (dress, diet, artistic/literature expressions, folklore, heroes) and implicit culture (values, beliefs, attitudes, tradition, mores, goals).
2. The material should reflect the pluralistic nature of our society, emphasizing cultural differences as positive traits.
3. The material should depict various cultures as dynamic and vital, as cultures where individuals can grow, be nourished, and be enriched as unique human beings.
4. Dialectic variations should be presented on an equal basis with the "standard" language.
5. The content and illustrations should avoid stereotyping and present a variety of role expectations for all groups.
6. Positive role models should be provided, e.g., minorities and women and disabled individuals are shown as leaders as well as followers and as characters with ideas and initiative.

7. The material should present all groups as being valuable without debasing one group relative to another, and present several role options for all groups.
8. The diversity of individual experience within a group should be adequately represented in terms of social class and religious and political preference.
9. Religious beliefs, symbols, and ceremonies should be presented in a nonderogatory or nondemeaning manner.
10. Historical events should be presented accurately and with attention to the contributions and perspectives of all groups.

Despite their importance, Chinn (1979a) reported difficulty in locating special education curricula developed for culturally diverse groups. Although over 100 assessment instruments have been identified (Oakland & Matuszek, 1977), a comprehensive search of computer databases yielded only a limited number of program descriptions and instructional strategies. No ethnic studies designed for culturally diverse handicapped students were located, although there have been multicultural educational programs designed to sensitize all students to cultural similarities and differences (Garcia, 1978). Chinn concluded that the "absence of literature pertaining to specific curricula and instructional strategies for culturally diverse exceptional children suggests that either they do not exist or that the isolated curricula and strategies that do exist have not been published or disseminated" (p. 50). A study designed to determine the extent to which noncommercial materials had been developed locally or regionally for use with exceptional children from Mexican-American and Asian-American backgrounds polled over 700 school districts, state departments of education, regional centers, research projects, and individual professionals (Cegelka & Pacheco, 1984). Results suggested that only a limited number of locally developed materials were available for use by others, and that most of these were reading and language development materials. Further, the study found no consistent pattern nationally as to the commercial curriculum materials utilized with these groups. Of the 89 commercial materials listed by respondents, only five were listed by five or more respondents.

By and large, special education curriculum practices are monolithic in terms of race, ethnicity, and culture. It appears that at present teachers must rely upon their own personal resources in providing culturally relevant instruction, from interpreting what is relevant and appropriate to designing strategies for delivering that instruction. To accomplish this, both inservice and preservice preparation of teachers must include strong components of multicultural considerations. Aragon (1973) asserted that "the true impediment of cultural pluralism is that we have culturally deficient educators attempting to teach culturally different children" (p. 78). In a similar vein, Rodriguez (1982) has suggested that "at the most basic level, the reason that bilingual exceptional children will be unable to achieve educational normalization is that at present trained personnel capable of dealing with the diverse educational needs of this group do not exist" (p. 45). Hence, it becomes even more important that special education teachers who are not bilingual develop the cultural sensitivity to work effectively with children from diverse backgrounds. Sensitivity to cultural differences is a prerequisite to valid professional practice (Hilliard, 1980). Ways must be found to address the values, attitudes, and aspirations of specific minority groups if the information and skills taught are to be meaningful to the culturally diverse student. Brode and Rodgers (cited in Plata, 1979) listed the following questions as important considerations in designing educational programs.

1. What are the attitudes modeled in the home toward academically related activities? Are there differences in attitudes (a) between socioeconomic classes within the ethnic community; (b) related to regional differences; and/or (c) as a function of length of U.S. residency?
2. What crosscultural conflicts might arise in teacher-pupil, teacher-parent, and/or pupil-pupil interactions in relationship to cognitive styles, social customs, value systems, and religious beliefs?
3. What are the common language barriers between the primary language and English that the students will face in the school curriculum (for example, for Spanish speakers, the differentiation of *i* and *e*, *ch* and *sh*, *b* and *v*)?
4. What psychological effects might the language barrier or bilingualism have on the students?
5. What teacher traits (psychological, emotional, and personality) are necessary in order to successfully teach the culturally diverse student?

A very important unresolved issue revolves around the question of which language should be used in instructing handicapped LEP children. In a study of communication disorders in LEP children in California, Carpenter (1983) recommended the study of the relative benefits of speech-language therapy conducted in English as opposed to the home language of the child. She questioned the notion that therapy can be conducted similarly with such children as with monolingual English-speaking students merely given interpreters and translated materials. Carpenter also recommended research to determine the minimum non-English language proficiency levels required by teachers and other instructional personnel to use the language effectively for instructional purposes.

Although insufficient research has been completed to demonstrate the preferability of either English-only or bilingual instruction for handicapped students who are limited English proficient, there exists considerable support for bilingual instruction. This is due, in part, to the recognition that problems may arise when "minority children from working-class homes are forced to accept instruction in the foreign, majority, middle-class language, and their own language has low prestige, both in the society and in the school" (Skutnabb-Kangas, 1979, p. 17). This has led to the conclusion that the affective benefits of instruction in the primary language are a primary consideration; academic success can be better facilitated through instruction in the most familiar language.

Expert opinion tends to support acquisition approaches where language is learned through usage as opposed to approaches involving the formal study or conscious learning of the language. Further, because data with nonhandicapped students indicate that it takes from five to seven years for language minority students to approach age-level norms in acquiring academic learning proficiency levels in English, it would appear that bilingual education support should be available for handicapped students throughout their educational program. At the secondary school level, students who have been receiving bilingual special educational services will continue to need this support if they are to acquire full English language proficiency; at the same time, additional students newly arrived in this country will also require bilingual special education services. For special education teachers who are not bilingual, strategies will have to be developed to facilitate their delivery of instruction to bilingual exceptional students. One set of such instructional strategies for the monolingual teacher of LEP students is presented in Table 13.4 (page 580).

While these suggestions, as well as others, appear to have some face validity and may provide direction for the practitioner who cannot wait for research data on instructional effectiveness, instructional delivery approaches for culturally/linguistically diverse exceptional children are essentially without either a well-articulated theoretical base or a convincing database. As succinctly summarized by Carpenter (1983):

> [We] do not know what kinds of educational programs will be most beneficial for LEP handicapped children. We are not sure how to assess these children in ways that yield maximum information for program planning. We do not know if our (educational) technology is adequate, given appropriately trained staff to implement it. And, conversely, we do not know, given such staff, if our technology is sufficiently adequate to impact on their educational lives. We do not know if different languages of instruction lead to different educational outcomes, and we are not even sure what the expected outcomes are or should be. (pp. 45–46)

FUTURE PERSPECTIVES FOR MULTICULTURAL SPECIAL EDUCATION

The influence of social and political trends on educational programs is always great. Given the political undertones of much of the bilingual education movement, this fact has important implications for the future of bilingual education mandates in this nation. During more conservative political eras, the notion of promoting and protecting the rights of minority groups becomes less compelling, with governmental energies being directed more toward facilitating the productive majority, assuming that the less enfranchised minority groups will also benefit. It is not surprising then that, under the conservative presidential administration of the 1980s, bilingual education came under attack. The emphasis shifted from bilingual instructional programs to those with a heavier ESL emphasis. At the same time, cuts in federal funding support for bilingual education have served to refocus program emphases to some degree. These efforts notwithstanding, in many locations bilingual education continues to develop and grow.

Table 13.4

Teaching a Bilingual Lesson

1. Develop a bilingual vocabulary list of 10–30 key words.
2. Summarize in English and the native language the key concepts of the lesson.
3. Utilize the bilingual aide or volunteer for preparation of written materials, tape recording, and classroom translations.
4. Prepare a few relevant English sentences that utilize the key words and concepts. The concepts should not be simplified, but the teacher should avoid conditional phrases and other complex grammatical structures. Concrete examples should be identified so as to increase the context relevance of the lesson.
5. Prepare written and tape recorded presentations in both English and the primary language of the key words and relevant sentences. This is a key role for the bilingual aide or volunteer who works with the teacher with limited English proficient students.
6. Practice pronouncing the translation from the tape. Even with the availability of a bilingual aide or volunteer, the teacher should attempt to use the student's native language as a means of indicating acceptance and recognition of the value of that language.
7. Have the bilingual students read the key word and relevant sentence lists in both languages while listening to the tape and then alone.
8. Keep classroom language constant and ask oral questions that do not require an extensive knowledge of English grammar (e.g., "Is this a _____ ?" "What is this?").
9. When questioning students, begin with *yes/no* questions, then proceed to *wh*- questions.
10. Use actions and concrete examples to reinforce oral statements.
11. Using the prepared English sentences, orally substitute native-language words for the English words (e.g., "The weather is _____ [frio].")
12. Provide oral and written instructions for each day's assignment.
13. When assigning silent reading, put the material on tape (either in English or the student's native language).
14. Plan group projects so that peer modeling and cooperative learning can be utilized.
15. Plan both verbal and nonverbal activities in each lesson and limit the amount of time spent on class discussions.
16. Use a controlled grammatical framework for class discussion questions (e.g., "Cars are made of _____ ." Books are made of _____ .")
17. When summarizing a lesson for the entire class, make use of the exact wording of the key concepts that have been translated into the student's native language.
18. When study or review questions are included in a lesson, have them translated into the native language of the students along with the answers for self-checking. Use a bilingual format so the students can follow class discussion of the questions and answers in English.
19. Whenever possible, arrange for a special grading system, such as an individual contract, pass/fail, or a monitoring grade.
20. Be realistic in your expectations, flexible in your approaches, sensitive, and patient.

Source: Adapted from A. Plata (n.d.). *Assessment, Placement, and Programming of Bilingual Exceptional Pupils: A Practical Approach* (pp. 46–47). Reston, VA: ERIC Clearinghouse on Handicapped and Gifted Children, Council for Exceptional Children.

Whenever state laws and regulations are more stringent than federal laws and regulations, state mandates apply. Whereas federal support and direction provided much of the initial impetus for bilingual education, in those states where large numbers of minority group populations provide a constituency, it is likely that bilingual education will continue to develop.

It is probable that in most areas of this nation the heightened appreciation for cultural diversity will continue to express itself in more pluralistic approaches to educating all students. It is essential that this happen, given the current educational reform movement. Many of the reforms undertaken to date are quantitative in nature, e.g., requiring more units for graduation, competency testing, statewide syllabi, and increased instructional time. Unless these quantitative reforms are accompanied by a qualitative accommodation in curriculum, instructional strategies, and in the attitudes and approaches of school personnel, additional numbers of children are at risk for both inappropriate placement into special education and attenuated academic opportunities.

Given special education's historic recognition of the influences of individual differences, it is probable that efforts to provide for the linguistic diversity presented by many of these students will continue to develop into a special education priority. Only now are we beginning to shift our emphasis from assessment and eligibility considerations to program planning and delivery concerns. Attempts to develop and validate approaches to meeting the educational needs of LEP handicapped and gifted students are quite recent and should continue during the ensuing years. The longstanding commitment of the field of special education to providing programs appropriate to the unique needs of individual students predicts a continuation of efforts to address the unique ethnolinguistic characteristics of culturally diverse, exceptional children.

SUMMARY

The United States is no longer the cultural "melting pot" that it was at the turn of the century; instead, it is a pluralistic society composed of many diverse ethnic, cultural and language groups. This change in demographics and attitudes has resulted in concurrent changes in the education of students from minority group backgrounds. There are over 2.7 million students in the United States who have limited proficiency in English. By the year 2000, it has been projected that over 50 percent of the school-age population in some states will be of minority background. This change is especially significant in special education since it requires an amalgamation of knowledge and skill in special education and bilingual education.

The identification of minority background students for special education programs and services has been a special concern over the past two decades. Traditionally, minority students have been overrepresented in classes for handicapped students and underrepresented in programs designed for the gifted and talented. The disproportionate representation in classes for handicapped students formed the basis for many of the criticisms and class-action litigation which resulted in special education reform. Many of the provisions of PL 94–142 were explicitly designed to address these inequities. Efforts to assure that assessment instruments used to determine special education eligibility are not biased continue along with efforts to see that these tests are not interpreted in a biased manner.

The school curriculum and its delivery have also presented problems for minority background students. The dominant Anglo-American culture has permeated textbooks and instruction often distorting or omitting the richness of other cultures and languages. The competitive nature of most classrooms is foreign to students from many cultural groups which value cooperation and avoid competition. Thus, what is taught, how it is taught, and the way that classrooms are organized has made it difficult for students from minority backgrounds to achieve.

One of the major controversies in the provision of services to students with limited English proficiency has been what the language of instruction should be. Many experts strongly favor continued academic instruction in the primary language simultaneous with the development of English language skills. Rather than interfering with learning English, continued instruction of the primary language seems to facilitate the acquisition of the second language. Although there are considerably less data on the most effective approach for limited English proficient students with handicaps, there is evidence that bilingual instruction can be used successfully with low IQ and learning disabled students.

Providing special education services to students from diverse cultural, ethnic, and language groups is one of the major challenges in the field. More research on effectiveness and best practices must be conducted to guide the development of programs. Improved instructional materials which are educationally sound and pluralistic in their depiction of the world need to be developed; and more teachers with competency in special education and bilingual education need to be trained. Bilingual/multicultural special education is a growing, dynamic specialty within special education.

References

Adler, M. (1968). Intelligence tests of the culturally disadvantaged: Some pitfalls. *The Journal of Negro Education, 37*(4), 364–369.

Aragon, J. (1973). Cultural conflict and cultural diversity in education. In L. Bransford, L. Baca, & K. Lane (Eds.), *Cultural diversity and the exceptional child* (pp. 24–31). Reston, VA: The Council for Exceptional Children.

Argulewicz, E. N. (1983). Effects of ethnic membership, socioeconomic status, and home language on LD, EMR, and EH placements. *Learning Disability Quarterly, 6*, 195–200.

Askins, B. E., & others. (1978). *Responsive environmental early education program (REEP): Third-year evaluation study. Final evaluation report, 1977–78.* Lubbock, TX: Texas Technical University. (ERIC Document Reproduction Service No. ED 157668)

Baca, L., & Chinn, P. C. (1982). Coming to grips with cultural diversity. *Exceptional Education Quarterly, 2* (4), 33–45.

Bailey, D. B., Jr., & Harbin, G. R. (1980). Nondiscriminatory evaluation. *Exceptional Children, 46*, 590–596.

Ben-Zeev, S. (1977). The influence of bilingualism on cognitive development and cognitive strategy. *Child Development, 48,* 1009–1018.

Bergin, V. (1980). *Special education needs in bilingual programs.* Rosslyn, VA: Inter-American Research Associates, Inc., National Clearinghouse for Bilingual Education.

Berke, I. P. (1982). The development of criteria for student participation in bilingual education in California and Texas: Federal, state, and local roles. *Bilingual Education Paper Series, 6* (1). Los Angeles: Evaluation Dissemination and Assessment Center, California State University–Los Angeles.

Bernal, E. M., & Tucker, J. A. (1981). *A manual for screening and assessing students of limited English proficiency.* Paper presented at The Council for Exceptional Children Conference on the Exceptional Bilingual Child, New Orleans. (ERIC Document Reproduction Service No. ED 209785).

Brode, J., & Rodgers, P. (1979). Personal Communication. In Plata, M., Preparing teachers for the Mexican-American handicapped: The challenge and the change. *Teacher Education and Special Education, 2* (4), 26.

Brown v. Board of Education, 347 U.S. 48 (1954).

Bruck, M. (1978). The suitability of early French immersion programs for the language disabled child. *Canadian Journal of Education, 3,* 51–72.

California State Board of Education (1979). *Ethnic survey of pupils assigned to special education classes for educable mentally retarded.* (EMR, school year 1977–1978). Sacramento, CA: Author.

Cannon, L. (1978). Latin influence mounts throughout the Southwest. *The Washington Post,* Sunday, March 26, 1, 1–10.

Carnegie Council on Policy Studies in Higher Education (1979). *Giving youth a better chance: Options for education, work, and service.* San Francisco: Jossey-Bass.

Carpenter, J. (1983). *Bilingual special education: An overview of issues.* Los Alamitos, CA: National Center for Bilingual Research.

Cartwright, C. P., Cartwright, C. A., & Ward, M. E. (1981). *Educating special learners.* Belmont, CA: Wadsworth.

Castaneda v. Pickard. 648 F. 2d 989, Fifth Circuit.

Cegelka, P. T., & Pacheco, R. (1984). *Special education curriculum materials for Mexican-American and Asian-American handicapped students: Final report.* San Diego, CA: San Diego State University.

Cegelka, P. T., Rodriguez, A. M., Lewis, R. B., & Pacheco, R. (1984). *Statewide status study: Educational services to handicapped students with limited English proficiency: State of the art and future directions.* San Diego, CA: San Diego State University.

Chinn, P. (1979a). Curriculum development for culturally different exceptional children. *Teacher Education and Special Education, 2* (4), 49–58.

Chinn, P. (1979b). The exceptional minority child: Issues and some answers. *Exceptional Children, 45,* 532–536.

Cohen, R. A. (1969). Conceptual styles, cultural conflicts, and nonverbal tests. *American Anthropologist, 71,* 65–73.

Cole, M. (1975). Culture, cognition, and I.Q. testing. *The National Elementary Principal, 54* (4), 49–52.

Costello, J., & Dickie, J. (1970). Leiter and Stanford-Binet IQs of preschool disadvantaged children. *Developmental Psychology, 2,* 314.

Cummins, J. (1978). Bilingualism and the development of metalinguistic awareness. *Journal of Cross-Cultural Psychology, 9,* 131–149.

Cummins, J. (1981). The role of primary language development in promoting educational success for language minority students. In *Schooling and language minority students:*

A theoretical framework (pp. 3–49). Sacramento, CA: California State Department of Education (Office of Bilingual Education).

Cummins, J., & Gulutsen, M. (1974). Bilingual education and cognition. *Alberta Journal of Educational Research, 5,* 91–100.

Cummins, J., & Mulcahy, R. (1978). Orientation to language in Ukranian-English bilingual children. *Child Development, 49,* 1239–1242.

DeAvila, E. (1976). Mainstreaming ethnically and linguistically different children. An exercise in paradox or a new approach. In R. L. Jones (Ed.), *Mainstreaming and the minority child* (pp. 93–108). Reston, VA: The Council for Exceptional Children.

Duffey, J. B., Salvia, J., Tucker, J., & Ysseldyke, J. (1981). Nonbiased assessment: A need for operationalism. *Exceptional Children, 47,* 427–434.

Dunn, L. M. (1968). Special education for the mildly retarded—is much of it justifiable? *Exceptional Children, 34,* 5–22.

Evans, J. S. (1974, May). *Ability development project for five-year-olds. Final Report.* (ERIC Document Reproduction Service No. ED 154577)

Feldman, C., & Shen, M. (1971). Some language-related cognitive advantages of bilingual five-year-olds. *Journal of Genetic Psychology, 118,* 235–277.

Feuerstein, R. (1979). *The dynamic assessment of retarded performers: The learning potential assessment device, theory, instrument and techniques.* Baltimore: University Park Press.

Garcia, R. L. (1976). *Learning in two languages.* Bloomington, IN: Phi Delta Kappa Educational Foundation.

Garcia, R. L. (1978). *Fostering a pluralistic society through multiethnic education.* Bloomington, IN: Phi Delta Kappa Educational Foundation.

Gardner, R. C., & Lambert, W. (1972). *Attitude and motivation in second language learning.* Rowley, MA: Newbury House.

Garwood, G. (1979). *Educating young handicapped children: A developmental approach.* Germantown, MD: Aspen.

Genesee, F. (1976). The suitability of immersion programs for all children. *The Canadian Modern Language Journal, 32* (5), 494–551.

Gonzales, E. (1979). Preparation for teaching the multicultural exceptional child—trends and concerns. *Teacher Education and Special Education, 2* (4), 12–18.

Gonzales, E. (1981). *Renorming and translation of existing tests.* Paper presented at the Council for Exceptional Children Bilingual Special Education Conference, New Orleans.

Good, T. L., & Brophy, J. E. (1974). Changing teacher and student behavior: An empirical investigation. *Journal of Educational Psychology, 66,* 909–405.

Grossman, H. J. (Ed.). (1983). *Classification in mental retardation* (1983 rev.). Washington, DC: American Association on Mental Deficiency.

Henderson, R. W. (1980). Social and emotional needs of culturally diverse children. *Exceptional Children, 46,* 598–605.

Hilliard, A. G., III. (1980). Cultural diversity and special education. *Exceptional Children, 46,* 584–588.

Hoge, R. D., & Luce, S. (1979). Predicting academic achievement from classroom behavior. *Review of Educational Research, 49,* 479–496.

Jensen, A. R. (1969). How much can we boost IQ and academic achievement? *Harvard Education Review, 39,* 1–123.

Johnson, E. G., Gerard, H. B., & Miller, N. (1975). Teacher influences in the desegregated classroom: Factors mediating the school desegregation experience. In H. B. Gerard & N. Miller (Eds.), *School desegregation* (pp. 243–259). New York: Plenum.

Johnson, J. J. (1969). Special education and the inner city: A challenge for the future or another means of cooling the mark out? *Journal of Special Education, 3,* 241–251.

Kagan, A., & Buriel, R. (1977). Field dependence-independence and Mexican-American culture and education. In J. L. Martinez, Jr. (Ed.), *Chicano psychology* (pp. 279–328). New York: Academic Press.

Killalea Associates (1980). *State, regional, and national summaries of data from the 1978 civil rights survey of elementary and secondary schools* (Prepared for the Office of Civil Rights). Alexandria, VA: Author.

King, E. W. (1981). The status of ethnic diversity in American classrooms. *Journal of Multilingual and Multicultural Development, 2(3).*

Kiraithe, J. (1982). Second language acquisition: Implications for assessment and placement. In A. M. Ochoa & J. Hurtado (Eds.), *Special education and the bilingual child* (pp. 38–55). San Diego: National Origin Desegregation Lau Center, San Diego University.

Kirp, D. L. (1973). Schools as sorters: The constitutional and policy implications of student classification. *University of Pennsylvania Law Review, 121* (4), 705–797.

Krashen, S. (1981). Bilingual education and second language acquisition theory. In *Schooling and language minority children: A theoretical framework* (pp. 51–79). Los Angeles, CA: Evaluation, Dissemination, and Assessment Center, California State University, Los Angeles.

Kunzelman, H., & Koenig, C. (1976). *Nondiscriminatory assessment using learning screening.* Kansas City, MO: International Management Systems.

Lambert, N. M. (1981). Psychological evidence in *Larry P. v. Wilson Riles:* An evaluation by a witness for the defense. *American Psychologist, 36,* 937–952.

Landurand, P. (1980). Bilingual special education report. In P. Landurand & others (Eds.), *Bridging the gap between bilingual and special education. Presentations from the Roundtable on the Bilingual Exceptional Child* (pp. 3–10). Reston, VA: ERIC Clearinghouse on Handicapped and Gifted Children.

Langdon, H. S., & Parker, D. (1982). Developing a bilingual individual education plan for language minority students. In A. M. Ochoa & J. Hurtado (Eds.), *Special education and the bilingual child* (pp. 56–61). San Diego: National Origin Desegregation Lau Center, San Diego State University.

Laosa, L. M. (1977). Inequality in the classroom: Observational research on teacher-student interactions. *Aztlan International Journal of Chicano Studies Research, 8,* 51–67.

Lau v. Nichols, 414 U.S. 563 (1974).

Lynch, E. W., & Lewis, R. B. (1982). Multicultural considerations in assessment and treatment of learning disabilities. *Learning Disabilities, 1,* 93–103.

Mercer, J. (1973). *Labeling the mentally retarded.* Berkeley: University of California Press.

Mercer, J. R., & Lewis, J. F. (1978). *System of multicultural pluralistic assessment (SOMPA).* Cleveland, OH: Psychological Corporation.

Meyen, E., Rodriguez, F., & Erb, K. S. (n.d.) *Mainstreaming multicultural education into special education.* Lawrence, KS: The University of Kansas.

National Association for Retarded Citizens (1971). *Policy statement on education of mentally retarded children.* Arlington, TX: Author.

National Coalition of Advocates for Students (1985). *Barriers to excellence: Our children at risk.* Boston: Author.

Newsweek (1982). California: Isla Vista Grande grade school's Tower of Babel. December 6, pp. 151–152.

Oakland, T. (1980). Nonbiased assessment of minority group children. *Exceptional Education Quarterly, 1 (3),* 31–46.

Oakland, T., & Matuszek, P. (1977). Using tests in nondiscriminatory assessment. In T. Oakland (Ed.), *Psychological and educational assessment of minority children* (pp. 52–69). NY: Brunner/Mazel.

Office for Civil Rights (1975). *Task force findings specifying remedies available for eliminating past education practices ruled unlawful under Lau vs. Nichols.* Washington, DC: Author.

Oxford, R., Pol, L., Lopez, D., Stupp, P., Peng, S., & Gendell, M. (1980). *Changes in number of non-English language background and limited English proficient persons in the United States to the Year 2000.* Volume 4: Fiscal Report. Washington, DC: National Center for Education Statistics.

Pifer, A. (1979). Bilingual education and the Hispanic challenge (Reprinted from the 1979 *Annual Report*, Carnegie Corp. of N.Y.).

Plata, M. (1979). Preparing teachers for the Mexican-American handicapped: The challenge and the change. *Teacher Education and Special Education, 2*(4), 2–26.

President's Committee on Mental Retardation (1969). *The six-hour retarded child.* Washington, DC: U.S. Government Printing Office.

Prieto, A. G., Rueda, R., & Rodriguez, R. F. (1981). Teaching competencies for bilingual/multicultural exceptional children. *Teacher Education and Special Education, 4* (4), 35–39.

Ramirez, B. A., & Tippeconnic, J. W., III. (1979). Preparing teachers of American Indian handicapped children. *Teacher Education and Special Education, 2* (4), 27–32.

Rodriguez, F. (1982). Mainstreaming a multicultural concept into special education, guidelines for teacher trainers. *Exceptional Children, 49,* 220–227.

Rotberg, I. S. (1982). Some legal and research considerations in establishing federal policy in bilingual education. *Harvard Education Review, 52* (2), 149–168.

Rueda, R., & Prieto, A. G. (1979). Cultural pluralism—implications for teacher education. *Teacher Education and Special Education, 2*(4), 49–58.

Sanua, V. (1975). *Bilingual program for physically handicapped children.* Brooklyn, NY: Board of Education of the City of New York. (ERIC Document Reproduction Service No. ED 137488)

Sedo, M. A. (1978). Special education and the Hispanic child: A ten-point action plan. In P. Landurand (Ed.), *Diagnosis and intervention in bilingual special education: Searching for new alternatives. Proceedings.* Boston: State Department of Education. (ERIC Document Reproduction Service No. 202245)

Sirota, N. (1976). *Bilingual program for children in bureau CRMD classes. School year, 1975–1976.* Brooklyn, NY: New York City Board of Education, Office of Educational Evaluation. (ERIC Document Reproduction Service No. ED 137449)

Skutnabb-Kangas, T. (1979). *Language in the process of cultural assimilation and structural incorporation of linguistic minorities.* Rosslyn, VA: National Clearinghouse for Bilingual Education.

Smith, J. (1979). The education of Mexican-Americans: Bilingual, bicognitive, or biased? *Teacher Education and Special Education, 2*(4), 37–48.

Stevick, E. (1976). *Memory, meaning, and method.* Rowley, MA: Newbury House.

Tempes, R. (1984). *Implementing theoretically sound programs: Do they really work?* Paper presented at the California Association for Bilingual Education Conference, San Francisco, CA.

Time (1984). In search of the angels. *124* (5), July 30, 1984, pp. 72–77.

Tucker, J. A. (1980). Ethnic proportions in classes for the learning disabled issuing on nonbiased assessment. *Journal of Special Education, 14*(1), 93–105.

U.S. Commission on Civil Rights (1974). *Toward quality education for Mexican Americans. Report VI: Mexican-American education study.* Washington, DC: Author.

Wong-Fillmore, L. (1979). Individual differences in second language acquisition. In C. J. Fillmore, D. Kempler, & W. S. Y. Wang (Eds.), *Individual differences in language ability and language behavior* (pp. 203–228). New York: Academic Press.

Resources

Organizations

National Association of Bilingual Education

1201 16th Street, N.W.

Washington, DC 20036

Publishes a newsletter, maintains resource files, disseminates information, and advocates for appropriate programs for children and youth from different language backgrounds.

National Clearinghouse for Bilingual Education

1300 Wilson Boulevard—Suite B2–11

Rosslyn, VA 22209

Collects, develops, and disseminates information on bilingual education.

Periodicals

National Association of Bilingual Education Journal

1201 16th Street, N.W.

Washington, DC 20036

Professional journal which publishes papers on a variety of issues in bilingual education.

FOCUS

1300 Wilson Boulevard—Suite B2–11

Rosslyn, VA 22209

A series of thought-provoking papers published monthly by the National Clearinghouse for Bilingual Education.

FORUM

1300 Wilson Boulevard—Suite B2–11

Rosslyn, VA 22209

A quarterly newsletter with information of interest to those working in the area of bilingual education.

Books

Baca, L. M., & Cervantes, H. T. (Eds.) (1984). *The bilingual special education interface.* St. Louis, MO: Times Mirror/Mosby.

Chinn, P. C. (1984). *The education of culturally and linguistically different exceptional children.* Reston, VA: Council for Exceptional Children.

Cummins, J. (1984). *Bilingualism and special education: Issues in assessment and pedagogy.* Clevedon, Avon, England: Multilingual Matters, Ltd.

Omark, D. R., & Erickson, J. G. (1983). *The bilingual exceptional child.* San Diego, CA: College Hill Press.

Chapter 14

PREPARATION FOR ADULTHOOD

One of the fundamental purposes of education is to prepare individuals to live a productive and rewarding life (Marland, 1971). Thus, special education and its related services assist handicapped youth in preparing for the roles and responsibilities of adulthood.

Exceptional individuals often need specialized and individualized assistance in the transitional stages from school to work and in their preparation for adulthood as a whole. Recent trends and legislation in special education and related service delivery systems have recognized this need as a priority within the general scheme of program development, research, and program implementation.

In this chapter, the rationale for the formal preparation of exceptional individuals for adulthood is presented. The societal view, both historical and contemporary, is discussed. The current perspective and efficacy of practices surrounding preparation for adulthood is examined. Finally, recommendations for the future, including research, changes in practice, and predictions of future activities, are considered.

Patricia L. Patton
San Diego State University

RATIONALE FOR
VOCATIONAL PREPARATION

Young people with disabilities face an uncertain future when they leave the nation's public schools. Qualification for employment is an implied promise of American education, but between 50 and 80 percent of working age adults who report a disability are jobless (U.S. Bureau of the Census, 1982; U.S. Commission on Civil Rights, 1983). Without employment, many individuals turn to community services only to find long waiting lists. Those adults with disabilities who do gain entry into publicly supported day and vocational services often experience low wages, slow movement toward employment, and segregation from their nondisabled peers (U.S. Department of Labor, 1979).

To become productive adults, exceptional youth must be provided with the necessary job training, job search, job placement, career development, independent living, and functional academic skills to prepare them for the world of work and independent living.

Approximately one school generation after guaranteeing the right to a free, appropriate public education for all children with handicaps, it is now appropriate that special education address the transition of persons with disabilities from school to working life. The cost of disability joblessness and dependence is high and rising. Approximately 8 percent of the gross national product is spent each year in disability programs, with most of this amount going to programs that support dependence (White House Working Group on Disability Policy, 1983). The public's investment in special education can do much to prevent dependence and lead to full community participation, if systematic attention is given to the transition of young people with disabilities from school to work and adult life (Will, 1984).

The public recognition that handicapped persons, regardless of the nature and severity of their handicap, have a basic right to be viewed as total human beings involved in community working and living is only beginning to make an impact. Recent legislation reflects that impact. Several public laws—PL 94–142 (the Education for All Handicapped Children Act of 1975); PL 94–482 (the Vocational Education Amendments of 1976, Title II); PL 93–112 (the Rehabilitation Act of 1973 and the 1978 Amendments); and PL 93–199 (Part C of the Education of the Handicapped Act, as amended)—have all mandated appropriate vocational and independent living programming for handicapped persons to be provided in the least restrictive environment. The mandates for vocational programming include the implementation of programs which provide exceptional youth with adult preparation skills. These skills include career awareness, career exploration, job seeking skills, job training skills, appropriate personal-social interaction, leisure activities, and independent living (i.e., mobility, time management, money management, independent domestic management, civil rights awareness, knowledge of benefits and tax laws, etc.).

Although legislation has mandated vocational preparation, recent statistics indicate the obvious need for rapid and effective implementation of programs.

introducing

JON

Jon Bradley is a 23-year-old, mildly retarded individual. He received his schooling in special classes for mildly retarded students, although in high school he was mainstreamed for physical education and vocational education. He is able to read at the third grade level and do math at the fourth grade level. Jon is in good physical health and has excellent fine and gross motor dexterity skills as evidenced by consistent average and above average grades in regular physical education classes. He lives with a friend in an apartment and is able to pursue an independent life-style. He has held "odd jobs" since graduating from the public schools at age 21, doing yard work and other types of manual labor. Previous employers describe Jon as a dependable and diligent worker.

Jon recently applied for a job doing manual labor with a local Navy contractor in his rural northwest hometown. Because of high unemployment in the area, more than 500 people applied for the 35 jobs available with the company. Based upon Jon's past experience, the interviewer determined that Jon had the ability to do the essential functions of the job; however, because of his handicap, he was afraid that Jon might not "fit in" and might be harassed by other employees. Jon was not hired; the job was given to a nonhandicapped person who had experience equivalent to Jon's.

This is a clear example of a person being denied employment, solely by reason of his handicap. Jon was qualified to do the job and should have received employment on that basis under Section 503 of the Rehabilitation Act. It was also improper to consider possible harassment by other employees. The regulations provide that the employer is "obliged to prevent harassment of employees through affirmative action efforts," and may solicit the aid of the contracting governmental agency in doing so.

Only 40 percent of the adult handicapped population is employed as compared to 74 percent of the nonhandicapped population (U.S. Department of Education, 1985). In 1972, Associate Commissioner of Education, Ed Martin, predicted that only 21 percent of the handicapped students leaving public schools would have full employment skills. The remainder, almost half a million, would enter society with little chance for achieving independent status (Beason, Heaney, & Stafford, 1980). In 1976, only 2 percent of the students receiving vocational education were handicapped, whereas the total handicapped population in the schools was 10 percent. It was reported in 1980 that 59 percent of the handicapped youth leaving school in the next four years would not be prepared for the world of work or community living; they would, therefore, need to seek solutions for unemployment in welfare, outpatient assistance clinics, social security, and other public aid programs (Miller, Sabatino, & Larsen, 1980). Razeghi and Halloran (1979) have estimated that the cost of dependency among unemployed, disabled individuals exceeds $115 billion per year.

Handicapped persons, like nonhandicapped persons, hold jobs which range from unskilled positions to professional positions. The key to job success with handicapped persons is the assurance that the job environment is adapted to minimize the handicap as much as possible. Additionally, the acquisition of work-appropriate behaviors is vital to career success. The more severely handicapped the worker, the more support services are required to obtain and maintain successful employment. Unfortunately, handicapped workers tend to be more prevalent among the unemployed and underemployed than do nonhandicapped workers.

Historically, many handicapped workers were engaged in sheltered employment. However, the future trend is to provide handicapped workers the opportunity for community-based employment, regardless of the severity of the handicap. The U.S. Department of Education (1985) views this trend as "supported community employment." Supported employment is used to assist students in the transition process; the amount of support needed as a handicapped student exits the school system varies according to the needs of the individual (see Figure 14.1).

There is an urgent need for programming to prepare exceptional youth to become independent adults who are tax contributors rather than tax consumers. Comprehensive programming centering around career preparation and independent living is costly in its early stages but it ultimately saves billions of dollars by preventing handicapped individuals from dependent economic lifestyles. It has been estimated that, for every dollar spent on the vocational habilitation of handicapped youth who would otherwise become institutionalized, fourteen dollars are saved in reduced future expenditures (Beason, Heaney, & Stafford, 1980). Vocational rehabilitation experts have estimated that, for every dollar spent on a client's rehabilitation, seven dollars are returned back into the economy. Furthermore, the vocational rehabilitation costs for school-age students graduating from a comprehensive vocational preparation program are two-thirds less than those for the typical adult client (Ashby & Bensberg, 1981).

The economic gain of preparing exceptional individuals for an independent adult life is clear. The human and personal gains for these persons are even more striking. Olshansky (1977) states that disabled persons continue to view work as one of the central facets of their lives. He presents eight basic assumptions about human behavior which emphasize the role of vocational preparation in the overall well-being of the disabled person. These assumptions are:

1. *Each person seeking help has some capacity and need for self-direction and self-determination.*
2. *The amount of self-direction possible for any person depends not only on factors within a person, but on opportunities outside a person.*
3. *Raised expectations tend to raise vocational performance.*
4. *Any process of labeling and segregation tends to lower expectations.*
5. *Growth and development occur best and most within natural vocational environments.*

Figure 14.1

Major Components of the Transition Process

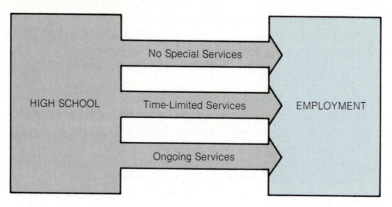

HIGH SCHOOL

No Special Services

Time-Limited Services

Ongoing Services

EMPLOYMENT

Source: From "Bridges from School to Working Life" by Madeleine Will, *Interchange*, June 1982. Reprinted by permission of the College of Education, University of Illinois at Urbana-Champaign.

6. *Persons are more likely to change through practice than through "talking" therapies.*
7. *Nothing motivates a person as much as opportunity.*
8. *Each person from the moment of birth, whatever his/her limitations, has a natural drive toward independence and normality.* (pp. 151–153)

Olshansky believes that only by acting on these assumptions via systematic programming and preparation for adulthood can exceptional individuals assume their rightful roles in society as independent, productive adults. This holds true for the mildly handicapped individual and also for those with the most severe handicaps.

The literature is filled with convincing rationales for providing such programming for specific disability groups. Included are descriptions of programs for a range of handicapped individuals: severely handicapped (Brown, 1983); learning disabled (Patton, 1981); mildly handicapped (Sitlington, 1981); gifted and talented (Hoyt & Hebeler, 1974); physically handicapped (Palmer, 1982); culturally diverse handicapped (Fair & Sullivan, 1980); deaf-blind (Patton, 1980); emotionally disturbed (Pooley, 1981); and cerebral palsied, epileptic, hearing impaired, and visually handicapped (Domeck & Konar, 1982). The recurring theme throughout is the obvious waste and loss that occurs without such programming and the economic and humanistic gains that are made with such programming. Olshansky (1977) captures the overall essence and trend of thinking, stating: " . . . without work they (disabled persons) feel as if they are nothing . . . they feel useless, abnormal, childish, and wasted . . . one must establish oneself . . . one must be useful . . . one must work" (p. 159).

The fields of special education, vocational rehabilitation, and vocational education are each responsible for providing services and programs to prepare exceptional individuals to enter adulthood as productive workers and contributing members of society. However, until the recent past, these fields have functioned quite separately with few formal linkages.

Historical Perspective

Special education services tend to emphasize academic preparation of exceptional individuals with the intent of providing the special resources needed by handicapped children to achieve their full potential (Weintraub & Abeson, 1976). Special education's primary population includes handicapped children and youth. The major curricular emphasis is the development of cognitive, social, emotional, and physical skills. As handicapped students enter adolescence and young adulthood, there is a greater emphasis on vocational and general life skills. This is commonly referred to as career education for the handicapped.

Career education for handicapped students includes more than just vocational training and job placement. Career education refers to the total process of preparing exceptional individuals for the many roles of adulthood. The Council for Exceptional Children Position Statement on Career Education (1978) captures the totality and the importance of formal adulthood preparation efforts:

> . . . *career education permeates the entire school program and even extends beyond it. . . . It should prepare individuals for the several life roles which make up an individual's career. These life roles may include an economic role, a community role, a home role, an avocational role, a religious or moral role, and an aesthetic role. Thus, career education is concerned with the total person and his/her adjustment for community working and living.*

In the early history of special education, the role of the federal government was limited, especially as related to vocational development. There was really no federal commitment to education for the handicapped until the late 1950s (Ashby & Bensberg, 1981). Then, in 1975, the landmark legislation, PL 94–142, the Education for All Handicapped Children Act, entitled handicapped children to a publicly supported, appropriate education of the quality equal to that afforded nonhandicapped children. The law required the Individualized Education Plan (IEP) with the inclusion of vocational goals and objectives, as appropriate. Also required was cooperation between special education and vocational education with joint development of IEP vocational objectives.

Vocational rehabilitation, on the other hand, has focused on assistance to handicapped adults to become vocationally productive and independent. The primary goal has been to facilitate optimal vocational development and adjustment of handicapped persons. For years, competitive employment was the only goal. However, noncompetitive employment and independent living have recently come to be viewed as acceptable outcomes of the rehabilitation process (Maki, 1978).

Historically, vocational rehabilitation began as a service delivery system for injured veterans returning from war. Physically disabled adults were the only persons served by that system. Then, in 1954, federal mandates established that socially disadvantaged and mentally disabled adults would also be eligible to receive vocational rehabilitation services. More recently, the Rehabilitation Act of 1973 redirected rehabilitation efforts to those persons with severe disabilities. The law also required the development of the Individualized Written Rehabilitation Program (IWRP), and included major civil rights legislation. The 1978 Amendments authorized a wide variety of comprehensive services for independent living.

The inherent philosophies of special education and vocational rehabilitation are identical. The goal is to provide handicapped persons the opportunity to participate in the mainstream of society to the fullest extent possible. The only difference is the age of the disabled population served. Special education believes in equal education for all handicapped students, from birth to the completion of high school; vocational rehabilitation believes in equal opportunity in the workplace and community for all handicapped persons, ages 16 and up. It would seem that, as handicapped students prepare to leave the school system, special education and vocational rehabilitation would collaborate services to effect a smooth transition for these students. In reality, this has not occurred, or only at minimal levels, in most areas of the country.

Technically, mentally disabled persons have been eligible to receive vocational rehabilitation services since 1954. This would include those students who have been classified as mentally retarded, learning disabled, emotionally disturbed, and/or developmentally disabled. During the late 1950s and early 1960s, there were some efforts at establishing work-study programs for these students, whereby they would receive special education services and also be active clients in the vocational rehabilitation process. However, these programs diminished, primarily because handicapped students were not found to meet vocational rehabilitation's criteria for high probability of success in competitive employment. This outcome did not fit with the accountability goal of vocational rehabilitation: permanent, competitive employment in the public or private sector.

Hopefully, this is changing with Public Law 98–199, which was passed in December of 1983 and is referred to as the Transition Initiative. This legislation is a renewed attempt to coordinate the services of special education and vocational rehabilitation. This coordination will be the key factor in effecting handicapped students' transition from school to work.

Special educators should be aware of the services provided by vocational rehabilitation. Available services include vocational evaluation, vocational counseling, medical services, vocational training, supplies and transportation, job placement assistance, and follow-up services. An individualized plan is written for each client to assure that services meet the unique and individual needs of the client. The Individualized Written Rehabilitation Program (IWRP) must contain the same basic components required in the IEP. The IWRP includes annual goals, short-term objectives, services to be provided, a person responsible for providing the services, time frames, and evaluation of outcomes. The current

Learning specific vocational skills while still in school will prepare young people to function independently when they enter the working world.

trend is to coordinate the student's IEP with his or her IWRP as the student prepares to leave the school setting and enter the work force and general community.

Vocational education has focused on assisting persons to choose, prepare for, and function in occupations not requiring a baccalaureate degree. Vocational education places emphasis on occupational areas for which a need is known to exist at a particular time in a particular locale (Bailey, 1977).

Vocational education programs have traditionally served regular class students at the secondary and postsecondary level. The major curriculum emphasis has been the learning of the specific skills needed for unskilled, semiskilled, and skilled occupations. Examples of these occupations include auto mechanics, carpentry, electronics, and others. Males have been the primary enrollees in vocational education classes until the very recent past. Also, handicapped students have been very underrepresented in these classes.

The Vocational Education Amendments of 1968 required that states spend at least 10 percent of their annual basic grants for vocational education on programs for the handicapped population. The law authorized projects to create bridges between public education and work, programs combining in-school and on-the-job training, and work-study programs.

The Vocational Education Amendments of 1976 mandated cooperation between vocational and special education programs. Vocational education planning for handicapped students was required to be consistent with the student's special education IEP (Ashby & Bensberg, 1981).

The above summarized legislation for rehabilitation and special and vocational education portrays the history of efforts of preparing exceptional individuals for independent living and occupational success in youth and adulthood. Moreover, in the more recent legislation, the common goals and purposes of the various efforts become more obvious. Finally, the legislative history reflects an assertive move to recognize the legal and civil rights of disabled persons.

Transition from Past to Present

Programs in special education, vocational rehabilitation, and vocational education have at least one important goal in common: to enable handicapped persons to live as much in the mainstream of American life as possible, whether that be through education or employment (Commissioner of Education and Commissioner of Rehabilitation Services, 1977). In addition, the programs share several more subtle and overlapping commonalities:

1. All employ the same definition of "handicapped."
2. Vocational rehabilitation services are likely to become available to handicapped students when a vocational or independent living goal becomes feasible.
3. All three programs must serve the severely handicapped as well as those more easily educated and rehabilitated.
4. The three programs duplicate some services and complement others.
5. The site of most special education and vocational education activities is the public school system, and many vocational rehabilitation services are also provided there.
6. Eligibility for special education and vocational education services may continue until age 21 (or age 26 in some states), and eligibility for vocational rehabilitation can begin as early as age 14.
7. All three programs employ an individualized program plan of services for the disabled person.
8. Program cooperation and collaboration is implied for fiscal viability and effective service delivery.   (Ashby & Bensberg, 1981)

Those commonalities have led to many forms of cooperation among special education, vocational rehabilitation, and vocational education at the federal, state, and local levels. A number of states have implemented formal, cooperative agreements to facilitate the delivery of appropriate and comprehensive career education, vocational-special education, and rehabilitation services to secondary and postsecondary handicapped individuals. However, current cooperative programs are experiencing a number of growing-pain problems. In vocational rehabilitation, most services are delivered to newly disabled adults, not to disabled youth who are still in the public school system. In special education programs (especially those for the mildly handicapped), most of the curriculum emphasis is on school skills, not life skills. In vocational education programs, most recipients are nonhandicapped, regular class students. Fortunately, these problems are beginning to be addressed. The Transition Initiative (discussed earlier) is creating a thrust for: (1) planned transition from special education to adult services; (2) joint vocational rehabilitation-special education programs; and (3) integration of handicapped students into vocational education classes.

A 1980 study of 31 state-level interagency agreements among special education, vocational education, and vocational rehabilitation revealed that the following were the most frequently cited provisions to assist exceptional individuals in their adult preparation:

1. Use of vocational rehabilitation funds and services for in-school handicapped youth, ages 14 through 21.
2. Provisions for joint client/child find activities.
3. Provisions for development and delivery of inservice training for professionals from the three agencies.
4. Establishment of state level interagency working or liaison committees and monitoring teams to: (a) coordinate planning and funding at the state level and (b) provide technical assistance to local schools and agencies.
5. Suggested policy statements encouraging the cooperative development of IEPs and IWRPs at the local level.
6. Suggested policy statements encouraging the involvement of vocational educators and rehabilitation personnel in special education staffing teams.
7. Provisions for funding and coordination of assessment services for high school age students.
8. Use of funds from all three programs to provide a continuum of vocational assessment services for handicapped students in regular vocational classes, special vocational classes, special programs, and special schools. (Ashby & Bensberg, 1981)

Current Legislation

Current federal legislation mandates that handicapped individuals are entitled to the rights of citizenship and independence, both in general and in regard to their special needs. Rightful citizenship, however, is not advanced solely as a result of law. While law is an essential prerequisite, it is not sufficient in and of itself to achieve the desired outcomes for adult independence. Of even more importance is implementation (Crosson, Browning, & Krambs, 1979). Appropriate implementation is dependent upon many sources including government officials, state agencies, professional service providers, the general public, and, most important, disabled persons themselves and their families.

The major special education legislation in effect today is the Education for All Handicapped Children Act, PL 94–142. The purpose of the Act is to assure that all handicapped children, ages 3–21, have available to them a free, appropriate, public education which emphasizes special education and related services designed to meet their unique needs. It assures that the rights of handicapped

introducing

LAURA

Laura is a 17-year-old, physically handicapped student. She became disabled at a young age due to a rare form of muscular dystrophy. She currently uses a motorized wheel chair, has no use of her lower extremities, and limited use of her upper extremities. Laura was in self-contained special education classes through junior high school. She then was completely mainstreamed into high school college preparatory classes and graduated high school with honors.

Laura recently applied to a local public university and met all admission requirements. However, she was told that several of her required courses are held in classrooms on the second and third floors of campus buildings and that it would be impossible for her to attend these classes because the buildings do not have elevators. She decided to complete her first two years of undergraduate schooling at a community college with accessible classroom facilities.

This is a clear example of a person being denied access to higher education solely on the basis of her handicap. Laura met the admissions criteria and should have been afforded the right to attend. Sections 503 and 504 of the Rehabilitation Act bind public universities to provide access to educational programs; thus, the university is obliged to either remove architectural barriers or move the classes to rooms which are accessible to a handicapped student.

children and their parents or guardians are protected. In addition, the regulations governing the implementation of PL 94–142 clearly recognize and mandate vocational preparation as part of the special education to be provided exceptional individuals.

The major vocational rehabilitation legislation in effect today is the Rehabilitation Act of 1973 (PL 93–112) as amended by the 1978 Amendments. The purpose of the law is to develop and implement—through research, training, services, and the guarantee of equal opportunity—comprehensive and coordinated programs of vocational rehabilitation and independent living. The law focuses primarily upon employment-related services for the handicapped. However, it does provide for a broader range of social services and civil rights such as accessibility and the guarantee of nondiscrimination. The 1978 Amendments place priority upon serving those with severe handicaps and authorize comprehensive services for independent living for this group.

The major vocational education legislation in effect today is the Vocational Education Act of 1963, as amended by the Vocational Education Amendments of 1968 and the Education Amendments of 1976 (PL 94–482). It establishes specific mandates for providing vocational education to handicapped children and youth. It requires that 10 percent of vocational education funds be allocated to handicapped students. The federal commitment to vocational education of the handicapped was reiterated in 1978 by the Commissioner of Education. In his statement, the Commissioner noted that a disproportionate number of handicapped persons compared to nonhandicapped persons were unemployed. In spite of federal legislation, handicapped students have not had adequate access to publicly supported vocational education programs. The Commissioner reaffirmed federal policy to provide such an education to every handicapped person (Boyer, 1978).

Current legislative mandates in special education, vocational education, and vocational rehabilitation reflect a commonality of purpose for serving handicapped youth and adults. A statement by the Commissioner of Rehabilitation Services, which outlines several possible future directions for the vocational rehabilitation program, demonstrates this common purpose. Among the directions mentioned are a "fully coordinated" nationwide program involving vocational rehabilitation, special education, and vocational education; a national survey of disability and needs of the disabled; and new emphasis on the multiply handicapped and culturally and economically deprived (Rehabilitation Services Administration, 1978).

CURRENT PRACTICES

In the past decade, there has been a remarkable increase in programs and practices centered around preparing exceptional individuals for adult employment, independent living, and personal-social adjustment in the mainstream of society. In 1975, the U.S. Office of Education developed a list of goals for students leaving the formal education system and entering the mainstream of society. These goals were written for nonhandicapped students but they also apply to exceptional individuals. Whenever feasible, exceptional students, like all others, should be prepared to be:

1. Competent in the basic academic skills required for adaptability in our rapidly changing society.
2. Equipped with good work habits.
3. Capable of choosing and/or have chosen a personally meaningful set of work values that foster a desire to work.
4. Equipped with decision-making skills, job-hunting skills, and job-getting skills.
5. Equipped with vocational personal skills at a level that will allow them to gain entry into and attain a degree of success in the occupational society.
6. Equipped with career decisions based on the widest possible set of data concerning themselves and their educational-vocational opportunities.
7. Aware of means available to them for continuing and recurrent education once they have left the formal system of schooling.
8. Successful in a paid occupation, in further education, or in a vocation consistent with their current career education.

Figure 14.2

Clark's School-Based Career Education Model

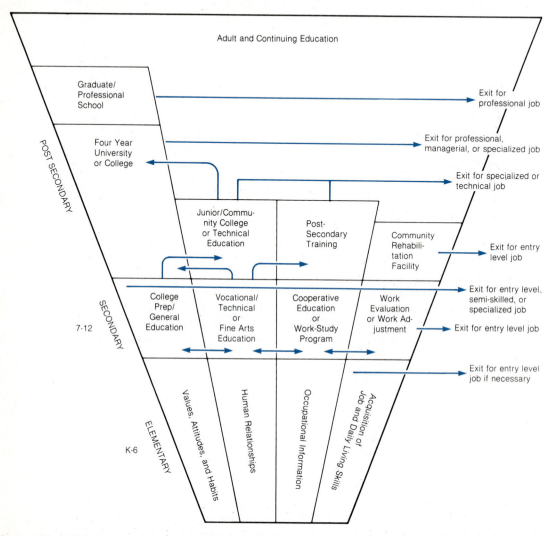

Adult and Continuing Education

Graduate/Professional School

Four Year University or College

Junior/Community College or Technical Education

Post-Secondary Training

Community Rehabilitation Facility

College Prep/General Education

Vocational/Technical or Fine Arts Education

Cooperative Education or Work-Study Program

Work Evaluation or Work Adjustment

POST SECONDARY

SECONDARY

7-12

ELEMENTARY

K-6

Values, Attitudes, and Habits

Human Relationships

Occupational Information

Acquisition of Job and Daily Living Skills

Exit for professional job

Exit for professional, managerial, or specialized job

Exit for specialized or technical job

Exit for entry level job

Exit for entry level, semi-skilled, or specialized job

Exit for entry level job

Exit for entry level job if necessary

Source: "Clark's School-Based Career Education Model" from *Career Education for the Handicapped Child in the Classroom* by G. M. Clark. Copyright © 1979 Love Publishing Company. Reprinted by permission.

9. Successful in incorporating work values into their total personal value structure in such a way that they are able to choose what is for them a desirable lifestyle. (U.S. Office of Education, 1975)

Current practices in adult preparation reflect movement toward the accomplishment of those goals. D'Alonzo (1977) emphasizes the urgent need to continue this movement in the form of contemporary theoretical models, public awareness programs, viable vocational preparation programs, advocacy systems, court litigation and legislation, and the restructuring of the preservice and inservice training of educators.

Models for Career Education

Two major career models have evolved within the field of special education which focus on the final goal of adult independence (Cegelka, 1985). The pioneering, competency-based model was developed by Brolin (1978), followed by Clark's (1980) developmental model. Cegelka (1981, 1985) analyzes the two models emphasizing the schematic, developmental basis of Clark's model and the pragmatic, functional basis of Brolin's model. A summary of her analysis follows.

Clark's School-Based Model.

Clark's (1980) approach to career education is a school-based, kindergarten through adulthood, developmental model. In this model, career education includes four interrelated components: (1) values, attitudes, and habits; (2) human relationships; (3) occupational information; and (4) the acquisition of job and daily living skills (see Figure 14.2). Individual student needs determine the curriculum and the relative emphasis of competency components at the secondary and adult education levels (Cegelka, 1981).

The emphasis on personal values, attitudes, and habits along with the development of human relationships is the major feature that distinguishes Clark's model from Brolin's model. Clark argues that basic educational philosophies support the importance of teaching the *process* of being able to select, defend, and act on one's values. He further points out that research literature on the adult adjustment of handicapped individuals, as well as firsthand reports of handicapped adults, are consistent in identifying those specific values as crucial variables (Cegelka, 1981; Clark, 1981).

Brolin's Life-Centered Competency-Based Model.

Brolin's model is based on the adult adjustment needs of handicapped individuals, and it includes 22 competencies and 102 subcompetencies relating to career education. These competencies are organized into three curriculum areas: (1) daily living skills; (2) personal-social skills; and (3) occupational guidance and preparation skills (see Table 14.1, page 602). According to Brolin, handicapped students should have acquired these skills before they leave school so that they are prepared to succeed in community living. The competencies are generic enough to be applied to all levels of instruction, from the primary grades through high school. They can also be incorporated into a variety of subject matter areas.

The reader is referred to Brolin's *Life-Centered Career Education: A Competency-Based Approach* (1978) for curriculum plan details, including student objectives, instructional activities, and suggested ways for families and people in the community to assist in competency development. This resource is an invaluable tool for the teacher or coordinator responsible for designing adult preparation programs and developing IEPs for exceptional individuals enrolled in those programs.

Table 14.1

Brolin's Career Education Competencies

Curriculum Area	Competencies
Daily Living Skills	Managing Family Finances Caring for and Repairing Home Furnishings and Equipment Caring for Personal Needs Raising Children, Family Living Buying and Preparing Food Buying and Making Clothing Engaging in Civic Activities Utilizing Recreation and Leisure Mobility in the Community
Personal-Social Skills	Achieving Self-Awareness Acquiring Self-Confidence Achieving Socially Responsible Behavior Maintaining Good Interpersonal Relationships Achieving Independence Making Good Decisions, Problem Solving Communicating Adequately with Others
Occupational Guidance and Preparation	Knowing and Exploring Occupational Possibilities Making Appropriate Occupational Decisions Exhibiting Appropriate Work Behaviors Exhibiting Sufficient Physical and Manual Skills Acquiring a Specific Saleable Job. (Skill is not included because the subcompetencies would be unique to the particular skill being acquired.) Seeking, Securing, and Maintaining Satisfactory Employment

Source: Adapted from *Vocational Preparation of Retarded Citizens* by D. E. Brolin. Copyright © 1976 Charles E. Merrill Publishing Company. Reprinted by permission.

Hursh (1982) has created a program development model for use by administrators in developing systemwide plans or by teachers who desire a format for classroom curriculum implementation. The model consists of a series of five sequential steps leading toward optimum adult preparation. The five steps are:

Step 1: Assessing Needs of Special Students
Step 2: Identifying Specific Career Education Goals
Step 3: Identifying Barriers and Facilitators
Step 4: Generating Intermediate Objectives
Step 5: Measuring Effectiveness of the Program

Each step includes: (a) a purpose; (b) an overview of relevant outcome criteria; and (c) a suggested sequence for satisfying outcome criteria. This model combines practical usefulness with a firm conceptual base. It is a step-by-step process to identify, define, establish, achieve, and evaluate goals (Hursh, 1982).

This does not by any means exhaust a review of effective career education models currently in the field. It is, however, representative of the variety of models which now exist to conceptualize and implement viable career education programs for exceptional individuals. Most current models contain several common elements: personal-social growth, acquisition of functional skills, community-based instruction, and interdisciplinary modes of implementation.

VOCATIONAL PROGRAMMING

Many current programs employ the theoretical constructs reviewed in the preceding section. The most successful programs are those which are a collaborative effort among special education, vocational education, and vocational rehabilitation. These collaborative programs have several major common elements. Those elements are discussed in terms of identification, assessment, and the delivery of services.

Identification

School-age, handicapped students participating in current vocational programs are those who have been found eligible to receive special education services as mandated by PL 94–142. This is estimated to be approximately 12 percent of the total school population. However, a major problem exists after students graduate from the formal education system because there is confusion regarding which postsecondary school or service system is responsible for continuing the adult preparation efforts. According to Bullis and Foss (1983), between 1977 and 1980 there was a decrease in the number of students served through formal cooperative work-study programs. They relate this decrease primarily to confusion over the implementation of PL 94–142 and federal directives for work-study programs. Hence, identification of students needing services does not seem to be a serious problem, but the smooth coordination of services as students leave the school setting is of major concern.

Handicapped students who have graduated from the public K–12 school system are no longer protected by the mandates of PL 94–142. However, these students *are* protected by Sections 503 and 504 of the Rehabilitation Act of 1973. Community colleges, four-year colleges and universities, and a wide array of adult services are bound by this act. Sections 503 and 504 guarantee:

1. A qualified handicapped person has a right to employment with reasonable accommodations. (A *qualified* handicapped person is one who meets the essential eligibility requirements for a position or service.)
2. A qualified handicapped person has a right to public educational services if he or she meets the age criteria for services.

3. A qualified handicapped person has the right to postsecondary and vocational services if he or she meets the academic and technical standards for admission and/or participation in such programs.
4. A qualified handicapped person may benefit from any right, privilege, advantage, or opportunity enjoyed by others receiving aid or services.

Sections 503 and 504 clearly mandate that a handicapped person shall not be discriminated against solely by reason of his or her handicap. This right to participate in the mainstream of society includes the right to employment, the right to public education, the right to public access, and the right to aids and services.

Section 504 applies to any individual who (a) has a physical or mental impairment which substantially limits one or more of the person's major life activities; (b) has a record of such an impairment; or (c) is regarded as having such an impairment. Any person who has been previously identified as handicapped during the K–12 educational experience is technically deemed protected by Sections 503 and 504 of the Rehabilitation Act.

Assessment

Determination of vocational and independent living potential is the goal of the assessment process in adult preparation programs. School psychologists are beginning to recognize the need for expertise in this area (Hohenshill, 1982). In vocational assessment, the purpose is to assess and predict work behavior and vocational potential, primarily through the application of practical, reality-based assessment techniques and procedures. The vocational evaluation process has been an important component of vocational rehabilitation for years. It is a recognized specialty within the field of vocational rehabilitation, with an active professional organization (the Vocational Evaluation and Work Adjustment Association), a national materials dissemination clearinghouse (the Materials Development Center, Menomonie, Wisconsin), and a recent certification effort (the Commission on Certification of Work Adjustment and Vocational Evaluation Specialists).

The traditional tools of vocational evaluation have recently begun to emerge in the school systems as viable methods for determining vocational potential of handicapped youth. These vocational evaluation tools are listed and briefly defined below:

1. History Gathering: The accumulation of background data including family, medical, social, education, vocational, and any other information pertinent to the individual's current functioning.
2. Psychometric Testing: The use of traditional standardized paper-and-pencil tests including intelligence, personality, achievement, aptitude, dexterity, vocational interest, and vocational values instruments.
3. Work Sample Assessment: The use of actual samples of work in a standardized fashion to assess the individual's ability to perform a variety of real work tasks.

A counselor holds an informal meeting with learning disabled young people to discuss a number of vocational training and career preparation options.

4. Situational Assessment: The use of simulated work environments to provide an assessment of the individual's capability of performing work and work-related tasks in a natural, ongoing (usually two-three weeks) work situation.

5. Job Analysis: The actual task analysis of a variety of jobs and the matching of required job tasks to the individual's job skills.

6. On-The-Job Tryout: The use of community-based work sites to determine an individual's ability to perform work and tolerate the stresses and strains of ongoing, competitive employment.

7. Adaptive Behavior/Independent Living Skills Assessment: The use of both standardized and informal measures of the individual's ability to live independently in mainstream society. Independent living skills assessment may include such things as the ability to manage money, travel independently, manage domestic affairs, etc.

8. Behavior Observations: The use of structured observation of work and work-related behaviors in simulated work environments, on-the-job tryout sites, and other real-life situations. Results of behavior observations, combined with results of the other vocational evaluation tools, are used to devise individualized behavior management plans to assist the individual in becoming a productive adult worker and member of society.

The primary purpose of vocational assessment in secondary level school settings is to determine current levels of vocational and independent living functioning and to establish vocational goals and objectives for inclusion in the student's IEP and Individual Written Rehabilitation Program (IWRP). Ideally, this is done jointly by special education, vocational rehabilitation, and vocational education specialists.

For an excellent review of current vocational evaluation practices being used in public school settings, the reader is referred to Bensberg (1981). That report contains descriptions of vocational assessment techniques appropriate for students with mild handicaps as well as for those students with the most severe handicaps. However, the sparsity of formal assessment devices for the severely handicapped is stressed.

Delivery of Services

Virtually all vocational programs presently in progress employ a reality-based framework of instruction and service delivery. There is a definite trend away from concentration on pure academic training and toward more practical interventions which will provide students with pragmatic, useful skills of adult living. The programs generally emphasize:

1. Career awareness about local employment options.
2. Training of appropriate personal-social and work-related behaviors.
3. The use of local community resources.
4. The use of community-based work sites.
5. An emphasis on including employers of both the public and the private sector in the training process.
6. An emphasis on a multifaceted mode of service delivery including the family, community, administrators, employers, and social and rehabilitation agencies.

Many current programs include academics along with practical knowledge surrounding general adult preparation. Ellington and Winkoff (1982) describe an elementary program for handicapped students which integrates academics while teaching about actual careers and employability skills. The approach is cost effective as it uses existing school resources such as the cafeteria for a source of information on food service, health laws, using equipment, and reading recipes. Thypin (1982) reports on the Adult Performance Level project. In this program, problem solving and interpersonal relations are skills that are taught directly and the curriculum infuses academic skills into areas necessary for independent living. A cooperative vocational program in Nebraska (Feis & Werbel, 1981) features classroom activities including an in-class employer program in which community employers describe their businesses to students. Students also learn how to complete job applications, develop employment resumes, and analyze job behaviors. This can be considered an innovative program because, traditionally, vocational development skills are infused into the academics. With this program,

High school students enrolled in this vocational development program practice
mail sorting and stuffing envelopes in preparation for similar jobs when they
finish school.

the academics are infused into the vocational development ·training. That is,
writing skills are taught via resume writing, verbal expression is taught via mock
job interviews, and reading is taught via searching through the classified employment section of the newspaper.

As mentioned earlier, the Transition Initiative has created the impetus to offer
a wide range of vocational services. These range from very minimal services for
a short time period to very comprehensive services over a long period of time.
For example, some handicapped students may need only career and academic
counseling to pursue regular education courses for their career goals. Others may
pursue regular education classes, but need very specific adaptations such as
interpreters (for deaf students), extended time for exams (for learning disabled
students), or readers (for blind students). Still others may need very specific
special instruction in vocational training using task analysis and very low stu-
dent-teacher ratio (i.e., the severely handicapped student). This will be the challenge of the future in vocational development programs for handicapped
students. Special educators must be knowledgeable about a wide range of services
and be able to plan and implement these services in the individualized programs
for handicapped students.

Project WORTH

Project WORTH is a vocational preparation project of the La Mesa-Spring Valley School District in San Diego, California. Mildly handicapped students (i.e., those identified as learning disabled or mildly retarded) are enrolled in Project WORTH during their seventh or eighth grade years after a thorough assessment by a child study team and the development of an IEP. The students continue in the project until they graduate from high school.

Project WORTH incorporates a sequential learning process for vocational and independent living preparation. The first sequence includes classroom activities which prepare the students for community job experience. Classroom activities include job-seeking skills, audiovisual lab experience on appropriate job interview and work behaviors, work adjustment training, and independent living skills training.

The second sequence includes a combination of relevant classroom activities and actual job placement within the school setting. These jobs include such things as cafeteria helper, groundskeeper, teacher aide, office aide, etc. The student is given regular supervision and feedback regarding his or her appropriate work behaviors via direct communication, videotape, and self-monitoring of work productivity.

In the final sequence, the student is placed in an actual job in the community. Community job placements include auto repair shops, service stations, medical offices, hospitals, pet shops, and retail stores. During this final sequence, the student's IEP goals and objectives are evaluated by both the classroom teachers and participating community employers.

Project WORTH has demonstrated that mildly handicapped students can be successfully prepared for work in the community. More than 50 percent have received permanent positions. Employers have been very positive in their response to assist in the job training of these students. Team collaboration among teachers, counselors, students, parents, and employers has provided a smooth transition from school to work. Finally, because of early involvement of nonschool personnel (i.e., vocational rehabilitation counselors or employers), students move quickly and easily from high school educational services to community adult services.

Current programs contain a strong emphasis on experiential learning, incorporating actual work experience, both in the classroom and in the local community. Schirmer and George (1983) describe a career exploration and awareness program in which the classroom is organized into work-stations in areas such as business, electronics, and mechanics. Project PICES (Simek, 1980) focuses on career awareness, vocational skill identification, and employability skills; it stresses communication between employer, teacher, team members, and parents. Project WORTH (Marinoble, 1980) is based on a sequential learning model for occupational readiness and success. The three stages it includes are (1) classroom activities which prepare students for community job experience; (2) placement in an actual job within the school environment; and (3) placement in an actual job in the community.

Programs also emphasize the vital importance of active employer involvement (Steinmiller & Retish, 1980) and the general use of community resources such as service clubs and governmental agencies (Green & Wing, 1980). Ford (1980) has developed an excellent model for the systematic recruitment of employer involvement with particular emphasis on employers in industry. Marinoble (1980) stresses that recognition of participating employers is vital to program success and recommends that the employers receive certificates of appreciation or some comparable award.

Individuals with severe cognitive disabilities are poorly served in current programs (Ashby & Bensberg, 1981). If they are served, it is usually through a traditional sheltered workshop experience. However, a study conducted from 1971 to 1983 in Madison, Wisconsin demonstrated the following:

1. Severely handicapped persons can be taught to perform meaningful work in nonsheltered vocational environments.
2. Public school programs can be engineered so as to provide rational and functional preparatory experiences for many of the lowest intellectually functioning students.
3. Adult service systems can be designed so as to arrange for a reasonable number of severely handicapped persons to function in nonsheltered vocational environments.
4. Functioning in nonsheltered vocational environments is clearly more cost-efficient than functioning in sheltered environments. (Brown, 1983; Pumpian, 1980)

The prime element of success was believed to be the heavy involvement of students in community-based work experiences.

Cooperative programs involving special education, vocational rehabilitation, and vocational education offer services with both in-school and community-based components. In Ashby and Bensberg's nationwide study (1981), 95 such programs reported the provision of work placement, vocational evaluation, work supervision, counseling services, job development activities, and other related services.

It is clear that coordination of efforts and interdisciplinary service delivery is of utmost importance to successful program implementation. Fenton and Keller (1981) offer these recommendations for cooperative programming:

1. *The educators and vocational rehabilitation personnel need to improve their familiarity with each other's missions, programs, organizational characteristics, and staff members in order to replace confusion and misinformation with mutual understanding and appreciation.*
2. *Awareness-raising efforts should help all concerned to identify the ways in which their missions complement one another and their efforts can dovetail to benefit eligible students.*
3. *All need to view the handicapped students in totality and design programs which will meet their needs through all stages of development, including job placement.*
4. *Rehabilitation counselors must get to know the vocational educators in the school district as well as the school psychologist. Also, they should be aware that in many areas, the role of the special education teacher is changing to that of consultant.*
5. *An important contribution of the rehabilitation counselor is to clarify eligibility requirements to ensure that all students who can receive vocational rehabilitation services are identified.*
6. *Rehabilitation counselors and vocational educators should participate in the development of the eligible student's IEP.* (p. 9)

Repeatedly cited in the literature is the gap between public policies and the actual delivery of programs for adult preparation of exceptional individuals. One reason for this gap is the inexperience of direct service providers, most of whom have not received any special training for the added responsibilities of implementing the new policies and programs. Many special education teachers are unprepared by either training or experience to teach a full range of vocational and independent living skills (California Department of Education, 1981). Conversely, many vocational education teachers are ill-equipped to instruct special education students; 67 percent of the vocational educators surveyed in a study of seven California school districts did not consider themselves to have enough preparation to teach handicapped students (Ellis, 1977). Vocational rehabilitation personnel are not well versed in the special/vocational education systems or in the instructional technologies and implementation strategies surrounding those systems. Although vocational development and adult preparation programs for disabled students are legally mandated, there is currently a shortage of school personnel with adequate training to teach practical competencies in independent living, vocational adjustment, and job experience to handicapped youth (California Department of Rehabilitation and Office of Special Education, 1980; Pennsylvania Bureau of Vocational Rehabilitation, 1980; Texas Education Agency, 1981). The need for qualified personnel who can provide effective career education and vocational rehabilitation options to handicapped youth, facilitating their smooth transition to the world of work, is a clear and undisputed issue.

Greenan and Larkin (1983) suggest that formal certification for this specialty is a very real possibility in the near future. They report that both special education and vocational education certificate programs are beginning to require courses in K–12 career development for exceptional individuals; however, no requirements yet exist for postsecondary and adult levels. They emphasize that vocational education, vocational rehabilitation, and special education leaders at the state education agency and higher education levels will need to collaborate to develop and implement effective certification policies. Only through effective and relevant personnel preparation for meaningful service delivery will exceptional individuals be prepared for adult roles and responsibilities.

EFFICACY OF PRACTICES

The effectiveness of past vocational programs has been documented mainly in terms of the economic savings that result when exceptional individuals are prepared to become tax contributors rather than tax consumers. This has been shown to hold true for the severely handicapped (Brown, 1983) as well as for the mildly handicapped (Ashby & Bensberg, 1981). The additional humanistic gains have been assumed but not validated from an empirical point of view. Most of the reported gains in psychological well-being are supported with testimonial and/or qualitative methods of investigation.

Because this specialty field is relatively new, present practices are only beginning to become a research concern. Much of the current research revolves around the outcome of in-class or school-supported activities. A study designed to develop and enhance career potential of physically and multiply handicapped children revealed that two-thirds of the students enrolled in the program felt either "moderately" or "very" satisfied with their learning across five areas (Gillespie, 1980). Career attitudes of learning disabled students in regular classes were "superior" to those in resource classes (Kendall, 1980). This finding was supported by Kendall (1981) when career attitudes of learning disabled students were studied further. Those in regular classes were able to make a more sound career decision.

In regard to the vocational assessment of exceptional individuals, Czerlinsky (1982) developed an instrument which reliably discriminates between students who are vocationally decided and vocationally undecided. A neuropsychological approach to vocational evaluation using the McCarron-Dial System has been proposed to predict work and independent living potential and generate vocational objectives for the IEP (Patton, 1981). Gannaway (1980) has demonstrated that a work sample approach to assessment has strong predictive validity when used with handicapped students. These findings permit greater confidence on the part of teachers, counselors, and job placement specialists in determining occupational directions for their students.

Focusing on general program delivery, Barba and Guzicki (1980) report that enrollment in a career education program increased the overall school attendance of special students. Mullarkey (1982) reports an 80 percent employment success of disabled students in a vocational preparation program in spite of such problems as failure in academic subjects and problems providing transportation to work sites. Chern (1980) reports varying success in vocational preparation programs and suggests improvement in scheduling with community facilities and involving more regular teachers in vocational preparation programs. To assist counselors and teachers in understanding motives of youth in the transition from school to work, McCarthy (1983) has developed a taxonomy.

Research reveals varying success with cooperative programs between vocational rehabilitation and special education to ease the transition from school to the independent work/adult world. Bullis and Foss (1983) report an actual decrease in the number of students formally served through these programs. However, they report an increase in informal agreements and delivery of services. In a nationwide study of cooperative programs currently in operation (Ashby & Bensberg, 1981), an average of 65 percent of students served were successfully placed on jobs. Job placements ranged from unskilled to professional, with most being in the unskilled and semiskilled categories. Exemplary job placements included food service, health care, skilled labor, custodial, industrial, domestic, and general labor. Most of the programs surveyed served moderately and mildly handicapped youth.

Community-based living and competitive employment is a very recent trend of programming for severely handicapped persons (Wehman, 1981). Bellamy, Rhodes, Bourbeau, and Mank (1983) report a number of studies verifying successful employment in competitive jobs for this group. Brown (1983) also reports success with such efforts.

Finally, from a survey of professionals who were asked to establish research priorities for career education for the handicapped, the following priorities were rated as needing the most immediate attention: (1) instructional methodologies; (2) settings for skills training; (3) delineation of essential competencies needed for vocational and community adjustment; and (4) attitudes which prevent entry into the world of work (Wimmer & Sitlington, 1981). A recent framework for research has been proposed to accomplish these challenging research tasks (Phillips, 1983).

FUTURE PERSPECTIVES FOR VOCATIONAL PREPARATION PROGRAMS

This chapter has presented the rationale for including adult preparation programs for exceptional individuals in the formal educational and related social service systems. Historical and current perspectives have been discussed. Current practices, including current theoretical models, current programs, and personnel preparation, have been examined. The efficacy of practices in the field, including current and projected research, has been described. From this information, the following conclusions can be drawn along with perspectives for future practice:

1. The history of special education, vocational education, and vocational rehabilitation reflects a growing commonality of purpose in serving handicapped youth and young adults in their independent living and vocational preparation pursuits.
2. The legislation in these fields also shows increasing similarities with current laws mandating similar, if not identical, service delivery systems. The areas of commonality are:
    a. Specific mandates for the vocational assessment, vocational training, vocational placement, and the independent living preparation of handicapped youth.
    b. Individualized planning to provide this preparation in the least restrictive environment.
    c. An emphasis on comprehensive preparation programs involving team efforts of an interdisciplinary nature.
3. Current adult preparation programs emphasize hands-on, community-based approaches for service provision. It is extremely important that the participating community members be formally included in and recognized for the vital role that they play.
4. With this community-based interdisciplinary thrust, it is of utmost importance that the funding mechanisms be restructured to make such efforts possible. Examples might include:

     a. Joint funding of school and community personnel who provide vocational programs.

     b. Joint funding for school-based vocational rehabilitation counselors which would increase early eligibility identification and promote joint development of the student's IEP.

5. It is clear that vocational preparation programs are rapidly being implemented in the formal educational setting. It is important that administrators and service providers actively promote extension of these programs so that they continue after graduation. The stage is set for this extension to occur via cooperative efforts of special education, vocational education, and vocational rehabilitation. It is simply a matter of making the system work to meet the adult adjustment needs of exceptional individuals in the future.

6. There is a need for research to be conducted regarding the follow-up of students currently enrolled in vocational preparation programs. Mistakes are going to be made; successes are going to occur. These need to be investigated so that the current efforts can continually be refined and proceed along a positive course.

7. Parents and disabled adults should be included in adult preparation efforts. They can make an invaluable contribution in the form of consultation and serving as positive and successful role models.

8. Efforts for training the severely handicapped young person for community living and competitive employment is a recent trend. These efforts and reported successes should be considered and promoted so that severely handicapped persons can continue their movement into the mainstream of society.

9. Finally, the vital importance of formal adult preparation programs for all exceptional individuals is now fully established. Parents, teachers, administrators, community members, employers, and disabled persons themselves will all provide the crucial energy needed to see that these programs successfully prepare handicapped young people for a productive, independent, and satisfying adulthood.

SUMMARY

One of the primary purposes of education for handicapped individuals is to prepare them for adulthood. Since working is one of the primary roles of adults, education must include instruction related to careers and vocational choice. It must also help students acquire the skills needed to seek, find, and keep a job. Recent legislation in special education mandates vocational programming and independent living programming for all handicapped students.

Despite the mandates for vocational preparation, the employment statistics for handicapped adults are not good. Only 40 percent of the adult handicapped population is employed as compared to 74 percent of the nonhandicapped population. Handicapped persons who are employed hold jobs which range from unskilled to professional positions; and each individual who is employed becomes a contributor to the economy rather than a consumer of services.

Vocational rehabilitation assists handicapped individuals to become vocationally productive and independent. Although the original goal of rehabilitation was competitive employment, noncompetitive employment and independent living have become acceptable goals for some clients. Like education, rehabilitation services are guided by individual, written plans and the overall goal is to enable handicapped persons to participate in the mainstream of society to the fullest extent possible.

In the past few years considerable emphasis has been placed on the collaboration between education and vocational rehabilitation and on the transition between school and the world of work. To reduce the likelihood that students will leave school inadequately prepared or "fall through the cracks" after graduation, educators and rehabilitation counselors work together with students and their families to assure a smooth transition.

Many handicapped individuals will enter college and complete undergraduate and graduate programs which lead directly to employment opportunities. Others will participate in vocational training programs and join the work force. Still others will receive more intensive training and services which will enable them to work with assistance or work noncompetitively and live more independently than they would have in the past. Regardless of the individual's handicap, employment opportunities and independent and semi-independent living arrangements are becoming more available. Although more needs to be done, this is an expanding area that links several disciplines in efforts to increase opportunities for adults with handicapping conditions.

References

Ashby, S., & Bensberg, G. J. (1981). *Cooperative occupational preparation of the handicapped: Exemplary models.* Lubbock: Research and Training Center in Mental Retardation, Texas Tech University.

Bailey, J. D. (Ed.) (1977). *Cooperative programming between vocational rehabilitation agencies and the school systems.* Washington, DC: U.S. Department of Health, Education, and Welfare, Rehabilitation Services Administration.

Barba, C. E., & Guzicki, J. A. (1980). Project Invest: Instructional network for vocational and specialized training. *Career Development for Exceptional Individuals, 3* (2), 83–86.

Beason, E., Heaney, J., & Stafford, T. (1980, April). *A personnel preparation program with emphasis in career/vocational education for the handicapped.* Paper presented at International Council for Exceptional Children, Philadelphia, PA.

Bellamy, G. T., Rhodes, L. E., Bourbeau, P. E., & Mank, D. M. (1983). *Sheltered workshops, day activity programs, and consumers with mental retardation.* Eugene: Unpublished manuscript, University of Oregon.

Bensberg, G. J. (1981). Vocational evaluation of the handicapped. In S. Ashby & G. J. Bensberg, (Eds.), *Cooperative occupational preparation of the handicapped: Exemplary programs.* Lubbock: Research and Training Center in Mental Retardation, Texas Tech University.

Boyer, E. L. (1978). Position statement on comprehensive vocational education for handicapped persons. *Federal Register, 43* (186), 10–12.

Brolin, D. E. (1978). *Life-centered approach to career education: A competency-based approach.* Reston, VA: The Council for Exceptional Children.

Brown, L. (1983). *Teaching severely handicapped students to perform meaningful work in non-sheltered vocational environments.* Madison: Unpublished manuscript, University of Wisconsin-Madison.

Bullis, M., & Foss, G. (1983). Cooperative work-study programs in vocational rehabilitation: Results of a national survey. *Rehabilitation Counseling Bulletin, 27,* 349–352.

California Department of Education (1981). *Vocational preparation for special education students at the secondary level.* Sacramento, CA: Office of Special Education.

California Department of Rehabilitation and Office of Special Education (1980). *Interagency agreement.* Sacramento, CA: Department of Rehabilitation and Office of Special Education.

Cegelka, P. (1981). Career education. In J. Kauffman & D. Hallahan (Eds.), *Handbook of special education.* Englewood Cliffs, NJ: Prentice-Hall.

Cegelka, P. (1985). Career and vocational education. In W. H. Berdine & A. E. Blackhurst (Eds.), *An introduction to special education* (2nd ed.) (pp. 573–612). Boston: Little, Brown.

Chern, H. (1980). *Evaluation of special education projects in career education 1979–1980* (Report No. 8126). Philadelphia, PA: Philadelphia School District, Office of Research and Evaluation.

Clark, G. M. (1980). Career education: A concept. In G. M. Clark & W. J. White (Eds.), *Career education for the handicapped: Current perspectives for teachers.* Boothwyn, PA: Educational Resources Center.

Clark, G. M. (1981). Career and vocational education. In G. Brown, R. L. McDowell, & J. Smith (Eds.), *Educating adolescents with behavior disorders.* Columbus, OH: Merrill Publishing.

Commissioner of Education and Commissioner of Rehabilitation Services (1977, October 17). *Collaboration between education and vocational rehabilitation agencies.* Washington, DC: Unpublished memorandum, Rehabilitation Services Administration.

Council for Exceptional Children (1978). *Position paper on career development.* Reston, VA: Author.

Crosson, A., Browning, P., & Krambs, R. E. (1979). *Advancing your citizenship: An advocacy manual for persons with disabilities.* Eugene: Rehabilitation Research and Training Center in Mental Retardation, University of Oregon.

Czerlinsky, T. (1982). *Assessing vocational decision-making in the rehabilitation process: Instrument development.* Research report. Menomonie Stout Vocational Rehabilitation Institute, University of Wisconsin–Stout.

D'Alonzo, B. J. (1977). Trends and issues in career development for the mentally retarded. *Education and Training of the Mentally Retarded, 12,* 156–158.

Domeck, A., & Konar, A. (Eds.) (1982). *Lifelong career development for individuals with disabilities: A resource guide. Cerebral palsy, epilepsy, hearing, mental, orthopedic, visual.* Columbia, MO: Missouri University.

Ellington, C., & Winkoff, L. (1982). Low cost implementation of a career education program for elementary school children with handicaps. *Journal of Career Education, 8* (4), 246–255.

Ellis, S. (1977). *Success criteria for the vocational education of handicapped students.* San Diego, CA: San Diego Unified School District.

Fair, G., & Sullivan, A. R. (1980). Career opportunities for culturally diverse handicapped youth. *Exceptional Children, 46* (8), 626–631.

Feis, P., & Werbel, V. (1981). *The cooperative vocational program: Project report.* Hastings, NE: Educational Service Unit #9.

Fenton, J., & Keller, R. (1981). Special education–vocational rehabilitation: Let's get the act together. *American Rehabilitation, 2* (5), 4–9.

Ford, P. (1980, April). *Career education and working with industry.* Paper presented at the International Council for Exceptional Children, Philadelphia, PA.

Gannaway, T. W. (1980). A predictive validity study of a job sample program with handicapped and disadvantaged individuals. *Vocational Guidance Quarterly, 29* (1), 4–11.

Gillespie, J. (1980). *Project CA-SA: Career awareness-self-awareness. A psycho-educational model designed to enhance career potential and self-esteem in physically handicapped children.* Final report. Fullerton, CA: Fullerton Union High School District.

Green, D., & Wing, J. (1980). *Tapping community resources.* Reston, VA: Council for Exceptional Children.

Greenan, J. P., & Larkin, D. L. (1983). Vocational/special education: State of the art. *Career Development for Exceptional Individuals, 6* (1), 43–50.

Hohenshill, T. H. (1982). School psychology and vocational counseling = vocational school psychology. *Personnel and Guidance Journal, 6* (1), 11–13.

Hoyt, K. B., & Hebeler, J. R. (1974). *Career education for gifted and talented students.* Salt Lake City, UT: Olympus Publishing Company.

Hursh, N. C. (1982). A career education model for students with special needs. *Teaching Exceptional Children, 15* (1), 52–56.

Kendall, W. S. (1980). *Affective and career education: Research implications for the learning disabled adolescent.* Paper presented at the International Council for Exceptional Children, Philadelphia, PA.

Kendall, W. S. (1981). *Career attitudes of the learning disabled adolescent: Research suggestions and practices.* Paper presented at the International Council for Exceptional Children, New York, NY.

Maki, D. R. (1978). The theoretical model of rehabilitation. *Journal of Rehabilitation, 44* (4), 26–28.

Marinoble, R. (1980). Community jobs for handicapped students: A career education technique. *The Vocational Guidance Quarterly, 29,* 172–177.

Marland, S. P. (1971). *Career education.* Washington, DC: DHEW Publication No. (OE) 72:39.

Martin, E. (1972). *Status report to the Legislature.* Washington, DC.

McCarthy, H. (1983). Understanding motives of youth in transition to work: A taxonomy for rehabilitation counselors and educators. *Journal of Applied Rehabilitation Counseling, 14* (1) 52–61.

Miller, S. R., Sabatino, D. A., & Larsen, R. P. (1980). Issues in the professional preparation of secondary school special educators. *Exceptional Children, 46* (2), 344–350.

Mullarkey, J. E. (1982). *Project career: Special vocational needs education support program.* Paper presented at the International Council for Exceptional Children, Houston, TX.

Olshansky, S. (1977). Changing vocational behavior through normalization. In W. Wolfensberger (Ed.), *The principle of normalization in human services* (pp. 150–163). Toronto, Canada: National Institute on Mental Retardation.

Palmer, J. T. (1982). A career education program for students with physical disabilities. *Career Development for Exceptional Individuals, 5* (1), 13–24.

Patton, P. L. (1980). *Proceedings and resource guide: Vocational rehabilitation of the deaf-blind client.* Region IX Rehabilitation Continuing Education Program, San Diego State University.

Patton, P. L. (1981a). *State of the art: Vocational rehabilitation for the learning disabled client.* Region IX Rehabilitation Continuing Education Program, San Diego State University.

Patton, P. L. (1981b). A model for developing vocational objectives in the IEP. *Exceptional Children, 47* (8), 618–623.

Pennsylvania Bureau of Vocational Rehabilitation (1980). *Field investigation and evaluation of learning disabilities: Project report.* Harrisburg, PA: Author.

Phillips, S. D. (1983). Career development of special populations: A framework for research. *Journal of Vocational Behavior, 22,* 13–29.

Pooley, R. C. (1981). *Career development for dropout LD and ED adolescent boys: Report.* Richmond, VA: Governor's Manpower Services Council.

Pumpian, I. (1980). *Vocational training programs for severely handicapped students in the Madison Metropolitan School District.* Unpublished manuscript. Madison: University of Wisconsin-Madison.

Razeghi, J. A., & Halloran, W. D. (1979). A new picture of vocational education for the employment of the handicapped. *School Shop, 37,* 50–53.

Rehabilitation Services Administration (1978). The Rehabilitation Services Administration plans for the future: A tentative agenda. In *Programs for the Handicapped.* Washington, DC: U.S. Department of Health, Education, and Welfare, Publication No. OHD 78-22000.

Schirmer, T. A., & George, M. P. (1983). Practical help for the long-term learning disabled adolescent. *Teaching Exceptional Children, 15* (2), 97–101.

Simek, T. S. (1980, April). Project PICES: *Career education curriculum and work experience for secondary emotionally disturbed/learning disabled students.* Paper presented at the International Council for Exceptional Children, Philadelphia, PA.

Sitlington, P. L. (1981). Vocational and special education in career programming for the mildly handicapped adolescent. *Exceptional Children, 47* (8), 592–598.

Steinmiller, G., & Retish, P. (1980). The employer's role in the transition from school to work. *Career Development for Exceptional Individuals, 3* (2), 87–91.

Texas Education Agency (1980). *Qualification of personnel providing vocational assessment of vocational planning.* Austin, TX: Author.

Thypin, M. (1982). *The education of mildly handicapped adolescent/adult students: The infusion of academic and essential living skills.* Paper presented at the International Council for Exceptional Children, Houston, TX.

U.S. Bureau of the Census (1982). *Census report.* Washington, DC.

U.S. Commission on Civil Rights (1983). *Legislative report.* Washington, DC.

U.S. Department of Education (1985, February). *Federal Register.*

U.S. Department of Labor (1979). *Labor trends report.* Washington, DC.

U.S. Office of Education (1975). *An introduction to career education.* Washington, DC: U.S. Government Printing Office.

Wehman, P. (1981). *Competitive employment: New horizons for severely disabled individuals.* Baltimore, MD: Paul H. Brookes.

Weintraub, F. J., & Abeson, A. (1976). New education policies for the handicapped: The quiet revolution. In F. J. Weintraub & others (Eds.), *Public policy and the education of exceptional children.* Reston, VA: Council for Exceptional Children.

White House Working Group on Disability Policy (1983). President's Committee on Employment of the Handicapped, Washington, DC.

Will, M. (1984). Bridges from school to working life. *Division of Career Development News, 8* (4), 5–6.

Wimmer, B. D., & Sitlington, P. L. (1981). A survey of research priorities in career education for the handicapped. *Career Development for Exceptional Individuals, 4* (1), 50–58.

Resources

Organizations

National Rehabilitation Association
1522 K Street, N.W.
Washington, DC 20005

> A national organization which focuses on activities, services, research, and publications regarding vocational rehabilitation of handicapped persons.

President's Committee on Employment of the Handicapped
1111 20th Street, N.W.
Washington, DC 20010

> A federal level committee which focuses on employment opportunities for handicapped persons.

Parents Advocating Vocational Education
1516 North Orchard
Tacoma, WA 98406

> One of the national parent centers which focuses on vocational training and employment for handicapped individuals.

Rehabilitation International USA
20 West 40th Street
New York, NY 10018

> Provides information and expertise in the rehabilitation of adults with disabilities.

Materials Development Center

Stout Vocational Rehabilitation Institute
University of Wisconsin—Stout
Menomonie, WI 54751

> A clearinghouse and materials dissemination center which focuses on materials and resources related to the vocational rehabilitation of handicapped persons with special emphasis on vocational evaluation and work adjustment training materials.

Chapter 15

ADULTHOOD AND MATURITY

In recent years, our society has made radical changes in its perception of persons with cerebral palsy, epilepsy, learning disabilities, mental retardation, and other developmental disabilities. Changes in perception have caused improvements in services designed to help developmentally disabled individuals achieve their maximum potential. However, an adult with mental retardation has a burden uniquely different from an adult who has any other developmental disability; he or she must cope with society's historic tendency to perceive such an individual as a "perpetual child" or "a child in an adult's body." This persistent perception is reflected in the lack of adequate, age-appropriate services for mentally retarded individuals of all ages; and it is a critical lack for older and elderly mentally retarded persons.

Every citizen should have the opportunity to achieve a fulfilled life and a dignified maturity. However, mentally retarded adults, aging and aged, appear to have been an invisible group until the mid-1970s—invisible in their whereabouts in the community; invisible in their unique needs; invisible in the rosters of funding agencies; and invisible in the literature of both mental retardation and gerontology (Dickerson, Hamilton, Huber, & Segal, 1979). The invisibility of older retarded persons is the result of several factors. Service systems do not track or maintain contact with former service recipients; mild or moderately retarded

Martha Ufford Dickerson
G. Allen Roeher Institute
York University

individuals are absorbed into the community and frequently are lost among the street people; most current programs focus on children or adolescents; and the adult retarded population has few advocates. Andrews (1983) commented on the insensitivity of professionals in the field of retardation who reported they had no knowledge of a large number of former clients, or indicated that they assumed some other agency would provide anything that was needed. Manson (1983) reported on the dramatic increase in the life expectancy for mentally retarded persons as a result of improved health services and medical treatment, thus increasing the number of retarded citizens who reach old age.

Society must accept two challenges: (1) to provide enriching, maturing, fulfilling services to a group of developmentally disabled people who have become middle-aged or older without having had the opportunity to prepare for this stage in their lives; and (2) to prepare developmentally disabled children and adolescents for a life of fulfillment as mature adults by providing them with training and skill development in such areas as sexuality and interpersonal relationships. This chapter will focus primarily on the first of these challenges.

DISABILITIES IN ADULTHOOD

Hitzing, McGee, Wood, and Keith (1978) identified five groups who are frequently mistreated or denied service: prisoners, children, mentally ill persons, mentally retarded individuals, and the elderly. Because both retarded and aged persons are often dependent upon others for their care, they are more vulnerable to alienation and mistreatment. According to Pezzoli (1978), "The two groups thus share many of the same problems of societal indifference, stinginess, and contempt, mixed with equally dehumanizing pity, patronization and, most annoyingly, a tendency to treat both retarded and aged persons as children" (p. 206).

Later, Flumenbaum (1979) asserted, "If social policy and service availability follows the public's stereotypic attitudes toward the various disabilities, and then we add age as a factor in the public's attitude, we see that AADD (aging/aged developmentally disabled) persons are in an unlikely position for becoming visible to service providers. Changes in the availability of services for this population may directly depend upon programs which change public attitudes" (p. 189). Lacking strong advocates and political power, minority groups do not receive an equitable share of public funds to improve the condition of their health and welfare (Cohen, 1983).

It is time to throw open the doors and help the invisible clients "come out of the closet." It is time for adult, aged, and elderly developmentally disabled people to become visible, conspicuous, and assertive so that they may begin to enjoy the rights and privileges accorded to other adults in society. It is time for professionals to seek out adult developmentally disabled persons and involve them as participants in planning and experiencing the rest of their lives.

In the past, there were as many definitions of mental retardation as there were professional disciplines dealing with the population. Some definitions emphasized etiological factors; others emphasized sociobehavioral factors; but several definitions have been recognized in current literature and practice. In contrast, Thomas and others (1979) found that there was no recognized definition of aging and aged, as applied to developmentally disabled individuals. This lack of clarity has resulted in the common practice of perceiving developmentally disabled individuals who reach the age of 45 or 50 as old, in contrast to members of the general population of the same age who are perceived as middle-aged.

According to Kriger (1975), comparisons cannot be made between the lifestyle of a nonretarded adult and the lifestyle of a mentally retarded adult because the nonretarded person has many social, educational, and vocational advantages not usually in the experience of the retarded person. Obviously, many nonretarded people acquire disabilities as they age due to accident, illness, or injury. These disabilities, while handicapping to the individual, are experienced against a background of so-called normalcy. The "normal" person who, during the aging process, experiences decreased mobility due to arthritis or diminished sight because of glaucoma endures these assaults of aging after many years of a handicap-free life. Conversely, a developmentally disabled person, who acquires additional disabilities as a result of aging, experiences these assaults as an exacerbation of a lifetime of coping with handicapping conditions.

In an effort to bring clarity to the consideration of aging in terms of the developmentally disabled, as well as to the so-called normal population, Thomas, Acker, Choksey, and Cohen (1979) described aging in terms of a lifetime phenomenon, consisting of biological, sociological, and psychological processes occurring during the progression from the physical maturity of the middle years toward old age and death.

Judging from the focus of services currently provided developmentally disabled persons, it would appear that they have an unusually long growth period or childhood, followed by an extended maturation period of adolescence, and at an early age slip into senescence, having never experienced the plateau stage of middle years. Increasingly, parents and professionals recognize the potential for the continuous growth and development of developmentally disabled individuals. Countless numbers of individuals are striving to understand and accept the condition of their births and are working valiantly to overcome the external handicapping condition that society adds to original burdens.

Recognition of New Concerns

Some parents and professionals have begun to recognize that developmentally disabled persons of all ages need training and guidance in the management of their social-sexual relationships. The Mental Retardation Program of the National Institute of Child Health and Human Development convened a conference on Human Sexuality and the Mentally Retarded. Specialists from the fields of biology, medicine, psychology, anthropology, sociology, genetics, education, social work, and law were invited to identify issues and share concerns. The proceedings of this landmark conference edited by de la Cruz and LaVeck (1973) formed the basis for teaching methods and materials (Kempton, Bass, & Gordon, 1973) now commonly used by parents and professionals to teach sexuality and human fulfillment.

Simultaneously, parents and professionals began to ask questions such as: "What is going to happen to these adult retarded people when they age and become elderly?" "Now that the institution does not provide lifetime care, where will they go?" The University of Michigan, through the collaboration of the Institute of Gerontology (IOG) and the Institute for the Study of Mental Retardation and Related Disabilities (ISMRRD), provided significant leadership in addressing the concerns of clients perceived to be in "double jeopardy," both aged and developmentally disabled. The four-member task force (two representatives from each institute) took their concerns to the 98th Annual Meeting of the American Association on Mental Deficiency (AAMD) in Toronto in 1974 (Dickerson, Hamilton, Huber, & Segal, 1979). The presentation was heard by few conference participants, which was an accurate indication of the low level of interest in the plight of older retarded individuals.

However, the Developmental Disabilities Office of the Office of Human Development Service, Department of Health, Education, and Welfare, was sufficiently impressed by the paper to fund a consultation conference on the gerontological aspects of mental retardation held in Ann Arbor, Michigan, in 1975. Seventy participants were invited from the 50 states, as well as districts under United States jurisdiction. Participants were representatives of administration and direct practice from agencies serving the mentally retarded population (Hamilton & Segal, 1975). Segal (1978b) continued to gather data on a national level while Sweeney and Wilson (1979) compiled the research efforts conducted in mid-America. As with the initial efforts in the area of human sexuality and retardation, these early efforts in the field of aging in developmentally disabled persons provided the basis for practice that was to evolve.

Acceptance Versus Rejection

Most developmentally disabled adults have had ego-shattering experiences of rejection. Some have never known unconditional acceptance from another human being. Many have been infantilized for so long that they are incredulous and distrustful when someone, anyone, encourages them to take responsibility for some aspect of their lives. Some individuals have been intimidated so thoroughly that their physical posture reveals their poor self-image, sending a negative message to people they meet resulting in further rejection. Thus, the cycle of disorientation, alienation, and patronization continues. Goffman (1963) has described the negative impact upon an individual when acceptance is withheld by another person.

In addition to the lack of healthy experiences with others who honestly accept them, most mentally retarded adults are ill-equipped to manage the many different socio-sexual relationships that are options for community residents. Sadly, too many retarded adults have been exploited or otherwise victimized because

introducing

THERESA

Theresa, 32, is a proud mother. Her 10-month-old daughter is healthy and shows no signs of developmental delay. However, her pride in her daughter does not ease the stress Theresa feels living in her parents' home.

Theresa is the youngest of five siblings raised by John (66) and Mary (65). John and Mary recall Theresa as a "slow baby—slow to do everything," and remember that she was classified as "trainable" and attended special classes. They are proud that as a family they took care of their own and never sent Theresa away. Theresa moved into a group home at age 20 when she qualified for a sheltered workshop.

During the following 10 years, Theresa was a faithful worker and a popular resident of the group home. She learned many homemaker skills and enjoyed a diverse social-recreational program. When she was 30, Theresa demonstrated her readiness to live in a supervised apartment with another woman. Her activities continued as before, with one important addition. Theresa developed a sexual relationship with a man from the workshop and soon she was pregnant.

Theresa and her friend were delighted with the pregnancy, but their parents were dismayed. For religious reasons, her parents supported her decision to refuse an abortion. Theresa was informed by the children's protective source that as a retarded woman she was a mother-at-risk and would therefore be monitored in the management of her baby. Arrangements were made for Theresa to spend the last two months of her pregnancy in a residence for unmarried pregnant women where she could learn basic child care.

Following an unremarkable delivery, Theresa and her infant daughter returned to the residence for an additional six-week period of instruction, supervision, and observation. At the end of this period it was decided that Theresa was incapable of caring for her daughter, and custody for her child was awarded to her parents, John and Mary. In order to be with her daughter, Theresa moved with her into John and Mary's home.

Theresa's daughter appears to be doing well in her grandparents' home, but everyone else in the household is under stress. When Theresa returned home, her parents curtailed her activities and actively discouraged any contacts with former friends. John and Mary are worried about the future for their daughter and granddaughter. They are concerned about Theresa's rebelliousness, which appears to be increasing. Currently, no services are utilized by the three-generational family; the expectation continues to be "we'll take care of our own."

of their naivete. Few retarded adults have had the opportunity to discuss the feelings and behaviors associated with loss, separation, aging, dying, or death. Imagine the vacuum in their lives, the feeling of never having been fulfilled in any way—socially, sexually, emotionally—and then to be informed, "now you are old." For most of society, the perception of age and retardation provides a doubled reason for rejection of the individual so described. According to Pezzoli (1978), "Mental retardation and old age are both handicaps in part because of social devaluation" (p. 204).

CURRENT PERSPECTIVES

Social and Political Trends

There are significant changes in the age distribution of the world population, and these changes are reflected within the mentally retarded population. The percentage of the population over 55 is increasing as is the average life expectancy; a child born today may anticipate an average lifespan of 76 years. According to the White House 1981 Conference on Aging, in 1976 there were 43 million people over the age of 65 and, by the year 2000, it is anticipated there will be 57 million people over the age of 65.

In spite of the emergence of an older society, a national preoccupation with youth prevails and impedes the public recognition of the needs of aging citizens. Cohen (1983) reported that older persons experience discrimination in employment and housing and do not receive their share of other public services. Additionally, older citizens suffer from false stereotypes about the elderly.

Self-advocacy groups have emerged to represent older Americans, and they have become a recognized political force because of their voting power. Their efforts in the past have brought about notable service improvements, such as the establishment of Medicare, a federal health insurance program for aged and disabled persons receiving Social Security disability benefits that pays for hospital and nursing home care. To date, the self-advocacy groups representing developmentally disabled Americans have not wielded comparable influence, partly because developmentally disabled adults, as a group, have a poor voting record.

Parents, professionals, and interested citizens are advocates for developmentally disabled persons. These advocates, through state and national organizations, have been largely responsible for the enactment of legislation on behalf of developmentally disabled individuals. A small but growing number of professionals are expressing concern for the increasing number of older developmentally disabled persons with service needs. A symposium on this topic at the 6th International Congress of the International Association for the Scientific Study of Mental Deficiency (IASSMD) attracted 75 participants (Cohen & Dickerson, 1983), in contrast to the eight participants who attended a session on aging at the 98th Annual Meeting of AAMD in 1974.

The National Administration on Aging, a unit of the Office of Human Development Services, provides grants to state and community programs on aging to ensure planning, evaluation, and coordination of service efforts. Additional funds are made available to establish gerontological centers where professional training and research may be conducted.

The Administration on Developmental Disabilities is also a unit of the Office of Human Development Services. Like the Administration on Aging, the Administration on Developmental Disabilities supports university-affiliated facilities where professional training, research, and demonstration may take place. This administration relies upon state planning councils to plan, coordinate, and evaluate the use of federal funds allocated for state and community programs.

Many older adults who are developmentally disabled require services throughout their lives so that they may enjoy the rights and privileges accorded to all adults in our society.

Relevant Legislation

In addition to federal legislation described elsewhere in this text, the various states have passed laws that are more or less supportive. These regulations generally pertain to the civil rights of retarded adults as citizens of the community. According to Schulman (1980), "Rights pertinent to retarded adults refer to the right to marry, to informed voluntary sterilization, to life, to bear children, to a barrier-free environment, to employment, to travel, to vote, and to drive" (p. 79).

According to Ackerman (1979), the Education for All Handicapped Children Act (PL 94–142) fosters normalization in that mentally retarded children are mainstreamed into the classroom and each child's educational program is based on an individualized plan. Ackerman also observed that, even though parallel legislation exists to foster the normalization of the older developmentally disabled person, the results have been less productive and lack focus on individual treatment plans.

Identification and Assessment

Demographic data about the adult developmentally disabled population are scarce, incomplete, and inaccurate. This is due to several reasons: unclear definitions of developmental disabilities, inconsistent classification procedures, lost or obscured records because of frequency of client transfer in and out of agencies, and lack of follow-up at termination of service. Attempts have been made in some areas to fill this informational void, such as the work done by Hanf and Keiter (1978) in Oregon, and by Sweeney and Wilson (1979) in mid-America (Illinois, Indiana, Michigan, Minnesota, Ohio, and Wisconsin). Although statistical data are incomplete, certain commonalities have been recognized which permit cautious generalization.

Adults who are developmentally disabled are like other adults in that they may range from young adulthood (18–30), mid-adulthood (30–50), and older adulthood (50–65), to elderly adults (65 up). Frequently, those individuals who are over 50 years of age are referred to as aging/aged developmentally disabled (AADD). As with the general population, retarded adults come from all segments of the community. Their collective family roots reflect the American mosaic in that every ethnic, religious, racial, national, and socioeconomic group is represented in the population of adults who are developmentally disabled. As with the general population, developmentally disabled adults are individuals with unique characteristics.

Developmentally disabled adults maintain their individuality and uniqueness, even when considering the one characteristic they appear to have in common— developmental disability. Such factors as cause of disability, sex, age, general health, degree of disability, and complexity of resulting handicap contribute to this dissimilarity. Each developmentally disabled adult presents a unique history of remediation and training. Cosmetic surgery; dental monitoring, treatment, and correction; and use of adaptive devices and equipment may have been more or less available depending upon certain factors, such as year of birth, family affluence, and place of residence during early childhood and adolescence.

Some individuals had the opportunity to develop vocational skills and hold jobs; others did not. Some maintained a strong connection with family members; others did not. A few developed a sense of personal worth and became accepted and respected; most were tolerated, ignored, or rejected. The younger adults were more likely to have lived in the community all their lives, while some older retarded adults seem to have led shadow lives for a few years following release from institutions, only to reappear with service needs when their support networks collapsed. Some developmentally disabled adults have suffered sensory or motoric losses typical of the aging process.

Some multiply impaired middle-aged adults appear so much older than their chronological age that no one questions their permanent residency in homes for elderly nonretarded persons. Ensor (1979), in his analysis of services to the AADD in Michigan, commented, "In the clear absence of categorical services for the AADD client, the 'masquerading' client—one who 'seems like' a member of the *served* population—may be in the best position to be served at this point in time" (p. 163).

Kriger (1975) and Segal (1978a) found that many AADD persons outlived the parents and other family members upon whom they were totally dependent and, thus, became even more vulnerable and needful of service. Scheerenberger (1977) found that previously institutionalized adults who did have family members presented additional service needs because the family members frequently needed support to accept the change in lifestyle of their retarded sons, daughters, brothers, and sisters. Hamilton and Betts (1977), in their work in Chicago, determined that retarded adults were underemployed and, in fact, lived in poverty.

Like other people, developmentally disabled adults have been influenced by the information or feedback they have received from significant others in their lives. Families, neighbors, professionals, care givers, and other retarded people have been providing conflicting messages about the community's expectations for their behavior. Television, radio, and movies have also contributed to shaping the adults' perception of themselves, their worth, and their place in a multicultural dynamic world.

When considering the need to assess the potential performance of a developmentally disabled adult, it is imperative to evaluate the individual's self-perception and understanding of his or her own situation. While it has proven valuable to use tests and other measurement devices to classify the level of retardation in order to appropriately place school-age children, such tests are of minimal assistance when dealing with adults. It is of greater importance to assess an individual's ability to adapt to the world.

Individualized Program Planning

In the past, program planning for developmentally disabled adults placed emphasis upon their maintenance in supervised, safe settings where little attention was paid to continuous education and training to support continued growth and development. Recently, most professionals and some parents have accepted the latent potential for progress that is existent along with the chronicity of a given disability. Adams (1971) expands on the concept of chronicity thus: "Chronicity is not related to disability but to vulnerability to stress; for their adjustment can at any time be undermined if the pressures of life become excessive" (p. 258).

Present practice in planning for developmentally disabled adults places the emphasis upon meeting the individual's needs as they are perceived by an advisor/advocate. In discussion about individualized program planning, Schulman (1980) identified three phases in the process: (1) *Development*, the time to gather facts and formulate a plan; (2) *Implementation*, the time to accomplish the plan, including monitoring and recording; and (3) *Progress*, the time to determine gains and losses, successes and failures, and otherwise prepare for re-entry into the phase of development. Thus, the process of individualized program planning (IPP) is cyclical and never-ending.

The goal of an IPP is to help the individual adult enjoy his or her mature and senior years uninhibited by infantilization and with the supports necessary to maintain the conventional standards of a secure, fulfilled life. They must be provided the diverse services needed to foster developing adequacy and independence; and it is essential to include and involve the developmentally disabled adult in every phase of the process.

Developmentally disabled adults, like other people, have needs in seven areas, as described by Dickerson (1983): income maintenance, home maintenance, health maintenance, vocational-educational opportunities, recreational experiences, interpersonal relationships, and crisis management. Each of these needs will be discussed in terms of the developmentally disabled adult, and each area should be considered when conducting the IPP process.

Income Maintenance. Every developmentally disabled adult is eligible for financial assistance in the form of Supplemental Security Income (SSI), subject to certain limitations. Monthly income varies depending upon place of residence (with family members or in an approved facility) and provides for board, room, incidental grooming, clothing, and recreation. The amount is moderate and frequently incidental expenses are not sufficiently covered. A recipient of SSI is limited to a financial reserve of $500 and there are limits on earned or unearned income. These restrictions, as well as low expectations for an individual's job performance, serve as powerful deterrents when disabled adults or their family or advocates contemplate self-support.

Currently, there is a trend to encourage mentally retarded adults to become partially or completely self-supporting. This trend is gathering momentum as a result of the enactment in 1973 of the Vocational Rehabilitation Act which introduced the rehabilitative approach to income maintenance. Subsequent amendments to the act have attempted to make it more responsive to developmentally disabled individuals.

Home Maintenance. As indicated above, the adult whose income is derived from SSI has limited choices of where to live—with family or in an approved licensed facility. Depending upon the community, there may be several, few, or no options other than living with family. The options—dormitories, shared apartments, group homes, adult family care homes, and nursing homes—provide varying degrees of independence. Such facilities may be adequate; but, in situations where several disabled adults live together, there is apt to be an overreliance upon rules and regimentation, thus decreasing the independence of the individual.

Health Maintenance. Any developmentally disabled adult who receives SSI automatically receives Medicaid, a federal program which covers essential medical expenses. For the chronically ill residents of nursing homes and intermediate care facilities, such coverage is generally adequate; however, the healthy developmentally disabled adult who requires medical monitoring or dental maintenance and repair may find the coverage inadequate and may need to seek supplementary aid from state or local medical services.

Vocational-Educational Opportunities. Developmentally disabled adults confront many barriers when they attempt to join the work force. Architectural barriers are a reality; however, negative attitudes of employers and fellow workers,

A developmentally disabled adult leaves his group home residence to go to his job; he learned the appropriate vocational skills through a career development program.

though less tangible, present even greater obstacles. In the current job market, thousands of nonretarded persons compete for unskilled jobs, making opportunities for developmentally disabled adults even scarcer. According to Schulman (1980), current programs designed to prepare individuals for the work force focus upon skill development with little attention to social and personal skills, which are also necessary in order for developmentally disabled adults to meet employment criteria.

Some of the middle-aged and older developmentally disabled adults have become mainstreamed into the American world of work and cease to be singled out because of their handicap. Some of them may be expected to reappear for services at the point of retirement or layoff, and they may be served by agencies for the general public (generic agencies), which is to be desired.

Increasingly, the community expects more training and rehabilitation as preparation for the complex demands of high technology, as well as to meet the learning/training needs for people who have more severe deficits and lower levels of competence (Adams, 1971). Severely retarded adults have demonstrated they can compete in this "high-tech" era (Gold, 1974). Bellamy (1976) based his work on the normalization principle as he provided vocational training for severely retarded clients; DuRand and Neufeldt (1975) have addressed the need for a career development focus in the vocational training of developmentally disabled persons.

Educational opportunities which are not vocationally oriented are expanding as well, and these serve to improve the quality of life. Adult education has become a method for developmentally disabled adults in the community to learn about available resources and the behaviors expected of community residents. Adult activity centers devote many hours to teaching the activities of daily living (ADL). These same educational methods are used within institutions to prepare residents for release and subsequent re-entry into the community. Hofmeister and Gallery (1978) have identified educational/training packages already in existence that are appropriate for use with homebound, elderly individuals.

Adult education for the mentally retarded has moved onto college campuses in several states, with the highest concentration in Colorado, which initiated a statewide program. The College for Living (CFL) is a response to the need of mentally retarded individuals to have access to a continuous learning experience in an environment appropriate for their age group. Dickerson and Eastman (1982) and Dickerson, Eastman, and Saffer (1984) have been developing materials for use in continuous learning experiences.

Recreational Experiences.   The more independence individuals achieve in managing money, using public transportation, and choosing friends, the more their recreational experiences will be like other community citizens. Any interest which they can afford can be enjoyed, including movies, restaurants, bars, arcades, sports, travel, crafts, or hobbies.

Recreational options are much more limited for homebound adults. Television remains the major source of entertainment, with few other activities available. There is little to encourage interaction with other people or involvement with a new activity, skill, or behavior.

Interpersonal Relationships.   Developmentally disabled adults find themselves limited in their options of personal relationships because of their living conditions. The more independent the lifestyle and the less screening and monitoring of behavior, the more freedom of choice an adult will have when selecting acquaintances, friends, companions, and sexual partners. By way of contrast, when a developmentally disabled adult lives in a supervised situation (parental home or approved facility), he or she is more apt to have immature relationships. It is usual for a retarded adult in such a protective environment to view all other adults, except the other residents, as authority figures from whom one must seek permission, sanction, and direction.

Obviously, the more fragile and dependent that developmentally disabled individuals are, or appear to be, the more they are infantilized, thus continuing a nonproductive cycle. It goes without saying that the more dependent a client appears to be, the less intimacy he or she is permitted to share and the less privacy he or she enjoys. There is little opportunity for the adult who is so protected to experience initiating, maintaining, enjoying, and terminating a relationship. Often disabled adults are not even permitted to choose the person with whom they share their bedroom! Dickerson (1981) has reported on the common practice of staff making room assignments on the basis of agency re-

A Community-Based Recreation Program

Eighteen elderly developmentally disabled individuals living in group homes throughout a large suburban county were in need of recreational activities. A few of them left their homes daily to attend sheltered workshops; however, most seldom left their homes. Each of them had lived most of his or her life in state institutions. Two women and one man were nonambulatory, one woman was blind, and two men were nonverbal.

Arrangements were made with a local department of recreation to integrate the 18 individuals into a community-sponsored multipurpose center for senior citizens. The developmentally disabled adults were prepared for participation in the program through the expertise of a social worker who was familiar with mental retardation. He arranged a series of biweekly Saturday meetings over a seven-month period. The meeting rooms used on weekdays by the senior program were made available for these special sessions.

The social worker, assisted by volunteers recruited from the nonhandicapped senior membership, provided a stimulating, interesting, and inclusive simulation of the weekday program as a vehicle for the developmentally disabled adults as they practiced new behaviors. They learned where to hang their coats and how to pay dues, serve themselves coffee, and participate in games, singing and other social behaviors typical of the multipurpose center member.

After the seven-month preparation, the developmentally disabled adults began attending regularly scheduled activities with the nonhandicapped seniors from the community. The president of the center arranged a welcoming affair for the new members. In her remarks of welcome, she commented, "We welcome you. We have come to know you as truly people first and senior citizens second. Your handicaps, which we recognize are minor difficulties, we can overcome."

quirements and available space with little or no recognition of individual social-sexual needs.

Those developmentally disabled adults who live freer, less monitored existences are less dependent and have more coping skills to rely upon as they negotiate relationships. There appears to be an increasing number of mentally retarded adults who enjoy intimate relationships, live with peers, marry, and become parents; but little data regarding the numbers of individuals so involved or the success rate of these relationships are available. As parents, retarded adults require extensive support services to create a healthy environment for their children; and frequently, children are removed from their parents because the home situation is found to be unfit.

Crisis Management.   Restricted living options and lack of meaningful peer relationships are deficits that make facing a crisis all the more formidable. Like other people, developmentally disabled adults may experience a crisis when they feel unable to manage their lives with the resources they have available. The crises in a developmentally disabled adult's life are not different because of his or her disability; they are merely more complex.

When crises occur, some developmentally disabled adults who have been "passing" as nonhandicapped will emerge and request assistance from traditional agencies. For less independent adults, crises are frequently "handled" by an authority (parent, guardian, caregiver, social worker, or doctor) with little consultation with the adult who is in crisis. This lack of involvement in crisis resolution is another example of infantilization and denial of growth through experience. Clients are frequently shielded from usual interpersonal experiences such as separation, loss, dying, and death.

Availability of Service.   Sweeney and Wilson (1979) reported that, in six states (Illinois, Indiana, Michigan, Minnesota, Ohio, and Wisconsin), the services most frequently offered older developmentally disabled persons were medical treatment, information and referral, adult activities, and recreation. The least frequently offered services were educational classes, sheltered employment, vocational classes, and counseling in regard to sexuality or interpersonal relationships. It appeared that the development of diversified resources in the community had not kept pace with the movement to desegregate the mentally retarded. Chinn, Drew, and Logan (1979) have described the challenge to service systems as a human problem incorporating a range of concerns—educational, social, medical, legal, and interpersonal—and, thus, requiring attention from a comprehensive perspective.

Other Issues

There are four major concerns that are rarely addressed with developmentally disabled adults: ego development, sexuality, emotional disorders, and guardianship. There is much overlap among the concerns, but an attempt will be made to consider each concern independently.

Ego Development.   It is important for every person to understand the conditions of his or her personhood—sex, racial and ethnic heritage, family, and his or her strengths and weaknesses. This is no less important for an individual who has a physical or mental disability; yet, many parents and professionals refrain from discussion with their children or clients about physical and mental disabilities, or they enter these discussions in a guarded manner relying upon hollow platitudes, half-truths, and phony optimism to get them through the experience. This evasive behavior on the part of the parent or professional serves to intensify the confusion the individual is already experiencing. Yet extensive clinical experience with clients suggests that they have known there was something undesirable and frightening about them that alienated them from other people. They have wanted to know about the undesirable differences.

Self-control or management of one's own behavior develops concurrently with self-knowledge and must be established in order for an individual to achieve responsible self-expression and fulfillment in adult life. In the past, practitioners have attempted to train individuals in the acquisition of socially acceptable behaviors without helping them make the connection between the behaviors and their knowledge of self and ultimate respect for self. Practitioners have traditionally placed more emphasis upon helping the person "get along with others," with little recognition of the need to "get along with one's self."

To fully implement the normalization principle, we must reverse the priorities and help individuals first learn to get along with themselves. Developmentally disabled adults must work on ego development as a basis for all other social-emotional growth, and this includes learning about their disability and understanding the impact it will have upon all social-sexual relationships. As the individual develops respect for self, he or she is better prepared to develop appropriate behaviors to ease interactions with others.

Sexuality.   Two civil rights accorded to mentally retarded people are frequently difficult to protect: the right to informed, voluntary sterilization, and the right to marry. In the past, it was common practice to forbid mentally retarded adults to marry and to make sterilization a condition of release from a state institution. Across the nation, many states still maintain discriminatory laws regarding marriage and sterilization in spite of federal rulings to the contrary. Currently, as a result of a more enlightened view of mental retardation and human sexuality, these restrictions are being removed.

Johnson (1975) comments: "More and more people, including parents and teachers, are increasingly able to perceive the incongruities and irrationality of many traditional attitudes toward the sexuality of special groups and strive courageously toward greater objectivity and rationality" (p. 61). McNab (1978), writing for educators, said: "The handicapped have the same sexual needs and desires as others; but lack of exposure prevents them from obtaining the skills necessary to function in society" (p. 305). Bass (1974) has stated that the sexual needs of the mentally retarded may be even greater than the needs of the non-handicapped because of limited communication, greater frequency of physical contact, and fewer opportunities to channel sex drives due to limited socialization with peers.

Like other people, developmentally disabled adults will continuously learn about sexuality and its impact upon the successive stages of their lives. Gustwick (1978) reminds us that it will take a lifetime of listening, answering questions, and guiding mentally retarded adults to help them achieve healthy sexual maturity.

The rights, privileges, and responsibilities inherent in an individual's role in relation to another person's role must be earned, and are learned through exposure to various stimuli and models in the environment. When these stimuli or models are inadequate or present defective or conflicting information, the developmentally disabled adult, already vulnerable, becomes confused.

Parents have the privilege of directly teaching and training their child, and consciously or not, influencing their child by their own behavior. Many retarded children and adolescents grow up in homes where parents are hesitant to discuss sexuality, and this behavior conveys many strong attitudes about sexuality. Other parents negate the sexuality of their children and strive to protect their innocence by perpetuating their ignorance. Still other parents support sex education for their children in the hope that some information will prove a behavioral deterrent and that they will learn enough to say "No" and, thus, avoid exploitation.

Professionals are influenced by parental opinion and often are fearful of addressing sexuality for fear of arousing parental criticism. Less often acknowledged, yet an important factor, is the ambivalence many professionals feel about the sexual expression of mentally retarded people. Many professionals support the practice of teaching mentally retarded individuals about body parts, body differences, body changes, hygiene, conception, and contraception. A small group of professionals believe that, like other people, mentally retarded individuals should have the right to learn about the range of sexual expression and the particular behaviors and responsibilities unique to an individual's sexual orientation. Members of this group usually perceive the goal of sex education and sexuality development as an intrinsic element in developing a healthy individual who experiences or celebrates a fulfilled life.

Some parents and professionals in the past have held the view, "What they don't know, they won't do." All evidence proves the fallacy of such an opinion. The great majority of developmentally disabled adults are capable of learning the concepts of privacy and mutual consent, which prepares them for sexual activity without fear of embarrassment or punitive action.

Some retarded adults have proven to be capable of practicing birth control and maintaining sex hygiene, thus avoiding unwanted pregnancies and infections. Some retarded adults who have had the opportunity for sexuality training have made decisions not to become parents, while others have decided not to marry. Ironically, these individuals have made decisions that please the general public, which historically has tried to mandate such behaviors; however, the individuals who have made such decisions enjoy the dignity of owning their own behavior rather than having it legislated for them.

Whether or not retarded adults are capable of providing adequate parenting to a child is a moot question. Johnson (1975) stated: "Parenthood is a most difficult undertaking, and decisions concerning whether or not to attempt it would seem to invite the most careful anticipatory education and counseling, for special group members even more than for others" (p. 206).

It may be that young adults will have had a better introduction to responsible sexuality than the current group of adults have experienced. In the meantime, those already in their adulthood must rely on settings such as adult activity centers for ongoing sex education and counseling (Secker, 1973).

Emotional Disorders.   Szymanski and Tanguay (1980) have been leaders in recognizing the need for treating emotional disorders in mentally retarded persons. Their work contradicts the popular view that retarded individuals cannot profit from the use of psychiatric interventions. Their work emphasizes the need for an interdisciplinary approach in the diagnosis and treatment of psychiatric disorders. They state: "Many studies have shown that mentally retarded persons may not only develop all of the types of mental illness found in the general population, but that as many as 50 percent may, at some time, suffer from some type of diagnosable psychiatric disorder" (p. xiii).

Turecki (1981) described prolonged dependency and the concomitant need for attachments to parental figures as factors contributing to the vulnerability of developmentally disabled individuals to experience exacerbated stress at times such as puberty or pregnancy.

It is a simple exercise to establish the relationship between lack of guidance in the development of a healthy ego, lack of accurate information regarding social-sexual relationships, and the evidence of emotional stress and mental illness.

Guardianship. Laws governing the appointment of a guardian vary from state to state; however, in each situation the laws are designed to protect the individual's rights and to protect society from the individual's antisocial behaviors.

Parents need to understand that their legal status as parents of a developmentally disabled child is no different from the legal status of parents of nonretarded children. When any person, regardless of competency or of functioning, reaches the age of majority, parental guardianship is terminated. In some instances, continued guardianship may be indicated, and legal counsel will be required to prepare a petition for the court's attention. The court will require evaluative material about the potential ward, in terms of physical, mental, social, and educational needs, and his or her ability to cope with the environment and make decisions. The court will determine the need for guardianship, the extent of guardianship, and, if indicated, appoint a guardian.

Many developmentally disabled adults will not need a guardian, but the court may recommend or appoint advocates to provide support to these individuals as they learn to manage their lives. Others will require some assistance in certain areas and the court may appoint partial guardians to be responsible for designated concerns such as financial management or health monitoring. A partial guardianship permits the development of a highly individualized plan which recognizes maturational needs and is subject to periodic review, revision, or removal. Very few developmentally disabled adults require total guardianship, which literally means loss of all personal rights and responsibilities for life, with no option of reversal.

Since the removal of rights is such an insurmountable barrier to the achievement of maturity, the move toward guardianship must be considered with great caution. Every responsibility or right assigned to a guardian is a responsibility or right removed from the developmentally disabled adult. Professionals must advocate for each adult client to ensure that the determination of degree of guardianship focuses on the client's maturational needs rather than the convenience to other family members.

EFFICACY OF PAST PRACTICES

As indicated earlier, until the mid-1970s the primary practice focus in the service of developmentally disabled adults was on custodial care in large institutions. This practice resulted in many adults having been trained to be obedient, passive, and quiescent, in exchange for protection, board, and care. Hartman (1969) described residents of institutions as overprotected, overroutinized, and lacking any power to affect their circumstances.

Practice, as described above, was the result of several interrelated factors. Myths about the developmentally disabled, which have emerged from distorted facts and incorrect assumptions, have been barriers in helping the community accept disabled individuals. Myths, such as "they're all alike," "they're better off with their own kind," "all retards are oversexed," "they'll always be a tax burden," "they're children who never grew up," and "they're apt to be criminals" have been all too prevalent. A popular perception of developmentally disabled adults during the '50s and '60s was of men and women who were incompetent, unlovable, irresponsible castoffs.

To be perceived as deviant is extremely destructive to the person so perceived, for behavior tends to be negatively influenced by the role expectations that accompany such a disparaging perception. According to Wolfensberger (1972): "This permits those who define social roles to make self-fulfilling prophecies by predicting that someone cast into a certain role will emit behavior consistent with that role. Unfortunately, role-appropriate behavior will often be interpreted to be a person's 'natural' mode of acting, rather than a mode elicited by environmental events and circumstances" (pp. 15–16).

Institutions have traditionally been overprotective, infantilizing environments. Staff members at all levels of the institution's hierarchy had low expectations for the residents' growth and development and provided minimal stimulation, constantly monitored or supervised the residents, and overused correction. Frequently the residents reacted to the staff's behavior with rebellion, resistance, and other acting-out behaviors. This, in turn, reinforced the staff's perceptions of the residents' incompetence. The end result was that developmentally disabled residents were situationally vulnerable and miserable; and staff, especially direct care workers, had few satisfactions from their job.

Cooper (1979) recognized that direct care workers had the most contact and the greatest responsibility for treatment of adult developmentally disabled persons, and yet were the most neglected members of the staff hierarchy in terms of financial reward, recognition, job training, and skill development. Rarely were direct care workers included in training opportunities and seldom were their observations given consideration. Frequent turnover of direct care staff precluded the opportunity for many workers to expand their knowledge and skill in their work with clients. Lack of training and supervision contributed to the perpetuation of misconceptions about developmental disabilities and to the workers' discomfort in dealing with handicapped conditions.

Levinthal (1979), in his analysis of community services provided aging and aged developmentally disabled persons in Indiana, reported that very little was offered to meet the needs of the individual. Rather, the services provided replicated the services provided to younger clients. This lack of recognition and attention to an individual's need is comparable to the service observed within institutions.

Sweeney (1979) reported that data obtained from 325 agencies in six states in mid-America revealed obstacles to service delivery to aging and aged developmentally disabled adults in three semidistinct categories: resources, attitudes, and training. Although this was a limited study in terms of geographical area

Living in a community group home allows for social interaction and normal life experiences for developmentally disabled adults.

and the client population identified as service recipients (developmentally disabled individuals over 35 years of age), the findings nevertheless are indicative of current opinions regarding obstacles to service delivery.

PRESENT PRACTICES

The current trend away from custodial care toward a normalized life experience is hampered by certain unresolved general issues. Several systems can provide service to developmentally disabled adults who live in the community. Lack of communication between these systems results in fragmented service delivery. For example, the selection, licensure, and monitoring of a community facility for adults (group home, foster home) may be the responsibility of one state agency, while a second state agency may be responsible for providing individualized programs for the residents of the facility. Conflicts erupt because the first agency tends to be paternalistic and overprotective, while the second agency advocates for less stringency in order to promote growth and development. La Framboise and Provencal (1979) recognized the need for coordination between the diverse state and local educational and vocational training agencies. This need becomes increasingly critical as available resources for funding decrease and demands for service increase.

The problems of coordination and communication are confounded by the wide differences in interpretation and application of the normalization principle. On the one hand, some professionals are concerned over the application of the principle for severely and profoundly handicapped persons as an invitation to frustration and failure. On the other hand, some professionals are troubled by the reluctance of their colleagues to apply the principle in an innovative manner. This confusion and lack of consensus is reflected in the range of different opinions held by professionals in regard to guardianship, and in the wide variance in the quality of worker-client relationships and patterns of interaction.

One of the great advantages to living in the community, as opposed to an institution, is the opportunity for an individual to develop interdependencies in a social network. These interdependencies complement and nurture the development and maintenance of a healthy selfhood; however, Kriger (1975) and Thurman (1983a) found that many retarded individuals placed in the community were not really involved in the community at all. In too many instances, the forms and patterns of institutional living followed the retarded individuals from one residence to the other. Thurman (1983a) found that, in three out of four group homes, residents were monitored and controlled in such a way as to limit a "normalized" style of life and to perpetuate the relationship distance between clients and staff.

In spite of confused and confusing agency conflicts, differing opinions among professionals, and continued infantilization from some workers, developmentally disabled adults are trying to find a place in a community that may harbor hostile attitudes toward them. They are trying to be recognized as individuals capable of having some control of their own lives.

One of the first steps toward meeting the needs of the individual is to involve that person in every step of the planning process; yet, in far too many instances, IPPs are conducted without the person for whom the plan is designed in attendance. Sometimes there is no advocate for the client at the meeting; yet, a plan is designed and the individual is expected to accept and adhere to it. Too frequently, IPPs reflect organizational goals and family concerns rather than the maturational needs of the developmentally disabled adult.

Ackerman (1979) believes that in the past the client's specific needs have been perceived as second in importance to what agencies had predetermined they were willing to supply. Ackerman states: "As long as consumers, practitioners, and administrators are kept apart, normalization is impossible" (p. 202).

Existing Service Needs

The above concerns have an impact in all systems, at all levels of practice, and in the provision of direct service. These concerns are evidenced in identifiable barriers in the seven areas of service needs discussed earlier.

Income Maintenance.   Under the present SSI regulations, there are few incentives for a recipient to move toward the independence of the world of work, for he or she realizes that earning a meager income will cause a loss of benefits and will be a gamble in an area where there has been little job security for the handicapped (last hired, first fired). On the one hand, a federal agency, the Social Security Administration, is practicing from a custodial frame of reference; on the other hand, a second federal agency, the Vocational Rehabilitation Administration, is practicing from the frame of reference of normalization.

Home Maintenance.   Although the 1970s witnessed a mass exodus from state institutions, placement in the community has not necessarily assured the assumption of the privileges of community citizenship. Too frequently, community placement of an individual has meant moving into a setting with fewer people, where life is supervised and monitored by a nonresident staff that provides routinized, boring, in-house programs. Occasional group forays out into the community serve to foster nonacceptance from the community, for these groups are perceived as alien and dependent. The aged developmentally disabled person is apt to be placed in a community nursing home where he or she tends to join a group of patients who are senile and subsequently receives no differentiated treatment.

Health Maintenance.   Medicaid coverage which is the primary resource for developmentally disabled adults does not provide comprehensive medical care and frequently must be supplemented by other resources which are more or less available, depending upon the community and the users' awareness of how to access them.

Vocational-Educational Opportunities.   Efforts in the area of vocational and educational experiences for developmentally disabled adults have been hampered by certain factors. Untrained staff in adult activity centers have relied upon programmatic materials and supplies designed for children which are infantilizing, nonproductive, and monotonous. Vocational counselors have been reluctant to spend the amount of time required to prepare developmentally disabled clients for job placement because the counselor's success is judged by the number and rapidity of job placements he or she secures. Finally, agencies are confused as to their purpose and, thus, staff vacillate between preparing clients for job entry and/or teaching skills to enhance the activities of daily living. Rarely is there a blending of the two purposes into one meaningful goal.

Recreational Experiences.   Although great strides have been made by public, private, and voluntary agencies in the expansion of social-recreational experiences for developmentally disabled adults, the mainstreaming of individuals into community recreation is superficial. Many programs, designed for the exclusive use of developmentally disabled people, segregate them from the community and

DAVID

In his mid-60s, David has achieved a life of independence since his 50th birthday. Prior to that time, he had lived in an institution for the mentally retarded for 35 years. He recalls long years of cruelty and abuse, and still mourns the long ago separation from his family and neighborhood chums. During the years in the institution, he developed many skills that prepared him for community placement. Once in the community, a social worker assigned to help him with his adjustment to a new lifestyle became his advocate and, subsequently, his friend.

David lived in a group home for a while, but he is alone now, living in an apartment in a resort community. Recently he retired from a maintenance job he held for several years. His income is adequate for his tastes. He enjoys taking care of his home, watching TV, fishing, and having a beer at a local social club. David has decided he is too old to marry, but he has a long standing social-sexual relationship with a woman he met in the community. David has no guardian and, thus, makes his own decisions. He has accomplished a career change since age 50.

David would be the first to tell you about the friend who has guided and counselled him through the years. When David was first released from the institution, the social worker spent countless hours helping him learn how to adapt to the strange community. The client-worker relationship became a friendship, and when the worker left agency service, he did not forget his friend, but rather incorporated David into his family circle. Down through the years, this family and a growing circle of nonretarded friends have provided David with the support he has needed to fulfill his life.

perpetuate their alienation. In those instances where developmentally disabled people attend public entertainment (e.g., plays, concerts, ball games), they are frequently seated in special sections or isolated from the general audience.

Interpersonal Relationships. Most frequently, developmentally disabled adults live in situations where they have little to say about selection of housemates or roommates. It is not surprising that relationships between housemates may be based on tolerance rather than acceptance. Previously institutionalized adults have an orientation toward dependency upon staff, which is hard to abandon, and they find it difficult to move toward mutually negotiated interdependent relationships. Thurman (1983b) found that home supervisors and caregivers encouraged previously institutionalized adults to rely on staff for decision making and problem solving, thus discouraging the development of autonomy and mutually supportive peer relationships.

Crisis Management. The delivery of service to developmentally disabled adults is contaminated by the need of parents and professionals to protect the clients. This is especially apparent when an individual must face a crisis. At such times, the usual action taken is for professionals and parents to handle the crisis on behalf of the client and protect him or her from the realities of the crisis, thus removing the opportunity for growth through the experience.

FUTURE PERSPECTIVES FOR DEVELOPMENTALLY DISABLED ADULTS

As we move toward the twenty-first century, a new group of people are emerging from the closets of the nation. As Andrews (1983) reminds us: "The aging and aged population represent the next major group to 'emerge.' They are coming forth in the general population and in the population of disabled individuals" (p. 34).

Innovative programs and services in every area of need must be designed, implemented, and evaluated to prove or disprove the validity of the designs and the appropriateness for replication. Demographic information is needed about those developmentally disabled adults who are in the various age clusters. These data need to be studied in terms of recognition of trends and general programmatic priorities for each age cluster. Data about developmentally disabled children and adolescents should be maintained and utilized to predict future service requirements.

Thurman's (1983a) study of group homes for adults is a pioneer effort that must be replicated and expanded. Community placements must be studied and restudied during the next several years in order to determine the effectiveness of such placements to enable developmentally disabled adults to achieve their maximum potential, as evidenced by the ability to manage social-sexual relationships, make decisions, and handle crises.

The content and methodology of the education and vocational training provided developmentally disabled people of all ages must be researched in terms of its lifetime effectiveness. Efforts to involve developmentally disabled adults in individualized program planning, group program designing, and materials development (Dickerson & Thurman, 1981) should be researched.

Practice must be modified in the following areas: attitudes, recognition of lifetime service needs, training, role of the direct care worker, and full implementation of the Older Americans Act of 1965.

Basic to all other practice changes is the need to confront negative, pejorative attitudes in every part of the community, from the legislator or bureaucrat to the agency board member, volunteers within the agency, administrators, and direct care workers. Parents, paraprofessionals, and professionals must confront the crippling, dehumanizing attitudes that shape their behavior. Vanier (1971) states a challenge: "The day must come when, instead of creating large walls around our houses, we open large doors to welcome at our table the lonely, the old, and the handicapped" (p. 102).

As our attitudes about developmentally disabled people change, we will begin to recognize that an undesirable difference is not necessarily an evil difference, and we will learn to refrain from labeling others with the tags of their differences. We will come to understand there is a purpose for each life and each life can be a fulfilled experience. Finally, we will come to accept that risks must be taken; mistakes can be corrected; and growth will occur.

As attitudes are modified, developmentally disabled adults, their families, and professionals will find it easier to implement a lifetime of service for developmentally disabled people of all ages—those presently old and growing older, and the young who will grow old. As bureaucrats, agency administrators, and program designers work together to eliminate fragmentation and duplication of service and to develop new options, they must actively seek the participation of developmentally disabled adults and their families. Anglin (1983) challenges us to learn from "today's untrained, lost older-retarded people so that the many more retarded individuals who will reach old age in the future will do so without fear" (p. 32).

In all planning for developmentally disabled persons as a class, recognition must be made of the improved preparation the youth have experienced. According to Cohen (1983): "As they become older, their improved functioning and more 'normal' life experiences make them closer in needs to the average aging person" (p. 17). As with other segments of the population, professionals and volunteer advocates must be prepared to provide support and assume responsibility for individuals whose family members may become less available.

The need for training and staff development is paramount at all levels of the community and agency systems. Professionals from diverse disciplines must learn to practice in an interdisciplinary mode by improving communications, clarifying definitions, decreasing use of disciplinary jargon, accepting accountability to and from peers, and abandoning traditional disciplinary "turfdoms." Gerontologists need to learn about the unique needs of developmentally disabled people as they age, and mental retardation specialists need to learn the growth and development patterns of people beyond age 25.

Educators must "adultize" the programs presented to developmentally disabled students and help them acquire skills to enhance the quality of life by presenting classes in the management of social-sexual relationships. Vocational counselors should develop curricula that emphasize career development. Life skills coaches and preretirement counselors should be assigned to adult training programs. Effort should be made at the administrative level to clarify the vocational counselor's role so it is not in conflict with clients' goals.

Administrators and supervisors need to learn how to recruit qualified or potentially qualified workers, provide orientation, emphasize working with people rather than systems maintenance, and provide support in tangible forms such as raises, promotions, participation in meetings, and ongoing training. This process is of critical importance in relation to direct care staff who, in terms of actual hours, exert the greatest influence upon developmentally disabled individuals.

It is time to recognize the residence as the place where an individual is going to learn the behaviors he or she needs in order to venture out into the neighborhood, explore the shopping malls, use public transportation, and gain access to all of the community's resources. It is in one's home where a person is going to learn to overcome, handle, or otherwise manage the real or imagined alienation that he or she feels from the community. The key enablers in this critical experience are parents or direct care workers. If a person is able to live at home, support services should be provided to the parents to address the above needs. If a person lives in an agency-supervised residence, the support will be provided by direct care workers.

Agencies must refine the job description of direct care workers to ensure their acceptance and understanding of their responsibilities, including the responsibility to encourage mobility and to guide individuals in the management of social-sexual relationships. Thurman's (1983a) research into the life experiences of mentally retarded individuals who live in group homes produced many insights into the powerful role of direct care workers. Specific criteria should be developed for the position of direct care workers that include a broader experience base and richer education than is currently required. Using new criteria, direct care workers should be recruited, trained, and supervised. They should receive respect for their position within the service system and receive equitable salaries and ongoing training as tangible rewards. We must reverse the pattern prevalent in the 1980s—where the poorest paid, least trained employees carry the heaviest responsibility for the most vulnerable members of the community.

Older Americans Act of 1965

The Older Americans Act, passed in 1965, is Congress's main vehicle for providing funds and services to meet the special needs of older persons. Subsequent amendments to the original act established direct service to the elderly through nutritional programs, Foster Grandparents, and Retired Seniors Volunteer Program (RSVP). The amendments of 1973 established local and state units called Area Agencies on Aging, which place emphasis upon planning and coordination of services to achieve the objectives as stated in the original act:

1. An adequate income in retirement in accordance with the American standard of living.
2. The best possible physical and mental health which science can make available, and without regard to economic status.
3. Suitable housing, independently selected, designed, and located with reference to special needs, and available at costs which older citizens can afford.
4. Full restorative services for those who require institutional care.
5. Opportunity for employment with no discriminatory personnel practices because of age.
6. Retirement in health, honor, dignity—after years of contribution to the economy.
7. Pursuit of meaningful activity within the widest range of civic, cultural, educational, training, and recreational opportunities.
8. Efficient community services including access to local transportation, which provide a choice in support of living arrangement and social assis-

tance in a coordinated manner and which are readily available when
needed.

9. Immediate benefits from proven research knowledge, which can sustain
and improve health and happiness.

10. Freedom, independence, and the free exercise of individual initiative in
planning and managing their own lives.

These are the rights of all older Americans, including those with developmental
disabilities.

SUMMARY

In the past many people with handicaps, especially those that were more severe,
did not live to be adults; and even fewer lived into old age. Those that did live to
become elderly received few, if any, services and were virtually unknown to
service agencies. In the 1970s, the aging and aged disabled began to be noticed,
and their plight in terms of inadequate health care, housing, vocational, recreational, and spiritual opportunities was recognized. This recognition brought
with it a new advocacy which has focused on assuring the rights of developmentally disabled adults, among which is the right to grow old with dignity.

The number of developmentally disabled adults is not known because of
unclear definitions, inconsistent classification procedures, and lack of systematic
tracking procedures. Consequently the range, number, and scope of programs
and services can only be estimated. However, like all aging and aged adults, those
with developmental disabilities may at some time need financial assistance, help
in finding and maintaining a place to live, staying healthy, contributing vocationally, finding recreational opportunities, developing and maintaining interpersonal relationships, and managing crises. Many can use the generic services
which are available to all people, but others need more specialized services.

The issue of sexuality and disability has received considerable attention in
the past few years. Like all people, developmentally disabled adults are sexual
human beings who often desire and establish intimate relationships. In the past
attempts were made to suppress all interpersonal relationships among handicapped people and to deny their feelings. More recently, programs that include
counseling, support, and education have been developed to help disabled adults
make responsible decisions about sexual expression.

As the age of the general population advances so does that of disabled adults;
yet the programs which they need are not there. The field of aging and aged
adults with disabilities continues to be one where there is great need for attitude
change, improved and expanded programs, and trained personnel.

References

Ackerman, J. (1979). Analysis of services to AADD persons in Ohio. In D. Sweeney & T.
Wilson (Eds.), *Double jeopardy: the plight of aging and aged developmentally disabled
persons in mid-America* (research monograph) (pp. 196–234). Ann Arbor, MI: University of Michigan.

Adams, M. (1971). *Mental retardation and its social dimensions.* New York: Columbia University Press.

Andrews, R. J. (1983). Focus on the aging and aged mentally retarded person: Implications for administrators and supervisors. In J. S. Cohen & M. U. Dickerson (Eds.), *Hey, look at me: I'm old and retarded* (monograph) (pp. 33–46). Downsview, Ontario: National Institute on Mental Retardation.

Anglin, B. (1983). Aging: The consumer's point of view. In J. S. Cohen & M. U. Dickerson (Eds.), *Hey, look at me: I'm old and retarded* (monograph) (pp. 21–32). Downsview, Ontario: National Institute on Mental Retardation.

Bass, M. S. (1974). Sex education for the handicapped. *Family Coordinator, 23* (1), 27–33.

Bellamy, G. T. (Ed.) (1976). *Habilitation of the severely and profoundly retarded: Reports from the specialized training program.* Eugene, OR: University of Oregon, Center of Human Development.

Chinn, P. C., Drew, C. J., & Logan, D. R. (1979). *Mental retardation: A life cycle approach.* St. Louis: C. V. Mosby.

Cohen, J. S. (1983). Programming for an invisible population: Aged mentally retarded persons: Public policy implications. In J. S. Cohen & M. U. Dickerson (Eds.), *Hey, look at me: I'm old and retarded* (monograph) (pp. 9–20). Downsview, Ontario: National Institute on Mental Retardation.

Cohen, J. S., & Dickerson, M. U. (Eds.) (1983). *Hey, look at me: I'm old and retarded* (monograph). Downsview, Ontario: National Institute on Mental Retardation.

Cooper, J. (1979). Criteria for designing training. In D. P. Sweeney & T. Y. Wilson (Eds.), *Double jeopardy: The plight of aging and aged developmentally disabled persons in mid-America* (research monograph) (pp. 312–317). Ann Arbor, MI: University of Michigan.

de la Cruz, F. F., & LaVeck, G. D. (Eds.) (1973). *Human sexuality and the mentally retarded.* New York: Brunner/Mazel.

Dickerson, M. U. (1981). *Social work practice with the mentally retarded.* New York: The Free Press.

Dickerson, M. U. (1983). Elderly retarded people and the seven basic needs. In J. S. Cohen & M. U. Dickerson (Eds.), *Hey, look at me: I'm old and retarded* (monograph) (pp. 1–8). Downsview, Ontario: National Institute on Mental Retardation.

Dickerson, M. U., & Eastman, M. J. (1982). *Training for parents of children with developmental disabilities.* Wayne, MI: Wayne County Intermediate School District.

Dickerson, M. U., Eastman, M. J., & Saffer, A. M. (1984). *Child care training for adults with mental retardation: Volume one–infants.* Downsview, Ontario: National Institute on Mental Retardation.

Dickerson, M., Hamilton, J., Huber, R., & Segal, R. (1979). The aged mentally retarded: The invisible client: A challenge to the community. In D. P. Sweeney & T. Y. Wilson (Eds.), *Double jeopardy: The plight of aging and aged developmentally disabled persons in mid-America* (research monograph) (pp. 3–35). Ann Arbor: University of Michigan.

Dickerson, M. U., & Thurman, E. M. (1981). *Working with aging and aged developmentally disabled persons.* Ann Arbor: University of Michigan Press.

DuRand, J., & Neufeldt, A. H. (1975). *Comprehensive vocational service systems.* Downsview, Ontario: National Institute on Mental Retardation.

Ensor, D. (1979). Assessment of community services for the older/aged developmentally disabled population: Report on services in Michigan. In D. P. Sweeney & T. Y. Wilson (Eds.), *Double jeopardy: The plight of aging and aged developmentally disabled persons in mid-America* (research monograph) (pp. 156–164). Ann Arbor: University of Michigan.

Flumenbaum, R. (1979). Minnesota: Analysis of the data. In D. P. Sweeney & T. Y. Wilson (Eds.), *Double jeopardy: The plight of aging and aged developmentally disabled persons* in *mid-America* (research monograph) (pp. 165–195). Ann Arbor: University of Michigan.

Goffman, E. (1963). *Stioma: Notes on the management of spoiled identity.* Englewood Cliffs, NJ: Prentice-Hall.

Gold, M. W. (1974). *The severely retarded in non-sheltered industry.* Paper presented at 98th Annual Meeting of the American Association on Mental Deficiency, Toronto.

Gustwick, G. (1978). Sexuality and the mentally retarded. *Journal of Tennessee Medical Association, 71* (8), 611–612.

Hamilton, B. B., & Betts, H. B. (1977). *A study of the medical and allied health services delivery system for substantially handicapped developmentally disabled adults: Chicago.* Chicago: Northwestern University Rehabilitation Institute of Chicago.

Hamilton, J. C., & Segal, R. M. (Eds.) (1975). *A consultation and conference on the gerontological aspects of mental retardation* (proceedings). Ann Arbor: University of Michigan.

Hanf, C., & Keiter, J. (1978). The Oregon aged developmentally disabled population: Getting it all together from a data base. In R. Segal (Ed.), *Consultation–conference on developmental disabilities and gerontology: Proceedings of a conference* (pp. 68–92). Ann Arbor: University of Michigan.

Hartman, V. (1969). The key jingler. *Community Mental Health Journal, 5* (3), 199–205.

Hitzing, W., McGee, G., Wood, J., & Keith, K. (1978). A survey of older mentally retarded persons residing in the community and nursing homes. In *National symposium on future directions for older developmentally disabled persons.* Omaha, Nebraska.

Hofmeister, A. M., & Gallery, M. E. (1978). Combating regression: An educational approach to the needs of the aging and aged developmentally disabled. In R. Segal (Ed.), *Consultation–conference on developmental disabilities and gerontology: Proceedings of a conference* (pp. 93–106). Ann Arbor: University of Michigan.

Johnson, W. R. (1975). *Sex education and counseling of special groups: The mentally and physically handicapped, ill and elderly.* Springfield, IL: Charles C. Thomas.

Kempton, W., Bass, M., & Gordon, S. (1973). *Love, sex, and birth control for the mentally retarded: A guide for parents.* Philadelphia: Planned Parenthood Association of Southeastern Pennsylvania.

Kriger, S. (1975). *Lifestyles of aging retardates living in community settings in Ohio.* Columbus, OH: Psychologia Netrika.

La Framboise, E., & Provencal, G. (Eds.) (1979). *1984: Where do we want to be in five years* (report). Traverse City, MI: American Association on Mental Deficiency–Michigan Chapter.

Levinthal, J. (1979). Indiana. In D. P. Sweeney & T. Y. Wilson (Eds.), *Double jeopardy: The plight of aging and aged developmentally disabled persons in mid-America* (research monograph) (pp. 125–155). Ann Arbor, MI: University of Michigan.

Manson, P. (1983). Unique community placement problems of elderly retarded individuals. In J. S. Cohen & M. U. Dickerson (Eds.), *Hey, look at me: I'm old and retarded* (monograph) (pp. 47–54). Downsview, Ontario: National Institute on Mental Retardation.

McNab, W. L. (1978). The sexual needs of the handicapped. *The Journal of School Health, 48* (5), 301–306.

Pezzoli, J. J. (1978). National Association for Retarded Citizens and the aged developmentally disabled person. In R. M. Segal (Ed.), *Consultation-conference on developmental disabilities and gerontology: Proceedings of a conference* (pp. 202–212). Ann Arbor: University of Michigan.

Scheerenberger, R. C. (1977). Deinstitutionalization in perspective. In J. L. Paul, D. J. Stedman, & G. R. Neufeld (Eds.), *Deinstitutionalization: A program and policy development* (pp. 3–13). Syracuse, NY: Syracuse University Press.

Schulman, E. D. (1980). *Focus on the retarded adult: Programs and services*. St. Louis: C. V. Mosby.

Secker, L. (1973). Sex education and mental handicap. *Special Education, 62* (1), 27–28.

Segal, R. (1978a). The aged developmentally disabled person: A challenge to the service delivery system. In R. Segal (Ed.), *Consultation–conference on developmental disabilities and gerontology: Proceedings of a conference* (pp. 5–14). Ann Arbor: University of Michigan.

Segal, R. (Ed.) (1978b). *Consultation–conference on developmental disabilities and gerontology: Proceedings of a conference*. Ann Arbor: University of Michigan.

Sweeney, D. (1979). Denied, ignored, or forgotten? An assessment of community services for older/aged developmentally disabled persons within HEW Region V. In D. P. Sweeney & T. Y. Wilson (Eds.), *Double jeopardy: The plight of aging and aged developmentally disabled persons in mid-America* (research monograph) (pp. 54–88). Ann Arbor: University of Michigan.

Sweeney, D. P., & Wilson, T. Y. (Eds.) (1979). *Double jeopardy: The plight of aging and aged developmentally disabled persons in mid-America* (research monograph). Ann Arbor, MI: University of Michigan.

Szymanski, L. S., & Tanguay, P. E. (Eds.) (1980). *Emotional disorders of mentally retarded persons: Assessment, treatment, and consultation*. Baltimore, MD: University Park Press.

Thomas, N., Acker, P., Choksey, L., & Cohen, J. (1979). Aging and aged developmentally disabled people: Defining a service population. In D. P. Sweeney & T. Y. Wilson (Eds.), *Double jeopardy: The plight of aging and aged developmentally disabled persons in mid-America* (research monograph) (pp. 36–53). Ann Arbor: University of Michigan.

Thurman, E. M. (1983a). *Exploring the experiences of mentally retarded older adults in group home settings*. Ann Arbor, MI: University Microfilms International.

Thurman, E. (1983b). A self-help model: Methodology for working with elderly retarded persons living in the community. In J. S. Cohen & M. U. Dickerson (Eds.), *Hey, look at me: I'm old and retarded* (monograph) (pp. 60–82). Downsview, Ontario: National Institute on Mental Retardation.

Turecki, S. K. (1981). The retarded adolescent's future. *New York State Journal of Medicine, 81* (11), 1680–1682.

Vanier, J. (1971). *Eruption of hope*. New York: Paulist Press.

Wolfensberger, W. (1972). *The principle of normalization in human services*. Toronto, Canada: National Institute on Mental Retardation.

Resources

Organizations

Association for Gerontology in Higher Education
600 Maryland Avenue, S.W.–West Wing 204
Washington, DC 20024

A center for the collection, maintenance, and dissemination of gerontological training and education materials.

People First, International
P.O. Box 12642
Salem, OR 97209
> The first self-advocacy group of disabled individuals to become an international movement working to change society's perceptions of disabled persons into a positive one: people first, handicapped second.

Books

Janicki, M. P., & Wisnieski, N. M. (1985). *Aging and developmental disabilities*. Baltimore, MD: Paul H. Brookes.
> Covers topics ranging from issues in aging and disablement, philosophical and legal considerations, and biological and clinical aspects of aging to approaches to services.

Perske, R. (1984). *Show me no mercy*. Nashville, TN: Abingdon Press.
> The story of Ben Banks, a 16-year-old with Down Syndrome, who struggles to be reunited with his father after tragedy shatters his family.

Perske, R. (1980). *New life in the neighborhood: How persons with retardation or other disabilities can help make a good community better*. Nashville, TN: Abingdon Press.
> A collection of anecdotes about triumphs with mentally handicapped people and their neighbors with ideas to help neighborhoods accept and welcome mentally handicapped newcomers.

Summers, J. A. (1985). *The right to grow up*. Baltimore, MD: Paul H. Brookes.
> A comprehensive book on services, stages in the adult life cycle, and policy issues concerning adults with developmental disabilities.

GLOSSARY

Acceleration A term used to refer to educational options where a student is taught and given credit for successful completion of material usually taught to older students.

Adaptations Materials, policies, devices, and attitudes that allow and enhance the inclusion of a person with handicaps in natural environments and activities.

Adaptive Behavior The degree to which an individual meets the personal responsibility and social responsibility expectations for his or her age and culture.

Adaptive Devices Equipment and aids for handicapped individuals such as voice synthesizers, specialized switches, etc., which provide improved access, independence, or mobility.

Advocacy A process used by an individual, group, or organization to protect the civil and human rights of an individual or groups of individuals.

Aging/Aged Developmentally Disabled Individual Based on the four major stages of the life cycle (growth, maturation, plateau, and senescence), this term refers to a person who was disabled during the growth or developmental stage and is currently in the plateau stage (aging) or senescence (aged).

Alzheimer's Disease Degenerative disease of middle or late age with a deterioration of brain cells and neurons and a biochemical deficit affecting the neural transmissions to the brain.

Ambulatory Able to walk.

Amniocentesis A medical procedure for withdrawing amniotic fluid from the uterus during fetal development to detect disorders in the developing fetus.

Anorexia Nervosa Self-induced starvation found predominantly in young women and resulting in a 25 to 30 percent loss of body weight.

Antecedent A stimulus preceding a behavior that may or may not exert control over the behavior.

Anxiety Apprehension or tension resulting from fear.

Aphasia A language disorder that severely limits speech comprehension and production.

Applied Behavior Analysis Systematic application of the principles of behavioral psychology to change behavior.

Aptitude Specific abilities such as verbal or mechanical reasoning.

Architectural Barrier An obstacle which prevents a person with a disability from access, e.g., stairs or high drinking fountains.

Assessment Information gathering and testing used to make decisions about education, placement, or treatment.

Astigmatism Refractive error which prevents the light rays from coming to a single focus on the retina because of different degrees of refraction in the various meridians of the eye.

Ataxia An unbalanced gait caused by loss of cerebellar control.

Athetosis A condition in which arms, hands, and/or feet move constantly in a writhing motion.

Attention Disorder Difficulty in paying attention to the task at hand sometimes described as distractibility, impulsivity, or hyperactivity.

Audiogram A graph of the sounds an individual can hear at various frequencies throughout the range of normal speech as measured by an audiometer.

Aura A sensation that precedes an epileptic seizure.

Autism Extreme withdrawal and lack of language or communication skills often including self-stimulation, self-abuse, and aggressive behavior.

Bilingual Education An approach that provides for academic and skill instruction in the primary language of the child while he or she is developing proficiency in English.

Binocular Vision The ability to use both eyes simultaneously to focus on and fuse the two images into one.

Braille A system for writing words, numbers, and other symbols using various configurations of six raised dots which blind individuals "read" by touch.

Bulimia Eating in binges followed by purging by vomiting or taking laxatives or diuretics.

Career Education Education that helps students understand their career options and make vocational choices.

Cataract A condition in which the crystalline lens of the eye, its capsule, or both become opaque with consequent loss of visual acuity.

Catheterization A procedure in which a slender tube is inserted into the body (usually the bladder) to allow fluids to pass.

Cerebral Palsy A disorder of movement and posture caused by damage to the motor areas of the brain before the end of early childhood.

Childhood Muscular Dystrophy A progressive muscular disorder which begins in childhood and is characterized by wasting of muscular tissues starting in the legs and ascending in the body until death occurs in late adolescence or young adulthood.

Cognitive Academic Learning Proficiency The level of language proficiency required for learning academic information; a higher level of language facility than that required for simple, interpersonal conversation or communication.

Common Underlying Proficiency Model The model of bilingual development that holds that language skills developed in either language promote overall cognitive development and linguistic competence.

Communication Board A device which allows a nonverbal person to indicate words, letters, or symbols he or she wishes to communicate to others.

Conductive Hearing Loss A hearing loss involving the outer or middle ear that can often be corrected surgically.

Cones Light-receiving retinal nerve cells concentrated primarily in the central retina concerned with color discrimination and detail vision in high levels of illumination.

Congenital A condition existing before or at birth.

Consequence A stimulus following a behavior that may or may not exert control over the behavior.

Contracture Shortening of muscles which causes a decreased range of motion and joint mobility.

Cornea The clear, circular, transparent portion of the outer coat of the eyeball.

Creativity The ability to produce or create something original and of value to society.

Critical Thinking Rational thought used to solve problems.

Cultural Style Background and heritage including ethnicity, religion, socioeconomic status, and geographic location.

Curriculum The content of the instructional program.

Cystic Fibrosis An inherited disorder that affects the enzyme production of the pancreas resulting in serious health problems and death in early adulthood.

Decibel A unit of measure used to describe the intensity level of sound.

Deinstitutionalization The reform to move mentally retarded and emotionally disturbed individuals out of large institutions back into small residences within their home community.

Developmental Scales Assessment instruments used to measure the physical, cognitive, and social development of infants and young children.

Diabetes Mellitus A disorder of the pancreas resulting in insufficient production of insulin needed to metabolize sugars.

Discrepancy The difference between expected and actual performance.

Distractibility Lack of attention to task.

Down Syndrome A genetic defect associated with mental retardation also called Trisomy 21.

Dysarthria An incoordination of the musculature used in speech production caused by damage to the motor areas of the brain.

Dysfluent Speech production characterized by irregular rhythms.

Early Intervention Providing services to children from birth to age three to increase their rate of development and prevent further disabilities.

Ecological Inventories Analyses of natural environments and activities used for prioritizing and sequencing curricular content and community-referenced instruction.

Education for All Handicapped Children Act Public Law 94–142 which mandates a free and appropriate education for all handicapped children.

Enrichment   A term used to describe educational options that allow a student to work on material not typically taught in the regular educational system.

Epilepsy   A central nervous system disorder that may manifest itself in a variety of ways including loss of consciousness, involuntary muscle movements, and/or mental disturbance.

Ethnicity   The sense of common identity that derives from shared experiences, religious beliefs and practices, languages, value systems, attitudes, and physical characteristics.

Ethnolinguistic Minority   Refers to any subgroup, who by reason of ethnicity or primary language background, is identifiable as a minority group.

Etiology   Cause.

Expressive Language   Spoken language, production of words.

Family   A group of people, usually related by blood or marriage and usually living together, who interact with each other on a long-term basis in order to meet individual and collective needs.

Fine Motor Activities   Those motor activities which involve the use of the eyes and hands such as tracking an object as it moves across the visual field or picking up small objects.

Finger Spelling   A form of communication used with deaf individuals using the American Manual Alphabet.

Fluency   The smoothness of speech.

Functional Skills   Useful, meaningful skills for the individuals and their current or future situation.

Generic Services   Services already in existence within a community for the use of the general population.

Genetic   Combinations of genes and chromosomes which determine heredity.

Genius   Individuals who have demonstrated extremely high levels of ability in some meaningful performance.

Gifted   Endowed with natural ability, able to do something well above the average; talented.

Glaucoma   Increased pressure inside the eye caused by accumulation of aqueous fluid in the front portion.

Grand Mal   A type of seizure in which consciousness is lost and the body goes into convulsions.

Gross Motor   Those movements and activities which involve the use of large muscles such as walking, running, jumping, lifting.

Guardianship   A process of total or partial protection and assistance established by the court for an individual incapable of managing all or part of his or her life.

Handicap   The result of a disability which interferes with an individual's functioning in a specific situation.

Hearing Aid   One of a wide range of amplification devices worn in the ear or on the body.

Hemiplegia   A motor impairment involving one side of the body.

Heterogeneous   Different from one another.

Homogeneous   Similar or alike.

Hydrocephalus   Significant enlargement of the cranial vault usually caused by excess, nonabsorbed, or blocked cerebrospinal fluid.

Hyperactivity   Excessive activity.

Impulsivity   Acting without thinking.

Independent Living Skills   Skills of daily living such as money management, domestic management, mobility, and others that are needed for independence.

Individualized Education Program (IEP)   The written plan designed by a team including parents specifying present levels of performance, instructional objectives, and the level of service for each student receiving special education services.

Infantilization   The tendency to perceive developmentally disabled adults as childlike and incapable of age-appropriate behavior and to treat developmentally disabled adults in an overprotective, condescending manner.

Integration   Including handicapped individuals in settings with nonhandicapped individuals; also called mainstreaming.

Iris   Colored, circular membrane suspended behind the cornea and immediately in front of the lens.

Learning Strategy   A systematic approach for beginning and carrying out problem solving.

Limited English Proficient (LEP)   Describes those individuals whose primary language is other than English and who have not developed fluency in speaking and reading English.

Locus of Control   A personality construct in which an individual tends to view life events as consequences of his or her own actions (internal) or as a consequence of actions over which one has little control (external).

Mainstream   The regular educational or service system where nonhandicapped individuals receive services.

Mentor   Tutor, but also implies that such an individual is a role model.

Metabolic Disorder   A dysfunction in one of the many chemical processes that break down food into usable nutrients.

Mobility   The ability to get from place to place, to move around in the environment.

Morphology   The smallest meaningful units of a language and the rules which determine the structure of words and their various forms.

Multicultural Education   Approaches that promote the appreciation of cultural and linguistic differences.

Natural Environments   Places where people live, work, play, attend school, and otherwise function.

Neurological   Related to the nervous system.

Noncategorical Programming   A service delivery model which integrates students with various handicapping conditions into the same classroom.

Nonorganic   Something that is not organically based, either environmental or psychological or with no identifiable cause.

Normalization   Creating opportunities for handicapped individuals that are as close as possible to those available to nonhandicapped individuals.

Nystagmus   An involuntary, usually rapid, movement of the eyeball.

Optic Nerve   The nerve which carries visual impulses from the retina to the brain.

Organic   Something that is physically or physiologically based.

Orientation   The awareness of one's position in relationship to all other significant objects/events in the environment.

Orthosis   An apparatus which helps a person function, e.g., a leg brace.

Osteogenesis Imperfecta   A disorder which leaves the bone structure brittle, resulting in frequent fractures.

Otolaryngologist   A physician who specializes in diseases of the ear and throat.

Paraplegia   A motor problem resulting in paralysis of the legs.

Partial Participation   Principle that maximizes the participation of handicapped individuals in settings where independent functioning is improbable.

Peripheral Vision   Ability to perceive presence, motion, or color of an object outside the direct line of vision.

Petit Mal   A type of epileptic seizure in which the individual briefly loses consciousness.

Phenylketonuria   A genetically determined, metabolic disorder that can be effectively treated with a special diet.

Phonology   The sound system of a language and the rules which determine combinations of sounds.

Photophobia   Abnormal sensitivity to and discomfort from light.

Positioning Chair   A specialized piece of equipment that holds a person in prescribed body positions which control abnormal reflexes and maximize functioning.

Pragmatics   The use of language in context.

Primitive Reflexes   Reflexes and reflex patterns which are present at birth or appear shortly thereafter.

Prompt   Any visual, verbal, or physical addition to instruction which assists the student to perform correctly.

Prosthesis   An artificial substitute for a missing part of the body.

Psychological Processes   The set of abilities used to receive, interpret, and respond to incoming information.

Psychosomatic   Physical disorders and illnesses which are believed to be caused by psychological problems.

Quadraplegia   A motor impairment resulting in paralysis of the arms and legs.

Receptive Language   Understanding and attributing meaning to words.

Residual Hearing   Hearing that remains following a hearing loss.

Residual Vision   Any usable remaining vision.

Respirator A mechanical device that supplies air to the lungs when the individual cannot breathe for himself or herself.

Respite Care Caretaking of a disabled individual for a specified period of time to provide separation from the family.

Retina The innermost, transparent membrane of the eye formed of light-sensitive nerve elements and connected with the optic nerve.

Retinitis Pigmentosa Hereditary degeneration and atrophy of the retina beginning in the periphery with main symptoms of night blindness and progressive contraction of the visual field.

Retrolental Fibroplasia A disease of the retina in which a mass of scar tissue forms behind the lens occurring most frequently in infants born prematurely who receive too much oxygen.

Rods Light-receiving retinal nerve cells sensitive to movement and light in low levels of illumination.

Rubella A type of measles which may result in mental retardation, deafness, and/or blindness in the developing fetus if contracted by the mother in early pregnancy.

Schizophrenia Incoherent thinking or loss of touch with reality and inability to perform expected responsibilities, sometimes including delusions or hallucinations.

Sclera The white part of the eye.

Screening An assessment program used to survey large groups of individuals to identify those with possible learning or health problems.

Seizure An alteration or loss of consciousness usually associated with a convulsive disorder such as epilepsy.

Self-Concept Individuals' feelings about themselves, particularly their self-worth.

Semantics Content or meaning of language.

Sensorineural Hearing Loss A hearing loss involving the inner ear or auditory nerve with limited prognosis for improvement.

Sequela The result or outcome.

Sex-Linked Recessive Conditions Genetically determined disorders which are carried on the X chromosome and occur significantly more often in males than in females.

Shunt A piece of tubing with a small pump implanted in the head which allows excess cerebrospinal fluid to drain from the cranial cavity into the body preventing hydrocephalus.

Signing A form of manual communication used with deaf individuals which uses standard hand shapes and hand movements to signify words.

Snellen Chart Lines of letters of decreasing size on a wall chart which are used to test visual acuity.

Sociobehavioral Retardation Mental retardation that is not caused biologically but is the result of inadequate environmental conditions.

Socioeconomic Status The classification of a person or family according to such factors as income levels, amount of education, standing in the community, etc.

Spasticity A condition in which the muscles are abnormally tight, often accompanied by exaggerated reflexes.

Special Education Instructional programs that are designed to meet the unique needs of handicapped students.

Spina Bifida A condition characterized by an opening in the spinal cord at birth.

Stress A physiological response to the environment that results in feelings of anxiety.

Stressor An event or chronic condition that causes stress.

Stuttering Repetitions and prolongations of words, syllables, or sounds which produce an abnormal rhythm to one's speech.

Syntax Word order and the rules which govern the relationship among the elements in a sentence.

Talented Endowed with natural ability; gifted.

Task Analysis The breakdown of any task into its smallest essential components to simplify instruction.

Total Communication An approach to teaching deaf students which combines the use of residual hearing, speech, speechreading, fingerspelling, and signs.

Transition Movement from one setting to another, for example from school to the world of work.

Trisomy 21 See Down Syndrome.

Vocational Rehabilitation Services provided to handicapped persons to assist them in becoming employable.

Voice Disorder Sound production that deviates from normal on the basis of quality, intensity, or pitch.

Work Adjustment Training Training in work-related skills such as punctuality, appropriate interactions on the job, appropriate dress.

ABOUT THE EDITORS AND CONTRIBUTORS

Eleanor W. Lynch, Ph.D.

Dr. Eleanor Lynch received her doctorate from Ohio State University in Exceptional Children with minors in Child Development and School Psychology. Before coming to San Diego State University where she is a professor of special education, Dr. Lynch was a faculty member at Miami University and the University of Michigan. Dr. Lynch's publications include articles in professional journals, chapters in books in special education, public health, and social work, and a series of booklets designed for special education teachers and parents. She has directed a variety of funded projects including studies of parents' perceptions of special education programs and services, the status of services for chronically ill children, and a model demonstration project in early intervention which focused on interagency collaboration and technology in the provision of services to families with high-risk and handicapped infants. Her writing, teaching, and research interests include early intervention, working with families of handicapped children, community collaboration, the change process, and cross-cultural teaching and learning.

Rena B. Lewis, Ph.D.

Dr. Rena Lewis is a professor of special education at San Diego State University. After completing her doctoral work at the University of Arizona with a major in Special Education and minors in Psychology and Systems Engineering, she served on the faculty at James Mason University until she joined the faculty of San Diego State University in 1978. Dr. Lewis is the coauthor of two popular textbooks in special education, *Assessing Special Students* and *Teaching Special Students in the Mainstream*, and a frequent contributor to professional journals. In 1985 she was awarded the International Reading Association Albert J. Harris Award for her contribution to knowledge in the field of reading disabilities. She has directed a wide range of training and research grants including a study of the use of technology in special education programs throughout California. Her teaching and research interests include learning disabilities, the application of technology to students with special needs, and assessment.

Richard C. Brady

Richard C. Brady is Associate Professor of Special Education at San Diego State University. He is the director of the training program for teachers of the physically handicapped, and Executive Director of the North County Career Development Program. Professor Brady's major research interest is in the transition of physically handicapped individuals from special education programs to the mainstream of adult life. Professor Brady received his M.A. from Fresno State College and his Ph.D. from the University of Southern California. Prior to joining the San Diego State University faculty, Dr. Brady was Associate Professor of Education at the University of Northern Iowa where he was the Project Director for a BEH sponsored program on the development of educational personnel for the severely, profoundly, and multiply handicapped.

Mary Jane Brotherson

Mary Jane Brotherson is assistant professor of Special Education at the University of Minnesota at Duluth. She received her Ph.D. from the University of Kansas and her B.A. and M.S. from the University of Nebraska.

Dr. Brotherson is coauthor of two books, and author of numerous articles and chapters with special focus on families, and the integration of persons with disabilities into the community. Dr. Brotherson is currently involved in personnel preparation for early childhood special education. Prior to that, she was Project Director of a U.S. Department of Education project that helped families with adolescents with disabilities plan for adult futures.

Dr. Brotherson is a member of the governing board of the Minnesota Association for Persons with Severe Handicaps, and the Products Review Board of the National Information Center for Handicapped Children and Youth. She is also a member of the American Association for Persons with Mental Deficiency, The Association for Persons with Severe Handicaps, The Council for Exceptional Children, and The National Association for Retarded Citizens.

Patricia Thomas Cegelka

In the past 20 years, Patricia Thomas Cegelka has served as a special education teacher of educable mentally retarded children, a resource specialist, a school psychologist, and a professor at three universities. She is currently Professor and Chair in the Department of Special Education at San Diego State University as well as Associate Dean for Research in the College of Education at that institution. A major consideration in her move to SDSU in 1980 was her growing interest in the issues involved in providing special education services for culturally and linguistically divergent students.

In the past few years, Dr. Cegelka has conducted research and developed programs in multiculturalism as it impacts on the delivery of services to special education populations. She coedited a special issue of *Teacher Education and Special Education* on Multicultural Issues in Special Education Personnel Preparation, and has developed chapters, articles, and presentation papers on aspects of this issue. Her other professional interests include parent/professional collaboration and career education, with her major focus being in the area of personnel preparation.

Catherine M. G. Cohn

Dr. Catherine M. G. Cohn is a Faculty Associate at Arizona State University, where she served as the Founding Associate Director of the Project for the Study of Academic Precocity (now known as the Center for Academic Precocity). When she is not instructing kindergartners through eighth graders in computer science or Algebra, she serves as consultant to the center's staff for academic assessment and mathematics instruction. Dr. Cohn's research interests have included research synthesis of the effectiveness of creativity training, development of mathematical and verbal reasoning ability, and reaction time among highly able youths.

Sanford J. Cohn

Dr. Sanford J. Cohn is Associate Professor of Special Education at Arizona State University, Tempe, Arizona, where he focuses fulltime on the educational and personal development of highly able young people. Along with William C. George and Julian C. Stanley, he edited *Educating the Gifted: Acceleration and Enrichment* (Baltimore: Johns Hopkins Press, 1979), and he has written numerous journal articles and chapters for books concerning the gifted. Dr. Cohn was the founding director of the Project for the Study of Academic Precocity (now the Center for Academic Precocity) at Arizona State University, an extensive program of research through service. Nearly 30,000 highly able youths have taken advantage of the Center's varied program of assessment services and educational options since its inception in 1979.

Martha Ufford Dickerson

Martha Ufford Dickerson, M.S.W., retired from the University of Michigan after completing a career as a Social Work Clinician, educator, lecturer, and author. Her professional commitment to the needs of individuals who have mental retardation was intensified by her experience as a foster parent to four mentally retarded adolescent boys. Her book, *Our Four Boys*, describes the family experience. This publication was followed by several articles, teaching manuals, and the popular text *Social Work Practice with the Mentally Retarded*. Currently a resident of Ontario, Dickerson is associated with the G. Allen Roeher Institute on Mental Retardation at York University, and serves as a board member for two agencies that provide assistance to families in crisis.

Donald H. Doorlag

Dr. Donald H. Doorlag is a professor at San Diego State University, where he coordinates a training program for teachers of the seriously emotionally disturbed and behaviorally disordered. Since joining the faculty in 1970, he has taught classes in the areas of assessment, behavior management, research, and mainstreaming with a specific interest in the areas of learning handicapped and behavior disorders. He also chaired the Department of Special Education for a three-year period.

Dr. Doorlag has taught students with learning and behavior disorders, as well as adjudicated delinquents. His current research, writing, and consulting interests relate to instructional techniques for students with behavior disorders, classroom management, management of violent individuals, teacher training, mainstreaming, and the role of resource specialists.

Lannie S. Kanevsky

Lannie S. Kanevsky has been a lecturer in the Department of Special Education at San Diego State University. Her interests include programs for the gifted and talented and the use of microcomputer applications in special education. Ms. Kanevsky received her M.A. in special education with an emphasis in gifted education from San Diego University and will be an Assistant Professor in the Department of Educational Psychology and Counseling at McGill University.

Donald F. Moores

Donald F. Moores is Director of the Center for Studies in Education and Human Development and Professor of Educational Foundations and Research at Gallaudet University. He is a trained teacher of the deaf, with five years classroom teaching experience. He received his Ph.D. in Special Education from the University of Illinois. He was a professor of Special Education at the University of Minnesota for ten years and Head of the Department of Special Education for three years before joining the faculty at Gallaudet in 1980. Dr. Moores' current research activities are in the reading of deaf adolescents and on the effectiveness of public school programs.

Julia Maestas y Moores

Julia Maestas y Moores currently is a Policy Analyst in the Department of Health and Human Services, Office of Population Affairs. She is a trained and experienced speech therapist, teacher of the deaf, and teacher of children with special learning and behavior problems. Dr. Maestas y Moores received her Ph.D. in Educational Psychology from the University of Minnesota, where her dissertation was in pragmatic communication of deaf mothers with their infant children. Dr. Maestas y Moores was coordinator of the teacher training program in the area of deafness at the University of Minnesota. Her writing has concentrated on the linguistic environment of deaf children and participation of Hispanics in special education.

Patricia L. Patton

Patricia L. Patton is currently a Professor of Special Education at San Diego State University. She is also the Co-Project Director of Project WORK, a transition from school to work project for learning disabled students. Dr. Patton has worked as a vocational rehabilitation counselor, vocational evaluator, special education diagnostician, and special education and rehabilitation counselor trainer during the past 20 years. Dr. Patton received her M.S. in Vocational Rehabilitation Counseling from Florida State University and her Ed.D. in Special Education from North Texas State University.

Ian Pumpian

Ian Pumpian is an Associate Professor at San Diego State University. He coordinates the teacher credential in the area of severe handicaps in the Department of Special Education. Dr. Pumpian received his training and graduate degrees at the University of Wisconsin–Madison and taught adolescents with severe handicaps in the Madison Metropolitan School District. His major training, advocacy, and expertise focus on school and community integration, functional curriculum, and the transition of students from school to a wide range of normalized living, community, and work environments. He has written on these subjects, as well as provided numerous presentations and consultations to many local, state, and national audiences. Dr. Pumpian is an active member of The Association for Persons with Severe Handicaps (TASH); he has served on the editorial board and as a guest editor for the Journal for the Association of Persons with Severe Handicaps and is a founding member of the California Chapter of TASH.

Jean Ann Summers

Jean Ann Summers is the Acting Director of the Kansas University Affiliated Facility at the University of Kansas. She is a doctoral candidate in Special Education, with an emphasis in special education law, policy, and families. She has more than ten years experience in administration and state-level planning for services to persons with exceptionalities and their families. Her research on families and family-related interventions has led to more than 50 books, articles, and conference presentations on that topic.

Carol A. Swift

Carol A. Swift is Associate Professor in the Department of Human Development and Child Studies at Oakland University in Rochester, Michigan. She received her Ph.D. in Special Education from the University of Arizona and her B.A. and

M.A. degrees in Speech Pathology from Southern Methodist University. Her areas of interest include educational assessment; language problems, particularly in learning disabled students; and cognitive development and instruction. Dr. Swift has worked as a director in a preschool program for children with learning problems and as a communication consultant in a Native American special education program.

Ivan S. Terzieff

Ivan S. Terzieff is director of Supported Employment Program for Sensory Impaired Multiply Handicapped Adults with Seguin Services in the Chicago area. Previously, Dr. Terzieff coordinated the teacher preparation program for the visually impaired at the University of Arizona. He has also taught courses in orientation and mobility at Western Michigan University. He has conducted numerous workshops and has done research in technology for the visually impaired. Dr. Terzieff received a M.Ed. degree from the University of Pittsburgh and a Ph.D. from Ohio State University in 1980.

Ann P. Turnbull

Ann P. Turnbull is a Professor in the Department of Special Education and Acting Associate Director in the Bureau of Child Research at the University of Kansas in Lawrence, Kansas. Her major interests in research and model program development relates to the needs of families who have a member with a disability. The major themes of her work in this area have focused on family-professional relationships in implementing the requirements of PL 94-142, developing support services for families consistent with a family systems perspective, identifying empirically the positive contributions that members with disabilities make to their families as a basis for planning interventions, and working to develop a model to assist families in future planning related to the adult needs of their family member with a disability.

She serves on the Board of Directors of the American Association on Mental Deficiency and has been the recipient of the "Educator of the Year" Award from the Association for Retarded Citizens of the United States. Her professional work in the area of family issues has been strengthened by the fact that she is the mother of three children, one of whom is a son with mental retardation.

Photo Credits

Unless otherwise acknowledged, all photos are the property of Scott, Foresman and Company.

PAGE 3 Alan Carey/The Image Works   PAGE 15 David M. Grossman   PAGE 28 Jerry Howard/Positive Images   PAGE 38 Alan Carey/The Image Works   PAGE 53 Alan Carey/The Image Works   PAGE 73 Jerry Howard/Positive Images   PAGE 81 Harriet Gans/The Image Works   PAGE 95 Bohdan Hrynewych/Southern Light   PAGE 110 Alan Carey/The Image Works   PAGE 114 Alan Carey/The Image Works   PAGE 120 David M. Grossman   PAGE 125 Enrico Ferorelli/Dot Picture Agency   PAGE 139 © Mickey Pfleger 1987   PAGE 150 Alan Carey/The Image Works   PAGE 165 Tom Tracy/Medichrome/The Stock Shop   PAGE 172 © Elliott Varner Smith   PAGE 194 Alan Carey/The Image Works   PAGE 196 David M. Grossman   PAGE 204 Alan Carey/The Image Works   PAGE 219 David M. Grossman   PAGE 246 John Griffin/The Image Works   PAGE 249 Bernell Corp.   PAGE 255 Alan Carey/The Image Works   PAGE 257 © David R. Frazier Photolibrary   PAGE 267 Dan McCoy/Rainbow   PAGE 285 © David R. Frazier Photolibrary   PAGE 292 Alan Carey/The Image Works   PAGE 298 Michael Philip Manheim/Medichrome/The Stock Shop   PAGE 309 © 1987 Steve Takatsuno   PAGE 326 Alan Carey/The Image Works   PAGE 336 Alan Carey/The Image Works   PAGE 338 Alan Carey/The Image Works   PAGE 345 Courtesy Sentient Systems Technology, Inc.   PAGE 358 John Bowden/© Discover Magazine   PAGE 370 Alan Carey/The Image Works   PAGE 375 Alan Carey/The Image Works   PAGE 388 Alan Carey/The Image Works   PAGE 421 Michael Weisbrot   PAGE 426 Michael Weisbrot   PAGE 437 Alan Carey/The Image Works   PAGE 473 © John McGrail 1985   PAGE 489 Michael Weisbrot   PAGE 493 Michael Weisbrot   PAGE 503 Alan Carey/The Image Works   PAGE 516 Bohdan Hrynewych/Southern Light   PAGE 526 Alan Carey/The Image Works   PAGE 532 Michael Weisbrot   PAGE 549 David M. Grossman   PAGE 558 David E. Kennedy/TexaStock   PAGE 576 Michael D. Sullivan/TexaStock   PAGE 595 Jerry Howard/Positive Images   PAGE 605 Michael Weisbrot   PAGE 607 Alan Carey/The Image Works   PAGE 625 Alan Carey/The Image Works   PAGE 629 Alan Carey/The Image Works   PAGE 637 Alan Carey/The Image Works

Name Index

Subject Index

Doman-Delacato patterning program, 392
Dopamine, 419
Down Syndrome, 103–105, 115, 189–190
  age of father and, 190
  age of mother and, 189
  early detection, 107
  early intervention, 62
  family and, 514
  mainstreaming and, 105
Dropouts, 425, 426, 551, 554
Drug Questionnaire, 435
Drugs, 188, 364
  abuse, 69. *See also* Substance abuse
  in pregnancy, 55
Drug therapy, 391, 443, 444
  behavior disorders and, 422
DSM-III. See Diagnostic and Statistical Manual of Mental Disorders
Dysarthria, 323, 330, 340
Dyscalculia, 363
Dysgraphia, 363
Dyskinetic cerebral palsy, 141, 144, 145
Dyslexia, 363, 368

E

Ear, 279–280
Early Periodic Screening, Detection, and Treatment (EPSDT) program, 39, 52
Easter Seals Society, 172
Eating Questionnaire, 435
Ecological approach, 439. *See also* Environmental influences; Sociobehavioral factors
  behavior disorders, 417
  inventories, 117, 208, 210, 214–215
Economic status. *See* Socioeconomic status
Edison, Thomas, 353
Education. *See* Remedial education; Special education
Education, crisis in, 458
Educational approach, 357, 359
  learning disabilities, 384–385
Educational services, 37, 47
Education Amendments. *See* Public laws: PL 94–482
Education Consolidation and Improvement Act. *See* Public laws: PL 97–35
Education for All Handicapped Children Act. *See* Public laws: PL 94–142
Education of the Handicapped Act. *See* Public laws: PL 93–199
Effectance, 112
Einstein, Albert, 353
Electroconvulsive therapy, 444
Electroencephalogram (EEG), 364
Electrophysiological techniques, 299

Eligibility, 52–53, 66, 67, 68. *See also* Diagnosis
Emotional characteristics. *See* Social/emotional characteristics
Emotionally disturbed, 184, 407, 408. *See also* Behavior disorders
  hearing disordered, 294–295, 296
Employment. *See also* Vocational programs
  behavior disordered, 422
  communication disordered, 332
  competitive, 611–612
  gifted and talented, 494
  hearing disordered, 309–310
  learning disabled, 376
  mentally retarded, 128
  noncompetitive, 593
  physically and health handicapped, 158
  rate for disabled, 590
  segregated, 589
  supported community, 591
  unemployment, 158, 589, 590
  visually impaired, 230
Encephalitis, 444
English as a Second Language. *See* ESL
Enrichment strategies, 483–484
Enrichment Triad, 485
Environment, 239–240
Environmental influences, 9, 137
  behavior and, 195–196
  cancer and, 154
  communication disorders and, 322, 323, 324, 340
  giftedness and talent and, 464, 465
  hearing disorders and, 277, 286
  home, 365, 366
  learning and, 58
  learning disabilities and, 358, 359, 365, 366
  mental retardation and, 106
  neonatal intensive care unit, 57
  school, 365
  severe multiple handicaps and, 187
  visual impairments and, 240, 259–260
Epidemics, 283. *See also* Rubella: epidemic
Epilepsy, 145–147, 444
Epilepsy Foundation of America, 146
Erikson, Erik, 57–58
Escala de Inteligencia Wechsler para Niños, 567. *See also* Wechsler Scales of Intelligence: *Wechsler Intelligence Scale for Children*
ESL (English as a Second Language), 555
Esophageal speech, 340
Ethnicity, 517–518. *See also* Culturally diverse
Eugenics Movement, 29
Examining for Aphasia, 336

Exceptionalities, 4. *See also* Behavior disorders; Communication disorders; Giftedness and talent; Handicaps, physical and health; Handicaps, severe multiple; Hearing disorders; Learning disabilities; Mental retardation; Visual impairments
  detection of, 34–35
  effects of, 18–23
  etiology, 8–10
  future, 41–42
  individuals with, 4–5
    needs, 10–12, 14–18
    number, 6–7, 78
    services for, 36–40, 46–86
  professionals and, 13–18
Exceptional people. *See* Exceptionalities: individuals with
Expectation hypothesis, 97
Exploratory behavior, 240, 241, 242
Extended classroom, 464
Extension thrust, 143–144
Eye, 231–232

F

Facilitation, 55–56, 58, 69
Falsetto, 323
Family. *See also* Parents
  behavior disorders and, 421, 442
  beliefs and values, 520–521
  change and, 533–537
  communication, 508, 512–513
  communication disorders and, 339
  cultural style, 517–520
  death of child, 159
  developmental stage, 529–531
  functions, 507, 524–529
  future, 537–538
  hearing disorders and, 282–283, 290
  ideological style, 520–524
  impact of handicapped on, 19, 504–539
  institutionalization and, 534–535
  interaction, 507–513
  involvement in education, 210, 505
  learning disabilities and, 393
  life cycle, 507, 529–537
  older handicapped and, 532
  severe multiple handicaps and, 181, 186
  siblings, 505, 514
  single-parent, 507, 515, 516
  social services, 51
  stress, 153, 514–515, 519, 535–536
    adaptability, 511, 512–513
    change and, 529, 533, 535, 536–537
    coping patterns, 521–524
    institutionalization and, 534–535
  structure of, 505, 513–524
  support services, 186, 443